EDUCATING NOAH...TRAVELIN'

First of Two

Noah

Copyright © 2023

All Rights Reserved

ISBN: 978-1-916954-60-1

Table of Contents

About the Author i
Preface iii
Chapter One 2013 1
    Last States West of the Mississippi 24
    Scandinavian Summer Trip 41
    Northeast Cruise and Tour October 14, 2013 54
    Vacation to Italy, Monaco, Spain, Tunisia, and Sicily December 5, 2013 66
Chapter two 2014 83
    First leg of tour 2014 Exploring Australia, New Zealand, Bali, and the US. 83
    Finish up the US; June, 2014 123
    The Turkey and Tanzania Adventure Sept. 9th -21st 2014 142
Chapter Three 2015 178
    Caribbean Cruise 178
    Florida Road Trip March 2015 199
    China Tibet April 2015 218
    Hawaii 2015 263
Chapter four 2016 294
    2016 Southern Caribbean Cruise, January 27, 2016. 294
    May 2016, our trip to Greece May 13th through the 23rd. 324
    Iceland July 2016 359
    Road Trip: Road to the Sun and Canada August 2016 386
    Russia and Finland September 2016 408

India 2016 460
Chapter five 2017 .... **517**
Argentina and Antarctica February, 2017 518
The Three C's Adventure April 2017 556
The Ark Encounter 602
The Far East Adventure October-2017 604
Cruise Lines and Where **662**
Countries and States visited: **664**

About the Author

Noah is a person that learns by doing; he is not a book learner and never has been, but doing something once or twice has been the best for him. Many put off travel until retirement, and for the most part, so did Noah; however, patience was never one of his qualities. To provide that wish to avoid traveling extensively, this is what one goes through, what is seen, and what happens.

Preface

This continues the autobiography and will be divided by years; the last was by decades and involved work, family, cars, and vacations. Now that we are both retired, we have progressed to leisure and vacations to finish traveling extensively the world by the time we are 70, then slow down to a vacation or two a year plus a road trip; we will see how this pans out, working on and off now and then to supplement our savings and social security and combat the boredom.

It turns out that this will be two editions, the first published in 2023 and the balance in 2024 after our last (?) cruise…It took a bit longer to see what we wanted to see; at this writing, both of us are now 75 and deteriorating faster than we thought. The writing was more extensive to give everyone a "feel" about traveling so much and to tell what we saw, given how much changes over time…saw this in the Philippines, Vietnam, Hawaii, and Alaska!

Chapter One
2013

I am now sixty-five, still working very part-time; I finished the book of my life and am waiting for my daughter Tiffany to edit it so I can publish it. I am not looking to make any money on it, but I am conversing with my tax consultant about any expenses I can deduct if it sells.

As I wait for the editing, I am questioning what I wrote and what I left out. I will add those items I missed and soften the book regarding those folks who did not meet my expectations or let me down. It is just "spilled milk," and I did learn from each experience.

I am working part-time ten to twelve hours a week as an aide. I like working with seniors, and it does get me out of the house. I am currently working four days and at hours when the pool at the club is unavailable, so my time for the last two weeks at the club is now once a week temporarily, and I am missing that second day a week. I will remedy that after returning from the road trip.

I am actually to the point where I want to work at most ten-twenty hours a week. It has taken two years to break me of that "have to work" ethic. It scares me a little, even though we are taking great vacations, seeing the world around us, and doing the things we always wanted to do.

I always wanted to ride "The City of New Orleans" from Chicago to New Orleans and back. (From the Janis Joplin song "Me and Bobby Magee.")

Since we did Route 66 two years ago, this is a logical adventure and a new experience taking a train for an extended period. We will not be taking a train for transportation for any length of time for any further adventures; however, we did have a great time!

Noah

March, we arranged with America by Rail for a four-day venture to the city of New Orleans.

We left from the Sturtevant, Wisconsin station at 1:25 PM; parking the car, there was only $4.00 for the duration of the vacation. The train was on time, and we arrived at Union Station in Chicago in a little over an hour.

A company representative met us as we entered the station and led us to a lounge where everyone was to meet. We introduced ourselves and checked in with our guide. I asked about the optional swamp tour we wanted to take, and she confirmed that I should call immediately to make reservations. I did; the reservations were made for eight thirty Saturday morning and to be picked up in front of the hotel. The City of New Orleans was scheduled to leave at 8:00 PM, so we had plenty of time to explore the station and get a bite to eat.

The station is considerably smaller than I expected, the food court was adequate, but nothing like any of the airports we have experienced, and everything seemed dated and worn. I opted for some cheese and caramel corn to share with our new companions; there was complimentary soda in the sleeper lounge where we waited, a late supper to be offered on the train.

The group met for final instructions and boarded the train on time.

Half of the group had sleepers; the balance was coach. Our coach seats were located in the front of the third passenger car. Lynn and I sat in the first seats, thinking this would allow for more room, and settled in for another adventure.

We opted to get a sandwich from the snack bar for dinner; the snack bar was located on the lower level of the observation car. We were the second customer, only one person in this, a very small and limited option snack bar. The server was pleasant but slow to serve and fill our order. When we paid for our two beverages and sandwich, the line to be served was back to the staircase. You should bring your food and beverage if you are in coach because the train is not set up to accommodate that many people with just a one-person snack bar and a dining car with less than twenty-four-person tables.

At ten, the lights were dimmed for the coaches to allow the passengers to sleep. In that we were the first seats in the car, every time the connecting doors were open, the front of the car was flooded with light, and a gush of cold air flooded in for the fifteen seconds it took the doors to close, oh, and the un-muffled, clickity-clack noise of the train.

John, the guy in the seat across from us, counted while he was awakened during that time, a little over one hundred openings of the doors, fifty percent of them by the attendants.

We were told if we went to the dining room for breakfast at six-thirty, being "coach," we could get into the dining car before the people in the sleepers. We were in line, then shooed out of the dining room, told that it doesn't open till seven A.M., and five minutes later, we were told we could enter. (They have been in business for over 100 years, this kind of service I can only excuse for a company that is new, or do they not care?)

Many times during the trip, we had to pull over on a side track to let a freight train pass; the time was made up by increasing our speed on decaying tracks, causing side-to-side rolling much worse than any cruise ship we have been aboard. One of our members fell down one of the staircases, gashed open her forehead, and had to be taken off the train to an emergency room at a hospital. Besides this unexpected delay, we arrived in New Orleans on time. The observation car also had limited seating; many of the twin seats were taken up by one person, and some other couples took three seats with their stuff between them. There was no time limit, and many were "camped" in those seats during most of the ride. This was just another disappointment. Others told us that a few people were sleeping in the narrow aisle, which sounded too incredulous!

Noah

Upon our arrival, we were met by a tour bus for a three-hour tour of New Orleans. The tour guide "Marty" was exceptional. She is a native of New Orleans and provided many insights into the various attractions of the city besides Bourbon Street, the lakefront, the French market, the different neighborhoods, parks, cemeteries, and levies. She wove history into the presentation and a lot of local color. We had a little extra time, so we did make a short stop at a park pavilion to enjoy coffee and beignets.

After the tour, we checked into our room and asked the concierge about being picked up for the tour; she said that would be new, that she was not aware of being picked up at the hotel, and that we would have to go down to the beach at the tour pavilion. We rested, placed our luggage in the room, grabbed a bite to eat, and toured the city on our own. We attempted to call the tour company to confirm our reservation but had to leave a message; it was after five.

We returned to the hotel after talking to another tour vendor, claiming the bus would pick us up at the hotel, totally confused and exhausted.

Saturday morning, we checked again with the concierge, and she confirmed that we would have to walk down to the pavilion, so we gobbled down a quick breakfast and hoofed it down to the beach. On the way, we found an open tour kiosk, asked him, and he confirmed that the beach was the place to go. Upon arrival, we checked in and received our tour tickets, and were told to wait for the bus.

We then received a call from a bus driver saying he was outside the hotel. I told him we were down by the beach, in front of the Jax brewery. He stated that he was to pick us up and would be there in five minutes, and he would wait for us. He did, we got on the bus, and we were off. He had to pick up three other parties around town; he needed to learn about the confusion regarding the pick-up point and stated he had picked up at our hotel before.

Educating Noah...Travelin'

It is a thirty-minute drive to the small town of Lafitte, where the airboats are based, on the corner of a very large swamp. We had opted for a small airboat for a closer experience. We entered a welcome center and saw two albino alligators in a pool, along with another outside pool that had turtles.

In fifteen minutes, we loaded on our airboat, our driver introduced himself, and off we went. Everyone was supplied with hearing protection for the high-speed ride deep into the swamp. We entered a number of small canals looking for alligators when spotted. Most of them dived, but some did not; they wanted what we had -- marshmallows -- " Gator cocaine." Twelve-footer ignored us and continued, but four-footers readily came and gobbled up three of the marshmallows.

We then proceeded further into the marsh; saw a Cyprus swamp with cypress knees and a lot of Spanish moss. We learned that Spanish moss is not parasitic; it only grows where there are no leaves and transfers with the wind; it does not hurt the trees at all.

In another canal, we came upon small floating black birds with red beaks; they also liked the marshmallows.

Our guide then reached into a small bag and brought out a small alligator. He showed us the flap they have in their mouth so that they can open their mouth underwater, passed him around so that we could feel his soft belly, stroke him behind his head (he liked that), and have a true up-close look at him. At about two feet long, he eats about twenty to thirty goldfish a week; once he gets big enough, he will be released back into the wild.

We learned that small "gaiters" mostly get eaten by birds, other reptiles, bigger fish, swamp mammals, even older alligators; they have a very low survival rate. There is an organization that harvests the nest eggs; they mark the eggs with an X. When they put them in the protected nest, the X must be up; otherwise, when the alligator hatches, the baby will drown. The most dangerous alligator is the one that is five to six feet long; they are the most aggressive. Alligators grow about a foot a year to about ten to twelve feet. They live to an average of sixty to seventy years old.

The tour lasted about two hours, lots to see; found quite a few alligators, including one that was six feet and called" Hollywood". He came up to the boat, the guide fed him chicken, and his head was in the boat! A good show, and we got some great pictures.

On the way back to the hotel, I asked the bus driver to drop us off at Mardi Gras World, and he complied. We walked two blocks to the entrance and bought a tour. We were shown a number of completed floats, figurines, the workshop, and the progress of a float from the ground up. We were shown the inside of a float; we found that many floats now have a small toilet on board. (The people on the float are there for six-eight hours) The tour included a film on the history of the company, inside views of production, and the increased complexity of the floats. We were also able to don costumes for pictures and treated to a slice of King's cake.

The two hours we spent there went quickly, we were able to take a free shuttle back to Canal Street to walk over to our hotel and drop off our gifts before continuing to the French Market and lunch.

On the way to the French market, we hired a three-wheel bicycle cab. We jumped in and were whisked away the last five blocks to the market. This was the place to get all of the additional trinkets we wanted and taste the food. There was also a food fair going on, so we ate at that also. We ate alligator sausage, Muffalettas, green corn tamales, and French fries with basil, garlic, and pimento cheese. All great! And exceptional!

We took another pedal cab back to the hotel, giving ourselves an hour before joining the group leader and another couple for dinner at the Red Fish Grill. We ordered drinks; most ordered the red fish with sauce, I had the gumbo appetizer, Lynn had the shrimp bisque soup, and we had fresh bread served, which was punched by the server to stop the rising in the bag. For dessert, we had their famous double chocolate bread pudding. All of the food, the drinks, the servers, and the waitress were exemplary! We could not find anything wrong with anything, the ambiance, and the entire experience was enjoyed by all!

After dinner, we walked Bourbon Street for one last time and then walked back to the hotel, exhausted and full.

Sunday morning, we had a small breakfast at the hotel and walked up and down Canal Street. We caught the trolley and rode it to the end, where we were told curtly by the operator that this was the end of the line and must leave. We walked back to the hotel, picked up by bus at twelve-thirty to be taken back to the railroad station for our train ride home. The part of the group that had sleepers could and did use the lounge; the balance of us found seats by scattering onto the few seats available.

Within forty-five minutes, we were grouped with the sleepers and ushered ahead of the crowd waiting to rush the train when the gate opened. This time we had a small cluster of seats at the very end of the car, and the car looked a little newer, maybe only thirty years old, but the carpeting and lights were still dingy.

We were able to pick our dining time after the sleepers chose and went for a beer with another group member as a snack for the trip back. We were first at the snack bar and ordered the beers, my buddy pulled out his hotel room key to pay, and the attendant did not accept it, so I paid! This was the first time I had seen this ploy to have me buy, and John, my bud, stated it really wasn't intentional and said he would buy the next round. We sat in the observation car, drank our beers, and then joined the women in our seats. Dinner was called at our time; we made it to the dining car and had a very good dinner.

Noah

We discussed the number of vacant properties and burned-up buildings on the route. The train followed the same pattern of pullovers and excessive speed on poor tracks again. I was determined to beat the system and thought I could fit behind the seats on the floor, with my legs extending under my seat. After four hours, I returned to my seat for another fitful night.

We arrived in Chicago at nine A.M., picked up our checked luggage, and proceeded to the lounge.

We were accosted in the lounge by the Amtrak Nazi, stating he counted four more people than the sleepers. The tour guide interceded, and with a frown, we were allowed in as a group. After settling in for the connecting train, I went out to the Amtrak help desk to confirm the train and where to board. The person behind the desk was short, offered the minimum information available, and made it clear that this interruption was an intrusion on her time.

They announced a train to Milwaukee shortly afterward, I found and asked another Amtrak employee, and he was nice enough to tell me that the tickets we had were not reserved seating and could be used on the earlier train. I thanked him, got Lynn, and we lined up and got on the train, arriving in Sturtevant by 12:30 PM.

Note:

We found New Orleans to be as friendly as Milwaukee, with very nice people, welcoming and very warm, and fun to be with.

We found the streetcar operator, along with the Amtrak station people, were rude and unnecessarily short. The Amtrak employees on the train were very nice, but the pace was slow.

This was a once-in-a-lifetime experience; it will be the last overnight train we will take. The Chicago station was small, dingy, and outdated along with the trains; the New Orleans station was newer but had inadequate seating, had older people and kids waiting in line for more than a half hour, and was poorly organized.

Customer service is not a priority with Amtrak; the station employees reminded me of the DMV. If you like traveling in the past in a barely comfortable crowded atmosphere, you may enjoy overnight train travel.

The train engines were filthy and had peeling paint; the cars were dingy and dated; the passenger control was poor; inadequate seating in the stations and understaffing at the snack bar and dining car. It is a monopoly; therefore, it will not improve, and there is no incentive.

No more train vacations for us!

We had a breather from vacations for only a short time. As mentioned before, I am starting to work nine hours a week, which seems a real inconvenience! I increased my withholding on the part-time job due to owing on my taxes from last year, and since the checks are so small, no taxes were taken out, I don't need an audit, and I don't need another thousands of dollar's taxes due notice! I also had the maximum amount of taxes taken out of my social security check, so I am also dealing with a few hundred less a month from social security.

Galapagos Adventure 04/30/ 2013

We started by getting up early at 4:25 AM on Saturday morning; it was going to be a long travel day! We packed the car, ate yogurt, and went out the door at 5:25 sharp. We arrived at the bus station, inquired, and there were three parking slots left, so we got the pass and parked the car at the terminal for the week. Loaded the bus and off to O'Hare in Chicago.

At 7:40, we arrived at the American Airlines terminal. There was an outside check-in for our luggage, and we were processed with another couple on the spot. With boarding passes in hand, we proceeded to the TSA lines to be screened. The lines were manageable, and we were processed and checked in a timely manner despite the signs stating the lines were longer than normal due to a sequester.

I proceeded to the gate and waited for the flight scheduled for 10:00 to Miami, a 3 1/2-hour flight. The gate opened late at 9:45, and everyone crowded the gate and rushed the plane; we were all finally seated, and the overhead cabinets were closed when the pilot made the announcement that the right engine was not operating correctly. Maintenance was called, and a valve was replaced in thirty minutes flat; there was hope, but the paperwork had to be completed, and the flight reauthorized another 45 minutes and, finally, we were off.

The flight took the whole three and one-half hours, plus additional time to taxi; we asked the stewardess about missing the connecting flight, and she told us they radioed ahead, but no guarantee. The captain requested that the passengers that were to meet connecting flights should be permitted to get off first, but of course, the first class were left out first, and the balance of the passengers ignored the request. We exited the plane and headed for the international gates. We arrived forty-five minutes late to the gate and found the plane still at the gate, passenger access ramps still at the front door, and the engine was not running. I went to the neighboring gate, but there were no personnel at this one; he told me to wait for the gate personnel, who would return after buttoning up the door.

Three people appeared; we ran over and asked to be put on; they stated that the plane was full and that they were on the final checklist.

Educating Noah...Travelin'

I told them they knew we were late; it was AA's equipment that failed, and this was typical horrible airline service. We were directed to the re-scheduling desk, and disgusted, we went to re-schedule our flight. (By the way, after re-scheduling, the plane we missed was still at the gate!) I complained to the re-scheduler, and he repeated, "You were late" to respond; I kept repeating, "It was your company's flight."

They re-scheduled us for a flight four hours later and gave us a food voucher for the inconvenience. We found a pizza place, ordered food, and waited for our new flight. There were ten of us on that flight from Chicago, so American Airlines disappointed ten passengers with their poor service and accommodation policies.

The re-scheduled flight called the first-class passengers to load at the time we were supposed to leave, so the plane did actually start to taxi out a half hour late. There were many families and children on the flight, so the noise level was higher than normal, people up and down the aisles, and loud Spanish conversations. No earphones were offered for the entertainment, you had to ask and pay $2.00 for a set, and then they were yours to keep. I saw very few people ask or pay.

The flight down to Guayaquil, Ecuador, was four and a half hours. Time dragged, but we made it in the time specified. We were tired, but all of the families were wide awake, roaming the isles, talking loudly, and flirting with the young male attendant. Our tour hosts were there to greet us at the exit to take us to the hotel. We arrived at the hotel at 11:00 PM, checked in, showered, and went to bed. Tomorrow morning is an early breakfast at the hotel, and then the flight to the Islands.

At 6:30 AM, we got up, took the luggage out, and went down for a very nice breakfast at the hotel. I boarded the bus, went through customs, and waited for the flight to Balta on the Islands. The flight left on time, just shy of two hours, and was uneventful. I did notice that the flight did have a large number of teenagers; they were well-behaved and polite.

Noah

The airport was just finished, very new and clean; customs was slow but manageable; we gathered our luggage and met our guide, Soto Uribe, for the week.

A fifteen-minute bus ride to the ferry took the ferry (wait thirty minutes to load, ten minutes to ride, then ten minutes to unload passengers and luggage). Boarded another bus for the forty-five-minute ride to Puerto Arora. We were scheduled for a stop at a restaurant featuring the "best chicken on the island."

The views from the open-air restaurant over the foliage were breathtaking, the hostess very accommodating, and the chicken was outstanding! Refreshed, we boarded the bus for the balance of the ride to our hotel. The hotel was very nice; we checked in and unpacked. The room was basic, with a twin bed slat innerspring, two end tables, a small alcove with a shelf, a table, and a very nice bathroom with a shower stall taking up one-third of the bathroom. A pitcher of "safe" water (Refilled daily) and two glasses, no chairs, phone, radio, or TV. The room did have air conditioning which we consider essential in equatorial regions we have visited!

We then proceeded to the hotel pool to be fitted for masks, snorkels, and fins for the balance of the week. Once everyone was fitted and instructed on the use of fins and snorkels, we all went into the pool to ensure people were comfortable with the use of the equipment in the water and answered any final questions.

We then put our gear into the supplied mesh bags, went back to the rooms to change, and walked into town to tour the harbor, restaurants, and shops.

We were still tired from the traveling and lack of sleep; we found a Gelato shop, had a few scoops, and headed back to the hotel, it would be a very busy week ahead, and we wanted to get a full night's sleep.

Educating Noah...Travelin'

Monday morning started with a very nice breakfast at the hotel, where we met to take cabs for a nature and beach walk, ending on one of the most beautiful beaches in the world, "Tortuga Bay." The cabs here are small crew cab pick-up trucks. It costs $1.00 per person to go anywhere in town, and you will see one every 1-2 minutes.

We were dropped off at the park entrance and walked the 2.2-kilometer trail through the local flora and fauna, including a cactus forest and a number of land birds. After the trail, we walked to the bay on white sand beaches, another half mile of beach. As we approached the hill, making the approach to the bay, I sat down on a small bench. As I looked down, a half-dozen three-four-foot-long black ocean iguanas were within easy reach! Looking out at the underbrush, I saw dozens more! (There was no fear or scattering, they just accepted the intrusion) Over the hill, we found our group, set up just another one hundred yards away.

After a box lunch of chicken paella and plantains (prepared locally and excellent) with beer, soda, and water, we stored our shoes and equipment, donned our snorkel gear, and swam out to the mangrove outcropping a couple hundred yards away.

The water was a little murky, limiting visibility to only ten to twelve feet, but we did have a marine iguana swim past us, saw several colorful fish, bright orange crabs, a few frigates, and a booby fly and dive into the bay. After over an hour in the water, we returned to the beach for a sack lunch and took pungas (a ten-passenger rubber boat with an outboard motor) to the yacht for a ride to the harbor.

We took a cab back to the hotel, rested for an hour, then gathered to walk down to the Charles Darwin Station, a quarter mile away from our hotel.

This station demonstrates the conservation efforts to save the tortoises. We came upon several iguanas lying around; we saw baby tortoises of different ages and various other tortoises up to and including one hundred years old.

We were also treated to several large gold-colored land Iguanas; we coaxed one to move and eat a prickly pear fruit we found that had dropped from a local tree. He slowly demonstrated to us how he peeled the spikes off the fruit before eating.

It was late in the afternoon, and both of us were tired and sore; we straggled back to the hotel. We rested and changed, then met for a walking tour of the harbor and downtown. The town is completely safe, with virtually no crime. Bikes are left without being locked; belongings are left outside rooms without fear of "walking away." It was a tour of about a kilometer, with small shops, a fish market complete with begging pelicans and sea lions, a playground by the harbor loaded with happy kids, and the pier where we watched pelicans drop into the sea for fish and sea lions play under the pylons. On the way to the restaurant, we stopped at several shops to price the products and see the variety of wares offered.

We had pre-ordered our meals; I ordered the grilled octopus, most others ordered the fish of the day, and the balance ordered the beef. My octopus was excellent! I did share with those brave enough to try it; the beer was cold, all of the meals generous with tasty compliments, perfectly seasoned, and attractively presented. We all had our fill, the conversation changed to what was to be tomorrow, and we walked back to the hotel. Another good night's sleep.

Tuesday 0600, nine hours of sleep refreshed us for another busy day! The swimsuits were not completely dry, so we used a hair drier to make them wearable. Here, as in the Amazon, toilet paper is not flushed, and we were finally placing the paper in the trashcan automatically. A good breakfast and meet at 7:45 to walk down to the harbor to catch our yacht for the two-hour ride out to Santa Fe Island.

We took a punga to the boat, kicked off our shoes on the back deck, and settled in for the ride. The sea was a little rough, which made the trip a little longer than originally planned, and a number of people got seasick in transit; we were disappearing in the swells!

We landed off a small cove, transferred to a punga, and ferried to the beach for a wet landing. The beach we landed on was covered with sea lions, two families with one bull on each side of the beach with females and young ranging from small babies to two and three years old. A narrow five to six feet "no man's land" between the two families is where we aimed.

On the way in, we sighted several sea turtles; near the rocks, we saw some young sea lions playing with a sea turtle. Several sharks were just off the beach, patrolling for young sea lions; we did notice some with irregular tails. We were told that the older male sea lions chase the sharks and take bites out of them when they can, the sharks swim faster, but sometimes the lions get a bite or so.

After landing, we wiped out our feet, put on shoes, and walked the area. We were basically ignored by most of the sea lions; however, if anyone did get closer than a foot or so, the bull would start to bark, and that member of our group would retreat. There were about fifty to seventy-five sea lions in each family. As we walked the beach, we also had to be careful around the low-lying bushes because there were sea lions under them too, and if you got too close, you would hear a low growl. We sighted a hawk in the trees, then the hawk flew to the top of one of the signs and perched. We all had our pictures taken, couple by couple, within two to three feet of the hawk.

We progressed down the trail to another beach that had another set of families with huge bulls. We passed by them, being very aware of the low bushes and occupants, then climbed up an embankment to visit some land iguanas. We found two; they have established territories with just so many cacti. They eat the cactus flowers. Both iguanas were at least four feet long, brown and golden brown, and were, as with all of these animals, unafraid of humans or a group of humans. The guide found a number of fallen cactus flowers and created a path me to sit on a rock. The iguana followed the treat path to within a foot or so of me for some great "photo ops"!

We returned to sea lion beach and were picked up by Punga to return to the yacht for our snorkeling gear. After changing and gathering our gear, we jumped back into the punga to go to an excellent area to snorkel. Over the side into fifteen feet of crystal-clear water. We followed the shoreline to observe sharks (four to five feet long), parrot fish, puffer fish, groupers, starfish, redfish, yellow fish, blue fish, big fish, little fish, brave fish, and scared fish. He came upon another sea turtle and got his picture. A few sea lions thought it would be a good time to play in front of us, coming within a few feet under us and around us. Several iguanas on the shore and a Blue-footed booby posed also!

We spent another one and a half to two hours in the bay, then swam back to the yacht for lunch. Another excellent lunch on the boat, then the dreaded ride back. The sea had calmed, and everyone was grateful for that; we landed two hours later with everyone smiling and not heaving!

We boarded the bus back to the hotel, had a short siesta, and met to walk the town for our included supper in an area where the street was blocked off; tables set up in the street with local open-air restaurants serving food.

Again, we had pre-ordered coconut shrimp, lobster, or beef. Lynn and I ordered the shrimp and lobster. Both outstanding! The side dishes of rice and beans, pork and beans, French fries, and salad filled everyone to the gills! I saw other tables order Inca Cola, so I ordered one (It tastes like liquid bubble gum). Even though the meal was exceptional, the lure of gelato called out to many of us, and we stopped for a scoop on the way back to the hotel.

Wednesday, a "dry" day. Early breakfast, I love these breakfast buffets! Always include a variety of juices, yogurt, granola, some type of eggs, some meat, fritters or potatoes, many types of bread, and a variety of fruits.

The first stop was two crater-sized sinkholes created by the volcanoes; we circled both, about a half mile each in diameter and depth.

The next stop was a tortoise reserve. The first thing we needed to do was change our shoes for rubber boots (fire ants!), then we gathered in an area where we took pictures of ourselves in a tortoise shell. Then off to locate these land giants in the park. We found four of them in total, one female (You can tell by the smaller size and flattened shiny area on the back of the shell) and four males. Two of the males were pretty shy and retreated into their shells when we approached, but the largest was hungry, and our guide found some fallen passion fruit and created a path out from under the bushes. He slowly lumbered out, eating the fruits on the way, and posed for pictures eating and extending to reach the fruits.

The next stop was a cave or properly called a lava tube. A flight of steps down to see what a river of lava leaves behind. This was a very interesting geological formation, relatively smooth and dank, not a normal "cave." There was also a smaller one you had to crawl through; two of our group opted to do it, and we picked them up with the bus on the other side.

Lunch was a buffet at a resort; Lynn sang Karaoke with the guide and also posed on the saddle bar stools; I had the tequila!

After the food, we went to a coffee and sugar cane farm. One in our group rode the burro driving the cane crusher, Lynn fed the cane in. We were then given a tour of the processing of coffee beans. I helped with pounding the seeds, and Lynn helped with roasting. We progressed down to the sugar syrup still and sampled the alcohol, one straight and one flavored with anise. Potent and good!

One last stop was the senior center; We had received a request from this tour company to donate to this senior center. The deal was that they would match any donation to improve the lives of these seniors. There is no social security in this country, and previous donations were for the schools for the children, but another real need was for the folks at the other end of the spectrum, the older folks. This senior center is basically a daycare, someplace to go during the day when the rest of the family is off to work or school. It is completely voluntary, with no wages or salaries for anyone. Previous groups of this tour company had contributed ceiling fans and an air conditioner for the community room.

We were greeted, each of us, with a hug by a line of residents as we arrived. We were shown to a large open-air covered area. We were treated to a solo song by one of the residents, two native dances in costume by two other residents, and dancing. We were served iced coffee; we shared the treats we brought them. We then were treated to local band music, and we (Lynn, me, and two others from our group) danced with the old folks; an older man liked to dance with Lynn, and I danced with the oldest member, then another. Everyone then cleared the floor to listen to some more music; a resident then made a beeline for me to dance with her. No one else joined us on the floor, so we danced the entire dance in front of the crowd, my previous partner glaring at her the entire dance. We were able to get them all up for a final dance, where Lynn and I formed a conga line and finished the dance with everyone tired and laughing. A local dance group came to perform a couple of dances for the combined group; then the dance group left, the band started packing up, and we left with much applause and more hugs.

It was a really nice time, and they really appreciated the gifts and contributions. We walked the few blocks home, it was after eight, and we retired to our room for the night.

Thursday, 5:30 AM, we got up; at 6:15, we left for the forty-five-minute drive to the boat, loaded the punga to get to the boat, and settled in on the boat for breakfast. The two-plus hour boat ride to Bartolome Island was calm; we saw a shark fin in the distance and some sea rays flipping out of the water. We took a punga driven by the captain around the island, found a couple of penguins, saw some boobies dive into the water, and some cranes on the shore. We inspected the cooled lava on the shore, which indicated the waves of rock as it cooled. I had never seen black lava waves before.

We found a lagoon and snorkeled in another crystal-clear bay, seeing an assortment of turtles, sharks, lots of fish, more starfish and frigates, gulls, and those boobies.

We returned to the yacht, had another delicious lunch, and headed back to our base island. I bused home to rest, then went down to the harbor to watch the pelicans and sea lions beg for scraps and guts from the fishermen selling their catch and the people with heaping dishes of fresh seafood cooked on the spot.

A slow walk home looking into the shops and enjoying the night air. Our tour leaders treated us to cheese, beer, and wine, followed by pizza and ice cream. After another long day, we went back to our room.

Friday 8:00 AM in the lobby. This is our last full day on the islands; today, we are promised flamingos, boobies, and frigates. If the water is calm, we may dive on some hammerhead shark haunts.

Bus to port, punga to yacht, one-hour boat rides to North Seymour-Bachas Beach. It is mating season, and the male frigates are displaying their big red pouches under their beaks. We landed to walk the front portion of the island, the path rocky and very uneven. The walk weaved in and out of various nesting areas where the frigate was showing off.

There are two methods these frigate males attract the females, one is the size of their bright red pouch, and the other is building up to three nests. If the female doesn't like the pouch, the nests may attract her. We found some successful males with a family and others still trying. We found several land iguanas also and then came upon the blue-footed boobies.

The boobie males build their nest on the ground; it only consists of a few assorted small twigs. When the male sees a female, he starts a little marching dance with his head up. It is something like a slow march. It works; we found nests with females and young.

The last part of the walk was past more boobie nests, a sea lion colony, and great ocean views. Punga back to the yacht, get snorkeling gear, and punga back to a diving beach. We saw more fish, sharks, and one flamingo.

After snorkeling, we loaded up the yacht. Another delicious meal; the crew even shared some of their fish ceviche with me; these people know how to eat! We then headed to the area where the hammerheads hang out; upon arriving, the water was murky, and the ocean was not as calm as needed for snorkeling, so we headed back. (It was too dangerous to go in.)

The meal tonight was included, all fresh, perfectly prepared, and very generous in portions. Lynn had the beef, and I had the grilled shrimp, the best shrimp I have had in a long time! We had been introduced to plantain chips with a sour cream dip early and looked forward to this appetizer with every meal. Tonight was our last night on the island; luggage out tomorrow at 7:15, leaving at 7:30.

Saturday; We stopped at the market this morning; this is the people's market. Fresh beef and pork butchers on the spot, fish filleted, fresh chickens cleaned and ready for purchase. All the fruits and vegetables were available, a stall where food was prepared, and small shops selling clothes. Gas prices on the island are $1.48/gal regular, $1.02 for diesel. (Home prices are $3.89/gal regular, $4.09 for diesel)

It was fun to watch and mingle; we spent a half hour here, then off to the airport—bus, ferry, bus, and customs. Two-hour flight, we gathered luggage and boarded our bus to the hotel for a fifteen-minute check-in and luggage drop.

Then, a walking tour of Guayaquil.

We were first treated to Iguana Park. Iguanas were hanging in trees, under bushes, sitting next to benches, on rocks, walking in front of you, and just lounging. As in all of our experiences this week, all of the animals disregarded the presence of humans (except for the male sea lions protecting their females).

We were shown brightly colored classical Spanish buildings, beautiful government buildings, and a nice riverfront area. We got off the bus at Santa Anna Hill and "Las Pena's" traditional, bohemian neighborhood.

We walked the cobblestone streets, admired the old architecture, and learned that the front doors of their houses judged the families; the more ornate the wood was, the more affluent or important the family was. We'd see some very interesting paintings and building features.

Next was a one-kilometer hike on the riverfront, people-watching, park structures, banyan trees, and a gelato stop for gelato. The walk ended with an hour pirate ship cruise up and down the river with drinks and appetizers.

We took cabs to the restaurant for the last dinner in Guayaquil, walked to the hotel for a quick night's sleep at 3:45 AM wake-up, and luggage out at 4:5, and took the bus to the airport at 5:00.

Noah

The flights home were uneventful, boarding pass and luggage check-in, customs, finding the gate and waiting, disembarking, customs, getting check-in bags, finding the domestic flight gate, checking in bags, wait for the flight. The best part was that we arrived in Chicago one-half hour early, were able to get our luggage, and went out to catch our bus at the wrong place; we called the bus company and were told the loading zone was three blocks away!

We rushed to the loading area, we were really late, but the bus was still there! The couple taking the bus with us had told the driver, and she was waiting for us. We saw her get out of the bus and look and then get back into the bus, our hearts fell, but we still kept on going and yelling.

She came out of the bus again, saw us, rushed to us to help Lynn with her luggage, then came back to help me! Her name was Ernestine, we gave her a nice tip and wrote a letter to the company about how much we appreciated her, and Wisconsin Coach should recognize her.

We arrived home at 10:00 PM Sunday night; we picked up a pizza on the way home, ate, and went to bed. This was another great vacation.

Mother's Day 2013

As I have done for the last ten-plus years, I put on a banquet for Lynn, my mother, and my daughters. I prepared Muffalatas (from the French Quarter) chocolate crepes with cherries and chocolate syrup, shrimp, shrimp with goat cheese, and basil wrapped with prosciutto. I also wrapped pepperoni and cheese with basil and prosciutto for my daughters. A veggie tray, plantain chips with dip, German pretzels, a peach and avocado smoothie, and Camille brought a lemon meringue pie... The day went well, three-quarters of the food was eaten, and everyone helped with the clean-up, which was really appreciated!

My knees have progressively worsened; the Galapagos trip highlighted the need to address the problem. I had my annual review with my doctor in March and set the wheels in motion to address the knees. She (My MD) and that was interpreted as a follow–up to my hip replacement. Put in the request for consultation, so I called and then had to have her request it again, with x-rays to show progression.

This was scheduled as usual three months out; since then, it has been canceled and re-scheduled twice. (It is the VA!) On the third re-schedule in August, just before my next adventure, the hip was to be x-rayed again, and I was told to contact my primary doctor to again, re-schedule the knee x-rays at the same time. I did, and she did. I have not received verification of the new appointments for the x-rays and appointment with "ortho."

Noah

Last States West of the Mississippi

June; Monday, we left early (gasp!) We left at 6:30 AM.

23540 miles on the van.

It was overcast but not raining. We made good time out of the city, even with the rush hour traffic and construction.

Out of the State by ten thirty, our first stop was Pikes Peak State Park just south of Prairie Du Chen, WI. We stopped in Spill Ville at the Billy Clock Museum to see some magnificent hand-carved clocks. We then drove for over a hundred miles out to mid-northern Iowa to see the world's largest Cheeto, but it was Monday, and the restaurant bar where it is exhibited was closed. On to Fort Dodge to see the 10-foot wooden man reproduction but arrived an hour and a half late, so we just checked into the motel for the night. The beef brisket and pulled pork for dinner were exceptional, we settled in for the night. Hopefully, we will be out of Iowa tomorrow and actually see more of the offerings.

Day Two, 24003

I had a great night's sleep; the Best Western had a large breakfast room and a good selection of food.

We drove East (yes, East) to Brandon, Iowa, for the world's biggest fry pan, then off to Gladbrook, the home of the Matchstick Marvels Museum. We got there a little after ten-thirty in the morning and found that it didn't open until one in the afternoon. We expressed our plight to the city clerk and left. As we approached our car, she came up to us and let us know that she had called the mayor, and that he would be at the museum within the next ten minutes to let us in and give us a personal tour. True to his word, he was there. (Midwest at its' best!)

He opened up the place and let us roam around; we were so impressed. There was a matchstick Notre Dame, the battleship Iowa, the governor's mansion, an SR22 spy plane, a dinosaur, a three-masted ship, a Conestoga wagon, the White House, and the World Trade Center (they had to remove the ceiling tiles for the towers.) Some of his works are at the Smithsonian Museum, others at Ripley's Believe It or Not Museum. We did take several pictures, the twin towers were taller than me, and the White House was a good eight feet wide to give you some perspective. We watched a short video about the artist and bought a small kit so I can try my hand at it next winter.

The next stop was Indianola for the Hot Air Balloon Museum. The museum was smaller than we anticipated but provided a good history of ballooning along with a variety of baskets and materials to observe up close and personal.

We are heading west again, stopping by Stanton to view and take pictures of their two unique water towers; one is a teacup and saucer (just on the southern tip of town) the other is a coffee pot. This one is located in a cemetery! Oh, by the way, this was Mrs. Olson's hometown, the actress and the spokesperson for Folgers's coffee in the '70s.

That was enough for Iowa; we headed north to Omaha, Nebraska, to find a motel and supper, a new state, and more stuff to see! We had an address of the Bohemian Café listed as one of Bon Appétit Magazines as one of the top ten family-owned restaurants. We got there late afternoon to discover that they are closed on Tuesdays! I looked up a motel and called it a night; Village Inn was within walking distance; another day was done; at least we were now in Nebraska!

Day three, 24434

We went downtown to find Sapp Brother's coffee display pot. The Garmin got confused, and the streets jumped out of order, so we went on to Boy's Town. We had the abbreviated tour and observed the world's largest ball of stamps.

We then headed down to Gretna to see the Lighthouse. (Nebraska is landlocked) In just about 8 miles west of Gretna, we found it, a full-sized lighthouse on the edge of a small artificial lake. Linoma, the name of the small town where it is, is lettered on the side. West to Hastings, where we visited the Hastings Museum, which is the home of Kool-Aid. General Foods bought Kool-Aid, and the son of the buyer designed three different logos for the product; all were displayed. Exciting history, an actual kit for a Kool-Aid stand was sold along with all types of sales paraphernalia. The museum also had an impressive display of pistols and weapons, including the actual arrow that pinned two brothers, the Martins (who both survived), during an Indian attack.

On returning to the freeway, we had to stop by the travel center to observe the Kool-Aid man footprints.

We continued West past Kearny under the impressive and ornate Archway Monument over Highway 80. It can be seen for miles, especially in this very flat and rolling land, that land remains indistinctive for mile after mile.

North Platte, our last town for the day, included The Golden Spike Tower, which provides a bird's eye view of the largest staging train yard in the world, along with a small museum. We found a swimming pool shaped like the State of Nebraska, found two muffler men at the municipal building, and stopped in at the Fort Cody trading post, learning interesting facts about Buffalo Bill Cody.

We found our motel, checked in, and then off to a local eatery Whiskey Creek for a great steak dinner. Another long day; we will be leaving this state sometime tomorrow!

1. 24797

We both woke up early, had breakfast at the motel, and were on the road by 7:00 AM!

I had gassed up the night before, so we were right on the road.

Educating Noah...Travelin'

Our first stop was to be Car Hedge in Alliance, Nebraska. It was a good three-hour drive, and for most of it, we were the only car on the road. We did see a lot of wild turkeys crossing the road, and in the pastures, we saw deer, horses with folds, cattle with calves, lots of calves, and many very "spunky." This was also our first experience with tumbleweeds crossing in front of the car and into the car as we progressed. We were able to stop three-quarters of the way at a gas station for a potty break and some cold tea.

Car Hedge is on the northern outskirts of town; most of the cars are painted light grey, half buried in the ground, with a few on top. Most of the cars were the 1950s and '60s Cadillacs, Desoto, and other large vehicles, about fifteen to twenty cars in total. Quite odd or unique. This was very similar to the Cadillac and VW ranches in Texas with a twist of being organized like Stone Hedge in England. There was very little graffiti here, contrary to Texas, and there was a snack shop here. Many trains were observed heading to North Platte, all with over one hundred cars, most filled with coal.

We crossed the time zone line, so we also gained an hour. We headed south to Chimney Rock. I visited the visitor's center and observed many signs warning tourists not to leave the path and that rattlesnakes were in the area and to listen and look for them.

Off to Wyoming, on the Super, the speed is 75, set the cruise on 80, and away we went; our average gas mileage so far is 24 miles per gallon; super is cheaper in Nebraska than regular with ethanol; regular gas is $3.74 and $3.53 for super per gallon, so we ran the super! Lynn had to check out the souvenir shop before leaving!

Through Cheyenne, then directly south to Colorado. In Boulder, we toured the Celestial Seasonings tea company. The tour was extensive; we were able to sample several teas, both hot and cold.

Very nice company, with courteous sales staff and an extensive gift shop. Their lines of sleep-assist/caffeine-free teas are extensive.

The tea leaves are sent to Germany and put into a liquid CO2 bath, which extracts the caffeine but leaves all of the flavors intact. The most popular teas in the world are black, green, and peppermint in that order, and their caffeine content is in that order also.

We called a specialty restaurant Lynn wanted to visit; they were only open mornings and afternoons till four. It was three fifteen when we called, so off to the mountains we went.

We finally located the highway to go south, fighting the rush hour traffic. Going through the mountains at sixty-five-seventy was exhilarating, and we were able to catch a few shots of the mountains as we progressed. But it was getting late, and we needed to call it a day; found a town big enough for motels and restaurants, excited to find exactly what we needed, and called it a day!

Friday, Day 5

25317

We were on the road again at 7 AM, driving through the Rocky Mountains, lots of tunnels, beautiful sights, winding roads, and courteous drivers. Everyone pulls to the right and in the passing lane or left lane when passing or attempting to pass. There are scattered homes built into the sides of the mountain. Our first stop was Vail, Colorado. It reminded me of Carmel, California. Very up-scale, beautiful, and luxurious. Even the town's McDonalds and Walgreens had stone and glass buildings. All the condos were "high-end," expensive looking, and classy. We drove to the quaint streets and took pictures of one of the ruins, the buildings, and the streets. We felt out of place, took our pictures, and left. We finished leaving the mountains and crossed into Utah. It's 11:15; the land is parched, with just brown cliffs in the background and no signs of people except those on the road.

We opted to skip seeing the Arch in Moab, it is on all of the license plates, we have seen it on postcards and documentaries, and it would take up another three hours to see, so no Arch.

On the way to Salt Lake City, we saw three antelopes, a number of cattle being herded by horseback cowboys, and small corrals where cattle were being loaded onto trucks. We also saw a sign on the highway warning to watch for eagles on the road. Salt Lake City was the next stop. We wanted to stop by the Mormon compound to see the square, church, and Tabernacle. We saw the chapel, the visitor's center, the library, and the office building. Everything was impeccably clean; the people were nice and easily answered all of our questions. Then we stopped at their genealogy center, where we both looked up information on some of our family. They were really helpful. We got local directions and off to the Great Salt Lake!

We found a parking lot and hoofed it out a quarter mile (the lake is low) to put my tootsies in the water; as I entered the water, I sank more and more into the silty grayish salty sand, so after only a few steps, my feet were under the mud and the water was only a little more up over my ankles. That was enough; my feet were now covered with silty salt sand, along with my shoes. We washed our feet with the drinking water we had left and changed our shoes. It was late, and we needed to stop for the night.

We drove for an hour and found a small-town advertising a place to stay and a restaurant. We followed a pickup with a trailer on the dirt road for a mile, then he turned off, and we could see! We preceded another mile, and a town was still in sight; the road turned right, and I could see a stop sign ahead, so hope arrived. The stop sign was for a road even less used. We were now over two miles out of our way, so I opted for another road that went up by the railroad tracks. This one did go parallel with the tracks but was of sharp stone and dirt. I could see propane tanks on the horizon, so we continued on the road only to find ruts much deeper and, in spots, much softer sand. We progressed about an hour with other hopeful signs always leaving to dead ends. Dusk was coming on quickly, and then, one last hope was a truck going across our path a mile in front of us. It was the end of the road, and there was a paved road at the end.

We were able to hook up with the highway, and it was an hour to Wendover. We opted for that; the land is very desolate and grayish-white; we saw many places where the names of people were outlined in rock, similar to when we entered California on ROUTE 66.

As we arrived at the Wendover exits, I saw an exit for the Bonneville Salt Flats, so I made a mental note to see that next morning. It was very late, the first motel was full, and a Mustang car club had booked the entire motel. We did find a Days Inn down the road, checked in, went down the road for a quick bite to eat before returning to the motel exhausted.

Saturday, day six, 25912

The first stop after breakfast was the Bonneville Salt Flats; the motel manager said it was only ten minutes away, and he was right to the minute. No real structures to see, just the "flats" that go on for miles, with mountains in the background. There are stretches of soft sand and signs warning those that venture out with their various vehicles.

The next stop was Reno. This was a long stretch of scrubland. No animals, very few dwellings, but we did see a number of dust devils. After four hours of driving, we pulled over to Winnemucca for lunch. We had seen an increasing amount of motorcycles on the road, and here we found out why this was "Run-A-Mucca" weekend, an annual motorcycle rally event. Bikes all over the place reminded us a little of the Sturgis Rally we attended when we still had the bike. It took another three hours to reach Reno: a little Vegas, gaudy downtown, lots of people, beggars on the street. We took a slow ride down Virginia Street. Then headed for Lake Tahoe.

We stopped at a candy shop to take a picture of a bigger-than-life prospector and get directions, then off to an extremely scenic ride around the lake on the Nevada side. Again, gold was running in the street, and the cost of living was reflected by the price of gas here at $4.48 per gallon for regular. We took pictures at several scenic turn-offs and headed east to find a place for the night. I located a motel and crashed for the night.

Sunday Day 7 26397 Left At 0730

Filled up at an ARCO gas station. I had trouble starting the pump, went inside, and discovered that only cash or a debit card would be accepted, no credit cards. I then used my backup debit card and agreed to the thirty-five-cent processing fee! We were on our way south, more desolation, few homes, very small towns, most without amenities. We rounded Walker Lake. No buildings on the lake, only one boat launch that we could see, only a few people in campers by the beach, no one fishing, no recreational vehicles on the water. It was in the 60's and on a weekend. We thought that was strange. Next up was an extensive U.S. Army Depot and Navy Training facility. Supposedly this was a range where the pilots trained on the bombers.

We saw many bunkers on many acres, again, very few people and relatively no activity. There were signs of driving with your lights on throughout this stretch; we complied and soon found out why.

The land was so flat that the road looked wet, and a haze seemed to hide oncoming traffic. Having the lights on made it easier to see traffic coming at you; this was demonstrated when suddenly, a non-compliant driver's car appeared suddenly. At seventy to eighty miles an hour, things happen really fast, and although traffic was really light, the highway does mesmerize you, and you get a little complacent.

Four hours of driving left us at Tonopah, Nevada. We filled up with lunch and also gas for the car. We asked the waitress for directions to Scottie's Castle in Death Valley, just over the California, Nevada border; she complied and said it was worth the visit and only about a two-hour drive.

On the last turn to go to the castle, we saw a sign on the road stating that the attraction was closed. (We found out later that there had been a fire at the castle, and they were still rebuilding the damaged areas before opening up for the season) We turned around and continued to Pahrump, Nevada, for the end of the day. Since we missed the castle, we stopped at a little town north of Pahrump to check out the "World's Best Jerky." We tried all the samples; they were very good, and we bought some bison jerky, dried mango, and toffee peanuts. We arrived at our final destination for the day at 15:10, their time, had the car oil changed (it was 500 miles past due), found a car wash, and scrubbed down the car! The outside was covered, full of dead bug carcasses.

We checked into the motel, went out for supper, contacted friends and relatives to inform them of our itinerary, and took the time for a nice swim in the pool and an early night off the road.

Monday, Day 8; No Mileage Taken

We located the lot we bought for investment eight years ago, for $60K, now worth $15K due to the devaluation of housing in Nevada and Florida. It was still there, with no real changes; I visited with my brother Ted and his wife Carol; His house is relatively easy to find, and you turn at the Chicken Ranch Brothel and drive to the end of the street. No, I didn't stop; I did last time we visited with my wife and her girlfriend just to see the inside. Very nice and clean, not much different than a bar with food; I guess you could say a bar "with privileges." I understand the basic rate is $300.00, and everything is a la carte from there. The food is good, reasonable; the décor is easy on the eyes.

I did take a photo of the outside. We visited with Ted and Carol for a couple of hours, caught up on family things, had a nice lunch, and then left for Vegas to visit friends there.

It took about an hour's drive to Vegas and another fifteen to twenty minutes to locate their house, and spent the balance of the afternoon visiting with them; they fed us too! So, the food today was free! We left their home at seven P.M. to find a motel in Boulder, Nevada. We checked into a local motel, but the internet connection did not work with their password, so I just documented the day's activity, took a shower, and relaxed with my wife. Tomorrow is Kingman Az. to visit a cousin, then Scottsdale to visit another cousin.

Tuesday, Day 9, 26887

We left for my cousin's house in Kingman, Az. An extremely enjoyable visit with him and his wife for five hours, a huge Philippine banquet for lunch, left late and stuffed. We drove the three hours to Scottsdale, Az. to visit another cousin, again, a very entertaining visit, out for food at a unique Mexican Restaurant, very enjoyable. Left for our reserved motel and crashed for the night.

We have not adjusted our watches or the clock in the car. We got into the motel last night a little after 10;30. It was after midnight "our "time, so we slept till 8 AM today. This is the best La Quinta motel we have stayed in; immaculate, friendly staff, and the beds are perfect. Complete morning breakfast in a well-laid-out breakfast area, patrolled by staff for cleanliness and assistance. I left at 10;30 local time and drove the two hours to Tucson. We wanted to try the cheese crisps recommended by the food guide, so I ordered the loaded one. Lynn ordered plain cheese. These were listed as appetizers, but when served, they were a full fourteen inches in circumference, and mine was heaped with onions, peppers, mushrooms, and squash. I will definitely make these at home for lunch; I will start with a light deep fry of a flour tortilla covered with Monterey Jack and Colby cheese! Simple and tasty!!

We were only ten minutes to my father-in-law's place; here, we settled until leaving Friday AM on our trip back to Wisconsin. We don't like to stay longer, because people like fish, get old, stale, and smelly after staying too long!

Friday Morning, Day 10; 27313,

0730; We hope to make Roswell, New Mexico, our destination. Said "Goodbye" to the folks; he looks good for ninety-two! He still has trouble with his left hand and carpal tunnel, so I promised to send him a set of utensils to help. It took us two and a half hours to cross into New Mexico, saw many border patrols, and even went through a checkpoint. We had little wait; however, the trucks were backed up going out of New Mexico with twenty-three trucks waiting on the highway. Our lunch was in Las Cruces for a recommended stuffed sopaipillas (recommended by our "500 places you must eat" book). We found the dish "okay."

I took pictures of the world's largest Chili pepper, went past the White Sands Missile Range, a number of pecan groves, and some areas where the hills look like they are snow-covered, only to realize it is white sand. We also saw a junkyard dinosaur, a roadrunner, and the world's largest pistachio in Alamogordo. We did pull off the road for ice cream and tourist trap shops to start buying Christmas gifts for each other and family, which made Lynn very happy, and emptied my wallet more so I was more balanced!

I made it to Roswell, checked in to the motel, toured the city, and took some pictures of the McDonalds shaped like a flying saucer and some various aliens in town. There were few stores open on Main Street, it was the Friday after Memorial Day weekend, and it was after 1800. (6 PM for those not used to military time yet!)

We found an open store and walked in, and talked to the owner. I asked how the last recession had affected business, and he said since the beginning of the recession, sales have gone up, renewed interest in the parks and natural wonders was being felt in that families that couldn't afford the theme parks and expensive commercial attractions but could afford going to the parks and small trinket stores.

This brought to mind the sequestration we are in and President Obama closing down White House tours and many park services. It seems this would impact the public the most, and I feel this tactic of politics to be especially sleazy. We had a bite to eat, monitored the weather (another tornado just went through Oklahoma,) and settled in for the night.

Saturday, Day 11, 27799

I had monitored the news channels the night before to preclude any difficulties; there had been some tornado and wildfire activities in a number of states we were going through. There were reports of wildfires in New Mexico, and we decided to re-route our journey to avoid any difficulty traveling or getting in the way of emergency personnel, so we ascended the route to Nebraska through the Texas panhandle and Oklahoma. The land is desolated, brown, and blah. Very few buildings, little traffic, just flat dry land with a haze. (We put our lights on!)

After a few hours, we came upon a number of wind turbines on some low hills, but none of them were turning. A few cows and a couple of horses could be seen once in a while, but still no buildings or signs of civilized life outside the fences on both sides of the road. (Nothing to get excited about, just wood posts and barbed wire.)

Santa Rose, we crossed our previous path of Route 66 and the deep blue hole; we stopped at a truck stop to stretch, relieve, and gas up before setting out for another hour on the road before lunch.

Observed more trains, these empty cattle cars, came across several cattle yards, stock yards as far as you could see both sides of the road filled with cattle being prepared to be shipped. Very dusty and odiferous.

Dalhart, Texas, Pee Yew!

Some fields are green now, very few, but those that are green are irrigated and sprinkled. We passed through Stratford, Texas, the pheasant capital of Texas (no, we did not see any!) Off to Oklahoma panhandle, dry, small oil wells, high winds, lots of dust, nothing to note.

Our stop today is Dodge City, Kansas. We arrived late, a wrestling convention was being held, and the first three motels we tried needed rooms. We did call ahead and found one room at a Comfort Inn. We checked in, drove over to Boot Hill, and explored the replica town and buildings; tired and hungry, we inquired about a restaurant and referred to one just up the road. I had a very nice meal, experienced a moonshine drink, and got the location of where to buy it. I enjoyed the meal, found the liquor store, bought a mason jar of hooch for myself and the two sons-in-law for Father's Day, went back to the motel, and checked in for the night.

Sunday Day 12; 28284

Passed by a number of huge wind farms, only half of the turbines were turning. Very light traffic, the land is getting significantly greener, more cattle, horses, buildings, and crops on both sides of the road, more small oil wells and storage tanks, grain elevators every ten to fifteen miles, the small towns neater and kept up better now.

Our first stop this morning was Lucas, Kansas, the home of the Garden of Eden. Just before Lucas, a beautiful lake appeared; the blue of the lake took both of our breaths away; what a contrast from the last few days!

The Garden of Eden is a limestone home and tourist attraction designed and built by one man. Lots of concrete figurines, a mausoleum, an arbor, and electricity were the first in Kansas. A great example of early folk art, the man portrayed a number of biblical themes, including Adam and Eve, Cain and Able, along with storks with lights in their mouths (Most babies are born at night) and edicts regarding the common person.

Educating Noah...Travelin'

We toured the property and watched a short film; the Kohler Foundation reconditioned the entire house and then turned it back over to the city to maintain. The one notable item was that the original owner designed a mausoleum for his wife to join him upon death on the property. The town upon her death, forced the relatives to bury the wife in the town cemetery. After a few days, the relatives and friends dug up the coffin, paraded it down Main Street, placed it in the mausoleum, and then sealed it up with concrete. Issue done and over with. She remains in the mausoleum to date.

As we progressed to our next sight in Kansas, we observed the limestone fence posts; the farther away from Lucas, the fewer limestone fence posts; however, some were observed a hundred miles away. Just before the World's Largest Ball of Twine, we stopped at a combination sporting goods store, restaurant, and gas station. Lots of cars outside and most of the booths are full of people.

We ordered the sandwiches and were told the food would come out and pay when we left. The sandwiches were hot, the condiments fresh, and when we had finished, we went to the register, told the cashier what we had, and were charged accordingly. All on the honor system and very nice; what a great experience!

The ball of twine is the central draw of Cawker. It is right on Main Street, covered by a small shelter. Frank Stoeber made it of sisal twine. In 1988, the circumference was 40 feet 3 inches, weighing 17,886 pounds.

Our next stop was the largest collection of mechanical working mini sculptures. The museum or showplace was closed, only open Wednesday thru Saturday from 1300 to 1800 and by appointment. However, we did stop at the visitor's center just a couple blocks from the showplace. The center had a good variety of local handicrafts, which let Lynn shop and purchase more Christmas gifts. It also had three examples of the mini sculptures that were on display and working, including a flying duck with wings and feet moving, a man riding a bicycle, and a woman churning butter next to a guy working on a still.

Just outside Maryville, we saw a police car on the side of the road where several buildings were turned over. Several foundations exposed, pieces of siding scattered over at least an acre, and this may have been a result of recent tornados both here in Kansas and Oklahoma. A little scary, it was very calm, now unnerving!

We are seeing a lot of brick houses, much more than wood ones. Along the highway, the houses are neat with neat and kept yards. We made it to our stop in St. Joseph, MO. By 5:30. As usual, we were both exhausted. We checked into the motel, filled the car, grabbed a bite to eat, and went in for the night.

Monday day 13;28742

We left for a final leg of travel; we left at 7:15.

It took only two and a half hours to cross the upper state of Missouri. We entered Illinois and stopped to stretch. On the road for four hours or so for lunch and then re-evaluate whether to push on and finish today or stay in Illinois for the night and finish tomorrow.

At lunch, I popped the question; Lynn knew I really wanted to finish for the day at home, so she agreed, as long as we stopped in Wisconsin for a nice supper.

In East Troy, we did at a great restaurant called the Gristmill. We arrived home from our journey at 7:30. We Took in the minimum amount of luggage and crashed for the night!

Facts:

Total mileage: 5769

Average mileage: 23 miles per gallon

Gas costs: $934.34

Educating Noah…Travelin'

Motel costs: $974.35

Food costs: $607.44

Noah

Everything happens for a reason, and I am stepping up my weight loss attempts to seriously lose more weight. I devote two days a week to the gym when I absolutely can, one hour working out on the weight machines, one hour on a slider (low impact on my knees), and an hour in the pool, either swimming or exercising my legs and hips.

I finally got to see the ortho specialist. He did give me a prednisone shot in both knees. It was great for about ten days but then seemed to wear off. I agreed with him that we should have a follow-up in three months.

I am working twelve hours a week now, continuing to go to the gym twice a week. I have also been asked to assist in teaching new employees about proper body mechanics and company policy. I agreed but also asked that when I return from our next adventure, to be used as an occasional employee only rather than be scheduled weekly with the same patient.

We joined our motorcycle group on a weekend trip to the quad cities.

We followed the bikes and joined them at the various stops visiting pre-arranged attractions, including a preserved village around the John Deere homestead. An armory was explored in the quad cities on a military installation. I had a great dinner, then joined the rest of the group for conversation and swimming in the motel pool.

The next day nothing was scheduled before lunch, so we led a ride to the Archeology Antique from a currently popular T.V. show. As with the pawnshop (from the T.V. series Pawn Stars) we saw in Las Vegas, the store was much smaller than portrayed, and a lot of exaggeration is employed.

Scandinavian Summer Trip

AUGUST 2013

Saturday and Sunday 08-17/18

Leave on the bus to O'Hare, on time, no difficulty with luggage check, and zipped through security. We easily found our gate and started the sit-and-wait routine. SAS Airline, 3, 4, 3 seat patterns, crowded and uncomfortable, nine-hour non-stop flight to Stockholm. Cleared customs and got bags, loaded bus for a 5-hour tour. Since Stockholm is a collection of fourteen islands, many bridges need to be crossed, lots of bicycles need to be watched for, and many people on foot.

The Stockholm city hall is where the Nobel Prize banquet is held. We toured the building; a Blue Room where the banquet is held has no blue in it, various halls and chambers, including a room that had gold covering the walls. Everyone gasped when they entered. The building is less than 100 years old and designed to look older. There is a depiction of mother earth (with big feet and big arms) in the gold room, along with various other pictures portraying various historical events.

The next stop was the Vasa Museum. This is a museum built around a 17th-century ship that sank on its maiden voyage just outside of the harbor. The 300-year-old ship was massive, very well preserved, very ornate, and worth the stop. This was the ship that the Black Pearl of Johnny Depp's Pirates of the Caribbean movies was modeled after. We grabbed a bite to eat at the cafeteria and were

Noah

introduced to our first price shock in Scandinavia; two small drinks and a shrimp salad to share were over $30.00 U.S.

A drive through Old Town (one of the world's best-preserved medieval centers, filled with narrow alleys and crooked houses) to acquaint us with the sites available and landmarks to navigate by on our next two free days in this city ended with dropping us off at the hotel that was to be our home for a few days. We unpacked, met everyone for Hors D Oeuvres and drinks, and went to bed.

The tour guide provided this information during the tour; there is a 29% tax rate on pay to a limit, then the percentage increases. There is a 25% VAT tax on everything but food, an eighteen-month maternity leave when a woman gets pregnant, nine months for her, and nine months for the father. This can be used in parts till the child reaches the age of eight and can be used more by them. It depends on the couple. Everyone starts with five weeks of vacation per year.

Monday, big continental breakfast and took a walk to the Royal Canal tours. An hour tour narrated in English, slowly passing past the major attractions of the city on the various islands. After the tour, we rushed to observe the daily noon changing of the guard. This was a lot of pomp and stance, taking almost an hour; it was interesting but tedious. Off to a church where the world's largest wooden statue of St. George kills a dragon. Pictures, visit shops, and grab a European hot dog and gelato for lunch.

Rested up, then tour the Royal Treasury, Royal Armory, and the coin museum. I walked back to the hotel, napped Hors D' Oeuvres and wine, then walked to the Gondlen restaurant tower to take pictures of the sunset over the city and end the day.

Tuesday, finally caught up on sleep and jet lag. Another great breakfast, Europe and South America offer breakfasts that rival cruise ships! There are always fresh fruits, meats, cheeses, fish, eggs, bread, cereals, milk, juices, and coffee. I can go on, but it can only be described as bountiful. I talked with the concierge regarding directions, and a group of six of us took off to the ferry to Djurgarden and discovered Skansen (the world's oldest 75 acres open–air museum) on a close island. Costumed guides stroll the park, reconstructed cottages and building from the past, farms with animals, a zoo where you walk inside a type of monkey cage, an extensive aquarium, specialized museums (Tobacco and match museum, and biological museum), specialty cafes, and restaurants. There were also extensive green areas, ponds, and a small carnival. The park is perfectly clean, and the guides and employees are helpful. We spent over four hours exploring about three-quarters of the park.

We decided to end the adventure, explored the souvenir shop, took the ferry back to the mainland and our hotel, and rested for an hour.

We then took the subway into Kungsbror, the heart of town, and walked a quarter mile to the Nordic Sea Hotel, the Absolute Vodka Ice Bar. We paid the equivalent of thirty dollars each for entrance and one drink per person. We were given a parka with hood and gloves, accompanied through a series of doors, and entered the bar. It is at 0 degrees. Everything is ice, the walls, the bar, the tables, and the benches. Your drink is served in a glass made completely of ice, and you are advised to wear your gloves to drink. We took pictures of one another posing in the bar and finished our drinks; I even ate part of my glass to say I did! It was not uncomfortable; cushions were on the ice benches for those who wanted to sit. After about fifteen minutes, we finished our drinks and left to take the subway back to the hotel; this was during rush hour, but everything was orderly, clean, and no pushing or shoving! We changed to join the group for a dinner of fish or steak at a nearby restaurant. (Great meals!)

Wednesday

I packed for the flight out, walked the city and canals, loaded on the bus to the airport, checked in, and flew to Amsterdam, Holland. Upon arriving, the hotel kept the hospitality suite open for us, including appetizers, with beer and wine; an exchange student that a member had hosted gave us a little brief on the city and customs of the country when the rooms were ready; we settled in for a busy day tomorrow.

Thursday

The first activity is a tour bus for a five-hour tour of Amsterdam, Holland, and the countryside. We saw a lot of bicycles; 30% of the population takes bikes to work. Drove out to a cheese factory, provided a lecture on cheese, and sampled more than 20 different types of cheese, all good! In another building, they had examples of wooden shoes in various sizes, they were comfortable, and I did a little soft (?) shoe dance for the others in the group!

After the cheese factory, we drove to Edam, Holland, for a stroll through a quaint little town having examples of cheese and chocolate, canals, and dikes. The last stop on the tour before heading home was a windmill village, with numerous windmills that have been restored in one area.

On the way back to the hotel, the tour guide told us that in Amsterdam, cars are closely monitored. Traffic cameras record any speed over the limit; even 2-3 kilometers per hour over the limit generates a fine (supposedly millions of Euros per year). The parking costs four euros per hour (a little over $5.00 US);

The coffee shops are places where you buy hashish and marijuana paraphernalia and supplies. There are more bikes in Copenhagen than people; our guide has had fourteen bikes stolen (yes, they were locked), and the license plates of her car. The police do not respond to "minor" thefts but will make out a report. (In Italy, pick-pockets are not persecuted unless the theft exceeds 500 Euros). The bikes have the right of way, and you may be run over if you stand in the bike lane; no regard for pedestrians in the bike lane, and if you are getting off a bus, make sure you look both ways for the bikes, even when you have the walk indicator, you must always check the bike lane when crossing, because it does not apply to the bikes! It is relatively safe in the city, including the red-light district, except between 0300 and 0700.

Upon returning to the hotel after the bus tour, we walked two blocks to the Blue Line canal tours and took the city canal tour. A narration of the different districts was included, we saw most of the city from the water, and highlights of the city were pointed out, with an impressive fish-eye display of buildings, boats, and areas. A lot of the history of the city was explained, and facts were given, including that most of the commercial warehouses have now been converted into apartments, the apartments are very small (This is in European standards, so it is really small), and usually only big enough for one person. Fifty percent of the population is older than 30, 50% live alone, and only 15% have kids. Six hundred thousand bikes; the canals are all freshwater; pumps are run 24/7 to maintain water levels, no mosquitoes because there is no standing water in the canals.

We headed back to the hotel for happy hour, grabbed a bite to eat, and then started down to the Red-light district to check it out. The hike was much farther than anyone anticipated; it turned out to be more than a kilometer, probably a mile! As we crossed the canals toward the center of the city, the roads became narrower, and the "coffee" shops and adult shops became more prolific. As we entered the "zone," the picture glass doors/windows with the girls behind them in bikinis slow dancing and attempting to stop men and offer their services.

At seven thirty, more than half of the windows were empty; I inquired and was told those girls were "busy." Wow, it was still early evening! In that I was in a group of women, I did not ask one of the girls the going price for services.

After walking a number of side streets, I started to feel old and dirty; the women in the group had enough also, so we headed for home. Lots of people on the streets, walking and bike riding, the electric trolleys all at least half full, the bikes have small lights, and I did forget once crossing in a crosswalk and saw a bike out of the corner of my eye and scrambled out of the way, it was the fastest I moved all day! We had left the hotel at 7:30; we were back by 10:00; for that time, it seemed we had walked for ten miles! And probably was!!

Friday

After breakfast, we headed out to the Rijks Museum, the Museum of the Netherlands. We wanted to get there before the cruise ship crowds, and it was only a few blocks from the hotel. We did beat the crowd, got our tickets, and visit most of the exhibits in about three hours. We had a pass for the Hop-on, hop-off canal boats, so we took them to the flower district. We got off, and we were within a block of the two-block-long collection of any bulb flower you could imagine! The district was easily walkable; we even explored another cheese shop for samples and inquiries on brown cheese. After a fun visual experience, we continued to a city flea market to see what would be offered. It was surprising how many vendors were offering bicycle locks; almost every vendor had a selection! All the prices were slightly lower than the retail stores, which is high for Americans. We were tired, hopped on another canal boat, and enjoyed a ride to the hotel—drinks and hors-d'oeuvres, then off to bed.

Saturday

I left the hotel at 7 AM to go to the airport. After arriving at the airport, we suffered through the normal "rig-a-marro," including now stopping at a kiosk and pre-registering for luggage tags. (Half of the group still had problems).

I took a bus from the airport to the ship for our cruise and boarded; the process was quick and efficient. We found our room, found the deck with food, had a bite, waited for our luggage, and unpacked for the next week's cruise.

Sunday

The first day on the ship. I had a great omelet and sausage for breakfast. The first tour started at 10:00.

For the tour of Oslo, we had pre-bought a package that had been negotiated by our Vagabond leader Bob Spindell, having a tour covering the highlights of each port for a fantastic price! The tour covered a city tour, a huge preserved park, a ski jump with a great city view, the Kon Tiki Museum, the opera house, and a harbor tour. I returned to the ship, had a late snack, sunbathing on the deck, and prepared for the formal dinner. There was a nice selection on the menu; we talked for a bit, took in the variety show, and called it a day.

Monday

Stavanger, Norway. We didn't dock until late morning, so we joined in on a trivia game at a lounge. We disembarked about 1130 and were taken by bus to visit one of the oldest churches in Norway.

We also visited the Three Swords monument dedicated to the last battle of Norway; it is said that the bay was red with blood due to all the men killed in battle. We passed long houses built in 800 A.D., long low houses with thatched roofs. The animals were housed with the people; the richer you were, the more animals in the house, the warmer it was, and, of course, even more odiferous, thus the phrase, "stinking rich." Saturday, translated to Norwegian, is wash day for both people and clothes. We then proceeded back to the harbor with juicier facts about Norway, including oil being the biggest export (Government keeps the profits to guarantee social programs). Norway is the biggest exporter of salmon in the world, and in just this city, there are eight culinary institutes; Stavanger is the culinary capital of Norway. The cost of living in Norway is 3Xs that of the U.S.; houses start at $600,000 US; it takes two incomes to buy a home, five weeks of vacation per year, 18 months of maternity leave, and 50 % of the wage when you retire at 67. A new car here is retail price plus 100% tariff plus 25% tax.

In the winter, there is up to four hours of sunlight, the summer, sixteen hours of sun. Norwegians, including the kids, are big on outdoor activities, hiking, skiing, and camping. We had a walking tour of the preserved houses upon returning to the city. It was very clean, and the houses are passed down from generation to generation; if one does come on the market, it is instantly snapped up with a price tag of over a million.

We explored a local flea market in the harbor after the bus tour; no real bargains, and even at those prices, the vendors would not bargain with me significantly. As we approached the ship, we got a close-up view of a number of jellyfish. I got some really good shots of them coming up from the bottom and opening up.

Back on the boat, a cocktail party by Vagabonds, an excellent meal including escargot in garlic butter, perfectly prepared fish, and always a good dessert. Music Trivia, Latin Fiesta, 50's-60's Rock and Roll night, bed by midnight.

Tuesday

The town of Alesund. This is the Art Nouveau city; the whole town burned to the ground in the early 1900s, with 10,000 homeless Norwegians. The tour bus took us to the peak of Mount Aksla to view the town below and the magnificent fjord. After an hour of looking around, we were off to visit a lighthouse and bought a local thick pancake and brown sugar for a snack. (Delicious!) Then through tunnels and bridges (this city consists of 7 islands) to the Borgund Stone Church, this is the only marble church in Norway, with the oldest parts dating back to 1250 A.D. On the trip back to the ship, we observed crab fishermen pulling and rebaiting traps.

I asked about the construction of the sod-roofed houses; after the boards, a layer of birch bark is laid, then dirt and seeded with wild grass. These roofs are cool in the summer and warm in the winter. In the town, the roofs are now fired ceramic high gloss black and are now being replaced by PVC half rounds, painted/powder coated gloss black.

Back on the ship, another excellent dinner, trivia with new friends, and a lounge show.

Wednesday

The most picturesque stop of the entire vacation is Geiranger, Norway. The bus tour was later, so we toured the town on our own. We bought a few souvenirs, looked at tanned reindeer hides, and tasted one of the best things I have ever had. It is called brown cheese! Milk sugar and cheese; Sweet, interesting texture, and delicious. I bought a small bag for about $15.00 US, and between Lynn and I and two friends, it was easily gone by the time we were done with the town, and the town is only a few blocks!!

The bus had three magnificent stops; the first was eagle road to Eagle Bend for pictures of the fjord, the town, and the ship below. The second stop was the Flydal View Point; this is behind the village, with a different view of the fjord, the town, and the harbor. The last stop was the Summit of Mt. Dalsnibba. It took us an hour to get there, driving winding 11-hair pin turn roads on the troll highway to get a view I cannot describe. WOW! Pictures were taken but didn't do justice to being there! I piled some rocks like countless others to mark the spot, indicating I would be returning in the future. We returned to the ship in time to see the floating dock retract to the shore and pass the seven sisters falls, racing across the ship to take pictures of the suitor and the bottle he had resorted to. (Rock formations)

Tonight, another excellent meal, 60's and 70's music in the atrium, where we caught and wore disco rings and necklaces, then attended the show, a dance and singing presentation. Afterward, we went to the stern of the ship to join a group of fellow travelers for

Quest. Quest is made up of various teams; we were lucky enough to recruit a younger couple to help in the event of items older folks may not have! The groups were to produce various items. The first team to bring the item to the moderator got 5 points, the rest got 1 point, and if not, bring 0 points.

Here is a list of many of the items: a man's belt, the currency of another country, an empty purse, a woman with a tattoo not on the arm or leg, and a woman with a thong on (Our younger helper provided these!) a key card, a daily program from the ship, two pair of shoe laces, a man doing the splits, a woman doing the splits, a woman wearing a man's pair of shoes, a man wearing women's shoes, a man with two bras on his head, and a man dressed up like a woman. I was the guy with the bras, Lynn contributed one of the bras, I was the one that dressed up as a woman, and my special name—Sweet Cherry—I earned a bonus for the group for "enthusiasm." Our team won the contest, lots of fun! Medals and umbrellas for all!

Thursday

We set out in Bergen, founded in 1070 A.D., and the main port of Norway. Our tour started early with a city tour; we took a cable car to overlook the city and wharf. We walked the town wharf and extensive fish market and flea market. We tried smoked whale (tastes like beef jerky), Fresh salmon with wine and lemon juice, and reindeer sausage (tastes like venison). Lots of caviar for sale (no samples!), and nothing was inexpensive, but the crabs were huge, and everything from the northern sea was attractively displayed and could be cooked up and eaten on site! A seafood lover's dream!

I walked the one-and-a-half to two kilometers to the boat, grabbed a snack, and took a nap. More Trivia, formal dinner, another outstanding show in the lounge, back the stern for a game of Majority Rules. No, we didn't win, we were too slow, and we didn't have enough answers right.

Educating Noah…Travelin'

Friday

A day at sea. We participated in more Trivia games, instructed in and participated in towel folding, Salsa dance lessons, Belly dance lessons, and napkin artistry. A final dinner, final show, back to room to pack, and off the ship between 8 and 9.

Saturday

Off the ship went well, on a tour bus for a tour of Copenhagen, Denmark, a country just twice the size of Delaware.

A scenic tour of the countryside, a visit to a community with older homes and narrow cobblestone streets, and the Rosenberg castle featuring small delicate rooms, jewels, and silver. We witnessed another changing of the guard (I have seen enough of these now) and explored the grounds. The third stop was Christiansburg Slot-Palace. This is the government's meeting halls, great parquet floors, lots of newer tapestries, well decorated ornate rooms. After the building tour, we explored the stables and display of carriages; there were only fourteen horses left and seven attendants. I dropped off at the hotel, napped, unpacked, and joined the group for dinner at a local restaurant. The beds felt great; neither of us had trouble sleeping!

Sunday

Our last full day in Europe. We joined a group after breakfast to walk down to the canal and take the Copenhagen canal boat tour. The group we were part of paced the walk way too fast and opted not to wait for us. We arrived about ten minutes later for the tour, and the first boat had already left, but we got a choice seat on the next cruise scheduled to leave in twenty minutes (they operate every ½ hour).

The second canal cruise was actually better in that the tide (these are saltwater canals) had gone out, and we could clear the bridges; as it was, we could touch the bottom of the bridge when we went under them, as well as the sides. We saw a few swans (the nation's official bird), the city from the canal, and various boats and buildings; all narrated bilingually.

After the hour cruise, we headed for the Round Tower, Europe's oldest functioning observatory, built in 1642. There is not a staircase in the tower but a ramp to get to the top. We continued on a pedestrian street to an Italian open street market featuring cheeses, sausage, bakery, olive oils, anchovies, and much, much more. We then progressed to the amusement park across the street from the hotel called Tivoli.

It is the oldest amusement park in Europe. We walked the entire park, missed the shows, dodged the short rain showers, and took in the gorgeous blooming roses, dahlias, and other flowers we didn't know the names of. We went past some carnival rides, explored the shops, and bought some black licorice. It was a casual pace, but that was enough walking, so we returned to the hotel. I asked the concierge questions; Here are the things he said: 5 million people, 8 million bikes, a bike cost somewhere between 200Eu to 1000 Eu, a pack of cigarettes $8.00, gas about $12.00/gallon. We had a final dinner at another local restaurant with the group and returned to the hotel for the final pack for the adventure home.

Monday

We left the hotel mid-morning on the bus to the airport, a trip to the airport normal confusion at the airport, wait for the flight and a nine-hour direct flight to Chicago back. We cleared the airport, got our luggage, took a bus from O'Hare to Milwaukee, picked up the car, and went home by 10:30 PM Milwaukee time.

We had perfect weather the entire trip, 65-75 (F) degrees, sunny and fluffy clouds. It rained twice in Copenhagen, but the showers only lasted about 20 minutes. No big problems; we saw four countries, had excellent meals, and enjoyed most of the highlights the various cities had to offer. The company was good, the guides knowledgeable, and the drivers on time. The ship was fun and accommodating, and we had a lot of fun with the staff, another great adventure.

We have three weeks before leaving for our Northwest adventure, so we are busy washing, setting up the house for fall, and setting up for the new adventure. I did get a call from the V.A., and the nearest time for an appointment for Ortho is in January (It is September now). I hope they don't cancel that appointment; we will return to Australia in February!

I experienced something new in the continued breakdown of my physical body. My mental body is strong lean, and attractive! For a few days, I had intense pain on the top of my right foot, then to the right great toe, then that pain subsided to jump to my left foot. I looked up gout symptoms and noted to check the uric acid in my blood at my next doctor visit. I called the V.A., asked for my nurse, and left a message to include testosterone, THC, and Uric Acid levels and the rest for my upcoming annual appointment in October.

Northeast Cruise and Tour October 14, 2013

We needed to finish up the States of the U.S., and this was an opportunity for us, plus Canada and another cruise!

On Monday, we got up early for a flight to Chicago and then transferred to a flight to Boston. We were met in Boston by company representatives and bussed to a motel to meet up with the group. It turned out to be a group of roughly 200 people from all over the U.S., and we had four busses assigned, we checked out the dinner options and settled for a lobster roll, salad and cheesecake from a grocery store.

Tuesday morning we started with a bus tour of Boston; we drove past the bar the TV series Cheers was based on, and included the Ivy League colleges of Harvard, M.I.T., and Cambridge, all in the same general vicinity. We also circled the Red Sox stadium.

Our first stop with free time was near the center of town; We stopped at Dirty Nellie's for the "freshest Guinness in town", walked a portion of the red brick trail in town, and then came upon the oldest

Educating Noah...Travelin'

restaurant in the U.S., The Union Oyster House. Lynn and I shared fish cakes, Boston baked beans, chowder, and a corn bread muffin, all excellent and I recommend the place! We then toured more of downtown, walked a food court (Quincy Mall) which is very similar to the one in the old French market in New Orleans, found another Ice Bar, and a restaurant that makes fools of their patrons by putting sacks over their heads, one patron was even carried out of the restaurant on her chair (she was tied to the chair and a white sack over her head, and left there!) Fun!!

We left Boston to drive to a Shaker village in Pittsfield, Mass. A religious-based community based on celibate, communal pious Christians. We were provided an extensive guided tour through the compound with all the history. There was also a gift shop. There are only one or two Shakers left, in their eighties, and I wondered who made these handicrafts and maintained the buildings. Nice story, interesting people, but if you don't reproduce, how long will your ideas really exist? Spent the night in Rutland, Vermont, big marble producing area, and birthplace of John Deere of the John Deere Company.

We loaded up and traveled north through the Vermont hills and valleys in full fall color on Wednesday. We visited a picturesque set of waterfalls and sampled various maple syrup products from a street vendor. We visited Lake Champlain for lunch, and stretching our legs, walked the pedestrian mall, explored the shops, had ice cream, pizza, and beer. We then jumped on the bus to arrive in Montreal, Canada, by 6:30 PM. I grabbed a bite at the Tim Horton restaurant/coffee shop next door. (They, "Tim Horton restaurants," are everywhere!)

Thursday, we loaded up the bus and had a four-hour tour of Montreal. The tour included stops where we explored the underground city (RES = underground city entrance), the subway, and the shops beneath the city. All purchases include a 5% federal ta and a 10% province tax. Personal income tax below $20,000 is negligible, but the amount above 20K was not disclosed, and property tax was not disclosed either. There was much graffiti; the bike lanes go both ways, and many bicycles. We saw an IGA food store; there is a law that no building will be erected higher than the local mountain. About $400,000 for three-bedroom, two-bath homes, and typical apartment rent is $800.00/month. Main exports are wood and grain; college costs about $300.00/semester plus books. The St. Lawrence River surrounds the island of Montreal—Arret=stop in French.

We drove past the Olympic Village; the main pavilion roof collapsed a few years after the Olympics due to the snow. The French engineer who designed the building did not take the weight of snow into the design. There is no snow in France; go figure.

Traveling through the town, staircases are outside the buildings to save space inside; all buildings are six feet from the street to accommodate a sidewalk and a small garden. After the tour, we got off the bus in the old town section to view the buildings, shops, and restaurants. We found a restaurant offering poutine, a local favorite consisting of French fries covered with brown gravy and a few pieces of bland white cheese curds. Lynn and I were unimpressed, but we had to try it! After lunch and walking, we mounted the bus for the 3-hour drive to Quebec. This evening, we took an optional excursion to a Canadian Sugar Shack—a short bus ride to the outskirts of town to this specialized restaurant. We were greeted at the door and set in a large room with benches to be served family style. Throughout the entire two-and-a-half hours, we were entertained by a one-person show, incorporating singing and participating with dancing and accompanying the music with spoons and singing. The meal included pickled beets, French Canadian pea soup, coleslaw, baked beans, maple smoked ham, meat pie, meatballs, potatoes, pork rinds (the best I have had in years!), crepes and maple syrup. We were also offered maple-flavored beer, liquor (I tried both…good!), and sweetened coffee with maple syrup (Tastee!!). The entertainment was fun, and the food was delicious and plentiful. The experience was well worth the cost, and I would highly recommend this.

Friday started with another four-hour tour of Quebec, including a walking tour of the harbor. We strolled along the Terrasse Dufferin, a walkway along the cliff's edge for great views of the Saint Lawrence River.

Quebec provides 80% of all the maple products in the world. This is one of the last North American walled cities. More shopping, then visited the Plains of Abraham and watched school children re-enacting the British and French battle. We explored the town, observed miniature electric buses, and boarded our cruise ship. Dinner was shared with a delightful British couple, we learned the ship, attended the shows, and retired for the evening.

Saturday, no ports, participated in a culinary demo and trivia, met the production staff in a question and answer period, attended a martini tasting activity ($15 for 5 Martinis!), participated at an Irish one-man show, not so newly-wed game, and a 70's disco party.

Sunday, port of call, Corner Brook, Newfoundland. We took the free shuttle around the town, had not much to see, walked a small section of town, visited one shop, and returned to the ship. There was not much there, no real significance except for being in Newfoundland, so we had to put our feet on the land. Participated in various ship activities, followed up on a lecture Lynn had attended the previous day regarding wrinkle reduction with a consultation explaining a procedure involving three injections into her face at $800/shot that would "transform" her looks and last six to eight months before repeating. After being told this was an exceptional price, we declined and left. Met another very interesting pair of folks from Virginia at dinner, went to all the shows, and ended the night at the 50's-60's night at the lounge.

Monday, the port of call in Sydney, Nova Scotia, required a shuttle boat to town. We only explored the pier shops; the town was only offering views of churches and municipal buildings. The pier shops also incorporated a hall of local crafters. We spent a few hours on the shore then returned to the ship. We played two more trivia, played wacky golf, which I was one of the winners, and ate lunch and dinner in the cafeteria so that we could get our fill of "greens". Also, attended all the shows and retired for the evening.

Tuesday, Halifax, Nova Scotia: Our first of three small ship excursions called "Lobsters and light houses". We boarded a lobster boat right off the pier. The morning was cool, and there was a light rain. Drizzle: Most of us went inside as the boat progressed out into the harbor. As we progressed, the drizzle quit, and a number of us went on deck to enjoy the crisp weather. We sighted a number of lighthouses, pulled up a lobster trap that had two lobsters and a crab inside. We passed one of the captured lobsters around for pictures, and the crab was put on a box on the deck. It seems that the lobsters enter the trap, feed on the bait, then retreat into the corner of the trap to nap, and then can't get out; if he or she is over one pound and does not have eggs, it becomes dinner!! Each lobster fisherman has about 300 traps, marks them with his branded buoys, and checks the traps every three days. The waves get up to 30 feet high, and the lobster season starts in December. After circling the harbor, we headed back past one of the Titanic victim cemeteries.

The tour ended at a restaurant where we had a whole fresh lobster each, cold slaw, and potato salad. Delicious! We decided to walk back to the ship on a boardwalk, came upon an interesting shrub, and engaged a local who explained this bush was a type of rose, and what we were seeing were rose hips. The reason we have never seen them is that they are found in salt water, and Lake Michigan is a freshwater lake! Returned to the ship to warm up, participated in more activities, visited the chocolate buffet, and went to the various shows and activities.

Wednesday, St. John, the weather is perfect, clocks back another hour. We arrived late; the crew blamed it on the tide, although the tide occurs twice a day every day. This harbor, however, has the largest tide swings in the world, up to fifty-two feet every twelve hours.

The tour included two visits to the reversing rapids; the first visit was our first stop, the last stop was also this site, and yes, the water flowed in different directions! We then stopped at the city market to grab lunch and see the different shops and vendors. This is where I tasted Dolce, a dried seaweed that the locals gather in the spring and then spread on the rocks to dry. It tastes like a little fishy beef jerky. I liked it; Lynn didn't care for it. I bought a bag full to sample at home. After an hour at the market to eat another lobster roll, samaras (similar to an empanada), and gelato and shop, we proceeded to the Bay of Fundy beach to observe the sea caves of St. Martins, beach comb for "lucky rocks" (rocks with a white band encircling the stone), and sample "the best seafood chowder in the world", of course I bought a small bowl, and it was extremely good!

We visited a small town with covered bridges and another lighthouse before stopping at a local pub for a "free" Moosehead beer and returning to the reversing falls to see the water flowing in the opposite direction. Back on the ship, went to shows and participated in white night. Lynn had packed a white outfit; I had requested an additional top sheet, put on my swimsuit and made a toga. We were an item! Had lots of fun, enjoyed dancing with the crew and others, and had a great time!

Thursday, back to the USA, customs came on board and processed everyone. We then left the ship in "BaHaBa," Maine. Visited the town, self-toured the shops and restaurants, had lunch, then jumped on one of the fastest, largest, three-deck catamarans in North America, whale-watching boats to drive out twenty miles to see if we could find some whales. The twenty-mile trip took us out to a shelf where the average depth goes from 200-300 feet to about 600 feet. There were lobster buoys all over the place on the way out, all over the harbor, all the way out to the drop-off. In our lecture about whales, we also learned that to become a lobster fisherman, you have to have a boat, cost from $75,000 to $150,000, have two years apprenticeship, and pay $50,000 for a license.

There were several spout sightings, some whale swales, some whale tails. However, I saw only one very distant tail; the balance was seen only by the folks in the bow of the boat, in that the boat was always chasing the spouts, and a distance of at least one hundred yards was kept. The boat was never turned for those inside or on the sides and stern to observe the whales.

The trip was very disappointing; Lynn didn't see any of the spouts, heads, or tails. The commentary was heavy on donating to whale funds, saving the earth, and how lucky we were to "see" a specific whale that only the commentator and the few on the bow observed; there was no real concern for the passengers seeing the whales. We did see some seabirds; a few dolphins were sighted, but nothing close, no sharks or tuna, no pods of pilot whales or seals. The only real highlight was a section of Bellin from a blue whale that was passed around. This is a structure in front of the whale's mouth to filter food for the whale, and it looked and felt like a car air cleaner.

We returned to the ship, and it was the last night on board, so we attended all the farewell performances and also participated in the quest game. Our team won! We were first with two belts, a tattoo on a woman that was covered up, two pairs of shoe laces, an empty purse, a program, and a medical card; the other first was a man wearing lipstick, where I turned to a teammate and asked her to put lipstick on me, without hesitation, she grabbed me by the head and planted a kiss on me and said there, now get our points! (I hardly knew her and was very surprised she would kiss a toad like me, but we did get the point, and I did thank her when I came back to my seat!)

Friday, we spent most of the morning getting off the ship and loaded onto the bus to continue the tour.

Educating Noah...Travelin'

The government shutdown kind of put a kink in our plans, but we did go to Cape Cod via Plymouth. We stopped in Plymouth to view a reproduction of the Mayflower and a view of Plymouth Rock. After Plymouth, we drove to Provincetown, MA. To walk the quaint village for lunch, we shared an Angus Boursin burger (Boursin is a herbed cream cheese). From a restaurant claiming the best beef on the East Coast (It was tastee!), a shrimp cocktail (fresh large shrimp), and a green monster beer. Mmmmmmm! We stopped at another beach before leaving Cape Cod to see a few seals in the surf before arriving at our motel in Hyannis for the evening.

Saturday, we are off early to Rhode Island. We stopped by the town of Bourne at the mouth of the canal known as Buzzard Bay. We witnessed one of the few vertical drawbridges in the U.S. in action, lowering to let the garbage train cross to get rid of the state's trash. This is also the home port of the ship that was hijacked by Somali pirates and is the subject of the new Tom Hanks, Captain Phillips movie. This canal was the brainchild of Miles Standish to shorten the distance across land rather than sailing around the Cape.

We had lunch and shopping in Providence R.I., then on to one of the Vanderbilt mansions. We took the audio tour through the mansion, marble, gold, silver, and platinum everywhere. The bathtubs had four spigots, two for fresh water and two for saltwater bathing. There were twenty bathrooms and fifteen bedrooms, with hidden passageways for the twenty servants. Mrs. Vanderbilt ran the house hold and was said to change her outfit five or six times a day depending on the function and scheduled activities; she had four closets. We saw more mansions and golf courses here than anywhere else.

Rhode Island is certainly a very wealthy state. After the mansion tour, we traveled along the coast to Bridgeport, Connecticut, passing the town of Mystic (made somewhat recently famous by the movie Mystic Pizza) and previously as a major shipbuilder. Our motel that evening was a Holiday inn, and they offered the best buffet of the trip.

Noah

It was limited, but the sole, asparagus, and Bar B Q chicken and saffron rice were cooked and presented perfectly. Bed early in prep for our last full day of the trip, New York City.

Sunday, our full day in New York City. As with all the other days, up at 6:00 A.M. and loaded on the bus by 7:45. It was Sunday, the traffic was light, and we arrived at New York in just under two hours. There are twenty million people in greater New York, and the city seemed cleaner than I had imagined. We entered through Harlem, and passed the Apollo Theatre, viewed the Empire State Building, and drove to Central Park for our first stop. We took pictures of the hotel entrance where John Lennon of the Beatles was shot, then across the street to one of the many entrances, entering the Strawberry field's area.

We progressed into the park to visit the Bethesda fountain and use the bathrooms. This also enabled us to purchase a New York Hot Dog, one of our goals. They were only $2.00 and were O.K... We then progressed back to the bus, passing pedal rickshaws charging $3.00/minute; we walked past these real fast!

Back on the bus, we traveled to Radio City Music Hall. We had two hours to explore, witnessed the small ice-skating rink, explored the underground shops, and walked the streets to find a New York Deli. We found one, and the food was reasonable and very good, large portions to boot! Walked past NBC, CBS, and Fox studios, and walked the two blocks to Times Square. Back on the bus, we traveled down 5th Avenue, turned on 42nd St., and drove past ground Zero of the past Twin-Towers location to explore more of the treasures the city had to offer. Passed Wall Street and found the Wall Street bull to be much larger than we thought it was!

We stopped in the harbor and went past a number of street vendors to a storefront complex still being renovated after the last major hurricane, Sandy, to provide a great view of the Brooklyn Bridge and the George Washington Bridge. Two more stops before the end of the tour, the first to Battery Park to view the Statue of Liberty, then across the river to New Jersey to our motel by the airport. It was later in the afternoon, and traffic had become increasingly heavier, even on this Sunday afternoon; we drove through Chinatown, the Bowery, Canal, and Broom Street, SoHo, Little Italy, Ott, and Mulberry St... We then got into the inching queue funneling us into the Holland tunnel. After maneuvering to the entrance, we sailed through the tunnel, drove the short distance to Battery Park, and walked out to a fantastic view of New York and the back of the Statue of Liberty. The views were great. We took the pictures and walked back to the bus and off to the last motel.

Monday morning, early pick-up, and off to the airport for a direct flight to Milwaukee. Home by 11 A.M., another adventure completed, only six more states to see, plus the revisit to Canada and adding Newfoundland.

Noah

Here I am, sitting at the pool in the timeshare community of Fox Hills. We bought this timeshare back in the eighties and make it a point to use it every year, the week we can.

We always come in late fall to avoid the kids, and enjoy either the Two River Apple Festival or the Mishicot Pumpkin Fest, where there is a small-town High school pumpkin pancake breakfast with pumpkin pancakes, sausage links, and a beverage for $6.50 each person, the pancakes are all you can eat, you just need to go up to the grill, ask for more and the grill master will flip them to you…stand back… he flips them at least six to eight feet, and if you miss one, he will flip you another.

After breakfast, we walked Main Street for the current crafts and food vendors. We then drove down to Two Rivers for groceries for the week. Piggly Wiggly food stores are always a great value, and we found one up there. I did notice that all of the employees were women or teenage girls. It seems the whoosification has hit the rural areas also. I asked one where the boys were, and she replied that some were at practice, others were playing videos at home. I thought this was rather a shame; boys becoming bums at such an early age, what a waste and lack of work ethic!

We returned to the timeshare condo to have lunch, and we had a wildlife channel on. I can relate; I am the old alpha dog who can hardly walk at times and sleep more; nature would deal with me by starving me to death. With my size it would take a while, but without these pain pills, it would have been over by now. My knees are worse; I received a shot in each knee early this summer, which helped for two weeks; the doctor told me that the knees hadn't gotten much worse (it must be me!), and my next scheduled visit with the ortho specialist is in January, Ibuprophen has become my new best friend!

On returning from our week timeshare near Door County, In Mishicot, Wisconsin. I found the colors of the trees bolder than those in Vermont and the Northeast. I found the people just as friendly, but here, the trees were three or four colors rather than one and more vibrant. I also learned how dependent I have become to the internet with faulty WIFI at the timeshare! I am recovering from the away-from-home syndrome, preparing for our next adventure back to Italy the beginning of December.

I have been experiencing symptoms of depression and have asked for additional analysis of my blood draw to include testosterone, THS, and testing for gout. I am not happy with my diet progress and seem to be tired all of the time. I have projects to do, both the carved fish and the Pachinko machines I bought to recondition to give as gifts. I did find out that the pachinko lights work on a 10-volt DC system that I will need to obtain.

My nurse practitioner thinks I have pseudo gout and low testosterone. The lab results came back with my urate at 8.7 mg/dl with a range of 3.5-7.2! Way high, I will be increasing my water intake and eliminating the liver sausage from my diet to bring that rate down; my testosterone is sitting at 229, with an acceptable range of 241-827. It did go from my low last year of 204 to 273 before the testosterone was d/c ed; we agreed that we would monitor and try to supplement until we were well within the middle of the range before allowing the supplement to be re-evaluated. I am also going to set up an appointment with an alternative medical doctor who specializes in holistic, homeopathic, and alternative cures. I am not myself; too tired all of the time, too angry, and I don't like me…. Lynn is starting to feel that way, too! (She doesn't like the new me either.)

Vacation to Italy, Monaco, Spain, Tunisia, and Sicily December 5, 2013

Typical beginning, we went through, drove to the bus station, and took the bus to O'Hare. I had registered and confirmed online, but still had to use Kiosk, for luggage, and then it would only issue tickets to De Gaul in Paris. Now, only American Airlines tickets can be issued by American, and our connection was with Air Italia, so we needed to find the connecting flight gate and issue tickets (uses different codes also). Every time we travel, we learn more; nothing is consistent except for small seats and cramped quarters.

We arrived in Paris about eight and a half hours later, as typical at De Gaul; the gates are poorly displayed. After asking precise questions at the security check, we found that we needed to take a shuttle bus to another terminal. We found the exit for the bus, took it to the proper terminal, and then had to ask where the gate was! (It was behind the security gates.)

We found a kiosk after clearing security to print our new boarding passes and sit at the gate till departure. The flight was only about forty percent full, and the flight to Rome was only two and a half hours. The flight on Air Italia is always nice; plenty of room and wine is included in the drink selection.

Educating Noah...Travelin'

We were met at the luggage retrieval area by the travel company rep, put on the shuttle bus, and driven to our hotel in downtown Rome. The trip lasted almost a half hour, and the driver was very animated and knowledgeable of Rome and the surrounding countryside. There doesn't seem to be a speed limit, and stop signs are an indication to stop. In Italy, we were told, "Don't watch out for you, you watch out for the other guy," "Yellow lines keep you on the right side of the road most of the time," and "The first one to get to a spot has the right of way;" motorbikes will pass you on the right, left, and into the crosswalk. They will also weasel into any spot in front of you, whether you are a car, bus, or truck, to get the jump on the traffic light change.

The hotel was right in the middle of Rome; we were within two blocks of walking distance to the coliseum, walking distance to Vatican City, and in the midst of various restaurants, coffee, and gelato shops. We took a brief nap after getting to our room, and then explored the surrounding area to "see what we would see".

Walked a while, then stopped at a small mom-and-pop restaurant, had a pizza and beer, and talked to another couple who were also booked on the cruise we were on. We were now exhausted, full, and somewhat non-functional. We walked the block to the hotel, went to the room, showered, and went to bed. Tomorrow promised to be a great day with the inside tour of the Coliseum, the surrounding grounds, and Rome highlights...

On day two, we are in Rome, the Coliseum and highlights of Rome. The day starts with a typical fantastic buffet put out by the hotel. We boarded the bus, took a scenic ride of Rome, and then stopped at the Coliseum.

The tour included a "get in front of the line" pass to go into the Coliseum, and in we went. The structure is really immense and is much more complicated than imagined. The staircases take you up and down the four-story structure, plus there is a basement catacomb where the gladiators and animals are staged. What we didn't know was when the events began, a platform-like elevator would raise a gladiator up from the lower level, and then another would rise up either another gladiator or animal to fight. The death of the loser was controlled by the crowd with thumbs up or down. The audience never knew where the gladiator or challenger would "pop up." It was very interesting; a lot of the structure was still intact, and most, if not all, was originally covered in marble.... wow!

After the Coliseum, we walked to the ruins of Palatino, Nero's family home, also that of previous emperors, Romulus and Remus. We transverse ruins of markets, churches, and various other ancient buildings. Two hours walking was relieved by boarding the bus for a further tour past Circus Maximus, where the center of the track was like a fish spine! It seems as though everything built in Rome was covered with marble or travertine. This was accented with red marble from Egypt in many places. We also drove past a pyramid that was erected in Rome to reflect the ones in Egypt when the Romans conquered Egypt.

We had a traditional feast served family style at a local restaurant, which included pasta with tomatoes and eggplant, sautéed chicken with rosemary and oregano, roasted potatoes, cookies and berries with cream, and plenty of red and white wines.

After lunch, we took the bus to another section of town and walked into the fountain of Trevi, made our wishes, and threw three coins each to the fountain. Visited a number of shops, too full for gelato, and then progressed down the streets past columned ruins to the Pantheon, which was originally a pagan religious structure and then changed to a Basilica and remains so today. The difference between a Basilica and a church is the centerpiece wave picture. After the Basilica, we progressed to the Plaza Narvon to explore the Christmas Street market, and view two additional fountains. Today, we walked a total of three and a half hours over cobblestone....... It was a long day!! We were still tired from the traveling yesterday, full from lunch, so a little gelato was supper, and early to bed; we transfer to the ship tomorrow!

Saturday morning, it was a rough night. It seemed that in Europe, after summer, the air conditioning was turned off, and the room became uncomfortably warm so we opened the window.

The problem was this is a major city and does not sleep, car alarms going off, people talking loudly, brakes squealing, motorbikes with loud mufflers, etc. We would open the window for a while, then sleep, and when it got too hot again, we'd repeat.

Ate another great buffet breakfast and then loaded the bus, we were number four of four bus loads, so we had to wait quite a while in the lobby, then loaded the bus for an hour and a half ride to the coast. The trip was pleasant, with a nice view of the Italian countryside. The check-in to the ship went very well; we deposited our carry-ons and had a salad lunch. We then re-familiarized ourselves with the ship (we had sailed the Norwegian Jade) before and waited for our luggage to unpack.

Attended the mandatory safety muster, participated in the sail away party on deck, and then changed for dinner. We always request to be seated with others to meet different folks on the cruise. We have never been disappointed and enjoyed the company of new acquaintances. Attended the show and ended the day.

Sunday, we docked at Livorno, Italy, and had a seven-hour excursion to Pisa and a taste of Tuscany. Early to the bus, drove to Pisa and toured the Pisa Plaza; the leaning tower looks more impressive from the back, huge when viewed close up, and I could have but opted not to walk up the stairs to the top of the tower, loaded back into the bus, and a tour of the Tuscany countryside to one of the oldest Tuscany wineries for a lunch and wine tasting.

We toured the winery, viewed some aging wine in huge casks, and viewed the olive orchard and vineyard, along with the processing plant. We were then seated family style at a long table in the cellar for wine sampling (basically how much you really wanted) of a number of wines, then sausage cheese, fresh bread, olive tapenades, biscotti, and desserts. None left hungry or thirsty, and everyone was a lot friendlier on the trip back to the ship. Back on the ship, we participated in trivia, with the help of two other passengers and a group of guys at the bar. Dinner with another interesting couple, 60's show called "Shout," a take-off of the old "Laugh-In" show. We attended the 50's and 60's dance party and called it a day.

On Monday, we have an all-day tour scheduled: Cannes, St. Paul de Vence and Monaco Rock. Monaco is the second smallest country, the Vatican being the smallest. The total area of Monaco is two square kilometers. After loading onto the bus, we drove the streets where the annual Formula One races are held; there are some sculptures that mark the event, the streets are narrow by our standards, and I have no idea where the people that park on the street put their cars when the race happens.

It only takes a few minutes to leave town and the country to be in southern France. It took a little over an hour traveling along the coast on the French Riviera to get to Cannes. This is the world-renowned resort town that hosts a variety of movie festivals.

We walked past the Casino that is attached to the festival hall and checked out the various handprints left in special concrete squares littering the walkway in front of the building. We took pictures in some posing boards, walked around the building, and across the boulevard to window shop the high-end shops, with display windows showing off their exclusive brands, not a price tag in sight!

We were able to walk through a section of outdoor shops, did some more shopping (Lynn found a custom-carved gourd), then returned to the bus for a trip to Saint Paul de Vence. This is a quaint village that has retained most of its medieval appearance, offering very narrow cobblestone streets, artist's shops, high-end clothing, and souvenirs. We had a very good French bread chicken sandwich (It's France, the bread and pastries are phenomenal!). All the streets inside were steep up or down and cobblestone. Most of these small ancient towns cannot be navigated by a large car, much less a bus. To most of these sites, we had to hoof it a quarter mile just to the entrance of the attraction.

After an hour and a half, we met again at the bus and returned to Monaco. There were a number of escalators and elevators to get to the top of the rock of Monaco; here, we had a guided walking tour of their oceanographic Museum, the cathedral, the Prince's Palace, and the prison where the "man with the iron mask" was kept. Asking about the rent in Monaco, it ranges from $46,000 per square foot; Yikes! We were within fifteen minutes to all aboard, so the option of walking back to the ship was not there.

Back on the ship, we played back-to-back trivia with the same couples, seven in our team total. Met a new couple at dinner, took in the show, I went back to the room with cramping legs, and Lynn went up to the top deck to dance with the crew and others.

Tuesday, Provence (Toulon), France. We are pretty exhausted from the non-stop excursions and activities aboard the ship, so a one and half hour boat tour seemed to be the answer to slow down! The tour boat was less than a couple of hundred feet from the Cruise ship; we were able to snag two excellent seats on the top deck. We saw a ship in a floating dry dock, the port mouth forts and protection, a mussel farm, exhibits of small submarines, underwater exploring machines, and a nice view of the harbor and shoreline. There was a small market right on the dock; we picked up a beautiful tablecloth and lavender essence. Back on ship, we partook in leisurely crafty activities, origami, a Martini tasting, and trivia. Dinner with a new couple, participating in a win, lose, or draw, the show, another game of majority rule, and then a county western-themed dance.

Wednesday meant Barcelona. We had been here two times before, so we opted to go ashore and tour the town on our own. We took a shuttle bus to the Monument Colum (the Columbus statue) at the base of the main promenade. (Las Ramblias) This street leads from the harbor to the town center. We enjoyed the market, lots of fruit, vegetables, meat, and seafood. This included things we usually don't see at home, such as a variety of seafood fresh caught and just gutted rabbits un-skinned, whole lamb legs with hooves, skulls, and heads of various animals.

Back to the ship for a light salad lunch and a nap (yes, a nap!). Joined Lynn wondering the ship for activities, another trivia, met an interesting Australian couple for dinner, show, and bed…Lynn went up to dance for a while but joined me before midnight for a good night's sleep.

Thursday means Valencia, Spain, we were here once before and had taken a city tour. We wanted more this time. Spain has so much to offer, and we can't seem to get enough! I had been weakened yesterday with diarrhea. I felt better this morning, and I believe the problem has been eliminated! The laundry offered a special of everything in the laundry bag for $24.00, so we carefully packed the bag tight and took advantage of the deal. Let's hope the Celebrity Cruise line offers something similar for our upcoming 32 days back-to-back cruise in Australia! Today is a five-hour tour including the 5th Century BC village of Sagunto and a visit to the St. Joseph Caves.

In Sagunto, we visited an area preserved under modern buildings that exhibit the ancient town, including roads, walks, foundations, and partial buildings. We followed steep, narrow cobblestone roads within the city, passing areas where Jews and Christians lived together in segregated areas. Found various examples of blended BC and AD structures, a small ancient theater with examples of travertine and marble, small courtyards, and winding narrow roads and sidewalks. Over two and a half hours of hiking and walking, the town concluded with a bus ride to the caves.

Educating Noah…Travelin'

We hiked to the entrance of the caves and took a short walk to the boats. The tour boats took about 12 people each, plus a driver who poled us through the caves. The crystal-clear water was highlighted by lighting hidden throughout the route. There were many areas where we had to duck way down to clear the top or stalactites, and the boat would scrape from time to time on the sides of the cave. This was definitely not a trip for anyone with claustrophobia!

After a half hour, we disembarked from the boat and walked in a dry part of the cave for a kilometer, where you could see how the water had carved the walls. The supplied tape and headset pointed out various points of interest throughout the tour. After the stroll through the dry cave, we were picked up by our boat and driver and poled back through the caves to the starting point.

Photography was not allowed in the caves, so I bought a set of photos from the gift shop to include with our photo book. Had a quick gelato, jumped back on the bus, and went back to Valencia. Here, we had an abbreviated tour of the opera house, City Park, and Aquarium. We found that just outside the town was a cave with glow worms. There are only two places in the world with these worms, here and New Zealand, and now we have a connection!

On the ship, again, we played crazy golf, trivia, and dinner with another interesting couple, then off to the games. We were picked as participants in the Newly Wed game, one of three couples, and took second place! They played the tape of the games in all languages for two days!

Enough was enough, and we went to bed; tomorrow was our only day at sea, and we signed up for a four-hour behind-the-scenes tour of the ship. Bedtime, we get to sleep in!!

Friday, we slept in till 7:30!! We paid for a four-hour tour behind the scenes all over the boat. There were about twenty in the group, and the first stop was a welcome at one of the restaurants, then off to the theatre. Starting in the control booth, we got a first-hand view of the control boards, spotlights, and the process of coordinating the sound and lighting. From the control booth, we proceeded to the stage, with more info, then behind the stage to the dressing rooms and complex labyrinth of corridors and closets. It was during a cruise, underwear was hanging from lines, and everything had its place but was cramped.

From then, on to the bridge. It was a lot larger than I imagined; we were under way and traveling at 18 knots under calm waters and weather. We talked to the navigation officer on duty, the pilot, and even the captain dropped by to talk. We were shown the radar, all of our questions were answered, then we were taken to one of the side posts where the floor was clear, and windows extended out to see the side of the ship when they dock.

I did lean against an accessory counsel but quickly retreated with the alarm sounding, and the security guard agreed not to put me in chains if I kept my hands and body to myself!

Down we went to the laundry room. We got the full tour, everyone working two guys on mangles, six large capacity wash machines, and numerous drying machines that then fold the sheets and towels after being fed. The machines are fast and easily fed, and there are mountains of wash. The operation is 24/7 and works like a well-oiled machine! We asked why there were no women. We were told that there were lifting requirements, and to date, no female has met those necessary requirements.

After the tour of the operating laundry room (everything we saw was under full operation), each tour was conducted by a supervisor - the person in charge of each operation. Next was environmental. We were given a tour of the water treatment and garbage disposal. The water on the ship was safer than most, if not all, the ports we visited; the average person on board consumes about 280 liters/day of fresh water!

The food garbage is separated and ground up to be discharged into the ocean for the fish. Nothing is left after seven days in the sea. The balance is separated and recycled. Each port wants a piece of the charge for the recycle pie, so the waste is distributed to keep good relations with all. There was no odor; everything was exceptionally clean and odorless, amazing!!

On to the provision area. We were introduced to refrigerated lockers filled with sea food, fresh fruit and vegetables, and areas for dry goods. We were then marched through the bakeries, the butcher, and finally, a brief galley tour, seeing all the kitchens and food prep areas. The total tour lasted almost five hours; it was continuous, and we were standing or walking throughout. It was an experience we will never forget and left a very positive picture.

Throughout the tour, all questions were easily and immediately answered, the areas were all spotless, and everyone we encountered was positive and helpful. No camcorders or video recorders were allowed, but still, pictures were allowed everywhere but the laundry and the environmental areas.

A little restful salad lunch, another Martini tasting, team trivia, Dinner with a very nice couple from Denmark, Watched the show for the evening, Lynn went up to dance, and I went back to the room to journal, relax, and prep for bed.

Saturday, Cagliari, Sardinia, Italy. We signed up for the Best of Sardinia eight-hour tour, so we ate our typical breakfast: Lynn, fresh fruit, a pastry, and eggs and potatoes; me salmon bagel, cream cheese, and a little potato. After lunch, disembark and load on a bus. This tour included a meal. I always try to opt for tours with meals to get a taste of the country or area we are in, and we have never been disappointed!

The first town we visited was the museum village of San Sperate. The town is an outdoor museum with sculptors throughout the town and many murals painted on the walls. All the buildings are/were painted white, and the artists were invited to paint on them. There were many examples, large and small, and many incorporated the features of the building.

We came upon two benches carved from volcanic rock, and then we entered the garden/studio of a famous sculptor named Pinocchio Sciola. He carves, amongst other things, singing stones. Although it is rare that he interacts with tourists, he did come out of his house, warmed a stone sculpture and his hands, then proceeded to show us how the stones "sang." It was beautiful!

After he amazed us, he moved to another sculpture and played that stone with a violin bow; it was incredible! What a treat! We thanked him profusely and headed back for the bus.

Our next stop was Barumini, a 1500 BC fortification. On the way, we saw fields of artichokes, thistle, and fennel. When we arrived, we walked up to the fortification, but after a briefing by the guide, we (Lynn and I) decided not to go inside. The steps are various in size, height, and depth. There were no railings, and many areas were tight to get around, and the lighting inside was poor. But we did tour the outside of the structure while most of the group braved the inside. After the tour of the fortification, we had lunch family-style at a local restaurant, which included sausage, cheese, cold cuts, various breads, thistle, fennel, lamb, cookies, and wine. No one was left thirsty or hungry. We went back to Calgary to shop a bit before returning to the ship.

We met our team for trivia, too full to eat a full meal; we had a snack in the cafeteria, saw the show, and called it a night.

Sunday meant Tunisia! We docked in LaGoulette. I don't care for upper Africa. The people are pushy with their wares, expect to bargain, and act insulted when you come in with a low start on the bargaining deal. I felt I paid too much for a couple of items last time in Morocco, and yes, I paid too much for two items here!

Anyway, we signed up for a four-hour tour to Medina and the Sidi Bou Said. The trip to Medina was a good forty-five minutes through town. Nice clean buildings but dirty streets. We went through an area where "anything you want" can be purchased, new and used. The guide told us you will find stolen items here also, so you can buy back your bike; he has done it twice!

When we arrived in Medina, we were treated to the history of the town; Tunisia was and still remains one of Italy's major suppliers of food and olive oil. (Tunisia ships to Italy to have the Italian firms label the oil as their own).

When the Romans conquered this state and city, they discovered that Medina had no good water supply, neither being one of the few major cities located on water! So, the Romans built the longest aqueduct from the mountains to this city to make it viable. We then proceeded to the shopping area with all of the souks (stores). The difference between the shops was explained with the souk hierarchy. We were taken to a shop where the typical Tunisian hat was sold, the process was explained, and Lynn modeled one. We were also treated to an explanation of various fragrances and oils and offered discounts.

We were then taken through the bazaar; it was Sunday, so the streets and alleys were not jammed with people. We explored a variety of shops and purchased some "bargains," half good, some not so good, but Lynn was happy.

Back on the bus, to explore another part of town with bright white buildings and bright dark blue accents. Free time to walk and shop, trapped by three guys with falcons; paid them too much for letting us pose with the birds; Lynn was afraid one of them on her head was going to leave a deposit! We took some great pictures, had more views of the coast, and then went back to the ship. Outside the ship were more people with camels and Roman uniforms asking for money to pose with them. We cleared them and got back on the ship.

Noah

Late lunch, trivia with the "team," small supper, then we got ready for White Night. This is a Norwegian cruise thing where everyone on the dance floor wears white. I had requested two single sheets, and Lynn had brought two plastic leaf wreaths. I fabricated a toga, and off we went. We were a hit! I was one of three guys that had fashioned togas, but mine was the best! (Staff consensus). I lasted four dances before my legs and knees gave out, but we all had a great time!

Monday, Palermo, Italy, Sicily. I wanted to see the real Sicily, so we signed up for a five-hour tour to a little town on the coast called Cefalu. It was explained as a seaside town where little has changed in centuries. This town is visited a lot due to the influences left behind by Syracusians, Romans, Byzantines, Arabs, and Normans. The origin of the name dates back to the Greek kephaliodion, a word referring to the rock above the city. On the trip out, the Mafia question was raised, and our guide gave us the inside scoop. The first day you refuse to pay, they ask if you are sure; the second day, the head of an animal is at the doorstep; the third, the family is threatened. The government does offer protection with escorting services, but it is much easier to pay for the protection.

When we arrived, the bus stopped about a hundred yards outside the city; the streets were much too narrow, and no place to turn around. We were escorted to a small restaurant to use the toilet facilities, and a snack was laid out for us, including a table and dessert wine, little open-faced sandwiches with fresh bread and cheese, sausage, olive tapenade, and a jam. This was very refreshing, and we promised to return to shop for their wares. We all walked into town to the town center, a little over a half kilometer.

The center features a large cathedral that dates back to 1131. It is a gothic Norman-style church still used today and the center of the religious community. Free time to explore the village included a visit to a communal laundry area, various shops, and a very quaint and peaceful village. We viewed the ocean from various vantage points and slowly walked a different route back to the bus, and as promised, we visited the initial shop. The trip back to the harbor was quiet, just more history and Sicilian facts provided by the guide. We did discuss that the atmosphere in Sicily was different than any of the other ports. It seemed "more friendly," a feeling of "home," odd but nice!

Back on the ship after the six-hour excursion, goofy golf (Both Lynn and I won!) craft boxes, team trivia (the third time we came in second!), dinner with another very nice couple, and then we attended the Element Show that had been hyped the whole cruise. It was the best show, incorporating dance, magic, and music. We joined into the "55" or less show and ended with dancing to another theme.

Tuesday was the last day out; tomorrow, we had to head home! This stop was Naples; two "musts" were a Naples slice of pie and visiting the lost city of Pompeii!

Due to our extensive walking and partying on the boat, we elected this tour to be the shortest offered, which was exclusively Pompeii. The tour was early, and the bus left promptly at 8:45 A.M. from the port. The ruins are only a few miles south of the port, and we were there in a little more than a half hour. As with everywhere else in Italy, Pompeii used to be on the sea, but the sea has receded here a few kilometers. (Global cooling??)

There is a large reception area for the busses to drop off the tourists, surrounded by trinkets, souvenir tents, and vendors. The tour started at a cameo factory, where we were given a guided tour of the process, the materials used, and how the cameos were cut. Then, we were taken to the lower level with multiple showcases and jewelry and sculptures ranging from 10 to 10,000 Euros.

We were given 20 minutes to look around, then through the gates to visit the lost city. The story goes that at the eruption, a cloud appeared over the city for a day or two, and then the eruption began and lasted two days. Pompeii was covered with volcanic ash to a depth of 20 meters in two days, and a sister city on the opposite side of the volcano was covered with lava.

We walked along the outside wall and entered the south end of the city. It is much larger than any of the group imagined; there were approximately 30,000 inhabitants at that time, which was very large in that time. We entered one of the smaller auditoriums, about 40 square feet in size, with ornate statues, columns, and some marble or travertine still gracing some of the walls and seating area.

We came out on one of the main (east-west) streets; there are sidewalks and a street level about a foot below the sidewalk, all cobblestone. Every 10-15 meters, there were three flat stones placed in the street so that one could cross the street when the streets were flooded.

Small doorways indicated a residence; a double doorway would indicate a shop. We walked the streets to an area where most of the house was intact. We entered one of the homes to find light-colored pictures still remaining on some of the walls, a garden area, an open area for collecting water, and a servant's quarters where the remains of two servants remain. I was surprised to see the extent of piping in the house, the stores, and the baths. It was all lead and about an inch in diameter.

Progressing east, we came upon a Roman bath complex with an exercise yard and three baths, one warm, one hot, and one cold. We also inspected two cases where plaster molds were made of other people that were lost that day. More shops, more houses, a house of pleasure (indicated in the street in front of the door by a representation of a penis and scrotum). This was one of the houses (everyone looked down to see if any more "signs" were painted on the road). The end of town had another auditorium, easily the size of our modern-day football field, decorated with columns and sculptures.

We had a little time before the bus, so I found a vendor and ordered a slice of pizza for Lynn and me. It was very good; it was spinach and cheese pizza with a chewy crust, a little cheese, and a good portion of spinach. There's nothing like our pizzas at home, but it's extremely good! We walked with the group a couple of blocks to the bus and back to the ship we went. We walked almost the entire time while in Pompeii on smooth but cobblestones, and nothing in Europe is flat; you are either walking uphill or downhill!

We played our final trivia games with our team, second place one final time, and headed back to the room to prepare our luggage for pick-up and had dinner with one last couple, which was another pleasant experience.

Wednesday, our bus to the airport was at 9:30. The trip to the airport was 1 1/2 hours, then our flight to England, where we caught our American Airlines flight home. There were small glitches as always, but we were back at our house by 1:30 AM, about 20 hours since leaving the ship………what another great adventure!!

We only had a week or so before Christmas and then the end of a fantastic year for traveling.

Both of us have been seeing a holistic doctor in addition to our regular MDs so that maybe we can both accelerate our recouping to "healthy people." I settled up with him for the treatments we had received, bought a laser to be applied to the joint, and scheduled twelve more visits in January to see if he could really do what he claimed.

Noah

Synergy wants to use me as a nurse to sit down with families and review the supplies of medications they have and hopefully dispose of those that are no longer effective (lost potency) or needed. I also agreed to attend a new class on body mechanics, even though I used to teach this to caregivers.

Christmas and New Year's Eve are over; now, to get ready for the Australian Adventure, check with the dietician and get another injection in both legs!

Chapter two
2014

First leg of tour 2014 Exploring Australia, New Zealand, Bali, and the US.

We are preparing now for our Australian adventure. We have seen the Holistic doctor for two months on a twice-a-week schedule. Results are mixed; we've spent over $1,000 in remedies and appointments (not covered by the VA or Medicare). I was asked to and proceeded to drink some of my own urine; both Lynn and I have decreased our use of analgesics, but this is the big test. We will be gone for almost six weeks, with sun for the vitamin D, salt water for my dry skin, and a busy schedule.

The "shot" in my knees lasted for two weeks. It is not as effective, but I haven't taken any Ibuprophen in weeks and can walk the three miles in the slider without quitting. I also was scheduled for an aorta scan by the VA. They do these for all vets. This is the second year since the program was started, and I passed with no problem.

New Zealand/Australian Great Adventure 02-02-14- 03-10-14

Two weeks before our scheduled departure, I posted three websites tracking the weather in Chicago, Sidney, Australia, and Auckland, New Zealand. Starting from ten days out, the long-range forecast for Chicago was either clear or light snow on the day of departure. On Thursday, two days before leaving, the forecast changed to four to six inches of snow because of the snowfall all day. So much for predicting weather, and they say we are warming globally???

We did have Tiffany, our oldest daughter, drop us off at the bus terminal for our bus ride down to O'Hare. The bus was on time; there were about four inches of snow on the ground all the way and some ice on the road. At times, you could feel the bus drift in the lane, but we did get to our destination in plenty of time. (We took a bus an hour early to make sure we had plenty of time at the terminal.)

Since a three-hour wait is normal now, we took our time through customs. To our surprise, it went quickly and without long lines, and into the secured area, we were whisked! Most of the ticket assignments are done by the traveler. Although we had preregistered, it was a little faster, with no real line, and an attendant came over just to tag and weigh the luggage, check the destination, and direct us to the next stage. This is just a cost-saving; another job is being eliminated.

The first flight was to San Francisco. It was to be about four and a half hours, with snacks and beverages. There was a minor problem with the electrical system, and we needed to be deiced before taking off, but we were taking off within 20 minutes of when we were supposed to. After take-off, they came through offering gourmet snacks for $7.00 - $9.00. This was followed by water or soda. We weren't told that the gourmet snacks were the snacks "included" on the flight. This is just another example of cost-cutting on United's part, lack of communication, and poor customer service that they have.

So, we landed a few minutes late, but there was a four-hour layover. We had plenty of time to find the international airport, grab a bite to eat, and then find the New Zealand check-in desk. People were lined up at the desk, so Lynn found a seat, and I went up to find out what was going on. Yes, there were no signs and no announcements, but we needed to get our tickets exchanged for United issued to New Zealand. Had all the paperwork issued, plus the cruise documents they also wanted.

Then sit and wait. Loading was chaotic, first class then preferred, then loading economy from the back of the plane forward. We pushed our way into the line when our row was called. Upon entering the plane, we found more than half of the seats filled all the way back to our seats, with the entire section behind us seated. We had a window and a middle seat. The 747 is designed 3-4-3 across, and we were told the plane was sold out. It was an effort for the woman sitting on the aisle seat to get out, leaving us in, but we had enough room for our carry-on in the upper bins and nested in for the twelve-and-a-half-hour fight to our next destination.

The premium economy seats did have a little more legroom, and the armrests were not fully retractable into the seats. Yes, it is very uncomfortable, close, and cramped. The seats reclined 3-4 inches instead of 1-2 inches. The woman next to Lynn whined about not being able to raise her armrest. The other couple in their party did find another seat, so she moved into the cattle corral in the middle of the plane with her husband, which gave Lynn a few extra centimeters of room and not having to deal with an ever-shifting seatmate.

Beer and wine were included in the meals, which were very good. The movies were free along with the other selections, unlike United, where any entertainment was an extra charge. I had nine different movies to watch TV shows and actually got three hours of sleep. Lynn was luckier and got about five hours of sleep.

We arrived at the Auckland Airport a little after 5 AM. Customs was easy, especially this early in the morning. Our luggage came off the plane quickly, and we were met outside the secured area by the cruise line for our bus ride to the ship.

We had crossed the International Date Line, so now it was Monday morning. The ship was not scheduled to load until 11 AM, so we were taken on a tour of the city. We stopped at an overlook to view the harbor and were then taken to a place called Winter Garden to have tea and snacks. We were then taken to a museum where we pre-registered for boarding to expedite embarkation. We then had a ride to the harbor, being treated to viewing the world's most expensive yacht, which was being renovated to the tune of several million dollars.

New word: "Kia ora." KA-OH-RAE means hello in Maori, the native tongue. We arrived to see lines to check in. We asked about the express check-in since we had stopped at the museum, which got us past a few, but once we had passed security, there were more lines. Then, finally, there was the last line, and we were given a shorter line…so much for pre-registering!!!

We were in our room by 11:30 AM, got a bite to eat, and started to familiarize ourselves with the ship. We stopped at the restaurant to confirm our table and make sure we were seated with at least four other couples. We took a nap, received our luggage, unpacked, and dressed for dinner. We had an excellent dinner, toured the ship one last time, and then went to bed. We collapsed into a nice, firm, and comfortable bed and were asleep within minutes.

Tuesday, February 4th, Glow Worm Day! We are anchored in the Bay of Islands, New Zealand. Our excursion leaves at 07:45, so we are up at six, have a quick breakfast, and go into the theatre for our excursion numbers and loading queue. We loaded into the tenders for the twenty-minute ride to the dock. As we disembarked from the tender, we were greeted by a tattooed Maori warrior, blowing on a conch shell and making a face with his tongue out!

We boarded our bus and proceeded to our first stop, to walk through the Kauri Forest at Puket State Forest. We are guided by a local botanist, describing the trees and plants. There are no snakes on this island, but there are a lot of opossums, of which there is a bounty! (The only native animal to New Zealand is a bat. All other animals have been introduced). The opossums have no natural enemy on the island; they say, "If you see a possum on the road, there are two hundred hidden! The guide traps possums for extra money, and in one week, he turned in 600 pelts, a cool 24K in New Zealand dollars!

The next stop was the glow worm caves. This place and Valencia, Spain, are the only locations where these glow worms have been found. You can only take pictures outside the cave; it was cool and damp inside. We were walking on a narrow wooden bridge and were guided in with lanterns for about thirty meters when we were told to turn off the lamps. As we look up, pinpoints of light start to show. Soon, the top of the cave looks like a starry night, and the glow worms get brighter and brighter. These glow worms get to be about an inch long; they glow to attract mosquitoes and nits and entangle these insects with a sticky filament similar to a sticky spider web. The glow worms are brightest when it rains, and the insects are driven into the cave; this is when they feast. We re-lit our lanterns and went in deeper; here we were within five to six feet of the worms, and you could see the worm. We were told that when the worm matures, it turns into a flying bug, has three days to mate, then the eggs are deposited on the walls and ceilings, and the bug dies to start a new generation. On the back of the cave is a steep climb to the surface, then a steep walk back down to the bus.

We returned to the ship by two in the afternoon, watched a vegetable carving demonstration trivia, and at five, there was a Martini tasting. It cost fifteen dollars, but you get seven ½ Martinis! The bartender mixes seven different variations and then pours them all out at the same time (I got pictures!) Wow, what a great show! Then I was topped when the couple next to me ordered a double, fourteen Martinis, all different, and all poured at the same time. He had to stand on the bar to pour, DOUBLE WOW!

I found that the café served Sushi starting at 5:30, so I went up to have an appetizer before supper… Mmmmmmm, good! I still had some time before dinner in the dining room, so off to the top deck to snap some pictures of this gorgeous place; this is truly "God's Country."

Down to the dining room, we had requested a large table to meet others; of the ten places, nine were taken, there was a single person at the table, and the rest one English couple and the balance of Americans. We enjoyed a great meal, lively talk, and good company. After dinner, participated in a yes or no trivia and won a deck of cards for my mother. The show didn't excite us, and Lynn was not up to "par" yet, so early to bed to catch up on sleep.

Wednesday, February the fifth. Tauranga, New Zealand, a new place and new excursion, Elm's Mission House and Kiwi farm. The first stop was Elm's Mission House and Gardens, founded in 1835 by missionaries. The buildings were well preserved, with beautiful gardens and the oldest library in New Zealand. A nice walk through the various buildings and through the gardens before loading back on the bus to go to the 260 Kiwi Farm.

We were taken out to the field to see the kiwi vines. There is one male vine planted per four females. The kiwi plant needs frost to bloom the flowers, and then frost has to be prevented for the fruit to grow. In years past, the farmers would hire a helicopter at $1500.00 per hour on nights that frost was predicted to fly over the field and beat the thermal rise down on the ground to prevent the frost from killing the fruit. After a few seasons with the helicopters, windmills were erected with a diesel generator to blow on those chilly nights, keeping the thermal rise down, paying for themselves in two seasons. The kiwi origin is the Chinese gooseberry; it has more vitamins and nutrients than any other fruit, three times the vitamin C of oranges.

The leaves on the vines are trimmed for the sun to find the fruit, rings are cut on the vine trunks to prevent sugar from running back down to the roots, and bee hives are brought in every season to pollinate all the flowers. All mis-sharpened kiwis are plucked early, and there are one thousand seeds in every kiwi fruit.

We were escorted back to the main building and treated to Kiwi wine, Kiwi tarts, and Kiwi juice. After our snack, we were free to roam the building and souvenir shop, get back on the bus, tour the city, and on the ship early by afternoon. Trivia's, sunbathing, watching the ocean balance of the day, dinner, show, and bed.

Two things we learned from the driver on the way back to the city. The unemployment recipients have to work when there is work (as in the orchards at harvest time); the minimum wage here is $13.50 per hour. We are currently discussing increasing our minimum wage from $7.50 to $10.00 per hour. The argument in the US is that the minimum wage should be a livable wage, but from what we see in Europe and here, the cost of living is much higher than in the States; it sounds like the higher the wages, the higher the costs, hmmm! Back on the ship, I went for a swim; to my dismay, the celebrity had freshwater pools. To eat in the main dining room, the dress code is usually smart casual, but donning long pants wasn't that bad, and a nice shirt change did feel good. I had escargot in garlic butter, duck pate', and grilled fish. Lynn had her new favorite, lamb shank. After dinner, we trolled the shops and attended the nightly show featuring a pianist.

February 6th, a day at sea. Sunbathing, trivia, signing up for the egg drop and the ship building contests, enrichment series lectures put on by a professor of history, a forensic professor, and a published naturalist, attended "Wildlife of the Ocean"; baby whale drinks 120 gallons of milk per day, and that milk is 50% fat!

Attended "Tastes of Solstice," a sampling of the specialty restaurants on the ship, sampled crab cakes and orange chicken, and watched how to bone a fish and properly prepare a lobster tail.

Attended a diamond lecture, Chocolate Diamonds, How do you tell if you have a real diamond? Place a dot on a piece of white paper and place the diamond over it. If you see the dot through the "diamond," it is not a diamond; the diamond refracts light, and you should not see the dot.

Another great dinner, between the two of us, we had frog legs, spinach salad, cold pear soup, salmon tartar, roasted duck, and a rack of lamb. Grand show with officer introduction followed by musical singing and dancing.

February 7th, Friday, Akaroa, the Akaroa Dolphin swim day. Off the ship early, the tender ride is choppy and almost a half hour. The excursion is located right on the dock. We are told there are only twelve of us, given boxes to put our valuables in, and then fitted for wet suits and wet boots. Fitted up, we walk across the dock to a large fishing boat, and off we go into the harbor in search of the Hector dolphins.

These dolphins are the smallest in the dolphin family, only about one and a half meters in length at full maturity. They are not fed by the operators, and even though they are somewhere in the harbor, you have to find them and then hope they want to play. We found a mother and calf, but she was not interested in the boat or us. We then found a small pod of twelve that were curious. The boat was stopped, and we quietly lowered ourselves into the warm water. (This is the ocean; the water here was about 30 feet deep, and near the mouth of the inlet, waves 1-2 feet).

The problem with wet suits is that they make you buoyant, and it is a real effort to stay upright in the water. You must move your legs either in a long swing or marching action to stay upright. Lynn had a lot of difficulty doing this the first time; she was close to a few dolphins but finally ingested too much seawater and got out.

I migrated farther out from the boat and found dolphins surfacing all around. They are very quick, and all of a sudden, there is one in front of you, behind you to your right or left, just beyond arm's reach, then gone. We were in the water for about an hour when the dolphins took off. We went back to the boat, searched for more pods, and saw a few single dolphins, but then none, so we headed back to the dock. Getting out of a wet suit is like peeling a banana; it is actually easier to get off than on. We bought the photo pack showing the size of the boat, the size of the group, and pictures taken by the crew when we were in the water. We were told that this was the largest pod they had found all week and that the dolphins stayed with the swimmers longer than usual. Go figure!

We then explored the town and shops, returning to the ship by one o'clock. Sunbathing, working on an egg drop project, and ship. Trivia's, great meal, this dinner group quite lively and animated, so dinner now is also a 1 1/2 to 2-hour event, good show, and the day was done.

Thursday, Feb 8th, Dunedin, New Zealand. (The South Island) Had a formal breakfast this morning with an Australian couple and a couple from England. Very interesting conversations! Off the boat later this morning, we toured the town, mansions, the Dunedin Railroad station (the most photographed building in New Zealand), and the Botanical Gardens.

We also stopped at the world's steepest street, Baldwin, to take pictures. Cadbury Candy Company once a year sponsors an event where 30,000 chocolate balls are rolled down the street for charity.

The bus driver did provide us with a sample chocolate ball. They were very good! Next, we were off to the Otago Yellow-Eyed Penguin Reserve. We ended up at the tip of the shore, looking for penguins on the beach from a vantage point well above. No penguins, but we saw a few sea lions. We then proceeded down to the nesting areas, heavily camouflaged runs single file to a number of nesting areas. We did find one female with a chick, and we were within three to four feet of the nest. We re-boarded the bus to go to the penguin hospital and saw quite a few "on the mend." Penguins may be cute, but they are picky eaters. They are difficult to feed, all the helpers have peck marks on their arms, and they only eat their own fresh catch and will not pick up dropped fish from other penguins. The young must learn to hunt on their own and need to swim 20 to 30 kilometers to feed in the ocean. After feeding, they come back to shore to sleep at night. Prior to mating season/molt, they fatten themselves because they don't eat till the molting is over. During the molt, they will lose 50% of their weight. These yellow-eyed penguins are the world's smallest penguins, reaching a mature height of only as high as a human knee.

On the way back to town, the guide pointed out where the albatross's nest was, stating that the closest we could get was on the ship as we left the harbor.

Back on the ship, we waited on deck as the ship set sail and passed the albatross nesting area. We saw some nesting birds, but not one albatross flew close to the ship as we went by.

February 9th, all day, we cruised through the New Zealand Sounds. Dusky Sound 9-10:45, Doubtful Sound 12-1:15, and Milford Sound 4:15-5:45. These sounds are very similar to the fiords we witnessed in Norway, except that these were a little less steep, not as high, and greener. Deep channels throughout lower New Zealand, we explored a number of them, and we were told that it was unusually calm and clear. I took quite a few pictures and saw a few sea lions, albatrosses, and beautiful waterfalls. After the third sound, we headed out to the Tasmanian Sea for two days before our next port of call, Sydney, Australia. The water became a little choppier, but very little motion was felt inside the ship in this crossing.

10th and 11th at sea, sunbathing, mild days, the temperature in the upper 60s F, ship games, walked the deck for a mile, worked on egg drop and model ship, more lectures (extremely interesting and very well presented).

The Lindberg baby kidnapping, the facts like it was more common during the depression that wealthy people were targeted by kidnappings. The kidnapper asked for $100,000, which would be equal to about a million today. The baby probably died when the kidnapper fell with the baby when he tried to exit the bedroom, and the ladder broke.

About every 18 months, there is a total lunar eclipse; tides are due to the wobble of the earth in its orbit along with the moon and earth's gravitational pulls, front, and back bulges; the new moon or full moon is when the tides are highest. During an eclipse, the earth cools slightly, which generates wind, so you will feel a breeze.

The sun flips its magnetic field every eleven years; it flipped last year, and no one other than scientists noticed!

Participated in a putting contest; we didn't place, but it was fun playing on real grass on the ship. Lynn also participated in Bache Ball completion on the grassy areas.

Attended the Corning glass demonstration, where glass blowers on the rear deck have a furnace and working area. Different art pieces are created with numerous steps, and each is explained by a narrator. The pieces are all unique, and many were auctioned throughout the cruise. Every day at sea, there was a demonstration.

Australian customs came on board to process us, our visas were recognized, and the entire ship was processed efficiently and comfortably.

Dinner on the 11th offered kangaroo. It was very tasty, lean, and delicious.

As we are crossing over to Australia, there are a few Maori phrases we need to remember:

Hello: Kia Ora

Goodbye: Haere ra

Welcome: Haere mai!

Very well, thank you, ok: Kei Te Pai

Thank you. Ka Pai

How are you? Kei Te pehea koe?

Ocean: Wainui

February 12th, Sidney, Australia.

We started out the day on a four-hour tour of Sydney. The ship was docked between the opera house and the bridge ("Aussies" call the bridge the "Clothes Hanger"). We opted for the tour of the opera house and Sydney rather than walk the bridge due to my knees and the number of steps involved. We boarded the bus and went right to the opera house for a fully escorted tour. The details are as follows: Designed by Jom Utzon, built on Bennelong Point, and finished in 1973 for a cost of 102 million Australian dollars. (The bridge was finished in 1932) 2679 capacity in the concert hall, 1420 in the theatre (was1500). The seats are designed to reflect the human shape, including shoulders and faces, orthopedically designed.

This concert hall has the world's largest mechanical tract organ in the world. Every piece of raw materials except for the outside tiles is Australian, two types of Australian woods. In regards to the ceramic tiles that cover the outside of the structure, there are 1,056,000 of them, two different white colors and designed to be self-cleaning. During the 2000 Sidney World Olympics, tourists were caught removing the tiles with hammers and chisels! This was the only time there was extensive vandalism to the opera house.

After that full tour of the theater and concert hall, we passed back our headsets, filed through the gift shop, and went back to the bus. Off to Bondi (sounds of water) Beach! This is the best beach for people watching, a half mile of pure white sand, next to a seawater pool at the Bondi Icebergs Club.

This provided us a perfect example of a friendly, energetic bunch of people who have a refreshing tell-it-like-it-is approach to life. We walked the beach, inspected the changing rooms, and had an ice cream. Although there were rumors that this was a topless beach, only guys going topless were observed. (☹)

Back to the coach, we returned to the city, touring the city. The buildings use a lot of decorative wrought iron railings and trim and neat homes. Also, the streets became increasingly crowded as we returned to the harbor. It has been a perfect day, sunny, light breeze, 26C/79 F when we return to the ship.

Had lunch on board and spent time on deck watching the ferries and people come and go from the opera house. Took second place in a trivia game, worked on the biodegradable boat for the contest (Morris and Lobo, our room stewards, provided cardboard and plastic bottles, and scissors, Nevena the cocktail hostess, extra swizzle sticks), changed for dinner, then went back out on deck to take night pictures of the bridge and opera house along with Sidney's skyline.

Thursday the 13th is a day at sea.

Trivia, lectures, walking on deck, sunbathing, working on the ship model, and signing up for the egg drop. The egg drop is another game where we are provided 3 raw eggs and 3 balloons. On a future date, we will be required to drop these eggs four stories to a target, points for hitting the target, creativity, and unbroken eggs. Participated in the battle of the genders and friendly feuds and attended a great one-woman show after dinner.

Friday 14th, Melbourne, Australia

A sign greeting us stating this is the "Best place to live in the world"; we have an excursion planned early in the morning. Before I go any further, Aussies call New Zealanders "Kiwis," and in answer, New Zealanders call out: "Aussie, Aussie, Aussie," to which Australians reply, "Oui, Oui, Oui."

Off to the Serendip Open Range Sanctuary, where we walk into the park in search of kangaroos, emus, and koalas. After walking a hundred meters or so, we approached an emu. he (or she) was a little skittish, and we were only able to get within about ten meters of him. (Or her)

Noah

We then proceeded into the bush. The guide asked us to be as quiet as possible, and we were able to see a few females with a couple of joeys. One male started to see us and took a defensive stance, and we needed to move on. We saw a few more kangaroos under the low bushes a few more emus, and then walked back to the bus. Loaded on and then went to an area where water, tea, and cookies wait for us. After our snack, we went off to the You Yang National Park, where we trekked through the park on the hunt for Koalas. After following a path to the left 150 meters, we located a female 10 meters up in a tree. No noise, shouting, or yelling. She did move, but only slightly. After everyone took their pictures, we returned to the parking lot and headed in another direction to find another.

One hundred and fifty to two hundred meters later, we found two; both were farther away and blended in well, but we took pictures of what we saw. Koalas sleep 16 to 18 hours a day; they usually move from one tree to another at night. It's not too active or exciting; more on Koalas later on!

Moving to another part of the sanctuary, we walked a path to a watering hole, crossed a bridge, and found Bull ants, one of the biggest ant species in the world, and skirted around their nesting area. We found two families of kangaroos, with joeys in the pouch, more emus, another koala, and a koala named Pat, and we discovered the plants called pig feet. Kangaroo males live about 8 years, and a group of kangaroos is called a mob; 35 days' gestation for a Joey, a mother can hold up gestation up to 8 months and can determine the sex of the Joey.

The Joey spends 12 months in the pocket nursing; the milk changes as the Joey matures, and after 6 months, the Joey does go in and out of the pocket. Young females bond and have daughters first to form their own mobs, then later have males who, when they mature, move on to join other males.

Great day! Taunted the guide and driver to reply when I called out

Educating Noah…Travelin'

"Aussie, Aussie, Aussie," and Lynn took pictures of us looking like kangaroos. We got her card, Echidna Walkabout Tour, at www.echidnawalkabout.com.au. Back on the boat, Supper, Hypnotist show, and done for the night.

Saturday, the 15th of February, another day at sea.

Today, I finished the paper boat, 50cmx160cm x40cm, and 2.3kg. Or 5 pounds, 236 programs, 15 stir sticks, one package of dental floss, and two and a half rolls of tape total. I have pictures. Attended trivia, a lecture on "Shaaaks," and another on "The dingo's eating the baby case in Australia." The dinner was great; the three-tenor show was enjoyable.

Sunday the 16th of February, Adelaide, Australia. Off the ship early for another excursion in Australia, a tour of aboriginal culture and winery tasting. We started with a city tour museum, where we were provided a lecture tour through the exhibits regarding the history of the Aborigines. There are about 500,000 left. Australia is about the same size as the continental United States, but most of Australia is arid scrub.

The interior suffers years without rain. It is hot, the soil is poor and sandy, and there is a large water reserve deep under the ground, but when it is drawn up, it is hot and brackish, so most of the coast is where all the Australians live. Australia is one of the richest countries in gold, silver, precious metals, and iron ore. Aborigines were communal people, drifting and drifting to find food and water. When you were born, you became part of your family's specialty. (Weavers, hunters, fishermen, water finders, etc.) If you thought you could be a better weaver than someone in another family of weavers, then you would have to find someone in that family to take your family job.

We viewed displays of all the animals found in Australia: lots of snakes, spiders, and small rodent-like animals, and mostly nocturnal. Of the 40 most poisonous animals in the world, Australia has thirty-nine of them!

After the museum, we were off to the winery. We were treated to a sampling of five different wines, each paired with a specific cheese. The wines we liked were a Savanaugh Blanc and their Muscat. On the way back to the ship, we noted that the houses are small but neat. However, there was more graffiti here than we saw in Melbourne. It was a very informative and interesting tour; back on the ship, Trivia started working on the egg drop project. Excellent meal, excellent comedian show!

Monday, February 17th, day at sea. At 01:30 A.M., We received a call from Tiffany, our daughter, that Lynn's dad, Peg, had passed. No funeral was planned. We told Tiffany to send flowers, call Dee, his wife, to check on her, and as we go on all our vacations, to do whatever she feels appropriate, and we would fully reimburse her for whatever she decides.

This is our tenth cruise and the first with a window to the outside. It's kind of nice waking up in the morning, opening up the drapes, seeing dark blue water, a light blue sky, and all sparkling. The temperature is only in the 60s F, and there is a wind on the deck at 10 to 15 knots; the sun is shining through a few puffy clouds; what a great day! Lynn is down due to her loss, so I left her to herself and her activities. Attended a mandatory meeting for all back-to-back cruisers (800 of us!), then met Lynn for the lecture called "Maggots, Maggots, Maggots" by Professor Haydn Green. Don't laugh. The theatre had over 400 people for this lecture! Lunch, then a second lecture on the animals with pouches by the Naturalist Milos. One more lecture (they are all only about 45 minutes in length) was The Man Who Wasn't Darwin" by Professor Lisa Didler. Alfred Wallace did all the research on animals and species; Darwin was the man with the money; he was the one who published all of Wallace's work. You publish, and you get the credit. There is a Wallace frog that glides in the air, and there is also a Wallace Line extending off the coast of Bali, where the species are different. One has tigers and rhinos in Asia, and the other has kangaroos and koalas in Australia.

Shallow water plus sunshine creates a coral reef. Coral feeds at night; the polyps come out of the coral and feed on the plankton that drifts down from the surface water when the surface cools at night.

Tried the Molecular Bar tasting, a high-end science of combining alcohol with various odd complimentary ingredients; the first night Lynn and I went, the two cocktails cost $28.00. She had Indulgence, Kuala, raspberry vodka, and light Godiva chocolate liquor, and I had a 3G Martini, vodka ginger, and Lychee.

On the 11th, they had a Molecular bar tasting where you got 5 half drinks for $18.00, so I jumped at it. Here are the recipes I tried:

Dragon Fly: Vodka, Cointreau, Aloe Vera juice, pink dragon fruit juice, raspberries, lime, hibiscus essence, and liquid nitrogen.

Scorpion Kiss: Scorpion Blanco Mescal, Gram and Marnier liqueur, Agave Nectar, Lychee puree, passion fruit puree, lime juice, pastille, and cinnamon salt.

Mister B: Jack Daniels, Domain de Canton ginger liqueur, agave liqueur, grilled pineapple, grilled grapefruit, lemon juice.

Tanned Russian: Russian standard vodka, Malibu/Coco Lopez, grilled pineapple juice, fresh lime juice, and grated coconut.

ALL tasted GREAT!! (Although each full drink cost $14.00 each!)

More trivia picked up the rules and eggs for the egg drop contest. Another great dinner, then treated by a violinist, Jane Cho, Electra; an outstanding show! Lynn went to the 60's party and danced with the staff.

Tuesday the 18th, day at sea, egg drop day. Lectures on body decomposition, Egg drop competition, you get three raw eggs and three balloons, you must construct a vehicle to be dropped four stories onto a target and have all eggs survive without breaking out of all biodegradable materials, and nothing from the ship that is Celebrity's, including decks of cards and pillows. I had the most elaborate device, constructed out of casino buckets, toilet paper daily programs (expired), toothfloss, and tape. I called it the Kiwi Express. I made a parachute out of a waste paper bag and a capsule out of buckets, toilet paper, and tape. A stuffed kiwi was strapped to the top of the buckets, and off he was launched from the seventh floor inside down to the floor with a target on the third level. The kiwi freaked out (being his first experience flying), and the parachute drifted to the right. Both the Kiwi and eggs survived without injury, but other vehicles landed on target without breaking their eggs, so we lost.

I had a little discussion with Karl (the Kiwi), and he indicated he would do better if there was a Kiwi II Express, and he kind of liked the flight! Of all the 8 participants, only two eggs broke out of the 24.

Put Karl on the top of the couch, where he likes, played trivia, had another great meal, and attended the show. It was a juggler/acrobatic show, and the house was packed.

Wednesday 19th of February Esperance, Australia. Earlier this week, I saw a flash on the excursion video showing a pink lake. This was one of the "Must-see" on my list, but I didn't remember if I signed up for an excursion that went there! I talked to one of the people at the excursion desk, and they confirmed that this port is where it is. I asked them to check to see if the excursion I was signed up for included this pink lake, and they said they would check. In the meantime, I also checked with the concierge about directions to the lake in the event there were no excursions, and I could take a cab after the excursion I had signed up for, in that my excursion was only four hours, and we were in port eight hours.

After the egg drop yesterday, I checked again and was told if I bought the afternoon excursion, I wouldn't miss the lake, so I did, with the guarantee that there was enough time to make the connection between my early one and this afternoon tour.

Early off the ship, on the bus, and guess what? The first stop was THE PINK LAKE! And it was bluish-green. The area had been through a heat wave followed by two days of torrential rain; although today was nice and clear, the blooms of the algae that turned the lake pink were gone. I took the picture of the lake the sign, and loaded back on the bus. (We did see a pink pond at the last port we were at on the way back to the ship; it is pink. I did see it along with Lynn, and so they do exist, but no pictures!

We visited a decorative flat glass production plant and were treated to how flat glass is developed for jewelry and art. It was an interesting, nice shop, and I was highly proud that this was a pure Australian product. Back on the bus and over to see the shark and fish skin works. Here again, the process was explained: what happens to the fish and the scales after the skin is taken. I bought fish skin bookmarks for the kids and a toad skin coin purse for me. (Yes, a real toad, with two front legs (having the front legs cost $4.00 more).

Got back to the port and waited for the second tour, wondering where we were to go and if another view of the pink lake was in store.

This tour was to Cape Le Grand National Park. The first stop was to the whitest sand beach in Australia. It was a 50-meter walk down to the beach, so the group left us behind. We arrived, and the sand was like powdered sugar; I put some in my pocket and brought it home. It feels very powdery. The group encountered two small wild kangaroos, but they were gone by the time we got there.

I did go to the water's edge and noticed many black gelatinous blobs about the size of a deflated soccer ball three to four meters from the water's edge. I didn't have a stick to poke and was slightly smart enough not to turn over with my shoe, so I looked around and saw Lynn talking to a local. As stated before, the Australians are very friendly, straightforward, and more than willing to talk and answer questions. He told us that those "blobs" were dead cuttlefish. Of course, I asked how they tasted, and he said they were better than squid, just that you had to eat them before they matured and got pregnant. Why? I asked, and he said that making the babies takes all the fat... makes sense!

Back on the bus, another beach, beautiful tones of blue in the water, the water 18 degrees centigrade, no animals to be found except for a glimpse of a lizard in the bush along the path. Our last stop was a full-sized replica of Stone Hedge. 137 stones of pink granite weighing 38 to 50 tons each, and 18 lintels at a height of 8 meters.

It is aligned with the summer solstice sunrise, as is the original Stone Hedge (22nd of December), which is the longest day of the year. (The winter solstice sunset (June 21) is the shortest day of the year.) Back to the bus (notice no pink lake!?) and just in time to catch the last shuttle to the ship, I registered a complaint about the miss-information given on the second excursion, promptly received a call from the manager and agreed to meet tomorrow at 10A.M. Changed for dinner, and after attended a Rod Stewart clone show. Long day! Then Lynn participated in Dancing with the Officers and was a participant! They danced on the other side of the floor, and I got some pictures but couldn't get close enough to take any great pictures. She did get eliminated in the second round; her officer was nothing close as flamboyant as two of the other officers, but one of them did win. It was fun, tired Lynn out quite a bit, enough, and went to bed.

Thursday, the 20th

The last day at sea before the end of the first cruise in Perth. Slept in from yesterday, had a formal breakfast and lively discussion with an English and Australian couple, and attended a lecture on a Judge's death and Forensics, Brothels in New Orleans, and navigation. Met with the excursion manager, and he was ready with an online description of both excursions and a smug smile.

Educating Noah...Travelin'

I let him start, and then after reading the descriptions, I asked him if those descriptions were available to his people and then to anyone on the ship with no internet connection. He said yes and no, to what I replied, they should have known, and how was I to know. He stated I had a good point and asked what he could do. I said I felt guilty asking for a refund since I did go, and he said I could have canceled on the pier. I then referred him to the policy of no refunds within 24 hours, and he said this would have been an exception; I said I didn't want to be out the $240.00 on an exception that I did take the trip. It was OK, and I would be satisfied if he would talk to his people regarding advising excursions, including sights not in the brochure or on-ship description.

I also brought up the fact that on all the excursions so far, the guide who led the party to the bus set a quick pace, so the fastest and fittest always got the front of the bus; anyone who had any walking difficulties was doomed to the back of the bus, maybe some effort should be made to keep the group together, and to reserve a few seats for "caned" people, those that don't want to admit they are "disabled." He thanked me for the meeting, and off I went. I had a boat to float!

Today was also the boat judging, so off to the pool. Our boat was the biggest, more than twice the size of the nearest contender. Each boat was floated to see if they were sea-worthy, and then a staff member with Bache balls attacked by throwing the balls to sink the boats. Mine was presented last; I gave a short spiel and, walked the boat close to the "pirate," and threw the boat right in front of him. It took a direct hit without phasing it! No true winner was announced. We "all won" and received T-shirts, certificates, and a bottle of Champaign.

Our team won the progressive trivia, more T-shirts, bags, and caps., After supper, we attended the Grand Finale, including acrobats, the comedian, jugglers, and the violinist. It was a great show!

There were 780 guests continuing to the next cruise, including us, and 2000 new guests for the upper part of Australia and Bali. Tomorrow we swim with the dolphins again, these guys are bigger!

Friday, February 21st, the last day of the first cruise,

The first day of the second cruise and the Dolphin Swim day.

We exchanged our cards at 06:45 and hurriedly left the ship at 0700 for the hour ride to the beach/ harbor, where we were to meet bottle-nose dolphins. We boarded the yacht; it was Lynn and I and one other person from our ship.

About 24 of us boarded the yacht, and off we went. The biggest wet suit on board was an extra-large, so my back would not zip up, but it didn't matter. We were all assigned a group, and when we were in the water, the guide with a water scooter would drive out, and we would hold on to each other's belts and be towed around in the water. There was also a scuba diver below, trying to help herd the porpoises to us. We were close to several on the swims we took!

Then we went to a quiet cove, and we could all try driving the water scooters, which was a lot of fun; I thought they would be a little faster!

After a couple hours, we returned to the beach and had an hour, so we sampled some Aussie beer while waiting for our bus back. Nice hour rides back to the port, back on the ship by three, nap, trivia, dinner, and show. This is the start of Cruise II!

Distance traveled:

Ports visited New Zealand

Distance	Ports visited
Australia	Distance
Auckland	
Bay of Islands	140

Sydney	997
Tauranga	210
Melbourne	552
Akaroa	595
Adelaide	461
Dunedin	147
Perance	887
Dusky Sound	254
Perth (Fremantle)	554
Doubtful Sound	23
Milford Sound	55

Cruise total: 4875 nautical miles, 1 Nautical mile = 1.15 land miles

Cruise II Upper Australia and Bali ... 02/22/14 to 03/10/14

We left Perth at 6 P.M. last night to start our new continued adventure for the second half of our "back-to-back." The first day is a day at sea. We lost our trivia partners; both the Aussie couple and the English teachers left in Perth. We coupled up with another New Zealand couple and a couple from America who are on their 30th cruise! One thing I didn't mention about the Aussie couple: Jeff's hobby was building quarter-scale steam engines! He showed pictures...WOW! He has a track in his backyard and gives rides. They are true steam engines, and everything is working and to scale.

I attended another lecture on animal life and the earth. The earth is 30% land and 70% water on the surface, but given an average depth of 11,000 feet of water, the earth is really 95% water. Life collects at intersections, where earth and water meet the air and where water meets the land. The Korman bird is known as shag in Australia; Nekton is the species of swimmers, dolphins, fish, whales, and plankton is categorized as floaters.

I had missed this one on the first cruise; I then attended an information session about the ship. The ship carries 2800 to 3000 passengers, 1200 crew of which 350 are female. The ship needs 30 feet or 10 meters of water to navigate and has two rear thrusters and two front thrusters. The rear is 360 degrees maneuverable; the front thrusters are only left or right.

I signed up for shipbuilding again on this cruise and promised a new design. We checked with the service desk as to when to call Dee, my mother-in-law, regarding Peg's passing. There is a 15-hour lag; we must subtract 15 hours when we call, so we calculated a good time, and this was really nice. They will not charge for the ship-to-shore long-distance call! (The usual cost is about $15.00/minute) Played another trivia, walked the ship, and supper was at a different table. We had requested a round table for eight. Our new member was a woman from Perth on her first cruise to see the rest of Australia, and very nice. The show was a repeat, so we watched a free movie in the room.

Sunday, February 23rd, another day at sea.

Trivia times three; it is 85-90 degrees (F), so yes, tanning is also on the addenda.

Saw some flying fish (the first time); they would show up in three and fours, skim over the water at a high rate of speed, and "fly" 10 to 15 meters! I also saw a small pod of dolphins off the bow for a while. We are approaching Port Hedland, so there are other ships within sight, all cargo and tankers. It's an easy day; we make port tomorrow.

Monday February 24th, Port Hedland

We called Dee, which would be late afternoon on Sunday her

time, checked on how she was doing, and asked if we should stop by after the cruise and fly from San Francisco to Tucson instead of home. She said "no," that she was doing alright and sorting things out. We wished her well and told her we would check up on her when we returned home after the cruise.

Today, it's 102 (F), hot and dry; it's time to go to shore and check things out!

There were no real interesting excursions, so none were signed up for; we took the five-minute bus ride to town. The town consisted of three blocks of stores, ½ closed or moved, and a small craft market set up for us. We toured the small aboriginal museum and the craft market and walked the town, which took the better part of an hour; the bus then took us to the shopping mall for anyone wishing to get sundries at a reasonable rate. Took some pictures of us sweltering and some flowers, and we were back on the ship by 11:00 a.m.

This port is one of the biggest iron exporters of Australia. There are lots of ships in the harbor, all transport, ore ships.

We received a call from Tiffany that Lynn's brother and sister decided to fly down to Tucson to see Dee the weekend before we returned, and we confirmed that Tiffany had notified all other concerned folks.

Spent some time in the sun, watched the ships load, and left port at 4P.M., just before dinner. After supper, we went up on deck, still watching the passing cargo ships going in and out of port, not to mention a number of them waiting in queue.

Tuesday, Feb 25th, a day at sea on the way to Bali.

We signed up to participate in the dance mob, trivia, lectures, and sunbathing. On a slow, relaxing day, I had another excellent dinner and a xylophone/synthesizer show that was highly energetic and fun.

Wednesday, February 25th, Benoa (Bali), Indonesia.

Noah

We signed up for a full day in Bali, The Balinese Way of Life, lasting 9 ½ hours! So, we were the first tour group to leave the ship, tendered into the port by lifeboats, and then onto our coach for a day in Bali.

Our first stop was the Kehen temple, still in use today, with beautiful statues and stone carvings. Then, off to a village called Penglipuran, where we were able to tour through a family's homes and compound (I got pictures including the pig!),

By this time, it was time to eat, so we visited the Kintamani village for views of Mt. Batur, an active volcano, and enjoyed an Indonesian buffet lunch. I took pictures of the snake fruit and the Lychee nut I had to peel for dessert. Yes, to the Lychee, the snake fruit was just OK, but I had to try it! The rest of the meal was very good, lots of rice and vegetables. The view of the volcano was outstanding.

We experienced a traffic slowdown with traffic and people in the streets, a beautiful terraced valley, a silver and gold sweatshop, a batik linen factory, and a painting gallery in the Ubud area. They were exceptionally friendly people, our guide was outstanding, and we learned a lot about the Balinese.

We got on the last tender to the ship, showered, grabbed a bite at the cafeteria, and went back to our room for an early night.

Thursday, 27th of February, a day at sea. There is more trivia. Actually, I am getting tired of them, but the group is fun; I worked on building the boat and saw some more flying fish. Now, there were a few fish, sometimes only one, they were very fast! And I was still surprised at how long they were in the air. Lynn went to her first flash mob practice, and later tonight at 10:30, we have a "secret" practice on deck.

Friday the 28th of February, another day at sea. Today, there was more trivia, another mob practice, and a crepe demonstration. Later, after lunch, about 20 of us flash mob danced on the deck, dancing to

Gang-man Style...We pulled it off in 90-degree high humidity afternoon, so afterward, we went down to the shower to refresh work on the egg drop project. Supper lost at Family Feud, went to the show, and Lynn went up to the Black and White dance to check it out.

Saturday, March 1st, Darwin, Australia. They actually close the beaches four to five months a year due to crocodiles! They lost two kids last year! We went ashore and had an excursion to Crocodiles Park.

We fed the crocs, saw wallabies, saw quite a few wild cockatiels, took pictures of flowers, handled a baby alligator (crocs are too dangerous), Lynn held an alligator also, and I also handled a five-foot snake (felt cool and reptilian?) Lynn refused the snake!

Back on the ship after touring the town, the temp was in the high 90s (F), and the humidity was high also, whew.... took another shower and toured the ship inside.

Sunday, March 2nd, Day at sea. We did Trivia, walked, and watched two movies: Lazy, Easy Day.

Monday, March 3rd. At sea, slow, easy day number two. I made a rack to hold the catamaran I had finished yesterday due to the keel. Walked the deck and stayed to watch the entering the Great Barrier Reef mid-morning. The navigational channel is rather narrow, so we see other ships on both sides, and the ocean has different colors of blue. It was a formal night; I attended dinner and skipped the show. It was a repeat of a show we saw on the first cruise.

Tuesday, March 4th, the third day at sea, high winds closed the outside decks, but the ship was still smooth sailing. Paper airplane contest, with about twenty entrants. I made a birdie design, had a lot of hang time, but veered to the right and smashed into the wall. This affected its flight; I just made the minimum distance on the next flight but spiraled down on the third, and I didn't place. Had my metabolism measured and analyzed my health and said that I was carrying 20 pounds of excess water and that I needed to be detoxed. The detox would free the water, and my metabolism would then help take care of the rest. Only $300 for a mini, $600 for a six-month program, and a special price of $900 for the one-year program. I told her I would mull it over with my wife. Another great meal, the menus in the main dining room repeated those of the first cruise, so we tried different entrée and appetizers, all excellent and beautifully presented.

The clean comic on the show was refreshing; off to bed, and tomorrow is Arlie Beach and the Great Barrier Reef expedition.

Wednesday, March 5th, Arlie Beach. Many of us were concerned due to the storm we came through to get here and how clear the water would actually be. The sea had 1-2-foot waves, so the ride out may be a little choppy, especially if the wind increased with us crossing the sea lane.

We were directly loaded onto the catamaran for our journey to the platform at the reef. The catamaran holds 300 of us has a crew of 15, and it will take 2 to 2 1/2 hours north to get to the reef, 90 kilometers from shore! As we take off, the seas are still a little high, and the captain asks if anyone wishes not to go to let a crew member know ASAP. No one opted to get off. On the trip out, only six to eight got physically sick; the rest were pretty quiet. I migrated to a seat outside the two-and-a-half-story deck to enjoy the air.

After a half hour, I asked a crew member how to judge where we were; she pointed out the island behind us and said, "When you can no longer see any land in the back, look for a speck in the horizon, that will be the platform," she was right. The water did get rougher in the shipping lane as the island got smaller, then got calmer as we entered the reef.

At 10:40, we arrived at the floating platform. It was a 2-story platform with an observation deck below that had windows. Tied up and providing rides for everyone was also a glass-bottomed boat. The very top deck was for sunbathers and a slide into the ocean for kids. The main deck had all of the wet suits, snorkeling gear, and fins, along with tables, chairs, changing booths, and two platforms to enter the outlined snorkeling areas.

We changed into our wet suits (these were lighter than the previous wet suits but supposedly better protection from jellyfish), got our gear, and got into the water. The water is patrolled with a small boat, and there is also a person on the platform who watches everyone in the water. We got in the water and started swimming along one of the areas and saw quite a few different corals and fish. However, the waves were pretty high. The storm that preceded us the previous 2 days had made the water a little murky, and after the second wave flooded out Lynn's snorkel, she decided to end her swim and headed back in. I continued out, swallowing more salt water than I wanted, but too stubborn to go in, I followed the reef. I experienced many different small fish (no jellyfish or octopus) and found that if I stopped swimming and just lay in the water, more fish would approach me just out of curiosity. Looking up, I found myself beyond the marked area and turned back on a tangent towards the platform before the "boat police" came after me. The fourth time the waves overcame the snorkel, I had enough, too! Back on the platform, I peeled off the wet suit and turned in my mask, snorkel, and fins. I changed into clothes, and Lynn had scoped out the action and directed me back onto the catamaran for lunch. The lunch served buffet style, included ham and prawns, along with bread, salads, and vegetables and fruits. There is plenty to eat, and it is very good! All on board was 2:00 o'clock. We toured the top of the platform and then went below to look out the underwater windows.

Back on the catamaran, we left the platform promptly at 2 P.M. after taking two counts, making sure everyone was aboard. The trip back was smoother; the sea had calmed a bit, the water deep blue against a bright blue sky. We offloaded right back onto the cruise ship and changed for dinner, supper, and a Neil Diamond impersonator show.

Thursday, March 6th, a day at sea.

Slept in, all that salt water and exercise. This was egg drop day; this Kiwi expresses II was designed like a rocket, with nose cones and fins. Karl sat on the back, no parachute this time, but I didn't weigh the front enough, and it drifted to the left on its 4-story drop. This time, one egg did break. We still got 20 points but no win again, and we did get a mention for the most creative!

Karl (the Kiwi) and I returned to the room. We consoled each other. He took his perch for a rest, and I went to the Martini bar for a drink. I joined Lynn for trivia, another great supper (the escargot in garlic butter is to die for!), and attended the best show of both cruises. It was a singer-comedian named Mike Doyle. He has an incredible voice range and connected well with the audience, and everyone enjoyed the show with a standing ovation.

Friday, March 7th, Brisbane, Koalas!

Today was our city tour and the behind-the-scenes experience at the Lone Pine Koala Sanctuary.

We were given a guide for the group and guided throughout the sanctuary. As we proceeded in, we came upon three-foot lizards scurrying across the path and blending into the rocks; I caught a few with the camera. We proceeded to the back of the park and were told that there are over forty types of eucalyptus trees, of which only fourteen or fifteen koalas are interested. The eucalyptus trees grow very fast, almost as fast as bamboo!

Lynn helped plant a tree for the Koalas, and then we moved back into an area where the wallabies and kangaroos run wild with the tourists. We found a wallaby by a shed, and both Lynn and I petted him; he was soft and fur-like a dog. Back to the park central, we found more koalas, some Tasmanian devils, and wallabies. We all participated in the weekly weigh-in and inspection of a koala; it was time for pictures, so we each had our picture taken holding a bear. Lynn's bear was named Utopia, and mine was Cinnamon, both females; you don't hold males due to the gland on their belly for marking trees.

It's like holding a little fat teddy bear; when I stroked her, she hugged me more, and when I spoke to her, she nestled. (P.S.) You can't eat Koalas; their entire diet is eucalyptus leaves, and it taints the meat, just in case you wanted to know!!) These little guys live about fifteen years and sleep 14 to 15 hours a day.

An Australian Bar-B-Q lunch was served, and this, as with all the lunches provided, was extremely generous, and everything was fresh and delicious. We had an hour of free time, so Lynn and I went back in with the Kangaroos, petted an Emu, then found a mob of kangaroos, hand-fed a number of them and petted them too. They, like the wallabies, were soft and very docile, a nice up-close experience. We toured the town, back to the ship, dinner and show.

Lynn decided to check out Dancing with the officers. She was chosen again as a participant, and she got one of the wild officers! She rode him like a horse during one song, threw herself into his arms in another, wore a cowboy hat in another, and in the final elimination, donned a life jacket; then she was in a lifeboat, then she received resuscitation. (Dancing to the "Titanic" theme song).

She won the competition!! All this is recorded along with the entire cruise by the Discovery Channel; look for a program this spring on Mega cruise ships; you may see her! She won a dinner at a specialty Restaurant and said she would share it with me…Yes!

Bed, Lynn was completely used up!

Saturday, March 8th, is the last sea day. We slept late and had trivia, brunch, and a shipbuilding contest. I showed up, and all the rest of the people who signed up didn't (eight of them). They were called but no show! They Bache balled this one also, and his aim was very good, although it did transverse the pool twice before the pirates destroyed her. Another T-shirt and certificate, plus a lot of compliments from other passengers. The Crew members debated among themselves about which ship was better but paid me the best compliment in that they said my boats were the biggest and best of both contests. Put my winnings away, got some sun, finished up with trivia supper, and watched a movie in the room. (The entertainment was another repeat.)

Sunday, March 9th, New Castle.

Today is an eight-hour tour followed by a meal at the specialty restaurant Murano.

We have a city tour to start out the day, then off to the Australian Reptile Park. We entered the park and had several paths to take; they only requested that we meet in the lunch area for our included lunch at 12:15. We first went to the platypus enclosure. He is really fast, and it is very dark, but I got a few pictures of him. He's only a little over a foot long. Afterward, we went past a crocodile pond, where you see various eyes and snouts all over the pond; we liked the fence!

We then watched a show with snakes and alligators. The trainer was holding the alligator's egg when it hatched; they have a relationship. I didn't think reptiles could be trained or trusted, but when he put the alligator down, the alligator started walking toward the crowd, and the trainer just said the alligator's name and told him to lay down; the alligator stopped and laid on his belly!

We went off to the Tasmanian devil enclosure, and I got two great pictures of the two. As we walked forward, a trainer left one of the Galapagos Tortoises out of his pen. He had a bucket of vegetables to feed the big guy, and we could touch the shell and, if we wanted to, touch the back legs (it feels just like an elephant hide).

We proceeded to the Dingo area and found a white one that looked a lot like a coyote, a little larger and, according to the guide, a lot smarter. The wombat (looks like a large groundhog) was elusive and moved too fast and then too far away for any good pictures! Followed a path, came across a wallaby in the path, and gave him a few strokes, then found more of the Emus.

Lunch was typical Aussie Bar-B-Q: large steak, large sausage, rolls, salads, and drinks. We shared the meat and salads. Pictures inside a set of crocodile jaws took pictures of a no-swim sign and back on the bus and off to the resort town of The Entrance. It was a little early for the pelican feed, but this is the home of the world's largest pelicans; we did get a couple pictures of these, too. Had some homemade ice cream, walked along the beach, then re-boarded the coach for a ride through the countryside and back to the ship. We quickly changed and went to the Murano for our special dinner.

Lynn's winnings covered the $45.00 per person cover charge for the meal. The menu offered an alternative for an additional $89.00 each, and an off-the-menu selection was available; this is a cruise ship......with excellent food to start, so we ordered off the standard menu. I did order a glass of wine that cost $17.00, just to give you an idea!

Here is what we had: the start was a one shrimp cocktail, followed by appetizers. I had a goat cheese soufflé, and Lynn had scallops in a puff pastry. For the entre, Lynn had lobster; it was prepared at the table, shelled, at the tableside, then prepared with chives, mushrooms, bacon, and parmesan cheese in a cream sauce served over grilled vegetables and mashed potatoes, perfectly done, everything cooked to perfection. I had Venison, also perfectly prepared and presented. Desserts were triple chocolate soufflé with coffee-flavored ice cream; Lynn had a trio of desserts, including figs and apricots in puff pastry, mouse on rice crispies, and a fudge roll. They offered a small cheese platter, but we declined; we had plenty to eat. Although the meal was perfect, we both felt a little "out of place," the waiters and table people were very nice but a bit "uppity," and I could feel Celebrity pulling on my billfold, so we left.

Suitcases out of the cabin by 10 P.M.; set up everything for the trip back home and went to bed. At 11:30, we received a phone call that our flight had been canceled and a new flight and tickets would be at the door in the morning.

Monday morning, March 10th, new tickets, new flight, this one leaving an hour later, and lands in San Francisco; the connecting flight to Chicago is only an hour and a half after we land, we are going to have to run! Off the ship by 9:30, pick up luggage, and find our bus to the airport. There was some confusion with the busses, but we got on the one to the international airport and arrived at 10:45. No gate was assigned until three hours before the flight, so we found a place to sit with our entire luggage till 12:30 when the flight gate should show up and we can check our luggage and get our seat assignments. Pick up something to eat, and finally, the gate is assigned, and the luggage and ticket stations open.

Another line: check in the bags, both just under the 50# limit, and get our tickets; we are stuck in the middle of the plane. I told the attendant that we had paid for a premium seat on the fourteen-hour flight back, but she said we were added to another flight, and those folks had all the premium seats and that I would have to request a refund when I returned. Not too happy, we went through customs and sat another two and half hours for our completely full flight.

It was with United, so I prepared for the worst. We were loaded in group four, second to last, so finding the above seat space was difficult, but it worked. I had the aisle seat; the tray would not come all the way down when the seat in front of me was back, and she had it back the entire thirteen-hour flight. We were all cramped, there were no empty seats, and the numerous times I was bumped due to the thin aisles, especially by the attendants, was stupid. The plane had central entertainment, which meant everyone watched the same programming. You could turn off your headphones, but the screens flashed white with the United logo after every program. The player skipped the entire time, so the voices were not synced with the shows, and all of them would start and stop throughout the program. Did the pilot turn off the programs for a couple hours and darken the cabin…NO! It was a long flight, physically and mentally.

At the airport in San Francisco, we went another slow line through customs, then went to the carousels to pick up our luggage. We were told carousel one, and we waited and waited; then the carousel stopped, and a shout from the other side of the area indicated that some luggage came on carousal at the opposite side of the room. We ran over, picked up our luggage, and ran to the domestic United Air. Outside the luggage depot, we checked our luggage and then ran to the gate for our flight; leaving in half an hour, we still did not have assigned seats.

We got there just before they opened the gate to load; we got assigned seats between two strangers in different rows, middle seats for both of us and again, there were no open seats on this flight. We only had a four-hour flight, so we didn't care. However, we were given last priority to load, so we checked our carry-ons so we didn't have to find space in the overhead areas.

We arrived in Chicago at 7:30 PM and recovered our luggage. Lynn's backpack strap was ripped out, but we were tired. We missed the first bus to Milwaukee and waited an hour and a half for the last one. With all the time changes, the waits in airports, and the flights, we arrived home at midnight on Monday. We had gained our day back from when we crossed the dateline and had spent thirty-six hours traveling home. It's good to be home!!

Noah

Distance traveled:

Perth Au

Port Hedland, Au	972
Benoa, Bali, Indonesia	710
Darwin, Au	951
Airlie Beach, Au	1510
Brisbane, Au	517
New Castle, Au	429
Sydney, Au	75
Cruise total	5,164 nautical miles (1 nautical mile equals 1.15 land miles)

It took us both almost two weeks to recover from those thirty-plus hours getting back. All the projects are done; we just received both photo books, and the entire day–by–day write–ups have been edited and printed. Neither of us gained any weight despite 35 days on a cruise ship, so I started back to the gym.

The autobiography was published and available either in the Kindle version or hard copy. I gave each of the kids a copy along with my mother, Ted, and my aunt Irene, the family "documenter."

I contacted the office at Synergy for work, and they know I am available. I also brought them some Australian candy and kangaroo jerky. I also tried to promote my book to friends on the East and West coast.

We followed up with Dee, Lynn's father's widow. She seems to be doing fine. It's been 6 weeks since his passing, and we sent flowers again "just because."

I am starting to work on getting supplies for our African

Adventure in September, using the laser on my knees a little more often to promote some healing, and taking cleansing capsules to start a serious diet.

On the ship, I attended the metabolism class and follow-up discussion, indicating that I needed a cleanse. I researched on the web, found a number of products, and got them in. I started taking this product.........I believe it is a natural diuretic..........and I am paying for it!

The pseudo gout came back with a vengeance; the ball of my foot felt as if it was an open blister, and my left foot puffed up like a small football. After three days of drinking copious amounts of water and tart cherry juice and elevating the foot every chance I could, I discontinued the miracle drug. The pain went from the bottom of the foot to the side and top, making putting any shoe on that left foot excruciating. After the fifth day, the foot started residing, and I was able to put on a shoe and walk. I had two job assignments, so off to work I went. Last weekend, I celebrated with an apple-Tini. Oops, re-engaged the gout, back to the "open sore "left football. With more juice and more water, after two weeks, I can walk again without a limp. The pain is in the middle of the foot, and the swelling is down to the area just behind the toes. It has been three weeks since this whole pseudo-gout thing started. There are some aches and pains in my ankles, yes, both, and the bottom outside of both great toes, too!

I finally got the dates available for our summer road trip to visit the last States of the United States. I made a trip to AAA for the atlases and State books to plot the course and attractions. I also reviewed the vacations folder to see what was on the horizon. The one I really wanted was the "Top of the World" trip with Vikings that included China and Tibet, with a five-day cruise on the Yansing River, visiting the Great Wall and the terra cotta warriors. I called my agent at Online Vacations, and she sent me the info on the tour; she said Viking had extended deep discounts and would add an additional

$550.00 off the discounted price. I sold Lynn on the trip and jumped at the offer. So, now we have the road trip in June, the African Safari in September, and next April, China and Tibet.

Lynn's dad passed away, and we received some money. Lynn added to the amount, and we gave it all plus extra to the kids.... something we could have used in our rush, rush past life.

So now I have enough to do: some new clients, routing the road trip and healing this foot.

I have also planned a cross-country Segway adventure in Door County for a number of us in May, and I need to figure out the Android phone I upgraded to!!

I started my blog today. Tiffany, my oldest daughter, has one called the Chocolate Diaries, and she gave me a checklist.

1. Go to the library and get Blogging for Dummies
2. Buy a domain name
3. Get a hosting account
4. Chose a template

I did it all, and after a few hours, I had a Blog. Floodman1.wordpress.com, let's see how this goes!!

Well, it didn't seem to happen on the blog thing; I renewed the book at the library but just couldn't seem to get it off the ground. I called a niece, and she knew someone who could help, but that fell through also; I considered it a sign, so I discontinued. Now I just ruffle some feathers on Facebook and have been de-friended by a few who just want to rant without reason!

The Segway Eggstravaganza (Eggstravaganza was my name due to its proximity to Egg Harbor, WI.) I put it together and went off without a hitch. The motel was reasonable; we basically had the inside pool to ourselves, and the group was willing to go along with the "program." We met at the motel to decide where we could eat. The first choice was The Wild Tomato, but when we got there, it was a half-hour wait and no bar to sit at. We found another restaurant down the road willing to seat us without a wait. We had a nice meal and returned to the motel for a gathering by the pool. Our final late couple joined us to participate in a Trivia game; a bottle was brought, and to finish off a bottle of Templeton Rye Whiskey.

Saturday morning, we met for breakfast and walked across the street for breakfast. The service was slow; this was the very beginning of the tourist season, and everyone wasn't up to speed yet. We then drove up to Sister Bay to participate in the Goats to the Roof Parade. Well...it turns out only one goat showed up, so the whole parade consisted of an old fire truck and one large black goat! Everyone joined the parade to the Al Johnson Restaurant to watch the goat walk up to the grass roof. Well.... The goat refused to go up, so a pickup truck disappeared and, fifteen minutes later, showed up with two white goats. These goats wanted to go up to the roof and easily did (The black one continued to refuse to go up). It used to be that the goats would stay on top of the restaurant all summer, but a few years ago, one fell off, so they are taken down every night now.

After the parade, we went to the tip of Door County, checked out a motel the motorcycle club used to take over once a year, and grabbed a light lunch before heading to Seaquist Segways.

Seaquist Orchard Market was not open yet, but the owner of the Seaquist Segways sent his wife to lead us to the jump-off point. We were greeted and assessed as to our ability. Anyone who had not driven a Segway before was given one-on-one instruction until they were confident. These were cross-country Segways with oversized knobby tires.

We were led down a path to the middle of a field and, with a little experience, shown how to dismount the Segway. Once everyone was confident, we took off. We went through woods, up and down hills, some very narrow paths, rocks, bumps, and roots presented challenges for all. Yes, three of us did fall off, but we had no lasting injuries. After an hour or so, we took a break, then another half hour, another break, then back to where we started. We learned a lot about the topography of the Door County peninsula and the reason why cherries are grown here (shallow soil and basic 7.4 PH), creating exactly what cherry trees thrive on. The trees only last about 30 years, and when they are that old, the wood is only good for mulch. Apple trees are being introduced now; however, they are much more expensive to maintain. (More fertilizer, late season, more bug sprays)

The entire tour was almost three hours, we learned a lot, and even at the end, we were provided an area where we could "open them up" and drive them straight at top speed! (12mph) Lots of fun, and now everyone was confident in their Segways!

One couple stayed for the weekend. The rest returned home for Mother's Day on the 11th. We arrived home a little after 8 P.M., put the beans in the oven, and I was toast; went to bed at 9:30 and went right to sleep.

Mother's Day will be the last buffet day. The theme this year was Boston. Food included Boston baked beans, ham, homemade cornbread, a veggie tray, a fruit tray, shrimp and polish sausage on a stick, and a clam and fish chowder. Camille located and brought a Boston cream pie. I know I serve too much and too much variety, but I also do like the leftovers!

Everyone ate their fill and sat around with little, if any, enthusiasm. After just a little over two and a half hours, everyone was ready to leave. I packaged up care packages for whatever anyone wanted, and at three in the afternoon, we had everything cleaned up and put away. I had proposed paying for a Bahamas cruise in January. I need to re-check with everyone if they can arrange the time off and dog sitters. So, that will be the last; next year, Lynn and I will take out my mother, and as always, I will send flowers to Lynn, my mother, and our stepmother Dee in Tucson and let it go at that.

I gave up on a family cruise; family difficulties and work seem to be a priority over the family get-a-way, so I cut a check to both kids, "to be used for vacation only," and let them apply to whatever they want with their own family unit.

I also started cleaning out all of the leftover nursing supplies I kept at home and in the car. I donated to a local senior home and a free clinic. Another container was emptied.

On June 17th

We started to finish the United States tour, the day designated by the last shot for my knees. I was also proactive with my Hepatitis A & B booster shots, getting one before the vacation so the next shot would be after, and the last shot after returning from Africa.

Finish up the US; June, 2014

Tuesday, June 17, 2014. I had an appointment for my last knee shots with the cockscomb stuff. This was the third in the last three weeks. The VA claims I only need 3; civilians get 5 in a row, but according to the VA, three are fine?!

I arrived early to see if my 9:30 A.M. appointment would be closer to time. No one is taken early; they are always running behind, but I considered myself lucky to be taken at 10:10. Five minutes for the injections, and off I went.

I called Lynn, told her I would be home to pick her up in half an hour, and left the parking lot. Arrived home in 20 minutes; I fueled up and left the house at 11:00.

We stopped at a rest stop just after Springfield, Illinois. We witnessed a young guy losing his balance and falling at the curb. We walked over to help, and between his parents and us, we got him up. He had just been discharged from the hospital and was still pretty weak. He was unhappy with himself and just wanted to return to the car. We think he was more embarrassed. He was about 6 ft. 220 # and quite a handful. The parents thanked us, and we returned to the van and off.

We hit St. Louis right in the middle of rush hour and crawled through town for almost 45 minutes; however, we got a few extra arch pictures to add to our collection.

Our first scheduled stop was in Cuba, Missouri. We pulled into the Best Western and got a great room. I went up to the Country Kitchen for supper (I had a cup of the best potato soup I have had in a long time, Ribs, and fries. Lynn had the steak). I tried to use the napkin coupon trick, but it didn't work; the waitress was very efficient and friendly, and I got back to the room by 7:30.

Time to shower, log the day, plan tomorrow, and off to bed.

Wednesday, 18. Turned on the news and weather, another hot and sticky day forecast.

This Best Western has the most choices for breakfast: scrambled eggs, sausage, biscuits, gravy, pastries, bread, bagels, waffles, cereal, milk, coffee, and juices. We filled up with gas before hitting the highway. Noted a sale on beer, a thirty-pack of Keystone for $15.00, and the gas was about forty cents less than home!

The St. James Vacuum Museum was still closed; I got there too early! We went past a Rt. 66 souvenir and antique store; I surprised Lynn, took the next exit, and backtracked to look over the stuff. There seems to be a demand for knives in this state. We stopped at three of these tourist traps, one a discounted cutlery, lighter, and walnut bowl shop. We bought a little at each shop, Christmas shopping, etc. Please note all the shops were neat well organized, and the people were very friendly and outgoing.

We landed at our first scheduled stop a little after noon. Lambert's Restaurant, "the home of the thrown rolls." This restaurant has been on Lynn's bucket list for years. We had to sign up to get in, but we were taken five minutes later. The place is very welcoming, lots of activity, a lot of smiling people,

I ordered a Dr. Pepper Lynn root beer. The waitress served us two-liter insulated mugs of soda. I ordered the JLT (Hog jowl, lettuce, and tomato sandwich) with a side of pickled cucumbers and onions. Lynn had chicken and flat dumplings. As we waited for our order, a guy came through the center of the room calling "hot rolls." Lynn caught his eye, and he tossed her one. I waved, and he threw me one. The rolls are fresh, hot, and delicious. People come around offering extra sides, including fried okra, fried potatoes and onions, sorghum, black-eyed peas, and macaroni with tomatoes. Then our dinners came, Huge! Lynn had beets and carrots on the side, which came in separate bowls; my jowls came in a separate bowl, two large cut pieces of Texas toast, lettuce, and tomatoes, plus my side of cucumbers and onions in a separate bowl. Luckily, there are rolls of paper towels at each table because it gets messy. Everything was made perfectly, hot and very generous! WOW, what a great place. There is too much food...

Neither of us could finish our meals; we were still amazed as we walked out on the perfect timing of the food, everything fresh, hot, and nicely presented, and by the way, the hog jowls were like thick bacon, the perfect balance of fat and meat, and I couldn't finish the jowls...and I love bacon!

We waddled out to the car, traveled south to Branson, checked in with the timeshare provider, got the information of when the presentation would be (tomorrow at 0845), got our tickets for the show, and passed for the motel. We found the motel, checked in, and moved into the room. We went over the literature and maps, rested like lizards on the beds to settle our still over-stuffed bellies, and took off for the Fantastic Caverns jeep tour. The maps down here are a little deceiving; it seems the place is north of Springfield. The Garmin didn't work, so I went back to Maps and stopped at a gas station. We found the place. The tour was over an hour, with very interesting stalagmites and stalagmites, interesting narration, and it was a unique experience.

We returned to Branson, had time to fill up with gas and ice cream for dinner, and then went to an ABBA and 60's-70's production of singing and dancing. The show lasted two hours and was very entertaining; they asked all the veterans to stand while playing military anthems. It still amazes me how few of us there were; of the five branches and half the auditorium filled with people, only a total of 20 of us stood up!

Returned to the room, showered, and finished notes. It's late, and it was another great day on the road!

Thursday the nineteenth, we had breakfast at the motel, and off we went for the required seminar on timeshares. A very pleasant person gathered information, drove us over to the timeshares, and then pitched us. It was low pressure; the price went from $37,900 to $16,000 in quick order, and then we were told our timeshare was worth about $16,000, so it would be a push after the condo was sold. When I suggested that the condo may sell for only $10,000, they countered with a $12,000 price. We told them we weren't interested, and she countered with a $ 1,500 offer to keep the offer open, and we declined that also. We collected our voucher for dinner and the motel voucher and were out in two hours.

Off to the butterfly dome, went into the frog and salamander room, and found them in their cages and terrariums. The enclosure for the butterflies was on the second floor, with a triple door to keep the butterflies in. They were flitting everywhere! I was wearing a bright blue shirt and was being dived bombed throughout the 1200 sq. ft. room. There were easily a thousand butterflies flying, resting on leaves, on the floor, and on the feeders. Lots of action all around, a real joy to experience!

Educating Noah...Travelin'

After the butterflies, we went to a small tourist trap village, half crafts, half consignment. Then, we went downtown to tour the area on the free downtown trolley. We also went into several stores, including Dick's Five and Dime. This was similar to Wall's Drug in South Dakota, but more crowded and narrow aisles. We saw an advertisement for "Jigglin' George" and thought we would give it a try. It is a machine that stimulates blood flow from the ankles up. We did the fifteen-minute demo, got up and walked to the front of the store, and back felt great, and bought one. I will let you know how it works out after a few days with it! Went back to the motel; high heat and humidity took its toll! Decided to go to the restaurant Whipper Snappers, which had all the seafood you could eat, including lobster and crab legs. OH, yeah, it was great, bountiful, hot, and fresh, WOW.

Toured one last consignment and craft place, back to the room, shower notes, and bed.

Friday, 20, we had enough of Branson. Too much like the Dells, actually, I believe a little bigger! Tired of the steep hills and crowded traffic, I left the motel at 8AM off to Memphis, Tennessee! After driving for over three hours, we pulled over for lunch. Had a bite; Lynn called ahead for tour reservations at Graceland. The gas in Arkansas was higher than in Missouri, about $3.53 to $3.73 per gallon; I noticed a lot of Dollar General Stores, and the two-lane highways have slow lanes every so many miles to get around the trucks; very nice!

We arrived at Graceland around 3 o'clock and had 3:30 reservations. Quite expensive, we took the mansion walk-thru for $30.00 each, and parking was $10.00!

Took pictures and walked the grounds; he was a very generous man to the families, staff, and community!

In Memphis, "ya gotta go" to Biel Street! The Graceland help desk provided directions, and off we went! It only took 20 minutes, and we parked a block away. Took pictures, walked up one side and back the other, visited two junk shops, and had a beer and cranberry at O'Sullivan's.

Loaded back into the car and took off to Tupelo, Miss. To see the miner's "shotgun" house Elvis was born in and the shrine. The place was closed, but I got to walk around and take pictures of what I needed, and we were done! We found a motel, checked in, went out for a salad supper, and came back to end another busy day!

We stayed at a Days Inn, it was cheap, but the lights next to the bed along with the clock had no outlet, so they didn't work, the light switch in the bathroom worked sometimes, the sink was slow draining, the door opened by pulling up on the lever, and there was no desk. Breakfast was sparse, and even at 6:45 AM, only one apple left. The waffle maker had no spray, so the waffle stuck to the iron; the desk clerk was busy with her phone…. So much for Days Inns!

Saturday the 21st, we were on the road by 7:00 A.M. It was going to be a driving day! (38779) The day started out hot and humid, haze over the rivers and wooded area. The trip from Tupelo, Miss. to Ashville, North Carolina, through upper Mississippi, Alabama, and Tennessee to end in North Carolina is a pretty ride, with lots of green, rivers, and mountains. What a beautiful, lush country we have! We stopped at a waffle house for lunch, got caught in several rain storms, and experienced the Blue Ridge Mountains firsthand. As we traveled through the mountains, we came across rivers and roads with unique names, like "French Bread River" and "Thompson's Holler Road." There was a motorcycle rally going on in a small town, so we saw lots of bikes to and from stands set up in the "one horse" town.

We lost an hour. We are now in the Eastern time zone, checked into our motel, and bought tickets for the Biltmore Mansion (built by the Vanderbilt's grandson). The tour cost $60.00 each, so I hoped it would be worth it. We dropped our gear and headed out for a bite to eat. We found a place called Rocky's Hot Chicken Shack. We had chicken and waffles, fried tomatoes, and a chicken salad sandwich. Everything was excellent, plentiful, and delicious. Tired, we had traveled four hundred seventy-two miles, showers and bed.

Sunday, June 22nd, nice breakfast at the motel, at the estate by 8:20. Gate opens at 8:30. (39251) We showed our tickets and drove two miles from the gate to the parking lot, a river on the side, bamboo growing, very peaceful and lush, for the shuttle buses. The estate is eight thousand acres; there are forests, rivers, stocked bass ponds, bamboo sections, and even a railroad spur. We caught the bus to the mansion for a quick 10-minute drive to the grounds. Biltmore is the largest home in the U.S. with 250 rooms, 43 bathrooms, an indoor pool, two-lane bowling alleys, billiard, and pool rooms' servant quarters for the 30 servants on staff.

When I asked for a brochure on the estate, I was told it would be a good value to rent the handsets as we toured the estate, so we shelled out another $10.00 each for the handsets, and it was well worth it. We walked from the first-floor atrium, dining room (dinner at 8PM promptly, formal dress, and 7-10 course meals, with a full-blown pipe organ in the balcony) and parlors, the second-floor bedrooms and porches, and parlors, and the third-floor guest bedrooms and lounges. The basement had a pool, changing rooms, bowling alley, kitchen, and laundry. It took us two hours to go through the mansion; we then visited the gardens, went back to the car, and drove to the winery and what they call the Antler Hill Village, four miles away. We had great ice cream at the creamery, toured the very exclusive gift shop, and left after three and a half hours.

Next, on our way to the coast, we found the Peachoid water tower at Gaffney, South Carolina, the egg-shaped water tower outside Newberry, and stopped in Blackville's God's acre Healing Springs to drink and rub the healing spring water on my knees. (The land owner is listed as "GOD Almighty" in the local property records, so its water comes straight from God!) Indians called the spring "Healing

Waters," The springs are funneled into piping for filling bottles, which are supplied to anyone wanting it, without charge to anyone.

We tried to see Bee City in Cottageville, but it was closed. It looked like a small zoo with bee hives in the back, with a souvenir shop specializing in honey. Since we were traveling on two-lane roads, we saw a lot of the real people's homes, small neat brick houses, many with large porches or verandas, and mostly one-car carports. One popular thing we noticed was gourd birdhouses hanging off metal trees.

It was getting late, and both of us were tired. We found a motel in Summerville on the outskirts of Charleston, found a great rib place for dinner, and called it a night.

Monday the 23rd, mileage 39610. We decided to see Charleston via horse-drawn carriage, so we drove downtown to catch the first carriage out. The first carriage available was with Big John the horse and a very knowledgeable driver. Big John had two sets of shoes on regular horseshoes and, over them, rubber shoes. I asked how long the rubber ones lasted, and she (the driver/guide) said 3-5 weeks. The tour was for a little more than an hour and toured the old section where the Ash family lived who founded Ashton, where Biltmore was yesterday. Lots of money here!

I was able to take a number of shots of the local buildings, reminiscent of New Orleans with narrow streets, porches, and long narrow houses. Regarding the porches, since it is so humid here, the key was that if the door was closed to the porch, do not enter. The wool clothes were hot, and when people came home to relax, they discarded their clothes, so the closed door meant that they were not decent, lounging in their "original suit." This is the only other place in the world with an unsupported spiral staircase, as in Santa Fe, New Mexico, where it was supposedly constructed by a "stranger." It is rumored that this case was built by a master carpenter slave.

After the excellent tour, we walked a half block to the marketplace. It was still too early for most of the vendors, but we found some beautiful sweet grass baskets, (These baskets are an ancient negro craft, which is not a weave, but more a sewing of rice grass, where the grass is wrapped and sewn in various unique shapes and baskets) Lynn broke down and bought one, they are beautiful!

We then started our upward trek to the north up the coast. For miles, the road was lined on both sides with thirty-foot pines; all the way past McClellan, the roads were in good repair and easy driving. We went through Myrtle Beach and North Myrtle Beach, like the Dells again, very commercial and gaudy. After we crossed into Northern Carolina, we saw a number of tobacco fields, traffic was good, there was only an occasional left lane speed enforcer (driver who drives two miles over the speed limit and stays in the left lane), and most drivers courteous and watching out for the other cars, lots of pickup trucks and Chevy Suburbans!

We had enough driving, so I pulled off the road. We had a recommended AAA restaurant called Sting Ray, but the desk at the Comfort Suite had no idea. By the way, we stayed twice at this chain; the rooms were just a little better, a little bigger, but not worth the average $50.00 per night premium they charged over the Best Western Motels we stayed at.

So, in typical fashion, we jumped into the car and headed for town. Took a wrong/actually right turn and ended up in downtown New Bern. We went down what seemed to be a dead main street, and then toward the end, on the right was the Sting Ray restaurant! They claim to have the freshest seafood around, and they have a seafood store next to the restaurant. Great food! Lynn had shrimp, fried green tomatoes, coleslaw, and fries; I had the crab bisque and a scallop sandwich. Wow, great!

Tuesday, June 24th, on the road around 8 AM, going to the outer banks and finishing up North Carolina, mileage 39901. Heading east, seagulls are bright white and black. This is blueberry country, with lots of stands on the side of the highway. There were more tobacco fields, other crops not sure of, but we saw a trimmer in action. A trimmer is a boom truck with a saw mounted on the end of the boom. They cut everything in a straight line up to thirty feet high for phones and power lines. It's interesting to watch, with a bouncing rotating 4-foot diameter spinning saw blade! Saw a round item in the road (a turtle) and straddled it as we drove over three-quarters of the way across; the pickup behind me also straddled him. I hope he made it!

We arrived at the outer banks and headed south first through the Cape Hatteras reserve (supposedly the graveyard of the Atlantic) and proceeded 15 to 20 miles down the coast. Snapped a few pictures of some inland walking areas and a lighthouse but turned around due to the lack of ocean view. The highway is under sand dunes; you have to get out of the car, walk up the 15-20-foot dune, then down to the beach. There was not much to see, so we turned around and headed up the coast to Nags Head and then Kitty Hawk. Starting at Nags Head, on the ocean side again, you cannot see the ocean due to two-story houses on stilts and rentals almost completely side by side just behind those sand dunes; the houses are unique, with many different colors and nice porches. We had lunch at Captain Franks, hot dogs, a 50's style beach eatery where the order person took the order then sent it down to the grill on a wire, the order attached to a clothespin hook. Fun place, then looked over the shops and stores.

Crossing back to the mainland, we saw a number of power lines with birds of prey nesting platforms; I think Lynn got shots of a few with active nests!

We progressed north through Virginia Beach and Norfolk to cross the Chesapeake Bay. The crossing started out as a long bridge; we saw ten freighters in the bay. Then, after a number of miles, we went down into a tunnel, then another bridge, and then another tunnel, a total of 20 miles (including two 1-mile tunnels!) Easy drive, the bridges were fairly high, and the corresponding tunnels were fairly deep, interesting!

After landing again, we stopped at Stuckey's to see if anything had changed. We don't have any left in Wisconsin, and it was a nice break and brought back good memories. Not much has changed; I bought a pecan log, and some Christmas presents for the kids.

Late in the afternoon, we stopped in Salisbury, Maryland, to eat and sleep.

<u>Wednesday 25th</u>

We were up early and on the road to Delaware and D.C. (40.299). When we watched the TV for weather in the morning, the weatherman referred to the DELMARVA (Delaware, Maryland, Virginia) forecast. This is actually the tri-state forecast, and when we were on the road, going north, we saw a lot of references to DELMAR. This was another hot and humid day, and quite a few pieces of chicken trucks took' the clucks to Purdue to meet their demise. According to the license plate, Delaware was the first State, a good thing to know for trivia; as we went through, we found lots of fresh produce and flower stands every few miles.

As we approached the border and crossed back into Maryland, the houses were getting bigger. Another thing we noticed was that since we started heading east from Missouri, we no longer saw any wind turbines, much less any solar panels.

As we entered Annapolis, the traffic increased significantly and really slowed down as we approached DC. The Garmin decided to cooperate and got us right from the heart of the city to the visitor center. In DC, the Garmin alarm went off almost constantly, and all of the intersections were photo-controlled, along with the speed monitoring. All the bridges had tents under them for the bums, and many of the city benches were occupied with one or two; most stop lights had one of these bums walking the median with a cup for change begging; he was just shaking the cup and looking at the drivers trying to ignore them. Gas was thirty cents a gallon more; we witnessed row houses similar to New York on our way downtown. I dropped off Lynn and found a parking structure a block away, tipped the attendant, and got a space close to the exit. Found the elevator and met Lynn at the center. We bought tickets to the Old Town Trolley for $40.00 each; this is an on/off trolley, with the ticket good for the entire day.

Our first stop was to be the White House, but that was cordoned off, so we would have to walk to it later. We drove to the National Archives, then to Union Station, took pictures, and stopped, then on to The Library of Congress and the U.S. Capitol. Next, we slowly passed the US Botanical Gardens, the Air and Space Museum, The Smithsonian Castle, and the Holocaust Museum. We passed the Jefferson Memorial to get off at the Lincoln Memorial.

At the Lincoln Memorial, we transferred to another bus to go to Arlington National Cemetery. I needed to see the tomb of the Unknown Soldier, but it was hot. A quarter mile hoofing it to the tomb, and Lynn stayed behind; I hoofed it just in time to witness the changing of the guard. It was quite a moving experience, and I walked back to the bus to go back to the Lincoln Memorial. Interesting facts: Over 400,000 are buried at Arlington, and they will bury up to four members of the family up to four deeps.

The bus had a mechanical problem, another bus was called so it looked pretty close to finishing the sights we had to see, so we hoofed it……. that was a mistake, the maps are not drawn to scale, and the distances were much further than portrayed.

First, to the Lincoln Memorial, took pics but couldn't do the steps; we walked over to a concession stand and sat down to hydrate and share a sub. After the respite, we walked to the Vietnam Memorial. Amazing as to the number of names! We found a few benches and worked our way to the White House; we got as close as we could, and then at the entrance, Lynn got frisked by the guard…she kinda of liked that!

Another five blocks to the parking garage, or so I thought, no addresses on the building or shops. I became disoriented; people were hurried and rude, and traffic was as bad as in New York. I was exhausted; Lynn was exhausted, hot, and miserable. I asked a security guard in one hotel, but she sent me to the wrong place. Asked the parking attendant where it was. He didn't know and didn't care because I didn't have a ticket for his lot. I asked another security guard on the street, and she sent me in the right direction. And finally, we asked a janitor, who indicated it was across the street. Four people to get to a place within ONE BLOCK OF THE FIRST REQUEST!!

We had to walk 6 flights of stairs down to the parking area, and then no one was around to find the car; we found it, got in, and got out...$25.00.

The Garmin couldn't find us, so I used the compass to go east and south. Found an expressway but was squeezed out of the exit south, so we went east. We followed alternative routes to work our way southeast, away from the city; I will never go back! Of course, it was rush hour, and people were not friendly, courteous, and worse than Chicago drivers! In DC, there were always sirens going off and more bums than in Chicago or New York.

We made it to Richmond, Virginia, by 6:30, exhausted, needing showers, food, and rest. Enough is enough!

This was the first day we slept in. Both of us are still a little sore, but we were on the road at 8:30 a.m. (40527)

We went to Monticello to see the mansion of Thomas Jefferson. The place was gutted and rebuilt when he returned from France after his ambassadorship, with a European flair, skylights, and double doors. We took the tour through the house; he was very creative and inventive and had to compromise on slavery when writing the Declaration of Independence. He did not like slavery and thought it was wrong, but he had slaves throughout his life. He was not good with finances and was in debt to what would be a million dollars today when he died. I was going to go on the slave tour, but Lynn never joined me, so I returned to the mansion to find her waiting for the bus; the heat and humidity had gotten to her. We did go back to the gift shop, and I purchased the book on the Jefferson slaves to get the whole picture.

On the way back, we stopped at a 300-year-old tavern and shop complex. It was called Michie Tavern. It was close to lunchtime, so we thought we would treat ourselves. Well, here goes: we had trays and a pewter plate, went along a line, and scooped what we wanted: coleslaw, pickled beets, green beans, stewed tomatoes, two kinds of fried chicken, pulled pork, mashed potatoes, gravy, gazpacho, beer, hard cider, and soda. We had a little of everything, all great; I especially liked the stewed tomatoes and the gazpacho! Oh, and we also had dessert. Lynn had peach cobbler, and I had Ice Cream Scotch John (Vanilla ice cream with butterscotch, raisins, and apple crumbs.

Stuffed, we walked the balance of the complex, bought some Christmas gifts, and actually found Knight's Popcorn being sold in one of the shops! And waddled back to the car.

We drove through the Blue Ridge Skyway (On a perfect day, gorgeous scenery, good roads, courteous drivers!) to Natural Bridge in Virginia to find the "Foam Hedge," a copy of Stone Hedge in England, but it was destroyed in 2013. We looked at the natural bridge shop, saw the pictures, weighed walking down the 137 steps, and opted out. One more stop: it was late in the afternoon, and we were still tired from yesterday; plus, we walked and climbed a lot more than we anticipated at the stops today, PLUS it was HOT and HUMID!

The last stop was the coal house in White Sulfur Springs, West Virginia. The Greenbrier Classics golf tournament was going on in the 1700's this was fashionable health and pleasure resort named after its mineral springs, which are said to have curative qualities. The site is still there, but the Greenbrier Resort surrounds it. We then looked for a house made of coal, which turned into a tourist information center and now a hairstylist place. The sign across the street was grown over. Finally, I asked, got directions, found the place, snapped a couple pictures, and went off to find a motel.

We were off the road at 6, tired, shower, room, notes, and bed!

Friday, June 27, 2014, (40779) Today is a road day with a stop at Hershey, Pennsylvania. Left at 07:30 AM. Drove up to Winchester, Va., to find the largest apples in the US. It seems there are fifteen of these all over town; we found the original and one that was red, white, and blue. We arrived at the Hershey Complex a little after 1:00 p.m. We had gone from West Virginia to Virginia, then West Virginia again, then Maryland, and finally Pennsylvania. We started with a lot of mist in the mountains; we went through the Blue Ridge and Appalachian Mountains, incredible scenery!

We ate at the park, rode the auto-tour, ate the free samples, toured the massive gift shop, and had our pictures taken and placed on chocolate syrup for Christmas gifts to the kids. We had enough; too many kids running all over, and it was quite crowded for an early Friday afternoon! Left, took the tollway to go as far as we could, and went through several tunnels, including the Tuscarora tunnel, before calling it a day. Stopped at Bedford, PA, the home of the first oil strike in PA. Took a picture of the first Billion Dollar Well in America and the rig, found and took a picture of a coffee pot building, crossed a covered one-lane bridge, and had a great supper at Hoss's steak buffet.

Saturday, June 28, 2014, travel 'in the day and the Museum of Rock and Roll. The motel was in remodel mode, so we had vouchers at Subway for $5.00 each. We both had 6" subs and a drink, quite good and under the money allocated by voucher.

We actually saw a small wind farm in Pennsylvania, but none of the rotors were turning...so much for wind power in coal and oil country! Finally, I crossed the border into Ohio and arrived in Cleveland at the Rock and Roll Museum at noon. Located on 1100 Rock and Roll Blvd., the giant 150,000 sq. ft. building is impressive on the lakefront. There was Rock and Roll music playing throughout the facility.

We happened to be here, at the lakefront, with a Gay Pride celebration, lots of characters, and a lack of parking, but we found an unknown parking area and were able to park within 3 blocks of the Museum for only $5.00!

The Museum was much larger and newer than anticipated, with five floors, and we started at the bottom. This is a mistake, you should start at the top, and work your way down, the first floor is the best! Toured the entire building, bought more souvenirs, and left.

We have one more stop before heading home, and that is in Indiana. The Garmin took us on a short route through the city to the tollway, and off we went! We passed the Duct Tape Museum but didn't stop and crossed the state line a little before 4:00 PM. We found a Ramada Inn in Angora for the night, filled up the empty tank, and went to the restaurant attached to the motel for dinner.

The dinner was excellent, and they boasted a collection of bourbons, one hundred and seventy-seven to be exact! I tasted two of the bourbons and two of the Dragon's breath stouts, all outstanding! I had almond perch, and Lynn had fettuccini carbonara, both cooked to perfection. The waitress was entertaining and gracious; it was a perfect end to the day!

This, the 29th of June 29, 2014, will be our last day on the road for this trip. (41657) It is Sunday. I read in the hotel brief book that the Shipshewana Outdoor flea market is open from dawn to dusk. (The largest flea market in the Midwest) We were on the road at 8 AM and only had a twenty-minute drive. This is Amish country, home of the largest Amish communities in the world. We saw quite a few walking and taking their carriages to church. We arrived at the grounds to find everything closed. The market is closed on Sundays, and although we were quite disappointed, I kinda like that this day is still honored by this community. We took a picture to show we were there and drove off to home. Shipshewana is only about 4 hours from Milwaukee. We stopped for lunch in Racine and went shopping at Aldi's for milk, bread, fruits, and veggies. We were home by 2:30 PM.

Total mileage: start   37605   finished 41926   Total: 4321 miles

Noah

It's been a month since we returned from our last road trip. I can understand now the problem people have when collecting unemployment for a long period of time! I am working only 6 to 12 hours a week and find it an imposition.... Me!

I had another bout with pseudo-gout; this time, it was on my right Achilles heel, the top of the foot at the base of the big toe, and the inside aspect of the left big toe's base. Very hard to walk, very painful! I drank over a quart of tart cherry juice a day, using "Jigglin George" and elevating my feet every night.

It took 5 days, five quarts of juice, and elevation to get relief. My knees are as bad as before. I talked to my Nurse Practitioner at the VA, and she told me that they are doing both knees at the same time! I contacted Ortho at the VA to set up a discussion and evaluation in October for replacing both knees next May after China and Tibet; I know the weight loss will be a theme here, but now I need to use a railing to go up or down any staircase.

We invited Tiff and her family over for dinner. During the discussions, she mentioned that she just finished the TSA Pre-Check to avoid the long lines.

I did the application on July 27th; they automatically set an in-person review for September 10th, seven weeks out, no alternative days, just a selection of alternative apt times. I e-mailed them for any flexibility and will see what happens.

I filed an amended tax return over confusion with what I received electronically and what was in the mail. I changed everything back to mail to avoid this again! Paid over $500.00 to have the taxes done and had to come up with a very sizable amount to offset the refund I was to get and pay the difference. I also sent back the amount they refunded to me, and now I am waiting.

They sent me a letter at the beginning of May that the matter would be resolved in six to eight weeks. It has now been eleven weeks, and the number they gave me does not connect; after five phone calls, there is no connection. I went to the website, but without an exact amount, it wouldn't connect, so I went to the general phone number; again, it was all electronic, with no real person and no help without the exact amount. This is the second try, and I am totally frustrated with the government having only a one-way relationship; WOW!!

I am getting ready for Africa. I have my Global Entry card and number. Lynn interviewed last week and should have hers by the end of this week. It is only $15.00 more for five years, and I hope it is worth the one hundred bucks each. It did include express check through the TSA and was considerably more passenger-friendly. The TSA didn't have an interview open until we were in Africa! Only three more weeks. I will finish packing tonight!!

I was challenged to the ALS bucket challenge by both my cousin Beverly and friends Sean and Melissa. They all had their heads dumped on by a five-gallon bucket of ice water as a challenge for donations. I had to top this, so I called up my cousin Jerry Moede in Mayville. He used to work for John Deere in implement sales and was the Mayor of Mayville, so I thought he would have connections for a front-end loader! I called him, and he asked that I give him a little time and said he would call me back. He did. He said my cousin John had a front-end loader on his farm and would be glad to help.

I called John, asked, and set the whole thing up for 3 days from now, a Thursday night just before the Labor Day weekend! I then called my other cousin, Barb, to ask her to come out and film and act as a backup filmmaker.

Thursday afternoon, I drove out to Waterford, picked up a pizza from a Mexican restaurant (Yeah, I liked the idea, and there were no chicken places on the way out!), and arrived at the farm. John already had the tractor out, poles to steady the arms so the bucket would not fall on my head, a tripod with a camera, and a hose to fill the bucket. It is a one-yard bucket, so I figured it would make an impression!

I challenged the Vagabond Club of Milwaukee, Chapter G GWRRA, Bill Lister, Jerry Moede, Jerry Bruchert, Fred Bruchert, Sean, Melissa, and Beverly!

John had an area marked where I was to stand. I made my spiel, and he dumped the water. Yeah, it was cold, but it missed half of me. So, he refilled the bucket and doused me again, and it turned out well! We stayed for a while after changing to eat the pizza and drink the beer. The next evening, Camille, my daughter, came over to show off her new Jeep Cherokee. After going over her new treasure, she helped me put the challenge on my computer, on my Facebook, and e-mail it to my friends! What a great two days!

After Labor Day, yes, we went as we have the last twenty years to the St. Martins fair! Worked for Synergy, and now we finally weigh our luggage. Both of us are limited to 33# of luggage each; we are both around 30#, started taking our Malaria pills, and luggage at the door!

The Turkey and Tanzania Adventure Sept. 9th -21st 2014

Day 1

The cab was twenty-five minutes late in picking us up. We had called for a cab for a pick-up at 5 P.M. At 5:10, we called and were told he was on the way; at 5:20, we called again, and we were told they thought the pick-up was for 5:30. The cab did arrive, with apologies, at 5:25. We still had time to spare (I usually build in a half hour buffer) when we arrived at the motel pick-up point.

Everyone was early, so we actually left the pickup point sooner than scheduled! It was a clear, cool evening, dispelling fears of heavy rainfall forecast for the evening. We made it to O'Hare in an hour and fifteen minutes, proceeded to check in, and went to the TSA checkpoint to get to the gate. There was no separate TSA or Global entry lane for Turkish Airlines, so we joined the rest of the "stiffs," removing our shoes, frisking due to my hip, and then off to the gate.

We loaded an hour before take-off; I got a window seat but also had the under-seat heater ahead of me, so I had limited legroom. I was just happy not to be in the corral in the middle! Turkish Airlines has excellent food! One of the stewards wears a chef's hat! We had both a supper and a breakfast, plentiful, tasty, and hot. We left on time, and the eleven-and-a-half-hour flight went on without a problem. We arrived at 5:30 P.M., their time. Cruise and Tour were waiting for us at the exit. There are thirty-eight in our group for the Istanbul extension, and another 10 will join us when we return to the airport in three days to continue to Tanzania.

As with most cities worldwide, this was rush hour, slow, cars cutting in if any space was available, so it took us an hour to get to our hotel in the center of the city. On the way, we saw Roman walls an aqueduct from 2 BC, and rebuilt in 4 BC. It no longer works. The Hotel Marmara is a four-star hotel, and we were to find that all the hotels are either four or five-star hotels, quite a difference from the Best Westerns and Motel 8's we are used to in our stateside travels!

We checked in and found our room (not with a view; we were across from a vacant, broken window building,) but the room was clean and inviting, and the bed comfortable! The rooms here have heating and cooling that is door key activated; the room was at 29 degrees centigrade, so we put the AC on full. Lynn collapsed on the bed, groaning, stating she was going to take a shower and hit the sack! I showered, changed, and went down to help the bell boys to bring up our luggage. By the time I brought in the luggage, Lynn had showered and was sleeping in the bed. The room had become comfortable, and I turned down the air.

I had heard that the rooftop view was wonderful, so I wanted to see this, especially at dusk. Took the elevator to the top floor and then had to walk up a flight to the roof deck.

It was really crowded, with lots of young people, and the bartender was swamped! The Europeans and Asians do not have the normal personal space wants as we Americans and are used to being bumped, so I had to readjust to this (it is their place!) I wormed my way to all four corners to snap some shots of the city; wow, fifteen to seventeen million people is a lot bigger than Milwaukee's 700,000!

A great combination of old and new, I counted at least six Mosques scattered in the city among the glass and steel modern buildings; the city was alive and throbbing! Istanbul is the largest city in Europe, with three-quarters European, one-quarter Asian, and a gateway, one way to Asia, the other to Europe.

I took the elevator down to the lobby and restaurant bar. There was nobody there at this time; they were all enjoying the view and night air on the roof! I called over the bartender and asked for the most popular local drink if I was Turkish.

He showed me a bottle and said it was Raki (also known as Araka or Araki) and wanted to know if I wanted a single or double. Yeah, I said double! He had a double shooter glass, filled it, and served it with a small glass of water. The drink tastes like licorice, similar to Absinthe and Anisette, both of which I have had in America and France. If I poured this over ice, it would turn a milky white, sometimes called dragon's or the devil's milk. (It is a distilled drink from grape residue.) I finished the drink and asked if there were any others; he said "no," so I signed the bill: 24 Turkish Euros (about 12 dollars!), went up to the room, and crashed for the night.

Day 2

We had an early wake-up; we organized the packing for the next few days, dressed, and went down to the restaurant for breakfast. The breakfast was typical European/South American; to say bountiful would be an understatement! Various cheeses, fruits, meats, olives, eggs, potatoes, breads, yogurts, cereals, warm pastries and salads. A honeycomb, juices, coffees, teas, and milk. We both love the selection and freshness!

We loaded up on the bus for the city tour at 9:00. Istanbul is a corruption of the native language; roughly translated, it is "the city." The local currency is the Turkish Lira: Two Turkish Lira to an American dollar and 100 Kuru (Kr) to a Turkish Lira. We were told that the dollar was accepted throughout the city, and it was, and given the two-for-one, easy conversion made it very easy to buy what we wanted.

The bus is split by two guides. Ours is Yaren, a historian and archeologist. The first stop was the Hippodrome. (Hippo is the Greek word for horse; "Drome" represents race). Istanbul marked the divide between the Ottoman Empire and the Roman Empire. The Hippodrome was capable of holding 100,000 spectators. Istanbul was built on an old Roman Port, and many Roman shipwrecks have been recovered intact; it was a Roman Capital for 800 years.

The Hippodrome was built for chariot racing. This was the most popular sport. Slaves drove the chariots. (And sometimes, they were able to buy their freedom with their winnings.) Most races were 7 laps. They raced counterclockwise. The size of the Hippodrome was 450 meters x 130 meters. The height was approximately the same as the coliseum in Rome and just as ornate. Only 2 Obelisk still stand; One is an Egyptian obelisk with a base showing Phoenicians, Romans, and Germans. This one is only 1/3 as tall as originally and stands 15 meters tall. The other, approximately the same size, is a Roman oblique and is just formed stone, plain and typically "Roman functional."

Istanbul is a peninsula with the Black Sea to the north, the Aegean Sea to the west, and the Mediterranean Sea to the south. It is one of the largest ports in the world.

After walking the Hippodrome, we toured the Sultan Ahmed

(Blue Mosque). We stood in line, and all women needed to cover their heads & anyone showing knees (men & women) needed a skirt. Lynn assumed her hat would suffice but was turned back to get a scarf by the gatekeeper. Everyone had to take their shoes off and place them in a plastic bag. Lynn detected a strong foot odor from the carpeting and was glad she wore socks that day. This mosque has 6 minarets. Only one is needed for the call to prayer 5 times a day over loudspeaker. There are designated women's areas in the back (like small cages). Men and male children are allowed throughout the interior. There are lots of stained glass and blue tiles, very ornate, and a lot of carved wood and stone.

After leaving the mosque, we put on our shoes and walked across the courtyard to St. Sophia Church. This is a large church with lots of tile and lots of stained glass. Very worn marble steps, similar to the marble in the churches in Barcelona, from years of people walking up and down and through the entrance doors.

We gathered at the bus to go to lunch at the Handi Restaurant. The 7-plus course meal included salads with tomatoes, cucumbers, olives, red peppers, and parsley, followed by tandoori bread with butter and goat cheese, walnuts, and a kabob with garlic mincemeat & spring lamb. A soup with tomato and carrot base, lamb & veal kabobs with rice, tomatoes, and French fries, with Baklava for dessert. This was served with beer, wine, or water. We all left stuffed.

After lunch, we traveled to an Oriental rug store. We watched a demonstration of how the rugs are made. The average rug has more than one million knots or more. We were given a history of the rugs, the difference in styles of rugs, the all-natural dyes, and various insects for color. We were treated to beer, wine, liquor, and juices while many different colors and sizes of rugs were presented. There was also a pottery and jewelry shop attached with all beautiful gold & ceramics.

We jumped back on the bus and went to the largest bazaar in

Europe: 400 plus vendors, lots of gold, food, spices, scarves, leather, rugs, lamps, and more gold. Lots of gold (yes, I know this is a repeat, but there was a lot !!) You need to watch the karat value; I saw some very glittery 4-karat pieces, though. (Gold is the "proper" gift for marriages, births, and circumcision.) The mall was extremely clean, and every so often, you may be stopped by a shopkeeper offering a product that will rid you of your mother-in-law or make your wife love you again. They would say ANYTHING to get you in the door. Not pushy, just friendly and funny. (There is a mistrust of banks here, so many keep their fortune in gold.)

On our way back to the hotel, we passed a pink train terminal, which is the Orient Express origin. No stop, no picture. (This time!)

We had 1 ½ hours in the room to rest before walking to our restaurant for dinner. We both showered and napped for an hour. We met in the lobby at 7:45 PM and walked ¾ kilometer through the streets...

The streets were crowded with people, and stores were all open and reminded us of New Orleans, Bourbon Street. We turned down a street filled with restaurants. Both sides, open air, one to three stories, were all restaurants. There was cooking out front and displays of seafood and meat kabobs. All great food smells.

Three-quarters down one street, we were escorted to the third-floor open-air feast. Here are most of the things we were offered: fish, chicken, lamb, salad, stuffed grape leaves, yogurt with garlic, mushrooms, beans, eggplant, a spice paste, calamari, bread, eggplant, beer, wine, and water. For dessert, we were offered grapes, peaches, and pears. We were all stuffed.

We found our way back to the hotel around 10:30, leaving the restaurant still full of people, along with all the other restaurants on this street. The main boulevard was less crowded but still busy; we watched an ice cream vendor putting on a show by the way he served his product. He played tricks on the customers, and quite a crowd gathered to watch.

Everyone enjoyed the show by the ice cream vendor; after three brave souls, we left to finish the trek to the hotel. We packed for the next day, an early pickup with luggage out by seven. Took our showers and collapsed in bed for a good night's sleep.

Day 3

This is going to be a loooong day! Another excellent breakfast, then all of us and our luggage on the bus. The first stop today was the Palace. Once inside the outer gate guarded by two soldiers, there was a spacious area. The main path continued a good half kilometer. To the right was a guarded garden gate, then a path down to boat docks. To the left was a reception area with tents, tables, and chairs, then on to a church that was ages old. Three quarter down the path, there is a souvenir shop and clean bathrooms (advised by our guide, these would be cleaner and less crowded than inside the palace complex).

We re-gathered outside the shop to continue the path to the main gates of the palace complex. Another elaborate gate and we entered the massive secondary courtyard. Inside, to the right of us, was a long building with twenty-plus smoke stacks. This was the kitchen building consisting of multiple kitchens, each one specialized, butchers, bakers, vegetable preps, breakfast prep, lunches, and dinner preps!

Ahead of us was another building containing the palace and audience rooms (gold gates, lots of inlaid works, and parquet). To the left was the harem with eunuch housing and additional meeting rooms. Most of the rooms were multi-purpose. They are arranged during the day with carefully placed cushions and tables. In the evening, the cushions and tables were removed and replaced with sleeping mats.

We then toured the inside of the Harem. As we passed through a smaller arch and gate, we started past the eunuch quarters. The path is rounded and polished by century's stone, all with intricate designs; everything is ornate and practical at the same time. A look into a small room exposes a simple bed, table, and chair. This is a eunuch room. Two eunuchs share a room, and they work twelve hours on and twelve off, so they only really see each other going to or from work.

After the harem, we visited other various buildings & rooms, including the spoon diamond (84Karet), as big as a fist! A pathway to the private dock, we walk on another path showing beautiful views from several porches over the sea.

Lunch was at the palace restaurant; again, various salads, meat, vegetables, and desserts.

After another stuffing meal, we walked out of the compound and down the street to the Cistern. This was an underground cavern that stored water from springs and the aqueducts that carried water to the city from the mountains. There were many columns, water still there, about a meter deep. The area we toured was about 150 meters long by 50 meters wide. When looking down into the water, quite a few 1 to 2-foot carp could be seen. (They eat the algae.) It was only 2-3 stories down from street level, and although hot and humid, it was quite well kept for being 100 years old.

We met the bus and drove past the Orient Express terminal, so I was finally able to snap a few pictures of that famous building. We were dropped off at the airport.

At 6:15 PM, we took off for Tanzania on Turkish Airlines. The air in the middle of the plane did not work well. We were right over the wing, so it was also noisy. I didn't sleep. Lynn slept but would not admit it.

We landed at Kilimanjaro Airport at 12:30 AM. Got our visas ($100.00 each cash, the bill must not be older than 2006, and no rips, tears, or markings) and luggage and were loaded onto the buses for a 1-hour drive to our first hotel. Lights out at 3 AM. Set the alarm for

8:15 AM.

Day 4

I was up at 8:10 to beat the alarm and ate breakfast at 9:10: custom-made omelets, fresh fruit, granola, yogurt with juice, and coffee.

We left the hotel at 11:45 to meet the balance of the group at the other hotel. We were given a brief of the itinerary. Our driver's name is Dominic. He will be our driver all week, #1 Land Rover. There were five of us in our group: Dennis, Bonnie, Barry, Lynn, and me. (I don't do last names well!)

The meeting hotel had a wonderful yard overlooking a lake with flowers and flowering trees. One had huge yellow trumpets 6" in length 5-6-inch diameter. It was an Australian Bombax. Another was all lavender, and there were 50-100 hummingbirds in & out of that tree. Another had orange & red blooming flowers on the ground & bushes, every color of the rainbow. We had a lunch buffet of lamb, fish, pork, beef, salads, and desserts. Yeah, too much. ALL GREAT TASTING!!

Off to Tarangine State Park game drive. The Land Rover always stocked in a cooler, 3 bottles of water per day for each person. The paved roads are no more than 2 lanes (one left and one right). They drive on the left side of the road. There are speed bumps in the road every 2-3 miles to slow traffic. On one 2 ½ hour journey, we slowed down for goats and people and were passed on the left & right by motorcycles. We saw bicycles and motorcycles with live chickens, stacks of eggs, roofing material, pipes, and almost everything else. Women were walking with material, firewood, banana stalks, and groceries, balanced on their heads. A few small towns had Saturday markets where people walked up to 10 miles to purchase/exchange/barter for goods.

We arrived at the park and started to drive dirt roads, like we would for most of the time here. One lane, domed, washboard, heavily rutted, this won't be the first time I will mention the roads!

We saw blue-balled monkeys and Lilac Rollo birds that are iridescent, with blue chests and wings. It's very pretty to watch them take off.

We saw zebras, elephants, wildebeests, impalas, giraffes, 2 leopards in one tree, a female lion in another, vultures with a carcass, various birds, a small deer species (tick, tick) hares, Guinea hens, jackals, and bull oxen.

A beautiful sunset, then on to a lodge just outside the park where we will stay tonight and tomorrow. We were briefed on our dawn departure, showered in our rooms, and then had a light supper at the lodge. Buffet of soups, salads, polenta, glazed carrots, local steamed beans, bread, rice, African guru, chicken, lamb, fish and sauces, and a dessert.

By 9:30 PM, we were back in our room (we were warned not to leave any windows or doors open at night because of the monkeys; they get in and wreak havoc & poop all over). I checked the conversion table 1USD=1200 TSHS.

Tomorrow is another early day, but we will get an 8-hour sleep first. Our next lodge is on the crater ridge of a dormant volcano. 7000 feet elevation crater is 5000 feet. We are shown little yellow apples (the size of a golf ball), which are used to cure upset stomachs and sore teeth by chewing the roots.

Tarangire Sopa Park and stayed at the lodge.

Day 5

5:20 AM, an early morning bang on the door, an early AM ride. Meet @ 5:50 to go on a dawn game ride. We left the parking lot promptly at 0600. We wanted to be in the park at dawn to see the animals early!

Noah

From black to full light took only 35 minutes! We saw more of those midget deer; we passed a burrow of mongoose, and about eight of them scrambled out and disappeared into the grasses. More birds singing and eating, a male ostrich, a couple of hornbills, and another African eagle. The road here is 1 ½ lanes of packed dirt and highly rutted. It was cool this AM; we all wore jackets. We only traveled 5-10 mph all the way down into the crater. It took an hour to get to the bottom. Here we saw hyenas in the distance, secretary birds, which are very large, black & white. The government wants to change the name to "Walking Eagle." A lion's territory is 70 sq. kilometers.

Our guide told us to say "Sawa, Sawa" when we were ready to go. It means OK, GO!

"Jambo" means Hello.

"La Salama" means good night.

Fewer teats-see flies and cooler in the early morning. As we enter the park, all the tires of the vehicles are sprayed down (that is where the flies rest).

We followed a riverbed, herds of Zebra, water buffalos, and, of course, wildebeests. The dirt is plentiful, lots of dust, brown dust, red dust, and black dust; none of the roads are paved, all are deeply rutted, and many holes and washboards; wow, what a workout just riding in the Land Cruiser!

We saw a large patch of destroyed shrubs and trees, half-eaten, stomped, and scattered, then came upon a small group of elephants; a large male and several children scratched themselves on a bent-over tree, one then another, then another, you could almost see their eyes roll back as they moved back and for the over the tree! Then the family crossed right in front of the land Cruiser! A female actually stopped in the middle of the road to nurse her baby, then moved on.

We were not seen as a threat to this group. (We were stopped, quiet, and moving inside very slowly!) After that show, we moved on to more iridescent birds, yellow and green birds (Green Bee Eaters). When they flew, the yellow feathers accented with emerald-green outlines were fantastic!

It was breakfast time, so we met with the seven other cruisers in an area that had primitive toilets and the drivers setting up tables for breakfast. The breakfast was served buffet style: hard-boiled eggs, bacon, veal sausage, fruits, vegetables, yogurts, juices, coffee milk, and rolls. After breakfast, we headed back to the lodge. When we arrived, we inquired if they had found the bat we thought was in the room with us last night, and they admitted they had not found it. We asked for another room, and they accommodated us and also provided folks to assist in moving from room to room.

On the walls of the path to the new room, we found two lizards, one blending in very well. On the grounds, we also saw a number of critters, Hyrax, that looked like a large gofer or muskrat. A tawny coat and a very short tail. There was a family of monkeys on one of the roofs, and we found that one couple last night watched an elephant walk by their patio!

Lunch was by the pool, buffet style.

The afternoon was ours, so I finished up the notes and started adding additional facts about where we traveled. The Acacia tree, when elephants and baboons eat the berries or fruit, they appear drunk. We always knew when elephants had been to an area, the small trees and shrubs were half eaten, stomped, and mangled, with lots of defecation, and they defecate two to three kilos every hour! They also eat bark off of mature trees and grass. They are vegetarians and eating machines.

A number of birds follow the elephants, picking through the poop or "scat" to find the bugs that were not digested.

The Baobab tree, referred to by Disney as the "tree of life," was selected for the cover. I took a picture of a skinny 16ft. tree that was planted twenty years ago; it looks nothing like the mature trees that are hundreds of years old, competing with our Redwoods in age. Wow, they can get to be 30 feet in diameter, and their leafless branches look like roots. African legend says baobabs were planted upside down! Very impressive. Lynn went out on the porch to read; I took a shower to get all the dust off and took a short nap. Late in the afternoon, we had a meeting as to the itinerary the next day or so, which included appetizers and drinks. From the lobby porch, we watched a family of elephants (got some great shots!) One of the females trumpeted and took off, but no one followed. When she returned, the other adult led a baby elephant in another direction, and all followed her. It was interesting listening to the variations of grunts they used to communicate.

We found more of those hyraxes on the adjacent roof and saw a couple wart hogs to the right, a few wildebeests, and a musk ox, all on the resort property and relatively close! We joined into a few conversations, a few more cocktails, and hors d'oeuvres. Then we all went to supper! This was a BBQ buffet with soups, salads, and vegetables. Back to the room, shower temp only cool, no hot water tonight (Lynn was not happy); she found a 5-inch African giant millipede (They can grow up to 28 centimeters (about 12 inches) and can secret a toxic liquid) I needed to rescue her from it and readily dispatched the monster with a flush down the toilet.

Tomorrow, we will be doing a lot of driving on dusty, rough roads, safari on the way, a place for the women to shop, more safari, and then the next camp. The room is very comfortable, the bed inviting, we were out like lights!

Day 6

Breakfast and early morning game drive to Lake Manyara National Park, then Continued drive to Ngoronogoro for check-in!

Educating Noah...Travelin'

We learned early how to identify many animals, and usually by the marking on the "Butt"! The Impala, for instance, has three vertical black stripes on a white base. We also saw a 500# male lion under a tree. He was sounding off; it sounded like a low (ehhhhhhh), and this growl can be heard for 1-2 square miles! And yeah, that is what it kinda sounded like! His territory is approximately 5 square miles; he drinks a lot of water because he regularly marks his territory.

Driving along, we next found a cheetah and her cub under a tree, so look closely at the pictures, and you will find a tree with lumps under it. It's them. She must not have been hungry because a number of impalas were grazing only 20-30 meters away!

More animals, these were water bucks; luckily, one or two were turned around, and we saw the toilet seat on their butts! Giraffes, zebras, wart hogs, and elephants scattered throughout the drive.

We (mostly the women) were promised a place to shop, so we stopped at a large store in the middle of nowhere. The big thing here is Tanzanite; there was also a large selection of carvings, bowls, jewelry, T-shirts, materials, sculptures, and artworks. We were allocated an hour, and you bargained for everything, 😊 We let Lynn haggle for once, then packed up the cruisers with all of our goodies, and off we went.

We continued the trek to Lake Manyara State Park, lots of small villages; many people waved at our vehicle; we saw many three-wheel Cushman-style trikes, motorcycle taxis, bicycles, and people walking along the dirt road. This main road is two-way, and there are speed bumps every mile or so to slow traffic. Turned off the pavement to Gill's Farm coffee plantation for lunch. Lots of dust and the now normal rutted washboard one-lane dirt road. The path to the restaurant is banked by blooming flowers of every size, shape, and color.

We had our own dining room overlooking the plantation; after sitting and giving drink preference, we were treated to a five-course buffet lunch! Pumpkin soup, loaves of bread, tossed salads with avocados, radishes, carrots, olives, and a variety of lettuce. Cheeses, lunch meat, samosa, clique, rice, curried chicken, lamb, a dessert bar with bread pudding, tapioca, a spice cake, and a rhubarb torte with three sauces.

Stuffed, we waddled back to the cruisers for the trip up the volcano, stopping several times to view the crater on our way to the hotel on the edge. The last eruption was three million years ago, so it is past due!

The Ngorongoro Serena lodge is built on the side of the crater; all rooms have an unobstructed view of the crater and no screens on the French doors that open to your own private deck. Please refer to the pictures again; this is another 5-star lodge!

At 7 P.M., the lounge show began and entertained us with local music and dance. Halfway through the show, a box was placed on the floor for donations. There was little participation, so Lynn picked up the box and circulated through the crowd; she encouraged everyone and filled the box with money!

The supper meal throughout this adventure was served around 7:30 P.M. Fish, tandoori chicken, and lamb, along with soups, salads, rice, and potatoes, with a selection of desserts. After dinner, we returned to our room with a glorious shower (the dust gets into every crevasse and opening), clean sheets, and a hot water bottle between the sheets on both sides to welcome us; a nice touch!

Tuesday, September 16, early breakfast, off we go, so see what we can see! We Safari-ed to find a hippo pool, lions and cubs in the high grass, thousands of wildebeests, hundreds of zebras, a few hyenas, and some acacia trees. These trees are special; the bark has a sour taste, so the animals leave the bark alone. If one of the trees senses that it is being gnawed on, it is rumored that the tree sends out a signal via roots or in the wind to the other trees to "sour up" the bark! The marula fruit on these trees affects the elephants and baboons like they are drunk. (Yup, worth repeating!)

Every so often, we would witness a Savannah Express! This is a group of wart hogs, running with their tails straight up and running at full speed, in a straight line, for quite a while, covering a considerable distance. Came across another hippo wallow; this one had around thirty hippos! Lots of birds, including pelicans, and we witnessed a few of them rolling completely over in the water. It was fun watching a pink belly and four short legs rolling from one side to another, the head submerged! We watched other hippos leave and re-enter the water and listened to the grunts, snorts, and swimming. CAUTION: You can SMELL the hippos before you see them, and it is far worse than a Wisconsin manure pile!

We then progressed to another lunch in the wild. As always, tablecloths, silverware, China plates, and glass. This one also had a cash bar set up with wine and cold beer. Porte-potties were set up for us also.

The grilled lamb, chicken, and sausage are accompanied by soup and salads with vegetables and rice. Dessert, of course! It was very pleasant, with no real irritation from flies, bees, or mosquitoes, a light breeze, sunny, under the umbrella of the trees, with monkeys scampering just outside the perimeter and guinea hens pecking alongside the road.

After lunch, we continued on safari to find a solitary male lion lying in the grass just off the road and, in the distance, two black rhinos. We were told that the baby rhinos stay with the mother for 4-5 years, and there will be no more calves until the end of the period, and the baby is weaned. More wildebeests, wart hogs, a large gathering of flamingos, zebras, monkeys, and baboons.

We finished this day's travels, stopped at the souvenir shop at the lodge, and bought pictures of the lodge from the crater to show how magnificent these accommodations really are!

Had a "Get to Know Us" meeting with our host and tour leader, followed by dinner, back to the room, shower, clean sheets warmed by those water bottles, and off to never-never land.

Day 7

Early up, bags out by 7A.M., another long day in Africa. We progress down new dusty one-lane, deeply rutted, washboard roads in our Toyota Land Cruiser to our first stop, Oldupai Gorge. This gorge is 55km (34 miles) long with two branches. (Shaped like a Y), and the depth ranges from 30 to 100 meters. It was cut originally by a volcanic eruption, then a river, followed by wind and dust. Africa gave the world humankind. We were "home". We overlooked the gorge, viewing the Oldupai Gorge "Castle." In 1911, a German butterfly man (entomologist), Professor Wilhelm Katwinkle, found fossil bones. He was followed by Professor Hans Reck two years later, and in 1931, Reck was accompanied by "This is the place," the Leakey's found the oldest bones of a creature nicknamed "Lucy," the carbon 8 skulls. (It was determined that "Lucy" was only an R. Louis Leakey discovery. Who was joined four years later by his wife, Dr. Mary Leakey, staying there for twenty-eight more years.)

Here, they discovered Homohabilis, "Johnny's child" due to John, the son, finding high, and was named after the Beatles song "Lucy in the Sky with Diamonds." Besides this, there was also a later dated African man skull (the nutcracker man). From the jaw bones of this skull, it is determined that this early man was 95% vegetarian and 5% meat. We were privileged to have a short lecture on the gorge, we are Homo sapiens, and the gorge was named after the ADLUP plant that is used by natives as an antiseptic and the animals as a source of water. There is some evidence that human evolution may be the result of two biological chains!

After the lecture, we strolled the grounds and visited the small museum and gift shop. I spied a small group of white-faced boys standing off in the distance, and we had seen a few small groups of three or four of these guys alongside the road. It seems that these boys had just been circumcised. After the circumcision, they must stay in the bush for three days as part of the rite of passage; when they return, they are given the implements of the men in the tribe.

After spending a while there, back in the cruiser, and another one and a half hours at 50-60 mph on domed dusty, rutted washboard roads. (Yes, I know it is a repeat, but it keeps happening!!) We pass a bus. It is the only once-a-day bus going east. There is one other that goes once a day west, yeah, no a/c, and yes, I took a picture of it!

We finally arrived at the Maasai village. The natives were waiting for us! The entire village was standing outside the confines of the village, separated into two groups, the males and the females. The males started dancing around to a monotone instrument for two dances, then a gathering where individual males would jump up to see how far straight up they could jump. The females then provided dance and singing, moving around in circles. The women didn't jump as much as the men, but they sang a lot louder. The entertainment was welcome; we were then escorted into the village to see how they lived.

The village is within a circle of thickets and thorns. Just inside this barrier are about 18-24 rounded dome huts 12 feet across by 6 feet high. Then, a 10-foot dirt causeway to another circle, with another low wooden fence to create a gathering area; the center was occupied by a large dead tree (on the inner low fence was a low set of benches where trinkets made by the residents were for sale) In the back there is an opening path to a structure 10X12 square, about 100 feet away, roof and half sides, that was the school. The children three to five years old go there daily, and there is one teacher to learn language arts (both Swahili and English), history, and art. When they are six to eight, they go to a primary school that services several villages.

The doors to the huts are on the side, with a narrow 2 ft. wide hallway to the center of the hut. I could not stoop low enough, so only Lynn and the others went inside. Inside, there was a fire in the center captured by cement blocks, a few cooking utensils by the wall, and a small pitcher of water. Three rooms total: one bedroom for parents, another bedroom for the kids, and the central living room. For the information talk, a few 5-gallon buckets were provided to sit on. (None of the guests and our guide could stand upright in the hut.) The huts are made from hides, reeds, grasses, mud, cow dung, and cardboard. The diet of this tribe is blood, milk, and meat.

Small groups of 5 or 6 were made and assigned a tribe member. He was responsible for showing the inside of the huts and the school and touring the village. He was also the one we needed to go to negotiate for the trinkets and wares offered by the village; no prices were displayed, and bargaining was welcomed. We did make a donation along with most of the group to the school; most of them bought some trinkets, and I did tip our "guide."

After a two-hour stop, time was up, and we left. I asked our driver about government assistance. He told us that the government does provide some food during extended draughts, but that is it, and yes, there is a charge for those two buses daily! These folks were genuinely content with their life, were very accommodating and friendly, and were the poorest people I have seen yet in the world; go figure!

We continued down the road to the Serengeti (literally means unlimited land) to stop for lunch; it was a shady area with concrete picnic tables, a light breeze, some starlings, mice, and black-faced monkeys in the trees. No, the lunch was not blood, milk, and meat; it was box lunches, way too much as always. We had beef, and the lunch consisted of 1/3# of beef, bun, water, juice, fork, knife, spoon, toothpick, yogurt, apple, two bananas, crackers, cheese, and a piece of pound cake…. still hungry?? All of the stops throughout the week had restroom facilities, which was really appreciated, especially after all that bouncing around in the cruisers.

Educating Noah...Travelin'

After lunch, we progressed into the park; the dry areas we had seen previously turned into greener, grassy areas. The land was very flat, so we headed for some out-cropping of rock looking for cheetahs!

Sure enough, at the second outcropping, we found a cheetah in a tree; progressing to another outcrop, there was a family of lions and, later, another cheetah (you have to look closely!) We then struck gold, with a family of lions in a small oasis, some lying in the grass sleeping, others lounging under the trees, with cubs repositioning being the only real movement!

Progressing toward camp, we came upon two male lions 15 feet from the road and thirty feet from a family of elephants. We stopped to watch; after a few minutes, the male elephant started to become irritated that the lions were close to his family, so he started snorting and walking toward the two lions. The lions did not want anything to do with this, so they got up and started walking away, five to six feet next to the cruisers. Talk about close-up!

That was hard to beat! As we progressed toward camp, we found another wallow hole with a number of hippos, herds of zebras, herds of water buffaloes, lots of antelope and impalas, a few singular secretary birds, a couple pair of ostriches, and a couple of wart hogs.

Due to the multiple stops to view the animals up close, we didn't arrive at our lodge until 5:30 in the afternoon. We were all escorted to our rooms, all with great views, unobstructed, on our individual balconies. The rooms were very comfortable, with hot water, a suite, mosquito netting around the bed, and spacious! Looking out over the Serengeti, we had a Dick Dick (Small 36" high fully-grown deer) grazing a few feet away, small monkeys with long tails jumping from 10-15 feet, tree to tree, and the start of bullfrogs singing!

We gathered in the main building for a briefing on the hot air balloon ride; the wake-up call was at 04:00, bags out by 04:30, and left promptly at 04:45!

Day 8

We left the lodge in the dark promptly at 04:45 A.M. The ride to the launch site was uneventful, the animals are already grazing. It took almost an hour to get to the launch site, we watched the four balloons being filled, got our assignment, two people per compartment, eight compartments for passengers, the middle for the pilot. We were all given waist straps, took pictures as dawn came, then after thirty minutes we crawled into our spaces, the pairs with the upper compartments first, then us with the compartments on the ground crawled in and attached our waist straps to the basket. The pilot fired up the burners, and slowly the balloon filled. As the balloon rose, a truck on the side, righted the basket, and we were told to keep seated (there is a small cushioned seat across each of the little cubes) until airborne and then instructed to stand. In a minute or so we were gently lifted into the air. During the experience, we were as low as 20 ft. above the ground, to 200 plus feet. There was absolutely no sensation of lift or descent or of moving across the land. There was absolute silence broken only by the heaters for the balloon.

We saw the Serengeti from a totally different perspective. There were narrow zebra paths, hippos in the river, impalas with two young bucks jousting each other, a lioness and her cub, zebras and wildebeests, hyenas, giraffes, wart hogs, and many birds.

The ride lasted a little over an hour and fifteen minutes, the landing was a little bumpy but safe. Lynn had a little difficulty climbing out, but one of our fellow travelers offered his back, and she "piggy-backed" out with ease.

All the people that were in the four balloons gathered for the Champaign toast, a tradition with balloonist, when they land. A couple of the pilots balanced the Champaign bottles on their heads, Lynn and I followed by balancing our glasses on our heads! The Champaign was easily poured and two to three glasses were common. Conversation easily flowed afterwards; we were given the history of ballooning starting in France, in the 1700's. We asked our pilot what it takes to be a pilot. What you need to do is fly a balloon solo for at least three months, you then need to fly passengers with an instructor for six months for a commercial license.

After the Champaign, we jumped into our cruisers to a proper English breakfast on the plain. Tables were set with cloth table cloths, China, and silverware. There were two "room with a view" three sided toilets set up for the men and women, with a turbaned man with a pitcher and wash basin to wash afterwards, with cloth hand towels. Oh, and what was served by the crew all in white and turbans? That would be fresh fruits, hot rolls, juice, coffee, and tea, sausage, bacon, eggs, potatoes, beans, mushrooms, and more Champaign.

After breakfast, we traveled to join the rest of the group that had chosen not to balloon. The trip was through the park, so of course we saw more of the animals; saw a Kori Buzzard the largest flying bird (the ostrich and emu don't fly!) We saw another secretary bird (The one the African government want to change its name to the African eagle), zebras and wildebeests are not even worth a glance any more they have become that common! A huge elephant male crossed the road just in front of us, without even giving us a second glance, a small herd of zebras did the same thing but they were a little skittish down the road.

One odd thing we did spy was a dead impala up in the branches of a tree. It was whole. So, it was fresh. The guide told us that it would be a fresh cheetah kill, that the cheetah was close, and that is how they store their fresh kills, no buzzards or hyenas, too fresh no decomposition smells.

We arrived at the hotel to rendezvous with the rest of the group for a late lunch.

We packed up the entire luggage into the land cruisers and headed on another game drive to our next lodging a tent camp!

Noah

On the trip, we saw the signature crushing, stomping and half eaten area created by the elephants. This would be a 100ft. square area just devastated, with the accompanying poop (remember they poop a couple pounds and hour!)

Larger herds of various antelopes (we now identified them by their butts), deer, (more butt ID), wildebeests, we were able to watch one young wildebeests "feeling his oats". He was running in the herd full speed, kicking his rear legs high, and circling in small and large circles all the time with an occasional soft butt with his head to another male, then off again! We watched him a full ten minutes, and he was still going when we left, guess he was one of those crazy teenagers!

We stopped to help a broken-down cruiser, and while waiting we remarked on how green the area and grass had become, no wonder the animals were migrating here.

Late in the afternoon we arrived at the tent camp that was to be our home the next two days, WOW.

Everyone was assigned an individual tent; ours was built on a platform. Now this is not a real traditional tent like we had in the Boy Scouts, this was on a wooden platform, up two small flights of steps ten feet off the ground. The open covered 12X8 front porch to a zippered front screen. The tent is about 12X24; the first area is two twin beds surrounded by mosquito netting, two dressers and a desk. A small hallway that leads to the bathroom, a shower stall on the left, a toilet closet on the right, and both faced by two separate marble topped sinks with a cosmetic table between them, flapped windows on both sides and between the shower and right sink is a rack with Turkish towels, and thick robes. This was just as nice if not better than the other accommodations so far and beats the crap out of Best Western!

We had time before our meeting to freshen up, (the water pressure in the shower was the best so far plus plenty of hot water!). We were filled in on the next two days' activities, I saw a couple drivers in the back, and bought them all beer. We had dinner after cocktails, menus, tablecloths, linen napkins, China and silverware. Soups, salads, a variety of entrees and dessert.

All the entrees were brought to the tables at the same time with silver domes covering each one; on a signal, the staff removed the domes at the same time; nice touch and a neat show!

Since all the animals in the Serengeti have free range, we required an escort, which was readily provided to our tent! During the night, we heard growls, grunts, and the croaking of some bullfrogs; it felt "natural," and we had no problem sleeping that night.

Day 9

At about 5:45 a.m., the birds start to sing. By 6:30, at least 6 different songs and one "wok, wok, wok" from a "nutso" Von Der Deckens Horn bill (looks like a toucan, red bill with a black and white body) who wanted, very loudly, us to know he was there! Yeah, he stood out, obnoxious, but where else would you hear this?

We had requested coffee and hot chocolate (it is included and free) which was delivered in a silver set promptly at 6:30 to the table on the porch. We then sauntered out and sipped our hot refreshments on our porch, watching a cape buffalo scratching himself on tree trunk 15 feet away, listening to the "wok. wok, wok" with a background of bird chirping and frog croaking.

Dining room for breakfast, now besides fresh fruits, juices, and bakery were prepared eggs. I had the eggs Benedict, the best I have ever had, and Lynn had a fresh croissant and fruit.

The morning drive, this is the Western Serengeti corridor at peak migration season, now till January and February, when they move back east following the fresh new grass.

January is the calving season, and they move east due to the shorter grasses and thereby less opportunity for the predators to hide. You can see your young from farther away. Even so as they migrate through April, May and June, half of the young are lost to predators. This park, along with the other two major parks we visited, is for animals only, the last Maasai tribe was relocated in 1951. The animals take the same path every year.

In this area, at this time, it is estimated 2.5 million wildebeests, 700,000 zebras, and 500,000 gazelles and antelopes, plus all the other animals!

We stopped next to an Acadia tree; it has a symbiotic relationship with a colony of ants. Lots of spikes on the tree but some animals will still try to eat it. When an animal brushes or starts nibbling on the branches the ants will immediately go to that spot and attack! They will not stop biting until the intruder retreats. Oh, and yes, it does bear fruit (Manula), it makes elephants and baboons act drunk when they eat them. (I know I stated this before, but it leads to the question) So, let's see you get bitten to death to eat the berries by the ants just to get a high, hmmmm!

We saw another herd of wildebeests, and yes, one "nutso" male was acting up, bucking, circling, and running at full speed. We just had to stop and watch the show. (This was the second one, "feeling his oats") We then progressed down to the river crossing. A group would cross, then there was hesitation, and they would withdraw from the bank. It seemed that one had spied our cruisers and made them skittish, so we waited.

Sure enough, a few minutes passed and one of the wildebeests came back, crossed in front of the vehicles and crossed back over the river. Then, there soon was a group on the other side, one started across and then started running. The leader went around the back of us to the herd, about a hundred followed until they stopped again, we figured it was a mom going back to get the kids!

Educating Noah...Travelin'

We followed the river for a while and found a rare leopard tortoise; he/she was young, only about a foot long. (These are the largest tortoises in Africa.) More animals, the zebras, make a high-pitched whiney; the wildebeests have a low two-tone grunt. At a crossing for the cruisers, there were 15-20 hippos; they would periodically drift below the water, then in a few minutes or so, you would see two holes in the water, sometimes a little snout, sometimes a portion of the head then down under the muddy water again.

There were fifteen to twenty storks walking the shore and shallow water, a few kingfishers in the shrubs and trees and two large Nile crocodiles, no one really active, and a family of baboons in the trees across the river and sitting on the bank picking bugs on their family. We just sat there quietly, what a placid scene, I think it was afternoon nap time!

There are 75 different species of Antelope in and around the Serengeti, some identified by the markings on their butt, others like the Topie Antelope gets its name for standing on termite mounds to survey the land. The heat is building, and when we were higher up next to the crater a few days ago, the flies are here and bothersome. Not as much as in Australia, but still bothersome. We slowly passed a den of tawny covered slender mongoose (about five or six) but they are quick! (The mongoose is the smallest carnivore on the plain.)

We headed back to camp for lunch, it is clouding up and if it rains the roads become impassable and slick for a while and may cancel the early evening drive, we will see!

Lunch, downtime till the 3:30 drive; this is the last real drive, so everyone showed up early, and the clouds have passed, so we are good to go!

In the parking lot a driver picked apart a small dung heap, and sure enough a half dollar sized dung beetle crawled out; he was shiny black, the "stuff" didn't stick to him!

Noah

Out on the plains, another wildebeest herd, a big one, from full left to right were wildebeests, some zebras intersperse, and an occasional warthog. Vultures on a rare carcass, another troop of baboons, water buffalo crossing in front of us (animals have the right of way along with all the other animals here).

We found two small piles of past animals; one was a zebra lower leg and hoof. Another was just some hide and the horns from a wildebeest.

On our way, back, we came upon a rather rare group of elephants 35 to 40, huge to baby, and all sizes in between, They just let us be, we let them be, it is the way of the Serengeti!

Back to the tent camp, received flight home info, another great meal, and then a procession of the staff, waiter's, chef's, kitchen help, and stewards, singing dancing and wishing us a good trip home, while thanking us for staying with them. Lynn got up and was welcomed to dance with them at this celebration that will leave an impression for life!

I settled up the bill, we were escorted back to the tent, and settled in for the night.

Day 10

Our morning started the same as before, the birds, the frog and that hornbill! Oh yeah, the coffee delivered again! The morning is cool, a slight breeze, what a great clear day! Luggage out at 7A.M. We found, from other guests, that a couple cape buffalos were sniffing outside one tent's front screen, another heard an elephant very close, and the low growl of a lion was also heard. All we heard was the low grunting of a wildebeests.

Breakfast, oh so good, load up the cruisers and off to the small airport. This is the last run with our driver; he will drive 18 hours home after we take off. He told us that if we wanted to see the most feared animal of the Serengeti and referred us to the u-tube video "Honey Badger don't give a shit" I wrote it down and did watch after coming home, I saw what he meant!

We saw more animals on the way to the airport, five mature giraffes munching on leaves, five lions under a tree a few kilometers later. Of the five lions two were off to the side, this would be a mating pair.

Lion facts: When lions mate, they do so every fifteen minutes for THREE DAYS! That made everyone sweat a little. When lions kill a larger animal, one lion gets on their back and bites the spinal cord to sever it and kill the beast.

After an hour, we reached the small airport, three of the planes were there, waiting for the fourth. The airport consisted of a restroom with holes in the floor for the men and women, and two picnic tables under a canopy. There is also a small building for? No-one was there.

We were divided into groups of 18; these are single prop 18 passenger planes, maximum luggage weight of 33# per person, that includes purse, carry-on, and suitcase. The cabin is tight, cramped and basic. The seating pattern in these planes behind the pilot, six rows of two small very narrow aisles and one ¾ seat. The flight to Arusha was only a little longer than an hour; we had a view of Kilimanjaro which is locally referred as the shy mountain because it is always shrouded in fog or clouds.

After landing, we all gathered at the small airport to be divided up into groups of 18 for a bus ride through town to our lunch restaurant. This was Saturday, shopping or market day, everyone is out, people all over, regular motorcycle "cabs", bicycles piled high with different items, hand carts made of car tires and a large box., roads dirt, lots of dust, lots of life!

The open walled restaurant offered a bountiful lunch, as usual a lot of fresh fruit, breads, and salad bar, choices of BBQ chicken beef or fish and finished with a dessert comprised of four small bowls, containing a cinnamon roll nugget, chocolate covered coffee beans, a fruit melody, and a small piece of coconut chocolate cake. There was a glass blower on premises and an ever-present gift shop.

We loaded up the buses and progressed to our original hotel rooms to rest up, shower, and relax before our farewell dinner that evening.

We opened up the multiple French doors on both porches, and enjoyed the sounds, one bird sounding like a coo-coo, another like a crying baby, and soft native music wafted through the air.

At 8:30 we joined the rest of the group for a farewell dinner, after which we left for the airport an hour drive away.

We arrived at the airport, just before midnight for our 2:30 A.M. flight out.

As we lined up, there were only two ticket agents and one pre-check. It was slow and when we got to the pre-check, my name wasn't on the manifest. So, I was directed to another airline officer that was training someone else, and finally after showing him all my identification, my tickets and my underwear labels, he approved me, issued me a seat assignment and then we got back in line again to be pre-checked to check our luggage. One of the agents didn't want to let us in, but the other agent reached around her for my documents. Checked our bags making sure they have tickets to transfer to Chicago, went through the exit visa, with declarations for each of us, failed the metal detector got frisked, and waited.

A bunch of younger back packers came in about a half hour before the flight, crowded the gate, and when the gate opened it was pure bedlam! When I got to the seat that was assigned, it was occupied, so the steward said to take the aisle seat, that lasted about five minutes when the couple that had those two seats showed up!

Lynn piped up and said the seat next to her was empty, so I wished the other couple luck and took that seat (I really think it was the original assigned seat) and was glad when the doors closed and wasn't challenged.

We had a short 30-minute flight to Mombasa, Kenya; we stayed on the tarmac for about 45 minutes, unloading and loading, then the six-plus hour flight to Istanbul.

At the airport in Istanbul, we went through one security checkpoint, yep, my hip again, another free feel, then we waited for our gate to be assigned, progressed for the gate, went through another passport, baggage screening and confined to a loading gate. As the takeoff time got closer, the whole area filled up; there were only seats enough for a full plane load. And people were starting to get irritated. Well, the gates opened and pure pandemonium again, no order, no first class first or families with children, just everyone for themselves, push and shove. We found our seats window and aisle, thank GOD, I didn't even mind the under-seat heater under the seat in front of me, blocking half of my leg room!

We were delayed for about 45 minutes, no explanation, then the flight back to Chicago, eleven and a half hours.

Upon arrival, thank GOD again, we progressed to the checkpoint. We had our new trusted traveler cards, but when we got to the machines it looked like they were roped off! So, we proceeded to the agent, he asked if we had checked in, we said it looked like they were roped off, he said that it was just a roped off thin aisle, but he got us in with an agent, I had filled out a form just in case and off to pick up our bags.

The group was waiting for us at the exit; we loaded up on the bus and were home in a little over an hour. Camille picked us up at the drop off, we thanked her, and thank you again, Camille, she opened the garage, took the stuff and us upstairs, we showered and collapsed in bed, what an amazing trip!

Noah

This was our fourth trip with Cruise and Tour and we will travel with them again!

Conversions:

2.54 inches = 1 centimeter

39 inches =1 meter

1 mile=1.6-kilometer   1 kilometer= 0.621 mile

Temperature

Centigrade	about	Fahrenheit
10 degrees		50 degrees
15 degrees		59 degrees
20 degrees		68 degrees
25 degrees		77 degrees
30 degrees		86 degrees
35 degrees		95 degrees

Educating Noah…Travelin'

It took a good three days to recover, but well worth it!

My review with the VA went pretty well. They agreed to a bilateral knee replacement, they didn't think it was enough time between the January Caribbean Vacation and China and Tibet, so we preliminary scheduled the operation for May 27th, they still did bulk at it, but finally agreed with my insistence, with me agreeing to lose 30 plus pounds so my goal for January is 275! I also e-mailed my nurse practitioner regarding my high creatine level.

I am going to mention this again; Mr. Workaholic is getting to a point where working more than 10-12 hours a week is too much. Wow, I can see how long-term unemployment destroys a work ethic! I will be working something like thirty-five hours the last two weeks and am; looking forward to going up to Door County for the week! I'm too busy, regret going to work; don't like the commitments I have made, even though the work is unchallenging, and enjoyable. Sad, very sad!

Lynn and I made friends with another vagabond person. She stated that she needed help with her animals that she would be going with the Vagabonds for three weeks to Australia. Lynn said I would be glad to help, so I said "sure".

Educating Noah…Travelin'

No good deed goes unpunished. The animals (at least 100) consisted of the following: four Emus, seven rabbits, two horses, a number of ponies, mules and donkeys, chickens, peacocks, geese, swans, ducks, guinea pigs, parrots, canaries, cockatiels, fish, and cats, lots of cats, on three properties, all needed to be fed and watered daily. I contacted my daughter to see if the grandson would like to help on weekends to learn commitment and learn about farm life.

Then the frost came, (third day), ice and snow. All the water hoses are frozen to the ground, and both of the houses are "hoarder" houses, with narrow aisles with unorganized miscellaneous junk on both sides knee high to the rooms. We located tank heaters after a number of days chopping ice for the animals to drink, blew a couple of fuses due to bad cords, and finally got the cold weather down to only three hot water pails to water the Emus, chicken's turkeys, and geese. Moved two outside cats inside; and our best time at the farms was 2 hours; coupled with the twenty-minute commute made for exhausting days.

Most of the time I am alone without the grandson Cruz, then it is 2 1/2 to three hours. She started to call every night and some nights 11 and 12 PM. I E-mailed her and asked her not to call that late, and then I told her that a couple guinea pigs froze to and I wasn't aware of some pheasant females and chicks she moved into a yard the two days between the three-hour orientation and her leaving. Then she panicked and I got a call from some guy she uses to repair tractors and equipment, and an Airline stewardess just back from China, both wanting to inspect the property because they got panic phone calls!

I met the guy the next day; he was there when I got there, we talked, and he was fine. Followed up with the stewardess, and she came after I was there and fed and watered all the animals again!

I e-mailed the owner that I would continue the work, that the peacocks (hens and chicks) were fine, and that I was extremely upset that she had so little trust in me, and I was done with her after she returns.

She e-mailed me that she would be returning Tuesday night and that she had arranged for someone else to take her home.

I fed all the animals for the last time Tuesday morning, gave them all extra water, hay and bread, filled all the troughs, cleaned all the cat boxes, so she would have the least amount of work acclimating back to her world. I left a note letting her know about the days the grandson accompanied me and requested he receive $5.00 per day, provided a note from him in appreciation for the opportunity to work with the animals. I also included a self-addressed stamped envelope to his house.

Four days following the experience I received a note from her, stating she had no control over the weather and included a check for $400.00 to cover the hiring of the grandson and pay towards the mileage incurred. I went to a hobby store nearby and purchased a Mustang model and put $50.00 in an envelope along with a picture album I put together of his favorite animals on the farm. I called him up and went over to surprise him, he was!

I also volunteered to drive Vets to and from the VA hospital. Another experience I needed to know. Getting to become a volunteer is like joining up again, including multiple tests, a physical, shots, and a road test to boot! It took two weeks to be to the stage where I could start driving. I get to pick the days I work, start at 0700 and work till 1400-1500, averaging 90-110 miles shuttling disabled vets to and from the hospital. I do get a $5.00 voucher for lunch, the volunteers are great to work with, and the vets we transport for the most part are very grateful.

I started a Nutri-most diet on the 15th of November. Pricey, at $1350.00 (original price was $2700.00, but I volunteered to be a guinea pig for the Vagabond Club), they guaranteed losing at least 35-45 pounds in 40 days. The diet is rigorous: two proteins, two vegetables, and two fruits per day. (Consumption averages less than 500 calories a day.) No sugar or fats, and negatively charged water, plus supplements. I must record daily in a journal plus e-mail morning weights daily. Occasionally, I get hungry, especially with the constant food commercials on TV or when I walk into a food store or anyplace with food displays.

Forty-four days of drinking lots of water; 500 or less calories a day. Only seafood, beef, veal, and buffalo, vegetables and fruits, limited to 3 oz. of protein, 3 oz. of select vegetables, and two different fruits a day, must not repeat any of these the next day!

I Lost 43 pounds in 40 days, three days without the formula, and now 3, weeks introducing oils and more food (2500 calories) but no bread or starches. It is actually very hard to exceed 1,000 calories now without feeling uncomfortable or full!

Chapter Three
2015

On January 2nd, I tendered my resignation to Synergy. I will be going on a Caribbean Cruise this month, will be on a road trip in March, and China Tibet in April, and then the bilateral knee replacement is really too much to schedule around. It was two years to the month.

Enough, time to move on to other things. Ruth, the owner, asked for a copy of my autobiography. I gave her a MATC pen set to pass on to an employee as a gift and asked her to provide me with a struggling employee who is in nursing school so that I could provide him/her with all of my remaining nursing equipment.

Caribbean Cruise

Sunday, the 18th of January, we got up at 3:30 A.M. to start our newest adventure. We had already packed the car and needed only to dress, make the bed and get out! We usually take the Coach USA bus from Milwaukee to O'Hare in Chicago to be delivered right to the airlines without the hassle of Chicago driving and leaving the car there. I always pre-buy the round-trip tickets, staple them to a schedule, hide the return in the luggage, staple to a schedule and put them with flight documents on the beginning trek, plus check the free parking areas (they don't charge for parking if you leave your car two weeks or less) to make sure there is room to park.

Anyhow, we arrived at the bus depot at 4:20 A.M. and waited for them to open up, get the pass to park, and park the car in one of the few spaces left. The bus arrived on time, and we left promptly at 04:35. The traffic was light; only one person picked up in Racine, and none in the Kenosha stop. There was no snow on the road, visibility was very good, and we arrived at a sleepy hub terminal and walked right up to the United area. We now have to log ourselves in at a

United kiosk to log in and pay our fee for our one shared piece of luggage, wait for someone to weigh our suitcase for another chance to make additional money, receive our boarding passes and off to the security check point.

Again, there was no special TSA line so we had to go through the same as everyone else, I got stopped, had to go through the screener again, then passed over by the magic wand, to discover I indeed had an artificial hip as I explained…twice!

I am still looking forward to using that $100.00 Trusted Traveler pass we both applied for and have yet to use! We hurried up to the gate to wait the 2 1/2 hours for our flight.

The old hurry-up-and-wait routine, but we were there!

As loading was announced, everyone rushed to the gate for their place in line, priority 1,2,3, or 4, those with priority 1 sauntering in the last minute to rubbed our noses in it. We found our seats, the bins were not complexly full, but most of the carry-on could never fit or comply with the true requirements!

We took off on time; it was only a 2 ½ hour flight, so there was only one pass for free juice or soda and snacks available for credit card purchase at about $7.00 per selection. The screen in the back of the seat in front is on a constant United American ad, to be watched time after time after time……. You get the gist. (No, you can't turn it off either!)

Oh, yes, the economy is still very cramped, and the "recline" is still only about 3"; you can opt for premium economy, which gives you six additional inches of leg room, or triple the fare for business class, which has spacious seating, and leg room.

The plane stopped, and everyone jumped out to stand while we all waited for the door to open. The first class/business class filed out, then the rest of the plane, front to back. Follow the signs to the baggage claim area, look for your flight, and wait at the specified carrousel to start delivering your luggage.

Oh, and again, everyone crowds the conveyor, waiting for their luggage. After 20 minutes, most of the luggage was taken away with no new items; I found an employee about missing luggage or if another carousel was used. He indicated that two different carousels were used, so sure enough, I walked over to the other conveyor to find our suitcase going around and round with a few other orphans.

Now, to find the cruise ship representative, We found her and the small group of ten escorted to an area on the side to wait for our bus. It seems that the biggest crush of passengers arrived between ten and one. With the hour change, we were now looking at 2:20 PM; it took a half hour for a full bus to come and load us for the fifty-minute drive to the port. The all-on-board was 3:30, and we arrived at the terminal a few minutes before. The terminal was virtually empty; we got our photos, signed our waivers, and received our sea passes. Obligatory photos, easy walk on the gangplanks and then on the ship; welcome aboard!!

We got in line to change our seating from late to early; there was a longer wait than we thought, so I went to find the steward to separate the bed (the inside rooms are so small, it is much easier and more spacious with 1/2 the bed snugged up on the walls of the room! I found out what channel the Green Bay Packer game was on, dumped off the carry-on, thanked Wendell (our room steward for the cruise), and went off to find Lynn.

At dinner, we were seated at a table for ten; there were only six of us, and one pair was a mother-and-daughter family. The little girl was fun, but she was very spoiled and very fussy, an only child.

The first night was always slow; it took almost forty-five minutes to get our appetizers. I screwed up my diet by eating two rolls and waiting for the food; it was my first food other than a snack bar that day. My appetizer was seafood spread with crackers, my dinner crusted salmon was perfect, Lynn had a cold peach soup, and a slow roasted prime rib, also cooked to perfection and juicy!!

At 7:15 in the evening, up almost 17 hours, we walked the inside promenade, took the elevator up to the deck, and walked in the night air back to the rear or aft to take the back elevator down to our room. Showers, night clothes, and at eight-thirty, this exciting couple hit the hay....out for the night!

Monday, January 19<u>th</u>. A day at sea.

Both of us were up at 07:30, refreshed. The breakfast on the buffet deck. As always, there was everything to choose from, including omelets with whatever you wanted in them. We always stop and get another ship daily activity program to see what each of us wants and determine where we will meet, and then off we go to our own needs and wants.

I chose to walk a mile, then my knees broke down, so I sunbathed for 15 minutes in front and then back; I made up a sign saying I was not Moby Dick, the great white whale, to prevent crew member from throwing me over the side (to save me!) It worked! Some pointed at my whiteness, but they all seemed to read the sign before calling the crew!

After the sunbath, I walked another 1/5th mile, but that was all my knees could take.

I then joined Lynn in the theatre to get the low-down on shopping at the three ports we were to visit. She had gone to a trivia and did her own self-guided tour of the ship.

Lunch at the buffet

Me, another 20 minutes on each side in the sun (with my Moby Dick sign very prominent!), then off to a Martini tasting event. The Martini tasting usually ranges from 4-5 Martinis, a history lesson on who created the specific Martini. This time, we were all able to mix the martinis, shake them, and dispense them to our neighbors. We were all very generous, and each ended up with 24-30 oz. of booze. (For $18-$24 ea.) By the third Martini, everyone was talking and laughing, and all of us were new friends!!

We were told by the bartender that this was the largest class in the past six cruises. We all had a great time, and including the two bartenders, we were all given souvenir glasses to boot!

What kind of martini, you ask??

Pomegranate, Coconut, Lemon, and Chocolate… yum!!

Lynn had gone to the line dancing on deck and played another game of trivia; we met back in our room to change for the first formal night. Sport coat and dress, I was wearing the sports coat…

The table for ten was now down to four. A single woman asked if she could join us, and we welcomed her; she was wearing a white tux with a red bowtie and cummerbund. We enjoyed her company the balance of the cruise!

What did we have, you ask? Between Lynn and me, we had pear and rum cold soup, shrimp cocktail, spinach salad, Duck, New York strip steak, BBB cream Brule, and lemon pie, all perfectly prepared.

After dinner, we attended a production show of show tunes of the 70's.; afterward, Lynn went to a game called 'Finish That Lyric' and had a great time; I went to a cigar and single malt tasting. NO ONE ELSE CAME! So, I had two fingers of Balvenie 12-year-old triple cask scotch (very smooth and oaky) along with a 1990 Rocky Patel cigar. (Also, it is very smooth mild, with an easy draw!)

I joined Lynn in the room, showered, journaled, and went to bed. (Royal Caribbean discontinued chocolate on the pillows at night three years ago, I asked!! ☐)

Tuesday, Costa Maya Day!

Up at 7:30, Breakfast on deck 11, the buffet; Lynn prefers this so you actually eat less, on your terms, and quicker in and out. After breakfast, we usually go out on deck to scope out how close we are to land and what the temperature is and get in a little exercise.

We then proceeded to the service desk. We had received notice in December that the ship would not arrive in Costa Maya on time and that we would arrive an hour later. I contacted the excursion company regarding the notice, and they relayed back to me that the tour scheduled at 10:30 was local time and not a concern.

Now, back to real-time, the day of the excursion, and sure enough, we will be docking not at 11:00 but arriving at 11:30. (Arriving! This means 15-20 minutes to put down the gang planks, fight the first of people, go through security, etc.!!) Since this excursion was booked through the agent's company and not the cruise line, the shore excursions office on the ship could not help; back to customer relations...... They have always been supportive and proficient on every cruise.

She dialed the number and handed me the phone. I was connected to a local service agent, explained my situation, and told to hold on for a transfer......... yep, disconnected! I called the desk person over, and we called again, four times, either busy or dropped calls! That was enough; my very helpful person was getting frustrated, and I was very frustrated, so I asked her to help me one more time and dialed the emergency number for the excursions. I connected and started to complain, but she cut me short and said, "What can I do to remedy this?"

I said to reschedule for a later time, and she asked that I hold. Ten seconds later, she told me we were scheduled for 1:00. Anything else? I thanked her profusely, told her she was a saint, and thanked the desk person for her patience with the phone use. (No charge to the room or me!)

We went back to the room, got ready for the adventure, and went down to deck 3 to pick up 2 towels (charged to the room, if not returned, $25.00 each charged to your credit card!) We got in line, checked out, and were on the pier by 11:50, now to find the dolphins.

The directions were to bear left as we approached the entrance to the market at the end of the pier. We watched the Indians dressed up in Mayan garb, posing for pictures with the tourists, passed a number of shops, and kept bearing left through a maze of shops, bars, and restaurants. Another ship had arrived before us, so everything was bustling; a large kidney-shaped pool between two bars was full of people, the paths crowded, and being lunchtime, most people drinking, eating, and laughing.

I found the dolphin pools but couldn't find the check-in point. So, I asked several folks on the way down the beach. (You can't be shy, always ask! Who cares if you are just another stupid tourist!!) Besides, the signage is usually poor, turned, or missing…too many of the attractions!

We found the place! Issued life vests (required), gave locker keys for our stuff, and told us we were in the next group of eight. We dumped our stuff, got to the dolphin pool, and then I was turned back to take my camera back to the locker; no personal cameras allowed. (No, there was not a sign!) I hurriedly picked my way up the beach, padded the distance to the lockers, deposited my camera, and hobbled back to join the group, proceeding into the water on a platform next to the wall supporting us in chest deep in salt water.

We were then introduced to "Danny," our dolphin of the day. We were briefed on what not to do:

1. Touch after the blow hole, not in front of the hole or close to the hole.
2. No sudden moves

3. No grabbing or pulling except when he expects it
4. The dolphins can sense anxiousness and relax!

We were then told to put out our hands in the water. Then, each of us took turns with interaction and photos in the order:

1. Put your hands palm out. Danny came over, and you got to stroke the inside of his flippers.
2. Kiss the dolphin
3. The dolphin kisses you
4. Swim to the middle of the pool, put out your arms, and hold the dolphin upside-down
5. Swim to the opposite side of the pool; the dolphin swims under you upside-down. Gently grab both flippers and ride him across the pool, belly to belly.

After we all had a turn with Danny, we all splashed him, and he, in turn, splashed us! He made a few passes by us for some extra "pats," and then he jumped a number of times to show off!

Danny was incredibly fast, very social, and reminded me of a very good dog. (He received quite a few fish treats between performing with us.) You could also see there was a very good relationship between Danny and the trainer. Halfway through the "work," he decided to make a quick visit to the side of the pool to check on his buddy dolphin in the next pool, jumped, then returned. I was also surprised that male dolphins were trained to be more aggressive than females!

After the encounter, we showered, changed, and reviewed the pictures for purchase, and of course bought them! Who wouldn't buy pictures of themselves interacting with dolphins!!

We then toured the various shops and tourist traps, looking for those unique items you can't find anywhere else, and headed for the ship. It was an easy walk on the pier. Went to our room and took mini-naps. We then proceeded to the pool, bought ice cream drinks, and sunned ourselves.

Took a tour around the deck, changed for dinner, and attended a trivia game (We won again, two more key chains for first place!) before joining our new table friends for dinner.

Dinners included garlic soup, strawberry soup, tiger shrimp, lasagna, a small rice ball, chocolate layer cake, and lemon tart.

We attended and participated in another trivia game and won pens, this time for first place. (15/15!)

After the trivia, we attended an Elton John impersonator comedian show that was very entertaining and fun.

We went to the newly/oldie wed game. Lots of fun to watch, the couples were funny and the longest married couple (over 60 years) actually won!

We walked the deck to the rear of the ship, took the elevator down to our room, and called it a night.

Wednesday, Cozumel

We're already in port when we wake up. We dressed in swimsuits under our clothes, grabbed a quick breakfast, and got off the ship. We went to find the park where our next excursion was planned. There were two other ships docked at the pier also, one Celebrity and one Carnival, a busy day in a busy port.

At the end of the pier before the major highway to town was a slew of shops and bars and a couple of restaurants. We threaded through the area; most of the shops were still setting up for the day, so we got by without much "hawking" calling out to us to buy. We had to find our way to the park, found it was four miles from the pier, and asked at the stand the cost of the trip for two. They all said $12.00, so we took the first cab. (It is actually $12.00 per ride for up to 4 people.) The ride was only 10-15 minutes, along the seashore, and very pleasant.

The park opens at 08:00. We arrived a little after 9, and we were some of the first to be welcomed. We posed for the picture with the Inca warrior, checked in for the Manatee swim, and signed the request for the pictures; no "selfies" or personal cameras were allowed during the experience. We saw a group forming, so we quickly dumped our gear in our locker, got in line, and received our vest. We received all the safety facts, checked our vest for fit, and then we were approached by a park person and culled out of the group. It seems that only one encounter was included, and the Manatee experience was at 10:30. These were dolphin swims going on; we saw at least three in progress. So, we went on a tour of the park.

There were a few zip lines just starting to open up; we promised ourselves to check that out when we finished with the manatees. Other activities were on the beach, including snorkeling on the reef just a few meters off the shore, cabanas, shore chairs, a bar, a restaurant, and a sea lion pool. We sat down by a lagoon and watched a couple zip liners fly overhead. Lynn was building her courage! It was approaching 10, so we headed back to the adventure pier; we briefly explored an ancient ruin replica and admired the different flowers and trees in the area.

It seems Mexico is not too time-conscious ; 10:30 passed, then 10:40, and then at 10:45, they started to gather people together. It was a very large group, but then they asked us to form four separate groups, with the manatee group lining up on the outside, followed by three groups of dolphin folks. The park has thirty-two dolphins and five manatees; each dolphin eats eleven kilos (22 pounds) of fish each day, and the manatees are fed romaine lettuce. The amount is regulated, especially for the manatees, who will over eat (like a horse or pony) to keep them healthy. There are two performing areas for the manatees and six for the dolphins.

We were refitted with safety vests and led out on the pier to an area where we descended into the water to a platform that again kept us chest-deep in the ocean. The procedure was basically the same as yesterday with the dolphins. This time, there were two manatees in the area. One, Angel, was the largest at about ten feet long, and the other, Edgar, was about seven feet long. They seemed to be not as "smart" as the dolphins; the closest I can describe them is two docile, friendly cows with flippers and a tail.

The manatees were coaxed to swim past us; they were dark-colored and felt rough, bumpy, supple, and spongy, kind of like a tire without enough air in it. They have a face like a walrus, two large flippers (with retractable nails), and a large, flat horizontal tail. They swim slowly and deliberately and seem to be social, docile animals. They are vegetarians and do not have teeth. When you feed them, they will gum you, trying to get the last scrap of lettuce. It is not threatening and very soft. Any lettuce not eaten is quickly gobbled up by the fifty or so small fish of various colors, shapes, and sizes accompanying the manatee when they eat.

One trainer was having difficulty with the small manatee; Angel wasn't a problem but seemed to take a liking to me.

We each did the routine with the animals: the kisses, the holding, and the stroking of the front flippers. In that the younger manatee wasn't cooperating, we were there longer than most, and then Angel would come and nuzzle me after finishing other people; she was very nice, but her bulk would pin me against the wall. And no, I wasn't encouraging her (they scolded me, but I was innocent!!), but I did give her a few flipper strokes when she came and fed her, too.

After everyone had a turn with the manatees, we were able to free swim with them; Angel got most of my lettuce and muzzled me against the side once (she must have weighed half a ton!) like swimming with a big friendly water cow! Great fun.

They called us out of the water, we all enjoyed the encounter, and both manatees were given a little additional romaine for their cooperation.

We changed back into our clothes, proofed the photos, paid for them, and checked the time. Due to the un-cooperation of the one manatee, it was well past noon. We didn't have time for zip line and shopping, so I asked Lynn what she wanted to do. She chose shopping.

I asked the cab stand person how much it would cost to go to downtown Cozumel. He said $16-18, so the next cab, I offered $16 to go downtown, he countered with $8, so I agreed, and off we went. The downtown areas were in the opposite direction from this morning, so we passed the pier as we went down the coastal highway to the shopping center downtown.

We started at the far end of town and worked our way back toward the pier two miles away. We had a list of items we wanted. Lynn wanted Ammolite for sure and souvenirs; I wanted a bamboo shirt, bamboo pillowcases, Del Sol products (color change in the sun), plus some hot sauces for the son-in-laws. As we worked our way down the strip, we were lured with "free" gifts, "lowest prices," and "special just for you" hawked out to us, vendors standing on the sidewalk trying to divert us into the store, and pitiful looks when you walk by.

Lynn found the jewelry store the ship's excursion leader recommended while I sat outside. She found the Ammolite she wanted and then started to bargain. $1600.00 to $700 to $445, $250 and finally $200. His final price, she said, throw in the necklace, and I'll take it! She then came out to get me; I said I wouldn't pay for it unless I got a beer, so a cold bottle of beer was quickly put in my hand. It was entertaining, and Lynn was happy, so her birthday present was bought.

We found the other stores, bought like drunken sailors, found the hot sauce shop, and bought a variety pack for one son, the hottest they had for another. My legs were giving out, and I asked a cabbie how much, and he looked at me: $8.00. We jumped in at the terminal, we climbed out, and I gave the cabbie a smile and a ten-dollar bill. Halfway through the tangle of shops, we were caught in a serious downpour. There was no place to sit, my knees and ankles barking; as soon as the rain started to let-up, we hobbled the rest of the way to the ship, deposited our loot in the room, changed out of our wet clothes, took the welcomed pain pills and rested for a half hour. We then went on deck for a light snack.

We watched the "all aboard" wrap up as the "lagers" strolled toward the ship; the crew was trying to wrap up the canopies, gang planks, and welcome back station. The ship was to leave at 4 p.m., and they left those behind that are not on ship-sold excursions.

If you are on a ship-sold excursion, they will wait for you. It looked like two excursionists were significantly late. The ship waited, and the gangplank was finally pulled aboard at 4:50! I figured there was some leeway because tomorrow is a day at sea, and the wait could easily be made up. Trivia, dinner at our table of ten with only five left.

After dinner, another trivia: the pain pills were not effective, even with the alcohol, so I went back to the cabin to shower, change, and add some more pain relief. Lynn went to a production of Jersey Boys and then went up on deck to join in a 70's costumed singing and dancing and finished with a conga line around the deck.

Another day is gone; this week is going too fast!

Thursday, Another day at sea.

We slept in till 8:00! Straggled to breakfast and checked the deck. 75 degrees with a wind of 10-12 knots. It's time to bake ourselves. We were up to 45 minutes per side.

This was the day Lynn wanted to try climbing the rock wall, so off we went to see what she could do. We figured most of the kids and adventure adults tried and did the first day at sea, plus this was the first available time today, so the late risers won't be there either. We were right; there was only one family there, so Lynn slipped on climbing shoes fitted with a harness and a helmet.

They helped hook her into the safety line, and she got up about two feet and stopped. They lowered her back down (the two feet) and showed her where she should put her hands and feet to get higher. She tried again, got four feet up, and just couldn't anymore. Well, that was that! She tried, and the people helping were very gracious.

We then went down to the pools and had ice cream drinks for Lynn to feel better and heal a bruised ego!

We went our separate ways, Lynn off to read her book and then play "Bago," a bean bag game with the crew to take third place to walk the deck, watch the ocean, and people watch.

We met at three, another trivia game (we didn't win), and watched an amazing ice production show presented on the ice rink on the ship. (Yes, an ice rink on a Caribbean cruise ship). Another trivia dinner, this one offered steak and lobster tail, more provided to each of us if requested. (Needless to say, we all requested an additional tail). After dinner, another Trivia; we won with a perfect score and added another key chain to our collections.

The production show was singing and dancing, then on to join the game of Quest, an adult scavenger hunt game.

Each section of the stands had four representatives, two females and two males. We had two females, but the men refused to go down to the arena, so after one younger guy finally went down, I hobbled down to the area to complete our forward team.

The idea of the game is to present to the narrator the items requested. The first person gets the most points, the second a few less, and then one point if you show up with the item. There were 9 teams.

Noah

Here are some of the items requested:

Two pair of shoe laces; Girl with two pairs of men's pants; Man, with a bra; Show a thong; Show a piercing not on the face; A six-person pyramid; Show six ships programs; One woman and one man sharing a pair of pants; Show a pair of boobs…The finale was a man with lipstick, a bra, jewelry, and women's shoesparading around and voted on.

We didn't win, didn't place or show, but had a good time, and I know we did better than a few of the others!

It was Midnight when we got back to the cabin; tomorrow is Coco Cay, the Bahamas!

Friday the last full day on board, and this is the private island.

We were up at seven, the first shuttle boat to leave at eight twenty, so, we dressed over our swim suits, crammed a brief breakfast, picked up our towels on deck three, and were in line for the first shuttle. These boats are quite large and can accommodate 200 guests each. There was one loading, one at another port to load after one was full, and another waiting 100 yards out, waiting to take the place of the full one leaving. The shuttles are scheduled to leave every fifteen to twenty minutes; the day is perfect: warm sun, light breeze, beautiful water, sparkling and dancing in the sun; it takes ten to fifteen minutes to get to shore and unload. We are then to report to the excursion hut; we do, we have signed in, and we have forty-five minutes to look around, check out the native vendors, and explore the beaches.

On the announcements after the Quest, we were told that Coco Cay was a private island and all we needed was our ship pass, we could charge our drinks, and the food was provided free from the ship. So, we didn't take any cash; the problem was the natives did not accept anything but cash, and how were we supposed to tip the excursion vendors!?!

Educating Noah…Travelin'

I determined to go back after our Sting ray excursion to get some money to tip the crew if warranted and buy something from the natives to help them out.

We were greeted by the captain and walked down the beach to a small boat waiting for us at the pier. There were eleven of us signed up for the first excursion. The boat rides to the small island where the rays were penned up, only about twenty minutes on calm seas. When we arrived, we docked on a small pier, were given goggles, safety vests were optional, and took steps down to the water, currently about chest deep.

Our cautions were: no sudden moves, shuffle when you walk, and relax; animals can sense anxiety. The barb that killed Steve Erwin, the Australian Zoo adventurer, is located ¾ of the way to the body from the tip of the tail. (Steve broke all the rules, approached the ray from behind, and startled him when he jumped on it for a ride. Mr. Erwin was known for tempting fate and pushing the limits, a shame it caught up to him.)

There were three staff in the water that we walked /shuffled over to meet some rays. They held the rays (most of them about three feet around, dark grey on the top and white on the bottom, weighing in about 50 pounds) and showed us how to feed them, tucking our thumbs in our hands and presenting a ten-inch squid to the area below the eyes by reaching under the handler's arm, move the food close. You feel suction, then more suction, you loosen your grip and the squid is sucked right out of your hand.

If your hand gets too close, you may get a Stingray "burn" caused by entering the ray's mouth. No one got that close; some didn't want to handle the squid! (The mouth can crush clam shells, krill, and lobster shells and pulverize them.)

Everyone got an opportunity to hold a ray, they are soft on the bottom, and have many sensors there, so I lightly rubbed mine, and he didn't flap as much as others. Both Lynn and I posed holding rays, a couple of conchs were found, we held them, a star fish was found, and we passed it around also. Then a sea slug was found, he was eight to ten inches long and about four inches in diameter, I was one of two who held the slimy guy, even the captain refused to hold him!

We were given free time after all the pictures to explore the area; I found a small reef with many fish, a number of rays swimming about, and a few buried. The pictures turned out pretty good.

We spent a total of forty to forty-five minutes then loaded back on the boat to return to the island. Every one, the captain and staff were especially patient, helpful, and easy to work with, a great experience!

We all thanked the captain as we disembarked and left. I set Lynn up on a beach chair, walked back to the shuttle area, caught a shuttle back to the ship, went to the cabin, got some cash, caught the next shuttle back to the island and was back with Lynn in an hour. We went to the excursion hut, gave a tip for the crew, shopped the native market, bought a few trinkets, then we went to have lunch at the provided buffet. We met some folks from the ship, swapped island stories, walked the beach again, and went back to the shuttle, back to our cabin, showered, changed for dinner, and packed our bags.

I signed us up for the Kennedy Space Center optional tour to get us off the ship early and our departure at the airport was 4:45, a long time to spend in an airport!

Had one last win at Trivia, said goodbye to the other couple at our dinner table and our waiter and assistant, walked the promenade once last time, took in the farewell production show, and went up on deck for one more "at sea" walk in the warm air and back to the cabin to finish the packing and sleep our last night on the ship.

Saturday, the last day, and going home

Since we were scheduled for an excursion, we were to be the first

Educating Noah...Travelin'

ones off the ship. The gathering point was the casino; we arrived a half hour early and joined the melee. I have never witnessed such confusion, people shoving and jockeying for position to get off the ship, elevators were blocked, luggage and people crowded the aisles, chaos, and you would have thought this was the ships first cruise and the captain and crew inexperienced.

Finally, fifteen minutes after we were told to disembark, they opened the doors for our group. We proceeded through the ramps and staircases to customs, welcomed back, and off to our tour bus.

The trip to the space center was forty-five minutes; we were briefed as to when we would be picked up for the forty-minute trip to the airport at two that afternoon.

This was a fully guided tour; we experienced the first shuttle; Imax was shown the actual rockets, a number of space shuttles, and a bus tour of the various launch pads; we saw the world's largest doors on the assembly hanger. The huge tractor that transports the rockets to the launch pads, each tractor tread weighs a ton!

I was able to ride a simulator in a simulated launch, lots of shaken' goin' on, and simulated G force! (Lynn chickened out)

We also toured the gift shop. (Like we could miss that!) We got shirts, souvenirs, and freeze-dried ice cream.

The park was very clean, the tour very organized, even the sandwich we bought at the commissary was fresh and good. We learned a lot, had some good experiences and lessons, it was just a bit cool, being in the high 60's, but I guess good for us to get used to cold again.

The flight back is uneventful, and there are lots of kids on the plane; if you don't pay for the entertainment, you are subjected to two and a half hours of United advertising, over and over again. (I know I mentioned this before, but it was that irritating!)

Noah

Came jockeying to get off the plane and, yes, again, told the wrong carousel for our luggage; United both ways was overbooked, crowded, uncomfortable, and clueless as far as luggage retrieval, not customer friendly, not even close.

We waited for our connecting bus back to Milwaukee; I bought a small pizza so we didn't starve to death. The driver of the bus seemed to expect us to put our own luggage under the bus and was not very friendly, so for the first time in years, no tip. We arrived in Milwaukee an hour and a half after leaving O'Hare, also the longest trip ever on this bus line. Loaded the car, and we were home by ten P.M., showers and bed, another great adventure!!

Educating Noah…Travelin'

Noah

It has been two weeks since returning from the Caribbean. I have lost the weight and water gained and am again on track to lose ten pounds a month. I made a mistake by taking a diuretic to reduce the ankle swelling and the gout returned for two days. I have not eliminated bread and potatoes from my diet but I am severely limiting them. I am watching what I eat, no longer counting calories and seeing if I can wing this effectively.

I am planning the road trip for March, tweaking the April China trip, walking 3500 steps or more per day, and still driving the Vets once a week.

I followed up on the China Visa, which cost us $450.00 each; I received our seat assignments for the fourteen-hour (one-way) flight to and from China and was not happy. I always compare the assigned seats to SEAT GURU to find out what we have. For both flights, we were at the very back of the plane and right across from the toilet. Along with the position next to the toilet, the recline on the seats is restricted. I complained to Viking and am awaiting new seat assignments. In my opinion, these seats should be discounted, not just assigned! I did not receive a reply for almost a month, so I went to the supervisor, who was curt, responded that seat assignments were to go through my agent online even though it was a Viking Booking, and lightly apologized for the MIA contact at Viking. I promised not to bother him again, contacted American, and upgraded the seats there and back for an additional $150.00 for seats in economy, but in the middle of the aircraft. The malaria pills cost another $160.00 plus the Diamox for altitude sickness, another $30; we are in the tank for another $800.00 for this China trip, and it is still a month away!

Took a road trip to Florida and the Keys; I will attach that after this paragraph. The diet must be maintained. I can only eat a little wheat, potatoes, or booze! I am bouncing back after vacations, but the amount of water I retain is huge, and I know if I take a diuretic again, the gout will return, and it is too close to China to risk it!

Florida Road Trip March 2015

I pushed up the date from starting on a Tuesday to a Monday just to give us another day as a bumper and relieve a little anxiety.

Since Mondays are horrible going through Chicago, I did not mind starting later; we were in the car and off at **8:50 AM, March 9th. (48554)**,

(this is the car mileage each day.)

I had talked to our friend Terry Werth (former truck driver) about the routes through Chicago, and he told me the difference between going around the city or through was only 4 miles; this was a no-brainer. We went around, and with the I-pass, never slowed to fewer than 60 mph throughout Illinois!

As we entered Indiana, we pulled over for our first "relief" break, stretched our legs, and discussed finding our first stop.

This would be a "Roadside Attraction". A giant woman's leg is used as a sundial. Since no address was given, only a general location, someplace outside Rose Lawn, Indiana, in a nudist community. 😊

Not being shy, we went to one nudist resort, and we were told this was not the one and that there were others "down the road." So, we took off, found a local restaurant, and asked there. Sure enough, "the leg" was at the Sun-Ora nudist resort, back about a mile. We entered and inquired at the gate, and they were gracious enough to let us in and take pictures. The leg needs paint, but it is a good thirty feet long!! (Yep, picture in album!)

Off to see the second Indiana "Roadside Attraction," the town of Santa Claus. It seems that this very small town was named on Christmas Eve, so the name Santa Claus seemed appropriate!

The entire town was really just a theme park, a campground, and a candy store; it was kind of a big disappointment, but who else has gone to a town called Santa Claus!

We drove a little further, just to cross the border into Kentucky, noticing a few oil wells in the fields as we transitioned to the south.

Tuesday, March 10th

We got up early and were all packed and fed and in the car by 7:30 (49013)

We left in mild rain, and throughout the day, it rained; sometimes, the rain overwhelmed even the fastest wiper speed! We made Nashville by 9:45 a.m. and went to the Ryman Auditorium. This place was built as a church, then used as the Grand Old Opry for twenty years, then went to waste for a while, to finally be restored as a historical site.

We opted to make a record (how neat is this!), so we signed up and went to a small recording studio in the auditorium. The engineer was very nice, very helpful, and pleasant to work with. He explained what would happen and what we needed to do, gave us each a set of headphones, and positioned the microphones for us. We were given two chances to record the song we selected, and the recording (us) was pretty bad, but we did it! Here are the excuses....

1. Only one side of my earphones worked.
2. There was no written music with the words, just paragraphs of words.
3. We picked a Willie Nelson song that we barely knew and didn't get to practice except for the first recording.
4. I rushed the words, and we both got lost a few times.

The compliment we got from the engineer was that we were the first folks who actually got on track again after losing our place during the song! (We still stunk; I kinda sound like Johnny Cash! Lynn, like a screeching owl!)

We stopped at the Alabama tourist bureau as we crossed the State line, looking for an artist (Joe Minter and his African Village) in Birmingham, but no one else seemed to know about him! However, they indicated we may be interested in the Vulcan statue in Vulcan Park in Birmingham and The Space and Rocket Center in Huntsville.

Since we had toured the Kennedy Space center in January, we thought this would be interesting also! We took a short detour and visited the space center. We drove past this last year while Lynn was driving and I was napping.

It seems this is one of three space centers; the third is in Houston. This one has the most engineers (even currently). It also has a space camp, training facilities for the astronauts, and extensive displays, equipment, and movies.

It was quite an extensive complex with a B1 Bomber (the Blackbird), some helicopters, missile launchers, and military and space vehicles.

We learned that after WWI, the German scientists who surrendered were housed in New Mexico. After a while, they were offered jobs. The Germans were allowed to visit 3 US cities in which to live and work. They selected Huntsville due to the mountain ranges that reminded them of Germany. This was how the space program was also developed in Alabama.

It was well worth the stop. It was only 3:30 p.m., so off we went to Birmingham, found Vulcan (the statue), got a motel room, and had an excellent meal at a seafood restaurant with an extraordinary waiter, matched by fantastic seafood! After dinner, we walked around a mall to get some exercise and experience the city.

Wednesday, March 11th: Back on the road by 8:10

(49385)

We ate breakfast. Actually, Lynn had breakfast, and I heated up my leftover redfish and enjoyed the remainder again!!! What a treat!

Noah

We left Montgomery in the rain, and the two-hour trip to Birmingham was all rain, from steady to downpour, we could hardly see!!

Birmingham is the place where Jefferson Davis had his white house, so we had to see it; very nice, nothing as grand as the northern White House, in D.C., but very nice; it is across from the new state office, which dwarfs the other buildings, there is also the Alabama legislature building and court house. We also saw some very nice churches, and going through the neighborhoods, typical southern shot gun houses with always a porch in the front, some with a porch in the back, and none with basements.

As we left Birmingham, the sun started to come out, and the temperature steadily rose to the 70s. As we drove to our next stop in Tallahassee, Florida, there were a few brief showers, but nothing that lasted more than 10 miles.

We were looking for an art park in Railroad Square as a stop. We stopped for directions and found the place, but only a few sculptures, a few resale shops, and a restaurant. We toured the resale shop, looked at the art, and left.

We didn't want to end up at Lee and Larry's motel (our friends from Milwaukee) during the weekend, so we opted to drive to Jacksonville; with the time change, we still arrived by 6 p.m.

Lynn spotted a LaQuinta motel, so we pulled over, asked where we could get a good Bar-B-Q, and were directed to Bono's.

We registered for a room and progressed to Bono's Bar-B-Q, where, again, the service was excellent, and the food was outstanding! Lynn had brisket, and I had pulled pork.... Wow! The onion rings were fantastic, and the sauces were great. We mixed some of them together to create our own sauce. Very yummy.

Thursday, March 12th

On the road by 8:17 (49860), the first stop today is St. Augustine (they are celebrating their 450th birthday, as the oldest city in the U.S.A. this month) and The Fountain of Youth.

This was a whole 15-acre waterfront village founded in 1565 by Spanish explorer Pedro Menendez de Aviles; we were among the first to arrive. (The founding of Florida was originally in 1513 by Juan Ponce De Leon searching for this place, The Fountain of Youth.)

This is the first and oldest continuous European Settlement in the United States of America. We first went to the actual fountain of youth. It is an artesian well and is still running! Of course, we took a drink; it is full of minerals and actually good for you.

The reason it was called the fountain of youth is because the Indians lived much longer than the Europeans, basically due to the good water, not fouled by human waste drunk by the Europeans due to poor sewer systems and poor hygiene in Europe.

Juan Ponce De Leon (This was his whole name!) and his crew made friends with the Indians; the land was fertile, the fish were plentiful, and the weather was perfect. We toured the area, went into replicas of the native Timucua Indian huts community areas, and saw a lot of peacocks, including albino peacocks similar to the ones we saw at the TIVOLI Park in Copenhagen.

We also toured the town. They have a Spanish fort, very similar to the one we saw in Puerto Rico, a house made inside of a log. We also visited a crafting area where we saw the first schoolhouse in America, and Lynn scarfed up on some nice Christmas gifts!

The next stop is Daytona Beach; oh, by the way, this is BIKE Week! From twenty miles out, there were bikes all over the place! All and any kind of motorcycle, trikes, customs, basic, odd, and straight. As we approached Daytona, more and more bikes, and most very loud!

The traffic lights are very long in Florida and coupled with the increased traffic with the bikes, it took us over an hour to do the strip, drive the loop along the beach, and out again. There was way too much glitz, no parking, nothing like Sturgis, and I didn't like it at all! And Lynn concurs!!

We decided to cross Florida to go to the Manatee Park on the Gulf side called the Wildlife Preserve in Homosassa.

This was a review. We had visited this park the last time we were in Florida to see Larry and Leroy quite a few years ago; not much remembered, so we re-enjoyed the park again! The manatees were a little larger than my good friend Angel, the manatee in Cozumel.

We closed the park and drove south, looking for a motel and someplace to eat. We found both a Microtel and another Bar-B-Q place called Sonny's (Another excellent waiter and meal).

Friday morning the 13th. Since it seems everything needs phone calls and has restrictions, we had to wait till nine o'clock to see if the cycle zip line adventure had any weight restrictions. We had tried last night (it is in St. Cloud and was supposed to be open from 9 till dusk, but at 6 p.m. it was closed?) As with yesterday, with the boat tours reserved a week solid from now, this was not available. As a matter of fact, it no longer was offered! We thought a bicycle zip line would have been fun! Unique, good exercise and no one we knew had done, now we joined their ranks since it no longer existed!

The plan was to drive back to the Atlantic side and south since the Wiki Wachi show wasn't till 11 A.M.

We finally got to use our sun pass, driving down to our next stop in Fort Pierce. We did stop for a small meal and rest stop on the way, the service plaza is much larger than in Illinois, offers four or five restaurants, a convenience stores large restroom, and very clean!

Two stops in Fort Pierce: a very nice Botanical garden called Heathcote Botanical Gardens that had a large collection of tropical flowering plants and ferns, plus an extensive Bonsai collection.

We also went to the Manatee Center on the Ocean. No manatees were in today. They had up to eighteen come in from 11 AM to 2 PM. We were late again, it being three in the afternoon. We watched a short informational movie, examined the skeleton of a manatee, and discussed the where's and whys of the manatee's habits. They can move each side of the upper and lower lips separately. The front flippers are used like hands, with finger nails, and they kind of walk on them on the bottom looking for food. Their closest relative in the animal world is the elephant; their gestation is a full year, and they have to be five years old to get pregnant. They only have one pup, and they live to 50-60 years old. It is very interesting and informative!

We had some time, so we decided to go down the coast a bit more to Boca Raton and found a motel and also a VERY French restaurant. The entire staff was French, with the attitude! But the meal and the wine were exquisite! Back to the room to plan our Saturday, so we end up in Lake City tomorrow night for our Florida Key Sunday.

Saturday the 14th at 8:30 a.m.

(50372)

We have three activities planned on our way to our motel in Florida City. As we go further south, the cost of everything is much more, along with the traffic. The investment in the sun pass was well worth the money, and the GPS is a God-sent. The drivers cut into the lanes, back and forth; some lights are "camera-ed," and exits are close to each other; you must watch both sides. They are passing both sides and cutting in front, and I do not hold up any traffic!

The first stop is Boca Raton, Gumbo Limbo Nature Center. (The name comes from a native tree.) We arrived ten minutes before opening, so we walked the butterfly trail (all outdoor and wild). The butterflies we saw were Zebra long wings and Monarchs, along with native plants, trees, and Indian structures.

We then went into the center. This is a turtle rehab center. When turtles are injured, they are brought here to be rehabbed, fixed, cured, or helped as much as possible, including new hatchlings. Many of the injured develop air bubbles under their shells; this cannot be removed, so weights are added so the turtle can dive effectively. There are a number of isolation tanks for new "patients," along with four large tanks that have a variety of fish, eels, and sting rays to acclimate the various rescued animals and serve as an educational resource. Some of the things we learned were that baby and young turtles are omnivores; they especially like jellyfish!

As they age, the turtles become more and more vegetarians. The research center here is trying to determine the sex of the turtles before they are five or six, it seems that the sex is determined by the temperature of the sand, and the egg itself. We had heard this before in South America. The warm sand means females, while the cooler temperature means it will be a male.

The next stop was in Fort Lauderdale. This is high end car country, Porches, Rolls Royce's, Bentleys, Maserati's, high end Mercedes, lots of Cadillac's, BMW's, Audi's and Lexus's. The traffic is also horrible; the drivers need remedial driving classes and courtesy refreshers!

This is the location of the Bonnet House and Gardens. Mr. Birch, a wealthy attorney from Chicago bought the 35 acres it is on and gave it to his daughter for a wedding gift. She married Fredrick Bartlett, from the True Value Hardware family. He married 3 times. His third wife was from the Eli Lilly family. The estate is named after a particular lily blossom found on the property.

The estate was given to the State of Florida Preservation Society in 1985 with a grant of one million dollars to keep the estate up, by the surviving widow who passed quietly at 109 years old.

The son of the founder of the True Value Hardware Empire did not want to follow in his father's footsteps in the business and at 19 wanted to paint. His father said that if he would be accepted in Germany at the best art school, he would accept the decision. The son got accepted and graduated in two years. The following year he painted art glass, ceilings, and various pieces of art, grossing over $65,000 which would translate to almost $2 million in today's money, so he was very successful. His art glass was so good that when Tiffany was invited to bid against him, upon examination, Tiffany refused to offer an alternative quote stating "why"? He specialized in painting murals.

The house is on 35 acres in prime ocean front property, a two story, classic with courtyard, three holding ponds, plants and trees from all over the world, three orchid hot houses and a number of out buildings including a boat house, a garage with a 1938 Cadillac, paintings, art works, sculptures and statues.

Orchids were blooming throughout the estate, there were examples of many world-wide plants all flourishing from a plant that only blooms at night, a poisonous tree, and a shrub called "yesterday today and tomorrow" where the flowers turn from deep purple the first day to light purple the second day to white the third day, and then sheds the flowers. Animals on the premises that we saw included a variety of lizards, swans, turtles, snake birds, egrets, and three surviving monkeys of the original fifteen.

Off to Miami, to the place called Jungle Island. We expected more, kind of like a zoo but it did have some highlights. We got up close to macaws, parrots, goats, and I got to hand feed a couple of flamingoes!

We found our hotel, a Ramada, and walked across the street to eat at a seafood restaurant. We had sautéed calamari in a tomato sauce,

Noah

which was excellent. I had grouper and Lynn had tilapia with fruit salsa. Both were excellent. We shared a slice of key lime pie for dessert.

Sunday, March 16th, we left the motel for Key West, 0745 (50464)

It was a beautiful day; the temperature was in the 70s, so I stored the hearing aids, and we drove with the windows open, enjoying the sea air! The trip through the various keys to Key West is about 125 miles, through 42 bridges, and an average speed limit of 50mph.

The first picture we took was of a giant roadside crab; the first stop in Islamorada was Robbie's Feed the Tarpons.

We bought two small buckets of fish and went out on the pier to feed the 100 or so 3-4-foot tarpons by the pier, along with watchful pelicans.

We were warned not to feed the pelicans but three snuck up on Lynn, grabbed her right hand for the fish she held; she suffered one gash and three small cuts, that is when she had enough, blood was on her hands, arms, and some on her blouse.

I finished feeding my fish to the tarpons, gave them the rest of Lynn's, and back to the boat house for antiseptic and band aids. We walked around the outdoor market, then back in the car to continue our trek south west to Key West.

The next stop was to be a Crane foundation, but it was not open yet and would not be open for another 2 hours, so, no go!

Off to the Walgreens across the street to get some triple antibiotics, clean up Lynn's wounds and continue our journey. We were to find the River Queen from the Bogart movie but we didn't find that either!

The bridges have areas where people can fish from, and we found fishing folks at each bridge. We saw advertising for a Sandal and T-shit shop claiming great bargains only to find that the only great bargains were one rack of t-shirts in the back of the shop and a small selection of flip flops to be the only bargain in the store! Quite a few buildings had murals painted on the side, very nice, and not too faded!

We finally made it to Key West, and like most tourist places, no free parking and you are lucky to find reasonable off-street parking! We did find parking in a structure, out of the sun, but it cost more than a few "sheckles"!

We first took the city tour, to get our bearings, note what to look for on our own, and find out anything new or interesting. There are no waves in the beaches, due to the reefs, many beaches are sandy only due to imported sand (no waves to bring in or make sand), there used to be a railroad track out to the Keys, but a storm took it out and it was not replaced.

Buildings are restricted to three stories, many porch ceilings painted light blue, to prevent ghosts, insects, and birds from gathering, Coke was bottled here using rain water, cigars were rolled here until most of the town burned down, (there was an ordinance for a long while requiring metal roofs on all buildings) the streets are very narrow, we found jewelry with butterfly wings, Duval street is the main drag, and I do mean DRAG, the most popular bars have female impersonator shows at night, reminded us of New Orleans! Duval Street also has a bar that serves 240 different rums. Key West was the only part of the United States that actually succeeded in seceding from the U.S., although it only lasted a few days!

04/23/1982 a five-minute war to stop the highway blockage, Key West was the Conch Republic with their own flag.

This is the end of Highway 1 and the most southern tip of the United States. This was Hemmingway's town, went past his house and bar; he had a lot of cats, so we also ate at a semi-famous restaurant called The Six Toed Cat. Good food but pricey.

President Truman also had a home here; it was sold in 1985 for seventeen million and is now called the Truman Annex.

We also had key lime pie on a stick covered with chocolate while touring Duval Street. (The original Key Lime Pie was made at the Corry Mansion Inn.)

We went through the main square, Mallory; the Aquarium was the first attraction, but we had seen quite a few, so we skipped that. We went through Mel Fisher's ship wreck museum, which was very interesting, and I learned a lot. Although I really wanted a piece of history, I was not prepared to pay thousands.... even a very small piece was in the hundreds!

When he announced the discovery, the government wanted it all, but after eight years in court, he got to keep it all.

Locals are called conch's (KONKS), being here less than 7 years, you would be a fresh water conch, over seven, salt water! There are lots of tourists, lots of stupid people cutting off buses with bicycles, crossing traffic against lights, slack jawed, confused, and standing in front of pictures or just walking in front of that perfect picture moment, and finally, taking five to ten minutes to take one picture with a point and shoot camera or phone, or I pad!!!

We headed back, stopped 1/2way for supper, and ended back on the mainland to rest at a "reasonably rated" motel in south Florida.

Monday, March 23, 2015, Left at 8A.M. (50718)

We are off to the Gulf Coast traveling hours through the everglades, lots of snake birds, vultures, cranes and crows. We also went through several areas warning to watch out for panthers. Our first stop was Bonita Springs Wonder Gardens, various tropical plants, alligators, (many were growling, never heard that before), turtle's, flowers from a shaving brush tree, more orchids, Banyan trees and vines. I had to have this knife made from an alligator jaw, so yep,

I bought it!

Next stop was the joint Edison and Ford winter estates. We toured the combined grounds the various houses and the incredible blooming plants and gardens. I got to see one of those shaving brush tree blossoms, trees, shrubs and flowers from all over the world, odd trees, bamboo clusters, splashes of purple, yellows, reds and blues, Access to the river on a pier extending over fifty feet into the river, huge trees, and manicured grounds. The compound had its own water system, pool, and power generator way before the public.

Our last stop for the day was the John and Mabel Ringling estate in Sarasota, called CA' D' ZAN. We just toured the mansion, a Venetian Gothic Palace. The grounds again are planted with exotics from all over the world, there is even a rose garden (a thousand plants) here, roses don't grow on the Atlantic side of Florida, but they grew well here on the Gulf side.

The building is very Moroccan, marble floors, painted ceilings, formal dining room ballroom with twenty-two couples painted on the ceiling from all over the world, (you can tell by their traditional countries costumes) over the top furnishings mostly from Europe, five sets of China, a massive tiled Venetian deck and dock overlooking the river. This by far was the most over the top house we saw in Florida!

That was all for the day; I found a place called Barnacle Buds, which had crab cakes and filo dough-wrapped seafood, and called it a night.

Tuesday St. Patrick's Day, March 17th, 0800 (50968)

Breakfast was great; the hotel breakfast person was outgoing and friendly and even made us a chocolate chip waffle. We were very impressed! She was also making cheese omelets; this was an included breakfast at Best Western! WOW!

Off to Tampa; Tampa was founded by Henry Plant (a railroad

magnate) and he was responsible to turning this once small town into a winter resort.

We went downtown to the Cuban section, Hyde Park; Ybor (E bore) is what the twenty-square block area is named. Here there are two large cigar stores, you can actually sit and have a coffee and watch cigars being rolled! As usual we were there in the morning in a place that starts jumping after two in the afternoon.

In our walking tour of the area, we encountered those two cigar shops, one offering alcohol and coffee with cigars, the other just cigars, Irish bars, Cuban bars, and coffee shops (I had a Ybor coffee, which consisted of espresso, steamed milk and sweetened condensed milk; Yummmmm!), tattoo shops, Columbian, Cuban, Italian, Turkish, and Greek restaurants. Took pictures, admired the buildings, and then, off through the horrible traffic to visit our friends who relocated to this area fifteen years ago,

Larry and Lee still own the motel/building, storage complex. New, is that they rent the pool daily to nude male swimmers for cash, repairs and help on a barter system, both developing health issues, the place is in constant renovation, and they both have adopted a slower pace lifestyle. A good visit and then we were off again to try to leave Florida behind and head for Georgia.

We made it to Brunswick, Ga. Another La Quinta and seafood for dinner; waitress refused the "napkin coupon", but the food was excellent.

Wednesday, March 18th, 8:30 AM, the car has a full tank; (51345)

Our first stop this morning is Savannah; we want to take a carriage ride, eat at The Lady and Sons restaurant (owned by Paula Deen), and tour the downtown market square.

We arrived at 9:30, found a parking lot, and walked to the city market tours booth to sign up and get directions. It is cool, upper 60's, nothing like home, but we were getting used to wearing shorts and T shirts! The information lady was very helpful; we paid for the first carriage out and proceeded to the pick-up point a couple blocks away.

The carriage was a bit late, caused by traffic, and there were six of us filling the buggy, we loaded and took off. We toured the historic district on the 50-minute ride, a General Oglethorpe founded the city, (he died of yellow fever, this is a high point that was surrounded by lowlands and swamps, in "bad" years a good part of the population did not make it to Christmas due to the yellow fever from the mosquitoes in the spring and summer.)

This is the second largest port on the East Coast, and for many years, Savannah was the place that set the price of cotton in the world.

There are many little (two square blocks) parks; one was the scene from the Forest Gump movie, a few buildings used in a Julia Roberts 1995 movie, "Something to Talk About," a verified haunted mansion, and a Baroque-style synagogue.

The buildings are all restored to original condition, lots of wrought iron, brick, and brick that has been covered with stucco to look like stone.

There was almost constant narration, all very interesting. Our driver was a retired chef, and we got a reference from him regarding an interesting meat dish. (Bobotie) Made with minced lamb, beef, raisins, almonds, and curry, we will try when we get home!

Our tour ended a little after 11:00 so we hoofed it over to the Paula Deen restaurant with her sons, "The Lady and Sons", a three-story restaurant made out of an old warehouse. It was early, the restaurant was already serving and they took us as walk-ins.

We had heard mixed reviews from friends and on-line but we HAD to see for ourselves and were very pleased and pleasantly surprised. There was a buffet offered, but it just looked like every other southern food buffet, and we wanted to try her food.

Lynn ordered her favorite fried green tomatoes, she also had crab stew; the batter on the tomatoes was light and wow, the onion dressing soft and rich, speaking of rich, that crab stew was smooth and full for flavor and crab!

I had a half asparagus sandwich with ham and potato soup, and a small salad with her blue cheese dressing.

The service was very attentive, everyone gets a pancake and biscuit with their meals, my sweet tea was bottomless, no need to remind, and the food was great!! (Hint…order off the menu!!!)

We then explored the area, we actually found a non-southern hospitality southerner, we were looking for the salt shop, we asked a passing security person where, he stated "I'm on lunch now" and kept on walking, so I guess it was too much to ask!

We then went into a Honey store (specializing in honey) and a salt store; you guessed it, specializing in all kinds of salt and spices. A candy store and watched them make pralines, oh yeah, tasted and bought, and a few other novelty gift shops.

Time to move, found the car, and drove to Macon Georgia for the night.

Thursday, March 19th, my birthday, left the motel at 8:30 A.M. (51592)

This was the nicest, cleanest, Best Western, most enjoyable breakfast room attendant of all the motels.

This weekend is the Macon Cherry festival, and all the trees are in bloom. It has started to rain again today, driving in drizzle to mild rain all day. Our first stop was to be Covington Ga., looking for the Hollywood square where movies have been shot. We couldn't find, GPS couldn't find, so we moved on to Atlanta, downtown, the Coca

Cola Headquarters and showcase, the World of Coca-Cola!

We parked a few blocks away, hoofed it past the Olympic Park and a huge Ferris wheel to the main building. Once inside, we watched two short films, one about the origins of Coke, the other showing Coke advertising ads throughout the world. Both very interesting, the one about the advertising was uplifting, enjoyable, and everyone left with a smile.

We watched a number of kids having their picture taken with a 7-foot Coke polar bear, watched a bottle cleaning machine, bottle capping machine, and a room with advertising through the decades. Finally, everyone ends up in the tasting room, where you can try over 100 Coke products offered in various countries. When you finished sampling, you exit through the souvenir shop, and receive a complimentary small bottle of Coke.

Interesting stuff for us, Dr. Pembenton created the formula, they have a statue of him; in the 70's they came out with the "new Coke", there was such a reaction by the public, that after only 79 days after introduction, the "classic" Coke was brought back and continues today, the public has spoken!

Lynn picked out what she wanted for Christmas, and we were on our way back North, we stopped for the night in Lexington Ky.

Friday, March 21st, left at 8:30 (52093)

I'm 67 for a whole day now, how depressing! And the weather agrees, foggy and rainy AGAIN!

There was nothing we wanted to see in Lexington, we left another message to Lynn's step mother that we would be dropping by on the way home (this would be the third call) and tried to stop at an Amish community in the town of Nappanee, where there are apples in front of a number of businesses advertising each business in their own unique ways.

Noah

We found Dee's daughter's house in the town of Granger, Indiana, on the river. We found Dee's daughter and her husband and Dee at home and had a very enjoyable visit with them. After the visit, we headed for the toll-way for home.

Lynn's dinner clock went off, and we found a very nice Italian Restaurant, Giannetto's.

Service and the food, were outstanding and impressive; we talked to both the husband and wife that owned the place, they ran it like a fine watch; the employees were attentive, the food served hot out of the oven, and even the other patrons were fun, friendly, and outgoing, much like the family you always wanted.

Three hours after leaving the restaurant, we were pulling into our driveway, another great adventure!

Mileage 52648   Total 4094 miles driven; Gas $442.55 Cheapest 2.13/gal   most expensive $2.89/gal   average $2.38/gal; Total gallons 173.22; Ave MPG 23.6; Motels $1276   Ave: $116 Stayed at Best Western, La Quinta, Microtel, Ramada; Food: $780

The diet is getting frustrating, weighed in again, kept steps up in the 5000 area, and ate about what Lynn did, but gained 18 pounds! Yes, I dropped 12 pounds in a week back here at home, but it is really frustrating! I am still at 254 and we will be leaving for China the end of the week.

I rushed to get my information in for those stinkin' taxes due on the fifteenth, my tax preparer is unhappy because I had to wait for three K-1's and it jams her up at the peak of her getting everything done by the deadline, then I need mine by the 2nd! I brought her a small bag of chocolate but she was not impressed!

China Tibet April 2015

This is the last trip we will be taking with my natural knees, so we wanted it to be something special, and it was!

There was a considerable amount of preparation for this trip, some problems with the poor seating assigned by the airline, poor customer service from Viking in resolving the seating problem, plus obtaining visas for China and Tibet; but with the help of Sara our Online travel agent, persistence, and involving a Viking customer service supervisor; the issues were finally resolved (with of course additional funds (mine) and a lot of frustration (mine).)

The Vacation package we took was the Viking Roof of the World package, and we also included a Shanghai extension. It included four hotel stays plus a six-night cruise on a Viking River ship on the Yangtze River. A number of internal China flights limited the amount of luggage taken by each of us, with a maximum size and weight of both carry-on and checked luggage. (Carry-on 8"X16"X22" 11 pounds' max, 16"X24"X39" 33# checked bag) We carefully packed and just resolved to use the laundry services on the ship and the hotels.

Our oldest daughter, Tiffany, was off the first day so she agreed to drive the van and drop us off at the bus station. We arrived five minutes before the bus and had an uneventful 80-minute ride down to O'Hare Airport, in Chicago, the air is crisp, no clouds, we were not going to have any problems with weather for take-off!

I had tried to check us in on the flight 24 hours prior, but I was not able to, with the airline claiming I needed to see an agent. We got into the line, only two agents and 12 people in line! (The line was moving slower than those at the DMV!), so I had Lynn hold our place and asked the kiosk agent why I couldn't check–in online or at the Kiosk. She stated that my Visa had to be checked first. I asked her if she could verify and then let me check in with the kiosk; she said yes, and I was able to check-in with the kiosk. Most airlines are forcing everyone to use the kiosks to eliminate one more service job; it just seems they still provide poor service, inconsistent assistance, and have an attitude of the airline first, not the customer, but I digress.

We now checked the bags, went through the abbreviated TSA due to our trusted traveler status and proceeded to our gate to wait an additional 2 hours. When processing our check-in, there was one last chance for the airline to make additional money.

They offered early boarding for a fee, or an upgrade in seating for a much larger fee. I opted for the early boarding; just to be sure our carry-on would be by us. Oops, yes, another delayed flight, mechanical, two more hours to wait, so we each took turns walking the airport, and watching the other people. Finally, we were then herded onto the plane, tickets and visas rechecked, and yes, everyone seemed to have oversized carry-on's (2 per person) even some huge backpacks that didn't seem to alert anyone at the gate.

We settled in for our 13+ hour flight, the first thing the guy in front of me did, as we lifted off, was to put his seat completely back, and only move it up for the two meals, and only after being reminded both times by the flight attendant, and for landing (he needed reminding again), lucky me! (He also "fidgeted" throughout the flight, like some 5-year-old kid, at 50-ish??)

Luckily, there were a lot of middle seats empty, so Lynn could move over, makes me question to original horrible seating, was this done by the airline on purpose?

The flight lasted a bit over the thirteen hours, took us up over Canada, into the Arctic Circle, over Alaska, and descended down over China to Beijing; population 24 million.

Noah

It was 9:40 p.m. by the time we picked up our luggage, we had crossed the international date line, (we now were 12 hours out of "phase") the Viking representative was easily spotted and the hour drive to the downtown Fairmont hotel was quiet; we showed our passports at the desk, got our key, and settled in for the first night, of our three-night stay. This Fairmont hotel like all the hotels was 4 or 5 stars, comfortable and well appointed, marble floors, a separate shower, bathtub, and toilet room; the toilet seat was heated, it was a combination bidet and toilet, phone next to the toilet, and a TV by the bathtub, lots of water pressure and plenty of hot water. On the bed, each night was a note as to what the weather would be the next morning, the drapes closed, (electric) and everything immaculate.

Day 2

Buffet breakfast at the hotel is extensive, with a complete selection of Chinese options with soup, wontons, noodle and rice dishes, eggs any way you would like, potatoes, vegetables, sausages, bacon, pastries, cheeses, cold cuts, juices, fruits, yogurts, cereals both hot and cold, coffee and tea.

First activity was a short bus ride to the Forbidden City. We met our own personal Viking guide "Jimmy" for the duration of the trip. He let us know that he would be our own personal resource throughout our trip, and that each city we would be also picking up an additional local guide to provide the most comprehensive trip possible.

In China and some other countries, the family name is first, then the personal name, the Viking representatives took on western names to make it easier for everyone to remember and pronounce. He also always wore a red jacket, a red cap, and carried a red flag with a glove on it; our group was about 24 people.

Here is some info on the Forbidden City, we walked it, yep, a good 175 acres surrounded by a 10-meter-wide moat, with an outside wall and an inside courtyard, followed by another wall and courtyard very much like a Russian stacking doll, where the more gates you go through and the more courtyards you transverse, the more there are inside.

This Forbidden City (entry forbidden to all except royalty), is a UNESCO World Heritage site. It was completed back in 1420, is the world's largest palace complex, consisting of 10-meter-high walls, courtyards, and 800 buildings with 9,999 rooms. (Yes, the number 9 is significant; it is a "special" royal lucky number). Each gate door has 81 door knobs; it is lucky to rub one so many of the lower ones are well "polished". The local guide was up on his facts, filling us with detail as we explored the grounds, (the bricks in the courtyards all had the name of the brick maker on them!) viewed the various treasures, inspected the living quarters, and admired the statuary and just starting to bloom gardens.

After the three hours of exploring, we left the complex for a lunch, Chinese style, at a local restaurant. We would find this to be a common theme, round tables with a large lazy Susan in the middle. Coffee, tea, soft drinks and beer included. Two or three different appetizers, six to eight main courses, and 1-3 desserts usually at least some watermelon slices, all served family style, with our guide specifying the main ingredients and whether the dish was spicy or not. NEVER was there a shortage of food or variety!

Next, we jumped on the bus and headed for the Summer Palace and Gardens. This used to be the summer retreat of Royalty during the end of the Qing Dynasty. This, too, was expansive, covering over 700 acres of carefully tended gardens, rock formations, pathways, buildings, towers, and palaces. We were scheduled for a boat ride, but it was too windy, and all the boat excursions were canceled that day. We were lucky enough to enjoy a bit more roaming time plus watch a man paint symbols on the walkway with colored water. It was like watching poetry and art in one, to be enjoyed for the moment. When the water dried, the creation disappeared. It was just another

Noah

"ya gotta be there experience!"!

On the way back to the hotel, we stopped to walk Tiananmen Square. At 100 acres (80X550 meters), 44 hectares, yep, this is the world's largest public square (440,000 square meters, or 4,736,000 sq. ft.!). Big government buildings, statues from the Mao era, I noted quite a few light poles with many light fixtures on each and asked, Yes, the whole square is lit up at times, and it is like daytime; The biggest square in the world and it lights up like an American football field! WOW!! Tiananmen, translated is "gate to heavenly peace," and is situated at the North end of the Forbidden City.

That was enough, some were still experiencing jet lag, others were tired from all the walking and the huge amount of information overload, and others just wanted a little down time. We had a great group, no laggards, everyone promptly getting on the bus, and everyone listened and paid attention to instructions. As a side note, some members of our group were stopped and asked if they would pose with some younger folks for pictures and selfies, Westerners are still a little bit of an oddity, and many of the young people want to have pictures taken with us!

Most of us opted to take the optional Peking Opera theatre package that included dinner, so we went up to the room, freshened up, relaxed for a bit, and then joined the group for the trip to the opera.

My theory is to experience as much as possible when we vacation. We can rest at home and may never be able to see what is offered on these trips again, and what is seen is not offered anywhere else in the world. Even if we aren't excited about the main event, there is always something unique or different we will always remember!

Just to give an example, the cost of this excursion was 150 RMB per person. Conversion at this time is 6 RMB per dollar; so, for roughly $25 bucks a piece, we got a bus ride, a show and a meal.... Duh!!!!

This Peking opera was traditional Chinese, music, mime, dance, acrobatics, and singing. We had a served meal, then witnessed three mini plays, some opera singing, an interesting variety, beautiful clothing, and you could follow along with the themes even though all was in Chinese, a unique visual and audible experience. After the event, we were taken back to the hotel for the night, it was really nice not having to worry about transportation, getting lost, or unsavory characters, with this door-to-door care and service, I could get used to this!! (And actually did!!)

Day 3 April 6th Monday

Early morning start, the bus left the hotel at 7:00 A.M.! It is cool, with the temperature in the upper 50s F, and there is fog. (Smog?)

Today is the "Great Wall of China Day"; the wall is less than an hour and a half drive out of Beijing! (About 40 miles) We were able to see more of the Capitol city of 24 million plus people as we drove through it and out, including our first viewing of the "bird's nest" stadium constructed for the 2008 Olympics a few years back and what we would see a lot of in China…construction!

The ride out after finally leaving the city progressed from flat to increasingly rolling hills, the hills were terraced at one point, this was promoted by the Mao regime to promote the land producing more for the people, the trouble was, the land was not fertile, the weather not cooperative, and the yield at best was poor, the roads are congested even though trucks only move at night, day time is for automobiles and buses. (it's the law!!)

There were a lot of apple trees planted, and it was the beginning of apple blossom time so many hillsides were speckled with budding and blooming white trees. The tour was at one of the highest points of the Wall, Badaling Hills, and the Gangue Gorge. This is where there is a cable car that takes us up 80% of the way to the crest, where you can continue up on the wall to the highest point or descend down the wall for further views. The wall itself is 8-9 meters high, wide enough for 10 people to walk shoulder to shoulder (about 10 meters) and rolling. (You're either climbing upstairs or inclines, or down, following the topography of the hills.) NONE is easy walking, steps vary in height, (some 6" high, some 10" high) depth (some shoe deep some shoe and a half deep), and slopes are steep, (30-35 degrees) and ALL is stone, all worn!) Yes, I climbed, a hundred or so meters (about 300 feet), but I had to use the railing both up and down, and even though we were there at opening, it was getting very crowded with today being a public holiday, and there are a lot of people in China!!

This will probably be mentioned more than once, and to me, it has become more and more irritating. It seems that the Chinese don't have much regard for personal space, and most do not respect lining up for events, cutting into lines, finding "family" that is already in line, with bumping, wedging, and brushing commonplace, as you walk down very crowded common areas, streets, and sidewalks. However, the people are really nice, one on one!

The view is fantastic, the wall goes on for miles and miles (more than 6200 miles!) and it is interesting how it snakes along the various hilltops and valleys. After seeing what I could, I walked back down to where Lynn was staying, took some more pictures, observed the ever-increasing surge of new folks, we took the cable car back down to the parking lot, explored the shops at the base and parking area, bought a Panda baseball hat for me, and a warm furry hat for Lynn and waited for the rest of the group.

The rest of the group soon joined us; we were then bused to a company that specializes in quality Jade. We had a guided tour of the company and observed how Jade is graded, the many different colors of Jade, and the quality ratings of Jade. Jade sculptures, a sailing ship, three-masted, four-foot-long by six-foot-tall, with chains, sails, and infinite detail, all carved from one piece of solid jade! There was a showroom full of jade jewelry, sculptures, book ends, and vases, from very small to very large, a full spectrum of colors and grades, plus paintings and silks.

Included was a lunch that was, of course, Chinese style, "Americanized" Chinese food, including sweet, sour pork, lemon chicken, shrimp prepared two ways, fish, veggies, rice, fried rice, noodle dishes, meatballs, dumplings, and fruit plates (dragon fruit, melons, grapes), excellently prepared and professionally served! (Including liquor and beer).

Back on the bus and down to the over 40-year-old Sacred Way of the Ming Tombs tour. This is the valley the Ming Dynasty Emperor's chose to have their burial places. A long stone walkway started with a grand marble gateway a large building housing a lucky stone turtle (rub his head for good luck, yes, I did!) this was followed by 18 pairs of stone sculptures, bigger than life, including depictions of warriors, and animals including elephants, camels, lions, and mystical ones, all paired and facing the path.

The walk started at one gate; a covered map showed where the various tombs were placed in specific locations in this expansive valley, each tomb positioned in the best place for proper Feng shui.

After that, we headed back to the hotel. Again, we took the offered optional Peking Duck Dinner at one of the few restaurants that offer this praised dish prepared in the same manner as it was originally prepared for royalty and explained completely by our host guide.

Ten people at a linen cloaked round table, the hour and a half presentation went by way to quickly and it was delicious! Basically, you take this wheat crepe thin pancake, place some oyster sauce on the top, then a strip of duck skin, a piece of duck, a scallion, a slice of cucumber, fold and eat…. repeat…. Dee- Lischus!!

Tonight, pack for tomorrow, flight out plus early bus ride to old Beijing, Rickshaw rides, local host, tea demonstration, and airport for flight to Xian!

Tuesday Day 4

Out by 9:30 AM, a late day! Luggage was out by 8!

Interesting things about this hotel: no 4th, 13th, 14th, or 24th floors; we checked, we were on the 15th floor, and there was no room 1514! In China, 4 is the symbol of death, and in Beijing, it is taken very seriously!

As we drove to the old section, "Jimmy," our Viking companion, let us in on his life as he grew up. And it was very interesting to see his side of a little-known country by the west, and we have no idea of what really may be happening around us!

The changes in China:

Aspirations of families in the 1960s and 70s.

To have a bicycle, to have a sewing machine, everything is rationed; you must have a ration coupon with money for ANYTHING. Clothes are all hand-made, only cloth is sold in the stores, and then only so much per person (coupons!) There is no excess food no way to keep leftovers.

Aspirations of families in the 1980's

A refrigerator, a washing machine, and a color television.

This was the end of the Mao regime; 1982 was the institution of one child per family. The left-overs could now be preserved, new clothes didn't have to be made constantly, they could be washed in the house rather than taken to the river or washed in a tub, and there was a window to the world with TV!

Aspirations of families in the 1990s

Telephones, computers, and air conditioning; since the 90's, apartments, and a car! As a note, one half of all construction cranes in the world are now in China, China is the world's largest car market.

Educating Noah...Travelin'

The Chinese just started buying cars a little over 10 years ago, and you can only buy an apartment for 70 years (The government owns all the land). Only 20 years ago, there was no privatization of land, and the average size of a bare-bones apartment, without furnishings, floor coverings, appliances, toilet, or sink, is 1000 square feet and costs about $500,000 U.S...

As we came to Old Beijing, we noticed what was common in many Chinese towns and villages. Each had a bell tower and a drum tower, with a non-political square on the meridian between the two; the bell would sound at 6 a.m., signaling the beginning of the day, and the drums would sound at 6 p.m.

We went to a small park area where we met a world champion shuttle cock juggler; he was in his 70s, tossed the shuttle cock from foot to back, to head, to foot, to back, to arm, back, hand, leg... you get the idea. We all received our own shuttle cock and received a lesson, most of us failing, not so gracefully, but it was a great experience! This was a nice way to start out and interact with the people.

Next, a bank of two-person bicycle rickshaws was waiting for us. Due to the narrowness of the streets, this is ideal! Since there is no room for cars and everyone wants one, the streets are especially crowded, even the tires of the parked cars have cardboard or wood sections covering the tires to protect them from dog urine. There are no bathrooms or showers in the houses. These are all communal and public restrooms, and showers are located on every block or so.

Our destination was Madam Wong's home, in the middle of the old section, once part of a larger complex. The family-owned the entire compound, but the government took most of it away, leaving only these two-and-a-half-room structures for the remaining family.

The size of this typical house is about 400 square feet, about 10X40. The half room is the kitchen; there is the living room and a sleeping room. The public toilet was only a few doors down, along with the public bath. Dirty water is recycled, the rooms were very clean, and she served us all tea, told us of what life was and now is, and also introduced us to her niece, who paints the inside of snuff bottles and other bottles for sale to tourists. Her niece's bottles were featured in the last Olympic catalog, and yes, they were beautiful. She even showed us the specialized brushes and how the bottles are painted in reverse. Yes, I bought a small snuff bottle along with others! Madam Wong also had a number of pictures with foreign notes displayed on them, so I brought out an American five and said she could have it if she displayed it. She gladly agreed and smiled a warm and friendly smile. We then jumped back onto our rickshaws and progressed through the balance of the area till we came to the bell tower. The bell tower houses a tea room, and we were treated to a tea tasting.

We were taught the Chinese way of drinking tea and tasted oolong, jasmine, pure Lychee, and a fruit tea. There was a showroom with many different tea sets, tea blends, and other products as we left the sampling to catch our bus to the airport.

We loaded up on the Shanghai Airlines to Xian. (Pronounced she-an) They confiscated my cane, but I got it back; everyone was padded down going through the security; they were very anxious about ni-cad batteries. They did not want any rechargeable batteries in the checked luggage!

It was an hour and three-quarter flight to Xian; we shared a daily Chinese paper translated into English. It was all about the world, only a third about local Chinese news, and little, if any, local negative news. It was like watching CNN and the BBC outside the US, much wider ranging.

It's funny how we never hear of the 35 million people in the world still in-slaved, the continued problem with the Greek debt, and how the standard of living is getting better in many places in the world!

We landed on time, and like before, the city center always seemed to be an hour or so away from the airport.

Our new local guide introduced herself and told us about her life and how much has changed since democracy took over in China. The farmers used to struggle to grow pomegranates, but now selling to tourists is better income and less risky. This was the capitol of China before it was moved to Beijing. We arrived at our hotel, and it was a five star. We were invited to eat supper there; this one even had a large selection of sushi, which I thoroughly took advantage of!

We met later to take a walking tour of the old Xian market area. Fresh fruits, various regional foods, noodles being made and stretched, souvenir shops, oddities, lots of people milling and looking, and many unusual foods offered.

This is where the locals go to get a bite to eat out. Half of the area was Muslim shopkeepers, and I was told that they were clever and shrewd, much like the Jews; there were few Jews in China and many more Muslims. I also asked about the fog/smog in Xian. There are five power plants surrounding the city, four coal and one nuclear. This location is very dry, and during the summer, it regularly gets above 30 degrees centigrade!

What is a happy room? One that has a western toilet that can be sat on; this town boasts 24-hour McDonald's and KFC's because now people love to eat, and no ration coupons are needed, they have extra money to spend, and Chinese love to eat!

The sights, sounds, and smells of the market were lively, cordial, and extensive. We were all ready to return to the hotel by 9:30 PM. This was another great day full to the brim of knowledge and history.

Wednesday, Day 5

The bus leaves the hotel at 08:15. The first stop today is the Buddhist's holiest place, The Wild Goose Pagoda!

As with all the tours included in our itinerary, the local guide was invaluable in providing what to see, what the significance of what we saw that was so important, and what to learn in the complex of buildings; this was a seven-story square tower (all wood) pagoda, gardens, and walks.

There were intricate wood and stone carvings, various Buddhas, and a peony garden (peonies are the national flower). The sacred number (especially Buddhist) is the number 5, less than the 9 of royalty, of course!

All the door knobs and locks are 5 times 5 or 25 per door compared to the 9X9, or a total of 81 on the Palace and Forbidden City doors. All doors have a high threshold to block the path of evil spirits, all paths incorporate sharp bends and 90-degree turns to stop evil spirits, and all doorways have a stone to block a clear path into the dwelling or garden when possible. (It must work, I didn't encounter even ONE evil spirit!)

During the Mao period, many religious artifacts were destroyed, and the monks were sent into the country to work in the fields. He did everything he could to destroy religions but failed, and some are returning now; Buddhism is the most practiced religion in China.

In Buddhism, the monkey king protects the monks. You cannot become a monk until you are 18. Fulltime monks and nuns are vegetarians. Part-time monks, nuns, and those practicing Buddhism are not required to be vegetarians.

China is trying to reinstall the values in the culture that are promoted by religion, in Buddhism it is not necessary or mandatory to go to temple weekly, but most celebrate the first calendar lunar day, the Chinese New Year; as a matter of fact, never plan a trip to China on the Chinese New Year, May 1-7th, or October 1-7th, these are big public holidays and trains, planes, and buses are full of Chinese going home to be with family. The Dalai Lama is head of the Tibetan

Buddhist's but he is in exile at this time banned from China, the most successful Buddhist branch is the Shaolin made famous by the TV show "Kung Fu", starring David Carradine.

We then proceeded to a site where the making of the terra cotta soldiers is shown, the Museum of Qin Terracotta warriors and horses. The methods in fabrication and a large collection of mementos and artifacts collected along with an extensive museum were highlighted, and lunch specializing in local foods was provided. We watched the chefs make the noodles that are famous in this area by pulling and spinning. We found the noodle soup to be very delicious, and the yak burgers to be tasty!

Having our bellies filled and wallets emptied, we went on to the UNESCO site with the actual soldiers and dug is. It is confirmed that this site dates to the Qin Dynasty 211-206. This is a relatively new site, discovered by a farmer in 1974.

The complex consists of four main buildings, three are buildings constructed over the actual dig sites (pit sites), and one building is dedicated to two 1/3rd scale bronze carriage and horse's models where they were unearthed, and other bronze discoveries.

The balance of three buildings where each is in the process of uncovering and reconstructing the soldiers, horses, and carriages from trenches that are seven meters deep and four or five meters wide. These are huge buildings. The first has the most reconstructed pieces, and placed back into the trenches where they were found are hundreds of soldiers and horses. All the soldiers are different, have different faces, different builds, and different weapons, and the include archers, swordsmen, and spear bearers. The theory is that the peasants broke and destroyed the soldiers and buried the pieces due to the way they were treated. Current total uncovered: 8000 soldiers, 130 chariots, 520 draw horses, and 150 Calvary horses!

The finished warriors are facing the front of the building. As you walk on either side, less and less of the trenches are exposed, and you can see the parts and pieces not yet reconstructed. At the rear of the building is a small section where a few pieces are in the process of being completed, piece by piece. These buildings are not small. I guess they could easily be 100 meters wide and 500 meters deep.

It is believed that the emperor at that time wanted to kill his elite army to protect him in the after-life but was convinced to have the terra cotta soldiers made instead. It is also believed that the artisans and those laborers who put this whole army together were killed to keep this place a secret. As the site is being uncovered, more is found, 100's of duck remains were found (food for the after-life). Many of the area's finds were looted for the weapons, pottery, and other items commonly used but scarce to the common people.

After exploring the various buildings, we set out for the buses, ran the gambit of shops and merchants, and headed back to the hotel.

Tonight was the Chinese Cultural Theatre. It started with a seven-course meal, rice, wine, beer and dessert. There were four different acts; each of these acts had sub plots. It was a very colorful combination of acting, ballet, gymnastics, and a little opera.

We didn't return to the hotel till 10:30. Early AM leave for the airport (Luggage out at 11:00 PM, wake-up at 4:20 AM).

Day 6

Left the hotel by 5:20 AM, box breakfast, an hour drive to the airport, then 2 hours at the airport, including typical airport security in China, everyone gets the "wand" and hurry up and wait lines. The nice thing is that most of the airports we used have "happy" toilets; there will be a stocked toilet paper dispenser just inside the main door for your use (none in the stall), just no hand towels, and the air dryers all seem to need repair.

Aircraft loading in China is first class first, then everyone for themselves! (In the middle, also) Two aisles back, but it all worked out. We arrived in Tibet, and as we left the airport terminal, we were all greeted with white silk scarves by the locals and ushered through the parking lot to our waiting buses.

We were supposed to have tea with a local family, but this was canceled due to extensive road work being done; everything was new, the tunnels, the bridges, and the highway, a parallel clearing, and tunnels were also being constructed for a railway! The countryside was brown, and we saw some vultures, some water buffalo, a few cows, and some tractors; with the improving economy, the water buffalo are being replaced by tractors, and it seems that the tractors are cheaper and easier to keep than the water buffalos! The rivers were low and very shallow; the spring floods were due in a few weeks; we drove to our Lhasa Hotel directly.

For some undisclosed reason, a soldier accompanied us on the bus from the airport to the city limits. (Don't ask, don't tell!) We were scheduled to stop at a local restaurant for lunch, and yep more food; tried yak burgers, which were really good, plus a noodle soup that was also outstanding! And lots of other Chinese dishes! All Chinese style with a Tibetan flair, exhausted and full, we waddled to the bus for a short trip to our hotel, and we all checked in.

This is Tibet and the famed city of Lhasa, the "City of the Sun," at an altitude of 12,000 feet. (Yes, Lynn and I both started taking our Diamox altitude drugs two days ago.) We were all affected in some way: tired, altitude, packing, and unpacking; everyone had an easy afternoon to get ready for some more sightseeing and adventure!

Dinner tonight was at a Tibetan Steak house. The meal served family style included beer, wine, and water, started with a very creamy tomato soup, a veggie pizza, Yak dumplings (the best!), vegetables, potatoes, carrots, meat in gravy, curried beef, rice, and fruit for dessert. Tomorrow is going to be a busy day; we all went right to our rooms when the bus returned us to the hotel after dinner!

Noah

(Hey, what happened to that promised steak?)

Friday, Day 7, Meet the Monks Day!

The very first stop with the group today is the Jokhang Temple tour. This 1300-year-old temple is the spiritual center of Tibet; it is one the most sacred sites, and Buddhist pilgrims from Tibet, China, and the world make pilgrimages here!

As we got off the bus, we got in line to get into the complex. This was one of the few times most respected lines besides the airport; I said most, but there were still some that disregarded or tried to disregard. We were passed several times by worshipers led by monks with rotating prayer wheels walking around the complex. There were others, with a mat on the sidewalk or ground chanting, some aloud, some silently, going from standing to kneeling then to full prostrate position, some using a wooden block to slide their hands in front of them.

These folks (Tibetans are darker complexioned and have higher cheek bones than the average Chinese) continue praying for hours, the same prayers (they don't count the number of prayers) (108 sufferings), and the crowds just walk around them.

The prayer is usually asking for a favor from Buddha.

It was still pretty early (Thank you, Jimmy and Viking, for impeccable timing!). The line was relatively short, and we proceeded to the inner court yard. Pictures can be taken here, but not inside the temple. A very large court yard is trans versed, and the temple itself is surrounded by a little city of vendors and stores. You can walk around the temple in about 20 minutes, but it is getting crowded, and watch out for the prayer people throwing themselves on the ground! I was approached by an older man with a smile and his hand out. I shook his hand, bowed slightly, and he walked away smiling even more. Westerners are still and oddity here, and I found out from our guide that that stranger just wanted to welcome me to his country, in all of our travels, that was another first. I kinda of liked that!

As we approached the temple to go inside, the crowd and prayer mats became increasingly difficult to navigate. Once in, the floors were a bit slippery due to the yak butter pilgrims bring to keep the candles glowing. Candles were all over the place, the crowd is now push and shove, try to go with the flow through the various rooms and expect to be jostled and bumped.

There are a number of Buddhas inside, each manifesting money, health, wishes, happiness, and so on. There was no real talking, just silent or barely audible prayers and the sound of yak butter being poured into many candle troughs. (After all, it is good luck to provide yak butter and feed the flames!) Money (sacrifice money, not a lot of real stuff!) is also placed all over the place near the statues, between glass panels in front of the statues, some even burned (yes, I bought a pack) for those that have passed on and are in need of extra cash. You may get a dirty look if you do not walk with the crowd clockwise; counterclockwise is not lucky!

We had an additional half hour or so to explore the shops outside. Nothing new, but the crowds were getting larger, more brushing, bumping, etc.

Lunch, gotta feed those starving tourists and provide as much Chinese food as possible! This time, a great mushroom soup, vegetarian noodles, spicy yak, spring rolls, cilantro broth on rice, stewed yak, egg rolls, and apple fritters for dessert.

We had a short ride back to the hotel for an hour's rest before heading out to the home of a local family to see a somewhat typical Tibetan life.

Greeting at home "Tosha Dahgal way" (Phonetic, of course). All generations live in the same house, the oldest female is the leader, polygamy, both male and female, is common, and in Tibet, there is no child limit. We were treated to butter tea (tea with yak butter in it). I really liked it. It tasted rich and a little salty, and there was also a good assortment of snacks, including yak cheese, which was hard and supposed to be. As a matter of fact, all the snacks were hard and had to be sucked on to soften. The house had a closet kitchen, a prayer room (A large picture of the Dali Lama was there, it was only permitted because Chairman Mao was in the same picture), a living room, a bed room, and a three-season room. There was also a small attached work room for making crafts to sell, the bathroom and shower facilities are communal and not in the house.

There was a solar water heater outside in the courtyard, and I actually spotted a kinda toilet next to the washing machine (I suspect it was one of those "I don't see nothing……) known worldwide.

Our next stop was the Sera Monastery (Yellow Hat Monastery), which was completed in 1419 and has been in continuous operation since. The monk population was up to 2000, but it has dwindled to the current 40 monks. In the upper court, we were treated to view a couple sand paintings in 3D relief. The sand diorama was protected with glass cases and was quite detailed. The complex houses three religious colleges and has an extensive collection of manuscripts and tapestries.

This was now a chance to watch the monk's debate. In a courtyard, for two hours a day in the afternoon, the monks gather to debate their individual religious views; the younger the monks and the less experienced in the front part of the courtyard, the older and more experienced in the back.

There were about 100 or so in one-on-one discussions, along with small groups clustering. A monk would make his statement, and if animated, he would end up making his point by slamming his fist on his open palm! It was very interesting watching from the sides as we circled (clockwise, of course) the enclosed courtyard on a path around the monks.

In Tibet, there are two main religions: Buddhism (4 different sects) and Tibetan Bon, a very simple religion. Here, 50% of the people used to work for the government, but it is now about 30%; working for the government has good pay and pension, but China and Tibet are promoting private business. This is the largest city in Tibet at 13 million and growing.

Tonight, we had a dinner show and buffet. I tried lung, but it was too fatty for me, fried lotus flower, which was very good, usual rice and noodle dishes, and cookies and fruit for dessert. The show was very colorful, singing, dancing, and quite entertaining. It was time for bed, back to the hotel, everyone dragging; altitude still affecting most, and everyone easily tires.

Day 8, Lhasa Tibet, Potala Palace.

The first stop today is the Potala Palace; the complex dominates the town on a hilltop in the middle of the city. This impressive compound, 300,000 square feet, is a monastery, seminary, palace, and former living quarters of the Dalia Lama, who is currently in exile. It is built on and a hillside, few hand rails and lots of steps; the steps are irregular in height, worn stone, and depth also varies.

We viewed a number of artifacts, walked in the lower courts, and viewed the museum. It was still in the 50s, although the sun was shining, it was cool, and after a few steps, most were having difficulty breathing. Many of the group climbed the steps to the top, but we didn't. We were told that halfway up the stairs got much steeper, had no railings, and were more crowded, so a number of us opted to mill around the lower sections.

Lunch at a local restaurant, lots of Chinese food, rice, and noodle dishes.

Afternoon, the Barkhor Market and the Tibetan Museum. Walked the markets and saw many different prayer wheels, prayer flags, jewelry, cloth trinkets, and produce. The museum displayed traditional Tibetan clothing, both past and present, cultural artifacts,

Buddha statues, imperial seals, and pottery.

Back to the hotel for the rest of the afternoon, dinner at the hotel, tomorrow we fly out!

Speaking of dinner, they had Sushi. Another traveler and I love sushi, and we tried it; the sushi was great, but the wasabi sauce was the hottest either of us had ever encountered! Both of us lost our breath when we tried it the first time, and then both of us were tearing up on the second attempt. Some bread and milk brought us back to kinda normal, and soy sauce and ginger were used for the rest of the meal!

Day 9 Sunday Airport and fly to Chongqing. (Sounds like "Chung quing") Early hotel departure at 8:30 AM.

We are promised that if everything goes well and on schedule, we will be able to stop and see the Panda, given a warning that usually only one or two will be seen!

We picked up our soldier at the city limits and engaged in our hour trip back to the airport; we did see some yaks in the fields, cows in the fields, and people working on the bridges, roads, and in the fields. I asked why they were working on Sunday, and I was told that the workers don't get paid till the work is done, so they work straight through till the project is finished and then go home for a while before coming back and signing on for another job.

It was a bright, clear day with no airport delays. We got some great pictures as we flew over the Himalayans', at 37,000 ft., snow caps and all!

We landed a bit early in this thriving 35 million-people province and were able to visit the Pandas! We were able to see a few red pandas'; they look like raccoons, and then five, yes, FIVE Pandas in their distinctive enclosures, some eating their bamboo and posing!! It seems that pandas, like Koala bears, are picky, each only liking one or two varieties of bamboo or eucalyptus, respectively! What a great treat, and I suspect it was due to that expert timing our "Jimmy" arranged. Wow!

Back to the bus and on to the river, where we checked in and slowly unpacked for the 6-night cruise on the Viking Emerald. We now had a little time, toured the ship, read the daily brief, and enjoyed a drink with another couple from our group. Dinner was relaxing, and we went to bed early.

Day 10 Shibaozhai Pagoda

This morning was river cruising. We have a small porch outside our room; it is bright, in the upper 60s, and the river is moving along quietly. Both of us slept great last night. It was nice to have our lungs full of oxygen again. Up at 0600 to try that Tai Chi* class offered every morning on the top deck. We lasted about half way through (the excuses....my knees, shoulder, and Lynn's back!), so off to breakfast!

- *This slow, graceful, continuous movement is supposed to be gentle on the joints, and I believe that daily practice could add a decade or more to your lifespan by reducing stress, improving balance, and increasing mobility and strength. I did get through a whole session on the second last day of the cruise but paid dearly both in shoulder and knee pain. (Whine, whine, whine!!)

At 9:15, morning briefing and safety instructions

At 10:30, a presentation on the Yangtze River.

The Yangtze is the third largest river in the world, preceded by the Amazon and the longest, the Nile. The Chinese call it the Changjiany River (long river). It is 3974 miles/6397 kilometers long (Navigate able: 1739/2800 kilometers). It starts at the Roof of the world, Tibet, where it is called the Red River due to the reddish sand and shallowness. Off of this river, 70% of the rice paddies in China get their water. When the rice patties are planted, they only take three months to grow. The Chinese also plant fish in the patties; carp grow fast, so when the rice is harvested, so are the fish, enough to feed themselves and take to the market; 30% of the Chinese population also live on this river. Our cruise will be in the middle section (known as the land of fish and rice), which is the most navigable, from Chongqing to Wuhan. In 1957, the river had its first bridge across it. Since then, there have been eighty-one total bridges and tunnels erected. We will be visiting three gorges (like fiords) on our journey. The first will be tomorrow. It is the smallest (about 5 miles), the Qutang Gorge, and we will pass by in the early am.

After lunch, we docked and walked through town, up to the pagoda, approximately three-quarter miles of vendors on both sides. We arrived before other river boats, so the vendors were a little sleepy, and the walk wasn't as crowded. Just after three beautiful Chinese gates, we came to a suspension bridge. We posed with our birth year signs and progressed across the good 100 yards of bouncing, swaying wooden planks.

After crossing the bridge, Lynn decided to stay and wait while the rest of us walked on to the Pagoda. In reviewing the climb inside, I found, again, steep stairs, no railings, and mounting crowds, so I opted to just circumvent the pagoda, take pictures, and tour the island back to where Lynn was waiting. My knees were getting progressively worse, but I did get to see this thing up close! Here's the scoop:

This all-wood Pagoda was built in 1572. It is listed as one of the top eight fantastic architectures in the world. The total area of the pagoda structure is 50,000 square meters. This was unknown to the world until China's reforms and the opening of China to the world in 1979.

Returning to the ship after some fantastic bargaining with the vendors, I caught them by surprise with my faint and heart attack bit and went to the room to relax on the balcony.

This is when I saw that we were docked next to another ship, and another one was docked on that one, side by side! I proceeded to the sun deck and found three more behind us. Wow, what great timing! I needed some envelopes and paper for notes, so I asked the young girl behind the desk if I could borrow a uniform and collect a toll when the people came back through our ship. She was quick enough to ask what her cut would be. I said 30%, and she then said for 30%, she would translate!! Wow…how clever and fun! (No, we didn't do it!) Back to the room to change. It is the captain's welcoming party tonight!

Day 11, On the river.

Got up early so as not to miss the first gorge. I wasn't disappointed; being the narrowest, shortest, and steepest, there is a lot of lush foliage. After breakfast, we docked to disembark onto small sightseeing tour boats that had glass ceilings, large sliding side windows, and small open rear decks. Five minutes into the tour, a frantic woman shouted that her husband had accidentally dropped his 100-plus-year-old family shillelagh over the side. (There are travelers and tourists this is an example!) Who in their right mind would take a family heirloom on a trip to a foreign country, climbing on boats, through airports, in and out of busses and cabs??

Anyway, this created quite a stir; the captain turned the boat around. The river was fast and murky, and the stick was not that easily seen! We couldn't see it; we thought the cane was just another casualty of circumstance and stupidity. However, a small sampan was close; they came aside, asked what was going on, and agreed to look further down the river to see if they could be of help.

Ten minutes later, they caught up to us again with the prized shillelagh in hand, smiled, handed it over, and waved goodbye, not expecting anything but a gracious thank you! This just reinforces what I tell people about our travels: most people all over the world are good folks, just look a little different and dress different, "People are people." The man and his wife were ecstatic; they borrowed money from our guide for the boat tip and also some cash to pass along to those who helped find the cane!

Getting back to this gorge it was beautiful. I took pictures of the steep sides and saw caves way up that had coffins in them. No one knows how they got up there or why, but I suspect that they were placed there to be closer to heaven. There were waterfalls, different foliage, and crevices and peaks with various names. The day was perfect; the weather was sunny, and the temperature was in the low 70's the 2-hour excursion was relaxing and enjoyable. We then returned to the ship to sail further down the river and attended a lecture on the locks and the four-hour lock transition.

We drifted past the computer room, and I broke my own rule of not using, sent an e-mail to the kids, and deleted 150 or so junk e-mails from my filling e-mail cache. The connection on the ship was as fast as dial-up; then we lost the signal, and it took another 20 minutes to reestablish and sign out…that was it. No more e-mails this trip!

Walked the ship, talked to a bunch of people, attended a Viking, returned to a guest party, and received small gifts and drinks. This ship, like we experienced in Italy, only had air conditioning and no heat, so we opened our sliding doors to freshen up the room without having to turn on the a/c or fan.

Day 12, The 15th of April

We woke up parked between two other ships, a riverboat like ours and a working flat boat. It is in the mid-70s nice, and we are scheduled to leave the ship at 0900 for the three gorges dam tour. This is the largest hydroelectric power station in the world and just became fully operational in 2011. The dam is designed to take an earthquake up to 7 on the Richter scale; the power produced by the 34 generators is equivalent to burning 25 million tons of oil or 50 million tons of coal.

In building the dam, over a million people were displaced, and there was some destruction of archeological and architectural sites. It is the most expensive dam in world history, at about 28 million dollars.

The three gorges consist of;

1. Qutang Gorge: (lesser) or Kui Gorge, the narrowest and shortest.
2. Wu Gorge (gorge of witches) This one is about 25miles long;

The third and largest (about 50 miles long) is the Xiling Gorge, and we enter that later at night. The middle of this gorge, the largest, is where we docked and explored the Three Gorges Dam.

This was one of those promised relaxing afternoons, floating peacefully down the river, viewing the Twelve Peaks shrouded in mist, watching the changing river sites, going through the mile-long locks (four of them) dropping 22 meters in all, operating 24 hours a day along with 120 ships, we reviewed the Viking CD and just a nice easy afternoon and evening, a crew show for tonight and off to bed.

Day 13 Jinzhou

We have been at anchor since last night due to some dredging, and then a heavy fog bank has prevented any movement. The school was contacted regarding a delay in the visit, and then, as the fog persisted, they were to come and join us for a program on the ship. Since the fog was so extensive, that was also canceled. At 11:30, the fog bank did dissipate enough for us to weigh anchor and progress downriver to our final destination, only a half-hour behind schedule.

We were treated to a lecture on Chinese culture, and here are the highlights:

When dealing with western tourists, many Chinese adapt western aliases like Jimmy, John, Henry, and Iowa and keep those names throughout employment.

Red is the good luck color.

Chinese = China = Middle Kingdom

Q is pronounced "chin"; X Is pronounced "shea," and the pictograms used by the Chinese are words, not letters.

Confucius promoted going to the middle on all matters, not to the right or left, harmony. He proposed that every person was born to play a role, and what your role is came from your previous life.

The main religions in China are Confucianism, Buddhism, Taoism, and Taoism, which teach that we should be good people; all the religions believe in heaven or an afterlife.

Buddhism, founded by the enlightened (Buddha), teaches that the current life is not true; we are living an illusion. A true Buddhist is a vegetarian and has 5 basic beliefs:

- Do not kill any animal
- Do not steal
- No sexual oddities
- No lies
- No addictions

Yin: feminine, passive, receptive, dark and soft

Yang: masculine, active, creative, bright and hard

Feng Shui: five elements in Harmony; earth to metal to water to wood to fire

In General, the Chinese believe in being a good person, thereby changing the environment yourself. The Chinese Culture respects the elderly; grandparents take care of the kids so the parents can work, and there are very few nursing homes in China because the Chinese believe the kids should care for the elders.

There is increasing concern in China regarding the aging

population of people over 60, which is now 12% and growing. They are rethinking the one-child rule.

The most important festival is the Chinese New Year in February or late January. This is a day of family reunion; 200 million people clog the trains, planes, and highways to get home and share at least one meal with family. The week before and the week after this holiday clogs the entire transportation system.

Most family tables are round to encourage interaction and sharing of food.

Chop stick bad manners: do not point with chop sticks, do not hit the side of the bowl with chop sticks, never stick the chop sticks into food, and must always be laid down. Wait till the food is in front of you; do not reach across from someone to get food. The chop sticks should match.

There are no corner bars in China, and alcohol is consumed after dinner at home or with company. Chinese Valentine's Day, the 7th day of the 7th Lunar month, is represented at night by the two brightest stars banking the Milky Way, one "parent" on each side. There are to be no magpie birds that day because they help form the Milky Way.

Paper money is burned to be used by those on the "other" side. (Yes, I bought some, remember?)

Both the Crane and Turtle represent longevity.

The cicada has the longest life span of any insect (up to 17 years), and it sheds its skin. It is the Chinese symbol of regeneration and rebirth. In ancient China, people would place a jade cicada in the mouths of the dead to impede the decay process and hasten rebirth in another world.

The phoenix represents the feminine power of the empress

Ducks represent happiness and marital faithfulness.

Dragon holds the first place among the four greatest Chinese creatures, along with the phoenix, tiger, and tortoise.

Carp represents strength and perseverance. The words "fish" and "abundance" are pronounced the same (Yu).

The bat is also a traditional good luck symbol.

Giant pandas (bearcats) date over 3 million years and were kept by early emperors to ward off evil spirits and natural disasters. They were considered symbols of might and bravery.

Chinese people have no idea of personal space in crowds, on buses, or with cars. With friends and family, "please" and "thank you" are not expected or used. The peony is the national flower.

Women do not change their family name when they get married since Mao.

There are 1.8 billion people in China (one out of six in the world).

Up to four generations live under one roof.

It is being considered that if the firstborn is a girl, after three or four years, another child may be permitted.

Divorce is only allowed if adultery is involved.

Cremation is mandatory

Best wishes: "Happiness, Longevity, and Good Fortune"

New foods I had an opportunity to try this trip:

Yak lung—fatty, very fatty …no

100-year-old egg—black, kind of clear, tastes of vinegar.

Pig's ear—fatty, no real taste…no

Jellyfish salad—was combined with coleslaw…good

Pig's tails—fatty, no real taste…no

Chicken feet—chewy, bony, gelatinous…no

Lilli root soup—excellent. You must try if you have a chance

Deep-fried lotus—very good…yes

Black donuts—very good …yes

Aquavit (Scandinavia's National Drink) 110 proof…good!!

Day 14, Friday, Wuhan and Shanghai

We had an early breakfast, checked out, and left the ship; the cruise portion was over. We boarded the bus for a ride to the Hubei Museum to review artifacts dating back 2400 yrs. Ago, dating B.C., where a 45-year-old man was very old!

This is a smaller city, only about 10 million, and it is also "Jimmy's" home town.

There were a lot of brass carvings, vessels, and artwork. We were also witness to a bell performance. Each bell has two sounds and three tones. The performance was accompanied by percussion instruments, flutes, and dancers.

It was very nice and very classy, and we had second-row seats! This is where Chairman Mao swam across the river as a show of virility (He did this every year until he died). It is also the first place where a bridge was constructed across the river.

Lunch at a local restaurant featuring local foods, again, outstanding!

Off to the airport for the second last time of this trip, the flight was delayed to Shanghai for an hour, but from what was said, this is not uncommon due to mist, fog, and smog both here and in Shanghai, a city of 26 million.

We arrived late in the afternoon, whisked through, our bags expedited and picked up by our Viking representatives, and we boarded the bus for the usual ride of an hour to our downtown hotel.

Shanghai is the "Pearl of the Orient" much like Paris is for the East. The Fairmont Peace Hotel is located right on the Bund, in the Phuong area it is a five-star hotel and has hosted both Presidents Reagan and Clinton. The room is spacious and welcoming, very nice indeed!

Day 15 First days in Shanghai

Many of us have sinus problems. It is smoggy, cool, and busy!

Breakfast in the hotel is grand, two fresh egg prep stations, pastries, a Chinese section, fresh fruits, salmon, cheeses, yep, whatever you want, and as much as you want!

This morning is a trip through Old Shanghai, one of the most beautiful gardens called the Yu Garden. This is one of the best classic Chinese gardens presently under State preservation. There are no straight paths in the garden, all doorways have high thresholds, (ghosts and spirits move only in straight lines, and cannot cross raised thresh holds.) All of the entrances have doors or will have a large stone to further deter bad spirits. (Keeps on working, still no spirits or ghosts seen or felt!!)

There are well-placed pools containing Koi and turtles, perfectly placed stones with formal rooms having Ming Dynasty furniture, round and shaped doors and doorways, and even an area outside with various-sized pebbles used to exercise the bottoms of your feet. (A massage with every step!)

After a leisurely informed walk through the garden, we drove down the Bund, to a silk company where we were given an explanation of silk thread pictures, and clothing and bed covers along with clothing manufacturing with silk. At this location was a restaurant specializing in Mongolian food. We loaded up our bowls and partook in a great meal. After lunch, we made a visit to the Shanghai Museum with four floors of Chinese history, bronzes, furniture, paintings, and even different forms of money.

Back to the hotel for a rest, tonight we were scheduled to see an acrobatic dinner show. The dinner was abundant, the show well put together, varied quite a bit, and showed both a lot of strength and flexibility, everyone enjoyed! The Main Street outside the theatre was banked with trees all of which had lights that slowly changed colors; these lit trees went on for blocks!

Back by the hotel at 9:45 PM, we were all tired!

Day 16 second day in Shanghai and we are off to a boat ride in the moat of a town called Suzhou (Sudo), I call it our moat boat ride. It was very relaxing, the little ferry boats held 16-18 people and we went up and down the moat/ canal system that averaged three meters deep and 15-20 meters wide and saw parts of the 2000-year-old wall. We also went up a small tributary that was narrow and witness's two weddings, one in traditional red, the other, the bride wore white, both grooms were in red. We witnessed the old style of living, the small shops and stores and the cramped living conditions in the past.

After the moat boat trip, we went to a more exclusive and extensive silk factory. We learned that the mulberry leaf used to feed the worms cannot be picked when wet; only certain mulberry leaves are eaten by the worms, the symbols for the plant, the worm, and silk in Chinese. What to look for in gathering the cocoons: This company shows the complete process of gathering silk after roasting the worms inside their own cocoon. We watched the cocoons being sorted, the good ones being roasted and checked, and then the multiple machines used to unwind that single filament from the cocoon. (One filament can be 100 meters long.) We witness how the defective silk is woven so that quilts, blankets, and comforters can be made from them. The extensive gift shop provided that last opportunity for those silk gifts and mementos we just had to have.

Lunch, Chinese style, and plenty as always!

Last stop was the Master of the Nets Garden. This garden emphasizes harmony. Here a blend of ponds, rocks and shrubbery blended with the wooden structures. We saw the world's largest Bonsai tree, viewed comfortable living quarters and peaceful court yards.

This evening we joined with a number of our group to take our tour guide out for dinner, his choice was Chinese, we let him order the entrees and we all had a great time. It seemed that he was a little embarrassed but with most of us if not all, we just over rode him! to pay for his meal.

Day 17 last full day in Shanghai and we are on our own. We started off with a walk to the Bund sightseeing tunnel, a visual effects ride in a small enclosed cable car type vehicle that transverses the river. The cost was 50RMB (about $10.00 US) each and it just being opened, we had the car to ourselves.

On the other side of the river, we hoofed it to the Jinmato building. (Called locally "the can opener" due to the square hole in the upper part of the building) This was the second tallest (at 2073 ft.) building in the world, now third, but still has the fastest elevator. (40.3 MPH) It was foggy and drizzling, which caused the views to be less than great, but we are here! Note: Tourist maps are NOT drawn to ANY scale; what looked like a two-block walk turned into a half mile!

The elevator ride was fast, at 9.1 meters / second the 95 first floors took less than 45 seconds. We then were directed to ride two escalators to the observation deck on the bottom of the can opener opening. It was not impressive, still foggy, rainy, but we did take some pictures. Then we took the elevator to the top of the building, looking down through the glass floor you could see the bottom of the "opener" and more panorama of the city, more pictures.

Next, we grabbed a cab and off to the Maglev. This is the world's first commercialized high speed magnetic elevated transportation system in the world. We bought round trip tickets to the airport and waited up on deck for the train. It came, we easily found a seat, and waited. The doors closed, and we quickly accelerated to a maintained speed of 300 km per hour (180mph); the trip took seven minutes! It takes 10 minutes to load and unload, then back we went; the whole experience was a little over a half hour! WOW Very quiet, very smooth, no real sensation of speed except when passing something close.

As we exited the train station, we were approached by a cab driver offering to drive us to our next stop, the French district. As we climbed into the cab and took off, we noticed no meter.... oops! He did take us to where we wanted to go, and did produce a receipt, but it was for 200 RMB ($40 US) about twice what it should have been, but we were happy just to pay and get out of the cab.

Walked around, had a quick lunch, and decided to walk back to the hotel, it had gotten warmer, stopped raining, and we didn't believe the hotel was far.... according to the map that was...

Yep, it turned out we had quite a hike, but with frequent rest stops and interesting neighborhoods we again came to the Bund. We walked on top of the Bund to see the river, and just to do it, and ended our two-hour trek at the hotel.

The 84 RMB bought a sandwich and chips for supper, and we went to the room to rest, pack and go to bed early for the trip home tomorrow.

Last day, we checked out at 9:30 AM, Jimmy picked us up with a van, we picked up another couple at another hotel and we were deposited at our airline with luggage by Jimmy. I thanked him handily; gave him his gratuity envelope and we started the final process on getting on our plane to Chicago.

Noah

The flight home was as good as can be expected, the seats were uncomfortable, lots of people up and down in and out of the overhead compartments, minimal customer care, rating American Airlines on the bottom with United. Comfort has been deleted in their vocabulary unless you have a couple extra thousand to fly business or 1st class; treat us like cattle, so mooo!

This ends the tale: I am grateful for being home; I do not want to be brushed, pushed, shoved, or crowded for a while. China is completely different and changing logarithmically, and people are people!

The Viking Experience after we were actually on the tour was seamless and very busy, but they did not drop the ball anytime!

The personal guide for the 24 or so of us was with us 24/7 throughout the experience, he was intelligent, warm, sensitive, and understanding. He was the most outstanding guide we have ever had and an asset to the company. The planned events were all at low times for us to navigate through the various sites and enjoy. The additional guides brought with us at each different city were very informative and worked well both with us and our guide.

We made it home by 8:30 PM; the van (Tiffany had left it for us) was waiting for us in the bus terminal parking lot.

Educating Noah…Travelin'

We were starving for American food, and I wanted to pick up some cough and flu medications for our expediting these flu symptoms. Next to the Walgreen's was a Taco Bell, and that was close enough. As we pulled out of the drive-thru, we had to make a hard left onto 27th St. to go home. We stopped for traffic at the median, and when there was an opening, we took off, or sort of, there was a large bang under the car, little response to the accelerator, so I cruised across the road to a closing Honda dealership, and pulled over to the side. Inspecting the car, I couldn't see anything under the car, or over the engine. I called my daughter to see if she knew of anything, she didn't and she had just dropped off the car!

So, then I asked to talk to Mike my son-in-law regarding the Kia. It was under warrantee (Mike works for a car dealership and sold me this and many other cars) so he said it was covered, to call Kia, and they would tow it to an authorized dealer, to have them tow it to Racine, close to the dealership he works for and he would watch for a good repair.

We found the Kia number, they arranged the tow, called my daughter back, and she picked us up and drove us home after the tow truck took off with the van.

I called the dealership the next morning to identify the van. When I got to the right person he asked if I had talked to Mike yet. I said "no", but now I wanted to know what was wrong. He told me that this morning, they moved a car behind the van, and the van brake was not set all the way, it seems that the van rolled a good 50 yards into their car and had significant damage to the rear quarter and back. That afternoon, I went down to see what happened, found that the axel spline had broken, and the rear taillight gone and damage to the rear quarter panel. I told them I needed a replacement, and there was one ready for me, no charge!

I then went over to Mike's dealership to discuss what had happened and goad Mike! I told him that this car no longer "wanted me" as an owner, after discussing a various number of options, and taking a few test rides, I decided to buy a new car, a Subaru Forester. In discussing this car, Mike told me it would be best to buy the car new, the resale is high, just like Honda, and the selling price is not with a huge mark-up to start, and the credit Union has a buyer that will do a better job at bargaining than I could. (Really?? So much for my ego!!)

I talked to Paul at the credit union; got the trade value of the van, got the best price from Paul, with the color and options I wanted and told him to make the deal, unless I call him in 24 hours.

Noah

I then went home, did all the research on the resale values, selling prices of the cars, and made cursory phone calls, I could not come to within $500.00 of what Paul had offered, so I called him back the next morning and gave him the "go", and to call me back with how much money I needed to make this buy happen. A week later, I gave the keys to the van to Mike, my son-in-law, walked over to the credit unions desk, got the check, and a ride over to the dealership. The salesman gave me an orientation, we looked over the new 2015 Subaru Forester and off I drove. I promised the salesman I would have the first oil change done by the dealership but did not expect to see him before or after that.

It took a week and a half to readjust from this trip also. Called about the taxes, they will be ready early next month, and I also waited a week to take my weight.

I also had my final appointments at the VA for the bilateral knee replacements at the end of May, passed everything, all set! Picked up the taxes, everything set, weighed in, I'm at 245. I still hate watching everything I eat; I am still forcing myself to drink lots on water, and not liking to have to know always where a rest room is as a consequence.

Everyone that I have talked to does a double take when I say by-lateral, but as usual, that is just their opinion. I increased the number of steps this month another 1000; that too is difficult especially since I discontinued my pain medications to toughen myself up.

It only took 10 days for the write up on China and the photo album so I am happy with that, had another Mother's Day at our house, prepared portabella sandwiches with Swiss and fried onions, prosciutto and cheese rounds, and roll-ups, almond squares with Nutella and blueberries, fruits, Cami brought additional rolls and sandwiches, Taffy brought fruit and a cake; nice selection, always plenty of food and variety, plenty to distribute when all went home. Mike decided to spend his Mother's Day with his mom, he and Taffy have decided to divorce and are trying to sell their house, it is taking longer than they anticipated.

I have returned home from the bilateral knee replacement. It took only three hours with two surgeons to replace both knees, I was in recovery later in the afternoon; doing fine, sent Lynn home. I had difficulty the first two days, my blood pressure was too low to do anything and over those two days I received 4 units of blood; the third day my systolic was above 110 so we could then start with recovery exercises, ice packs for swelling and such things. After a week in recovery, they transferred me to another floor for rehab; I pushed every limit and got discharged home on Monday the twelfth day!

At home, I started my rehabilitation. I had talked to PT before leaving and we agreed on seeing them once a week for three weeks to check on my progress and work with me on strengthen exercises. I started the second day home to start walking and working the 15 step stairs at home. I started at 475 walking steps, and up and down the stairs two times, and I also stopped using the OxyContin. I continued to do all the exercises indicated three times a day and increased my walking to over 5000 steps a day and doing the stairs 4 times a day. After our first meeting, my physical therapist set additional goals of standing on one foot for at least 30 seconds, then the other to improve my balance, this was a late afternoon appointment and we had to limit my exercises due to my blood pressure dipping below a systolic of 90.

The day after our first meeting with PT, I started doing the walks without the walker. Beginning again from 3000 steps to a goal of 5000+ steps a day and a minimum of five times up and down the stair case. The second meeting was late morning; I did the one leg stands per leg for 30 plus seconds and bent myself to pieces! She told me to work on 30 seconds per leg with my eyes closed and assigned additional exercises. I continued to do all the exercises plus my 5000 steps and average 5-6 staircases a day.

Our next PT was only 4 days after, I told her I couldn't stand on one leg for more than a few seconds and told her that we had a dinner meeting with the motorcycle club, and no one could do it longer than a few seconds………. I think she was "pulling my leg"!

We worked an exercise bike; she went over a number of machines that I can use at my gym club to strengthen my muscles. I then had a whole week to work out at the gym and hopefully make the third meeting with PT my last!

This is after the last meeting my third and final PT class. Sue, the PT person, put me through the ringer on this class, I had to walk through a rope ladder placed on the floor, stand on a half ball, and multiple exercise machines (I was early as usual so she assigned projects for me while waiting for my time.) and then we went for a walk with walking sticks up, down, and around, in the hospital, and then outside, halfway around the hospital. She noticed I was getting tired so we turned around, went through a sandpit, gravel pit, and grass; up and down grass covered hills and areas, and finally she gave me the "OK" after measuring the angle of my knees to assure I have full flex. She asked me how many more appointments we had, if this was our last one or a few more. I said no, we accomplished all we were scheduled and I would appreciate it if she would pass me. She said yes, but she wasn't kidding about the eyes closed standing on 1 foot so I promised her that I would accomplish this at 30 seconds each foot and report back to her when that was done……………. I'm free!

Since the last time, we had PT I have tried to get at least 10,000 steps per day is not easy, and I'm also going to the gym more often using exercises the cross-trainer with the cross ramp that exercises the "glute's", "Quad's", Hamstrings, and the calves, plus trying to get those additional steps in and using the indicated machines to further strengthen my legs from the "glutes down seems to be working this is my job now. Now I have to start on my weight again when I got out of the hospital, I was at 243.6 pounds, we have been going to the restaurants using up gift certificates which packs on the pounds I'm

Educating Noah…Travelin'

currently at 245.6 got to get down to my next level which is 225.

I am doing these reports now through my Dragon voice recognition system my wife says it looks a little goofy but I kinda like it; it kinda spells like I do so I will have to do the spell check and correction later on as usual. I just need to get the recorder working so I know how to use that for our next vacation trip, I am learning but I'm slow.

I came across a great deal to revisit the Hawaiian Islands. It was with Your Man Tours, a kind of a discount tour outfit. Lynn wanted to revisit, we were there courtesy of Uncle Sam with the R&R program, and they flew me from Vietnam and her from Milwaukee for a week on Oahu.

That was in 1969, we want to see all four islands, spend a little more time there, and see how much has changed. The deal was only a little more than $200/day with air!! This was one of those last-minute deals; had to pay everything up front, but we leave the end of September!!

I couldn't get the list of optional tours from the YMT website even though I requested twice, but then I contacted my travel agent, and she responded and provided everything I needed; it will be another memorable adventure!!

It is now the end of August 2015 this is a 14th week after my knees were replaced, the swelling at the ankles no longer plagues me at night, everything is working well and I've been averaging 11,000 steps a day for the last four weeks. I do have some soreness but I expect that and I'm getting a lot firmer now, I now have to start really concentrating on my diet, haven't lost any weight, but haven't gained any either.

I got bored and anxious so I started planning out our new vacation schedule. While I was nursing these knees back into production, I sent out the passports because the passports were going to be expiring next

July. When traveling, they won't accept the passport if it is going to expire within six months. We had a window, so I took it! It took exactly 4 weeks we got them back, I paid for expedited overnight delivery and we received them in two days, I guess that is the new overnight standard by the post office!

Regarding Hawaii, I finally called Your Man Tours when I got our airline information, this is usually sent a month before so that I looked over the seats and then I upgraded and we got premium economy seats. We will see what Delta's premium economy seats are now compared to United and American since this is the first time we flown with Delta. An interesting comment is that they don't serve food, so we got six-hour flights without food, actually it is longer, we just land in California for an hour and a half and then continue to Hawaii. On the way back, we have a plane change in California and they wanted to charge more for the upgrade due to the change, when I objected, they only charged me for one upgrade for two seats, so I didn't push it.

We went to an Iceland seminar by Fox travel. Iceland on top of Lynn's list, so next July will be going to Iceland and we made the initial payment.

I also found a Russian excursion with Viking and they included the air with the price, so even though it was a year ahead, we bought into that too. They do guarantee that if Russia closes their border, we can apply the monies to another Viking cruise.

For January, I was looking into Jamaica as far as an all-inclusive for a week. The all-inclusive prices were high (for my taste), I can't drink that much and I don't drink that much anymore, so it really didn't make a lot of monetary sense. Lynn wanted to go to Aruba so I found a cruise through another discount outfit for an exceptionally low quote. I called, and I said as long as you can give me a good price on air there and back and transfers, I'll take this one. So, they did, quickly and I got the cruise. However, they didn't quote taxes and everybody else quotes taxes so it wasn't as fantastic of a deal but is still a very good. You always, always, have to question "Great Deals"!

A lot of money went out these last two or three weeks.

I bought a new Subaru before I went in to get my knees done, and I can't tell you how much we both love that Subaru. It is really nice, it's handy, it's the right size, it's easy getting in and out of.

Subaru called me last month, said that when I scheduled an oil change, they would like me to be a mystery shopper for them. I made the appointment for the oil change and on to be a mystery shopper for Subaru and I should get $40.00 for my trouble!

I re-started driving for the VA last month once a week, it is nice to get back there with having fewer people doing the north side because of the unrest but it doesn't bother me and I drive one of the Ford flex's which is like a little tank.

As I mentioned before about getting bored, I'm trying to deal with it and plus I'm walking 11,000 steps per day and that takes around three hours. I bought a $10 radio and I change different routes and places.

We also went to a church festival last weekend and I got to dance, and I'm telling you that it is so different now that I've got the new knees, I almost cried; that's not characteristic for me and I hid my face and stuff because my eyes were welling up. What a great feeling! I can actually dance again so this could be big surprise on this cruise with Lynn in January to Aruba (Maybe in Hawaii too!)

My daughter went through a hell on a home sale. They were trying to sell the house because they are getting divorced. The deal fell through the same day as the closing and so the other two houses they had lined up fell through do the contingency.

The buyers came to the house the morning of the closing unannounced. As a final inspection, as they toured the back yard, my daughter mentioned that the highway behind the property might be expanded or improved. That blew the whole deal, they refused to close, so I'm not sure yet if they ever got the money back, but the whole deal stinks!

The house Mike wanted to buy, canceled their closing also and to date refuses to return the earnest money. None of the stuff makes sense and I'm blaming it on the real estate agent who supposedly has years of experience with what I think, he had his head up his ass!

We had Lynn's sister-in-law Janelle, and their son, Matt and daughter Karla with her husband Ian, along with Camille and her husband Kelly, move Tiffany's stuff to the new house the previous Saturday. Mike moved his into a U-Haul truck. With everything exploding, Lynn, I, Linda, (Mike's sister), Mike and Tiffany moved all the items back to the house that black Monday, five trips with the U-Haul, and we also helped Mike empty his U-Haul, the rest of the furniture was returned two days later, that was stored in the moving van……Lynn and I helped there too!

Mike was a wreck; everybody was tired and exhausted! We all pushed on to finish.

After discussions, it was decided that Tiffany would find a new place, and Mike would buy her out of the house and re-mortgage the house.

Mike contacted the credit union he works for and an appraiser was sent out.

The appraisal came through $40,000 less which nobody believes, so they are having the place re-appraised. The closing on the condo my daughter was buying was delayed due to the poor appraisal.

The divorce did go through, however, and that actually went smoothly.

So, we wait, I will start packing and re-checking everything about the Hawaii vacation the end of this month, we are also going to the annual Konk-A-Pot weekend later this month with the motorcycle club, it is just one weekend before leaving for Hawaii.

I had to call the company (dragon recording) to find out how to transfer the recorder info to the computer, it took FIVE phone calls but I got an answer and now know how to do it without paying more for the advice!

August 2015, this is a 14th week after my knees everything is working well, I've been averaging 11,000 steps a day for the last four weeks I do have some soreness but I expect that and I'm getting a lot firmer.

I haven't lost any weight but that'll come, I'm replacing some of the fat with muscle I hope the knees are doing fine, no complaints, I'm just walking up and down stairs.

Hawaii 2015

Day 1 Friday

This is the first day of vacation and we are in the hotel. It's about 1:00 o'clock in the morning here, or five hours earlier on my watch.

We left the house at 6:30 P.M. Friday; the cab driver got there exactly at that time. We are leaving from Milwaukee this time.

As we approached the check-in counter, Lynn discovered that she had left her coat in the cab. She called the cab driver, he said he would be back in an hour, so we checked in, processed our bags, and waited. He did return in 50 minutes and was very nice about it. We then proceeded to the TSA checkpoint knowing we would be expedited due to our pre-approval. Got to the line, told that the TSA line was under man-powered and stretched thin because the Pope was in Washington and supposedly all the TSA people went there. But, due to our delay waiting for Lynn's jacket, the lines were again open! So maybe it was lucky (or Karma) that we were delayed!

Noah

Everything went well, got to the gate, got on the plane. Delta loads airplanes like they did in Istanbul basically everybody runs and lines up into the hallway, no real order, as they call out families and disabled who have to push through the lines, then first class, then preferred, the groups three and four, everyone struggling to get on the plane as soon as possible due to overhead storage limited spacing and most everyone bringing two carry-ons! (With some exceptions, including us!)

We did not have the upgraded comfort economy class at the beginning or the end on the jump from Milwaukee to Minneapolis and the return from Minneapolis to Milwaukee because I just didn't think the 45 minutes warranted the extra cash for the upgrade.

After we landed, we disembarked and found our new gate for the second of three flights to finally arrive in Hawaii. I did some walking around to get my steps in, we now had the "comfort seats" upgrade, so we had over 4 inches of extra legroom and priority seating which we both enjoyed and were now toward the front of the plane. We also got to push through the crowd at the gate earlier, had space in the storage compartment, and settled in for the five hours to LAX.

There was just supposed to be an hour and a half layover, but they made us get off the plane with our carry-ons, wait in at the gate, and then reloaded very similar to Milwaukee cattle car kind of loading except for our priority again. No incidents on a layover from LAX to Honolulu. We landed, got our luggage, found the YMT (Your Man Tours) representative, received our Lei's, and directed to a waiting bus to take us to our first hotel.

There were 13 people on the bus, and he was going to make four stops. The bus driver announced the first stop, and one guy got off. He then asked if anyone else was to get off; I said I wasn't sure which hotel we were going to, and the bus driver said he didn't know either, so I told him I would get out from then on to see if we were registered at the hotel stops, he kind of groaned, but agreed only if I was quick

Educating Noah…Travelin'

about it, otherwise we could ride to the end, and he would help us resolve the problem. At the second stop, three younger guys got off, no women, and none of the group we entered the bus with, so I told the driver to go on to the next stop. At the third stop, a number of folks from our group got off; I got off with them, telling the driver I would be as quick as possible. I asked the bellhop regarding all the YMT people, and he stated this was the place for all YMT tour folks in Waikiki, so I told the bus driver this was our stop, got Lynn off the bus, got our luggage, and checked in. This was the first time in all of our tours that we were not taken to the hotel or ship without a guide! (Or specific bus)

This was a long day, basically what they served on the plane was peanuts and pretzels and potato chips but no real meals except for our meal at home, and we had packed crackers, fruit, and smoked sausage, which helped.

While we were being driven to our hotels, the driver had some interesting facts about Hawaii that usually aren't told. The sand in Hawaii is so fine that he sticks to your skin so they imported all of the sand on Waikiki from Australia. The plants are mostly from other places, Europe, South America, China, and Australia; very few plants are indigenous now because they have gone extinct.

He also said that Hawaii has about 1.1-1.3 million people, with 800,000 or so on Oahu, which is the most industrialized island, thereby providing the most jobs. There are almost as many cars here as there are people; they have a light rail system

in place, it may take 5 to 6 years to complete, costing billions of dollars.

The natives in the original alliance are not too happy with that. They've also discontinued the ferry line between the islands because of the fuel used, claiming it was inefficient and harmful to the climate. So, it's not all roses here in Hawaii, but it's beautiful. The "VOG" (a kind of fog or smog) we were in tonight is fine volcanic ash mixed with water vapor.

Day 2 Saturday

Saturday morning, I took off and walked; our internal clocks screwed up due to the time changes, both of us were up at 4 A.M. their time. So, it is walking; we walked down to Waikiki Beach, only about two blocks away, and there were a lot of early A.M. biker's, (bicycles) preparing for a rally tomorrow. A mix of pedestrians, surfers and bikers, runners and walkers, at the break of dawn. A few bums on the benches, but nothing to be concerned about, we watched dawn come up over the ocean and we also saw a bunch of surfers paddling out for the surf at the breakwater.

You can rent a surfboard for five bucks an hour and they have them a block off of the main drag; It was humid, warm, and was sprinkling lightly, and as a matter-of-fact, most the day today was sprinkling and light rain, on and off.

There are lots of tourist traps and lots of tour shops on the main boulevard. An ABC Store is located every 1-2 blocks, similar to a large 7-11 on the mainland. We walked past those (they were already open) and proceeded back to the hotel. There wasn't much open it 5:30- 6:00 A.M. in the morning, so we stopped at Burger King and shared a Burger King breakfast for eight bucks; (In all of the Islands, there is no such thing as a dollar menu at ANY of the fast-food places).

We had a general organizational meeting at the hotel, giving everyone a rundown on the days' activities, what optional tours are available during our 12 days on the islands, and to sign up and pay for those options.

Of the fourteen excursions offered, we opted for eleven of them, skipping the Best of Beatles show, the legends concert, and the Kauai Movie tour, the movie tour was an on-land duplication of the helicopter tour.

At 11:00 o'clock we loaded up the bus and off for an included tour of the Punch bowl crater, Pearl Harbor, China Town and the Capitol.

The Punchbowl Crater was our first big stop. The Punchbowl is one of the dormant volcanoes now covered in vegetation which was made into a graveyard for the soldiers from the attack on Pearl Harbor, The National cemetery of the Pacific.

We couldn't get to the main monument because a park ranger stopped us as we turned onto the road; we even had to back up the bus. The tour companies were not notified of the closure to buses and that for the weekend, only cars were allowed. So, we drove slowly past the entrance, and were able to just view the everlasting flame monument.

We then drove past the capitol building, built in 1969. It is the only U.S. capitol completely surrounded by water, it was also built to honor the land, with columns shaped like palm tree trunks supporting a second floor to minimize surface area contact with the ground, to respect the land. They designed this building to look as natural as possible.

Next, we went down to Chinatown. It was the first Chinatown in the United States and that was in the 1840's. It was kind of a place where ill repute, gambling, "anything goes" went on. Due to wood construction, fires were plentiful and with crowded conditions, it burnt down twice.

The Iowan Palace was the next stop, it was built in 1881 and had electricity and phones before many in DC on the mainland, and the White House! That was due to the visit of Thomas Edison. They had electricity and phones in Hawaii just in the palace though and there were no other phones on island so we don't know what they did with the phone, but they had a working one!

Across the street is a government building shown on the new Hawaii 5-0. In the original series, with Jack Lord, they used the palace as the headquarters! The Hawaiian's are very proud of the original 5-0 series; it plays every week on one of the TV stations episodes after episode.

The bus system here is named "the bus". There was a referendum on what to call the bus transit system and the main answer was "the bus" so all are called to "the bus". One of the taxi companies is called "the Cab"; kinda simple isn't it!!

Pearl Harbor; the attack started 12/07/ 41 at 07:55 the first airbase on Oahu was attacked, Army, Marine, Navy, and the Air Force airbases were hit first, so basically, they crippled all the aircraft and the runway. With aircraft destroyed, crippling the ability of the U.S. to defend itself from the Japanese when they next bombed Pearl Harbor.

Then they went after the ships in the harbor. The concerns with Japan were brewing since 1923, they had warnings that something might happen, and it would happen on a Sunday morning, but the warnings were ignored, so it was no big surprise attack as claimed, just the concerns were negated by the upper brass, and powers that be.

We spent about three hours at Pearl Harbor, it was too windy to be ferried out to the Arizona, but we did tour the grounds, the submarine, torpedoes, shops, museums, displays and watched a documentary. Since we had toured the Arizona last time we were here (in 1969) we didn't have that eerie feeling again, and both of us did not miss that!

After Pearl Harbor, we went to a jewelry company called Maui Pearl Divers. They specialize in black coral, and very expensive black coral! They had pearls, all different shades and hues, very similar to the Jade factory we saw in China and the marble factory and jewelry store in Rio called Stearns, in South America.

The sales techniques are similar; we had to tour, got free gifts, free wine, and plenty of people behind the counters to answer any questions we had about any piece of jewelry shown. We were the first couple out, found the shuttle bus, talked to the driver and a sales associate until the rest of the folks in our group found us and we were taken back to the hotel.

The evening was on our own, we found a place that was like a 50's dinner. We had a nice meal there, a good waitress, Mai Tai's for five dollars and we shared a hamburger and pulled pork nachos. We took a walk to a hotel that was recommended called the Pacific Beach. Inside, next to the restaurant, is a large aquarium that was just unbelievable; Multi story, like a museum aquarium, with all kinds of fish, big and small, shellfish, lobsters, and stingrays.

With temperatures in the 80's and humidity to match, we headed back to our hotel; we had been up almost 16 hours. We found out that our tour leaves promptly at 6:45 A.M. so we went to bed early.

Day 3 Sunday

Sunday morning, we are on the first YMT optional excursion on the island of Oahu! This is an all-inclusive, full day tour and left the hotel at 7:00 A.M. till 4:30 P.M. We got up "later" this morning, around 5:00 o'clock this morning. I went for a morning walk while Lynn got herself ready, then we did the trip down to the lobby to the coffee shop. Had coffee and tea, shared a donut and a bagel.

Our bus driver/ tour guide was friendly, very experienced, native to this island, and full of information; he talked most of the time we were on the tour bus. This tour covered one hundred and twenty miles.

After leaving the Waikiki beach area we traveled the coast; stopping briefly at the Nu'uanu Pali Lookout, Hanauma Bay, viewed the area where some of the original Jurassic Park movie was filmed, and the TV series: Gilligan's Island, and Pleasure Island. Then to the macadamia nut company. Macadamia nuts is the second largest industry here now; (the trees came from Australia.)

Noah

We were treated to samples of all the coffee's they produced, and all the different macadamia nut varieties, including onion and garlic, (my favorite), salted, unsalted, chocolate coated, honey, cinnamon, and spicy to mention a few. After multiple tastings, of both the coffees and nuts, I went out to the back where they had bins of nuts, a couple tree stumps, and a few rocks. This was for "do it like the natives" area.

I dug out a couple of the nuts from the bin, placed one on the stump and smacked it with the stone, this cracked the outer shell (looks like a walnut) to reveal a hard-walnut shaped inner nut. This nut required a lot more force to break open, after three attempts, it did smash open to yield a lot of pieces of the nut.

I repeated the procedure to finally get an intact inner nut, then gathered a complete nut, the inside hard nut, and the inner edible nut to show Lynn and the others!

Although it was drizzling all day, the Chief wanted to put on his show for us, so we obliged him by heading down to the stage area. Chief Sielu has been featured all over the world, including the Oprah Winfrey Show, the Tonight Show, and Good Morning America, amongst many others. You could tell he enjoyed what he did and was very entertaining!

The show included how to open a coconut (the coconut has a face!), The stem is the front of the coconut; look for the belly button and locate the face. Between the eyes is a line; hit across the line with a rock or the blunt end of a machete. We had a sampling of the coconut water, coconut milk, and the meat of the coconut, and how everything of the coconut is used.

He then demonstrated how to make a fire with sticks and coconut fibers, performed with lighted torches, and explained native traditions. The show was informative, entertaining and everyone loved to watch a man who truly enjoys practicing his art. In the early days, the men did all the hunting and cooking. Wonder who did the clean up??

Time for lunch, special arrangements were made for a restaurant to open just for us called Tita's Grill!

Orders were taken on the bus, Lynn ordered the garlic shrimp, and I ordered an island favorite, Loco Moco (beef chunks over rice with gravy on top). The meals were served in Styrofoam take-out boxes; choice of soda or water was included. A Porta-potty for the men and one bathroom for the women. It was a little primitive, but the staff was very nice, fun place to eat, and we got to try some local fare!

Next stop was the North shore beaches where the surfers enjoy waves of 6-8 feet on a consistent basis. Oh, by the way, the water is consistently in the upper 70 degrees to the lower 80's!!

There were many beaches and grounds for nesting for the green sea turtles, but it was constantly drizzling, and no turtles to be found!

Our last stop before heading home was the Dole pineapple plant. On the way into the store, I took a picture of a variety of Eucalyptus trees that has a smooth bark that is multi-colored; I hope it shows up in the pictures!

Inside was a huge store, we had the pineapple ice cream, Mmmmmmm! Bought a few souvenirs and posed inside a pineapple for austerity! We couldn't believe the amount of pineapple stuff available!

On the way back to the hotel, we were told that Pineapples are no longer a big export due to labor costs, and sugarcane also due to labor costs. Now tourism is the most valuable commodity, also as some coffee.

We were dropped off at the hotel, put our gear in our room, and went out to find the night life on the strip. We explored the beach again, looked at the various sculptures, small decorative pools and rocks, walked out on the one pier, people watched, and then headed back to the hotel. We picked up some juice, a banana, and pastry for breakfast, the lunch was plenty food for the day! Still suffering from Jet lag, we showered and off to bed.

Day 4 Monday

We had the morning off this morning, so I took my walk down to Waikiki Beach, saw the morning dawn on Waikiki Beach, and returned to the room to make coffee and eat our breakfast.

This morning, the two of us were on a mission to find the Surf Rider Hotel we stayed at when we were on R&R back in 1969. Since I had been exploring the beach to the left when we came here, we went right on the main drag. The hotels butted against each other; a block down was the Surf Rider, and across the street was the International Market Place!

The hotel was extensively remodeled ten years ago, and according to our guide, one of the most expensive on the beach! We did go into the open-air lobby and shops, all new, then went out on the beach. What was then a long expanse of beach is now all hotels, so now Waikiki is mostly hotels with a beach open to all, only a few blocks!

The International marketplace was under construction. It used to be a square about four blocks away with a large park in the middle, stores banking on the left and right, and a dinner theatre in the back, where we saw Don Ho, the "Tiny Bubbles" guy! The area currently under construction was only one square block, surrounded by stores and an open market. We walked up and down the main drag and then explored the market, mostly Chinese vendors selling "collectibles," jewelry, trinkets, and souvenirs.

I also checked out the local KFC, Burger King, and McDonalds. The menus were different, no dollar menus, NOTHING to eat was under $5.00, and quick service………forget about it!! It's not fast food at all, more like, "hope you have time to be patient and wait for your food".

Educating Noah...Travelin'

Back at the hotel we prepared for the second optional tour, the Polynesian Cultural Center Tour. This Center is staffed by students from the Brigham Young University; they work here half a day to offset the cost of tuition. What a great idea! Wouldn't it be nice if the Universities here coupled up with industry? Teaching work ethic, fiscal responsibility, and business and entertainment skills!

It was a three-quarter hour drive, and we spent a total of eight hours! We met another tour guide who kept control of our group of 30 plus folks in this 42-acre park. Many varieties of plants, flowers, trees and shrubs though out the park.

First, to a viewing stand along a river where we witnessed the Rainbows of Paradise show, consisting of six canoes each representing different Polynesian villages (cultures) including Samoa, New Zealand, Fiji, Tahiti, Tonga, and Hawaii, their type of dance, dress and music.

After the show, we move to a stage where we were shown a dance, coconut shelling, music, a performer climbing a palm tree, and some comic relief.

Next to a theatre where we watched an IMAX show, showing the forming of the islands, the arrival of the different people to the islands, and the Polynesian cultural mix that was the basis of the people in Hawaii.

After the IMAX show we went on a canoe ride down the river to the villages, where several representative cultures were displayed, in one of the meeting houses, we were lectured on the Samoan building, where the chief would sleep, which doors were used for whom, (different door for different types of people) and typical meals, and how they were prepared. Moving along, we were then conducted to a dining hall, buffet style with a huge salad bar, including Huila salad, island dishes including Teriyaki Mahi, Maui blend vegetables, different breads, and an assortment of desserts....... yes, I tried a little of everything, including Poke' which is a fish that is citrus cured similar to Ceviche. EVERYTHING was good-to-excellent, perfectly seasoned and moist!

We had an hour and a half free time to discover the shops around the theatre, so off we went. Lynn and I split up agreeing on a time to meet and where, so then I went to the henna tattoo place to get my tattoo, a warrior facial tattoo, which turned out like the real one Mike Tyson has. I had a lot of fun with it, a lot of second looks from others, especially in our group, amazingly accepted by most, even the kids! I kept it for three days, and then I scrubbed it off with soap and sand. I was even asked if I came from New Zealand by a bus driver, which I answered "Aye Mate"!

We met as arranged, Lynn liked the tattoo; the best $15.00 I ever spent, and yes, we took a photo! We met up with the group at the designated area, and went in to see the show, in our reserved seating section. This show, "Ha: Breath of Life" a story of passion and love through dance, song and fire, about a family that came to the Islands, accepted by the natives, and the life cycle of the boy born to the family. The show was very colorful, dramatic, and promoted openness, acceptance, and family values. A well-presented show, professional, flawless and well-practiced.

We were out of the show at 9:00 P.M. easily found our bus, and shuttled back to the hotel, what a great full day!

Day 5 Tuesday

Tuesday morning flight to Kauai (the oldest of the islands) about 45 minutes away but we left early in the morning by 7:00 AM on a bus and off to the airport. We arrived at the airport, checked in, took about two hours to wait for the airplane. Thirty-five minutes later we landed, they served a small drink on the plane. YMT took care of the luggage, we just got on the plane after TSA checks (Trusted traveler not honored, but I am used to the frisk!), we got off the plane, met the group, and loaded the bus. The YMT package included a tour of the Island, Kauai is known as the Garden Island. We briefly witnessed the Opaeka falls, then off to the Wailua River Marina. Here we boarded a boat to cruise up the river through lush foliage on both sides of the banks. The trip to the Fern Grotto was a very nice leisurely forty minutes. Upon reaching a dock, we disembarked and walked through lush forest to the Fern Grotto. At the Grotto, we were treated to song and a dance by a small quartet. After the show, we progressed via a different path through the foliage to our waiting boat, to be ferried back to the bus. We even were treated to a duo with song and dance on the trip back, what a nice bonus!

Landmarks, as always were pointed out with a running commentary by the excellent bus driver, of where some movies were shot, even a story about Frank Sinatra getting caught in a rip tide!

We were driven to a shopping center where there were several restaurants and a food store for those who wanted food in their room. An hour and a half later we were driven to our beach hotel for the next three nights. Nice place, two outdoor pools, and right on the water!

We were warned that there was a severe rip tide just off the beach, there was sand but also a lot of coral and volcanic rock, nice to look at but I did not venture into the ocean here!

After returning from my exploration trip, Lynn now rested, we went exploring outside the motel complex. We knew of a small shopping mall down the road, and after exploring the shops, Lynn was starting to give out. Just 100 yards back was a luxury hotel with a dining room, so we decided to treat ourselves.

We sat at the bar, I had a specialty Martini, and Lynn had a cranberry juice. We talked to a few guests and the bartender, one of the guests was from our home town of Milwaukee.

We were then seated, had a wonderful meal, the house special fish for me, (WOW), and Lynn had lobster and goat cheese stuffed wontons with a plum sauce, she says WOW also, we actually bragged about the food to all the others in our group the rest of the time on this island. After that fantastic meal, we waddled back to our room.

Day 6 Wednesday

Two optional tours signed up for, the Waimea Canyon Tour, from 8:00 A.M. to 1:00 P.M., and the Smith's Hawaiian Luau from 4:30-9:00 P.M... A breakfast was offered at this hotel consisting of bagels, and sweet rolls along with coffee and juice, and bananas; so, I made up a bagel for us to share and a juice for Lynn when I returned from my morning walk. (I got a very nice picture of the sunrise, so you can see it in the album.) The bus loaded and took off promptly at 7:55 A.M.

Again, our driver was extremely knowledgeable, her name was Nani, she must be in her seventies, and she seemed to know everyone at all the stops, she was fantastic! Running commentary with a flair! Our first stop was the Hanapepe lookout.

After spending a half hour there including a restroom break, we proceeded to the Spouting Horn, where the surf comes up through the volcanic rock. We witnessed it a number of times, trying to catch the spout with the camera.

Next, we took a winding narrow road to the Grand Canyon of the Pacific, named that by Mark Twain. The canyon is about ten miles long, 3,000 feet deep, shows various colors, shades of greens, browns, and orange, and has a wonderful waterfall, and we didn't see a rainbow today, but we did see one on the helicopter tomorrow!

We stopped at the Kauai Coffee Company for more samples, a sandwich, and information on coffee growing, and varieties of coffee offered, a nice relaxing break before heading for the hotel.

Some information on this Island; It is the oldest Island of the eight islands known as Hawaii; it has one half with the most rain in the

Pacific if not the world, while the other half has considerably less. (All of these islands have a rainy side and a dry side; this was the rainiest!) South Pacific was filmed here, along with segments of Fantasy Island, among many other movies. There is one highway that circumvents the island, and it is mostly a two-lane road. There are about 600,000 people on this Island; there are more than a million cars.

We were dropped off at the hotel; Lynn went to the room to rest, and I went for a walk and swam in the pool. Lynn came out later to sunbathe and talk to others, and then we got dressed for the Smith's Luau.

Today was a perfect day, it was warm but not too humid, no rain today, which was surprising but it might come back because rain comes and goes and it will shower really hard for 15-20 minutes, then it'll wean off, and then go away.

We opted for this Luau because it is supposed to be the best of all the Luaus; it has not only Polynesian food but has Japanese and Korean! So, we were really kinda looking forward. This was little pricier but it includes all drinks, food, and entertainment, it ought to be interesting.

At about 4:30 P.M., we got together again and went to the luau. It's on 30 acres of land. The trip was only a 15-20-minute bus ride. The park has ponds, all different kinds of the local flora and fauna everything, in blossom. After a greeting with a Lei and a picture, we loaded onto a trolley, which took us around the entire park, showing different areas of interest, the restrooms, the arena, and the food service area. After that, we waited for the ceremony to remove the pigs out of the pit. This is called the Imu. The ceremony with the blowing of the horns, and the drama of uncovering the pig, presenting it to the crowd and then conveying it to the kitchen.

There were 400 people attending. As we entered the open covered area, we were directed to the Mai Tai table, the soft drink table, and a bar for special drinks and beer. There were three bar tenders tending the Mai Tai table, constantly restocking, most people taking two drinks. The people at each table were brought up when called, two buffet tables with two lines per table, moving quickly, well stocked, and another great variety of choices! In forty-five minutes, we were all finishing our desserts! Plenty to drink and eat, (all you wanted in both), then the announcement to progress to the open-air show arena.

The show lasted a good hour, had a great variety of cultures represented by the islands, was very colorful, and had a great production. After the show, we walked out to our waiting bus and back to the hotel at 10:00 p.m., another full and interesting day!

Day 7 Thursday

Early morning walks, stop at the room, and pick up Lynn, down to the breakfast room for coffee and juice plus roll because today is the 7:30 a.m. pickup for the Kauai Helicopter Tour.

We were told to wear dark clothes, so we did. We were driven to the airport, where we were dropped off at the heliport. We signed in and were assigned to a 6-person group. The previous day, we were asked what our weight was for weight distribution (I'm glad I lost that weight; any passenger weighing greater than 260 pounds is charged an additional $120.00!).

We were assigned seats on the helicopter. We watched a film on safety, issued float vests and instructed on how to use them. I wasn't happy with my seat assignment back and middle, but I was told that all seats had great visibility and not to worry. Our group of 6 were called out to the pad and lined up according to number. We then were assisted to the chopper, assisted in buckling in, and ready to lift off. My position was behind the pilot and Lynn was on the outside seat next to the left window. (I had to lean across her for all the pictures I took, and the pilot favored the other (right) side for dipping and picture taking.) However, it was a good experience, we circled the entire island, witnessed the Na Pali coast, saw great waterfalls, (including the view of "Jurassic Falls") flew into the crater, flew through VOG, explored Mount Waialeale, the wettest spot-on earth, with an average of 400-500 inches of rain annually, saw great landscapes, valleys and beaches. The flight lasted about an hour; we had a gentle touchdown, and then waited for the rest to join us, afterwords, a ride home to the hotel.

We were both fired up and wide awake so we took off to a small shopping restaurant complex pointed out by the bus driver about three blocks away. We explored a bakery, an antique store, a hippy café that offered vegan food at outrageous prices, looked at a Korean restaurant, and settled on a pizza for lunch at a pizza place.

We then took a leisurely walk back to the hotel, Lynn insisting that she could walk the 6-8 blocks to the fish restaurant we had passed earlier for another special supper.

I went for another walk along the beach and went swimming in the pool. Lynn rested, sunned herself, and talked to people at the pool. Finally, we decided to walk the walk to the restaurant. Lynn kept up well, especially when she saw the restaurant in the distance, pushed on, and finished at the goal!

The effort was worth it! Drinks here are any simple mixed drink and only $4 bucks! We ordered the Poke' as Hors d'oeuvres, which turned out to be half a fish! The main course for Lynn was a seafood fettuccini with mussels, shrimp, clams, and scallops; I had an Ono burger (Ono is a local fish). Both were excellent! I got the mussels; Lynn got some of my steak fries, and a bite of my fish burger. No room for dessert, the walk home to the hotel was welcome. Packed before going to bed, luggage pick-up at 6:00 A.M.; off to sleep.

Day 8 Friday

Quick breakfast, turned in keys, and on the bus by 7:00 A.M., and off to the airport to Maui, the Valley Isle. YMT took care of the luggage, then the frisking, the two hours wait to get on the plane, the half hour flight then unloads to a waiting bus. Same routine, different day and island.

This morning was another included tour with the package. Back on the bus, we proceeded to Iao valley. This is the definition of lush tropical foliage. We were allowed an hour to explore, a narrow-paved path over a small bridge where the 2000-foot Iao Needle Rock formation could be seen, a waterfall, and tranquil river. Limited hand rails on steep stair cases prevented Lynn to progress any further than across the bridge, but I struggled up to the lookout point, took the photos, then down winding steps to the river, to follow it back to the parking lot. Lots of steps without railings☹, but what a beautiful place!

Everyone was on time meeting back at the bus, we had an option to stop at Bubba Gump's for lunch, a list of choices was sent around so that the order could be called in. When we arrived at the town of Lahaina, a picturesque old whaling capitol of the Pacific, we were given two hours to eat and explore the many shops up and down the main street.

The group, except for three people, had chosen to eat at Bubba Gump's, so that was our first walking stop. I took a picture of one of the waiters carrying mugs of soda. We had our own area assigned and just indicated which dish we had pre-selected and what we wanted to drink. Lynn had the garlic shrimp; I had the fish, and both were very good! The waiter played a game of Gump Trivia with the group. We answered a lot of questions and won a ping pong ball and a bunch of Gump pencils. One question Lynn answered correctly was, "What was Lieutenant Dan's first name?" Hello, a trick question… Dan is the answer.

Then we were off to explore the town and shops. There were some people on the beach with large sieves, I asked them what they were looking for and they explained that this was a good location for sea glass, sea glass is small polished rock that are like crystal, and she was an artist that used the glass in her creations, which we found several in various stores.

We also explored a scrimshaw shop; I was and am fascinated by this old art form. Lynn fell in love with a necklace that had a butterfly wing encased, so I got it for her for Christmas. I found a necklace made out of a walrus tusk with a turtle image on it for myself, so we both made out!

More stores, a couple more T-shirts, then back on the bus to be taken to our new hotel, on another beach for us to enjoy! The Kaanapali beach is one of the best beaches in Hawaii; in December through April the migrating whales can be seen just off shore! We were here too early for the migration; no whales were seen!

Day 9 Saturday

This was scheduled as a leisure day, but we can sit around at home! So, yes, we had another optional tour. This one was an eleven-hour tour called the heavenly Highway to Hana.

Another early departure, this was a three-quarter island tour, fifty plus miles of coastland, over 625 turns! We were on a 16-passenger van, the largest allowed on the road, many (54) one lane bridges that were barely wide enough for the van, sharp hairpin, blind corners.

We stopped after an hour at a lookout, for driver supplied breakfast, (coffee, juice, and doughnuts) he had also provided each woman in the group a flower for her hair at the start! Then off to find scenic beaches, waterfalls, rivers, and blooming plants and trees, everything is growing here!

As we approached noon, we stopped at Wai'anapanapa State Parks black sand beach, I went down to get a sample, feel it and explore a lava tunnel, we then all met at the picnic tables to enjoy box lunches, which were exceptional and included water or juice.

The next stop was the seven sacred pools, more water falls, and more coastlines, greener!

As with the other tour bus drivers, this one was knowledgeable, entertaining, and had a running commentary throughout the entire trip.

He pointed out many of the properties owned by movie and TV stars. Here is a list of a few of them: Bill Bixby, Bill Hanks, Tom Hanks, Woody Haroldson, Oprah, Pat Benitar, Ted Turner, Crazy Al Yankovich, George Harrison, and Bill Dana (José Jimenez), an acre of land here starts at $1 million!

One of the unique things this driver did was at many stops, he provided examples of different fruits, nuts, and seeds for us to eat or feel; he would also pull over to the side of the road for pictures to be taken, at stops, he offered to take pictures of couples in front of various backdrops.

He also relayed the story of Captain Cook, who met his demise on this island. He just happened to come during the season, and the direction as a god was prophesized; he would, on islands (huge ships), have cannons, his hair came off easily (wig), and his hands disappeared on his sides (pockets). What happened?

When he left, he was honored, then he came back, <u>from the wrong direction</u>, when he landed, the native stole one of the row boats (nails were wonderful and completely foreign to them. Cook then captured their king and tortured him, so they had to kill him, "no one touches the king". They killed Cook, burned him (did not eat him) and preserved his ashes as "noble" ashes.

"Mouca" is the mountainside

"Macee" is the seaside

Educating Noah…Travelin'

There are only 12 letters in the Hawaiian language, and all the words end in vowels.

All porta-potties are international…….Russian to get in, European inside, then Finnish when you exit!!

We also made a final stop before heading home to an old general store. Run by the same family since the 1920's. A very quaint, quite small, very friendly person, the register was a hand crank one!

We arrived back at the hotel just after 7 PM, grabbed a small supper, went up to the room to pack, and went to bed.

Day 10 Sunday

October 4, we started out this morning at about 07:00 A.M. in the morning, transferred to the airport to fly twenty-five minutes to Hilo on the island of Hawaii, called the Big Island.

When we arrived in Hilo, we all boarded a bus and took an all-day tour, first, another Macadamia nut company. We were the second bus to stop there. As we looked around the store, five more buses pulled up. I selected the items I wanted, gathered up Lynn, made the purchase, then ushered her to the patio in the back, got into line for two scoops of Macadamia nut ice cream, one chocolate, and the other vanilla, found two of the few remaining chairs and watched as all those tourists crowded into the place designed to handle only 75-100 people at a time!

The next stop was an orchid nursery. So many varieties of orchids and other exotic plants! The colors, the shapes, WOW! What an experience! I took quite a few pictures; I hope the pictures are able to convey even half the vibrant colors we saw!

Next, on the way to Volcanoes National Park, we stopped at Thurston's Lava Tube. (The Hawaiian name is Lahuku) The trail down to the tube is on uneven ground, handrails are absent in many places, and the walk to the tube is about 100 yards. We both wanted to see it. It was very similar to a cave we saw in Australia. The floors were wet, there were puddles, and it was a little slippery. It was a true tube, so you needed to watch your head as you walked the 200-300 ft. total length of the tube. At the end of the tube was a staircase with railings that led up to a trail, another 100 yards back to the parking lot. Yes, I took pictures!

Next stop, the Volcano Park. On the way, I was actually able to remember some of the information given to us. A current hot spot is located in the middle of this island. Lava is at a temperature of 2000 degrees, lava rocks are the most porous rocks on earth, there are millions of lava tubes, magma is underground, and lava is above the ground. Some tubes are 20 feet off the shore of this island; the volcano is 3000 feet below sea level. 1970 was the last blow-out of the caldera we will be visiting. A caldera is an opening two miles in diameter or larger, and craters are less than two miles in diameter.

The islands are moving. Kawai, the oldest, used to be where Midway Island is now; there are 132 total Hawaiian Islands, and the Pacific plate moves 2-4" per year northwest. The big island of Hawaii is the largest of the islands; it is 2 times the mass of the others combined and has the highest mountain in the U.S. Most of this mountain is below sea level, and there is snow on the top!

There are more pigs on this island than people. Many trees in this rain forest area approaching the park will form root bundles up in the branches among the leaves to help absorb moisture and prevent them from drying out.

We arrived in the park and hiked up to the observation deck to observe the smoking, steaming Kilauea Caldera in the Halemaumau Crater. Our driver also showed us what the volcano looks like at night when it flares, which is much more impressive. We toured the Jaggar Museum and Visitors' Center, providing different views, history, and facts. I did take two pictures of a painting that, when looked at from one side, looks different from the other side!

On the way out of the park, we also found steam rising from the ground in a number of areas!

We had lunch at a stop and then continued across the island to our last hotel, the Marriott King Kamehameha's Kona Beach Hotel, late in the afternoon.

Day 11 Monday

The World's Iron man contest will be run here next weekend. The streets are filled with people running and biking, an area of the beach is buoyed off for people swimming back and forth, and the chatter is in different languages and accents!

We had the submarine ride this morning. It was started about 10 o'clock. We first had breakfast; we found a place that actually was $8.95 for breakfast!!

Lynn had the special of two eggs, bacon, and toast, and I had some fried rice. The bill was under $30 for breakfast! (Remember that all European and South American hotels include a full buffet lunch.) This may seem almost incredible here, but you can tell that I'm a little disappointed with Hawaii. We are just about Hawaii-ed out! We have one more luau tomorrow night, which we paid for before we found out that it was basically the same as the other two we've been to; it's the same dancing and probably the food.

The submarine ride was close, right on the end of the pier next to the hotel. We walked out, waited for a while, and then entered a shuttle boat that took us out to the submarine. When we reached the submarine, we crossed over and climbed down the ladder into the hull. The submarine is electric; we went for a cruise and were down from 72-100 feet, then 1020 feet under the ocean.

It was kind of nice there, cool and quiet, but there were an awful lot of kids! Lots of "Oohs" and "Ahhhs." We saw a number of fish, nothing really large, no stingrays or sharks, but we saw a lot of feeder fish, and we viewed three wrecks. It was kind of interesting; they even had a make-believe skeleton tied down to one of the wrecks, funny! The tour lasted about an hour and a half; it was well worth it.

We were back on shore, went walking down the beach, watched the people swim and bike, and went past the new vendors setting up specifically for the marathon.

It is very hot and humid, and everything clings to our bodies for fifteen minutes outside. We came back to the room and had snack bars for the little lunch we brought from home; the rest of the afternoon, I went for a swim for about 20-25 minutes and had my saltwater treatment, and Lynn took a nap.

I then came back, changed, and we got ready for the Booze Cruise at 5:00 P.M.

Most of the people in our group signed up for this, and the boat was only ¾ full; Marathon people don't drink or stay out late, especially this close to the race!

The drinks started being served as we left the dock; the food was excellent. Chicken and beef, chicken was boneless, very flavorful, full salad, mixed vegetables with eggplant and asparagus and zucchini, was followed up with three or four different kinds of mixed drinks and all-you-can-drink beer and wine.

During the entire cruise, a duo was playing tunes, and a dancer would dance to a few songs, changing her costume with each different song. There was plenty of room on the boat, very comfortable. We sailed to a specific area where stingrays fed, hoping to see a few through the glass bottom. We couldn't find stingrays, nothing but a few garfish! So, I went up on the front and looked over the bow; there were a bunch of gars zooming around on the surface, and then all of a sudden, I saw a stingray, about six feet across, coming right at the boat from the front starboard! As he glided under the boat, I could hear the "Oohs" and "Ahhhs" from the others as he passed under the glass. I was too slow to get a picture; everything happened too fast! Anyhow, we watched a show they had, one hula girl and two musicians, and we danced along with her. Actually, I went to the dance with the little girl and with Lynn. Everybody seemed to have a good time, and we did a conga line just before we came into shore. It was a lot of fun. Lynn enjoyed herself a lot! It was a nice evening; we only had two more days left in Hawaii, so it was a good way to start winding down.

Day 12 Tuesday

This morning, we went snorkeling. Again, the boat left from the pier right outside of our hotel! We were at the boat by 08:00 AM and boarded; there were not too many from our group, just us and another couple. They gave us a little breakfast and later a nice lunch, and we got out there. We had the option to upgrade, and so I took the upgrade to SNUBA. This is snorkeling with a hose. The hose is connected to a scuba tank in a small raft.

Of everyone on the boat, four of us signed up and paid the additional $85.00 for the opportunity! We received our briefing, and the other guy from our group backed out. So, then there were three! The other two were doctors from the mainland, and they asked if I would share the pictures that I took with my underwater camera; of course, I agreed, and I got their e-mail.

We were first to go in when we arrived at the snorkel point. We received our gauge flippers and washed out our masks. Since I was the only one who had scuba-ed before I was first in the water, I then hung onto my tank raft until he (the dive master) hooked me up and gave me the O.K. sign.

The other two then came in, and he attached them up. We were off, or kinda…the wind was picking up, the water was choppy, and we were in about 50 feet of water. We could just make out the bottom, like in the sub. Only a few small fishes could be made out. Besides that, our rafts got tangled, our hoses also wrapped, and then the rafts tangled up with the snorkeling buoys.

There were no really good underwater shots, but I did get some picks of the couple. He was having difficulties and went to the surface a few times; she had no difficulties. At the end of our half-hour of air, we were all being dragged by our hoses toward the boat. The dive master indicated that our air was just about gone, so we surfaced and swam to the boat. The dive master unhooked us, gathered and untangled the rafts and hoses, and we all got back on the boat.

The winds were accelerating, the boat bobbing, causing a number of guests and snorkelers to get seasick. It was so rough Lynn had not gone into snorkel due to the waves and chop; I grabbed some grub and secured a seat in the front of the boat, being warned that the waves may come over the bow, which I had no problem with! I sent Lynn to the back to prevent her from getting sick or wet.

The captain called in all the others that were in the water; the waves were getting too high, the sea too rough, and a storm was coming fast! We pulled anchor and headed back as fast as we could. Yes, I did get a couple doses of water, but it was refreshing!

Back to the dock, safe and sound, we went walking through the town, watching the kid Iron Man qualifiers and the new vendors, selling shoes, bike parts, slick suits, and souvenirs. We returned to the hotel in time to change and meet down on the beach for our final farewell to King Kamehameha's Farewell feast.

Since we had the largest group signed up for the feast, we were seated before others. An open bar was set up at 5:15, and the programs started at 5:30. A procession from the harbor to the stage kicked off the program. Separate classes offered included palm leaf fish making, henna tattoos, and Hawaiian dance lessons. Everyone stocked up on more drinks as we were called back at dusk.

Tables were called to a double buffet line. Salad, salmon, poke, poi, three bean salad, chicken, pork, shredded pork, and loaves of bread, all hot, all delicious, and all you could eat. After dinner, a dessert table was put out, and that, too, was as much as you care to eat. A dinner show followed, dance, men only, men and women, with and without fire.

9:30 P.M. ended the event, we all went back to our rooms, and tomorrow was "go home" day.

Day 13 Wednesday

I was not happy with our guide or YMT. We had to check out at 11:00 A.M., and our pick-up for the airport was at 6:00 p.m. Our checked luggage was taken care of by YMT, but what about our carry-ons?

Most of us had PM return flights; an optional activity would have been nice, at least offered! One of the other couples extended their room for another day and gave me a key so we could put our carry-on in their room, which I gladly accepted. I asked when they were going out for lunch and asked if we could join them.

Later, we were told that arrangements were made to store the carry-ons, but I guess that was announced at the meeting scheduled during our snorkel event; not too professional on our guide's part!

Anyway, we had lunch with the couple that extended the room, and I picked up the tab.

We walked around, lounged around the hotel until 6:00 P.M., then boarded the bus, checked in with the airline, and waited in the open-air waiting area for the 8:30 P.M. boarding time and 9:30 P.M. flight out.

A six-hour flight to LAX had only one hour between flights; our tickets had the wrong gate printed, so we ran to another terminal only to find that the gate was changed to the terminal where we came in. So, we ran back, got there about ten minutes before they started boarding, and then boarded. We arrived in Milwaukee at 1:30 P.M. our time. Neither of us had any sleep on the plane, plus we had been up 12 hours before our flight. We're glad to be home. Hawaii is nice, but we like the change in seasons, and it is way too expensive!

The last wrap-up month. I explored an alternative program to lose the additional sixty pounds; I want to be in the 180's by the time I'm finished, and to date, with the holiday meals and the cold weather, the calories have increased, the exercise decreased, and the angst is what I feared! The program was very similar to Nutri-fast, with

Noah

acupuncture and shakes added, but I can do this myself; I just have to get pissed enough!

I hate this! I don't like being afraid to step on the scale, feel guilty when I eat a whole sandwich or eat starches! Enough…again!

I am in the 240 to 250# range, vowed to restart monitoring daily in 2016, committing to more frequent gym visits, and drinking more volumes of water.

I am not keeping myself busy enough. I looked into day trading with an outfit called Online Trading Academy. I attended another session of introduction in 2012; however, they would not disclose the cost unless I attended an additional three days of orientation. I smelled something fishy! After waiting a few weeks, I watched the zip drive provided, which was just another sales pitch.

I sent a fiery e-mail to On-Line expressing the problem I had with the zip drive promising lessons and then getting a zip with sales pitches, asking to answer two questions: how much for the course, and then the specialty in Forex trading. After two days, I got my answer: $2,000 for the course and $7,000 for the specialty. I was willing to gamble ten thousand but not willing to pay $9,000 of it on education!

I will be calling AAA regarding driving for Uber next year!

Tiffany was to set up at her new place, Mike keeps the house and bought out Tiffany, Cruz is bounced between the two households, and all three are slowly adjusting to new circumstances.

I have five slots assigned for vacation already for 2016 and 2017: South Caribbean, Greece, Iceland, Russia, and Antarctica, with a two-week road trip in August to travel the Road to the Sun, Canada and U.S. Glaciers, and Vancouver Island.

My mother is having increased trouble with her eyes. She is losing sight in one of them and may lose her good eye. We are seeing specialists monthly. She has gone through two minor operations in the last 3 months, and I will accompany her in January. I filled in Ted. Hopefully, he will come up so that she can see him before anything happens with her site.

Chapter four
2016

2016 Southern Caribbean Cruise, January 27, 2016.

We left on Sunday; we were going to leave on Sunday because the aircraft leaves at 7 o'clock in the morning on Monday. With Wisconsin weather, we didn't want to risk it, we would have to get up at 3AM to take a bus get down to O'Hare by 5:45AM, it would be just too many chances we didn't want take.

Sunday morning

I called to confirm the airline. When I printed the tickets, all of a sudden, our seats were different, changed from 27 E and F to 30B and 32B, two crappy seats farther back, in the middle, and not together!!

I tried to call after printing, however, what happened was I was put on hold because of a big snowstorm on East Coast. They were being flooded with phone calls, after 45 minutes I gave up, I figure I would call later. I next called Coach USA to make sure there was room to leave the car as we always take the Coach USA down to Chicago and back.

I dropped Lynn and the luggage by the door, Lynn got the slip of paper you put on the dash, and I pulled the car around the back and locked her up.

We were waiting at 2:45 PM, and the bus, on schedule, picked us up at 3:00 o'clock. It took us an hour and twenty minutes to get down to the O'Hare Hilton.

In the morning, I had checked us in and indicated that we would arrive between four and five PM. We checked into the O'Hare Hilton and went to our room. I opened the door and found the bed was not made, sheets and pillows on the floor, and a bathroom with towels on the floor. I went over to the phone and called. The operator apologized and told me she would give us an upgraded room and would send up a bellhop with a new key.

The bellhop arrived and handed over a key to the new room, on the opposite side, and supposedly an upgrade. I guess that an upgrade is a chair. Everything else was the same except that the thermostat was 70 degrees, but the room felt like 60! I cranked the thermostat to 80, and we went downstairs to get something to eat.

One sandwich with chips and a drink, was $15.00. We took our meal to the room, it was a little warmer, but next to the windows the wind was howling and it was cold! I tried calling the Airline again, and this time I stayed on the phone. It took 50 minutes before I got a live person. I explained my dilemma, she said she couldn't do anything for me, but just see the counter clerk to change the seats back, I said O.K. and trusted that she would take care of things on her end.

By the time we hit the hay, it was livable, but still was kind 'a cool; so, after that we couldn't sleep much that night and we were up-and-down, with potty breaks, we finally got up about three- three thirty, packed our bags, called the front desk, told her we were going to check out, and asked if I should just leave the key in the room; she said O.K. and go, so we left the room and went over to terminal one, the United Airline kiosks in terminal one.

I checked in on in the kiosk, then and I wanted to check about these seats. We went over to the counter person and ask about having the seats changed. The counter person said I would have to do this at the gate, so we proceeded through the TSA checkpoint. I had to go through the tunnel because my hip and my knees!

After the check and small pat down, we headed for the gate. I did some walking; we are now at the gate, two hours before loading so I walked; Lynn sat down with the carry-ons and read. I found a chocolate croissant and milk for Lynn. This made her breakfast.

About 45 minutes before the plane was to take off, the gate person finally came up. I waited till she settled in and I walked up, explained my dilemma, let her know about the last night's conversation, and that I was unhappy with these crummy seats. She told me "I'm sorry sir but our plane is full and I can't do anything for you. The phone representative didn't know that this was the plane was full. There is nothing I can do."

We were stuck with the seat change, we were stuck in the back of the plane, between others, these are fill in seats, last one to be filled, we were also the last loading group, so there was no carry-on space left in the bins!

But it was only a two-hour flight so we just grinned and bared it.

At Fort Lauderdale, we retrieved our luggage, found the person from the Holland Cruise Line and set out for the bus. Our bus came, actually drove past us first, and had to circle the airport to come back. It was only about a 20-minute drive to the port. We got off the bus, then another line, another half an hour to get up to the check-in counters for our picture I.D. cards.

We checked in, found our cabin, and checked out the dining room seating. This was different from the other cruise lines, here we had open seating, where you show up between 5:15 to 9:00 o'clock and they'll find you a table, either for two or a group.

They took our luggage right from the bus and delivered to our cabin; that takes a few hours, Lynn was tired and hungry, we went up to the Lido cafeteria to grab some pizza slices, then I dropped her off at the room and I went exploring the ship forward and aft, found which the decks had what to offer, checked out the dining room, checked out what was going on with the bars, the main desk, locations of all of the elevators.

They offered a martini tasting at 5:00; three different martinis for $9.00, a great deal and a chance to taste different drinks, so yeah, I was in, three different kinds martinis that are mostly a Caribbean rum and vodka. Lynn met me after the tasting, and then to the dining room, for dinner.

We had very nice dinners, I had the red snapper, Lynn had a pork chop with cherry sauce and polenta, and green beans. Each had a small dessert. We were seated with two couples from Canada, very interesting, very good conversation. We discovered more of the ship, our room being in the bow, restaurant in the stern, both of us tired since we got up at 3 o'clock in morning and we have the jet skis tomorrow, we unpacked, showered and went to bed.

Tuesday, Half Moon Cay, Bahamas

This is a private island owned by the shipping line. I think it is a shared island but it was flying a Holland America flag. Since we signed up for jet skis today, we went on a first shuttle ferry. Most of the folks were confused and disoriented.

So, we basically just walked down the glass staircase; went down to the lower deck and walked onto the ferry. After loading, the ride was about seven to ten minutes into the bay. We got off, checked in with information booth; confirmed our reservation, we were an hour early, so we had 45-minutes to explore the island. We walked around on the beach, it is a gorgeous beach with all the different hues of the ocean.

It's a big sandy beach and since we're the first ones there, very quiet, and perfect sand, not a footprint! So, we walked the beach and then we checked out the souvenir shop, of course Lynn found some earrings and a couple things that we wanted to pick up, a deck of cards for my mom, a thimble for my boss, a bracelet for a daughter, and so on.

Back to the staging area for the jet ski people. Off we went in an open truck down the beach to a cove, we were the only two on the first excursion so we had a guide, we had a guy who followed us behind, and us. The jet skis were some of the larger ones, 135 HP, we were fitted with life jackets, given instructions as to how to operate the machines, pushed out into the bay, and told to play a little with the skis to orient ourselves and meet out at the buoy.

After a few minutes, the leader came out, Lynn followed him, and I followed her, a tail-gunner followed me. We went all over the bay back and forth, in circles and zigzagged. Once we got our sea legs, we actually went out into the ocean, the waves were four and six feet high, we were flying these things, and Lynn got scared and throttled down, but she was a good trooper, and she stayed on her jet ski. We didn't stay out there because we were getting battered pretty badly. We came back into the bay, did a couple more zigzags and loops. We were out a good hour and a quarter, got sprayed with a lot of seawater, had a great experience, and followed our guide back to the beach.

There was another couple now waiting, I asked them about anyone else, they thought they were the last, so out of some 2000 people on the boat, only four opted for the jet skis, not too many people went snorkeling, we only saw a dozen or so in the water, this seems like an older crowd, but we had fun!

The ship had a barbecue on the island. Chicken, mahi-mahi, short ribs, hamburgers and hotdogs. Salads, a seafood salad, potato salads, all kinds of fruit salads, and fruits.

We had our fill, walked the island some more, and then we took the ferry back to the ship by about 1:00 P.M. We had a trivia at 2:00 P.M. found some folks to join us, and placed pretty high, won the first of token prizes.

Wednesday, January 27

This is an at sea day, which means no port, as we head for Aruba. I took some pictures of Cuba, way off in the distance and it basically looks like a Misty Island. We also saw a squall out in the distance and took pictures of the storm off in the distance. I realize that many haven't seen this so I took some shots for the album.

We had breakfast, went through our programs, we get two daily programs and decide what each is going to do and arrange times for lunch and joint activities. We decided to meet for the coffee chat with the cruise director, to find out about him and how he got into the business. After that we went to a culinary course on spices and foods put on by the chef. The room was crowded, very interesting and we learned a little more.

Lunch was at the cafeteria, a great selection including an awesome salad bar and SUCHI!!!

During lunch, we went out on the back deck to enjoy the steel pan player, Kevin. He was so good and so entertaining, the island music with the steel drums, I actually bought an album! At 1 o'clock there was a cooking show, we attended, received a number of great recipes, and again the culinary room was overflowing.

The next event was a mixology course that gave recipes for three exotic drinks and of course we had samples! Next, yes, we are pretty busy on these cruises.... you can always relax and sleep at home!

The steel pan player offered a session on playing the steel pan drums, and both of us wanted to try our hand; we were a little late, but we watched seven passengers try their hands at rhythm with drums! Both of us decided right then and there that we would come earlier the next time the lessons were offered to try our hands! After the session, we cornered him and asked if he would be doing this again; he said "yes," so I bought him a beer and told him to watch out for us!

Lynn then went off to a Tanzanite seminar, Tanzanite (was created by the ocean to oceans colliding and it's around the foot of Mount Kilimanjaro, three deposits, one is almost totally empty and only two left, she also found out about Amalite, turns out to be shells of a sea animal under pressure found only in Canada).

I went off for a walk around the ship, both of us agreeing to meet for the afternoon trivia. There was the time change today and with what happens was at 3 o'clock we all moved our clocks ahead another hour so then all the paperwork and set up for tomorrow would work, and no complaints about getting up too late!

What would become a routine for the rest of the cruise, we attended a trivia session, change for dinner, Martini tasting, dinner, trivia, show, then Lynn got sick, motion sickness, rough seas, so we took her to the cabin, got her green apples, ginger ale, and put her to bed. I completed the routine of going to the B.B. King Lounge and followed it up with the disco area.

So, it was an early night for me and of course a really early night for Lynn, she's been a little better and hopefully should be a lot better tomorrow because tomorrow we go on shore for our first ostrich farm!

Thursday, January 28; Cranjestad, Aruba!

We were supposed to enter port at 1:00 P.M. but due to the rough seas and wind (70 MPH Gale force winds), we were two hours late, the arrival time was moved to 3:00 P.M.

Breakfast, smoked salmon has become my breakfast of choice, Lynn is having different egg preparations. We split up, I am going to another coffee with the operations manager (of the 900 employees on the ship he is in charge of 400, kitchen and housekeeping staff), Lynn went another jewelry seminar. We met for morning trivia, and we won! Lunch was Sushi and some rice noodles, Lynn had pork and gruyere-cheesy potatoes, just to give you a hint of the offerings!

We toured the decks, listened to more steel pan music, and prepared for the shore excursion, now at 3:00 P.M.

We jumped on our bus, and our first stop was an ostrich farm. At the ostrich farm, we met our guide named Gina and she told us that we're in the middle of, guess what, mating season for ostriches!

On this ranch, there are two kinds of birds, ostriches and emus. An emu egg is about 1-2 pounds (blue) with ostrich eggs at 5 pounds (whiter).

It takes 42 days for the egg (ostrich) to hatch; the females lay the eggs, and then the males sit on the eggs, rotating them every so many hours. The females can have eggs once every five days! That male is busy! Sit on eggs, rotate eggs, fertilize another female, sit on the eggs, ETC. they must be exhausted after a couple of months!! (Mating season is from August to March) The fresh ostrich eggs can withstand up to 300 pounds on top of it.

I got to feed a few ostriches, you basically back into them holding a bowl of seeds about belly high. They look around you when you get close to the fence, and then they peck like crazy in this bowl, their necks are really kind of soft but there they really want that food, so you can have your fingers, anything close, can get jabbed! Hold tight!!

After that we went on a drive through the island and got some history. As the guide was talking to us, he told all about Aruba. Aruba is actually 19 miles from Venezuela and it used to be that two Dutch men would transport freshwater, because it's all coral and rock. Now Aruba has the world's second largest diesel DE-saltation plant in the world. Fourteen million gallons a day! Everyone is allocated so many gallons a month at one rate, if they use more, the rates go very high! Power is a by-product of de-saltation, so the company wins two ways, with the water bill sometimes exceeding the power bill!

The winds on Aruba are always out of the Northeast, always, they don't change, they have a certain plant called the DI VI DI VI (dee vee) tree. Which always goes from northeast to southwest so if you look at the tree where the main branch comes, the rest of the tree points to the southwest so everyone on the island always knows which direction they are going. Also, the ocean, when you see light blue means white sand underneath, the dark blue means coral underneath. We learned in Hawaii also that the parrotfish are the creatures that create sand. One fish can generate 1 ton of sand a year so they're lucky they have a lot of parrotfish! Great white sand beaches!

The next stop used to be a natural bridge, but it collapsed in 2005. (Naturally??) Luckily it collapsed at night. Some more cracks are forming by the bridge so they're thinking that more of the bridge will collapse soon. There were a lot of little stones piled on other stones, very similar to the ones we saw in Norway, the guide said he didn't understand the meaning, so we explained that back in Norway we were told they were totems for people to return to later on in life.

Next stop was the Cassie Barry rock formation. Of course, I climbed it! There were no railings on the first side, that was kind of a challenge, then the steps were uneven in height and length, stoop through rocks, narrow passageway, and steep! But I made it to the top! Lynn saw me, I took some pictures so I can verify I was there, luckily, on the way back down, there were railings! I posed with the Blues Brothers down below, Lynn posed with an old truck and off we went!

The next stop was a 1913 lighthouse (California Lighthouse) that was being completely renovated; the keepers house now a restaurant.

On the way, back to the pier, I took some pictures of the beach. We went through the high-end of Aruba where all in the big expensive hotels were, we stopped at the beach. Aruba has the second-best beach in the world, seems like their second best in beaches and De-Saltation.

One of these beaches is also known for the sea turtles. They come in to lay their eggs, the water is very shallow, you can walk out in the water for 100 meters, and the water is still only chest high. So, a lot of people go there.

The last thing we learned, was that in Aruba you go to school and you learn four languages. The child begins with the local language, (popliteal) then they learn Dutch, because all the school books are in Dutch so they learn Dutch. By fourth grade the students are proficient in Spanish and English also, makes you think about our system!

We finished up the day on the ship by eating dinner, participating in Name That Tune, sat for a set at the BB King lounge, and attending a special show put on at 11 P.M. by the Filipino Crew Show. It was a great show, put on by the staff with cultural dances and singing, nicely done and very informative.

Friday the 29th

We woke up and went to breakfast. The ship was already docked at the pier in Willemstad, Curacao. Our excursion today started early, we were off the ship at 8:15, and were the first for our tour to line up so we got to talk to the guide while waiting for the rest to straggle off the ship.

We drove out of town over the Queen Julianna bridge that spans the inlet which is also the tallest bridge in the Caribbean. We noted the above ground grave yards here, the multicolored small row houses on the way to our second ostrich farm encounter. The weather is in the 80's it is comfortable.

At this farm, (largest ostrich farm outside of Africa) they had ostriches, emus, pot-bellied pigs, and a few crocodiles. We toured the farm, in an old military open truck, getting off a number of places for closer looks at the animals and interact with them. Both Lynn and I actually stood on top of an ostrich egg, it was about three or four weeks-old, wasn't fertile so they were going to basically just drill it and then save the shell to sell in the souvenir shop.

The easiest way to tell the difference, besides size, between ostriches and emus is the number of toes, ostriches have two per foot, emus three. We also got to watch a male go into an allegro theatrical dance; a dance to frighten others away. He spread his wings, ducks and rolls his body and neck, back and forth, quite a show. As we passed by other ostriches, it looked like a pouch was in the lower portion of the neck. What it was, is water, the ostrich will gulp down a large amount of water at a watering hole quickly, then run to where it is safe, then swallow, it's a natural safety adaptation.

Many of the ostriches had missing feathers in the backside. It seems they pluck each other's feathers and eat them for the calcium in them. (Watch your butt!!)

At the main building, it was too early to try eating an ostrich egg, but I did get a great shirt, and Lynn got a nice picture.

Next was the Aloe Vera farm. This island is perfect for this plant, originally imported form the far east. We sat through a presentation on how the plant is stripped for its product, this was the purist form of the "miracle plant" and Lynn scarfed up a bunch of aloe products for her, the daughters, and friends.

We had the pleasure of a "question and answer" period driving back to the pier. Curacao was conquered by the Spanish, looking for gold, silver, and gems, there was none; only giant natives (six-foot-seven-foot) compared to the Spanish low 5 feet tall.

This island was known as a "worthless land of giants".

The Spanish enslaved the natives, decimated the population from 300,000 to 600, in a matter of 100 years due to the disease the Spaniards brought with them; sound familiar? When the Dutch came, they saw value in the ports, they realized that this natural harbor was the biggest natural harbor in the Caribbean, no major storms, a warm climate perfect for a European to South American trading port. They engaged the natives, educated them, and employed them to construct the infrastructure.

This island, like Aruba, has no fresh water, the land is all volcanic rock and stone. Here too, is a large de-saltation plant, here too, the graves are above ground. We asked about the bright multi-colored homes and buildings. We heard a similar version in Aruba of a governor claiming migraines from the brightness of the buildings and the constant sun, recommended that everyone paint their business and home any color but white. Later afterwards, there was a rumor that the governor had "very friendly" relations' with the paint companies.

Upon returning to the pier, Lynn and I set off to explore the city. Lynn really wanted to walk the pontoon bridge that closed behind our ship. "The shaky grandma bridge" this extended a good 100 yards across the inlet. When ships came in, it would swing in to one side, and let the ships and tugs in. There is a flagpole on the end of the bridge, if there is no flag, the bridge will only be open for a few minutes, if there is an orange flag, it will be open 15-30 minutes, if a blue flag, it will be open for an hour or more. When the bridge is open, two ferries' go back and forth to facilitate pedestrian traffic, actually the bridge does not support vehicles except for bicycles.

We took a ferry over to the other side after exploring the stores on the ship side. There was only a short wait, the ferry filled up quickly, and the transit took less time than the loading. Once across we explored the shops, vendors, and Lynn found the stores that offered the coupons, then I took over and haggled with the salespeople for the best price. After we had our fill of shopping, the pontoon bridge was open again, and we walked back to the ship side over the bridge. Yes, it did sway and rose and lowered with the water waves. We did take pictures! Back on the ship, sail away party with harbor lights, steel drums, 80 degrees at 10:30 at night! (In January!!)

January 30, Saturday another day at sea. It's warm, it's humid. One of the first things we want to do is make sure we have a steel pan lesson, the steel drums you see in the Caribbean with Kevin the performer. We showed up 45 minutes before it was scheduled and of course, a couple people tried to step in front of us (many on cruise ships are oblivious to what is going around them, some, just plain rude or stupid!) but we got two of the seven openings for the introductory lesson.

For 40 minutes, we practiced playing. It is very interesting; it's like the inside of a turtle shell, and since mine was damaged and out of tune, I had to play the inside dents, which would be the sharp notes;

We played a four-sequence note pattern a number of times, then another four-note sequence, then another, and finally the fourth sequence until all of us had it down. We then put them all together with him leading for a song! It sounded pretty good! As a final song, we all played our sequences, and he added background to the song. All of us left smiling, what a great experience.

After the lesson, we joined others on that deck to a session of "name that tune" and invited Kevin, the entertainer to join us, we even bought him a beer. After the game, we talked, and got his background, he gave us a little history on the knowing how long he's been playing the drums; he's only 24 years old, he's been playing drums since he was 15. He has a girlfriend, enjoys what he does, and enjoys traveling all over the place. One drum cost about $1200, then you have to buy the stand and everything else. When one of these drums goes out of tune, re-bending them costs about 250 bucks; so, he's very careful on how he handles those drums. You don't throw your sticks in the drum! He was a very interesting fellow, friendly and open.

We had a small lunch with the salads; and of course, they always have sushi.

Off to the Queens lounge to learn to practice up on our cha-cha's. The lounge was crowded, being a sea day, and those not hogging the sun on deck looked for something to do. The ship swaying, a lot of un-practiced people, lots of bumping and amazing how many folks this age can't do a simple cha-cha!

We then went for a bean bag toss by one of the pools; We played two games one team won one, the other won the second, no time for a rubber match, so we all got a prize!

Educating Noah...Travelin'

We checked out other activities, then decided on just a cafeteria supper, play another trivia, see the highlight of the day, Safira, two dueling sisters on violins, WOW, what talent, and a great show! We listened to the Blues and checked out the disco to finish up the day.

Sunday, January 31, 2016, this was Columbia day. We are only in port for 5 hours, the Zuiderdam (our ship) casts off at 1300, (1 P.M.) so we leave the ship at 0800 to find our excursion, a horse drawn carriage ride in the city of Cartagena, it is a balmy 80 degrees.

The carriage ride took us all the way through town from the rich districts to the poor districts and the middle-class districts. Bougenvelia, all colors, are all over the place.

We went past the government buildings, the main churches, and the upper end of the villas. We stopped for 20 minutes for shopping at a place called Las Bovedas (the dungeons), we got some cigars, vanilla, coffee, a shirt, and a basket. After the shopping we caught up with the group for a bus tour. The next stop was at the Fort of San Felipe de Barajas, a 17th century fort. Although we didn't go all the way up the top or go inside the massive structure, Lynn actually got a nice tablecloth and she did a good job bargaining for! We ran into a movie set that was filming a movie in town and it just stopped traffic; it slowed us down a couple times, when the bus diverted to take a shortcut, the street was too narrow with a car parked on the sidewalk, so we had to back the bus up.

In Colombian culture, children are required to go to school till high school, not required to go to high school but strongly encouraged. All boys must join the military for 2 years at 18; the government will sponsor a college education, and when you graduate, you must use the degree in Columbia for at least two years. If you do not graduate or fail, your family is responsible for the costs.

Back on the ship, lunch, trivia, chat with the cast, then on to a seminar.

Noah

Tongue and Pulse Analysis. This was put on by the Acupuncturist, Dr. Carolina. Eight people showed up, she said that was too many, so she took the first person that showed up, then took us, the rest were asked to make appointments for later.

Me: tongue is dark tipped which means I have good sleep, and since I remember my dreams, I sleep well. However, she felt my pulse, and indicated that my liver and kidneys need attention. I will be looking up Chinese medicine for liver and kidneys.

Lynn: dull tongue, indicated trouble sleeping, which she does, and tongue and pulse indicated circulation problems. I asked "How much?" She stated the acupuncture treatments start at $165 for the first, and a series would be discounted, however, one treatment wouldn't do much just like everything else…….so we told her we would think it over and left!

Martini sampling, dinner, a trivia, the lounge shows by the BB King ensemble, and an all-request show at the piano bar ended the day.

Monday, February 1, entering the Panama Canal locks. We were told that the bow would be open for the passage through the locks. So, everybody was told that the front decks would be open to watch the boat going through the locks.

As we arrived, they opened up to the front doors at exactly 6:00 o'clock. I got up at 5:30 A.M. to get ready for this thing. Half the boat did too! They did open up at six, I was about a third of the way to the back of the ship. All the people crowded on the bow, by the time I got there, they were four-deep, and no one budging to allow others to take a quick picture. I took a couple quick shots, then I looked up and saw that the bow was open on the third, fourth, and fifth floor. So, I grabbed a Panamanian roll (a cream filled sweet roll) for Lynn, fought the constant crowd like a salmon swimming upstream, dropped the roll off in the cabin for Lynn, and strolled to a higher deck to take more pictures.

As we entered the locks, and I went down to the deck three, the open deck for joggers and lower observation which is about 20 feet above water. I got some good shots of the tugboats and the locomotives as we came in, tied up, and pulled us through the locks.

We also found out and got some history about this. It cost about $500,000 to go in (must be paid 6 months in advance) and out of the Panama Canal. Passenger ships have priority; some cargo ships may have to wait a day or so just to get in queue. There are two side-by-side locks, three locks to get up or down. No pumps, basically, all gravity. The lake Gatun and all the streams and rivers are, fresh water.

We docked in lake Gatun, Panama, for an hour so that we could disembark for the shore excursions in Panama. This was the jungle monkey watch!

At the pier, we loaded onto tour buses for the hour and fifteen-minute drive to the jungle docks. We then loaded onto some sightseeing boats, drove another half hour on a lake to a tributary and looked for monkeys. There was one place where a crocodile was sighted, but he sunk by the time we got there, we saw a little taper, it was like a little pig.

Later on, we found a monkey in a tree and a monkey with a baby in another tree and we finally came around to a place where the monkeys were coming down by the boats. One jumped on our boat, and then jumped on the other boat. We got some pictures of them all within 5-10 feet.

We only had one banana to lure the monkeys, so they left, and then "the show was over," so we headed back to the pier.

The bus then took us to Colon, Panama where we did a little shopping before jumping back on our ship that had come to pick us up. I swam in the pool during the passage through the locks, so I got a certificate for swimming in the Panama Canal!

I did some walking and while walking I saw a whole bunch of black and turquoise butterflies! Now I was on the 10th deck, which is about 12 feet per deck, that is 120 feet, about 12 stories! These butterflies were flying over the ship and there were more than just a few! I never thought butterflies would fly that much and are so many butterflies especially in the day time!

We attended the formal tea on board, sat on the rear deck and participated in the sunset sail away, dinner, pub trivia, saw a very good comic. Tried to participate in a "Tatoosh" tasting (Bourbon, Rye, and single malt whiskeys) but no one else showed up, it was canceled, but the bar tender let me have a sample of the Rye, and it was quite good!

Checked out the Disco and danced to a couple Michael Jackson tunes, then called it a night.

Tuesday, February 2

it is Costa Rica time. We are off the ship at 0900 for a half-hour bus ride to the jungle and the zip line adventure. On the way, the driver told us only about 40% of Costa Ricans voted. They realize the government is corrupt.

Costa Rica is now the largest producer of pineapples. It's a WG IW D2 hybrid; there are no dinosaurs in Costa Rica because Costa Rica was actually under the water at that time; it only surfaced about a couple million years ago or so. There are iguanas, sloths, and jaguars, but no dinosaurs.

We arrived to the outfitting area, they fitted us with harnesses and we each received our pulleys. The first group of eight walked to our first launch platform. We were all told what would happen if we missed the platform. You have to turn around grab the cable and pull yourself hand over hand back to the platform, we were all given gloves. One group saw a 4-foot green iguana, another group and I, just we saw the rustling of the leaves, another group saw a small orange frog. We were told those frogs are very poisonous but by the time I got to him with the camera he was gone.

I got a picture of Lynn, she was in front of me, she hooked up and zipped down; we zip down 11 platforms. I followed her, there are about 40 in our group and we were two of the youngest, and I was one of the few men, we thought this very surprising… go figure!

At every platform, there is a zip person who attaches you to the pulley and safety cable, as you approach the next station, you raise your legs and there is a cable pushed out to slow you just before you reach the landing, since you are 'zipping" pretty quickly, this slows you down very fast, kind 'a like jamming on the brakes, the harness is greatly appreciated!

Now we went from platform to platform and actually the 10th platform I missed. I didn't put my feet up high enough and I hit the platform and even with the brakes on, I went backwards. GOD, it was horrible! I drifted back a good 50-60 feet on the cable. I finally stopped, turned myself around and started pulling myself, hand over hand to the platform. I really started slowing down, so the zip line person told me to hold my position, that she was going to pulley out to me and attach a rescue rope. She came out, wrapped her legs around me, attached a rope and pulled herself back to the platform. She then told me to turn around again and pull myself to the platform with her helping by pulling the rope Yep, I am here, so I made it! We were both out of breath, I told her we shouldn't meet like this again, and she agreed!

The last zip is to the ground, only a couple hundred feet. There you are helped out of your harness and give back your pulley. They offered cold water, fresh pineapple, watermelon, and Lynn bought us both, a homemade cornmeal-based empanada which was excellent!

You're supported in a harness like a chair, but the heavier you are, the more the cable sags, I was near the limit of 260 pounds, running 245 before we left on the cruise, in the 250 range now, that's why I had to pull my legs up higher in and of course I was a little apprehensive because of the knee thing, but we made it and it was great!

I took some more pictures of the flora and fauna on the fourth or fifth landing, we also saw a two-toed sloth, he was looking down and probably actually sleeping. They sleep someplace between 20- 22 hours a day. They come down every 60 days to mate, lay eggs, and sometimes eat. They also eat up there in the canopy, their bones are like a bird's bones, hollow, they are very light so they can go on real narrow branches to stay away from predators. In the jungle, if you aren't careful you are eaten. Two toed sloths are brownish, three toed are in a grayish color, this was greyish; he was about 50 feet away, so I'm hoping that the pictures will come out.

We went to a final market, this one was very extensive, had a lot of different products, coffee beans, coffee, all kinds of sculptures, all kinds of paintings and carvings. It was a great market and the people were willing to bargain.

Back to the ship, went to our room and started to organize the "loot" so we knew what we had for who. Lunch, then went to the team trivia week scored 10 out of 15 which is getting close to the winning couple. Then off to a culinary arts center with the assistant program director and she explained a lot of things that were in the kitchen for a beauty product of facials, I got recipes for both daughters. Lynn helped mix some of the potions with avocado and olive oil; she received recipe book for her assistance.

Martini sampling, (yup, love those martini's), supper, trivia, a fantastic show by a pianist from Cuba named Juan Pablo. He was very entertaining; we had some apprehension about going to a show but he was very good.

Lynn went to the marriage game; a game show and I joined the pub crawl. The pub crawl was $20.00, I got a free glass that is all kinds of lights in the base. We started out with about 20 people, four bars were involved, different drinks, mixing beer, wine, and hard stuff! By the time, we made it to the last bar, we were encouraged to sing along, we were noisy, lots of fun! We went from the 10th to the 9th to the 2nd and then the 1st floor and that was it; Some people came to the pub crawl half in a bag, if not three-quarter the bag! There were some younger people there which is kind of enjoyable and was actually one crawler on a scooter! We all had false names, mine was "Sir mix-a-lot", the one on the scooter was "apple pie". I met up with Lynn at the disco, it was late, we called it a night.

Wednesday, February $3^{rd,}$ a day at sea.

We will be at sea today, tomorrow, and dock early Friday morning. Today was supposed be a relaxing day as it didn't have much as far as programs are concerned. We got up late had a late breakfast then basically we played games; Cruise bingo; we got close I mean I stood up with one number to go, but no cigar! This is my second last day of salmon for breakfast and sushi for lunch; and then we went and had team trivia at 1:00 P.M. and we got 12 out of 15 questions right, so we didn't do as good as we wanted to and one team actually got 15 out of 15. We went to the afternoon tea, they were insistent that we do not enter before 3 P.M. but at 3:30 we got the bum's rush, kind of wrong if this was to be a relaxing spot in the afternoon, but the other couple were nice and the time spent, pleasant. We returned to our cabin, we started looking over the stuff, we had our formal dinner tonight at the Pinnacle Grill which is one of the perks thrown in, and we were looking forward to this special dining event.

We arrived early for our 6:45 reservation and the Maître's expressed concern that we were "so early" he sounded and acted French with that kind of attitude. So, we retired to the bar for twenty minutes, to return exactly at 6:45.

We were seated in a booth, we thought it was a little uppity, but when we started getting the food, our waitress a charm and very personable, from Bali; the food was insane, the best food we've had on all the cruises!

We had a shrimp cocktail and steak tartar to start it; the shrimp were perfectly prepared, flavorful and large and we just can't say enough, the tartar was tastee. Lynn ordered a steak which was seasoned and grilled perfectly and had probably one of the best flavors she had ever had in a steak, I had a seafood carpaccio, which was plentiful and rich. We shared a dessert and felt overstuffed, we will both have to go on diets when we get home! We then checked out the Blues club, sat for a set, then the Northern lights disco, nothing happening tonight, so back to the room.

Thursday, February 4

T his is the last day of the cruise, tomorrow morning will be disembarking between 0700-0900 in the morning, so there will not be much time for anything. Our flight is at 11:30, so we need to get off the ship quickly, gather our luggage, go through customs, bus to the airport and take off for home.

This morning I signed up to be on a walk for cancer. This was for six international cancer organizations; We met on deck three, 100 people showed up and we all wore T-shirts, it was a 5KM walk which was 6 laps of the ship. I completed 3 laps, because I had another activity lined up, but by the time I left only 15-20 people were still walking.

The next activity was a Chinese acupuncture medicine lecture at 10 AM. Lynn joined me in the lounge at 9:50. The odd thing is that the person that was supposed to do the seminar didn't show up and so, at 10:10 we left. At 11:00 we went for the $25,000 jackpot bingo and win a cruise lottery in a Vista lounge. We were there, we tried, we lost.

We grabbed a quick lunch, listened to the poolside jams by the steel pan player Kevin; we asked him about the other lessons he had on board, he said the last time he only had two takers too many competing programs going on including Bingo. He stated that with this cruise there wasn't a lot of participation.

At 1:00 o'clock we had our favorite team it was our last afternoon trivia with the cruise director Jeremy; trickier questions, only knew 10 out of 15!

Next activity was the photo scavenger hunt. Lynn and I were the only ones there for a while, then three more people showed up. We broke into two teams, we had a list of 15 places to take selfies cameras, then meet back in 25 minutes. This was "stem too stern" 10th deck to 1st deck run! The list included: eating cookies; using exercise equipment, pictures of us with crew, playing ping pong, showing something long, picture with a bar tender, etc. We got back on time but 3 minutes behind the other team. Both teams had all the 15 pictures, both were creative, but since the other team beat us back, they won! Both teams received a drink as a prize!

Next, we went to a recipe collection culinary arts Center by the assistant host Alice. She promised us that since we showed up, we can have recipes of all the stuff that they had shown on the ship during this cruise. We asked if we could have an additional copy for our daughters, she agreed! So, Camille gets is set for sure, Taffy yes, and Ian gets any we don't need. We also got two of the ships cook books!

Back to the room, start packing. I went to the sip and savor that was with the guest chef Diane with a pre-dinner appetizer was a Panamanian Ceviche, paired with a Blanche, a white wine. I found it quite different in that lemon juice was used rather than lime.

I went back to pick up Lynn had a little bit a supper. After supper we went and played the last pub trivia with the show host, Kass. We spent a little time with our new found friends Brian and Bill and we discussed the Canada versus US; it was kind interesting especially on how Canada treats gay couples, they're married now, and how they are afraid to go to US cities because the guns.

We went to the BB King blues club and watched a set with them and after that set from the blues club we went to the final Showtime variety show with comedian Mike Robinson who is a ventriloquist and the dueling violinists Safira.

<u>Friday morning</u>

Our luggage was gone, we grabbed a bite to eat, we had grey luggage tags, we were to be called between 8-8:15 AM so at 8:00 we went down to the lounge to wait. We waited in a secluded area with another couple, and at 8:25 the woman got impatient, went to the disembarking area and returned to say there was no line, no one was checking and they were leaving. I said O.K. let's go, we will back you guys up! So off we went, showed our room key for the last time and walked off the ship. The luggage for the cruise is arranged in color coded areas, as you enter the warehouse, you show your tag, and then they will tell you where your grouping of bags is.

As we walked from the first section to the next, I saw three bags on the side, and one, looked like mine! I went over and verified that yes, it was mine, and it was soaking wet!

I was approached by a service representative that verified that the bag was mine, that it had fallen into the harbor and asked that I provide her with my address and phone number. I filled that in, she gave me the carbon copy, and circled the address and e-mail of Holland claims. She told me to claim a total loss.

We then located Lynn's luggage, and proceeded to line up for the customs, no trusted traveler side, so we had to wait in line, both of us had to produce our driver's license along with our passports to get through. All this time, my luggage is very heavy, leaving a water trail all the way, and a puddle when I stop! Time is short for our

Educating Noah...Travelin'

connection, find the bus to the airport and we are on our way. The bus stops between the terminals so everyone has an equal distance to walk. We tried to check our luggage outside, there was only one couple ahead of us.

I told the agent that the suitcase weighted 45# when we left the room, that it may be a little heavier due to the soaking......it weighed 83 POUNDS!

He said he would have to charge me $200.00 for my bag alone and $25.00 for Lynn's. I asked him where a garbage can was, he indicated that there was one on the other side of the entrance. I told him I would throw out some of the contents to get it down in weight, so I pulled the suitcase to the side, opened it up, everything was soaked, through and through! I took out the suit, Lynn's suit, the underwear and laundry bag, shirts and pants, leaving about a third left. The agent weighted the bag again, looked at me and said it was close to 50#s, I gave him an exasperated look, a twenty-dollar bill, and he said, "good enough". And in we went.

The flight home was short, we had our original seats, the luggage came promptly on the carrousel, and off to the bus pick up area. Within 20 minutes the bus showed up, we threw in our luggage, an hour and 20 minutes later we were at the bus station, loaded up the car, and headed for home. Stopped at KFC for supper and drove home.

At home, Lynn set up supper and two throw rugs, one in the bedroom for the suitcase, the other in front of the fireplace to start drying the remaining contents of my suitcase.

The suitcase was completely submerged, and for a while, several things including cigars and decks of cards were wet inside the cellophane. We saved what we could!

Glad to be home. Another interesting adventure!!

Noah

After a week of documenting for the cruise (above) for later review, and making the photo album, I am now "normal" again, and approachable. I was up to 258 #s and that just added fuel to the fire. I am now down to 250.2 so that is going well, I have initiated three e-mails to United regarding the seats they switched on us, they actually called me, and after the back and forth, I asked her who can tell me why I had lowest priority on seating and boarding while having paid four months in advance. That was two days ago, still waiting.

I also made a claim on the luggage they dumped into the salt water. I have sent four e-mails looked up and provided SKUs for the thrown away clothes, an estimate on the luggage, and an O.K. for Holland to compensate me monetarily for products bought on the ship.

They will not cover electronics, jewelry, hearing aids, medical devices, money, credit cards, and on and on, they wanted pictures of everything, after the fact she said they would have covered the $200.00 charge(?) for overweight, which I find questionable. We may be settling on something between $400-$750. We will see!

I am now working on the cruise to Greece, waiting for a gondola ride in Venice, but to date, nothing. Going back and forth with Royal Caribbean, so I can arrange the air and book some of the shore excursions. I like doing this by e-mail so I have written proof of what is said, offered, and denied. I asked for an excursion brochure to be sent, I don't want to print that too! I contacted Craig, our Edward Jones broker, for the cash needed for Greece and later on for Russia and Antarctica in September and a year from now February 2017.

I now have to work on getting down below the 240# mark, wheening myself from the cruise. Have to do more research on fiber and drinking more water.

We will be doing activities from the Franklin Seniors Club, and other organizations, including the Chapter G Goldwing club and the Vagabonds.

An interesting occurrence happened yesterday. We were attending a Franklin Senior sponsored trip to Sheboygan Falls for a Dorf Kapelle-Fasching Celebration (this is the German Mardi Gras (Pre-Lenten) Celebration. It involved music, dancing and traditional food.) My favorite song is "Alice" and it was the second from the last. However, in Germany, it seems you call out: "Shikee shakee, shikee, shakee and the response from the audience is Oui, Oui, Oui! Both very loud and with exuberance! Now, in Australia, you call out: Aussie, Aussie, Aussie! And the response is OUI, OUI, OUI!

It is a small world indeed!

We have 60 days till or next adventure. We finished another Milwaukee Tour tour this weekend. Lynn has attended four. Together we have attended three. This was a pizza tour! We asked all of our friends and acquaintances to join us, of those, we had a total of ten on the bus of twenty-four. These tours are very informative with a running commentary on the various neighborhoods, plus we stopped at four places for different styles of pizza, and the last stop was gelato! After that, we went with my brother and sister-in-law to the re-opening to the Safe House, downtown. It wasn't much different, crowded, and very loud, we stayed for a couple of drinks and left, finishing up another great evening!

Taxes are done, I owe the State, and now have to make quarterly payments, our incomes from work are under $5, 000 but the investments on money previously taxed are working and we have to pay for what that money earns, I guess we are lucky we don't have to pay social security on our investments too!

I have been having increasingly difficult time with my shoulders, the right more than the left. I had physical therapy late last year, that gave me most of my range back, now the pain is waking me up at night, and I am taking too many pain meds, treating the symptom, not the cause! I e-mailed my nurse practitioner and asked her to set up a meet with the "Osteo-folk", and she did. Within six weeks I had an appointment! They at first wanted only to work with the right shoulder, but I persisted that both should be examined to set up a base line. When I showed up for x-rays, my request had been considered, and x-rays were taken of both shoulders. The results, you guessed it, osteoarthritis in both, the surprise was that the left arm was almost degenerated as much as the right. I guess that since I use the right more than the left, I feel it more.

The doctor examined both, I asked to see the x-rays (it is so neat now that they are available almost instantly) and he pointed out the wear in both, the cushion almost gone, with bone on bone soon. He asked if I wanted the prednisone injection, I said, "Yes, this is going to be the same as the knees?" To this he agreed, so I asked him to inject both, hopefully this will last a few months, and we will play it by ear. He agreed, shot me in both shoulders, and scheduled some three months out.

I also signed up to drive for Uber, provided all the requirements, and was authorized to drive. I attempted to drive a couple times during the day and searched for rides but I couldn't find any even in Wauwatosa or the city of Milwaukee, I was also transporting ma to the doctor weekly, the shoulder problem, and my brother came up for a visit!

The brother visit did not go well. He and two of his kids live in Nevada. They have been away from Wisconsin thirty some years, returning three times, the last, about 15 years ago, I had e-mailed him in January regarding ma losing the sight in one eye, and possibly starting to lose sight in the other, that it may be a good idea to see her before she could no longer "see" him, and his wife again.

He e-mailed me, asking me not to tell our mother, to surprise her, that he would be up here the week of my birthday and anniversary, and to let him know about accommodations.

I provided the information for the room at the building I lived in and motels in the surrounding area. I also informed him that they should not expect to stay at Ma's apartment due to her night-timer's sleeping difficulties.

They arrived and checked in at Ma's around eight P.M. on a Sunday night. Rang her door bell, and definitely surprised her! At 86 she was surprised, confused and upset all at the same time, not the reaction my brother, his wife, one daughter, and son! She invited them in, he asked if two of them could crash there, she said "no", and after an hour they left for the small apartment in the building.

Monday Evening

He was back, and this time, his other daughter joined them (with her two 5 and 6-year-old daughters and 17-year-old son! (a total of 8 people!) They stayed for another two hours. Ma asked him to call me, and he did when they returned to their motel room. (The guest apartment in the building is only meant for two people, and there is no microwave, so they canceled the rest of the four-night stay in the room and moved to the motel.) He then called me at 9:40 Monday night. "We are here!"

Due to our experiences with Camille's difficulties in her college days, any call after 9 in the evening keeps us both up all night! Then, he wasn't happy that she was not over-excited to see them. I tried to explain to him that surprising 86-year old's later in the evening is more confusing to them especially on a routine Sunday night.

He continued that they couldn't stay at her apartment, and the room they had rented was too small and that they had to rent a motel room! So, I blew up; I was not in the mood to have him bitch and moan, this late at night, after not participated in anything with his mother for years (except for a monthly phone call) The inappropriate language lasted only a few minutes resulting in his hanging up.

I found out from ma that Cindy, Ted's oldest daughter with her kids had rented a motel room for her and the kids at an economy motel farther away, and that she was looking for something to do other than visit relatives here. I reached out to her via Facebook, she called me, I asked what I could do. She told me she and her son wanted to see the lake, and some of the highlights in Milwaukee.

Wednesday

This was Wednesday early afternoon; she was to meet with her family and uncle from her mother's side for dinner.

We agreed to meet on Thursday morning; later, I called her back and asked if the motel offered breakfast. She said, "No," so I asked her what they liked to eat?

She immediately said," bacon and pancakes!" I asked if they were early risers, and she said "yes," so I told her Lynn had to work, "so come here between 8 and 8:15, and I will have their order on the table". She agreed!

Thursday

On Thursday, as Lynn was leaving to go to work, they arrived. We had never seen the girls, bundles of energy, giving kisses and hugs, and her oldest son, last time we saw him was when he was two! Off Lynn went to work, I had everything set up, fed them all to the max, cleaned up, toured the house, then off we went in "Suzy" my Subaru!!

We drove down to the lakefront, visited the ferry station located next to the Coast guard station, over-looking the South Shore Marina, then over the Hoan Bridge (the bridge that went no-where) to downtown Milwaukee. We stopped at the Discovery World, no time for them to explore, took pictures of the Calatrava, progressed to the Bradford beach area, the pumping tower at the end of North Avenue, the church I had worked at (It has Tiffany glass), then on to the downtown Cheese store and Usinger's sausage company. I sprung for the cheese and sausage for them to take home and share. We then proceeded to the baseball stadium, the VA (we have historic civil war buildings on the grounds) and off to Ma's for "goodbyes". I asked what they wanted to eat before leaving, they asked for French fries so …. we stopped at Culver's, another Wisconsin institution. Back to the house, I gave her a copy of my book, gave everyone a hug, and off they went!

I was exhausted! Two little girls again! Wow! Was that great!! They were so outgoing, so lovable, so full of energy!!!! This was more for me than them, and her son, Devon, at 17, was so mature and gracious; she is truly "rich" in her immediate family!

It has been two weeks since "the call," and I haven't heard from my brother. I have never seen any of them since we visited Nevada a couple years ago, and probably not again. Enough of family dynamics!

Forty days to the Greece adventure!

As I await a new opportunity, I signed up to work at the polls this year. I believe I was one of the youngest, went to an hour orientation, and manned the polls, 0600 to 2130! Only a few breaks, food and potty, but the time went fast! This primary was the first major test of requiring an ID to vote. Most people presented their ID as they approached the table, there was no problems, none; another political myth!!

I also started the process of possibly driving for Uber. I did get a little confused, so I attended a class. About twenty people showed up with no tax advice to speak of. These folks had little to no knowledge of being an independent contractor and the need to estimate quarterly; they were vague as to what expenses are deductible, and it seems like you make "arrangements" with riders to sit outside their house and go online just after they request a ride! We will see…….

I did put together my Mother's Day banquet menu. Started my preliminary planning for the road trip in August, signed up for excursions on the Russian trip, and am exploring glass igloos for early November.

Tiffany is dating a marine reservist. They invited me to go shooting at a range. I was surprised at how accurate I still was, clustering 29 of 35 rapid-fire shots in a target. It reinforced that "manly" feeling I needed, so for a month, I got two shots in vitality: this for my manhood and the kids for my energy!

May 2016, our trip to Greece May 13th through the 23rd.

It is 13 days out, and as usual, I am getting antsy! I have gone over all the documents, checked and double-checked all of the departures, arrivals, duplication of anything I think I will need handy, and copies to Lynn.

The carry-on is packed with all emergency stuff included, including money, passports, and main luggage checked and re-checked and weighed.

We attended another Vagabond meeting. There was supposed to be a presentation on Master Gardening, but it was more about how to join and sounded like a clique. It was also election night. Bob Spindell didn't show, and he is in charge of the India trip; nothing as far as dates, length, or costs. Now Online Vacations has a VIP deal to India, Including cruise and air. I will be dropping our agent a note to see how little I need to reserve.

The night before the adventure, I checked out the parking at the bus station to ensure plenty of room for parking. To my surprise, only two slots were available, so I guess we need alternatives. The first attempt at Uber was not good. Lost a signal with my phone while driving to find a fare. I tried numerous times to get a signal and even called home, but it (the phone) said to drive further for a signal. I e-mailed Uber with the results, and they e-mailed me back that I needed so many gigs of data, but I had no answer. I tried calling Tracfone, but they put me on hold and never called back. I figured this was a sign, so I e-mailed Uber and told them I was leaving for vacation and dropped me as a candidate to drive. They responded that they would and then stated that the Uber application would be inactive, the entire account. So, the use of the free ride Uber offered was now gone.

I saw our neighbor Bill working on his car. He has been on and off working lately, so I took a stroll over, started small talk, and asked him what he was doing on Thursday. He said it was his day off, so I asked him if he wanted to make a quick twenty bucks to drop Lynn and me off at the bus station. He asked when, and I said to be at my house at eleven thirty sharp. He agreed, and we made final preparations. Actually, everything was packed, and most were in the front hall, but there was always check and re-check!

At 11:30, Bill pulled up to the garage. I opened up the back, it was all cleaned out and threw in the bags I had put on the driveway. Lynn came out, locked the garage, and off we went!

Half an hour spent at the bus station was spent talking to the agent. The bus came promptly at 12:00, and we were off by 12:10. The drive to O'Hare was the customary one hour and twenty minutes. Although I had pre-registered us, we had our boarding passes but had to wait in line to check our luggage, no kiosk, and still had to show ID. The agent reminded me that there was just a short time between flights, and I acknowledged it.

The security lines were just stupid! Austrian Airlines does not honor the Trusted Traveler program, so it took us two hours shuffling through the security, both of us being pulled aside for additional wanding, me due to the knees and hip. For some reason, Lynn gets pulled out, too!

Just a short wait for boarding, Austrian Airlines uses the A, B, C, and D method of loading and actually enforces it. Of course, many Europeans crowded the line, not wanting to honor the cue.

I paid extra for exit aisle seats but got the middle aisle plane seats. I was up against the wall, with no window and a space where people gathered for the rest rooms just forward of us. This meant the entire flight, there was someone either looking out the window in the door or just standing in front of us, with the restroom door opening and shutting, flooding the area with light and toilet flushing. The flight was about nine hours. With the time change, we had left O'Hare at 4:30 p.m. and were supposed to land at 8:35 in the morning in Vienna, Austria.

We arrived at 9:10; the flight from Vienna to Venice was to leave at 9:10, so we had to reschedule. We were told our luggage did not transfer, so then, we had to find the Austrian Air service center. We told them our dilemma, she did find a flight out at 12:00 for Rome, then one to Venice from Rome getting us to Venice at 3:30. I asked to use their phone, called the Royal Caribbean hot line and told them the plan, they said it should work, and would have a transfer ready for us at the airport, I thought all on board was 4:30; I found out later it was actually 3:30, with ship sail at 5.

So now we had our tickets, but we had to arrange for luggage transfer and get boarding passes. It was now 9:50 a.m. It should work!!

First, we had to find luggage, and we did. Airports do have a lot of similarities. We found the carousel, no luggage, to be lost and found. They told us the luggage was being held for the substitute flight, would use the same luggage tags, and just let the gate agent know so they could be transferred to the new plane.

We then ran up to the Austrian gate service and were promptly told that the tickets issued were for NIKI Air and that we had to go to their agent in terminal 1; we were in terminal 3. She was very nice and gave us directions, and off we went to terminal 1. There was a long row of ticket agents in terminal 1. None that I could see had NIKI airlines, so once again, we had to find an information booth. She indicated that NIKI was part of Air Berlin and indicated a bank of agents with a huge crowd in front. We jostled into a line after being wedged and playing chicken with other people. We were inside the rope lines. It took an hour and a half to get to an agent.... tic...tic...tic; we were both getting anxious. We explained our story; the ticket agent had to call his supervisor about the luggage, then issued us the boarding passes for the two flights and assured me that the luggage would be on the planes!! We had just minutes to find the gate and use the rest room! We did both with about five minutes before loading the plane!

The first flight was an hour and a half. We easily unloaded and found the AB Airline gate, waited 15 minutes, loaded onto that aircraft, seats tight, knees touching the seat in front, and of course, this being an Italian Airline, left a little late, so of course, landed late. We touched down at Venice airport at 3:40. We Grabbed our gear and hurried down to baggage, hoping that our luggage was with us and someone from the ship would be waiting for us.

As we entered the baggage area, Lynn said, "There is the person from the ship!" We met her, then went to the carrousel to wait for our luggage. For once, our two pieces came with the second load! We pulled them, the Royal Caribbean called for the car, we went out to the parking area, and a black Mercedes van pulled up. We jumped in, he put the luggage in the back, and we sped off to the dock. I asked how far it was, and he told me about 20 minutes, which seems to be a standard. All airports seem to be between 20 minutes or more from our first destination!

We arrived at the building in front of the ship; the crews were pulling all the guide posts and banners, no-one was in the building except for the clean-up crews! We were rushed through x-ray and security and met by an officer who welcomed us and ushered us up into the ship from the dock on the only remaining gang plank.

I was told that all on board was actually 3:30 and not 4:30; the ship sail was, and is at 5:00, 20 minutes from now! It was extraordinary that they waited for us and made that accommodation. We were virtually the last two people on the boat, including the crew!

We headed for our cabin, dropped off our carry-ons, met our room steward, asked that he separate the bed and provide two ship activities daily, and asked about muster. He told us that it was at 4:00. So, we still have to make that up! We checked at guest services to ensure everything was in order, walked the ship, and watched the shoreline of Venice and the various canals and bridges entering the older section. As we cruised by on the first leg of our journey, at 7:30, we ended the day!

Saturday

1st day on ship, and the first stop, Bologna (Ravenna), Italy. We were up at 6:30. Still a little shell-shocked from traveling, we grabbed breakfast and went down to the theatre for our excursion called "The Taste of Ravenna." We met at 8:00 in the theater and were down to the waiting buses by 8:25.

The first stop was just a photo-op of the Baptistery of Neon, built in the late 300s A.D., a 25-30-foot-tall octagon-shaped domed building, the oldest building in Ravenna. The next was a walking tour of the Basilica of St. Vitale, which is known as the best-preserved example of Byzantine architecture and art in the world! The church itself is really not that large and has three floors, but it is totally mosaic on the inside, with arches, domes, ceilings, and walls, not to mention the floor! Lynn and I have been all over the world, but this church with the mosaic tiles was the most beautiful! There were several crypts on the grounds, including the Mausoleum of Galla Placida from the early 400s A.D. UNESCO designates this small mausoleum as "Artiisticallt perfect"! With more mosaic tiles covering the interior and three coves housing the sarcophagi of Aelia Galla Placidia, one of the last regents of the Roman empire, her husband and son. The stained-glass windows were blown out during World War II, so the glass was all replaced with gold-tinted glass to highlight the mosaic tiles in both the church and the mausoleum.

After walking the grounds, we walked a couple hundred meters through the city, typical narrow streets, small shops, and little open markets. We smelled fresh fruits and spices as we passed. There were lots of bicycles and young and old riding them past us.

Our last stop was a taste of Ravenna food at a restaurant set up with a buffet of local cheeses, sausage, and meats, served with mineral water and a nice light bottle of wine. After the taste, I asked for and received copies of the typical menu both in Italian and English and then we had an hour of free time to explore the town before meeting back at the restaurant for the bus home.

I noticed some of the older men were making a "statement" by wearing a scarf with their shirt and slacks, always leather shoes. I don't know if they even have a pair of gym shoes? We also walked by a real-estate office advertising apartments; most apartments were in the 250-350,000-euro range!

On the way back, we saw a number of fishing shacks on the shore with large nets raised out of the water. In the past, and even today, this is how they fished, lowering the nets at low tide, then raising them at high tide to catch the fish. Now it is trendy to own one of these shacks, and expensive, one recently sold for a million euros!!

Back on the ship, a short nap before a Trivia game, then a snack, documentation of events and activities before walking the ship. Lynn joined a group that was line dancing, and I checked out isothermal applications at the health spa. It seems the isothermal treatments are for those models that have just a little fat to remove and kinda wanting to get skinny or skinny-er.... a treatment costs about $160.00, with 3 treatments recommended for a quantity discount of just under $400.00 dollars. It is an external cleanse using seaweed and a wrap that has electrodes to stimulate specific areas.

We played another round of trivia with our new-found friend and another couple from New York, decided to eat casual again, and went back to the room to prepare for the evening.

One of the main reasons we decided to eat dinner casually in the buffet was tonight was formal night, and most were dressed up in evening gowns and tuxes, and we were still suffering from jet lag.

After dinner, we went to the show. There was a singer, Austin Drage, who won the TV show X-Factor. He was a fairly good singer, the show was O.K.........next off to the centrum to participate with a mother, daughter, couple in Majority Rules, a game where the groups that answer the question the same win. We didn't win at that either!

It was now almost 11:00 P.M., so shower and bed; perhaps tomorrow would find us bright-eyed and bushy-tailed. The port is 10 a.m., and our excursion starts at 10:45. This is a tender port.

Day 3, Sunday

May 15th is Lynn's birthday! I had a card and a gift tucked away in my carry-on and got up early in the morning and put them both by the sink, then let her get up first.... :)

We had a late breakfast, strolled the ship, and watched the shore line. To get to Kotor, Montenegro, we traveled an inside passage for almost two hours, passing Dubrovnik, Croatia, and many small towns hugging the Adriatic Sea.

The air was heavy, 62 degrees F, cloudy, and raining lightly with the humidity in the 80's. The transit reminded me of the fjords in Norway and New Zealand. The towns are very similar: a road just off the shoreline, two-story white or cream buildings with tile roofs, and at least one church in every town. The towns were mostly at the very bottom of the mountains, so most of the mountains were covered with trees and shrubs, occasional outcroppings of stone, accented the green with cream and slate.

The tops of the mountains were hidden in a shroud of foreboding, ominous dark clouds, but in the south, some sunlight was beginning to break through.

Since I had the camera in hand, I took pictures of the ship and deck, along with some inside pictures, just to provide a little insight into this floating city.

We met for the excursions in the theater. There was no room on the dock, so we were ferried in via life boat, the transition lasting no more than 15 minutes.

Our bus was waiting for us; the first stop was the town of Budva. On the way to Budva we did stop for some pictures of the beautiful coastline, the different shades of blue and green of the ocean was hopefully caught by the camera.

The total population of this little country is approximately 620,000 people; all the roads are two lanes, and we went through two very long tunnels and rode along the seashore about half of the time. This country and both Budva and Kotor are resort places for many Russian languages are a mix of Russian and Italian. The kids start school at 6 years old, have to attend school for 9 years, and have the option of going to high school. If they wish to go to college, it will cost them $1500-3000 Eu per year.

We arrived in town after about 45 minutes, got off the bus, and hiked downtown to the old city. As in all the European cities, parking is tight, hard to find, and the streets are narrow. The city is walled, has six entrances, very narrow streets, small shops, and restaurants. I took several pictures. One of the squares had stones that looked like the symbol of pi and a flattened stone in front of it. This was an executioner's stone.........quick picture and go....... Budva is the oldest existing city in the Balkans. It was very similar to the one we visited in Canes, France, and it brought back welcome memories!

After walking through the various streets and visiting a number of shops, we wanted to try the local fare of food, at least I did! We were told to go to the restaurant next to the place where we were to meet and order the Montenegro sampler. When the waiter approached us, I asked for the sampler, and he gave me "the look" and said he did not know what I meant, so I asked for a menu; he promptly asked the people next to us if they were done with theirs's and gave us a food and wine menu and promised to be back.

Five minutes later, he returned. I could not find anything close to a "sampler," so I ordered the grilled squid and French fries, water for Lynn, and a red house wine for myself. Now understand we had used up a good 20 minutes of our free time exploring the old town, and time was ticking, ...ticking...ticking!! Finally, he returned with a wine glass 1/3 full of a very robust smelling wine (it was very good!) and a plate that had five squid bodies, with detached tentacles, roasted and fried along with a good handful of French fries, and yes, I did take a picture.

I took a bite of one of the squid's bodies. It was sweet and was as good, if not better, than the grilled octopus I had in the Galapagos Islands. After severe pressure, Lynn did take a bite, but it was a small bite. The look of the little squids just turned her off, so she just ate most of the French fries. I polished them off. They were very filling, but you must squeeze them to get the oil/water out of the body first, or it will be all over the place!

We joined the group and walked back to the bus. We then drove back to Kotor for a walking tour of that town. As you look up, there is a wall and stairway to the top of the mountain, where another fort stands. There are 2350 steps! Half way is a small chapel; two of our trivia team went up, the wife only halfway. He went all the way up for the view and just to prove he could. No, neither Lynn nor I attempted it!

This was another walled city, shops, squares and a lot of churches inside, yes, I took lots of pictures of the interesting buildings and churches. We asked why some of the umbrellas in one section were inverted to catch rain. We were told this was on purpose, that they funnel all the rain to the sewer system to flush the sewage down to the sea!

Back on the boat by four, we opted for just a salad for dinner, of course, after our team trivia at 5!

We met another English couple, and our team mate's husband had not shown up after his trek up the mountain, she told us he would show up, he always does!

We lost at that trivia, went for food, had a great salad, then found out there was a song Trivia, attended that with two other couples, they had to leave for dinner, we finished, and we won!!

Each of us won a Royal Caribbean pen, so I dropped off Lynn for the "If you know it, sing it" participation game, tracked the two couples down in the main dining room and gave them their prizes, extracting handshakes from the men, and hugs from the women.

Joined Lynn and another couple at a table for the game, Lynn participated in two songs, "Killer" by Michael Jackson, and a Brittney Spears song, but the activity person ran out of prizes. It was great fun anyway! A lot of people started to really get in the swing of things, but the time was up, and the activity ended.

A three-piece band set up, started playing 50's and 60's songs, I stayed for five or six, then called it a night, went to the room, set up the shower, went over the next day's planner, and completed my notes. Lynn joined me soon after, took advantage of the set shower temperature and another day done. Tomorrow is a day at sea, we will see what that brings.

Today

Today is a day at sea. Lynn made an appointment for a facial I gave her for her final birthday gift, I attended a gambling seminar and excursion briefing. The only reason I attended the seminar, was that they were combined. I did get a free pull at a slot.... nothing!

I then attended a sushi competition; afterward, they provided samples, the real reason I was there! Since it was "free," everyone crowded the table, which had plenty to share. Some just stood in front picking, choosing, and then asking for teriyaki sauce, ginger, and wasabi, blocking all those behind them. (This is not unusual and seems to be more and more prominent.) After that, I walked a couple of rounds in the sun, amazed at how many people were there sunbathing, with the same spot every day and hours on end. Most, if not all, retired, most "overflowing" the two and one-piece bathing suits.

Lynn went for her facial, she arrived early and after waiting 20 minutes past her appointment complained. She was told that the person in front of her had forgotten the overnight time change and asked for her understanding. Well, that did not go over well, Lynn told them the time change was announced twice the night before, and the daily program also stated the change, they provided her with an additional massage, and gave her a facial, with her scalp massage, that was extended.

We then met for a light lunch, and walked the ship, to compare afternoon activities and our next meeting.

Personal note: The more cruises and vacations we are on, the more I am convinced that many if not most people are cows and sheep. Many are selfish, petty, and "me" people that want everything to be free, want to be at the head of the line, and could care less for those behind them or with them except for immediate family or close friends. On cruises, they eat like pigs, heaping their plates, and then discarding half, I was asked if I wanted to have a beverage package, I told the bartender that it wouldn't pay.... He asked how many alcoholic drinks I intended each day, and when I said maybe one or two, he shook his head and served me my drink for the day! I asked, he said most take the package price and consider it a bargain! Enough of that, on with the day!

We met for a light salad lunch, then Lynn was off to Visual trivia, and I was off to The Art of Making Cocktails seminar. My seminar was canceled; I was the only one that showed, and they needed at least 5; there are 1900, give or take passengers. Do they all have liquor packages?? So, I just nosed around the ship, found the sushi restaurant, and had twenty bucks to throw at the casino. I quickly lost it. All of it! I lost the first $ at a draw poker machine, then thought I would move over to a penny machine, where I went to forty cents in about ten minutes. I went over to the desk and asked for some clarification. They sent over a mechanic, and I asked how to play 2 lines. I lost so much so fast. It seems that there was a multiplier, and my bets went from $1.20 to $6.00 per pull!! Lesson learned! I thanked him and once again left a casino $20.00 poorer. (I usually limit myself to twenty bucks; usually, it lasts about a half hour, and the gambling itch is satisfied; this time, it was only fifteen minutes, and I am good for another 6-12 months!).

I met Lynn on the way back to the room, she had played the trivia with another couple, then came back to the room for a nap. I changed and we both went to the salsa dance lessons put on by two of the dancers. We are getting old, we did most of the dance, we were better than some and much worse than others!

I went down to the bar to reserve seats for the five o'clock trivia and Lynn went to the room to change for dinner. Tried two new drinks, one was a habanero and grapefruit daiquiri, rum habanero and grapefruit syrup; and the best was a Sandy Collins, whiskey, maple syrup, and ginger ale soda! Lynn had a strawberry daiquiri tonight also, the second one in a row, and she usually never drinks alcohol. We lost again, but the conversation was great!

Tonight was our first night in the formal dining room. They gave us a table for two, Lynn had cold mango soup, and I was lucky enough to enjoy escargot; wow, what a treat. Her entree was steak, mine was Mahi and shrimp, and the desserts, of course, were excellent also! (Banana foster and triple B Brule.)

Lynn went off to watch "Dancing with the Superstars," and I toured the ship and caught up on this documentation. Lynn joined me in the room so that we could watch the late show of a comedian/magician called Mel Mellers, a very clever and interesting show. The time went by too fast! Off to bed, set the clock for 06:30. The meeting for the Santorini shuttle is at 08:00 sharp!

Tuesday morning already

Up at 6:20, dress, and check out the seascape of the Greek island of Santorini. Gulped down breakfast, the salmon is never out; if so, they will get it for you if you ask! Gulp down a coffee and go down to the theatre to join our group. Had to wait about twenty minutes, then off, down 4 sets of stairs mid-ships for the waiting port shuttle boats. The water is running a little rough, and the gunnels rise and lower 1-2 feet as we cross into the boat. It is only about ten minutes to the dock, but even in a sheltered harbor, we have to time our exits on the rise and fall of the boat, but no mishaps, and we head for the bus.

Now as we approached the Island we went past the old port to the other side of the Island to the new port, so we had a ship's eye view of the island from east to west, the new port accommodates a dock and a road down to the very small docking area. The old port is only accessible by cable car, walking down, or donkey. We will get to that story later!

The bus ride to the Akrotiri ruins is about 20-25 minutes, the ride up the sides of the volcano is narrow with many hairpins turns. The country side is pleasant, no trees except in a few towns, where they imported trees from Australia, the gum trees, smooth white bark and control the mosquitoes!

There is very little water, and the soil is mostly volcanic ash but full of minerals! In the winter, they may see a little snow. It is white and powdery due to the dry air. There is no pollution, but it doesn't rain much, so most if not all, plants need to absorb water through the air, like succulents. Caper bushes grow wild here, and I did take a picture of one outside the ruins.

These islands are part of a couple volcanos, one active and the other dormant, there is a location where the ocean is over 200 degrees F. As we went into the ruins, the structure over them is very similar to the structure over the Terracotta army site in China, the inside is computer controlled as far as temperature and humidity. It is also lit well. All work has stopped on the find due to the Greek financial crisis now four years old. The village was covered with volcanic ash 3600 years ago, similar to Pompeii, but much smaller and predates Pompeii by some 1000 years! Estimated at 1650 B.C.!!

There were only about 3500-5000 people in this ancient town, a complete sewer system below the streets, the women were light skinned, and pictures depict some in silk, so they had contact with the Orient! Also, trade was a big thing, the boats depicted had 21 sets of oars, and the art was similar to that found in Rome and Pompeii.

We circumvented the town, then went down inside some of the streets, the buildings were two or three stories high, the walls got thinner as they went up, and the door jams were about 5'10" high. A cache of 1200 urns were found intact, containing grains, oils, cured meats and fish, and nuts.

The guided tour lasted almost one and a half hours, we visited the gift shop run by the archeology society, to help out, since the government has put the receipts from the tours in the government coffers, to offset the debt of the government.

We then drove to the other side of the island toward the old port at the Oia village. This is all above the sea 20-30 stories, sheer cliffs down to narrow black pebble and sand beaches. The buildings are all a stark white with blue tops, done by the natives when they were told by the Venetians, they could no longer fly their flag. (Guess what color their flag was!)

We passed a beautiful resort on the side of the road, extending down one side of the cliff; we were told the cost to stay there was $800 EU. Per night, and may sometimes go to that per person staying!!

What little rain is captured on the roofs? The roofs are domed since there are still tremors, and the dome shifts more easily. Plus, everything is in stone due to no trees! There were a few windmills; we passed ten or twelve, but they, too, were shut down with no government subsidies. Two major religions are Roman Catholic and Greek Orthodox. The population of the island swells during tourist season and dwindles to a few thousand in the off-season.

As in America, many Europeans migrate here for the seasonal employment. There are lots of churches, the catholic churches outnumber the Greek orthodox three to one! The locals have a saying, "There are more churches than people, more wine than water, and more donkey's than men!

After a beautiful drive through the center and side of the island we reached our second destination of Fira.

We walked a quarter mile through the narrow streets to the edge of the cliffs. Here we had an hour to take pictures, visit the shops, and explore the town. Not only were the streets narrow, the town is pedestrian only, and the paths there were narrow for people!

We met at the bus after our exploration to our final destination, Oia. Here is the famous town that all the pictures around the world are taken... We bid farewell to the bus, walked a couple blocks to the edge of town, received directions on how to get back down to the shuttles, and bid our guide goodbye! Now, there are three ways to get down to the port; walk (about 1350 steps), donkey (they actually use the same steps, we were warned that you may get scraped along the wall, and watch out for the poop!), or cable car!

There are no railings on the steps, they transverse the side of the cliff back and forth, and you have to watch out for those donkey boobie traps! The cable car was donated by a benefactor's foundation along with a free airlift to the mainland for anyone needing a hospital, since there is no hospital on the island, I thought that was really nice, and we did appreciate the cable car!!

Noah

The ride down was only ten minutes, six to a car, and the loading was easy and efficient!

Back to the ship, drop off our souvenirs, grabbed a hotdog for me, a burger for Lynn, and we went on deck for the line dance. The line dance guy showed up, determined there were not enough people and canceled the event. We went back to the room and changed into long pants and nicer shirt, for me, Lynn, nice blouse and slacks, we were set for the night.

Five o'clock was celebrity Trivia. We had dinner and played Family Feud. Both Lynn and I walked away with prizes;

One of the questions was "what the first thing you do when you get up in the morning?" The answer, the most popular answer, wait for this...."check my phone!!"??

Participated in the "Who wants to be a Millionaire" game show, watched the production show put on by the singers and dancers called, "Pure Country" then went to the center of the ship to play "Battle of the Sexes".

Lynn had to stop off at the room, so I told her I would get us a seat. When I entered the room, there were only a few seats to be had, but I was grabbed by a staff member (female) dressed up like a guy and recruited to be on the men team, Lynn was also absconded to be on the women's team.

First competition was a guy dressed up as a girl, stuck a microphone in our face having us instantly come up with a song, it got down to one guy and one girl and she won, but at least Lynn was eliminated before me!

Next was pass an orange from guy to guy and women to women without using our hands, the guys won; next blow up a balloon, and smash it against another in various positions, the guys won, last was a conga line; all men with men recruiting men, then all women,

women recruiting women, the women won that one! We all got prizes, was a lot a fun, and we went back to the room ...long day, and a busy one tomorrow!

May 18th, Wednesday

We got up at 0615, dressed, gobbled some breakfast, toured the deck, and checked out the harbor. We were already docked; three cruise ships also docked, and a number of local ferries, including a twin-hulled hydrofoil, that zipped by pretty fast!

We were on the dock by 08:20, on a shuttle bus to the dock terminal, then, on the tour bus. The first stop was to be the Acropolis at 30 minutes away, but it was rushing hour, so the time it took was more like 45 minutes, so on the way, here is what we learned.

Athens, Piraeus in Greek, has four ports, Greece includes the land mass plus 6000 islands. This port is the 2nd biggest port in Europe next to London which is Europe's first. Piraeus now refers to Athens "old town" Greece has a population of about 20 million, with Athens harboring 4.5 million. It is the oldest continuous city in Europe at 5000 years old. Since the shore line is extensive, and there is sunshine 300 days a year the Athens folks come out at night, some of the bars don't even open till midnight. Many of the locals find that owning a large boat is cheaper than a summer residence, and so the slips are full. The tops of the apartment buildings all have water tanks, and a solar panel for hot water, there is a lot of graffiti, but the population just considers it as an indication of a younger crowd. The apartments sell for about $200,000 euro's, business space is $100,000 per 100 square feet, 80% of the people own a residence or apartment, it is considered an investment, 30% own a summer residence. The population is 90% Christian Orthodox, pollution was a problem in the 50's and sixties, but an underground sewer was installed and the cars pollute much less since then, the pollution is well controlled now.

There are many tangerine trees now blooming, this variety is very tart, and when used, the entire fruit in ground to make a jam. We did arrive at the Acropolis after touring the coastline, seeing the Olympic stadium, and observing motorcycles weaving in and out of traffic, and bumper to bumper parking with few if any parking spaces anywhere!

Taxis in this town are relatively cheap, a ride back to the pier from any of the locations we would be, would only cost $10-12 Eu.

We were about the fifth bus to arrive; two million people visit this Acropolis a year. Every city used to have an acropolis, to honor the gods, acropolis means "top of the city".

Legend says that three gods were fighting for the honor of having the city for themselves, Poseidon and Neptune; both due to the bounties of the sea, but Athena presented the olive tree, and it was determined that due to everything the olive tree provides, she won, so the Acropolis was dedicated to her. Athens has been dedicated to her for 28 centuries, the restoration of the Acropolis is the biggest on the planet.

The emphasis on the restoration is original material, since there were no straight lines, each block is exacting, and placed back exactly where it was, it took 18,000 rocks to build the original Acropolis. The walk up to the multiple structures involves many steps, all marble or polished stone, the surface uneven, pitted, with some loose stones or gravel. There are infrequent railings, and you must watch where you step all the way up and around the structures. We could not imagine if there was dew or rain on the polished stone, and many places were very uneven. None of the buildings were complete, none had roofed any longer, columns were missing, stones still placed alongside the structures. We toured the structures for about an hour, then headed back to the entrance, on the way we were able to view the structures from various vantage points, we also came upon a carob tree.

Carob trees are the basis of cocoa; the pods have 24 seeds per pod. We were lucky that we came early, it was a national historic holiday and all the parks and museums were admission free, so there were a lot more people coming up, along with classes of students crowding over all the walkways!

The next attraction was the museum. There we encountered long lines due to the holiday, but we did get in in a timely manner. The floor in front of the museum is glass, so you can observe a dig directly (about 20-25 ft. below the glass) One of the first items we came upon were multiple reliefs of gods. We were told we could not take pictures, but I had my flash turned off, and walked over to shoot the first of three gods. Welllllllll... I was approached by a security guard and he stated no pictures were to be taken. I told him that the flash was inactive, but he just repeated "NO pictures, delete the picture"; He looked over my side, and watched as I deleted the picture, gave me a disgusted look and said "NO MORE PICTURES IN THIS AREA! I said I was sorry and moved on to rejoin the group!

The gods were 1. a multi-headed god representing the four powers, fire, earth, wind, and water, with all the faces smiling, which is supposed to be rare, a horse, and a man with an eel body. There were various other statues in fairly good condition for being 6th century B.C., most missing noses, ears, fingers, and or hands or arms. But you could see quite a bit of detail. On one, there remained an inscription on the base. It seems that even back then, rich folk donated to make statues to honor people or gods. Patrons of the arts even existed then! We toured the balance of the museum. There were places where photos were allowed, so I took some of the many statues and reliefs.

Since there were tons of people and kids, the security folks had their hands full cautioning the kids "Not to touch" but I saw even a couple adults touch.... go figure! We then left the museum, walked a few blocks and ushered into a souvenir shop, given time to explore and spend some money, then back on the bus. The bus just stopped in the road and loaded us on, both sides of the road were parked tight, even yellow curbs were parked full, and corners! The side mirrors were very close to the bus when we passed the parked cars and trucks, and every opportunity, a scooter or motorcycle would pass us, or cut in front of the bus.

We passed by the Zeus temple, of the over 30 original columns only 16 are left, and they are twice as tall as Athena's, but they are in the valley! We passed a number of old arches, and lots of churches.

The tour included a restaurant stop to have a taste of local food. At the beginning of the tour a count was asked regarding pork, chicken or vegetarian. Half wanted pork, I took the chicken since Lynn took the pork and there was one vegetarian. The bus left us out after driving 20-25 minutes back in the direction of the port, and we walked 4-5 blocks through a pedestrian shopping area to the restaurant. Here we had a salad per table consisting of lettuce, tomatoes, cucumber, onions, and feta cheese. A choice of soda, and a gyro, that was very tastee!!

We then had a little over an hour to explore the shops before the bus picked us up to head back to the ship. We were lucky enough to find a shop that provided us the items we needed to finish our shopping. One thing, before we left the restaurant, I wanted to use the rest room, along with two women from the group. We did locate it, it was marked both men and women, with two small rooms, a stall in each, I guess whoever got there first just closed the stall, like we did......there is currently a big concern in the U.S regarding transgender people using different bathrooms; I don't seem to have a problem with it unless it includes locker rooms and showers, then if I were a woman, I would have a problem with a guy being there, especially with kids! But we will see!

Lynn did get approached by a gypsy when I was out walking, and finally gave in and bought a tablecloth for all the money she had on her, so of course I got blamed for not being there, it was my fault!

Educating Noah…Travelin'

The Syrian war has sent many refugees throughout Europe, Greece agreed to house and process 50,000, in areas north, by the border, the guide stated that there were still some 10,000 refugees still in Athens, they don't trust the government to provide them what they need, and are hoping everything will be over soon so that they can return home, or go further into Europe to join some other family members or friends.

Back to the dock, through dock customs, stopped and frisked (knees); bus to the ship, on the ship, stopped and frisked (knees again!)

We rested and changed, attended the five o'clock trivia, lost, went up to the grand dining room for our now, standing reservation, had another great meal, and talked to the excursion folks about cancelling our Venice excursion. Due to the problems, we had getting here, it being Italy, Italian time is a little less ridged than American time, and the excursion folks specified that the excursion was only to be taken by those leaving after 3:30 (ours was leaving at 2:30). Then we had to see customer service to get a transfer from the ship to the airport, which was also done.

Next was the "60 seconds or less game show" which was fun to watch, off to a music trivia, we lost again with new team players from Holland and Scotland.

Next "Finish that Lyric" game show, they were having difficulty having people volunteer to participate, so I volunteered, was the second last, they gave me a song from the 90's, and I blew it! 2nd place!!

Last but not least, we attended the "Love and Marriage game show." We really didn't want to participate; one other couple was married as long as we were, so we asked to let them play. A couple that had been married ten years later played, and a couple married 8 months ago played. It was a lot of fun, enjoyed by all, all of the contestants received a bottle of champagne, and the winner a souvenir pack.

Then an odd thing, to me, happened, an announcement was made that these shows were all in good fun and not meant to embarrass anyone on stage or in the audience, this happened with a few other games and a trivia or two, all telling everyone that the prizes were minor and that the object was just to have a little fun. Are people that sensitive, petty?? I will find out and report back later! Enough for this day, tomorrow is Ancient Deleos!

Thursday, May 19th, Mykonos, Greece. We arrived in Mykonos at 6:30 A.M. and we docked, we were to anchor in the harbor, the captain got permission to dock at the only slip, so we were able to gang-plank off the ship.

The first excursion was at 08:00 so we toured the upper deck before breakfast, it is sunny, not a cloud in the sky and in the high 60's. What a beautiful day! We ate, and toileted, rounded the upper deck again and down to the meet point. At 8:15 we were herded mid-ship, down 5 staircases, out on the dock, pictures as we left, (ship's photo team always has an actor or a life preserver to pose with), across the street where we met our guide for the day, received our headsets, and boarded a small ferry to take us to another port. There, we transferred to a sea-going ferry that took us to the currently uninhabited Delos.

The water is crystal clear, not much of a beach, and besides a museum, ticket office, souvenir shop, and a very small snack shop, there is nothing but ruins. This at one time was the busiest, sunniest and brightest ports in the world, from the seventh century B.C. to the seventh century A.D. There is no wall to this port, that is because it was a port protected by the god Apollo. As we exited the ferry and entered the gate, we were briefed as to where we were, times the tour would run too, free time, and ferry schedule in the event we wanted to stay any longer or catch the first one home. All the streets were narrow and irregular, the house we toured was large and comfortable, luxurious, at least 5 stories, and 5000 square feet. None of the roofs or second story of these buildings were still intact, but many parts are still outlined by the base, this one had a large open courtyard, to provided light and fresh air, a complete drainage system, a gathering room, a latrine, a bathing room, cooking room and small bedrooms. The inside walls were plastered and painted, there were also relief sculptures and paintings. The floors were wood and slate, the men slept separately from the women, since marriage back then was a contract with a man and his wife's father to support and sustain him, he usually upper 20's to early 30's she being about 16. It was also common for men to have concubines, and prostitutes. The idea was to maximize the children in the household.

Rain water was collected from the roof tops, and run into cisterns below the house, holding 100 kiloliters of water each. Water was accessible with each family having a well, the well water was only 8-13 meters deep. (There were also several public wells, and baths, as well as a community cistern, 250 cubic liters!) In this house, there was a grand entry hall, maintained by a slave, with a staircase to the rest of the house. The latrine seats were heated for the owners by slaves prior to the use. Metal was used to anchor windows and sills, also thresh-holds, iron or lead, in-cased in copper for a decorative effect.

On to the theatre, the first-row seats had backs to them, those were for dignitaries, the programs were for providing news, and some entertainment. This was the start of democracy, women could attend educational dramas plays, however not the comedies since the language was rather "free"!

On the island, there are venomous snakes, so we were warned that we should keep close to the group, and not go wondering too far off the paths! (I got "that look" from Lynn!)

On the way, back from the theater, there were a number of ruined small shops with marble table-top, used to display wares, the second shop had table tops with cleaver slices in it, so it is assumed that this shop was a butcher shop. Amulets were carved into the corners of some paths to protect the traveler from evil.

Just before Apollo's temple was a large market square, this is the place that sold the grains and barley. Hermes, the God of Commerce, ruled the square.

Along many of the low walls were benches to enable people to rest, there were many places in the square for people to sit, there were several public wells, and as before mentioned, a public bath. The Apollo sanctuary had three main rooms; everything was marble!

Down the road from Apollo's sanctuary were lion statues, still mostly intact, very impressive!!

The extensive ruins found, only account for 1/7 of the city! The island is deserted, lizards, insects, spiders and feral cats live there permanently. Park staff and museum staff work the open seasons, there is currently not enough money to continue the restoration at this time given the financial difficulties Greece is encountering. I did get a book that gives the history of this port, it is a very good read, and great pictures and maps of how things were.

We checked out the museum, shot some interesting photos. We walked the narrow alleyways of white walls and polished stone floors, many shops with friendly people. The water here is very clear also, no ocean smell at all and the restaurants line the beach, all open, all serving under canopies outside, the smells and the ambiance was great!

We then took the boat ferry back to the ship, grabbed a salad, worked on notes, changed for dinner, had a great round of trivia with three other couples, and had a wonderful supper. After supper, I asked our attendant for some white bags and top sheets for white night. He quickly provided them, and we were off to watch the second elimination of Dancing with the Stars, one more finale, down to three couples, very entertaining!

Back to the room, custom made our Toga's, caught up on some rest, and the "White Night" starts at the Centrum at 9:45 P.M.

We were the only ones with togas, but with dancing they kept coming apart! The activities guy tried to fix Lynn's but it worked for only a little while, mine kept sliding off my shoulder, however, we did make an impression, and we stayed for the line dancing, which was a lot of fun! You could tell who was from South America, they knew all the steps, and really got into it! Another great day, maybe I'll get more than 5-6 hours' sleep tonight!

Tomorrow is an "at sea" day, Lynn has a massage lined up, and we have a behind the scenes galley tour with the chef followed by a brunch buffet with him.... Yum!

It's Friday already, wow! I got up late, had coffee and a little fruit, walked the deck, and went down to the cabin to see if Lynn was up, and get the camera, we are cruising off the Greek coast, and it looks like the Misty Isles!

Yup, Lynn got up and we planned to meet after she had breakfast on the deck to coordinate meeting for the galley tour at 11; I walked the deck, watched a Brazilian Capoeira class, then joined Lynn for the galley tour. Lynn felt much better after her massage, I believe she is now convinced that the massage package we talked about a massage a month, is well worth the expense.

We met in front of the dining room on deck 5 for the tour. We initially were seated at a table with two other couples, given a disclaimer to sign, and then off to the galley, behind the dining areas. We went through two floors of areas from salad prep, soup, bakery, meat and starches. We were shown how the biscuits and tarts were made with special presses, gluten free area, the locked wine cellar, huge coffee urns, displays of how the finished plates were to look, plus actual plates made fresh for examples. We walked past the staging areas, areas for employees showing performance charts and reviews.

We then went back to the table and the other two couples sat at separate tables for two? We thought nothing of it, as we dove into a basket of various breads, a plate of 8 different sushi rolls, and antipasto salad, and a cheese plate. We saw another waiter going around asking about the main course, so we called over the waiter and asked if he was going to take our order. He told us that we had to wait until our table was full, we told him about the other couples, and that all of our group was seated and if we could move to a table for two so we could place our order. He called over the head waiter, and he quickly agreed to the move, apologized profusely, and kept sending a server over to refill our Champaign glasses while he personally took our order. Lynn had beef tenderloin, and I had stuffed chicken, both with mashed potatoes, carrots, and broccoli all perfectly seasoned and cooked. Dessert, we both had crepes, again, perfect. We waddled out of there, a great meal and an interesting insight to the kitchen, well worth the $30.00 price per person!

Two o'clock was another trivia, Lynn went to the movies to see "Concussion" and Lynn met me at the Captain's Corner, an open session where the captain, the engineer and the hotel services officer took questions from the passengers.

The captain and the main officers have their wives and family with them on occasion, there was no hesitation with any questions and answers, the captain had a good sense of humor, and seemed like he had a very good relationship with the officers. I did make a point to thank him for letting us on 15 minutes before actually setting sail in front of the group, and Lynn asked if he had ever left anyone behind at a port, and he said "No, I have always made every effort to bring back all of my passengers" which I thought was admirable!

Participated in "Split the Difference" game show, I was eliminated early, Lynn lasted two questions longer! (There are three optional answers to questions, and various people line up in a group they believe have the correct answer.)

Another trivia, this time we had two Latin America couples, and a family of 6, grandma, husband and wife, two young boys and a young girl all from South Carolina. It was a Disney movie and song quiz, and the kids came in handy, but yeah, we lost again!

Dinner, beef wellington, and Lynn had vegetarian chili in taco shells, and gazpacho green soup which she shared and was amazing!

A guess which diamond was real contest, I picked the right one, along with about 30 others, no, I did not win, watched a production of singing and dancing to show tunes, the main dancing couple are world acclaimed, and their dancing was a true art form! The next game show was the "perfect couple" four couples competed, it was a lot of fun, and the whole group of us enjoyed the antics.

Following the game show, we played quest. We recruited the two couples in front of us and two younger women next to them for our team. We chose the big swede guy, who was a little reluctant but then gave in, he was pretty reserved, but he could run faster than me, and his buddy was very reluctant!

We had to send a representative up with items, or actions, five shoe laces, gold key card, sea pass with a name starting with "R" on it, a guy with five bras on his head, one guy in women's shoes, guy with lipstick (that would be me, and I kissed his cheek!) one person doing the worm dance, a guy with a hairy back, and a person with a contraceptive device, so I ran up with a wedding ring! A number of other things, plus every so often the whole team had to go on the dance floor and do the Macarena dance! It was a lot of fun, everyone enjoyed it!

That was enough, it was almost twelve, so we called it a day, tomorrow is our last Greek port of call, Corfu.

Noah

Saturday, May 21st, we are slowly approaching the dock of the last Greek island we are to visit. We signed up for the Panoramic Corfu. We left the ship at 8:20, the bus was loaded on the pier next to the ship. The Queen Mary was docking on the other side as we boarded our coach. As we drove through town, we noticed all of the apartments had porches to enjoy the outside air. The weather is cool, low to mid-sixties, a 10-12 mph wind, and overcast.

This is a very lush island, with many Cyprus, Kumquat, and Lemon trees between grooves of Olive trees. As we drove through several small towns, I noticed again the extremely limited parking; the two-lane road we were on just accommodated the bus and a small car in the other direction, with inches to spare. One town, one lane wide, with only 2-3 inches on either side of the bus, many corners scrapped and chewed up, and the sides of the buildings showed numerous paints and scrapes. As the road zig-zagged up the mountain, there were many hairpin turns, and in a number of cases, a car had to back up just to let us swing through the tight corners. I know this was a holiday, but very few people are out and about!

Corfu consists of 6 islands, on the northern border it is only an hour away by boat to Albania, and 6 hours by boat to Italy, the main commerce here as in many islands now, is tourism.

This is the greenest of the six-island group and used to be a quarantine island. One of the legends here is that Poseidon was upset with Ulysses and destroyed his boat here. Athena felt sorry for Ulysses and built him another boat, and a small island vaguely resembling a boat is said to be it, and yes, I took pictures.

Every family has olive trees, and grape vines, when a family had children, Cyprus trees were planted, when the daughter was of age and got married, the Cyprus trees were given to her as a dowry.

How do you harvest olives from an olive tree? You spread a fine black net under the tree, and in fall the olives drop to the ground, where you harvest them, by gathering up the net.

We stopped at three little towns, got some beautiful pictures of the sea and seashore, finished up our shopping, and were back to the ship early in the afternoon. It was raining lightly on the walk back to the ship, back to the room to change, drop the last of the treasures, and off for a warm lunch.

After lunch, we checked out the photos in the gallery, we will add a few to the bill tomorrow, walked the ship, and pulled a current bill to see how far in debt I was from the charges.

We met at 4:30 for the second last trivia, our Scottish friends, our English friend, (her husband wasn't back trying to win at ping pong), and the two couples from Atlanta joined us. The subject was 60's and 70's music, "name that tune".

We aced it, 14/14! Pens for all of us!!

The dinner was exceptional, Lynn had lamb shank, I had fish, scallops, and shrimp, and yes, we splurged on dessert, key lime pie for me and apple strudel for Lynn.

We checked out the production number in the theatre, watched a show in the atrium, walked the ship, then attended the line dance class.

The 70's Disco Inferno Street party started next, the cruise director, the disco divas, and the macho men from the activities staff dressed up and performed, while leading us in dance. Of the three couples, we danced the most, Lynn and I even took the glass elevators up to the 11th floor while dancing, we punched every floor, so we could dance to the music and put on a spectacle, and yes, our friends saw us. We called it quits at midnight, found the information for debarkation in the room plus luggage tags, took showers and called it a day. Our last day on the ship is a sea day as we journey back to Venice.

Noah

Sunday, May 22nd, last full day on the ship, and a day at sea.

A day in the sun!.......no, I can do this at home! We actually slept in till 7:30, began to pack, and then went off to breakfast. It's always a great selection, but it's actually too much of a good thing. We went off to walk the deck; it was in the high 60s with a brisk wind, but it felt great! Lynn sat outside for a while until the wind got to her.

At 10 o'clock they had the second session of the Brazilian Capoeira Class. This is like an energized Tia Chi, here comes the excuses, too much for my shoulders, too tricky for Lynn, but we watched and even that worked up a sweat..........

Lynn went off to read some more, and I attended a Chinese Jou Herbs and acupuncture seminar. I was the only one to show up, but as I suspected, it was an herb sales job, along with the alternative Acupuncture treatments. I was told the natural cures were not as effective right away; it takes time to aid the body in healing itself, and treatments should be from one to about three months for effectiveness. The supplements were available only on the ship or through their website. I didn't even ask for the price!

Next, we met and attended the "Chef Tasting Table" presentation which went well, we met the head chefs of each department and they presented their best selection for the day. Then they invited us up to taste, we were all given five or six plastic spoons to taste, using a new spoon for each selection. The risotto was great! Actually, everything was!

We checked out the auction, but it was too pricey, most works started at a minimum bid of $1000.00 So we left without the free print if we would have stayed. Dropped by the buffet for a quick lunch, they were making panini's, so I had a small one, some fries, and some salad, Lynn had some Bolognese spaghetti, and half of my panini, and we shared a small dish of desserts.

I went back to the room to pack, Lynn back somewhere to read, then off to the Selfie Scavenger Hunt. We had a list of things to find and take selfies with the team, a list of about 20 items, including, but not all listed, seven bare feet, not our own with a selfie of all team members, selfies with all team members were the stipulation for all the items, two people in a shower team, passenger eating a cookie, two passengers in life preservers, sexy man, sexy lady, passenger with a napkin on their head, our team with the art work, and on and on.... most passengers cooperated with us, some refused. There was a total of four teams, we won!!! That is why we try to team up with another younger couple, more energy, quicker minds, much more flexible, and significantly more "selfie" knowledge.

Took a couple rounds in the sun, wind calmed down, and the temperature now in the 70's, I counted deck chairs, only three not tagged, both decks, about 350, on the top deck, about the same near the pool, 60% occupied, the balance with towels or personal items on or near. I did run into the head chef and complimented him on the positive and happy attitude of his chef's, he told me that a happy chef makes 'happy" food, and then the customer is happy also.........kinda like Karma!

The Grand Finale. Art Auction, it was still going on, about 10-12 couples bidding, I told the guy at the desk that we were called away, and if it would be alright if I received the "free" art picture promised for attending. He asked me why I got called away, I just gave him "the look" and he just shrugged and handed me an envelope. Lynn wanted it, so I made it happen, I went down to the room and hid it in the bathroom as a surprise.

I made it back to the Schooner lounge to meet Lynn for the 5 PM trivia, "The Beatles Hits," we lost with 14/15; what a tough crowd!!

Dinner, had a nice conversation with a newlywed couple from Oregon, and wished them the best of luck in their life together and gave them a "million dollars" worth of advice on life, jobs, and marriage at no charge!

"Where am I" trivia at 8, we won that one!!

Nine o'clock was a show featuring a woman who was a ballerina and contortionist, amazing how she could bend her body, choreographed to music, incorporating, hoops, ribbons and drapery.

Ten thirty was the finals for dance and karaoke singers, the dance partners were passengers, each pared with an entertainment staff member. The karaoke were three very talented passengers. After judging the winners, the entire staff paraded in to the auditorium for us to give them a hand of appreciation.

That was it for the day, got back to the room, checked luggage that was left in the hallway was gone, showered, checked all drawers and closets, set everything out for our travel day and off to bed for our last night on board the Rhapsody of the Sea.

Monday, bid our ship Good bye.

Time to go home. We toured the boat before breakfast, I had my last salmon breakfast for a while, Lynn ate a good breakfast since we didn't know when we would eat or where next.

We canceled our excursion, our flight was scheduled for 2:30 in the afternoon, the tour included transfer to the airport, but we were skid-ish especially with missing the connection flight on the way here, especially when the tour was recommended for flights after 3:30!

We were in a group to be let off the ship at 9:15. The disembarkation went well, and we found our luggage easily, and went out to the parking area. We found out then that the bus would be there at 11:00, and if we wanted to, we could walk a few blocks to a restaurant to wait. Oh, by the way, it was drizzling, with rain, off and on. So, we, with most, walked with our luggage to the restaurant with a canopy over tables and signs reserving the tables for customers only.

I bought a double expresso and nursed it for an hour and a half. As 10:45 approached, we walked back to the bus staging area and fought with those that stayed under the small shelter there (enough room for about 10 couples) too get our luggage on the bus, and then find a seat on the bus. There was nothing to see on the half hour trip to the airport, it was mostly freeway, skirting the old town.

At the airport, we found the line for Lufthansa, checked our luggage, and got our boarding passes. Went through security, and I get stopped for my knees; Lynn gets stopped for?? (We still don't know why she gets stopped and "wanded" almost as much as I did.) Made it to the gate with an hour to spare, found a sandwich for us to share, and waited to fight in line to get some storage room for our carry-ons. As in China, no queuing is honored, and many try to get in line when the planes start to load; the only people who do not have to fight are those with business or first-class tickets. Guess what....... the flight to Amsterdam was canceled, so those were transferred to our plane to Frankfort, AND the flight was delayed an hour.

Yes, we arrived in Frankfort and hour late, BUT they did delay the flight from Frankfort to Chicago for us and about 20 other people! Yes, we had to run from our gate on one side of the terminal to the other side, no rest room stop or resting, but we made it!

The flight was about 9 hours, about 30 minutes were made up in the flight, but we made it to Chicago, used our "trusted traveler" to by-pass the long re-entry customs line, picked up our luggage, made our way to the bus pick-up point, and had 20 minutes to spare!

We called Tiffany to pick us up at the bus station, we were a half hour late there too due to a 4-lane crash on the way back, but we were home, by 11:30 P.M. Another great vacation! We were tired, showered, and hit the hay!

Noah

It took about a week as always, to put ourselves back in sync with our lives again. As usual I immediately started to finish up on the vacation notes, have Lynn proof them and add them to this document. Then, the task of reviewing all the photographs, editing them, enhancing them, sending them to Shutterfly, and creating another album.

I also had limited time to get the visas for Russia added to our passports. It usually takes thirty to forty days, and we were leaving for Iceland in July, the two-week road trip including Canada in August, and then mid-September, Russia!

I have used Generations Visa service in the past with China, but this was even more extensive, six pages of questionnaire each, everything checked and rechecked, including everything on the passport, verification of spouse, education above high school, military service, occupations, and dates of when and where! Plus, photos, and $640.00; Fed Ex to D.C., including $40 expediting fee; sent the day after we returned, taking a total of 4 hours to "dot the "I's" and cross the T's"!

I also drove for the VA on one day, visited Ma, completed the album and ordered it with Shutterfly, took a road trip to upper Wisconsin to check out a weekend trip for the motorcycle club to a farm that offered home grown pizza, and back and a badly needed haircut all by Saturday night, five days…. a new record!

Iceland July 2016

Iceland, our third adventure this year, (2016), and Lynn's top pick. We signed up for it with Fox travel last fall after a presentation. We will be circumventing the island, eight days.

As soon as we returned from Greece, I sent in the passports, as previously stated so that they will be set for the rest of the year, then I started pestering Fox travel regarding seating on the aircraft, updates, and changes.

The first change was, instead of a seal watch; we are now on a whale watch. I asked about optional tours, especially for the Blue Lagoon thermal mineral excursion. This is now included, but after many tries, the other optional tours by Globus were not available.

I finally got our seat assignments, tried to upgrade to economy plus, but I was told no upgrade was possible except business class, and that would cost us an additional $2000 each. That would be almost what we paid for the vacation per person, so we passed on that upgrade. We will be bussed down to O'Hare, by Globus, and fly to New York. The flight to Iceland from New York is about five and a half hours. It will be cramped, but at least we are seated together, middle and aisle seat with a three-three configuration on a 757. (Watch those elbows when the cart comes through!)

In that we are in and out of busses and multiple hotels, we opted for two smaller bags, especially with no dress-up nights.

This is 34 days out; we converted $290.00 to ISK, I guessed at the amount needed in local currency, the tip for the guide and bus driver should run about $150 US which in ISK is 20,000., The rest I can use for tips, change to the toilets, (yes, like in Europe, it costs about fifty cents US in their money to "go").

We received our passports last Friday; it only took three weeks to process the visas for Russia and alleviate some of the usual pre-trip stress. I conferred the amount of ISK with Lynn and we decided to convert an additional $100 worth just to make sure we have enough cash on hand.

My Aunt died, there was no funeral, there was just a "family" service which was only for her kids. I researched and confirmed, and gave my mother the information available, so she could pass it on to her sister June. I discussed my mother's situation, we decided to close her safe deposit box, and keep everything in our safe deposit box, I then gave all the information to both Tiffany and Camille, since we are traveling so much, to be able to handle anything when it comes to my mother and we are on the other side of the world.

It is now a little more than two weeks out, we haven't received the final package from FOX Travel, but I am sure it will come soon. Last week we attended our fiftieth high school graduation celebration. 50! WOW!

Lynn recognized two people, me, none. There was a graduation class of 600; about 150 attended the dinner. We were able to tour the school in the afternoon, only about 20 people showed up for the two-hour tour, of a school that has been expanded and modernized, this year only graduated 150 kids! Very interesting, kind of depressing, and we both can't believe it has been that long ago!

It is two days before leaving, bags are packed batteries are charged, everything checked and rechecked, e-mail of phone numbers and flights to the kids, visit to ma done, only confirm air Friday, and be at the park and ride at 10 A.M. Saturday.

<u>Sunday Evening</u>

We are here! Another adventure in travel! Taffy picked us up just a little after 9:15 (she did that just to "get" me) sat at the College exit till 9:45 when the bus came to pick us and another couple up, the final two Wisconsin couples, we were to meet ten more people at the airport in Chicago.

The hour-plus ride down was uneventful; upon leaving the bus, we entered the terminal and proceeded to the check-in kiosks. I, along with two others from the group, attempted to check -in, but the "quick" time-saving check-in didn't work, so we joined the rest of the group in line. I had tried the night before to check in, but like the kiosk, I got only so far and stalled. I called Delta, our airline carrier, and waited for 20 minutes, and then my check-in timed out. I discussed the problem with the agent, and she suggested that I put in an emergency contact. I said it would take me a while to re-enter the data, thanked her, and tried again. You guessed it, entered the additional data, and yep, stalled again! I called again, and while waiting the obligatory 15-20 minutes, I got another agent keeping the check-in open by toggling back and forth. We could not finish the check-in together. He told me it was probably due to the group booking, and we would have to do this at the terminal.

After 20 minutes, the counter people finally figured out what to do with us, opened another line and proceeded to process the group. Then the dreaded TSA! Since Delta is an airline that recognizes Trusted Travelers, we had a very short line, and went through in less than 10 minutes, only one knee showed, and Lynn this time wasn't stopped and wanded at all!

We found our gate, took our bathroom breaks, and settled Lynn in and I went for my walks. Yes, it seems with Delta there is always a delay, this one was 45 minutes, so we were in O'Hare for about four and a half hours.

The commuter plane was very crowded, all seats taken, and the smallest seats we have had. It is only a two-hour flight, so it was no big thing........oh, yes, it took us almost 30 minutes after landing to get to the terminal. The aircraft was backed up that much.

Now we were in New York, the connecting flight to Reykjavik, was three hours, we found our gate, I went out for another walk, and food, and we enjoyed a margarita pizza flat bread and a health drink ($15.00) (Nothing is cheap in an airport), had a gate change, so we moved after the snack. FOUR more gate changes and a total of five hours, we were herded on to the plane, basically just the priority people, business and first class, family and kids, then a free for all. It seems there is no concern for order with Delta, since this happened exactly like this with Delta when we flew back from Hawaii!

We all settled into our slightly less cramped seats, backed up, and taxied to a waiting area, where we waited...........for almost an hour on the tarmac, supposedly for weather concerns. Finally, we took off just before midnight for our direct five-and-a-half-hour flight to Iceland.

We were served one meal two hours into the flight, and we were warned by the pilot to close the windows because sunrise in Iceland at this time of the year is about three thirty A.M. and the brightness is unforgiving!

This was a 737 jet, 180 passengers, only one galley, in the back, we were in the third last row, and being in the aisle seat, constantly bumped by service carts going to and fro, and passengers using the restroom.

Lynn got some sleep, I stayed up all night, the passenger at the window did not bother us at all, and actually slept most of the time.

We arrived in Reykjavik at 10 A.M. their time, no problem with the luggage, loaded the bus, and drove to the city an hour away from the airport.

When we arrived at the airport, we were told that the hotel would try to have our rooms available by 1300 (we are now using military time as they do), they provided us a lounge to wait. We found Lynn a comfortable chair, and I with another passenger left for a walking tour of the town.

We asked directions, and here they give distances by time, downtown was to the left "a good 10 no-more than 15-minute walk". My partner walks fast, like a European, so we covered the distance in about 20 minutes, toured a bit of downtown, and returned along the ocean front, great views of the ocean, and the snowy mountains on the side.

We returned to find both mates, her husband and Lynn propped up in chairs still waiting for the room. It was a little after one, so I slipped over to the bar to check out the local brews. I heard about a schnapps called "Black Death", ordered one of those, (Islenskt brennivi) asked about anything else unique to Iceland, and was given one made from Birch bark, (Bjork liqueur); and a local beer, stout if possible.

The Black Death tasted a lot like the French Absinthe, the liqueur had a very subtle sweet aroma and was quite good, the beer was almost black and had a hint of sweetness. I was warned by the items I read about Iceland, like Europe, was expensive, especially with alcohol, but I put a 5000 ISK note (about $45.00 US) and received back, 375 ISK as change! Three small drinks......$40 bucks....no more alcohol this week!

I finished the drinks, went to the desk, got our room keys, picked up Lynn and the carry-ons, went to the room, and both of us slept till five, freshened up, and joined the group for the tour company included welcome dinner.

We wrapped things up. We leave tomorrow, a.m at 08:00 sharp, luggage out at 07:00, breakfast buffet starts at 06:00, and we were told that there really isn't any "night" during the summer and that it gets "dusky" after 11p.m. (I will check that out some other night!)

The dinner was excellent, a salad, a dinner of baked cod on a bed of barley, and vegetables on the side, and an ice cream dessert that was on a bed of granola and fresh fruit served in a mason jar (or their version). We talked for a while, then all of us retired to our rooms to get a full night's sleep, and me an hour to type up the day's activities, set up the shower (it still was too hot) for Lynn, and open a window to the warm room.

Day 2 Monday, July 11th.

When I went to bed, it was still light outside. That was about 22:30. I woke up at 11:30, and it was still light! I then could not go back to sleep when I woke up at 04:00, got up, went to the potty, took my pills, shaved, put on deodorant, brushed my teeth, dressed, and snuck out of the room and asked the desk clerk where the botanical garden was, got a map and went out. It was 04:37, 11.3 degrees Celsius, a light overcast, and a slight breeze...life is good!

I walked around, nice and quiet, the air fresh and sweet; I followed the directions to where he circled the location on the map, and there was only an indoor swimming pool (I took a picture of the street sign and the "UT" sign in the parking lot) UT=out!

I then studied the map, there was a dot that actually was labeled botanical garden, only a few blocks away, located it, took pictures of some nice flowers, and a cluster of mushrooms. On the way, back, I went through an art park and got some really nice sculpture pics. Went back to the room, Lynn was almost ready, checked and rechecked the room, put the suitcases out and we went down to the included breakfast buffet.

This was a typical European buffet, strong coffee, tea, yogurts, fruits, hot and cold cereals, salmon, herring, cold cuts, cheeses, various breads and muffins, two types of eggs, sausage, bacon, and pancakes. After breakfast, we checked out, loaded up everything on to the bus, and out of the parking lot at 0805.

We took the city route, past the old capitol house, which was shipped piece by piece from Norway, through the streets, a concert hall that is an art piece itself, with glass walls, on the shoreline. We also drove past two lagoons just outside the city central and a beautiful church that was built only 20 years ago,

All the while, we were informed on the island. There is a population of 330,000 people, two-thirds live in Reykjavik. Iceland won its independence after the Second World War from Denmark. They are very proud of the country; 80% are protestant, 10 % catholic, and the balance practice the old religions or various others, if any.

It took only an hour to get to our first stop, the geothermal heat and electric power station in Hellisheioavirkjun. We were provided a tour of the grounds, the four generators, on a plant surrounded by old lava beds, situated on a fault line (the headless cat fault line, looks like a sitting cat w/o a head!) and generates over 300 megawatts of power. This power is the cleanest and most efficient generated power in the world, second only to hydroelectric power. They have also designed a system to take the CO2 out of the discharged stack and inject it back into the ground with calcium to change the gas into stone. Neat!

After the tour, we had some time, so I went out to the lava field to gather stone souvenirs and see what it was like to walk on the lichen-covered fields. It was like walking on a very thick, soft carpet; what a unique feeling! I selected and gathered my treasures for home, met up with Lynn, and bought a magnet and postcard for $10.00! And joined the rest of the group on the bus to our next stop.

On the way to the geysers, we learned and saw more; Iceland is at the 66th parallel, about the highest for human occupation, the last two years, they have experienced the coldest temperatures since they have been recording temperatures. (Global warming?) Usually, they get 70 centimeters of snow during the winter, (2.54 cm.=1" about 28 inches) and only 111 days with light. Since the growing season is short, and such a long time without light, trees are small where there are some, plus there is a lot of volcanic activity, the last eruption was in 2012.

The snowcapped queen mountain was, per legend, the gate to Hell. A bishop had a small church not too far from the mountain, and when anyone landed on the island, they had to pay homage to the bishop and let him know the purpose of the visit and the length of time they would be there.

The basis of the island is Danish, German, and Swedish. The first settlers were around 870 A.D. These settlers brought horses, sheep, and cattle; one of the few indigenous animals is the Arctic fox. The sheep, horses, and cows are to forage in the countryside for food, so the meat is all-natural. The country is very environmentally conscious and very proud of the way they respects the earth.

The second stop was the hot springs geyser. The first thing off the bus we were guided over to the chef, where we were treated to taste freshly baked bread, which was cooked for twenty hours using the geothermal hot springs, served with hardboiled egg, butter and herring, and a shot of Black death schnapps. (brennivin, "drekyist Is kalt" drink ice cold printed right on the bottle!) The bread was a rye bread, filling and sweet; I had a couple, with some of the other guys along with a few more shots, very good and filling!

We then walked the spring area, several bubbling pools, and steams of water, all at least 100 degrees Celsius, progressed to the main geyser, and waited for the big blow, and yes, after a few false starts, it did blow water and steam about 70 to 80 meters straight up into the air! We walked around the area, and I did it about twice; Lynn explored the extensive, expensive (all money under five hundred ISK coins) souvenir shops and restaurants and got back on the bus to our next stop.

Iceland has a land mass the size of Kentucky and Michigan; it is 15 degrees Celsius now, and with a light jacket, it is very comfortable. We pass by areas where there are farming, then there are horses, and they are harvesting the hay already, wrapping the bales in yellow, blue, or white plastic, very colorful. We can also see the glacier in the distance, an interesting sight. The next stop was the magnificent Gullfoss waterfalls. I was able to take a number of pictures from a number of angles. Just beautiful.

The next stop is Tingvellir, a geological Enesco area, where the separation of the North American and European tectonic plates shifts. Most of us walked through the valley. This is where the earth's crust just breaks, shifts, and pushes up; it is hard to explain; the black lines indicate rifts, broken rocks pushed up and aside, huge boulders split, and crevices all jagged. What a wonder!

We are now on our way to the next stop, our motel and dinner. We go through a 300-meter tunnel under a fjord where whales frequent (no, we didn't see any) a beautiful clear lake with a new island being pushed up from below, mostly rain-fed and incredibly clear, listened to more legends, and actually stopped at a local grocery store for jams, chocolate and rheumatism supplements the guide swears by.

We check into the hotel, get to our rooms, and prepare for supper. I put yellow caution tape across our guide door, and we joined the rest of the group for drinks. The guide comes in and shows everyone a picture of her on the floor under the tape in the doorway (supposedly dead or fainted); it really warmed up the group!

Lamb for supper was excellent, and then a few of us headed for the hot tubs. What a great feeling! 15 degrees Celsius and 90 F water!! Stayed there till a little after 10:30, went back to the room, showered, and typed up the day....it is now midnight, and it is getting a little dusky outside! Time for bed, up at 6, we leave at 8!

Day 3, Tuesday, July 12th, 2016.

I was up a bit later this morning, 0530. I dressed and let Lynn sleep till 0600, woke her up, turned off the alarm, and went for a walk and a little coffee. Nice and quiet, and of course, full light; I don't believe it gets any darker than dusk, and our tour guide confirmed that!

It is overcast and seven degrees Celsius, with light winds. Breakfast was another buffet, smaller but offered different items. I had cod liver oil, sardines in a tomato sauce, a melon slice I didn't recognize, olives, and some cheese, with a few whole grain crackers, and, of course, some herring.

After we ate breakfast, we loaded up the bus and were gone, on the road, by 0805. We passed marshmallow farms (baled hay). They have a short growing season; some places on the island can get three cuttings of hay, and the other half gets two. Horses, cows, sheep, and goats in the pastures. Every so often, we have to stop for a couple sheep crossing the road.

After an hour of driving, we stopped for a WC (restroom) break. I bought some fish jerky recommended by the driver to pass around, but the guide refused. She said it would "stink up the bus," so I still have the package and will probably take it home. After traveling another hour and a half, we made a ten-minute "pit stop" by a pasture to meet three "Islandic" horses in a field.

They came over to us, expected more than petting, and actually nipped my hand. We petted them, used them as a photo "op," and climbed back on the bus to continue our journey.

The temperature has climbed to 9 C, and this is as high as it will get today. Some occasionally light sprinkles of rain, but that is it!

More information as we travel: the high salaries here are about 475,000 ISK ($5,000 U.S.) per month. Taxes were a straight 37%, now it is three tiers: the first 280,000 is 37%, the next 280 K is at 40%, and everything after that is 47%K (and it starts at dollar one, for all employed.)

There is a VAT tax on everything but food; of 25%, food is about 10%. Nothing is cheap except for water and power. Checks are monthly, the income tax is now taken, and the accounts are settled every August 1st.

Sweden, Denmark, and France work a 36-hour week; here, a 40-hour week is expected.

The family structure changed in the sixties before the men worked outside the home, and the women were the domestics, taking care of the house and the kids. That is not so any longer.

Our next stop, a house, was a grouping of small sod houses, a look into the past. Everything was small and efficient; they wanted to charge $10 U.S. a piece to go into the living quarters, so we skipped that, even though the church was small. Everything was characteristically neat, clean, and orderly. They didn't charge to use the WC, so we all took advantage.

We had a drive to go, so we stopped at a small bakery and gas station to try the lamb hotdogs and bakery. I ordered my dog with the works, Lynn just ketchup. The works included bacon crumbles, mustard, mayo, relish, and ketchup. It was a little longer than an American dog but also skinnier. We both liked them.... eight bucks for two! Then we went to the bakery, two items, another six bucks!!

On to the whale-watching expedition in Hauganes! When we arrived, everyone got into a weather suit, a cold weather fisherman's suit, and off to the boat.

The recession of 2008 was worldwide; many lost their homes and businesses, and over 9000 Icelanders left Iceland to find jobs in Europe and North America.

The trip was billed as a one-and-a-half-hour tour of the largest fjord in Iceland. It was cool, even with the suits over our clothes and jackets! But after a good forty-five minutes, we got pretty close to two, then three small (20-25 foot) humpback whales. They actually swam under the boat, with no breaching, but they spouted several times, and you could see their backs. And we also had two tail flips! We tried to chase them. We had some more sightings, but I think they were playing with us, and soon, they were gone.

We then looked for some more, and none were to be found. We threw a couple of lines in the water, and two of us caught cod. I was not one of the lucky ones; the cod were "keepers," but after everyone saw them, they were released back into the ocean.

Back to shore, changed back into our regular clothes, and a short drive to Akureyri for our supper and hotel.

This was a very cute town. I took pictures and shopped, and dinner was gourmet: a salad with salmon, hardboiled egg slices, spring lettuce, and a green dressing set off by a small bagel chip. The main course was a perfect boned chicken breast on a bed of risotto and vegetables, followed by pancetta (pudding with strawberry, blueberries, and chocolate shavings) Plenty to eat, the strong coffee was excellent, and we then took a short walk in town, returned to the room, to shower, and hit the hay, after journaling.

Day 4 Wednesday, July 13th

After another great European breakfast, I had a full night's sleep, loaded up on the bus, and off to a Botanical garden located in the city limits. What a great selection of island flowers, most of them, if not all, imported to the island. It is 10 degrees C., but we are promised a "warm" day!

I noticed a lot of kids working in the gardens and the night before at the hotel. So, I asked what was going on and was told that the minimum pay for kids was a few hundred Kroners per hour, and from 8th grade up, the government sponsors programs to employ the young folks so that they "Earn their money!", "No sitting at home!" They are expected to work 4-8 hours a day in either the public or private sector. Now we saw some kids that were 12-13 years old working; what a nice concept, and not one of them was looking at a phone!

After a good 45 minutes in the garden, we were off to another waterfall and learned more of the Icelandic culture. 80-85 % own their own house or apartment. Most of the towns or villages are located over hot volcanic water sites, so hot water and heat is very economical.

Just across the river from Akureyri, they are trying to tunnel through the mountain; there have been two problems: a cold-water shaft was hit on one end, and a hot-water shaft hit on the other; both are causing millions of Kroners to fix before proceeding, and this has delayed the project by two years already! On the way back onto the bus, I told a veteran story, and I am still surprised at how few vets there are in a group! There are about 30 of us and only 3 vets!

I asked about the Icelandic horses lying down in the fields. The ones we saw were small horses, and I was told that the ones I saw lying down were probably young colts. When horses are content and happy, they sometimes just lay down and roll in the dust. I will have to check further on this. I am not convinced!

More marshmallow fields, now there are white, pink, blue, brown, yellow and black bales. Some have markings on the ends, so I guess those indicate which were harvested first. I also thought black would be a wrong color, but with only 111 days of sun, plus the cool weather, spoilage would still be at a minimum!

Back to housing, it used to be that the banks required 35% down, but then private banks came in and offered loans with little or no money down. Then, the 2008 crash happened, and it was worldwide. Many lost their houses and walked away, leaving their homes with the banks.

Unemployment in Iceland rose to 10%, unheard of here! It is now back to 3%. However, the currency fluctuates.

They have/had one small railroad, but the winds pick up very high, the temperatures get very low, and the snow very deep. It is impractical for a railroad here.

We drove by Mirror Lake, which is very clean and clear! Old customs included executing women who became pregnant when they were unmarried. Until the 50s, the husband worked outside the home, and the women took care of the house and kids; this has changed here also. In the past, in the old times, many people became paralyzed in the winter when they did not sufficiently clothe themselves when they went out into the weather; It really gets that cold!

The second stop of the day, Gooafoss, is the waterfalls of the Gods. The temperature outside had risen to a comfortable 12.9 degrees C, and the hike to the falls was only a few blocks. Lynn opted to walk it with me for a while. It was very nice. Took a number of pictures. I then went back another route downriver for more shots, meeting Lynn at the gift shop. I bought a bag of candy horse do-do to pass around the bus, and I kept the balance for the grandson; Lynn found a pair of reindeer slippers, but I was conveniently nowhere to be found. ($60.00 US for slippers!?!) I also bought sorcery neck bones, which I will read up on and try to start a game before we leave.

We are off again, a trip by Lake Neva; legend says it was a lake created by the devil's urine because he was jealous of God for all the beautiful lakes God created and getting all of the praise.

It is a 20-minute hike to the lake, over rolling paths, so Lynn opted to stay by the bus. The lake is beautiful, and I took several pictures of several areas of this very large lake, BUT... the lake is surrounded by swarms of small black nats/flies! Some locals had nets over their heads, the flies were all over, consistently, not millions, but BILLIONS; nice lake but not worth it! Now I know why the legends believe it was created by the devil's urine!

Back on the bus, saw a number of table-topped mountains, old volcanoes where the snow cooled the top, and flattened it. There are actually ten kinds of lava, the lakes are usually all fed by melting snow, and very clear, only 5-10 meters deep with lots of vegetation under the water. As we drive, there are steam vents every so often, we pass a black crater, 2000 years old, that is only a kilometer across, many hikers come to transverse this one!

It was time for lunch, and we stopped by a restaurant known for its lamb burgers. Lynn found a table, and I got in line to order. One register, one order taker, three cooks, and a barmaid. Service was characteristically slow, just like in Europe. The items were ordered, you got a receipt and a number, then sat down and waited again for the order to be delivered; no tip is expected when they deliver the food. The bill, one lamb burger, a handful of fries, a glass of draft beer, and 7 oz. Soda $30.00 US!

Lamb presented and served like a sloppy joe, a little dryer than pork, but good! I took a picture of a sign indicating a church, grave yard and a dead-end road, with a word longer than the symbols!

Back to the bus, traveling on two lane roads with no shoulders, and an occasional tractor we had to pass when traffic cleared. The next stop was an overlook with multiple vents, another volcano located on tectonic plates, rumored to be the next one to erupt. The tour guide was actually nervous, so we were hustled along for only a short ten-minute photo "op". There is a heavy smell of sulfur in the air, there is no vegetation, and a lot of yellow earth (the color of sulfur). On the other side of the mountain/volcano, bubbling pits of black ooze! We had to stop, the smell was even worse, vents working, hot water and tar bubbling, took pictures of all of it, a pretty active place, and we were vigorously warned to watch our step! The vents spewing sulfur, silica, and gypsum, the ground is soft, baby craters, and mist from the baby crater pots bubble busting and rolling...seemed like a very evil nasty place! Pictures, inspection of the craters and off we went!

More desolate land, upheavals of rock and ash, no trees or shrubs, worse than the Outback, in Australia, where at least there were some grasses, and small shrubs! Trees on this island are treasured, and due to the extended nights, the ones they have managed to grow are mostly stunted. The last stop before heading to the hotel in most powerful falls in Europe, Dettfoss!

It takes a good twenty minutes to get to this fall, black packed volcanic dust on a narrow path, up and down, with rocks in the path, watching your step all the way. Once you get there, a narrow path leads up, and down, these are only one-person paths, with rocks in them, not far (usually only a foot from the embankment or edge) oh, and not a hand rail in sight! Picked my way around, took a number of shots, played "chicken" on the narrow path with some others, then headed back. The falls are about 2/3 the size of Niagara, but very imposing, powerful, and stunning. On the way, back, I found a few more falls in the distance, I hadn't noticed on the way to, due to concentration on not tripping on the path (or climbing up and down small hills.... without a railing!)

However, it was well worth it, total of about 1.5 kilometers, or

5000 steps and when we got back to the parking lot, except for the path, you would have never guessed something that spectacular was only 15-20 minutes away! It is 15 degrees C, sun is shining, and the air is fresh and clean! Lynn had opted not to walk the distance so I showed her the pictures and told her this story when I returned.

We are in North Eastern Iceland, as we travel to our final destination today, grass is being joined by shrubs, then trees are actually starting to come into view. We are only about 38 meters above sea level, only 600 miles from Reykjavik.

Natives call this island "Eesland." Our new hotel promises truly native food, so this ought to be an interesting evening. We reached the hotel at 17:30, yesterday we left at 08:30, and breakfast started at 07:00.

Dinner offered the following, of which I tried all: lamb tongue, horse meat, horse jerky, horse heart, lamb, beef, potatoes, calamari, herring, salmon, plus vegetables, salad fixings, and breads. All of them were well prepared and tastee! To finish it off, rhubarb torte, fresh whipped cream, and three flavors of gelato. Globus also includes one glass of beer, wine or soda every evening meal.

After the meal, we walked around the facilities with a few of the other couples, chatted, visited four horses on the premises. Then went back to our room, shower, do notes, and off to bed, another unforgettable day!

Day 4, Thursday, July14th

We did not have to have our luggage out until 07:30, buffet breakfast and a nice walk around the area. It is 14.9 degrees C, and this will be the warmest of the day, although last night, we should prepare for a warm day in the 65-70F range. (No, it never got there!)

The first stop was just down the road a bit, a walk through one of Iceland's rare woods. We were shown a 100-year-old white oak, but it was only fifteen feet or about 5 meters high! The rest of the forest consisted of Aspens, and Poplars, that were 25-30 feet high. This part of the island is the place the islanders go to be amazed by trees.

As we moved on, we were riding along the third biggest lake, it is very long, 55 square kilometers and it is fabled that a sea monster similar to the loch ness monster lurks below its surface. No, no sightings today!

The mountain sides are green topped with ever melting snow, every few kilometers there will be a trickle set of falls with a river of clear cold water running down the mountain, sparkling and joining a small river along the road.

Traveling along, this will be mostly a travel day following the narrow road on the various peninsulas, along fjords and inlets on the rugged eastern coast.

More information on the schooling, the schooling starts at six years old, books and school are free, but there is no free lunch. At twelve to thirteen you go to high school or technical school. Then specialty school for three winters, the family is charged $70-80, 000 ISK, per student, and books; then to the universities for doctors and master degrees, unclear as to what that costs.... seems we are fed "free" in America, with a different definition of "free" here and else ware!

We stopped for lunch in a small town, Lynn had leek soup, and it was quite good, I ordered a fish and chips lunch which consisted of a handful of seasoned fries, a small cup of coleslaw, and three nicely sized pieces of deep- fried fish. The fish were coated first in curry powder, then battered and fried. This was supposed to be the best in the country, "Scottish style" and were delicious! Even with water to drink, cost about $32 US; I still can't get over how expensive stuff is here! (like in Europe!)

The next stop was a short visit to an artist's studio, lots of huge eggs on posts, decorated differently, a chicken wire ball with different lights shining through it, a movie about two women's feet on a round clay ball, moving feet and toes, and another you watched a woman on a screen going uh, uh, uhh, uh, uhh, at different intervals and timing. Odd, but interesting!

Stopped at a bird-watching area, saw small ducks, larger ducks, some loons.... then off!

The side of a cliff was pointed out, an abandoned cabin that was just a collapsed frame now seemed to project the coming doom. We also had our first picture of glaciers, at least the exposed tentacles in the valleys, four of them.

We were at our hotel at 16:30, unpacked for the day, set out clothes for tomorrow, and got notes before happy hour. Happy hour here is 100 ISK less per drink, so it is only ten dollars vs. eleven (US) for a beer!

I took a few more pictures of the four glaciers, joined everyone for "Happy Hour", limited bar, had them make a peach schnapps and orange soda for Lynn, and then I found a pomegranate liquor that was Icelandic, and combined it with a shot of tequila...very good.

Joined other couples the "regulars" to talk, then up to the included supper. This was the best one so far, beef carpaccio salad, and langoustines (small lobster tails) with sweet sour sauce, salad greens and potato rounds, followed by a raspberry blend with cream topping. If more lobster was wanted, it was provided...wow.

The tour director put me in charge of the luggage by putting on the notice board that I was in charge, so I asked the bus driver what time. He said eight, leave at 0830, so I made the announcement that the luggage would be out of the room by 07:30 and leave promptly at 08:30; we will see tomorrow a.m. how this works out!

A walk around, then to the room, finish up the notes, review the pictures, and off to bed!

Day 6, Friday, July 15, 2016

It is rainy, overcast, and cold, 11.9 degrees Celsius; no walk this morning. The buffet had sardines, herring, salmon, and omelets along with the breads, cold cuts, and cereals pancakes, yogurt, and juices and coffees.

Everyone was ready at 08:30, and luggage was outside their rooms at 07:30 ☺; it seems we were the only ones to have smaller suitcases; everyone else brought two full-size ones plus carry-ons. I guess Americans do over-pack. We did have to pick up some of the group. A few of the women did not want to walk across the parking lot in the wind and rain to the bus, so the driver drove over for the five or six princesses and two of their slaves.

As we travel, we are told that Iceland has 11% of the Lava fields, and also 11% of the world's glaciers. When it rains, the fields and mountains covered with moss turn a beautiful green, what a sight!

The folks are also kind of co-operating on the seat rotation, but some seem not to be able to count, or "forget" with a favorite seat, or just refuse, funny how even with a small group there are always some assholes!

Since it is raining this morning, no pictures can be taken through the bus windows, hopefully this afternoon it will clear up.

On the way to Vatnajokull, the largest glacier in Europe and the one featured in the James Bond movie Die Another Day, we opted for the Duck ride on the lake formed by the melting glacier. The water is clear and cold, and the floating calved glaciers are beautiful. A piece of 1000-year-old ice was chipped with an ice pick, and we treated ourselves to "old ice," just to say we ate a glacier! (It tasted like regular ice.)

The Duck ride was an hour in the rain, sleet, and heavy winds, but we got to see glaciers up close; what an experience! Oh, by the way, yes, we were all soaked to the bone, and we still had a good three-quarters of a day before the tour ended for the day! :(

Looking at the glaciers, the black lines are from lava, Clear means that the ice has been above the water for a while, and blue ice is the portion recently unattached from the glacier, highly compressed water.

Traveling on the bus past three of the largest volcanos, with a glacier weaving through them, the blue-white of the smooth glacier, against the now green and black volcanoes with the outlets of the glacier descending, and waterfalls cascading down the side...how wonderful and peaceful!

Lunch was at another truck stop, very crowded with three tour busses arriving at the same time, very slow service and typical push and shove by the European tourists. I got out of line, picked out some cookies, hot chocolate, coffee, dried fruit and the Skye yogurt, that Iceland is famous for, enough lunch for Lynn and myself!

We traveled a bit further, walked to see the front of an outlet up close, took some very good pictures, and collected a few more Iceland rocks. On the way, back, I took the picture of a young guy in front of the glacial outlet, asked him where he was from, he said Australia, so of course I said " Aussie, Aussie, Aussie" to which he replied "Oye, Oye, Oye." We walked back to the area swapping stories and wished each other well, I then took another picture of him in front of the glacier and left.

Down the road, stopped for ice cream, then walked down to a black sand (lava) beach, scooped up some for home, and jumped back on the bus to end up in Vik.

Drinks, and dinner, this place had bartenders that were a little faster, although no snacks offered, that would cost you! (When available, about $5.00 U.S.) for a small dessert bowl. One double southern comfort and a cranberry drink cost about $18.00 US! Dinner was served, appetizer plate with brown bread, peaches and beef, white bread on the side, entree: trout, sweet potatoes, salad and pickled onions, and ice cream over fruit dessert. All timed well, hot and perfectly cooked.

Back to the room, type up notes, need to get out swimsuits for the Blue Lagoon tomorrow, lay out clothes, 08:00 we leave!

Day 7, Saturday, July 16th, 2016

Early morning takes off, the group is very punctual, and there are no stragglers. We are moving at 08:03, all fed, packed, and ready to go!

It is 15.9 degrees Celsius; it is overcast, but a lot of light, our first stop is the shore line where puffins have their burrows, hopefully some will be there!

This the southernmost part of Iceland, the same area where the movie "Noah" with Russel Crow was filmed, and yes, I did get a lot of ribbing!! There was only one puffin in his/her burrow, and she soon ducked back in, we waited, a few did come back to the nesting area, but if we saw five birds, we saw a lot! We did get some very nice pictures of the shore, and all the beaches here are comprised of volcanic ash.

We continue on our way; the bridges are narrow on these two lanes; we have to take turns crossing the bridges because the bus takes up a little more than a lane wide. We passed the Eyjafjallajokll Volcano, the volcano that erupted in 2010, and the ash cloud shut down a number of air routes when we were in Europe. Many planes were re-directed for quite a few days! By the way, 1/3 of the lava in the world is in Iceland! (Much larger % than mentioned before) So, there are many fields of lava and rock, and those waterfalls are fed by the glaciers melting from the heat below.

We next visited another waterfall, we were able to get pretty close to the bottom of it, and some great pictures! I asked about some very small camper vans, the guide, Holm, said they are rented. Not much larger than a compact car, they are the size of the very small step van, very small! I went over and asked if I could take a picture of the inside and they agreed, inside was a wall-to-wall mattress, smaller than a twin, and underneath was a tiny refrigerator, room on the other side for a small gas grill, TV table, and minimal storage, I documented this with photos.

One more stop for ice cream, then off to the hotel. This is Blue Lagoon day, it was an optional tour, but Globus actually included it with the tour. All but two on the tour went for it, we dropped off our luggage, and had a bite for lunch, then loaded back on the bus for the 50-minute drive to the lagoon.

The Lagoon is located behind the power plant we visited the first day. It is a natural geothermal pool in the middle of a lava field. It owes its existence to the power plant, less than a kilometer away. The water is a blue green, and you can only see about 20 cm. (8 inches) below.

You are issued a high-tech waterproof band, walk up to a locker room, find an open locker, strip down, wave your band in front of an electronic eye, and your locker is latched. Then off to a communal shower, (men and women are divided), you must shower! Then down the steps to the pool. At the deepest, the pool is maybe 150 cm. (4 1/2 to 5 feet) deep.

The warm refreshing mineral water ranges from 37-39 degrees Celsius (98-102 F), it is reputed to have healing powers, with the mineral salts, silica, and blue green algae, is very relaxing, one station offered a silica scrub for facials, and we had our picture taken with the facial masks on! Another section was shallower; you are offered foam noodles to float.

Noah

After, we showered again, turned in our bracelets, and joined the rest of our group, everyone felt clean from the inside out, and very relaxed.

At 1800 we gathered for our farewell dinner. The tour director called me to the front of the bus, and simulated slapping me back and forth, then told me I had to sit in front of the bus and guide us to the restaurant. I grabbed the microphone, narrated the trip, mocking her accent, used a number of her phrases, and goaded the driver. It was a lot of fun, and we were all laughing when we got off the bus in downtown Reykjavik.

The Fish Company is the name of the restaurant; it is reputed to be in the top three restaurants in this city. AND IT WAS! Included was wine or beer, an appetizer, a salad, a small fish plate, a lamb plate, and a dessert. Well-spaced, it took two and a half hours, EVERYONE loved the food, the staff were also very professional and proficient. P.S. At the beginning of the meal, we were all provided wine or beer, the guide toasted us, then our buddy Mark toasted her, and I toasted the driver and the Globus guide. I was then served a plate of that fish jerky I bought the second day, with a shot of that Black death schnapps. I promptly passed the plate around so everyone that wanted it could try it. The plate was returned with four pieces left; it was quite good!

Back to our hotel, bid everyone goodbye, and we are off tomorrow for the trip home at 06:45.

A few final notes for tonight: Skyr yogurt, well known here for quality, is a "Greek" thick yogurt, a little bit sour but very good and filling. All waiters, bartenders, and cashiers wear all black to identify them. The only thing I didn't get to try was the putrefied shark. (It was out of season.) It is 23:00 hours; the sun is going down, and dusk is approaching. Have to get up at 05:00, so this is it. I will be finishing this and correcting it at home tomorrow.

Educating Noah...Travelin'

Up at 0500; finish packing for the journey home, sort and pack the suitcases, lightened up the carry-ons, and down to the restaurant for out last Euro style breakfast. After breakfast, took all luggage down to the bus, checked out and handed in key; (hotel keys are a very favorite souvenir for tourists!) and as amazingly noted, everyone on the group were on time and we are off as scheduled.

The driver relays that a polar bear arrived on the northern side of the island. They shot him, the reasoning, he was on the ice flow for unknown days, he was very hungry and thirsty, a threat to livestock, and especially humans, this is common procedure, per our driver "we don't mess with hungry bears!"

The lines are relatively short both for check -in and security, waited about 2 hours for our flight.

Typical for Delta, a big rush to the gates when they opened, crowding the gate, what made it worse was two gates opened within fifteen minutes, the corridor was blocked, people pushing and shoving to get to either gate, Delta has the worse loading of the American airlines. There was room in the overheads, many people carrying two carry-ons, plus large bags, including men, so overhead room is at a premium.

Settled in for the same narrow, uncomfortable seats, cramped, and it seems that the Delta employees make it a point to brush the people in the aisle seats (the only exception to this was the last flight, both stewardesses were very cognizant of the narrow aisles and made it a point to not brush, jam, and were exceptionally pleasant, more later).

The five-and-a-half-hour fight turned into 6 hours, the planes always took off late, this time, the crew came from another late arrival- so I made a note to make sure all transfers are at least two hours.

TSA worked...kinda, Lynn's top of her head was only shown, and my fingers too cool to read my prints. However, we were put through a priority line and did get through quickly. We claimed our luggage and carried it to the domestic terminal to turn in to the connecting flight conveyor, had to go through security again, only one line open, no TSA line, long line, very slow, seemed to be one supervisor for each TSA agent, signs all over warning passengers not to argue or harass TSA agent, and yes, got patted, then to the connecting flight gate....40 minutes away! We met up with another couple, they were grumbling too, and one of the employees with a go-cart, offered us a ride. It was worth the $5.00 tip, we were to depart from gate 47, he took us to gate 40, the top of an escalator.

Now we had 3 hours, bought a roll-up and chips, the last connecting flight, a commuter flight same herd of people crowding the gate, this jet actually had a little more leg room than the international 757…go figure. This was the best flight we have had in years, the crew was friendly, joked around, attentive, and careful! I presented one of my napkin coupons, and was confronted by the pilot, who smiled and commented he would look into a pizza maker for the aircraft, and corrected his name to Thomas, not "Bob" as I had indicated.

Collected our luggage, said good-bye to our new friends that were not continuing on with us, jumped on the bus, and were home by 8:30 P.M. Taffy picked us up at the park and ride, we brought up the luggage, grabbed a bite to eat, watched the early news, showered, and went to bed. With time changes about 30 hours; and oh, yes, nice to see dark again!

It will be a short time now for our road trip to the "Road to the Sun" in Montana. We went on a motorcycle club trip to Pontiac, Illinois. It was rather strange, the only bike that went was Russ, a past member that drove up from Kentucky. Everyone else had excuses not to ride, "it might rain", It is too hot" ………. I don't think the club will last too much longer. We did however, get to eat at the Historic Route 66 diner, and it was worth it!

We just found out that our grandson will not be with us on the road trip, we thought it would be a great thing for his education, experience, and under different rules, but he pulled out; this, is his loss, the offer will not be extended again.

I needed to wrap things up at home, re-checked everything for out Russian trip in September, and am currently negotiating flight upgrades for the 12-hour flight next February to Buenos Aires, and the South Pole.

I am trying to work at least 4 days a month for the D.A.V.; and now I am also signed up for going to India for three weeks with the Vagabonds in November. Lynn has decided not to go; so, at the Vagabond party on Tuesday night, I will be looking for a roommate.

The introductory party was attended by about 40 people, I along with a vagabond friend, Fran and her roommate seemed to be the few committed to go. The group is limited in size to 30 people, I am not sure if that includes the leader and his guest; I asked for quotes on upgrades on the flight, I also gave Bob (the leader) the first installment for the trip, since it was due in three days, and we would be on the road then. I also requested a meet with any potential roommate before we leave.

Road Trip: Road to the Sun and Canada August 2016

We left McDonald's at 7:00 A.M., 12,122 miles on the odometer, and we were on our way. This will be one of the most grueling days, hoping to get to Fargo, North Dakota for our first night stop. The grandson, (twelve years old) bowed out of going, he did not want to be away from his parents that long; so, we took a picture of him with us for some photo op's.

It was a hot August day, 78 (F) degrees when we left and the humidity was higher. After 4 hours, it was "that time" so we pulled over in a small town in Wixom, WI. To use the water closet. (Sounds classier than toilet!) They had a large Mr. Bass outside along with a few carved bears, so we had "The Boy's" picture with the bass and also a nice young lady taking a break.

At a quarter tank, we pulled over at a Quick Trip, filled up, bought a hamburger; and off, again! I started noticing that the day was getting darker, the cars coming at us had their headlights on, not a good sign, at high noon! Sure enough, we drove right into a storm, dark, high winds, driving rain, we saw many cars pulled off the road, we were driving at 30 mph, and being passed by the trucks we passed before.

It took us 20-30 minutes to get through the worst of the storm, then the sun came back, then a drizzle, then nothing, a bright afternoon, and back up to speed.

As we drive east to west in Minnesota, there are lakes everywhere, both sides of the road, small, medium, and large, if no lakes in site, there is a river, this truly is the State with ten thousand lakes!

Our first stop was in Alexandria, Minnesota; I wanted to visit the Viking Museum, see the ruin stone, get filled in on how far and when the Vikings were here, and of course, get a picture of Ole the Viking statue.

On the way to the museum, we passed a field of sun flowers, wow, just a field of yellow, bright yellow; Yep, got a picture to show. We later passed a few more sunflower fields, but now it was not a shock and just noted!

It seems the Vikings were here a couple hundred years before Columbus, And since we learned that Juan Ponce De Leon landed in Florida in St. Augustine, who gave Columbus all the credit?? The more we travel, the more we find how little we were taught! (Or revised history we were fed)

We pulled off the road in Fargo, North Dakota at 5:10, enough for today! We had called ahead for reservations at La Quinta; and they had a room for us. As we checked in, we were pleasantly surprised to find that the manager had a complimentary dinner for us, salad, mashed potatoes and meatballs; so, we had dinner too, not bad, not bad at all.

After dinner, sat down to confirm our upgrades in the flights for South America and Antarctica, checked the upgraded seats with seat Guru, and gave the final "go" on that too! (So much better taking computer with us and having internet!)

Took a walk, typed the notes, and the first day is done!

Day two, Friday

We drove 580 miles yesterday; we will see what we do today! North Dakota has a speed limit of 75; Montana 80, gas mileage will not be so good… but we will be travelin'.

We had another very good breakfast, and on the road at 7:05, so far, pretty consistent! Today we cross North Dakota with a few stops planned, there are more sunflower fields; the heads of the flowers still drooping as they were last afternoon, the rest are wheat fields, hay fields with the unwrapped bales of hay, some fresh, some stacked, some brown and aged. There are round bales, square bales, and even some of the old-fashioned small bales we were used to. When we saw them in Iceland, they were all wrapped, here, none of them were wrapped. As we traveled west on I-94 we passed the continental divide just west of Valley City.

We needed to stop at the biggest buffalo statue in the world, of course, so we pulled off at the Jamestown (Buffalo) North, Dakota. There is a small complex resembling a western town, old caboose, country store and a museum. We walked the complex, visited the buffalo, poked around the buildings, and took pictures with the picture of the grandson, spent money at the museum and general store, and returned to the road, our legs stretched, and wallet lightened.

At 10:00 the sunflowers are raising their heads, the bright yellow contrasted by tans of wheat, and the green of corn, with accents of soybean dark green is beautiful. The road is banked now by ponds, rather than lakes, and a lot of them; the flat lands are graduating to small rolling hills, most exits display "no services"; farms are large, few towns, traffic is easy, no lane sitters, most if not all courteous drivers, moving at a 75 -80 mph pace.

We passed the enchanted highway, with a road having birds on every post, ending with a giant sculpture, a round good 30- foot circle with birds inside, visible for miles right off the road, and yes, we got the picture. Just past this on the south side is the largest cow in the world, about a half mile off the road, this was a black and white Guernsey, no, no picture, and then a stop for gas and the Dickson Dinosaur Museum.

This is one of the best dinosaur museums we have visited, local artifacts, well-constructed exhibits, and very informative, well worth the stop, plus some pics with the picture of the "boy", one of the staff, even thought he was cute and wanted to hold him; I tried, but she would only hold him!! (Lynn was around, I think that is why she wouldn't hold me!!)

On westward, crossed the border to Montana, to Glendive, Montana; Home of the Glendive Dinosaur and Fossil Museum. This museum has more than 24 full sized dinosaurs, (the pterodactyl had up to a 50-foot wing span!) giant sea turtle skeletons, all from the local fossil digs in the Montana badlands!

It was interesting in that they had a number of people to interact with, to explain and point out different features and facts, another great stop.

Although we gained an hour by going to mountain time zone, we did not have enough to explore the Little Big Horn battle ground so we opted to drive a little past to Billings and hit this "must-see" tomorrow morning. We checked into the motel, asked for a good steak house recommendation (we are in beef country you know!) and we went to a place called Gusick's Restaurant & Lounge.

Lynn had steak and shrimp, I had country fried steak. Both were full meals, beef barley soup, salad, meat (perfectly cooked, and seasoned), choice of potato, and a scoop of locally made vanilla ice cream. I asked for the bartender's favorite drink and was brought a drink called "Green Tea" it was a scotch drink, with sweet/sour soda and other things, and was very refreshing! I pulled the old "BOGO" request, she asked where I was from, I told her, and she says" For friendly out of towners, here is another, on the house!" WOW; persistence pays off!!

The staff worked together like a well-oiled machine, from the host, bartender, waitress, and bus-man, efficient, very friendly and fast, proficient, and everyone positive! I told them I would recommend them both on Yelp and Trip Advisor and did just that before I started this note for the night.

That is, it, for tonight, busy day tomorrow as always, Lynn is watching the opening ceremony of the Olympics, I am finishing this, checking tomorrow's route, I will make reservations for tomorrow night and off to bed!

Day three Saturday

We drove a total of 611 miles yesterday, and it may be topped today!

We both slept like logs; Lynn watched most of the Opening Ceremonies until the American's paraded by and she then called it a night too. The breakfast provided was basically a full range as it was yesterday, and we were easily on the road by 7:30.

Traffic was light, and we were at the Little Big Horn earlier than most. We showed our senior park pass and got in for free, grabbed a good parking spot, used the facilities and started at the visitor's center.

A twenty-minute movie was run in a loop, a large room filled with artifacts and a gift shop.

The self-guided tour takes about twenty minutes, accessible with a phone. Grave markers are provided where the bodies were found, and the areas where the horses laid after the soldiers killed them for shelter. The Indians gathered their own dead and burned them, according to their beliefs. The casualties were about 10 soldiers (or civilian) to one Indian, it was a massacre! The area is on a grassy knoll, there is really nothing within miles of the place! I bought a book on what really happened here, actually Sitting Bull was with the women and children during the fight! (Again, there is so much we really were misled with back in formal school.)

We finished the walking tour, went back and bought souvenirs, and we were off! But there was also a Crow Indian store we HAD to stop by and spend some more cash! Everything in the store was pretty expensive, to very expensive, Lynn found a pair of moccasins, but luckily none in her size. We left with our scalps, and with only a relatively small "deposit".

Now was the longest drive of the day, from Little Big Horn to Helena, the state capitol. On the way, we had lunch and a fill-up at a bakery filling station. Great sandwich, plenty of bakery, and shared a huckleberry soda that was out of this world!

We arrived in Helena a little after two, found the capitol and asked about the one-hour tour of the highlights of the town. Although we were 30 minutes early, the ticket person said they were "full". We told her that we came from Milwaukee and how many people had she told that to or turned away. She told us that we were the first, but to stick around, and if there were any empty seats, we would get them.

We went over and took a picture of the capitol, a few mocking birds, some flowers and returned to see if there was any room, and sure enough, room for just two more.

The one-hour tour covered the government area, the old part of town, and the downtown. The government buildings are massive, the old mansions seemed to have been mostly owned by politicians, and lawyers, imagine that, and the downtown was centered over a place called "last chance gulch" the story goes. It was late, starting to rain, so some miners decided to camp for the night, and tried one last time to pan for gold. It worked! From start to finish 10, 000,000 ounces were found, and that, at about $3.00/oz.!

We saw one five-point buck roaming in one alley, and a doe walking across a front lawn, in downtown! We were shown the sleeping man mountain, I think I got a picture, and oh, by the way; it started raining at the start of the tour, and by the end, the rain was coming down in sheets! Yes, we were in open trolley cars, and yes, we got very wet!

We had reservations in Missoula, about an hour and a half away, made it through the mountains, took some wonderful shots, and checked in at 6:20.

Changed clothes, walked over to an Irish Pub, Lynn had pasties with mashed potatoes, and I had fish and chips (the best I have had in months!). Back to the room, planned out the next two days, Lynn set up the reservations, after I calculated the distances, tomorrow is the Road to the Sun, and Canada!

Day four Sunday

The miles we drove yesterday: 472! It actually felt like more, but maybe we are getting tired of "the road."

Nice breakfast. This motel either had very thin walls, or the trailer park had a fire! People were loud in the halls till after 10, loud in their rooms, and loud outside with motorcycles coming and going till the wee hours, and of course, they were loud pipes……… we were out of there by 7:20.

Educating Noah…Travelin'

The drive north was sparsely dotted with little strip towns, one store deep on the highway. The signs indicating scenic areas were in American Indian, with English sub titles. Creativity was evident also, we saw a full-sized Dutch windmill, signs that played on words, houses high on the top of mountains, and a lot of open space.

It took us three hours to get to the western entrance of Glacial Park and the Road to the Sun. Our senior pass got us in here too, as we entered, a deer crossed the road in front of the car that preceded us. The "road" follows a river for a while, many rapids, falls, red rock, trees of all shapes and sizes. The mountain tops are snow covered, the two-lane road gets very narrow, with a steep drop off on one side, and a sheer jagged wall of rock on the other. There are many turn off spots and you have to watch for others turning off and coming back on the road. There are also quite a few park cars carrying people back and forth who came in campers, or who preferred a ride through the park.

We started out on a bright sunny mid-morning, went through a fog bank, and a cloud, then back to a cooler but clear road on the other side. It took us a total of three hours too transverse the "road" with stops at the lodge, and various turn outs along the way. It was time for a reward, so we asked where we could get some Huckleberry pie; and a place up the road called Two Sisters, was highly recommended.

To say the stop was a worthy reward would be underselling it! The small restaurant was very eclectic; posters, bumper stickers, toy animals decorate the walls; the place was sparse, simple, and laid back. They have a shirt they sell, "Be kind to fat people, they may save your life someday" showing a bear chasing two people, the middle one being heavier than the other. As I checked out, I asked where the bathrooms were, and he said "follow the yellow brick road". I then asked why there was no tax added, and he told me there was no State tax. Lastly, I leaned over and told him never to go hunting with a fat person. He asked "why?" I told him that "we know we are fat; we will just shoot the skinny one in the leg when the bear comes"! The yellow brick road led from the front door to the outside door to the respective men's and women's room on the side of the building.

It was a short drive to the Canadian border; we showed our passports and off we went. The speed limit varies from 60 to 100 Kilometers an hour; 40 MPH to 60 MPH! We followed this closely and were passed by others like we were standing still. So, we did keep up with traffic instead of creating a hazard, however, in the towns EVERYBODY slowed down to 25-35 MPH; so, assume the towns are all speed traps!

We pulled into Calgary about 4:30; compared with the cities we saw the three hours on the road in Canada; this place is HUGE! More like Quebec and Montreal, but more spread out. Not too well organized, no rhyme or reason, lots of Tim Hortons and A & W Root Beer Stands. Gas runs about $.95-1.10/liter, no one takes American money, have to use a chipped credit card, Visa or MasterCard, no Discover.

We will be using this motel as our base and return here tomorrow night after walking on the glacier in the Canadian Banff and Jasper National Parks, and Lake Louise.

We asked the clerk for a recommend on dinner and went to a Vietnamese Restaurant a few doors down. Lynn had fried sausage wontons; I had a chicken and sausage noodle dish that was fantastic.

The sign on the door stated "Bathrooms for customers only...Don't even ask!" and back door to the motel was always locked, the front door after seven had to be opened by a room key or the desk clerk, we assumed bum or more politically correct "homeless" problem in this downtown location.

We need a little down time, hopefully an early start tomorrow, with long pants, and jackets ready!

Day five, Monday

The mileage yesterday was 388; but it felt like a lot more! Both of us were exhausted, so early to bed was welcomed, Lynn actually got a good night's sleep, I did too, but I have a clear conscience, so yeah, I can sleep anywhere! We got up a little before 6 A.M. Sloshed down some breakfast, made our last potty stop and we were off by 6:45!

We missed a turn on getting out of the city, but after 45 minutes, we found our way to the freeway, Canadian Interstate 1; so much for a quick start! (The GPS didn't work in Canada.)

The signs in Canada, this province, are in English, with subtitles in French. This would be a killer day, and we knew it; we pushed until we got to Baniff, where we entered Glacial National Park. We bought a pass for two for this and Jasper National Park; along with a minimum two-day pass, and the receipt is taped to the left side of the windshield.

The road is just two lanes, posted speed usually 60 to 80 kilometers per hour, and everything is in kilometers so 100 kilometers equals about 60 miles......Lake Louise was one of the three objectives; and it was time for a bathroom break; so, we took the exit. We stopped at the information center, then checked out the shops, again, they only accept chipped credit cards here in Canada, so my debit card was useless, and we were quite a way inside the border, U.S. dollars were frowned upon, they would have to convert, currently the Canadian dollar is worth about 75 cents. So, I had called Chase as a back-up, and I used that card for souvenirs, food, and gas.

Lake Louise is ......WOW! The lake overlooks a glacier; picture perfect! The blue in the streams and the lake is a light color, I hope it turns out, I also took a picture of a sign with English and French; went down a short path, took a close-up picture of roadway flowers; and came upon a closed path, due to bear sightings ....time to get back to the car!

Noah

Oh, Yup, road construction here too! Twenty minutes to dump a load of gravel, jockeyed our way to the Glacier Park by noon. I purchased tickets for the glacier walk and the glass floored overlook for both of us; The bus for our tour left at 1:45; buses leave every 15 minutes, so we had a little time to stretch our legs, and yes, go through the gift shop! I did ask the gift shop clerk about where she lived, she told us that they work a 6-month contract that included room and a subsidized board plus pay. They live in a dormitory close to the center, and both male and female are trained and work a variety of jobs, including driving various vehicles.

I ran the "loot" back to the car, and after watching the other load, we started hanging around the entrance 20 minutes early. It paid off, we were third in line, at exactly 1:45 they checked our tickets, and loaded the bus for the 10-minute ride to the Glacier Vehicles. The drivers of all the vehicles are young and try very hard to be entertaining; which they were!

The Glacier Vehicle is a six-wheel drive, has 6-foot tires, and can climb or decent greater than a 30-degree slope. They have twenty three of them, and the cost was over a million apiece! The tours were started in the early 1900's, the current building where everything starts was built in 1996.

So here is what happens, you get on one bus, that bus takes you to a terminal above the glacier, then everyone transfers to a glacier vehicle and we slowly go up an embankment, then almost straight down to the glacier, then out to the middle of the Ice, yes, I said Ice…….and it is slippery! We get 20 minutes to roam around on the glacier, some scooped up some of the water, most just posed on the ice. We were warned about crevices, and ice bridges that form and may drop 100 meters; so, we had to stay within the roped off area. As the snow and ice compresses it turns blue, we will see how that turns out! The road to the area is scraped daily by a grader so it is somewhat smooth, but the ride there and back is still pretty "bumpy".

At exactly 20 minutes we were transported to the terminal. We did come across some wild dahl sheep, we didn't hit them, but they have no fear of vehicles. At the terminal, we transferred to another bus that took us to the overlook. The overlook is a couple hundred feet over a valley, with a glass floor. Lynn actually braved it and came along with me…. Woo-Hoo! She even looked down through the glass!

Back on another bus to return us to the lodge, on the 6 km ride we saw additional sheep on the cliffs next to the highway!

Back at the lodge we grabbed a bite and headed for home, it was already 4:25 P.M and we had another interesting drive back to our motel in Calgary. The trip back seemed a little faster, not as much construction, not as many gauwker's, and only a few actually driving the speed limit. We did see a good-sized black bear along-side the road, checking out the cars parked nearby; there are signs posted everywhere, about not feeding the wildlife.

Back to the motel by 8 P.M.; this is the apex of our journey, now the trek home, we may even sleep in a bit tomorrow!

Day six, Tuesday, heading home

We only drove a total of 375 miles yesterday, but it was a full day!

Canada is different, in towns, the speed limit is 35-40 mph, everywhere, and camera enhanced; so, everybody creeps around the streets, and boulevards. If you are in a crosswalk, the traffic stops, most pedestrians don't even look! When Interstate Canadian Highway enters a town, the same applies, and yes traffic lights on the highway. After Calgary, the speed limit between towns is 90-110 kilometers per hour, before any major intersection is a sign "Caution Important Intersection". This was a drive day, Calgary to Moose Jaw, mostly Canadian Interstate 1.

We left a little after seven, both of us slept like logs! August 9th, 57 degrees, bright and sunny. As we traveled, it was a lot like North

Dakota, wheat, hay, and cattle, a few horses once in a while, few houses, fewer towns and very few cities.

It warmed up to the mid-sixties, and we were driving into the sun. We noticed the clouds were very low in the sky, and then, sure enough, we were in a cloud or fog bank. It lasted a good twenty minutes, and it was hard to see more than 20-30 meters (60-90ft.) ahead, and the temperature in the cloud was 5-6 degrees lower. Then it lifted, and the sun was shining on the highway, dry and clear.

We passed Redcliff, the Canadian "Green House Capitol" and stopped in Medicine Hat, to stretch, fuel up, and visit a pottery factory. We took a picture of the World's Largest Teepee (Saamis Teepee 20 stories high); Medalta pottery, one of the founding industries to this town. It went out of business in 1954 when the third-generation owner decided to stop making bowls, dishes, and vases, and retool to make giveaways for theatres, the company was on the brink of bankruptcy, the cost of retooling and time were both underestimated, and that was the same time television kept people home rather than go to the movies. The place had three large kilns, all the equipment was intact, and many of the products on display. Glass and plastic took the place of pottery, much cheaper, and then there was the imports that did the industry in.

Medicine Hat got its name from a battle, in which one tribes medicine man lost his head dress or hat, and left the area, the warriors laid down their weapons and were all killed.

Back on the road, the train tracks run parallel, tractor trailers and now stacked two high on the flat beds, the four-lane road separated by a median sometimes has pastureland between the East and West lanes, sometimes as much as an acre or two; we found this a bit odd also….

We made it to Moose Jaw by three fifteen, stopped by the visitor's center and got the information on the "Tunnels of Moose Jaw", and the wall art information. We took the picture of the world's largest

Moose statue and proceeded downtown.

We toured the downtown areas, the population is about 33, 275, one main street that dead ends in front of the train station. Back in the 20's Moose Jaw was "the other side of the tracks", the red-light district for the adjoining city of Regina. There are over 30 building murals, very reminiscent of the wall dog paintings we saw in Pontiac, Illinois. Yes, I took a few pictures of them, and then we parked the car and walked over to a non-descript store front with "Tunnels of Moose Jaw" painted on the windows.

Upon entering the two-room area has pictures and souvenirs on all the walls, they are of the late 1800's railroad days, through the 1930's and the prohibition years in the U.S. A lot of history on the Chinese; the indentured servitude, the abuse and the discrimination; It also described the head tax charged for Chinese who brought family to Canada, from $50 to $1000, to $5,000 per person in the early 1900's!!

But the real attraction was the tunnels, so we paid for the actor's guided tour. We had to wait for 20 minutes for our tour, and then a small group of us were led across the street to the second floor of a small clothing shop. In the back of the shop, we were greeted by a young lady dressed like a 30s flapper. (Fanny)

She took our tickets, made us promise not to tell anyone, and not to take pictures, and led us through a back-wall panel, to another room that was set up like a saloon. An animated piano player and bartender, then introduced a short movie about Al Capone. It seems Al was a number 2 man in New York, so he moved to Chicago to become a #1 there. Then prohibition started! He needed a source, and Moose Jaw was right on a rail line, and close to the U.S!

After the short movie clip, we were shown to his office, complete with a sliding fireplace with escape hall way behind the wall, and one of his "special" chairs, (had a bullet proof plate in the back of it); his bedroom with a secret sliding door in the back of the closet that led to a basement where the transactions were made, with wholesale buyers.

We were then turned over to "Gus" who finished the tour with us, all campy, and fun. The special knock was needed to enter where Gus was, and Fanny said it was Monday so she had one of the kid's knock, the door did not open, she then explained again, and that is when Lynn spoke up and said "It's Tuesday!" she then corrected the knocks to four knocks and Gus opened the peep hole and asked the appropriate questions to let us in.

There was a separate room with a switch board which Fanny showed us how to use, and where the "proper" books were kept, a small gambling room, and finally the tunnels that went under main street to the original place we started.

The young actors were quite good, entertaining, and the sliding doors, secret entrances well maintained, fascinating! VERY; enjoyable, educational, and revealing. In his "heyday" Al Capone made a Million dollars a week, (after considerable "shrinkage") In the 1920's and 30's! He was the richest man in America!

Al Capone died in prison, the syphilis he contracted as a young man, worked its way to his brain, and he died of a heart attack. His sentence had been reduced before he died to six years, due to him being a model prisoner…go figure!

We had supper at a local Canadian-Asian dinner, checked into the motel, and called it a day; tomorrow, we should be back in the U.S.A.D.

Day 7, Wednesday

We drove a total of 444 miles yesterday, and we are feeling the effects of the road trip, along with our butts!

I had it with the price of Canadian gas, had it with conversion of kilometers to miles; so, we were off a little after 7A.M., drove southeast to the border. This was a two-lane road, the fields were greener, more farm houses, and the rain. We could see the rain as we drove, there was an area where there was a break in the rain, took some great pictures of the rain front far away, and the sun trying to break through. Traveling around 60 miles per hour, we almost made it, but no, we were hammered, the windshield wipers could hardly keep up, with both heavy rain and increased winds, we were down to 30 miles per hour, and the white lines would still "disappear" for a while! That lasted 20-25 minutes, and really slowed us down, time wise, however, we made it to the border, it took a good 15 minutes to get through, showed our passports, the border patrol guy opened the back and checked the trunk, asked where we were, what we did, and how long we were in Canada. He was very pleasant, and efficient. He then gave us back our passports and a ticket with "Released" on it and we drove through the checkpoint, came to the final gate where another guard reached down with a grabber for the ticket, and told us we could go.

We drove another half hour, found a gas station with reasonable prices per gallon and filled up, glad to back in America!!

Our first stop in America was Minot, North Dakota. This town is referenced when we are in the middle of winter as the "coldest" spot in America. We checked out the Norwegian Heritage village, a beautiful full-scale church, house, and store room, along with a working windmill used in America, constructed and utilized by a Norwegian immigrant at the turn of the century and donated to the park by the children. Of course, we toured the tourist information and souvenir shop too! And yes, we lost an hour in Minot going back to Central Standard time.

Our last stop was Grand Forks, North Dakota; had problems locating the hotel, but after two phone calls and a lot of frustration, we made it. The GPS stopped working when we went into Montana, all of Canada, and even upper North Dakota, hopefully when we re-enter Minnesota, it will kick back in, I didn't realize how much we depend on that thing!

Checked into our room, dropped off our stuff, and headed for the Japanese garden with directions provided by the desk clerk. We found the garden, were very disappointed, it was very small, was a donation from a sister Japanese city, and was not well cared for, scum on the pond, only a few flowers, and overgrown. I took a few shots of interesting flowers, the ones I could find, then off to downtown for dinner. On the way, took a picture of a winking water tower.

The restaurant was called the Toasted Frog. It was very busy for a Wednesday night, we had to wait a half hour, so we walked the downtown area, we talked to two local artists, and one about 35 years old, from Somalia, was named Noah too; so, I introduced myself, we sized each other up, shook hands, and went back to the restaurant.

The wait was well worth it. I had a butter pecan martini, and an egg white sour, Lynn had a Virgin Daiquiri; we had pork belly for an appetizer, and seafood lavosh (thin crust pizza) and a lemon cake, all of which we shared; all perfectly delicious, and we actually took four pieces of the lavosh back to snack on tomorrow. Stuffed, we waddled out to the car, drove back to the hotel, and done for the day!

Day eight: Thursday

We traveled 494 miles yesterday. Lynn does not want to "iron butt" it home, so we will see how far we get; I do not like to re-trace routes, so we headed for Duluth, then down toward Milwaukee.

We left at 7:50 A.M.; the motel actually charged us for breakfast! We have stayed at Comfort inns, Best Westerns, LaQuinta, and a variety of three star and four-star hotels, and motels around the world, and everywhere outside the U.S. and Canada, the breakfasts were banquets, especially in Europe, China and Africa! The TV didn't work initially, the water pressure was low, and the adjustable bed didn't…. this is a Hilton?

It was cool, and we drove into another rain bank. We could find no interesting places to stop on our way to upper Wisconsin. We made it to Duluth at 12:30; Projected to be in Eau Claire, by 2:30. Lynn then stated "If we find a moccasin place on the way, and a dinner club to eat, we can drive home"; I readily agreed!

We stopped for gas outside Eau Claire; and as we approached Madison, I handed the GPS to Lynn to find a supper club; she found one, and we soon left the freeway to find it. It was in a small town, and yes, it was closed, it seems that in all the small towns we were in, both Canada and America, a lot of store fronts were closed or vacant, and help wanted signs all over the place!

We found a "Homey" sounding restaurant/bar in another small town a few miles away; it was open, and a small crowd of old folks were watching TV. We ordered two of the "specials" which were good, but just warm, not hot, and the people were nice.

We then headed for home, we parked the car at 8:30 PM, Both of us tired, sore butts, with a total mileage driven these 8 days of 4,084 miles.

It was a lot easier finishing up the notes, since I took my computer with me. The making of the photo book and the notes were done in three days rather than the normal week.

Little Big Horn

Noah

Educating Noah...Travelin'

The world's largest Moose; a glacier, me on the glacier!

I was not happy with the fire tablet and portable keyboard; so, I started looking on line for alternatives. I am learning, slowly, not to jump and do, but to seek alternatives before jumping. I ended up finding a used notebook computer on Craig's list, it had Window's 7 with office, and WIFI...$75. I bought it! I asked him where the best place was to find a battery...he said "Amazon" ☺ I ordered one the next day, received in a week, and everything is set up for our next adventure, Russia and Finland, in a little over two weeks.

I confirmed the hotels and the resort and started my checking and re-checking of information for the trip.

I have also booked another cruise for May, this one is from Miami to San Francisco, and should finish the west side of Central America. It will be busy, September Russia and Finland, October will be Fox Hills, and November, India.

Next year, February, Antarctica; May, Mexico, and September, Japan and Korea; January 2018, the big one, Miami to Singapore, 72 nights in Oceania, to finish up the major travels.

My shoulders are getting worse; even walking now, one or the other will start to shoot pain radially. I have an appointment in December, and we will see about treating the problem vs. the symptoms!

We skipped the Wisconsin State Fair this year with really no enthusiasm. It has been getting smaller with fewer vendors and less innovation; however, the St. Martin's Fair on Labor Day weekend also has shrunk, with few baby kittens, chickens, ducks, and dogs, some food vendors no longer participate, and the prices are higher than the dollar stores. We also went to the Walworth County Fair; it was $20 bucks for two, with no senior discounts. We had to pay for parking, and it has become more commercialized. We spent a couple hours and left. We are good for fairs for a while.

Noah

We have been attending the monthly motorcycle club meetings as associate members; the meetings only draw 12-15 of the same people, little enthusiasm, and it seems that the few "rides" that still are planned, are taken in cars.

Lynn planned "Pizza on a Farm," an overnight ride to a five-hour north of Milwaukee outside a small town of Athens, Wisconsin.

A few days before the event, one couple backed out, leaving us and a couple that are in the process of selling their bike, so we carpooled. (This was a motorcycle event?)

I had planned the route, it was along winding roads, quiet county side, and small towns, off the super highway.

We left a little after ten. It was misting and overcast. As we drove the route, traffic was light. We did see some wild turkeys, ducks, geese, cranes, and a few deer. The weather went from sprinkling to light rain to clearing.

The women got hungry, a small restaurant next to a gas station looked interesting, so we took the chance. The restaurant happened to be a Polish restaurant; with soups a specialty. We all ordered soup, Lynn had pickle soup, Art, beet soup, Pat barley soup, and I had tripe soup. All of them were served in generous bowls, with homemade bread on the side. All of them were excellent, brimming with flavor, hot and delicious. Next to the restaurant was a Polish shop; and a wide variety of items very reasonably priced and a little different from the run of the mill shops.

We arrived at the motel just before four in the afternoon, unpacked our overnight bags, and headed out to the farm only a half hour away. As we turned into the drive we were greeted by a young lady and a dog, "Goldie" who was laying on his back with his eyes closed. The young lady directed us to an area behind a barn to park, and we then proceeded to an area where picnic tables and three outdoor grills/ovens were smoking away.

Educating Noah…Travelin'

There were a number of people already eating, very casual, and we walked up to the grills to find out how to order. The people working the grills were very friendly, welcoming, and helpful. They directed us to another barn, where we were to specify the pizza we wanted, and pay for our meal. We claimed a picnic table, went into the indicated barn, and placed our order. There was water available, and a number of tables set up, along with a small table with produce if we wanted to take something farm fresh home.

We returned to our table and remarked on how the sky had cleared up, the sun was warm, and the smells of the cooked pizza made us anticipate the meal even more. Not ten minutes later, the cook called out Lynn's name and brought over the pizza. Piping hot, thin-crust whole wheat, it was gobbled down. We had brought ice tea to drink and a cherry crumb pie to share as dessert. We are all members of the "Clean Plate Club," so there wasn't much too clear. As we were eating, people were coming and going, and a couple dressed up like pirates walked past, so we asked, and they turned out to be the parents of the family putting on the event. They had just returned from a local Renaissance Fair and were here to offer help and eat. He explained how he had built the ovens and sold the farm to the kids. She told us that we should "Take advantage of ear piercings from the pirate because it was only a Buck-an-ear!" We all groaned, wished them the best, recommended the Polish restaurant and cleaned up the table, deposited the pan and waste in the designated areas, gave Goldie a belly rub and dog treat, and left for the motel.

We swam in the pool, soaked in the hot tub, and played dominoes with the other couple, at the motel to finish out the night. Had a motel breakfast, stopped at an Amish store on the way back, and stopped for lunch, to be back at home by 1 P.M., 27 hours of good fun, with good friends!

We leave in less than a week. I am all packed. I just need to recheck one more time, drive for the DAV one more time, visit ma, send in the last deposit for India, and do the year-end review with Craig, our broker, to ensure we have enough money in the account for the trips and taxes.

Russia and Finland September 2016

I have put together everything I can think of. I even purchased a notebook computer to make the notes. I am typing on it now, and it works great.... $75.00 for this convenience, WiFi, Word, and e-mail.... wow!

Tiffany, our daughter, came by at exactly 12:15, the time we agreed on for the transportation. WOW, again, right on time...a good omen. She dropped us off at the bus station and promised to water the plants once a week, and I gave her the deposit for the paintball event that Victor (her boyfriend) and I are planning. We need at least 10 people, but he and I agreed that 12 would be best in the event there was a cancellation.

The free parking at the bus station was full, with only one spot available. I commented on this with the attendant, and she agreed that this was unusual, but they had been busy all month. This is the only terminal that offers parking, but you cannot park there longer than two weeks, hence the drop-off.

The trip down to O'Hare was longer than anticipated; traffic was stopped, and we went on the tollway at 2 p.m.! However, I always plan a three-hour slot, and when we exited the bus, it was 2:15!

Now, here is the rub, we walked right up to the ticket agent, walked right through security, and we were seated at our gate by 2:40!

Since there was no loading group, I asked. It seems this airline (British Airlines) boards Premiere, Business, and 1st class, then rows 50 and up, 40 and up, and so on. I asked, how many cheats?

The attendant said, "We checked at the gate". They just wheeled the jumbo Jet up to the gate. It reminded me of the movie "Airport,"

Educating Noah...Travelin'

Yeah, and I took a picture of the nose just outside the window!

Well, the loading went well; the seats closed and pinched, and the eight-hour flight had little turbulence. Customs and finding our gate for the next step weren't difficult. I believe there is only one set of water fountains in the whole airport, none by the bathrooms. At Heathrow, the connecting flight gates are posted only an hour before takeoff, so everyone finds a seat somewhere close to a "flight status board" and waits. The shops, for the passengers, are mostly high-end; Tiffany's was one of them.

The one thing that I had a hard time observing the other travelers was the lack of compression socks. Many, if not most travelers, wore regular socks; some no socks at all, even flip flops, and sandals!

There was a small restaurant that was decorated with giraffes, one of the items a friend collects, they had giraffe stir sticks; when asked, they gave me one, I hope it survives the trip! P.S. Heathrow only takes pounds sterling, no EU's.

Loading of the second leg was to be by row only. When I called, I thought this would be nice. Everyone was seated outside the gates until the first class was called, and then, as usual, everyone rushed the gate, so yup, we got into the rush. This was a smaller plane, seats the same or worse, first and business and premium seats were all taken. This was only a four-hour flight; we both slept a little this time!

Moscow airport, is different from all the others, a noticeable lack of shops, we are herded down corridors that are very clean, but just walls. Customs was horrible, it took us an hour to get through, each person at a time, must stay behind the red line, (strictly enforced) there was a stern officer to enforce even one step over, as a few folks found out!

After the full five minutes of standing in front of the boxed customs agent, she or he looking at you, then the passport, you, then the visa, they handed you a slip of paper indicating to sign your full name twice on a half-inch line. With the attitude of a DMV clerk, you are handed back your passport and indicated you were done with a nod to the exit. Oh, and yes, there were several rifle-armed guards standing around; all the Russians were somber, and all directions were shouted.

We gathered our luggage, easy to find in that the two cases were the last two on the carousel, and headed for the exit. We put on our I.D. stickers and luggage tags, went through another security check, and easily found the Viking escorts. It was nice to see someone smiling! A quick final bathroom (WC) visit. In the men's WC, only one soap dispenser was just barely hanging on the wall, and two others missing; neither of the two hand air dryers worked. I looked at the other guy in the room. We did the "hand jive"; we smiled and laughed at each other as we wiped our hands on our pants, shaking our heads. Lynn had to wait in line, but everything worked in the women's room!

The ship was located two hours from the airport. There was a lot of traffic for Saturday, 6:30 to 8:30 at night, stop and go, nothing was in any language but Russian (signs); we saw two power plants, a couple of car dealerships, and some enclosed shopping centers along with many very new high-rise apartment buildings. The street lights here are a yellow-gold glow. We will find out more tomorrow.

At the ship, another check point, soldiers standing outside with police. Everything was set up, but I guess they were tired. We easily passed through the maze, passports out, but no one looked, and walked through the trailer, then along the dock, to the gangplank. You go to the reception desk, turn in your passport, and get an escort to your room. We were told that the luggage would be in the room soon and welcomed by our guide.

It was late, almost 23 hours since this started. We dropped our carry-ons and proceeded to deck three aft for something to eat. We shared a table with another couple from New York, had a pleasant conversation, had a nice meal, and returned to the stateroom.

After unpacking the toiletries, jammies, and clothes for the next few days, we showered and crashed! It is Saturday night, 10 P.M. their time, and we are here!

Sunday the 18th

We woke up once last night; the internal clocks were off, but we easily returned to sleep. I bought my regular watch, so the time was wrong. The TV has major European networks but no local time and temp, with the forecast, and I will have to find out about this when we go for breakfast for the time we are here.

I now have internet access, but my e-mail wouldn't open this morning. The breakfast on the ship is a typical European breakfast buffet, with special orders for those not wanting the buffet. After breakfast, we toured the ship for orientation. It is cold outside, 8 -10 degrees C (upper 40s F).

It is a lazy morning, and I am still trying to adjust the time, body, and jet lag. At 10:00 A.M. is the life vest practice. Everyone is required to go back to their room, put on their life jackets, and stand outside their stateroom for inspection. Just note that the life vest chord around the back and tied in front should only have one loop...we were instructed and had to re-tie.

An orientation in the Sky Lounge included what souvenirs to buy where it seems nothing from the street vendors (all amber is actually glass, and other souvenirs are Chinese or Japanese knock-offs). I/we are not interested in stacking dolls (started here in the late 1800s, or Amber (bought enough for Lynn on previous trips, and she agrees?!??)

In Russia, Red = Beautiful, there by Red Square is: "Beautiful Square". Icon's paintings of the holy family are protected by the state, so if taken out, you must have the "proper paperwork" that comes from the state department, which takes weeks, so good or great pieces end up confiscated at the border.

Zavtrack: (Breakfast) in typical Russia is Kefir (Yogurt), bread, cheese, and sausage, and, or kasha (porridge); Zakuski; (lunch) pickled mushrooms and sauerkraut, theirs is made with carrots and cabbage, which makes them sweeter. They also have herring, noodles, bread, cold cuts, and sausage or meat.

Drinks, vodka (Rice or wheat) served cold, the best brands Russian Standard, and Tsarskaya. If you are buying from a kiosk, you are warned to make sure the seal is not broken! The Fermented rye drinks "Kvass." Russian saying, "If you spend a long time eating, you will have a long life." Both have high alcohol content and should be paired with pickled mushrooms or other food to coat the stomach.

Caviar is best from three different sturgeons and salmon. The three best caviars in order, Beluga, Osetra, and Sevruga, are judged by size. The bigger the better, the more the taste and expense go up. (Up and including $150.00/oz.) The salmon caviar is acceptable. We went to lunch, a nice buffet, plus an order menu, back to the room to get our stuff together, jackets, and off to the Moscow "Up-Close City Tour."

We met on a bus, were given bagged lunches for later, picked seats, and then disembarked to hoof it to the Metro station, a few blocks away. Took a tunnel under the highway and then went down other steps to the Metro. This was the farthest station out. The metro only stops for a few minutes. We were told to get on, find a seat, and hold on, to "act like Russians" and push if we had to because the train would not wait!

The train does go up to 60 Km per hour and accelerates very quickly, and after the first stop, it decelerates quickly also! We stayed on till the 7th stop and got off to admire the mosaic tiles in the arches, each arch having a different picture, very beautiful, with contrasting white marble, NO graffiti! and spotless!

We then got back on another metro, got off two stops down, and between these arches were statues representing different people at different times. The two statues with dogs, the dark patina was polished off by a passerby who rubbed the dog's nose for good luck, and yes, I did too!

We then rode several escalators. These were extreme escalators, very steep, and we had to hold on tight, going up and down. (I have pictures of all of this!)

We then exited the tunnels and walked from Revolution Square, past some quaint shops, to Red Square. As we passed through the main gate to Red Square, we looked back to see the icons (religious pictures) above all the arches for the protection of the people. Once on the square to the right are the red Kremlin walls, straight ahead is the St. Basil's Cathedral with the colorful onion domes; halfway across, to the right, in front of the red Kremlin walls is a two-story rectangular building, Lenin's tomb, and to the left the massive GUM Department store.

We had an hour of free time to explore the square, tomb, and store; we were told where the WCs were and where to meet, and then we were on our own for an hour.

The shopping center GUM (pronounced "goom") was three stories, two major corridors, horizontally with three connecting halls, boasting 1000 plus stores! Resembling a palace on the outside, spacious on the inside. Mostly high-end stuff; the grocery store had caviar, at $100+/tin, Champaign for almost that much, and chocolates.

There was a Jimmy Chow store, a lot of stores, a lot of people in the halls looking, few people IN the stores, not a lot of bags being carried, just ice cream cones, and lemonade; supposedly the best in the world. (per our Russian guide).

We toured the building, then toured the outside, found some trinkets, and met the group for a walking tour along the river, got on the bus, and stopped at the White Cathedral of Christ the Savior; this is the tallest Eastern Orthodox Christian church in the world and holds 5,000 people.

We were lucky, it was open! The same door is used to go in and come out; you need to be assertive and have NO pictures inside. This was the most beautiful church we have ever been in, including the ones in France, Amsterdam, Barcelona, and even Rome. It actually made our mouths drop!

We toured the church (self-guided), and there were no pictures even to be bought! Trust me, I checked all three souvenir stands inside and out! WOW!

After the church, we walked around the church to cross the river again, see a statue of Peter the Great on a sailing ship, across Patriarchy Bridge to the Sofiyskaya Embankment, and through Bolotnaya Square. We caught up to our bus, ate our box lunches which included the following, ham sandwich, potato chips, juice, water, a pear, a banana, and a snack bar. Our guide also passed out some Russian candy....no one left that bus hungry!!

We then got off the bus, crossed back over the river, several "lock" trees were loaded with locks (pad locks) are put on bridges to symbolize togetherness by couples, forever.

We continued through the Tretyakov Gallery to attend a special performance of original Russian music and dance, utilizing the traditional instruments such as balalaikas, banyans, domras, and guslies. The performance was varied, stimulating and there was a lot of enthusiasm! What a great show! Everyone enjoyed it, standing ovation!

On the way back to the ship, we were told that the cars had been selling too much, that is why the streets are so crowded, the infrastructure is not there to handle the volume!

We were turned away at the first of the two entrances, and we were told no one knew which entrance would be open. The other entrance was open. The guard just let us in. We had to go through another checkpoint and basically just walked past everyone...I guess they only check sometimes...just you don't know when!

We were told supper was ready, but we were stuffed. We went back to the room, set out clothes for tomorrow, showered, and I wrote up the day, we walked more than seven miles; we are tired, tomorrow is another day!

Monday, September 19th, a down day, nothing going on during the day, so we caught up on sleep, typed up notes, talked to other guests, and just lounged around, it is cloudy and 8 degrees Celsius (40's F).

Russia, known as the "lungs of Europe," has the largest forest in Europe, second only to the Amazon, in trees, is the largest country in the world, 6.6 million square miles, or 17.1 million square kilometers, almost twice the size of the United States. The population is only 143 million. (As of 2012) Religions: 72% Russian Orthodox Christian,5% Islam,8% atheists, and Catholic, Protestant, Judaism, and Buddhism each 1% of the population. The Soviet Union was dismantled, and Russia became an independent federation. In Russia, visitors are always offered a cup of coffee or tea and sweets; it is considered rude not to feed your guests.

Moscow has been the capital city since 1367, with one move for two hundred years when Peter the Great moved the capitol to St. Petersburg to try to westernize the Russian Empire; in 1918, the capitol was moved back to Moscow.

Moscow's city traffic is officially ranked the worst in the world; the city boasts 2,500 historical and architectural monuments, 70 museums, 50 theatres, 4500 libraries, and 500 college and research institutions. It is considered the center of Russian culture.

There are more billionaires living in Moscow than in any other city in the world. In 1918, women were granted equal rights. A full two years before America, there were 10.5 million residents in Moscow (expected to rise to 16 million by 2020). Most, if not all, live in high-rise apartments, and it is the biggest city in Europe.

I caught up on sleep; we nosed around the ship, talked to a number of passengers and at 5, headed for the bar. I asked for a "good" Russian Vodka. I was served the Beluga Vodka, and I can see why they drink this like water, it was served on ice, and very smoooooooth! I did relish it, but it soon disappeared, so I asked the bartender for his favorite flavored vodka, and he poured me a honey and wheat flavored vodka, it was good, but I preferred the Beluga! Time to go back to the room; we have dinner, and then Moscow at night! The mistake I made was to return to the room past the souvenir shop on the ship, yup, more Christmas gifts for her and one more item off the "must get" list for those that follow us on our travels.

We went on our first optional tour (one not included with Viking; these you pay extra for.) Moscow at night. This was a tour that started at 9:30 P.M. and was a three-hour tour; we actually were the first bus back at 12:15!

We left at exactly 9:30, we take our headsets with us on all the tours, and we charge them when not in use in the room. As we progressed to the central part of the city, we took the main boulevard, Tverskaya Ulitsa. The islands between the streets are lit up in greens, reds, blues and yellows. All of the major buildings are lit up in different colors.

We boarded a boat, to tour the city by water; this looked a lot like Amsterdam! The boat ride lasted a good 45 minutes, it was a rainy night, most stayed inside the boat, and I ventured out on the open back deck, to take better pictures. Back on the bus, we progressed to Red Square, to see the Gum building lit up, along with the onion topped domes of St. Basil's Cathedral. We then re-loaded the bus for an alternate ride back to the boat, stopping briefly by one of the major universities that were setting up a light show, using the main building as a display screen.

Some more sites, a McDonalds, the first one in Russia, opened in 1989, a KFC, and a Starbucks just opened, although the Muscovites complain about the cost of a cup! We are told that Moscow is erratic, what works one night doesn't another night, we had to pass one gate that was opened before we got there the other day, tonight we had to wait for a guard to open it, then we went back to the street to enter at another entrance, the guide jumped off the bus, and we were lead passed the final check point without having to pass through an inspection trailer, to re-enter the ship.

One of the phases the guide told us, is that the optimistic Russians see life as a zebra, some black years, but the white years will follow, I really like the analogy!

Moscow is very resistant, both Napoleon and Hitler tried, to take this city, but both stopped at Moscow. There are five rivers that intersect here, including the Moskva canal.

Tuesday, Sept. 19th, breakfast early, I just can't seem to pass up the salmon, I will pay for this with weight gain, I know it! Today is the included Moscow Kremlin Tour. This afternoon, is a "Russia and your Cruise "presentation and we set sail north.

At 1:30 we leave the ship for the one-hour drive into the city and see the inside of the Kremlin. The traffic was slow, congested, and it seems only the police and fire departments have Russian cars, all the rest are imports.

The current wall is 400 kilometers long and surrounds 32 hectares of buildings and lands. Inside, after passing through detectors you will find the Russian Palace, one of several places that president Putin resides, various office buildings for conducting government business, and churches. At one time, there were 21 churches; and the entire city of Moscow was within the walls; Now there are only 8 churches.

Many of the diplomats live here, on display is the world's largest cannon, each cannon ball weighs a ton, and the largest bell in the world, which also cracked, the pieces are on an outside display.

In walking, you must stay on the walk, if you walk in the street, a guard will motion you to go back on the sidewalk, and he will be insistent! (Yep, I found out, got the wave motion, …and the look!).

In the cathedral square are the churches, the domes are to represent the flame of a candle, we were able to view the inside of two of the cathedrals, no pews to be found, you were expected to stand during the 2-hour service, in one church, the alter is just visible at the beginning of the service when the priest walks out. The actual entrance doors are on the sides, they are short and narrow, short so that you automatically bow when entering and narrow to preserve the heat inside. Walls inside are full of murals and icons, it is forbidden to take pictures inside. On the domes, there are crosses, at the base of the cross is a crescent, this represents an anchor and hope.

The gold and yellow trimmed flat top building is the current presidential palace, the grounds are immaculate, and I saw only one trash container, there is absolutely no trash, refuse, or plant out of place, exceptionally clean. It is a grey, cool and drizzly day, and even though it is a week day, there are quite a few tourists.

BbIX0A with a green background means exit, this is one of the first things you find out in Russia. Everyone lives in apartments here, the cost ranges from $300-500,000 U.S. and since it is now allowable, people can and want to own their own apartment, and their own car. The average age of a car in Russia is 18 years old, except in Moscow, Moscow is where the money is, we saw all makes, including Roll Royce and Jaguar, Lexus and BMW, Toyota and Honda. You have to be 18 years old to drive; the boys are expected to serve one year in the army or military.

As we returned to the ship, we were amazed on the size of the apartment buildings. We also drove past Russia's Pentagon. We were the second bus back, the guard this morning let us pass through the gate as we did last night, I asked, and the guide told me that they never know if there will be an inspection, or not, they just respectfully ask to by-pass if possible, sometimes it works, sometimes not.

A quick lunch, a little down-time and then at 3P.M. we attend the presentation on: Russia and Your Cruise.

The presentation involved the summary of our journey in Russia, and details of Russia.

As we left Moscow, we will be moving North, on the Volga-Baltic waterway through 17 locks lifting us a total of 150 meters (500 ft.) during a sum of 1100 miles.

Russia is the largest country in the world, 6,592,800 sq. miles, $1/8^{th}$ of earth's surface, 9-time zones, and 143 million inhabitants. 73% are urban dwellers that are currently averaging less than one child per family creating concern for the government.

Russia borders 14 countries, 12 oceans and seas and has 9-time zones. There are 185 ethnic groups 81% Russian, 4%Tartan, and 1.4 % Ukrainian.

1991 was the year the Soviet Union collapsed. Siberia the largest portion (75%) holds 20% of the Russian population, contains the world's largest oil reserve, and fresh lake water. The longest railroad in the world, the Trans-Siberian Rail Road takes a total of ten days from end to end.

St. Vladimir in 987 established the main religion of Orthodox Christianity.

The lecture was comprehensive, but the tone was monologue, and a few folks actually nodded off, Lynn says "that was the last one she is going to attend!" I'll go just because I like history!

Noah

A captain's party with Champaign and appetizers preceded dinner, dinner was excellent, slow night, bed early, we are sailing north, and the locks are very noisy at night.

Wednesday, Sept.21st, another lecture about Russian History, this time I almost fell asleep, monotone, little enthusiasm, we will be docking around noon, have a planned shore excursion to visit a Kremlin (fortress, every major city in Russia has one) and a visit to a home of a Russian family.

This afternoon was a shore excursion to Uglich (Ouglisch) This town was founded in the 10th century, currently 35,000 people, we were given a tour of the Kremlin (fortress) and the main attraction of course, was the church!

Inside the church, again there are no pews. You are expected to stand. The walls are covered with pictures and icons all displaying the critical parts of the Bible, the Adam and Eve, the life of Christ, and the crucifixion. Under communism, church was discouraged, so most of the common folk went to church only three times a year.

In order to accommodate the communist political regime, the celebration of Christmas was engaged with the New Year that seemed to make everyone happy. (Christmas trees were forbidden in the Soviet Union from the early 1900's to 1935).

Alongside the church was a small building displaying Lacquer boxes, these are actually made of paper mâché, then boiled, then coated with black paint, hand painted and then coated with multiple coats of clear lacquer.

The barrettes were the cheapest at about $7.00 U.S., the boxes ranged from $60-$400, U.S... The second half of the tour was a visit to a local home. The owner (Nadya) was a widow, a grandmother who provided us local fare, tomatoes, cucumbers, cheese, bread, pickles, coffee cake, and a home brew.

The custom is three toasts, the "brew" was quite strong (80% alcohol) and the first toast was "To friendship, despite politicians, may we all get along", the second one was "To good health, to keep traveling "and the third; "To safe travels and good weather".

Following the meal, she brought a huge beautiful ornate tea pot called a samovar, treating us to a light, flavorful tea. The house was built by hand by her mother and father, the garden, not a weed in it, was hers, flowers on one side, vegetables on the other, the heat is turned on by the government, higher education is paid for by working in the town where the industry is located for three years.

She had interesting tire art, so I took a picture of it for further reference! The interaction on a small 15 people group with a local is what I enjoy the most on these Viking tours. We were then picked up by the bus, transported back to the dock area where we walked the gauntlet of vendors back to the ship, having to relieve my wallet of Rubbles to make it back.

All on board, at 4:45, set sail at 5:00.

6:15 tonight is "Meet your Neighbor". This is the time when there is an informal gathering outside the staterooms, we all enjoy a glass of champagne together with your neighbors in front of your stateroom door. Nice and inviting, another plus to promote the small ship atmosphere!

We shared a table with a couple from Scotland, very nice discussions, interesting views on traveling inside and outside the U.S.

Tomorrow morning at 8A.M. the Yaroslavl City tour begins, so we went to bed early so that we could get up early.

Thursday, September 22nd; we got up, both of us had trouble sleeping last night, it looks like today will be similar to the last few days, mid-forties, and off and on drizzle, and light rain.

The city tour includes both the farmers market, and a visit to the

Noah

Governor's Residence. This is one of the Volga River's most significant ports, the population is similar to Milwaukee, 600,000; the unemployment here is 1.6%!

Our first stop was the Church of St. Elijah the prophet. Impressive icons, unique frescoes including one showing workers gathering wheat; this is rare, working people were rarely depicted! After progressing to the last area, we are treated to a quartet of singers, whose voices resonated richly in the hallway.

We then walk a couple blocks in the light rain to the marketplace. It is indoors, and warm, very welcome! Viking has arranged a sampling of sausages, cheeses, pickles, honey, and various nuts, we then toured the area, and I bought a few of the chocolate bars the guides have been promoting as "the best in the world".

We headed back to the bus, (it is still raining and windy) for a short drive to the Governor's Palace. This is a living museum, where we are greeted by an escort, who takes us through the palace, explains the subtleties of the women and men of the past. This includes the following: white rose means, "1st love", Red Poppies;" I dream of you"; a peony; "I want to spend my life with you"; and a sunflower; "Happy family life"; there were others but I can't remember the types and meanings.

We were then led to a ballroom; we were shown the subtle sign language used by the women, using a hand fan, foot signals, and subtle body movements. We were then treated to a three-piece chamber music ensemble; this was then joined by several of the costumed staff that danced to the music and then went into the group of visitors to engage them in dance. (Lynn and I were too far back in the group to be invited to join.)

It was a very pleasant experience; time went by very fast, we loaded on the bus back to the ship, and we were going down the river by noon!

We had a light lunch, another lecture on Russian History, another promotion regarding the different cruises available through Viking; a daily briefing on what to expect tomorrow, and a Viking Explorer Society cocktail party at 6:30 for guests that have sailed with Viking previously.

Dinner and a program at 9:15 finish out the day. The program included a game of "Name That Tune", which country it came from, and a specific question for the country, with extra points for dancing to the music, it soon became apparent that the dance floor was too small. The enthusiasm grew, the room became increasingly louder. The winning group won a bottle of Champaign, a pianist with a vocal accompanist played on; it was a good day, hopefully tomorrow will be warmer and we see a little sun!

Friday, September 23rd; I got up early, it feels a little warmer, but it is still in the mid-forties. By the time, we had breakfast, (it is time I start cutting back on the salmon on half a bagel) and get ready to disembark for our tour of the Kirillo-Belozersky Monastery, a local school, and small town.

The first difficulty was we were assigned to a home visit and the Monastery, when we wanted the school, since we had missed the school visit in China. They worked with us, our headsets worked on the new assigned bus, and off we went. The roads are not the best, mostly two lanes outside the major cities, and have considerable wear, holes, deteriorating shoulders, and bumps; we got our "exercise" bouncing inside the bus for 45 minutes.

The monastery started out as a cave, to wooden structures, to a fortress built in 1494, containing the largest church in medieval Russia. The complex was a fortress, protecting, monks and peasants; it was also the main place for religious knowledge, documents, and library, to say nothing of Icons.

Just a note here, icons are said to be the souls of Russia, for centuries priests carried these portraits of saints into battle for the fighting Cossacks to kiss-the right icon might bring them back from battle safely from the war. They are actually considered to be the Gospel in paint, so they are preserved, and closely scrutinized.

The Complex is quite large, cobblestone roads, not handicap easily accessible, including stairs without rails. There are eight guard towers, two monasteries, and eleven churches. In 1764 Empress Catherine the Great, stripped the monastery of its lands and turned sections into prisons; in 1924, the atheist Bolshevik government closed the monastery down, the monks were executed or arrested. However, unlike the monasteries in northern Russia, which were turned into concentration camps for political prisoners, this one has been kept as a museum.

Both Lynn and I agree we have seen enough churches, along with the artwork, the painted walls, and icons.

Next, we were driven through town to the grade school, a block two story building, facing a large soccer field and field house. We were taken into a classroom, it was sparse, but in the corner, was an example of uniforms they are no longer required to wear, the room was comfortable, about 35 chairs, with desks, and a projector in the ceiling. Not much different from home!

The differences are that another language is taught starting in second grade; they have a choice of English, Spanish, or French, along with Russian. They go to school 6 days a week, and are fed twice a day, most are subsidized meals. When the kids are 14-15, they are tested. They must make a choice as to a trade or further education, the grades also being considered in the choice.

Crafts are also taught, heritage crafts, woodworking, doll making, paintings, and lace making to mention a few since preserving their heritage is important in the Russian society. The bell rang, and the kids, changed rooms, it was fun to watch, they were just like kid's everywhere, they were well behaved, noisy, the girls all had neatly done hair, the boys in shirts and slacks. You can still tell the nerds and geeks from the rest, the popular girls, and the shy ones. We were treated to a student guide, and a student that sang and danced a traditional song and dance, along with a display of arts and crafts we could purchase on the way out, it was fun!

As we drove through town, we were told that here and in most small towns the people live in single homes, they prefer to build them themselves, most are heated with two or three wood burning stoves. It costs about $5000-6000 for the whole house, some don't have running water, but are you ready? They all have internet, and phones; the world is changing! P.S. A face cord of wood costs about $8.00, and they go through about 8-10 face cords per year.

We meet up with our ship, go through the gauntlet of shops, stock up on more souvenirs for us and friends, and then back on board. We have a lunch, attend another lecture on Russian history, then attended a cooking class on Russian dumplings that was exceptional, and included samples!

Back to the room, a briefing about tomorrow before supper, and tonight is typical Russian fare, so it ought to be interesting!

The briefing we attended, indicated that another night tonight through the dreaded locks...noisy, and a bit of soft rocking, there is little room between the sides of the lock and the sides of the ship!

Dinner! We had a table set for three tonight; we won't do that again, no one to talk too! However, I was able to get a copy of the menu to add to the picture book, and I will briefly describe what we had now:

Noah:

"Stolichnaya Salad" is a traditional Russian vegetable and meat salad (it was formed in a mold, and you could taste the celery, carrot, and chicken)

Russian "Koulibiaca" puff pastry stuffed with salmon and spinach in a white wine sauce

"Sir Niki" Russian curd blinis with strawberry Mélange

Lynn:

Borsch: Russian beef broth with beets, carrots, & piroshky

"Polansky Koteletti" Pork & Chicken Meat Loaf; mashed potato, zucchini, and bell pepper sauce

Russian Honey Cake

We slowly walked away…. both plates, all plates licked clean!

One more activity to wind up the day: Vodka Tasting (Noah, that's me☺ only).

The tasting started promptly at 9:15. The panorama Bar was full and 2/3rds women! I found a table and I recognized a guy that had a room just down the hall from us, and called him over, that balanced out the table with two women that were open to fill a table.

On the table were four sets of six shot glasses, a center plate with four pieces of bread with something spread on it, four pieces of pork belly, and four pieces of herring; around the outside of the plate a bowl with pickled mushrooms, one with green and red peppers, one with pickles, and another with green and black olives.

We were all given two sheets of paper; one had an abbreviated history of Vodka, the other a description of each of the six vodkas we would be sampling.

The presentation was provided by the Maître d' Anastasia, and Assistant Maître d' Marina; both wisps of women, but I believe either one could out drink anyone at this gathering!

The first vodka tasted was the "Russian Standard". This brand, the most popular premium brand has sales of $3 million, 9 liters per case. We are all poured a shot, some waving to have only half of the shot glass full. The first of six toasts repeated, and then down the hatch. This one very smooth, expressions around the room varied, but no one left any in the glass!

The balance tasted were "Five Lakes", from Siberia, "Pertsovochka" pepper honey vodka, (good for when you feel ill); "Baikal" a thyme and ginger organic Vodka, "Slavyanskaya" a birch bud infused Vodka, and finally "Tsarskaya Original" very smooth, supposed to have healing powers.

Between each tasting was a short story or joke, we were also encouraged to clear our pallet with a snack between each tasting. The atmosphere was very relaxed; the hostesses were entertaining, welcoming, and proficient.

After the last tasting, we were told one final story about how Russians do not let anyone leave without one final drink, so yep, one, more, round was poured, and a final toast, what great fun!

Back in the room by 10; 30; no problem at all going to bed, we hit the set of 6 locks at 2 A.M. We are raising the ship a total of 30 meters for the lake that is about 90 feet, it took almost 4 hours!

Saturday September 24th; Morning, up at 7, let Lynn sleep in, dressed and took my morning tour. Very quiet this morning, maybe ten folks in the dining room, no one outside. Toured aft, then toured the bow, it is crisp upper 40's, and actually partly cloudy, NO RAIN!

Took some early morning camera shots, talked to a few of the staff, went down and Lynn was up! Had breakfast, still very few folks around, then a leisurely game of scrabble, (I won!) Back to the room to clear e-mails, catch up on documents. The activity today is at 2:15 Kizhi Island; I will also see if I can find someone to help put this document in "documents" so I can find it easier!

Noah

The desk person was very helpful in moving this to documents, it took less than a minute……. Duh…. sometimes I feel way too stupid!

Every day there has been a lecture on Russian history and culture, quite informative, much different from what we seemed to learn, I guess the perspective is considerably different; I keep thinking what the people here think of our history, and what goes on in the U.S.A. In watching CNN here, it is different than at home, a bit more news, a lot less politics, however the liberal slant is obvious.

A wheel house tour is offered, we have seen bridges before, so we took a pass on that; lunch, then we turned in our paperwork for optional excursions Sunday, I signed up for the Banyan experience, Lynn took the Matryoshka Doll Painting one.

This afternoon we had the Kizhi Island experience. We docked a little before 2 P.M. and disembarked to this small island community. This island's main attraction is the two-multiple domed wooden churches, the Transfiguration 22 dome church, and the neighboring Intercession nine domed church.

This is an included tour, so most if not, all passengers gather off ship to be split into manageable groups to walk the ¼ mile to the church and small village complex.

This area has many legends and myths, as we walk a board walk on an earthen /gravel path, we are told of mermaids, magic rocks, and not to worry about the snakes, since they are currently in hibernation (I believe the guide was pulling our leg as we travel).

The main attraction is the 22 domes wooden transfiguration Church. Legend claims that in 1714 a carpenter erected this church, from Pine and Aspen. Once this church was completed, he threw his ax into the lake so that it would not be duplicated. The church is actually shaped on the inside like an octagon, and if viewed from the top, resembles a cross. UNESCO designates this church as one of the most complex structures in the world.

The two churches together, both shaped and build by axe have aspen shingles on the domes, these must be replaced every 70-80 years, the largest of the structures is 37 meters high (about 120 feet or twelve stories). The difficulty is the lack of a deep foundation, a shallow rock base with a birch bark water barrier is the base for both of these structures. The weather here is cool to cold. The smaller church (of Holy Mary) was the church that was actually used, easier to heat, more comfortable, the large church for warm weather use and for show. The altars are always partitioned off.

In 1982-1984 a metal structure was built inside the main church in order to save the external walls, when the walls are repaired, the metal skeleton will be removed, and the icons put back in their former places.

At the turn of the century, many parts were also covered by iron to preserve the churches, but it was decided that the church as it was originally built should be shown, and all the iron was removed.

Beyond the church is a large farm house, a wind mill, thrashing house and a sauna.

The farm house was very large; it did contain a living area, work shop, tool shop, and stalls, actually a combination barn and house, due to the long winters, and extended cold and darkness. Shutters were put on the windows for the summer white nights; the trim on the outside of the windows replicated that seen in the cities by the farmers. We were shown two pictures, of two families, asked the difference, when told, we could easily tell which family lived in the city and which lived on the farm, the reason for moving into the city was obvious, and farmers were poor! In the barn section, there was a small boat with an outrigger; the reason for the outrigger was that the cows were transported across the river to graze; there wasn't enough pasture land on the island to support the cows!

In the winter, the women would gather at one house or another to weave and spin; the men would work in the barn mending and building for the summer; in one corner of the house an icon was hung. This was the most honored spot, and any guest was to sit in that area, this was also the spot where the household money was placed, "God would watch over it".

The river and lake nearby had 47 varieties of fish; children were given chores from the age of 4-5 on up.

The fences were made so that you could create an opening by just moving five or six of the slanted poles.

There is also another small church, kept/preserved as one of the best examples of the early church structures because of the best proportions of the churches built. The windmill was on a pole that could be turned to catch the wind.

It was an hour tour, we had free time to go back and review the different structures, and hit the various souvenir shops, and I needed to get a stone that is found only here, in the world, got a necklace for me and a ball for Camille, along with other various trinkets.

We were back on the boat for the aft deck party, snacks, band, vodka, beer, and juice drinks for everyone. I started to attend another lecture, but the monotone and heavy accent drove me nuts, so that was that.

A briefing on the events tomorrow, dinner with another very nice couple, then the evening entertainment of "Call my bluff" ……it was fun, our team was bluffed.

Sunday, September 25th

Last night was rough, had sinus problems two showers, countless meds, but made it through the night.

There was a daily briefing regarding the remainder of the trip, St. Petersburg, and the details of disembarkation on Thursday.

Educating Noah...Travelin'

We arrived at Mandrogy just before ten o'clock. I am still amazed how fast everything is set up and passengers off the ship. Being a small ship, we just pick up our passes at the front desk and walk off the ship either forward or aft. The coming back is just as easy, no lines, no inspections, no crowding, just hand in your pass and board.

I had the Banyan experience, we were in a group of eight guys, the right size for a group. We were taken down a path along the river about a quarter of a mile, past some very ornate houses, and a vodka museum, making a note to check that out on the way out!

A small meeting room with a table and chairs, a changing room where we were provided paper slippers, a regular sheet to use as a wrap, and a towel. We all strip down, put on our sheets and walk into a small ante room just before the sauna. We waited a bit, then just walked into the two-tier benched wood lined room. It was close, but comfortable. An attendant walked in, made a welcoming gestured, said something in Russian, poured water in the steamer, and showed us what he was going to do, then proceeded to hit us, one at a time, to stimulate the back, chest belly and legs, going up and down the group. It felt very stimulating, refreshing, and smelled great! After every two guys, he threw another cup of water on the rocks.

He repeated this once more, and then led us outside, and pointed to the pier, he indicated that the water was deep at the end of the pier, so, one by one; buck naked, we jumped off the pier into the Volga River. Wow, what a great feeling. The water was about 8 feet deep, so there was no problem with hitting the bottom, but once in and after surfacing, we climbed back on the pier, and put our sheets back on. The fifty-five-degree weather seemed warm. We then all went back in to repeat the ritual, and felt great after the second dip, we sat around a table, enjoyed a cup of warm tea, some water, and a little strawberry preserve, simple but refreshing. We then dressed and headed back to the ship. I stopping at the Vodka Museum, 300 Rubles ($4.50) to try 3 different shots of Vodka, and three hundred more for a sample to take home, the place was full of different vodkas!

We then stopped by a garden to get some flower shots, for the album.

Here is what Lynn experienced. "We met our guide just off the ship and he introduced us to our instructor, Lena. There was a short walk to her shop. Her assistant was Olga. Lena spent a lot of time talking, explaining that the Matryoshka doll was the mother, and the smaller dolls inside, were her children. Not many of these dolls hold a rooster by the neck, but the ones that do are actually holding the father. She also explained what each color represented: Red for the mother, white for purity, etc. She spent way too much time on this. We had 3 brushes. The large brush is used for painting the dress, scarf and sleeves. The other brushes to be used for smaller parts of the doll. The opposite ends of the small brushes also were used to make dots on the clothes. She taught us how to clean and wipe our brushes and had us put on an apron and plastic sleeves to protect our clothes".

"Of the 4 men in our group one needed help putting on his apron. Olga modeled the scarf, showing us the knot and ends of the scarf had to be painted the same color of the scarf. Also, showed us the under garment and sleeves which should be painted white. There was a white plastic plate which we could use to blend colors. I really wanted my doll to be purple, but with all the blending to be done, red, blue, and white, I knew I'd never get the same color with multiple blending of these colors, so I did the traditional red. I only made the flower purple".

"The paint dried rather quickly, but as we put on the dots, we knew it would not be completely dry when we left. Lena gave us a plastic bag with a brush and more paints to finish our dolls at home. She also let us keep the plastic sleeves. We had to roll our painted doll in a napkin to place in that bag, but the dots weren't dry so I will have to correct that at home too".

Educating Noah…Travelin'

"She told us the real dolls that are not made in China have the artist's name and date of completion is on the bottom of the doll. In China, there is mass production. The colors are not as bright, and each person paints only one part of each doll, as in a mass production factory. She also told us not to buy from the open-air merchants, but I did anyway."

"As I looked around the class at the other painted dolls, I was very surprised to see how gaudy they were. They used all the primary colors in a very unattractive fashion. I guess my love and skill of working with crafts has given me a very good eye for what is attractive".

"She took most of the group to the actual artist factory to see them painting the dolls. I had to meet Noah, so I skipped that part, and waited at our meeting spot."

At noon, a "Ship's Quiz" was available at the reception desk; it is to be returned by 7P.M. to test our knowledge of the trip, Russia, and the ship. The noon lunch was on a Russian theme; many different dough items wrapped around different meats, as well as roast pork and chicken. As usual, many types of salads, cheeses, cucumbers and tomatoes served. There was a beverage made from bread, and as usual beer, and wine. The desserts were many, torts, blintzes and sweetbreads. When we thought, we were done, a young man came around with a cooler full of packaged ice cream treats.

The Russia today lecture, I lasted about ten minutes, more monotone, heavy accent, had to pass again, would have loved to stay, about 2/3 of the passengers filled the room. I did watch some on the internal TV and did get the gist; there are more similarities to Russia to the U.S.A. than anyone in the U.S. realizes.

Tea time at the Panorama bar, but we were still stuffed from lunch, plus this provided some additional time to catch up on journaling. The dinner, captain's reception, and farewell dinner was the closest to a formal dinner; sports clothes and dress shirts were worn, and women were prettied up also. This was a special menu; we were able to take one as a souvenir, so yes, that will be with the photo album. (Here it is in brief: Tandoori chicken, with parmesan foam, or Tuna Avocado, Tartar; Grilled Scampi with saffron risotto, with lobster sauce; entrée: Whole Roasted Beef Tenderloin, or Grilled Fillet Norwegian Salmon;

Dessert: Chocolate and cherry Surprise with vanilla ice cream

Memories of our cruise: a work in progress of the video of our trip provided by the Viking Cruise Line. We are on a number of the shots. It is offered now on a USB stick. We have tons of photos no one but us will look at, so we are going to pass on that!

We have two tours tomorrow, so we have to go to bed early (before ten), so that is it for the day!

Monday, September 25th

Breakfast early, we have our first excursion at 07:45; alarm set for 6:30, and we go from there!

We kind of have a routine, Olga, (I love you, Olga!) Desha, and Nadia are the waitresses we prefer for breakfast, they are always friendly and always there, and just a pleasure to visit with in the morning!

We pick up our cards and go out to our assigned bus. Our guide greets us; she is articulate, engaging, and well informed. Our first stop, and the main stop, is the Catherine Palace in Pushkin.

We thought Versailles, was opulent, but I must admit, the Russians have it on this one. We get there a little early, and are treated by a uniformed brass band, that plays a variety of songs along with a marching show that was not only a delight for the ears, but the eyes also.

The gates are opened and the expanse of the residence is mind blowing! We walk a full half block to get to the entrance, we are told to check all jackets, coats, and back packs.

The turquoise outside with gold guild, statue columns and buildings just does not stop. Inside, after shedding our stuff, we start up a grand staircase, gold, opulence, parquet floors (we all had to wear booties) and ceilings and walls with gold guild, paintings and mirrors, WOW! The most impressive to both Lynn and me was the Amber room. You can only take pictures prior or after the room, describing it would not do it justice, I have to refer to the photos! UNBELIEVEABLE! There were many tables, desks, and bureaus with inlaid wood that were polished like ice, just beautiful.

Many rooms also had multiple and very tall Dutch porcelain heaters that were blue and white and really did not go with the other décor. But, "What Catherine Wanted, Catherine Got".

During the war, much of the building was destroyed and burned. It is unbelievable the amount of restoration that has taken place. We would not want to know the costs for that rebuilding. But it is magnificent!

Many other rooms, (have photos), then outside to the garden, other buildings, and the grounds. Yes, I did get a whistle blow, and waved off the grass (oops) there was also other buildings we toured on the grounds along with several formal gardens.

Back to the ship for a lunch break, then in the afternoon we are off to the St. Petersburg City Tour, a five-hour tour! We took lunch on the panorama bar, it is an abbreviated lunch, salad and 1/2 a roll-up, but more than enough, plus the folks there, Gabriel and Jerica who seem to know your name after meeting them once!

This small ship ambiance and the attentiveness of the crew are just unbelievable!

Had our lunch, checked everything in the room, and then off to the City Tour. We opted for the bus tour since Lynn could not/would not be able to make the walking tour, and we figured we would get a better taste of St. Petersburg on the bus tour! (Besides that, it was a five-hour tour).

The first stop was the Somolic Convent; it took 80 years to build it, Peter the Great sent his wife here so he could marry another woman. She stayed there then changed her mind, but that is a history lesson....

The gas here is 35 Rubles per liter which comes to about what we pay per gallon in the States! 70-75 % of the population here still smoke cigarettes, politically correct restaurants enforce the no smoking rules, but per the guide, "that depends on the policeman" as far as enforcement. I am also finding a lot of Japanese and Chinese tourists here, and many of the signs have subtitles in English, where everywhere else, it was Russian or nothing!

We drove past the KGB building, which was very imposing, not ornate, and we were told that the basement is the place you go if you are brought there, and the only way out is Siberia! (NO ONE MESSES WITH THE KGB) The buildings we pass are very reminiscent of those throughout Europe. We do pass the smallest one, a yellow two-story with a large doorway. Got a picture of that one!

Next stop was a very Ornate Spilled Blood Church; the ornate structure, the columns, just beautiful! I took pictures of each face, the iron fencing, and the vender row along the canal. There were people with raccoons, owls, and doves to take pictures with, the gates and fencing in ornamental iron were fascinating!

On to the bus and off to the four seasons hotel, cost for two nights…$1300 U.S. we didn't stay but used the W.C.

Next to the hotel is St. Isaac's Cathedral; I also walked and took the four walls of this one, on one side the columns are pitted; this was from machine gun fire from WWII; what a shame!

I asked about a grey and black bird that looked and acted like a crow and was told "It is a crow!" I also asked about why people were picking up leaves and branches with leaves and told that a lot of people want something natural in their homes with the turn of seasons.

One stop for a picture of the light house poles, and a war ship, then off to Basil Island.

Basil Island is home to the Peter and Paul Fortress. The main attraction here is the church…. go figure! More gold, but here is the rub, very few icons, and half the floor has sarcophaguses of the dead rulers. Each ruler has their place, two of the marble sarcophaguses are different, instead of white, one is green, another is red, small place, for a church, or any building in Russia.

This was the last stop of the afternoon tour, on the way back to the ship; our guide filled us on more Russian life. Driving licenses can be obtained at 18, on the back of the car, there is an exclamation mark indication a new driver; the license numbers have gone to the Finnish letter and number system. Due to the difficulty of the Russian symbols, the Finnish style plates are easier to read.

St. Petersburg is a planned city, looks more like a European city, and is not just a city that has overgrown the original Kremlin or fort. The Russians prefer foreign car makers over the LADA. Many jokes about the reliability of the LADA Russian car; we were told one: "How do you know it is a LADA with 4 people? One is steering the other three are pushing!"

Flats or apartments are where most people here live; they are not cheap, ranging from $100,000 U.S. to 250,000. Utilities, internet, phone, light, and heat averages $150.00/month. Mortgages 12% to 15%, apartments are handed down generation to generation, multiple generations live in the housing, some boys are questioned if the girl they have with him loves him, or the apartment they are living in. (This of course may just be mother's speculation about how special her son is!) Tax rate is 13%; teachers make about $900.00 per month, people here are paid by the month.

Ninth grade you are tested to see the career paths available, the better the grades the more you are qualified for, and the more support the government will provide. Your options include trade school, institutes, and State Universities.

Unemployment stops after six months, you must accept a job offer, the State will help, but after so many rejections, or your six months, you are no longer supported by the State.

Babies, when the baby gets delivered, the mother gets $600.00 and her employer pays her about ½ her wages while she stays at home up to a year and a half; the second baby, the State pays her $6000; to pay only for the baby's needs. Now, I am old, my hearing isn't the best, and my memory suffers, but this is what I believe I heard, and it should be close, I am not picking and choosing only the good and bad, every society has its good points and bad, I just found these items interesting, especially the gouging by the banks on the mortgages!

Tuesday, September 27th. We actually slept in, we topped 11,000 steps yesterday, and we were worn out!

Our first excursion of The Hermitage isn't until 10:15, so we have a little time for leisure, documenting, e-mail catch-up, etc.

The one of the best things on this vacation is that everyone is cooperative, everyone was on the bus and we promptly left at exactly 10:15. The drive to the Hermitage was slowed by road work, yes, it is the same everywhere in the world, two workers were smoking, two were talking, and one was watching another one work. It took a half hour, the rain did stop, gloomy but we were to be inside for the entire tour.

As we pulled up, there was already a long line, and buses took most of the parking spots, so as in all European cities, we double parked since there was no parking available.

We received our tickets, and we actually passed two groups in line, since our entrance was timed at 10:30 (thank you Viking!) and after only 15 minutes we were ushered into the building. Next, we were directed to go down to the lower level to check all of our coats. Another line, and yes, bumped and pushed, especially from those accustomed to being close to a lot of people, there is no "personal space" here or in Europe!

I checked our coats, got in another line, and we went through another security check and finally in. With Viking, we all get voice boxes, and chargers in the room. This audio system has a charger in the room, and each night we recharge them. All of the excursions include them, so we are always in touch with our group leader, turning on the receiver, it hunts for the closest frequency and WA-LA has hearing! SOOO much easier, Viking really has these excursions down to a science!

We spent four hours touring this extensive palace/museum/collection. We thought the collection at Versailles, the Louvre, and the Smithsonian in Washington D.C. were extensive, but they actually pale to this! Marble, Gold, Jade, Paintings, Tapestries, Antiques, parquet flooring everywhere! Opulence, extravagance, and indulgence…. wow!

I know that America has only a few hundred years' history, we are so blessed to see what the world has to offer!

We were tired, it is way too much to take in, and I even took a few pictures of the court yards inside and outside this place!

The tour ended with all of us exhausted, walking through for four hours, listening to explanations and details of hall after hall, and room after room of treasures of the world, from all over the world, and especially from centuries of Russia. This includes portraits, glimmering marble, gold leafed stucco-work, gilded columns, and

13th through the 18th century works of art, including the best from Italy, Spain, France, and Scandinavia.

We finally had a few minutes to check out the shops, fight to get our coats, and meet outside to rendezvous with the bus for the trip back. I had had an eye on a Russian hat, another person in the group wanted one also, and we were approached, a deal was struck for two, yup, got a great deal!!

On the way back, took some pictures of "regular" St. Petersburg, traffic is thick, since the opening up of this country in the early 90's visitors have been flooding in, to see this wonderful country and its people. Remember, people are so much the same; it is the politics that screws everything up!

Back on the ship, they skewed the lunch/dinner hours and combined them from 4:40-6:30 so everyone has a chance to attend the ballet tonight. Another great meal, catch up on the journaling, just a bit of problem with e-mail, too many on when we got back. Next will be the ballet, 6: 45-11:00 P.M. tonight.

Everyone was on the bus at 6:44; and we were the first bus of three out. It seems that there is some roadwork being done even at this time of night, we had to jockey from 3 lanes to 1 lane, small cars challenge the bus!

After a little more than a half hour we arrive at the theatre, and again we double park to unload. The guide passed out the tickets and showed us how to read them. We walked a half block, went through metal detectors, and were told to enter from the left. It is a relatively small theatre, maybe 300 seats on the main floor, and then there four floors of balcony seats, at an ordinate and of course opulent setting. The ballet was three acts, this one was Swan Lake, the tunes were played from an orchestra pit, there must have been 20 musicians, and 35-40 dancers. The ballet was perfectly executed, and after the second curtain, we got up and left. When we got out in the parking area, Lynn said "I think it is too early, no one else followed us", so we went back in, no one challenged us ringing off the metal detectors, as we re-ascended the steps.

We stopped at an attendant, and she reinforced what Lynn said, so back into the theatre we went. We still had a few minutes, I wanted to check out the men's water closet, because there were guys lined up to use the one-on-one side of the building, so I waited outside the other, sure enough, the water closet was the size of an aircraft bathroom and no larger!

I confessed to the other members of our group, they got a good laugh, and then we all settled in to watch the final twenty-minute act. We were second to fill our bus, but we passed that bus on the way back. Snug and in bed by 11:15, another great day!

Wednesday, September 28th. We have two excursions today, the Peterhof Palace and Park, from 8:45 to 1:00, and our last excursion the Kommunalka Visit; I wanted to compare the small town visit we had earlier to the Big City visit today.

We received our disembark time, it is 4 P.M. tomorrow, we are the last ones off the ship; I don't know how long we will be able to use the cabin, but we will find out. I tried to break a small bill, it seems in Russia it is very hard to break big bills, even small ones, and no one wants change; it is a hundred Rubles or more and multiples of 100's. I guess I am still thinking "old" with change.... especially in Europe, except when we have to use a public WC!

We are the first bus out, and the trip to this palace is about an hour. Traffic is a fight, even for a bus! There are now nine river boats docked at a place for four, we are the closest to the dock, again, like the tours, Viking has this well planned!

St. Petersburg is the closest Russian major metropolitan city to the Arctic Circle, and supposedly cloudy dreary days are the norm, I will check today the forecast for Ivalo, Finland, where we will be spending the next 5 days.

Back to the excursion, this was an extra, we paid for this and three others, Viking usually includes at least one excursion per port, plus expert planning, exceptionally friendly staff and fantastic food...sounds like an advertisement? Enough!!

On the way to the palace, we are told apartments are all heated with hot water, and this is also where the hot water for faucets comes from, city supplied, just as Milwaukee was back in the 20's and 30's. After the break-up of the Soviet Union, everyone was given small parcels of land outside the city for Dacha's; a cottage, a retreat, whatever they wanted to do with the land, and most erected small houses and root vegetable gardens.

We were of the first groups to enter the grounds, there will only be outside and garden shots, no pictures inside. We wait in the Upper 40's-lower 50's, cool dreary grey day for twenty-minutes in line. Finally, at exactly the precise time the one of seven doors were opened, and we are crowded one at a time into the entrance. Once in, we have to check our coats, (no large bags or backpacks allowed), proceed to another room where we put on ugly brown covers for our shoes, and we are the second group to tour. Like the Hermitage, this description will not help, so we bought a book for a buck!

Sasha, our boat tour guide walked us through the rooms, one wonder after another, he is very knowledgeable, and no notes, of course if it was B.S. we wouldn't really know anyway, but the presentation was excellent, so who cares!

After the tour, through the gift shop, and the visit to the WC, we retrieved our coats for the outside tour.

The grounds are expansive, we were out in time for the start of the fountains, there are 168 fountains in total, and just below the palace is the centerpiece Samson Fountain. We toured the grounds, too much for the 45 minutes was only good for about 1/3 of the grounds, and we had to hustle, past a few fountains on the way to return on time, we did it, with one minute to spare! P.S. There are no pumps for the fountains!

Back to the ship, still no e-mail, had a light lunch, a little rest, then on to the visit!

These visits are what making Viking trips the best! Nine of us had the pleasure of talking over tea and cream or and meat filled pastries. Since there was such a small group, we had a small van; and treated to a "Mr. Toads wild ride" to and from the location.

The apartment/room, living quarters was part of the hold-over of communal apartments from the post-civil war era. It was located "downtown" in a five-story building that was a warehouse at one time. A hallway, a total of eight rooms, with a common shower/bathtub room, toilet room, kitchen, and laundry room, the four burner stoves, two burners were assigned to a room. The rent charged to those that did not own the room is $13,000 rubles /month ($200 US) for single, 15,000/ month ($240 US) for a couple. The building is hot water heat, per Irena; it is never cold in the rooms, when it gets too warm, they open windows. Electricity and gas, internet and phone are charged per room.

From the outside and hallway, the building is not attractive. The kitchen and bathroom areas are adequate. Everyone has their own kitchen pots and utensils at their own work tables. Once inside Irena's private area, it was quite lovely even though very small. She had a large refrigerator and 2 twin beds in one area. The next area held a couch, desk and chair, numerous bookshelves which held a very new TV, a microwave, family pictures and brick a brack. The ceilings were very high, her son and daughter helped her wallpaper the rooms very beautifully.

We sat for over an hour asking many questions of her, which she answered cheerfully. As to our host, she only wanted from us, our names, hometowns, and occupations. Everyone enjoyed the visit immensely.

Our program director, Yulia also joined us for this visit. We found out she lives in Moscow, in a 1-bedroom apartment with her husband in a very nice area. On board, since she is in management, she has her own quarters. Sasha, our usual guide, lives in Pushkin, just outside of St Petersburg. When the ship is docked here, he visits his home between assignments.

Tonight, we get the final disembarkation briefing, included were some interesting consumption facts regarding this cruise, we drank 350 bottles of the complementary red wine, 290 bottles of the white, 255 bottles of the complimentary beer, and utilized 1010 rolls of toilet paper.

We had our last dinner, attended the piano bar since the singer came up to us and told us she found "Soul Man", and "Car Wash". She did play them; we danced with the few that were left in the lounge to close the place down. After going to our cabin, I realized I forgot my camera in the Sky Bar. Lynn went back up to get it, and Ronaldo, the bartender was already calling our room to let us know they had found it. That is just how the service has been on this ship. When the crew gets to know you, the service gets even better; and this is the best we have had yet!

Thursday, Sept 29th debarkation, here are some final notes on Russia.

It is cold and raining. In St. Petersburg, it is said, "If it is raining when you leave, the sky is crying and looking for brighter days."

The ornate decorations around the windows on so many of the homes; Karniz; the bottom sill, Nalchik; the top, and shutters are called; Stavni.

Lynn went down to use the restroom by the restaurant since we could no longer use our cabin. She grabbed a cup of hot cocoa and 2 cookies for us. She didn't think she could make it up the steep, narrow stairs with those items, so she was going to use the elevator. The doors began to close, and the right door hit her very hard on her right side. What pain!! One of the crew saw this and came over to help. She took the cocoa from her and brought napkins. She then disappeared to get cleaning items to clean the mess on the elevator.

Meanwhile, Lynn grabbed the cookies and half a cup of cocoa and made it up the steps and back to the lounge. After sitting for a few minutes, the pain was hard to bear. She told Gabriel, the bartender, and he made her a glove full of ice to sit on. It did help, but when we went to lunch, she had to use the cane again. After lunch, she would read for a while and try walking, reading, and then walking. It got better, and eventually, she was able to pack the cane away again.

We needed to be out of our room by 10:00 a.m., so we left the ship for the airport at 4 p.m. To our delight, Viking not only offered coffee during the day and all the lounges on the ship but also provided us lunch! Our flight leaves at 7:40 p.m. to Helsinki—a long day…on a dreary, typical rainy September day in St. Petersburg ☹

I had planned this extension to Finland myself and arranged with Viking a five-day gap on returning home flights. The glass igloo and reindeer farm were too much to pass up, especially being this close. The only drawback was that this was just the beginning of winter and a season with noted cloud cover.

It was a short flight; it took longer to get through the airport (The only one in St. Petersburg), the initial airport security, and wait the two hours before flight to get into another line to get our tickets. I was able to talk the ticket agent into having the checked luggage transferred to the Finn air flight tomorrow to Ivalo; saved us lugging both suitcases back and forth through all the lines; then through another security line, then a passport checkpoint (very stern, look at you, look at passport, look at you, look at screen, look at you, look through passport, again and again.........(DON"T SMILE!), but I gave her a wink as I left; then they pass the passport back and a nod "you're done!" On to the gate, wait a half hour, yes, it took that long! Pushed and shoved to board the bus, push and shove to get off the bus, push and shove to get on to the staircase on to the plane.

The plane took off, we each had some free blueberry juice and after an hour and ten minutes, we landed in Helsinki. No luggage to pick-up, went through a friendly customs agent, found the rendezvous spot, and the hotel bus driver picked us up and drove us the ten minutes to the hotel.

Check in was a breeze, the room was ......to say "compact" would be generous.

The room was 10ft. X 30ft. Including two single beds, a desk, and a wardrobe. AND the bath that included a shower corner, 5 tiles by 4.5 tiles (5" tiles). It was very clean, neat, and efficient. All the lamps have cord switches, there is no air conditioning, a window is open on top, there is no screen, and it was comfortable. The internet was there but weak, eliminating about 20 e-mails before it froze. It's time for bed anyway; tomorrow will be another long day!

Friday, Sept. 30.

I'm up, both of us well rested (beds were very comfortable), and we have breakfast, quite good and complete. The last ride offered to the airport is at 9 a.m.; our flight, the only one to Ivalo, is at 5 p.m. :(

So, before leaving, it was time to take a stroll, it is in the lower 50's, partly cloudy, and I ask the desk person" What's to see in an hour" she tells me that there isn't much, we are too far from downtown Helsinki, "but go left" ....

So, I walk out of the front door, take a picture of the motel, and head into town. This is a small suburban town, took a picture of typical signs, see a number of people on bicycles, walk past a line of modern stores, a Chinese restaurant, a modern office furniture store, (has egg chairs, work loungers, odd lamps), and then a sauna store, with displays of different rocks, furnaces, and some bath tubs.

I found an outlet bakery, bought a doughnut to break a large Euro note, then a grocery store to check out what they offer and the prices of the same. (I usually find about the same things offered at a small convenience store with prices about the same as at home!)

At nine, we were quickly picked up and driven to the airport, went through security, and got fully scanned twice. This time, he found the knees and the hip! Now starts the "wait." We found our first chairs, and then I was off for a walk to check out the stores and the lunch offerings and get some steps in. I found a book exchange room for Lynn, found a room with free sleep modules during the day, and you can rent them overnight. I will go to the website for more details and price out all of the souvenir shops, cosmetic shops, and restaurant offerings.

We settled on splitting a Panini for lunch, set up by the gate that was posted early, and the gate opened on time; we wandered into the herd mid-way, which got us at the end of the sardine can bus, herded out to the plane, found our seats, and off we went.

The one-hour flight northwest was uneventful. Nothing was heard since the two women and the pretty boy across were talking non-stop, loudly (over the engine noise) the entire time. Ivalo has a very small airport; half of the plane pushed and shoved to get off. We retrieved our luggage to join the group, a total of 11, for the resort.

The drive to the resort was a little over a half hour, it is now after 6:30, we check in, and are the first to be dropped off at our cabin, home, for the next three nights.

This is a four-person cabin, one main room with bunk beds, a large bedroom adjacent, with desk; king sized bed, and a sauna with shower room at the end.

We went in, dropped our luggage, familiarized ourselves with the switches, and walked back to the main lodge for dinner. There was one choice, so we took it, I wanted to try some of the local alcohol, so I ordered Salniakki a salted black licorice flavored shot (Very good!) and a dark beer, that was tastee and not bitter!

The meal was a salad, curried chicken with rice and vegetables, and ice cream for dessert. We asked about tipping the waiter after the meal and were told there was no obligation…….. so I will make it up to our server tomorrow.

Walking back to the cabin in the dark produced a reason for the small flashlight attached to our key. (No street lights, it is overcast……) We got to the cabin, the key did not unlock the cabin, went back to the lodge, and the manager walked back with me, inserted the key, bumped the door with her butt, and WALA it worked!

I actually read the directions, but the sauna furnace was too slow so, after 20 minutes I shut it down, time to shut everything down; did the minimum of unpacking and jumped into bed.

Saturday, October 1

Here above the Arctic Circle! Kakslauttanen Arctic Resort we are 250 plus kilometers above the Arctic Circle, in the section of Finland called Lapland. The Hotel and Igloo Village is located 30 minutes north of the town of Ivalo.

We dress warmly; it is overcast and light rain. We walked up to the lodge, a typical European breakfast buffet, and then I asked about the rest of the stay. It seems that all of the outings are jobbed out, so actually, the times do change. The Visit Santa and the Reindeers tour was now 1 p.m. rather than 11 a.m.; the outing for chasing the Aurora was changed along with the husky's farm visit, so I revised the times…. subject to change, and also confirmed the glass Igloo, for Monday night.

Back to the cabin to catch up on notes, set up Lynn for her to have a comfortable read, then set a time to return to the lodge to delete and check e-mails, and a walk before the 1 o'clock excursion.

The "Visit Santa's Home," Celebration House, Kelo-Igloo area, Aurora Restaurant, and Feed the Reindeer at Sami village were well worth the money and undersold!

The group consisted of us and a family of three (two adults and a college student), so the tour was up close and personal. It has been overcast and raining lightly all day, and it did the same throughout the tour. The first stop was where the glass igloos are; we will be there on Monday night, and I will hoof it over tomorrow to take outside pictures. We are promised sun tomorrow! Next, we passed an area that had a good 100 Huskies; each one was chained to an individual house. They saw we were there, and we were able to walk up and pet them but were warned that they jump up, and yes, they were wet, and yes, the young one of the other group petted one, and the dog shook, water everywhere.

Then, a tour of the property where more igloos, the small ones, and ones attached to cottages; there were many!! We then toured the main celebration house and then on to "Santa's Village."

We are pre-season (no snow). We pass by a moss-covered shelter with no doors. This is a reindeer shed; they are built by the natives for the mosquito season. During this three-month season, the reindeer look for these sheds and stay inside. The urine from the deer repels the mosquitoes until the season is over. We drive past elf homes. There are little houses, like a big birdhouse along the road, that actually have lights inside for the night; I will see if I can get a picture of those, too!

Santa's hall is grand; his chair is on one side, a huge fireplace on the other. It has a capacity of 300 people! Next to the hall is an elf tower and then a bridge to Santa's house. The bridge Is unique in that it is a wooden structure, is arched very high, and offers a fantastic view. I was the only one willing to walk it, and it was agreed that I would meet the rest of the group at the house. They arrived by van just before I got there.

Santa's House was very quaint; it had one main room with a small kitchen, a tree, and a table with a heating and cooking hearth facing a wall display of dolls. The bedroom showcases a king-sized bed with swans carved into the base, which is very nice.

We stopped by a large corral with four reindeer. They could not be bothered to come closer to us. No matter what whistle, grunt, or coo we made, we were completely ignored, so we continued on our way.

Next, a new restaurant, which was an earthen restaurant, was built into the side of a hill. It was dark, lamps formed from reindeer hides, owls positioned in the massive fireplace, and wood columns all carved with images. The building is heated with geothermal heated natural water, which contributes to 70% of the heat. Outside, the restaurant is banked by two huts' that could hold 15-20 people easily! There is a long grill in the middle where food can be prepared, and even though the top is open, the grills stay lit in the rain or snow. Seats surround the entire perimeter.

We stopped at a pipe near the road. Our guide jumped out of the truck with paper cups and filled them, and then she passed them around. The water was excellent. She told us that this is done throughout the country for hikers and woods people for fresh water; it is clean, fresh, and delicious! She also pointed out a moss-like growth on the trees (Nava). A local boy makes dolls out of them. She told us that this plant cleans the air, and this is the cleanest air………think about that: this is truly Nirvana.

Last but not least, we visited the younger reindeer. These two females were shy and only came within 10 feet; the three males, one albino, came up to us and let us feed them lichens we had picked off the ground. One actually ate out of Lynn's hand and made her day!

That was the end of the tour. It was only supposed to be 1 ½ hours but lasted over 2. Our guide was gracious, informative, and very accommodating!

Back to the cabin to document and then a walk before supper; I will definitely stoke up the sauna tonight!

The walk brought back so many wonderful feelings I had as a Boy Scout when trekking through the various trails and woods. The sounds of branches, water flowing in the streams, the life underfoot; and yes, I took pictures of different mushrooms (80% of them are edible here, so you only have to learn the few you don't eat!) lichen ground cover, streams, and even the glass igloos we will stay in. There are still blueberries to pick and eat, along with little red Linden berries that are tart but taste good!

Dinner, the one and only option, was reindeer. Lynn was a little apprehensive, but then, she enjoyed her meal. The wild taste or gamey was there, but just a hint, it was a little above shredded, served with Linden berries and on a bed of mashed potatoes. We talked to the personnel about the reindeer jerky we saw on the tour, and we were promised some would be available here tomorrow.

Tonight, I did fire up the sauna. The directions weren't the clearest, but it worked. Lynn even joined me! (Only for a very short while) Then off to bed. We are promised the Sun tomorrow and a bit warmer weather. No phone, no internet, no radio, no TV, it's kind of peaceful.

Sunday, October 2nd

The alarm goes off, we awake refreshed, look outside, and see blue sky and in the east…THE SUN☺

We have only the Aurora Hunting scheduled for 9:30 p.m. this evening, so walks in the woods are our primary activity today. Breakfast was fine. We walked back to our cabin and "chilled" all morning. In the afternoon, we took a walk for as long as Lynn could hold out, returned to the cabin, and then took off again, checking out the whole complex.

There are two complexes, East and West; we had a West map, and we are in the East. We were already planning for our Igloo stay when I walked past them; at least the front row had people in it. I noted the variety of mushrooms, found a small bear print, and just enjoyed the clean, fresh, crisp air. The sun is still out; it is partly cloudy. And still looks good for the hunt tonight!

Dinner was fish, mushroom sauce, boiled potatoes, and, of course, a tossed salad with dessert. I thought I had paid for the suppers when I asked for the quote since there is nothing within walking distance as an alternative, but we will see when we settle–up. The dark beer is better than the amber; neither is bitter.

We were scheduled for the Aurora Hunting at 9:30, but that got moved up to 8:45; lucky I checked. (There is no phone in the cabins.)

We arrived at the main building promptly at 8:35; someone had just driven up in a van and was at the desk. As we checked in, we were introduced and shown to the van. He tells us it is a perfect night, although a little cold (0 degrees Celsius), but our snowmobile suits will keep us warm. We ask if this is the horse-drawn Aurora Hunting event, and he says, "No, this is the ATV trek," that is what is available.

So, we are driven to a building with a number of ATVs outside, brought in, and sized up for snowsuits. Lynn is very apprehensive, wants to be on the back of mine, and shakes her head regarding the paperwork and explanation regarding accidents, hidden stumps, and running into other vehicles. Then the phone rings, the operator hangs up and says, "There has been a mix-up. The driver from the other company is on his way to pick you up, and we picked up the wrong people!" So, to Lynn's relief, we changed back into our clothes, headed out the door to another waiting van, wished the others "good luck," and off we went to the horse ranch a few miles down the road.

It is a very clear night, and yes, it is cold! We are shown a wagon that has reindeer fur spread on the benches and blankets next to them. It is hard to see since there is no light except for the stars, but we hoist ourselves into the wagon. We are the only couple tonight; and we are off!

The roads here, except for the two-lane highway, are just dirt, and there are many potholes, which we feel… every one! We are taken into a cleared area off the road about a half mile. We get down and walk over uneven ground to an area with a circle of stumps cut for seating. It is cold clear, and the stars fill the sky. We are told the mystical version of the Northern Lights and the technological one, but we prefer the first one.

A young man is engaged, and she wants the pelt of a well-known fox in the area known for his beautiful coat of fur. The story goes on; the fox finally has no other option but to jump from the highest peak into the sky, and the colors are from the snow. His tail shakes as he traces through the sky to elude the hunter.

We saw a greenish hue develop on the horizon, then get bigger and bigger, swirl, and change size. After a half hour of watching and conversation, we loaded back on the wagon for the twenty-minute ride back to the barn, then got back in the van for the 15-minute ride back to camp. When we got out of the van, the sky was full of green trails. It was breathtaking. Even the driver said this was the best this year! We thanked the driver and made our way back to the cabin, watching the lights shift and flow, banks of misty green in the sky.

Monday, October 3rd.

This morning we slept in till 7:30; took a leisurely walk to the main building to have breakfast, check on what to do at check-out, time for check-out, where luggage is to go, and confirm Husky Visit time. It is -.5 degrees Celsius, but the sky is blue, the air is fresh and clean, what more can you ask?

Breakfast...I love the herring, tomato sauce, mustard sauce, and plain, plus the cold cuts, cheeses, yogurt, cereal, tomatoes, cucumbers, pickles, soft-boiled eggs, pastries, fresh bread toast, and fruits! There are a lot of Chinese tourists here; they are easily the majority, and for their size, they fill their plates twice! I would love to have that metabolism!!!

We are packing, so we live out of our carry-ons for the next two days. We checked out, waited for our transportation, and were whisked off to the west village and our igloo.

We have #34. We are given the key and a small map, and they will bring the luggage later. It turns out to be only a couple hundred feet from the igloo farm. It seems much larger when we get in. The beds face the North and are adjustable, higher than the beds in the cabins, and the shower and water closet are larger than the motel room in Helsinki!

We receive our luggage, set-up and acquaint ourselves with what is where, and oh, it now is raining...what happened to those nice clear blue sky and sun?? (Yeah, it happens that fast!)

We waited, yes, the rain stopped, then we walked over to the main building to take our last optional excursion, "Meet the Huskies".

We met our guide. We were the only ones on this trip, so like last night, we felt kind of special; we could ask any questions, and we had the guide to ourselves.

The drive to the farm was only ten minutes on rutted and rough roads, our guide made the comment that it all gets much better when it snows and freezes, which should be in a week or so...

As we drive up, we are directed to the same dressing room we were in last night. She tells us that it has been raining the last two weeks and the dogs may jump, so we all put on snow suits, boots and jackets, and then take a stroll.

We go to an area where a dog sled is displayed, we are told that there are eight dogs that pull the sled, and they train them by putting 16 dogs ahead of a quad that is running in 2nd gear. The dogs work every other day in season, each has a certain amount of food, and each has his own house and run. The houses are completely cleaned weekly fresh bedding and wash them down, if any dog shows any sign of difficulty, it is reported and if a trainer cannot remedy the situation, the dog is taken to a vet in Ivalo.

Each dog has their own personality, and that is seen as we walk among the 240 kennels. Yes, they were barking, and no they don't bite; some curious, some shy, some barking, some stayed inside their kennel, some anxious to be petted.

It was fun! We walked and talked; we even saw two hitches of 16 dogs pulling quads go past us. After the tour, we sat around a fire, talked over linden berry tea and cookies. The last few weeks there were a majority of people from Dubai; this is such a cross section of the world, and I believe that this Aurora has many meanings to many different races and religions; just fascinating!

Back to the main room, deposit all those now muddy clothes, the short trip back to the resort, and our guide even dropped us off at the door.

Now, a little time to relax, supper is at 6, pay up, get the information for the drive back to the airport tomorrow, then back to the igloo for the full night show. I do not think my camera is good enough for this, but I will try. Everyone we talk to that are guides or residence, still enjoy the nightly show by nature!

We went to supper at 6:30; we had the place to ourselves. So, we were shown to a table for two, a description of the entre was provided, and I ordered a dark beer and a shot of Salmiakkikoskenkorva, the black licorice heavy salted shot I love!

Salad was great, we had curried chicken with rice and vegetables, and a mixed tart berries with whipped cream. It was served by our favorite hostess's male friend Michael, a really nice guy, and talked to us as if he had known us for years!

While waiting for dessert, I asked for the drink menu again, there was something on it that bothered me through the meal; it was a drink, under hot drinks, called Reindeer Piss. The description was as follows: 4cl Jaloviina, warm meat consommé', served in a Lappish wooden cup. I ordered it, drank it, Lynn wouldn't and yes, the description was kind of accurate!

Suzy; (our guide) he is a catch, let him "land" you and marry him! Both from the Czech Republic; both extremely personable and capable! After dinner, we settled our bill, confirmed meeting time for departure and went back to the igloo, to watch our last show, the beds are fully adjustable; we made ourselves comfortable, and let the show begin!

And what a show it was! About 9:30 P.M. a low green glow expanded, then in the center it spiraled up and feathered out, then everything disappeared. At around 10: 45 we had one form on the left, and another form on the right, both sides grew, then merged, then disappeared, at 12, there was another show, and 2:30 one that expanded throughout the sky. This was the second of perfect nights, and the best shows, per the staff, this season. It was overcast the last two weeks and therefore no "show" was seen!

Tuesday October 4th; paid all the debt; said all of our good-byes and take the shuttle on a half hour drive back to the airport. We wait around a few minutes, then they open the gate, they are weighing everything and also measuring the bags, we check out bags, go through security, they got both knees and the hip! Lynn actually breezed through, and then we sat waiting for the plane. I bought some final trinkets, oh, by the way, 24% sales tax.

We walked out to the plane and headed back to Helsinki. The Airline magazine, Finn Air had some interesting Finish Facts! The total population of Finland is 5.5 million (this is just a little more than St. Petersburg, Russia), had an interesting article on the new Finnish education system, seems only one out of ten teachers that apply as teachers gets the job, most Filander's have some sort of secondary education, either formal or trade, and at fifth grade are proficient in reading and writing in their native language and their choice of one other. Finland is very ecology conscious, and also has a strong work ethic.

We landed in Helsinki, got our bags, Lynn spotted a Burger King, ($5 EU for just a burger) and waited for the first hotel pickup at 5. Checked into our room, went to the restaurant for food, Lynn had a meatball casserole, and I had a fish sandwich with a beer; ($43 EU) and then we took a walk. We again checked the prices at the little grocery store, (it was about $1.25 for 10 eggs at home here it is $0.59/dozen) the clerk looked at me and knew immediately that I was an American and said yes when I presented a 2 EU coin for a $1.80 Euro item. We then walked back to the motel, I have our pick-up set at 5:20 A.M.; we both showered and prepared for a very long next day.

Wednesday October 5th; We got up at 4 A.M.; it was a little warm in the room, even with an upper window open, plus we were anxious to get going. The cold breakfast they provided was cold cuts, toast, cheeses, fish, cereal, and yogurt. Plus, juice and coffee; not bad! The ride to the airport was quick, we shared with two other couples, I was the only one to tip the driver, he was surprised to get it but was appreciative.

Checked in and went through security again, this time shoes, belt, and yes, they also got both knees and hip. However, it went well, and the time before flight went fast. It is only a one-hour flight to

Noah

Heathrow, the London England airport. We had to find where our connecting flight was, took a bus to that terminal; it was tricky but we got there in time. We easily loaded, not as much push and shove as on some flights and set in for the eight-hour flight. We landed, pushed and shoved to get off, found the trusted traveler kiosks, and walked past the security to claim our luggage. We showed our tickets, passports, and were out waiting for our bus, loaded up and were at the Milwaukee Airport to take a cab home. Did you know, the airport charges $3.00 per ride for each cab, so it cost us more for the convenience. The ride home fast, nice Cabbie, we walked in, I took off to pick up a pizza for dinner, and the mail. We didn't last too long after dinner, internal clocks are off, early to bed, we are home!

Educating Noah…Travelin'

A week and a half, later, we spent a week at our time share at Fox Hills. This is the perfect time for the fall color show, Wisconsin has the best, reds, oranges, greens, and yellows, far better than the east coast! We made the mistake of going to Door County on Saturday, after the annual Mishicot High School Pumpkin Pancake breakfast. It was Mobbed! One of the towns actually closed the highway for a festival, we came back on the other side of the peninsula, stocked up on wine, cheese, fudge, and tasted all, of course!

It has been 30 years that we have owned the time share, as we did the tour of the attractions, many are now closed, the only things left to do are OGAN the restaurant our son in law's brother and wife own, Door County, and Gibb's on the Lake.

We will be looking into selling it, will offer it to the kid's first...

India 2016

Up at 5:30 A.M., shared a fried egg and cheese sandwich with Lynn, and we were on the road as planned by 6:15. We had made arrangements to pick up two other travelers, we pulled up early to their house, loaded them in, and were on our way to the pick-up point before 6:45, we arrived at the motel/pick-up area at 7:00; we were to leave exactly at 7:45, so we unloaded, I kissed Lynn good-bye, and the start of another adventure begins.

There is a total of 24 in our group, my roommate is to meet us at O'Hare, and so as soon as the 23 of us got on the bus, we were off. Saturday morning, early, bright, (7:40) is great for the trip to O'Hare, we were there in just over an hour!

We got in line to check in, then they started us in another line, so us in front ended up in back, then they let the business class use the one check-in agent we were assigned to, then they had us fill in with the rest again, no one used the kiosks anymore, must be an electronic lag for the airlines. We finally got through, then the TSA lines, no TSA bypass, only two lanes open, but finally they did open two more, belts, shoes off, computers out, this was the first-time I wasn't wanded? After passing through the metal detector, told them of the knees and hip, he just asked to see the back of my watch. (Made me feel so much safer??)

We all gathered at the gate, too many people, not enough seats, but with all the previous lines we only have an hour before we start fighting for assigned seats on the plane and precious overhead room.

I am sitting at the desk (Sunday evening) in our hotel room in Kolkata (Calcutta to the rest of the world) I used this spelling because I saw it on a police car on the way to the hotel!

We have been gone since 6:15 yesterday, and not much if any sleep, so this will be short, and sweet.

ETIHAD was the United Arabic airline we used; they brag 5-star food, comfort, and service. The seats were basic standard economy seats, tight, uncomfortable, and no room. The food was rice with vegetables, and some meat, they didn't have fish when I asked, I took "whatever", which turned into vegetarian. When I asked for the lamb shank, they were out of that also, so I think I got chicken. Hit in the head with a tray, bumped many times, and there seemed to be a shortage of overhead space, and both planes left at least 40 minutes late. The people here are worse than the Chinese in exiting the plane, push, shove, crawl over other passengers, male or female, and impatient with the stewards and stewardesses, I will report if this is common on the rest of this journey. (The 5 star is for first class only!)

We were in the air 12 ¾ hours from Chicago to Abu Dhabi; waited 3 hours for our 4-hour flight to Kolkata, (the City of Joy). The bus to the hotel was the typical hour drive, in India, they drive on the left, call bridges "fly-over's", and here in this city, on weekends and holidays, the population goes up to 17 million! (From a constant population of 14,000,000, Milwaukee is 600,000 in comparison.)

Monday, November 14, 2016... Both of us are up early, (6:00 AM) Frank (my roommate for this trip) is easy to get along with; we worked out shower times, who got what bed and closet quickly. The forecast for today is 66-85 F, it is currently overcast. Last night, the guide mentioned that only one or two tracked trolleys are still in service, busses have taken their place (funny how we are putting one in Milwaukee). The hotel is in the middle of old Calcutta, the streets are narrow, the traffic was even high especially at 9:30 at night, cars, bicycles, three-wheel bikes and motorcycles, and cabs, literally thousands of car-cabs. Shops are small; it reminded me of small cities in Africa. This as with all the hotels we stayed at has an ex-ray machine for carry-ons, a metal detector, and person with wand to greet you every time you enter. (Will this be coming soon to America?)

On the way to the first attraction, a little history…Calcutta was a trading post, fishing, and farm goods, one of the world's largest producer of rice, plus fruits and vegetables, for 150 years it was the English capitol of India and considered the most valuable city of the English empire next to London. (In 1857, the capitol was moved to New Delhi).

The Ganges River, runs through Kolkata and is considered sacred, if you bath in it three times your life will be better, per the teachings, however it is heavily polluted and the government asks the bathing be restricted, and to rinse with clean water after going in. The name change (to Kolkata) was in 2001, to signify the change from agriculture and fishing to Industry and education. (The name Kolkata actually means harvested yesterday).

The university here is accredited throughout the world, specializing in medicine and education. The town is divided into three major districts, North, South, and Middle, the middle is where the English lived, and it also was called "white town". There are 30 different and distinct cultures here; the city is 185,000 square meters, many religions, only 1% Christian, less than 1% Jewish, main religions, Hindu, Sikh, and Muslim.

There were also a number of flags with the hammer and sickle, representing the Communist Party, we saw a number of buildings with a swastika on them (this was a religious symbol before the Nazi party). We asked about religious conflicts in India, and told that the religious tolerance is quite high, no difficulty between teachings.

First stop was Mother House; this was the sect Mother Theresa worked from. Her tomb is here, we were not able to take pictures anywhere else within, but up a staircase was her room, a small single bed, desk, and chest of drawers. The room was barely 10X12 feet. Below was a wash area where a sister was washing, by hand, some robes, all the sisters wore the same, the robes were clean, but not pressed.

There are 65 sisters at this site, which houses a school for sisters, the crypt, and a museum, along with living quarters for the sisters. There are 4,500 sisters of this order in the world, dedicated to helping the poor.

On to the next attraction! The schools here are government and private. The private are better, and those that can afford them go there, the government schools teach English as a primary language, Bengali the second, the private schools are just the reverse. I asked about nursing care with male nurses and females due to religions; I was told that only strict Muslims limited care of females by males here.

The reason for less traffic today is that today is GURU Holiday, celebrating religious leaders, many of the various churches and sects had festivals today.

The bus fare is 6 Rupees (about ten cents) for the first 2 kilometers, and a money collector actually rides in the stairwell as the bus goes from stop to stop. There was a problem with Taxi's, where they refuse going short distances. This was solved by the government imposing a 3000-rupee fine if a customer is refused, and a photo of the cab with license is sent in.

A red dot on the female's forehead symbolizes they are married. Depending on what sign you were born under, dictates the month you should marry. The daily food diet of the folks in this city is rice and fish. The area is still recognized world-wide for spices, sweet yogurt, and a dessert made from the water separated from milk, a custard style dessert. (Yes, I did try it, and yes, it is very good!)

One of the most curious exports from America to India in the past, was ice! We shipped it from Massachusetts (actually Walden Pond). Almost ½ of the cargo melted on the way, but it was considered a luxury item back then, and much better than sending over an empty ship for the India exports! People here drive on the left side of the road (most of the time, sometimes bicycles, motorbikes and cycles go on the right;) It seems like anything goes, lots of horn blowing, bikes and motorcycles weaving in and out, very few cars with dents, signs at gas stations "No Helmet, No Gas". The price of gas is not posted, but it was about the same as in Russia.

In the Central district, only white people could use the central main cistern, no Indian people were allowed, that changed with the

Educating Noah...Travelin'

Indian Independence.

Our next stop was the Flower Market. This open market sells flowers by the kilo, (2.2 lbs./kilo) very crowded, no consistent direction, you just dodged folks going both ways up and down steps, people overtaking you, crossing in front, many times bumping lightly, saw a small tea stand, beautiful flowers, people bought with putting the flowers on a scale than dumping them into bags!

I asked about some vendors selling balls of clay/mud… these are from the river, the sacred Ganges, right behind the market… (I guess it is a religious moment.) At the end of the market, we were on the banks of the Ganges River and saw a few people in the water, lots of trash floating by; one guy on the side with his back to the crowd was urinating on the bank. This side of the Ganges River is called the Hooghly, the spiritual side. (And a guy was urinating on it??)

Back on the bus, most of the time we had to wait for the bus to return, little if any parking for busses, actually any vehicle!

On the way to the next attraction, we asked about health care. It is free here, as in Europe, and like Europe, only the poor use it, the rest opt for private care, better doctors, equipment, and drugs, plus the wait time is much less for appointments.

Holidays in India change dates every year, so everyone gets a book published yearly specifying the dates due to the star and planet positions.

Currently 80% of H1B working Visas issued by America are to Indian citizens.

St. Joseph's Church, next attraction. This church has an outside clock that works, inside there were icons behind the alter very similar to the Russian Orthodox ones in Russia, the church was impeccable, a few sculptures on the wall were dedicated to lost spouses, and the bench outside the church was dedicated to a husband who happened to be named "Peter Pan"!

Outside I took a picture of another woman washing clothes by hand, there was a sweet smell in the air, but we couldn't track it down, the inside of the church was impeccably clean, and there were many ceiling fans to keep the inside cool.

Back on the bus... a lot of fences and buildings were painted blue and white, we asked what the significance was.... political... this is the color of the current political party, the mayor stated that if you paint your house blue and white, you would not be taxed one year! (Not wanting to pay taxes seem to be universal throughout the world!)

When the Communist party was in power, (for almost 30 years!) the elections were "rigged" so that only communists won. She didn't explain how they were overthrown, but it sure seems that every place that has tried Communism, really flourishes after dumping them. From China, Russia and now here; we just went through an election where a major candidate was a Socialist; I guess history repeats if not heeded!

India has a GDP growth of 7 1/2 %; our growth rate for the past 8 years has not even exceeded 2%, India is growing faster than any other country!

The Kahl Temple was the next stop, 16th Century temple, outside pictures only, we were told not to give the beggars money, they are an "industry", and there is almost full employment in the city. The walk to the temple was about six blocks, past shops lining the streets. The temple itself had long lines to view the deity, (you get a red mark on your forehead, males and females, and very lucky if you view the deity). We were led as a group to view from the side; they were actually pushing people aside for us to have a glimpse! WOW! (I really was not that impressed, but then again...) Also, goat sacrifices have been banned due to animal rights people.

We then walked the gauntlet of beggars, vendors, and traffic of cars, bikes and motorcycles back to the bus.

On the way to the restaurant, there is a crisis here. Pakistan, and from what I heard later Saudi Arabia; has flooded the Indian markets with counterfeit 500 and 1000-rupee notes, so now no one will accept these, the ATMs have lines at one in the morning for bills lower than the 500 and 1000 bills, the government is determined to fix the problem, but until then, few if any are taking them, and there is a limit to how much you can withdraw.

A note here, a number of us commented on the friendliness and smiles on many of the people. Also, the cleanliness of the people and the clothes they are wearing. A large variety of styles, some men even wearing skirts, women from burkas to skirts.

Restaurant: Barbeque Nation. We had barbeque chicken, fish, lamb, and shrimp, each person got a skewer of three pieces each, a couple chicken wings, and roasted kernels of corn; we were told not to eat the salad, but the chicken and corn soup was excellent. There was also a large assortment of desserts including ice cream, cakes and fruits.

Some of us went outside to check out the small shops, some were selling cigarettes three and four at a time, books, none would accept US dollars, or those 500 and 1000-rupee notes!

Our last stop for the day was another church, a Christian Cathedral, St. Paul's. What is unique with this one is all the stained-glass windows are black on the outside and colored on the inside. The best and most colorful are the largest on each end of the church, front and back. I wanted to see if indeed all of the windows were blackened outside so I took a quick look inside, then toured the back and rear of the church. To my surprise there was an area being set up for a wedding later on today. The drive to the reception had lights over the arbor of greenery, yellow and white table clothes and white globes.... how cheerful!

Noah

That was it for our first day; we arrived back at the hotel at 3:30 and told a cocktail party with Hors D'oeuvres was from 7-8. We took a vote, and since we had all filled up on lunch, we decided the "free" booze and appetizers were plenty for the day.

We bid farewell to our tour guide, and I and a few others struck out to visit the local markets surrounding the hotel. Most of the shops were clothing or shoes, no prices on anything, and very crowded. We circumvented the shops around the hotel, and by then there was only two of us, both of us tired of the crowd and not knowing what prices to compare and our 500 and 1000-rupee notes in question, we went back to the hotel empty handed and exhausted.

I journaled and talked to Frank until 7, went over to the pool for the hour party, Bob Spindell had met the U.S. Ambassador on the flight and invited him and his wife to join us and share some experiences with us during the cocktail hour, What a bonus!

Party over at 8, we all still had some jet lag, called it a night, everyone back to their respective rooms, and tomorrow we are to meet at 9:30 for another interesting day!

Tuesday 11-15, 2016. I tried the eggs Benedict this morning; they were perfectly done! I also went down to the front desk to have them get to the page where the ID could be given and the internet could be used.

Everyone was ready for another day of stops; we were off at 9:40! On the way to the first museum, we also had a herd of goats walking on the side of the road, I also spied a cow calf lying alongside the curb, watching traffic, and mind you we are still in town! We also saw a number of people washing from water flowing from fountains powered by the tide, the overflow goes to these fountains, and mostly men use this as a bath/shower, including soaping up and rinsing. We came across one of the working trams, they are divided into 1st class and 2nd class, the difference is that 1st class has two fans in the compartment, they are old, at least 40 years, 2nd class, no fans at all! Most locals prefer local shops, these are all small, and of course most of the sidewalks have vendors, street food, shoes, and clothing.

Some history, when the Mongols conquered, they converted most of the population, then the English came, and took over the country. The English did torture, did treat the Indians badly and exploited them, there were areas where Indians could not go, water the Indians were not able to drink; and the Indians only had limited rights.

First stop today is Tagore House. This was a well-recognized songwriter from a family that had extensive properties in Kolkata, he also wrote the current national anthem, and received the Nobel Prize in 1919.

Here as in many of the attractions, pictures are only allowed outside, and here also, no shoes inside! We visited a square in the middle of the extensive house, walked up two flights of stairs to view the living areas. This included a dining room with a very low table and accompanying stools, a room that displayed an extensive set of robes, his bedroom with a very low single bed, a room with a marble floor and an urn with his ashes in; then to the other side, with a reception room that showed a picture of him and Albert Einstein, a model of a river boat, and the hallways and rooms covered with pictures of him, and that time period.

You must watch out for the picture police (from now on to be referred to as the PP) ... They will yell at you if you attempt to take a picture, (even w/o a flash) and this is all the employees and caretakers!

We put our shoes back on and walked several blocks to the Marble Palace. These were the back streets, lots of trash, garbage and rubbish, narrow streets and honking horns. You could take a picture of the palace outside the gate, but NOT inside, several folks were brow beaten and yelled at for attempting such a dubious deed (Not me this time, really!!)

From the open-air porch, there were two mounted Moose Deer Heads, and given the size, these were very large deer! Again PP, and no shoes, only a specified area to leave your shoes, and no railings or benches to remove the shoes, but we all managed.

There was a smaller house to the right of the gate where the family regularly provided meals for up to 400 people daily, nice flower beds, water system with culverts for rising tide water to be distributed to the flower beds on grounds, kind of interesting in itself.

Inside the mansion, a huge billiard table, many sculptures, in the first room, the second had intricately carved rosewood and mahogany statues, and a heavily decorated exposed ceiling joist walls and a marble floor. The third room had additional sculptures, marble floors and decorated ceiling with display cases shown period relics, walking back through the inner open courtyard, a collection of exotic birds in cages.

A short walk back to the bus, I am really getting to hate the constant Beep, Beep Beeping! and having to look constantly forward, back, and side for people, bikes, motorcycles, cars, busses and trucks!!!

More India information from our guide; "Good and Bad, Extreme rich and poor, weak borders, and annual floods". We passed several banks, all had long close lines waiting to pull out money in anything but 500 and 1000-rupee notes (most of my rupees are 1000 notes), most venders and shops will not take these or U.S. Dollars, and the credit card transactions are slow because of the bank runs, what a mess!

Now this wild traffic…here is how it works, if you hit a person or another car, bus, or truck, you go to court, if you are judged at fault, you get beaten by your peers, severely, and some die from the punishment. We noticed very few dents in the cars, and of course people everywhere!

Educating Noah...Travelin'

Jain Temple, built in 1868. This temple is surrounded by ten-foot walls covered with relief pictures, I did get a few pictures of these, and yes, we had to walk a few blocks to get there, sharing the one lane road with cars, bicycles, motorcycles going BOTH ways, and beeping!!

Inside there are a few buildings very bright and colorful, formal gardens, sculptures, and ponds. This religious order predates Buddhism! A 5000 BC religion that may be the oldest world religion. The people that practice this are strict vegetarians, exclude even root vegetables like onions, garlic, and potatoes basically teach complete non-violence not only to mankind, but animals, insects, and all living things.

The temple, yep, no shoes, no cameras on the inside, was marble the inside walls covered in mirrors, highly polished ceramic, and gold trim, very bright, very intricate! The grounds were clean well-manicured and pleasing to the eye, outside several of the building were a number of mosaic pictures, the columns on the low wall were all decorated individually.

On to lunch and more Indian facts, this is about the religions. Hinduism is the first or largest religion, Muslim the next. In Hinduism, it is believed that God is in everyone. One God, we all have a piece. Spiritualism is looking into oneself, and meditation is to explore yourself from within to learn the answer; therefore, millions of gods since we are all part of one.

Lunch was at a high-end shopping center. Another security check to get in, escalators to the 4th floor. There as always, was a buffet. What the buffet offered, soup with two small pieces of chicken in it (they actually looked like dumplings) A salad that no-one touched, chicken served in many ways, fish, rice, and vegetables. Bottled water at the table, a small dessert table with brownies, a dessert coffee cake, fresh fruit and a scoop of ice cream.

Noah

After lunch, we were allowed to walk the mall, most of which were high-end suits, shoes, jewelry, silver, and even a haunted store attraction. One thing I did note was that all the advertising showed white males and females at this mall, no Indians. Near the entrance was a McDonalds, an interesting menu, no pork or beef, and there was even a Mc Veggie sandwich! A help wanted sign on the outside when asked, and the guide reinforced that there was work for everyone, also a free school to improve them, so there was no reason to give to the beggars! (The school also provides free lunches to the kids during school.)

Second last stop was the Indian Museum. This time the men and women were separated to go through metal detectors and wanding, this too is tiring!

I took pictures of some very interesting carvings; there were several sections including stuffed and skeletons of fish, and reptiles, a room dedicated to textiles, and another to coins. Any transactions I was able to manage never involved coins as change. There were large samples of petrified wood, skulls of extinct animals including a mastodon.

The last stop was The Victoria Memorial and formal gardens. The government did not have enough money, so the young people chipped together enough money to build it, it is quite extensive, and outside where some heavily ornately decorated horse and carriage offerings, almost came too close to another car, (I actually felt the car go by!) he came from a lane I didn't see!

Back to the hotel, this will be our final night here, another cocktail party from 7-8 with Hors d'oeuvres, so we all again voted to forgo dinner. It was another great time, as usual, I asked the bartender for his favorite drink, this time it was a JIZ; vodka, mint and lemon; wow, smooth! I had FIVE women check it, they ALL ordered one, nice party, 9:50 is check out tomorrow, we are leaving for the Sunder Ban's Cruise!

Wednesday, on to another adventure! We were all fed and packed, had plenty of time, so Frank and I took off for a little walk, to explore the area beyond the hotel and the park across the street.

Even at 8:40 A.M., the beggars attack as you leave the security gates of the hotel. We walked a few blocks, shrugging off beggars and merchant's eager to get you into their respective areas. Now crossing the street is an adventure in itself. We found a break and what we thought was a crossing area, hoped that a few locals were crossing, looked both ways, and with a break in the traffic quickly walked across to the meridian…success!! We then found a path across the 12-foot meridian, and then looked for another break in the traffic, looking both ways, constantly; we quickly made it to the other side.

The park has vagrant families, the small kids, as soon as they see a white person come running with hands extended, when you "shoo" them away they laugh and disappear.

Looking through the park, there were a lot of rat holes, yes, we saw a couple, lots of garbage, open sewage culverts, and a lot of green foliage growing and competing for the fertile land. The smells range from a whiff of delicate flowers, to decomposing foliage, to sewer. There were three-sided open-air urinals for men, but we didn't see any facilities for women. We found a path back to the street, successfully managed across; returned to the hotel, got our bags, checked out and everyone was on the bus, accounted for and rolling by 10:10.

The bus drove about 20 minutes and we were at the river, Millennium Park, to board our river boat. It seems that we will be here 2 ½ days and three nights, with the boat returning to Kolkata for us to continue our vacation.

Set sail at 12:00; drill at 12:30, lunch 13:00-14:00. (Had to explain military time to a number of our group.)

Standard life preserver explanation; there are only 30 passengers plus crew on the boat, so no real security when we leave for tours and return; we locked up the valuables and passports in a secure drawer in the cabin. Lunch was a very good chicken soup, a buffet of various chicken, a lamb stew, and fish, yes, fish bones, tail and head. Desert was a pudding and mango/pistachio sorbet.

As we left, we watched the shore go by! Waived at fishermen and saw many small villages. Formal Tea and cookies at 4 p.m., played a little sheepshead with some others; of the 30 passengers on this trip, 23 are Vagabonds! (Our group)

Evening entertainment scheduled at 7 PM; this was also the cocktail party; we were shown a number of native dances, two girls and one guy; very entertaining, the girls opened their eyes so wide, it even made me sit back a little! Dinner at 8; I just had soup, a little fry bread, and some pudding, too much food!

A very nice relaxing trip down the river! The nicest thing is there is no "river" smell, but I did notice that there is quite a current, the tide rises five meters in the spring (this is spring) and only two meters at the lowest tide, the average depth 5-10 meters, salt water inlet, freshwater as you go inland, so salt, mix, and then fresh water inland.

Tomorrow is early call, schedules are set by the tide, and we leave the ship at 7:00 A.M., breakfast when we return.

Up this morning at 4:50, it is Thursday; the boat is dead in the water, in the middle of the river. The crew started appearing at 5:00, no one in the wheel house; I heard a morning prayer from the shore, a few barking dogs and a bird, everything else is silent and calm. I was anticipating a great sunrise, the orange ball did appear a little before 6 AM; it is cool, (about 60 degrees) a little misty, (or is it smog?) and visibility is a little over a mile.

We are at low tide, ships are resting on the mud along the shore, completely out of the water, and both exposed river sides have a significant amount of trash.

Educating Noah...Travelin'

The boat has two main decks and an upper deck, the only toilets for the passengers are in their respective rooms, and only one key to a room; everything is clean but worn.

Tea was available with cookies for a half hour, and then we gathered at the desk area to disembark. The 14-ft. skiff was only able to carry 10 people at a time, getting into the boat was a bit of a challenge for most, but there were two crew members offering assistance both from boat to boat, and then with the aid of a two-step ladder or secured chair, back into the skiff.

The trip to the bank of the river was less than ten minutes even with maneuvering to get as close to the stairs as possible. The four flights of stairs were not in good repair, the bottom three coated with mud and silt, no handrails. (After the walk and view of the crocodile hatchery, we came back up the river, two hours later to see that the entrance now was only one flight, the rest submerged by the tide!)

To get to the crocodile hatchery, we walked a brick 6 ft. wide path for almost ¾ mile. Although the path was put in just 5 years ago, the path was already in disrepair, sunken in some areas, uneven in most. We saw very little wildlife, some tracks, some quarter size red crabs. The plant life was dominated by Cyprus, knees were pointed out, some burrows (rat or snake or?), and deer tracks, garbage brought in by the tide, lots of clay, and even though the path averaged ten feet above the vegetation, during these spring tides, the path becomes awash with water.

We arrived at the hatchery, bins of 5-12 crocs sorted by age, all within pens with close meshed fences 8 feet high. There were also fenced areas where we did see a 10-12-foot croc swimming along the bank, the museum was closed, no monitors, snakes, lizards, butterflies, dragon flies, birds, to be found. We did all gather behind one fence, and one of the employees was throwing in a stubby piece of wood, and a huge crocodile mouth would emerge from the murky depths to go after it. There was no souvenir shop, another first…Garbage, disrepair, nothing to help support the activity to be found, and nothing!! No locals trying to sell crafts, junk, or anything…

We then walked a much dryer concrete path back to the river, this time only about a ¼ mile to the muddy banks. We did see a woman bathing in the water, fully dressed, I didn't get the point…at the end we all had to walk two ten-foot 14" concrete timbers (no railings just one guy to help steady you across) to get to the steps, negotiated our way back onto the tender, then back on the boat. Breakfast was waiting for us, (everyone was hungry), and the servers kept bringing more eggs, sausage, and rolls; I joined a group playing sheepshead, then leisure till that afternoon.

We ate lunch, and sat around until we got to visit a typical Sundarbans village. One of our group had picked up a shell this morning, and when she showed it to us, a hermit crab started coming out. We played with him, took pictures, and after almost an hour he was completely out of the shell; fun to watch!

The ferry to take us to shore was larger this time, however the steps up were more treacherous, uneven, various heights, slippery, of course no railings! There were a number of crew members that did help us get off the ferry, and later get back on. We walked the road into the village, interacted with the villagers, I flapped my arms and made duck sounds at the kids, they picked that up quickly, and when we came back the same path, they were waiting to "quack" back at me, smile, and giggle.

Huts were made of clay and dung, cooking in clay ovens using dried dung patties as fuel, lentil gathering, paddy husking, cutting hay for cows, a very basic store, roofs with Jack fruit growing on them, cows, goats, sheep, chickens interspersed between the buildings. Some of the houses even had a solar panel, and some a TV dish.

The people were all working, seemed content and industrious, mostly women and children, the men out fishing. The men go out fishing for two weeks, every night the designated "collector" comes by and picks up the fish, after two weeks on a little sampan, they came in to rest with the family. (Again, there were no souvenirs, local handicrafts, just simple people getting by.)

Back on the boat for tea at 5; this time they had Indian tea, which was very good!

7:00 P.M. is happy-hour with a mythological drama by local artists, followed by a traditional Bengali meal to wrap up the day.

Friday the 18th; Breakfast early, off the boat on a ferry to explore the Sundarbans, a collection of 100 islands, 48 inhabited, 2 underwater, and 50 uninhabited. This was the tiger sighting trip. We started out at 6:45 A.M. and were back on the main boat by 12:30. We made two stops, yep, those stairs again, narrow, silted, and varying in height, 3-4 flights, but we all made it there and back. Two observatories, and an elevated walk with both observation tower stops; All we saw were four deer, a small poisonous green snake, more red crabs (non-edible), and mud skidders.

Traveling between these two stops, we saw a variety of mangrove trees, with roots and knees of various configurations, an eagle, egrets, sand pipers, a crane, a monkey, a couple wild pigs or boars, and a crocodile.

At the second stop, with the elevated walk, we were told that deer were imported for completing the wildlife, and support the tigers, it took three years for the deer to be able to adapt to drinking salt water, since most of the uninhabited islands don't have fresh water, so the question is…why can't humans adapt? (To drink salt water?)

Lunch was spectacular; I would pay extra for this! Boned fish cooked in banana leaves, prawns, tomato soup, and mutton, all perfect, yum!!

Noah

Attempted for 20 minutes to get internet, logged on but couldn't get e-mail, and after ½ hour this new battery is low; I am so frustrated! This happened on the Russian River ship also.......!!!!!

Saturday, November nineteenth, it is late so there will not be much said. Today we left our river ship and after a short sightseeing trip to the airport, spent 1/2 the morning and 1/2 the afternoon in the airport, being checked in, searched, and finding the proper gate, yup, the last hour the gate was changed! Yup, the typical push and shove to get on the plane, I drew a middle seat, only people who paid for a snack were offered drinks, even coke was charged!

The two-hour flight to New Delhi went fine, took off fifteen minutes late, and when landed, people were shoving to exit, shoving to enter the bus back to the terminal, and shoving to claim their baggage. Everything went relatively smoothly, the bus picked us up at a far parking lot, and we had to risk a run or die five lane road; those cars that stopped for the last of us were treated to horn blasts by those behind! RUDE is the word!

We got to the bus, shooed away helpful people wanting to help with the checked bag the last 10 feet for a tip, then the hour bus trip to the hotel. Very fancy hotel, seemed to be unorganized as to small groups, all luggage was x-rayed and we were wanded before we entered the hotel. We got our keys, put our luggage in the room, and went down to the bar for cocktails, only ½ hour left; 8:30, supper at the Chinese restaurant in the hotel.

On the bus, we asked about a typical work week here in India, we are told it is 10-12 hours /days, with a 5 ½ days a week. We were reminded again not to tip the beggars, there are plenty of job openings; even the airline was looking for stewardesses! The first tour tomorrow is at 10:00, a city tour by bus, it is late, and that's all folks!!

The happy hour was only ½ hour since we were late checking in, but it included Sushi; so, who cares! Dinner was at the Chinese restaurant in the hotel, Frank had the lobster, I had the spicy lobster… don' t get excited, it was about 4 oz. of lobster, the balance was tofu cut and creamed to look like the lobster. One of the women ordered duck, a half duck, the carver came out and carved it at the table, she didn't want the crispy tastee skin, so Frank and I got that, the balance of her duck was served on little lettuce shells, she wasn't happy, but we were stuffed!!

P.S. I was able to have Wi-Fi again, so I got to catch up with Lynn also!!

Sunday, November 20th, 2016.

Last night was not the finest; loud music till 1:30 a. m., started again at 5:50 a.m.!!

Head stuffy, smoggy; and tired, should be an interesting day. Frank was up too, so we dressed and went hunting to find out what was going on; we played run or die with the roads and followed the noise.

It turns out it was a charity Run, for "Educate the girl child". We followed some of the route, found three DJ's pumping out tunes at full volume, and a stage with cheerleaders dancing and encouraging the runners; (note: for the route, there was a couple cleaning the gutters, so from the road and ten feet from the road, it was clean!!) There were even receptacles for the plastic water bottles… We were accosted by a Tuk-Tuk driver and found out that a ride to the market was only 20 rupees, (about 35 cents) if you pay the guy 40, (75 cents) he will wait for you! We also found an underground shopping center, but it was mostly oriental rugs…. (When someone approaches you here, it is a sales job, he will be friendly, ask where you are from, then ask you for your business as in a ride in his Tuk-Tuk or he will help you find what you want, and lead you to a shop he is "bird-dogging" for.).

Back at the hotel, a huge breakfast buffet, basically anything you could want of dream of was available...over-eat anyone??

First stop of the day is the Jama Masjid Mosque; this is the largest mosque in Asia, built in 1650. I have several pictures of the outside; none on the inside, no cameras allowed w/o a fee, it wasn't worth it to me. Had to remove shoes outside, women were issued sarongs, along with men with shorts; women enter on the right, men on the left. Extra charge to go up in the towers and only women accompanied by a man can go up in one. Inside, a large shallow square pool of water, four walls, a prayer area that is just a glorified hallway, with designated areas (outlined in the floor) for prayer rugs.

I asked the guide if he knew of any Muslim hospitals, and he said, "no", but there are a few Muslim charities; there are 21-22 million people in New Delhi; Tuk Tuk's cost 400,000-500,000 rupees, a rupee is 1.6 cents...a cost about $3000 U.S.

The next stop is the Gandhi Memorial, a large park surrounding a small square where the ashes of Gandhi rest. (Hindus cremate, Christians and Muslims bury)Remember, New Delhi is 85% Hindu, 10% Muslim, and the balance of the various other religions. I asked about the Jain religion, and he stated that it was one of the richest religions and only a small percentage of the religions in this country.

As we waited for the group, there were many school children there to visit also, a number of us were asked to pose with them, and along with a number of adults... being white here is a minority!! (This was very similar to the experience we had in China, where people wanted us to pose with them for photos.)

The last attraction was the Swaminarayan Akshardham, "eternal abode". A 100-acre tribute to Indian culture. Again, no shoes, no cameras, security tighter than an airport. The main building is carved marble, walls, and ceilings, domes, inside and out. This was the most extensive display of exquisite carvings I have seen, and we have seen a lot of churches, monuments, and tributes. Inside the carvings are accented with gold, and in some areas, pink and turquoise jewels and paint.

That was it for the day, back by 4:30, cocktails and appetizers from 6-8, then done!

Monday the 21st of November 9 A.M.

And off to the sights; here is more on India;

Placing your hands together with fingers pointing up; you return the same, with bow; meaning I bow to your soul within me to the soul within you, shows humility, respect, and peace.

India made cars, (Ambassador's), like the LADA in Russia are used only by the government, the vehicles are unreliable and no one wants them when other brands are available.

Our first drive by was the Embassy row, ours (U.S.A.) was one of the nicest!

We tried to get closer, to the American Embassy gate, but the local police through a fit, so no stop, they did not care who we were.

Road signs here, are in four languages: English, Hindi, Punjabi, and Arabic.

The first real stop is the "tower" Qutub Minor; build in 1192-1210; it is 72.5 meters high, there are 379 steps; lowest story angular and circular flutings, the second-round flutings, the third, angular, then all is repeated.

A second one was started, and the construction was started twice the diameter. They got about 10 meters high, 30 feet, and the emperor died, so construction stopped. (Ali Minor)

The pole in the courtyard has no rust! This iron pillar was built in the 4th century, it is 24 feet high (3 feet are buried), modern science still can't figure this out!

Noah

There is also a number of Neem trees, this tree, all parts are used medicinally! The seeds, leaves and bark, described in 4000 BC as "the curer of all ailments". (Look it up to see what products come from this tree, amazing!)

A guard signaled to me to join him, he showed me the best places to take pictures, took a couple of novelty shots, and then asked for a tip, I was more than happy to help him out, and a 30 Rupee tip ((.45) U.S. was enough???)

Next was supposed to be a lunch stop, but it was the wrong place....as we were waiting, we saw four business men get out of a Tuk-Tuk, and thought that was amazing, until a family pulled up in one and emptied out...NINE people in ONE Tuk -Tuk!!

There was also a restaurant sign, I had to take the picture, "Fork You" Steak restaurant, no need to go any further...

Lunch was actually an hour away through traffic, and it was the now, regular fare... a buffet consisting of chicken two different ways, a veggie mixture, rice, bread, and a dessert of a donut hole soaked in honey; back to the bus, vote for last attraction, and off to Huma Yun's Tomb.

Forty-five minutes later, fighting traffic and constant horn beeping we were there!

Seems that this guy was a direct descendent of Kahn, this structure and associated buildings were built in the 17th Century and took 9 years to build. The Muslims came along and added domes, made a Mosque, and added another Mosque.

Here are some more India effects:

The six-sided star (Jewish) in India is the symbol of the God Shakti

The lotus flower represents the flower where the Goddess Shakti sat

The Swastika is Hindu for positivity; in the Jain religion, it points the way to heaven

I asked why many of the Indians were dressed up, and was told, when they go on vacation, this is a special event, and they dress up for it.

On the way, back to the hotel, we passed the Indian War Memorial to the soldiers that served in the first and second war. This attracts thousands every day! As respect for those who served India in these conflicts; A bit different than the ones in the U.S.A.!

A short rest in the room, cocktails, and Hors d'oeuvres for dinner, answering e-mails, typing up the day, and off to bed.

Tuesday, 22nd of November, 2016

6:30 breakfast, at 7, we are on the bus on the route to Agra to visit the Taj Mahal and the Agra Fort.

This early affords quick passage out of the city; we are beyond the city limits in just a half hour! On the way, especially in the city, men urinating with their backs on the road has become common, and litter and trash are constant. As we left the city, it seemed cleaner, rivers and farmland all relatively clean, the crops growing in straight lines and kept weeding. The road signs are in English and Arabic, and the billboards are in English only.

On the way, we can see small cities on both sides, lots of construction, new apartment buildings. There are also quite a few kiln smoke stacks where families make bricks to sell at the market. Our guide tells us that this is being discouraged by the government since it is using up the soil and encouraging farming of vegetables instead. As we travel from city to city, there are many vegetable fields; common veggies include cauliflower, broccoli, carrots, onions, and cabbage.

Noah

Along the highway, there are many flowering trees and shrubs, a very nice contrast. There are little horns blaring. What a nice contrast to the city!

We made a pit stop about two hours into the drive, I was approached by two men dressed in white, they talked very broken very fast English regarding something about hearing, body and soul, I tried to listen, indicated my hearing aids, but I believe they were like our Jehovah Witnesses, after a while having shrugged many times, telling them I did not understand, they moved away...

Another hour and we were on the outskirts of Agra, we see stray cows, buffalo, and goats alongside the road, and they lay there because the wind from the traffic helps keep the flies away. As we drive over a large bridge, we see people washing clothes and linens, then spreading them on the flats to dry, after the bridge, in town, a few of the buildings have monkeys chasing across the roof tops and sides.

We arrived at the Taj Mahal a little after 10:30; we are coached again about ignoring the street sellers, beggars, and guides, and never showing them where your money is kept.

Our guide procures two large golf carts to take us to the entrance gates. (Yes, all 21 of us fit on two carts!)

We waited for the tickets, as we waited our white faces gave us away as those "rich white tourists", and we were set upon by vendors hawking key chains, snow globes, and carvings.... ignore, ignore, do not recognize them, they are aggressive and persistent, would make great sales people in the US, men, women with babies in arms, teens and preteens.

We all receive our ticket from the guide, and proceed to the gate, where security is again, women checked on one side, men on the other, then we see it! In the very large court yard there are three gates, east, west, and south, the north is the entrance to the Tag Mahal.

Educating Noah…Travelin'

It is almost noon, the sun is out, and the white marble glistens…wow. There is no paint involved, just carved white marble with different colored marble and stones to set off this piece of art.

Everything seems to be done in 4's or multiples of 4, and symmetry is perfect!

There are two buildings banking this icon. They were used by visitors to rest before going home after visiting; no one has ever slept inside this building. There are 16 gardens and some multiple of four fountains, with reflecting pools from the entrance gate to the Taj.

All of the iron rings that hold the marble in place are lead covered, so they will never rust, inside (need to put on supplied booties) was a bit of a disappointment, no pictures are allowed, there is one hallway what surrounds the inner chamber where another marble lattice wall surrounds two sarcophaguses; very little light, pushing crowds, and where you can actually see into the inner area, people are studying the inside. We are then ushered along and went into the halls around the center. All the entrances have high thresholds, and there are low steps where you do not expect them. The halls are carved, but nothing like the outside.

If you look across the river, there was supposed to be a duplicate Taj in black marble. However, the son of the emperor scuttled the building due to the cost, and against his dead father's wishes.

Looking at the Taj, the large platform is about 30 feet or 10 meters high; the only access was three small staircases, all monitored by guards.

We took a group picture at the Taj; Bob Spindell, our leader and organizer sprung for the copy of one to each member of the group…Thanks Bob!

Lunch was in town: a smorgasbord, chicken done various ways, mutton, rice, noodles, a fish dish, and those doughnut holes dipped in honey, bitter orange, or lemon.

The next stop was the fort. This, as the Taj, is open from sunrise to sunset, no charge for children under 15. There is a draw bridge over a moat, when the moat had water; crocodiles are kept in it, when dry, tigers and bears. This is the largest fort I have ever been to, many acres, gardens, fountains, courtyards, we toured for over an hour, stopping at special places for explanations of where we were and what function these areas served. We were only given access to 20% of the area, it seemed to never end inside! I took many pictures, again, no paint, and although most was of sandstone, there were buildings and areas of marble, beautiful arches, and platforms, all with the characteristic of symmetry, grace and beauty.

Back on the bus and back to New Delhi, another quick pit stops on the way, we picked up two of our group before proceeding to a tour company hosted dinner that lasted from 9:30 to 11:30. We were all taken to long tables and served various appetizers, there was a spinach dish I liked, plus okra that was crispy and thin, and the chicken was exceptional, dessert was an Indian ice cream.

We were back at the hotel at 11:45 P.M., and all of us were tired; tomorrow is an off day, and we will see what we will see!

Wednesday 23rd, 2016

We both slept in! We got up at 7:45!! Down for breakfast, we looked for the two women who wanted to come with us, and they were nowhere to be found. We went and got a map from the front desk, went back to the room, hats and sunglasses, and struck out for another adventure.

You cannot go more than a quarter block before being joined by a Tuk-Tuk driver offering advice on where to shop and where to go. They will walk with you for a block or so, do not give up even with more than several denials of their services.

We were looking for the local bazaar, we found the Chinese one, but it was too early in the day, we walked and walked some more, the sidewalks are crowded, irregular, vary in width, and height, I stumbled and went down once, Frank tripped a couple times also, but didn't go down.

We finally did find one, (bazaar) we went from area to area, high pressure, not cheap, they would convert to US but the 1000 rupee notes I had from home were not. I did find the spices my one daughter wanted and got them, so at least one thing is off the list!

We had twisted and turned a number of times and had walked over two miles per the pedometer. I was hurting due to shoulder and hip difficulties so we agreed to take a Tuk-Tuk back to the hotel.

We asked a driver how much to go, and he said 30 rupees. I offered him a U.S. dollar, and he accepted. The ride back was surprisingly comfortable; he took us right to the gate, and he was happy with twice the fare. We were happy to be back and considered it a true bargain and a win-win for us and the driver.

It was after lunch, I sat down to journal, Frank went down to check out the pool; we receive a note that there would be pizza party for us at 8 P.M. Walked around, then I checked out the pool, checked the elaborate settings for two weddings, happy hour, snacks, then pizza.

Thursday 24th of November

We are to be packed, eat breakfast and down to the lobby for the bus to leave at 7:30 A.M. As we checked out, there was a charge to our room for pasta at 6AM… We denied the charge, the breakfast included buffet was more than enough for anyone, a manager was called, we asked "why on earth would ANYONE order pasta at 6A.M"., when a banquet awaited then every morning? He had us write down that we did not order, did not receive, signed our names and finally were able to leave.

Noah

We were on the road by 7:40 and did catch a little of the beginning rush hour. This was going to be a six-plus hour bus ride. Jaipur is only 130 miles away, but even though the bus seems to be flying, the roads, traffic, two potty stops, and a lunch stop take a while.

Here are some India facts from the guide: Cities ending in "bad" were named by Muslims, and those ending in "pur" were founded by Hindus. India has a current population of around 1.3 billion (the U.S. is only 330 million). This is one of the most diverse countries on the planet, with fifteen languages and many religions that all seem to get along. The Flag consists of three stripes: the top orange, representing religion; the middle, white, representing peace and purity; the last, green, stands for agriculture.

As we leave the city, we pass a park area, a loose pig, and several monkeys on the sidewalk.

Tea is one of the major exports, along with food. Pakistan and India have been fighting with each other since they both gained independence at the same time from the British. There is so much "black" or underground money it has become a big problem. As mentioned before, very few business owners accept 500 or 1000-rupee notes. Most of my money is in 1000 notes (worth about $16.00 U.S. each)

Most of the highway has three lanes going each way with a divider in the middle. Sometimes, it narrows down to two; three lanes usually mean nothing. There are 5 vehicles abreast, all jockeying to get ahead of one another, and of course, the constant beeping of all the horns! Not only do the lane lines mean anything, but there will be an occasional car, bike, or motorcycle going the wrong way! Many times, a cow will be lying down in the median; along the road, we see cows, goats, monkeys, dogs, a few boars, and a pig now and then, garbage and trash constantly.

At the state line, we have to stop and pay a tax. The driver's helper has to run across three lanes of traffic traveling at highway speed to go into the building and pay the tax, then try to get back; no slow signs, no one slows down…he was quick! His only fear is if someone is driving the wrong way and he doesn't see him!

Vehicles on the highway include tractors, trucks, buses, cars, camel carts, horse carts, tuk-tuks, motorcycles (some with three people on them)

The gas price here is 75 rupees for a liter (about 3.75 liters per gallon, and 100 rupees equals about $1.50 U.S. $4.30/gallon)

Indians say they have three mothers: their birth mother, a cow mother, and India is their third mother. In the country, cow dung is prized; it is picked up and formed into cow dung patties and used as fuel for cooking.

As we enter Jaipur (known as "the pink city" do to the color of the buildings), we stop at the City Palace. A very large area divided into court yards' gardens and buildings, an elaborate wedding is being set up that will occupy three of these courtyards, flowers everywhere, bands setting up, sound systems, red carpeting, couches, 100's of workers, everyone working furiously to get this done for tonight!

A number of the arches feature peacocks, the national bird; there are also two large glass cases housing silver jars. They were each made from 14,000 jhar shahi (silver coins), each weighing 345 kg, height 5'3", 14'10" circumference, and held 900 gallons of liquid, yep, in the Guinness book!

As we left, we were attacked by the vendors, and even though we were told not to buy, I got a wooden cobra for my grandson for a very good price!

We check into a beautiful hotel, of course, as with EVERY attraction and hotel, we have to go through metal detectors, pick up our keys, and be provided with a glass of juice called Jamun (healthy for us, strange taste even for me), and find our rooms. THERE IS NO WIFI here. Lynn will not be happy!

Since this is Thanksgiving back home, Bob made arrangements to have boned chicken breast, mashed potatoes, and green beans for dinner, very nice and filling. The ritzy, marble, 5-star hotel charges for WIFI??? They did offer ½ hour free computer use in the business center. Of course, since it was 9:30 PM no one was around, then someone came up and logged me in……after 25 minutes with finally getting connected I got a message that it would not securely connect to roadrunner. I did not know the G-mail passwords, screwed and disgusted, quit, can't wait for the flak I will get when I get connected? At the next hotel…fancy yes, worth it…….NO!

Friday, November 25th, 2016, Jaipur.

Breakfast and on the bus by 8:30; everyone is ready for the elephant rides! We had a photo stop at Wing Palace and had to cross the road one way and then the next. A vendor was very helpful in getting us to the other side and back, and no, they don't all stop! It is early in the morning, and the five-story building just shines! It is basically just a wall, built on bed rock and with no real foundation. It was built in 1790 and was actually built for the women to have some privacy when bathing in the river.

Run or die, looking both ways and constantly watching traffic, we all made it back to the bus. Our guide offered the wares of the vendor that helped at a negotiated price, and several of us took advantage of a "thank you" for his help. (Note: one of his feet was facing the wrong way; he was very adept with moving with a large walking stick and had a very positive attitude!)

On to the Amber Fort; as we approach, there are actually two forts, one on the crest of the mountain and one about 1/3 of the way. A six to seven miles long wall, very similar to the Chinese Great Wall, brought back fond memories of our China trip. We also saw a family of wild boars, two adults, and about 6 piglets scampering. Fun to watch!

We got the cue to go up on the platform, and true to form, others pushed their way into our line to gain a few extra minutes. A good 5-8 dozen elephants, with a small cage for two people on each, lined up in two lines for the ½ mile journey to the lower fort. It was an interesting ride, a walk, swaying forward and sideways; once we started getting used to it, it was fun. Fran and I even hammed it up for a photographer as we passed by him…yes, we got the photos! The elephants only make the trip 5 times per day per the Indian Government so as not to stress the animals.

There is a platform similar to the one for loading in the courtyard, a relatively easy dismount, forming another great experience!

This fort was built in three sections between the 1600s and 1700s. It was abandoned late in the 19th century due to the lack of water. There are a number of sections, courtyards, and living chambers, all sandstone and marble, all intricately carved. We explored a couple of domed rooms on the top; these housed cisterns, and the open areas had grass shades when wetted, providing cooling with the frequent breezes. The fortress is also riddled with ramp tunnels for escape and hiding armies between the three sections, coursing all floors and even leading to the fortress on the crest. There was a large garden area just inside the main courtroom and one outside the walls next to an artificial lake. A lot of planning went into this, to say nothing of the beauty.

The next stop was a carpet store, Persian, camel, and silk, the same pitch we have seen in Morocco and China. The difference here was that after the carpet sale job, we had to go through the linens and clothes, then carvings and jewelry.

I escaped with my wallet intact, and we were off to lunch. This was a typical Indian buffet. I felt the spinach soup to be the best part;

no one was left hungry.

The Royal Observatory has a replica of structures to determine the time and placement of the planets. We checked, and the sundial was dead on to the minute! This was a perfect afternoon, sunny, warm, not a cloud in the sky!

I looked and found the planet indicators for Lynn's Taurus sign and my Pisces sign. It seems remarkable that this technology existed in the 1700s!

Our last scheduled stop was a jewelry store; again, it was rather high-end. In exploring the various floors, Frank and I found two different tiger knives. They were broad, one for each hand, and held with full hands, the width of the blades the width of a fist. The other was a knife that opened to have three blades.

Unscathed, we left to talk outside while the others were involved with sales and their head shaking.

It took us a good fifty minutes to return to the hotel; one of the interesting Indian Holidays is the Color Festival. During this festival, you put colors on one another, forgive, and vow to forget the past and have a positive future for both the offender and the offended. I thought this was a great idea!

Back at the hotel, Bob arranged a two-for-one drink happy hour with snacks; as with much of the other things with this place, the appetizers ran out early, very early, and only a very few were replaced; the drinks came slowly; they seemed very overwhelmed, and made little effort to alleviate the situation, very disappointing. I hope our new hotel tomorrow will have free WIFI. I am sure Lynn has news about Thanksgiving!

Tomorrow, we leave at 9 A.M. sharp. Some wanted to sleep in…this will be another 6-hour bus drive (or more). The women were already pestering about potty breaks along the way… we will see!!

26 November, Jaipur-Jodhpur

Frank's key stopped working. To add to the frustration, the "free" ½ hour internet would not connect to roadrunner again. This is getting really frustrating! We were all ready to go; we were seated for breakfast at the restaurant, and then we were told it was the wrong one, even though the group had eaten there yesterday. They said it was okay. But shunned us regarding extra coffee and taking plates away.

With the bus loaded up, we were on the road a little after 9 A.M. A potty break at 10:10 (I finally found some of the souvenirs I needed for home, only Lynn and one other to go!), we had lunch on the road, at 2:30 P.M.

Did I mention pigeons? They feed them, so many of the squares are covered with pigeons. We see many animals as we progress on our trip, along with many dogs, cows, Brahma bulls, pigs, and boars. Some of them are lying in the median, some on corners right next to traffic, and occasionally one walking in a lane or crossing the highway. This is marble and granite country, white, green, black, and pink; large slabs are displayed as we cruise past the stone cutters. Up on a ridge is a grouping of 24 temples across the ridge and on the path from the road. We are told that in the small villages, everyone knows everyone and many times the buildings are not locked, drugs at present are not a very big problem.

Our guide also explained about the caste system. It mostly depends on what you do for a living. Professionals and politicians are an upper caste, Skilled tradesmen another, and unskilled laborers the lowest. This is still promoted since each caste worships differently, dresses differently, eats differently, and has different values. The grandparents are the main ones who pick who is to marry; an individual's horoscope is very important as to when the ceremony is held, and it is unusual for the boy and girl to meet before the arranged marriage. The schools are trying to integrate by setting one set of standards and scores depending on caste. The example he gave is to get into an elite school, a score of 92 on the CAT exam was required for an upper caste, and a score of 45 for a lower caste. Many of the upper castes say it is not fair. Quotas give advantages to those with less preparation and background and draw down the quality of education, and they are still working on this.

Schooling is from pre-nursery to nursery and up to high school. At graduation, (16) you are required to take the CAT exam to determine if you go to a professional school or trade school. In the small towns, the children and parents are rewarded for good attendance with additional grains and food to supplement the harvest. Public school is free, but in order to get into the colleges, you must have a passing score; many of the upper castes elect private colleges. College is three years; MDs are 4 years; the military is by choice, and after 4 years, you may qualify to be an officer.

Jodhpur is known as the blue city; it seems that Krishna was bitten by a snake. However, since he was a God, he couldn't die, but he turned blue, and many of the buildings in this town are painted blue in his honor. This area gets very hot in the summer, with temperatures of 48-50 degrees Celsius, and it rarely rains, so this town is also called Sun City. It has a population of 1.5 million.

We saw our first train in days; India has the largest train system in the world and is India's largest employer. As we drive, the driver switches lanes, sometimes driving in the wrong lanes for extended periods of time, the horn constantly beeping; on the two-lane roads, there are severe speed bumps, and in other areas, the roads are not the best, towns are congested, and jockeying for position is constant, from there we went to the Mehrangarh Fort.

Another large fort, many steps, confusion on who will go up, who will partially go up, how many headsets… (This tour guide is a saint!) We cleared up everyone's needs and took an elevator up to the first level after receiving our audio guides. Pictures are as follows: Outside of the fort, there is a picture of the Blue City, Royal elephant seats, a palanquin (seats carried by slaves for royalty), a Hookah they really just smoked flavored tobacco for the most part!), a unique cannon, a bedroom, spiral staircase, an armory with a collection of tiger knives, firearms, and swards, and cradles.

Getting back to the meeting area was steep staircases and ramps, and I do mean steep! The trip to our hotel took longer than expected due to bridge clearance; we saw a number of Gypsy camps along the road, open fires, with ragged, dirty material open tents, and many waved at the bus.

We finally arrived at 7:30, had dinner at 8:30, wrote up notes, and tried to get to my e-mail till 11:45. No luck; pissed; I will try to have someone text Lynn about the no e-mail situation!

Sunday, November 27th, 2016. Jodhpur to Rajanpur.

This is another bus travel day, and I am getting tired of the travel. This morning is a 3 ½ hour ride, to a Jain temple, then a quick lunch, (1/2 hour) then travel to meet a ship on the lake at 4P.M.

Rajanpur is the Venice of India, with a population of 600,000, and a number of artificial lakes were established in 1569. This is a center for art; artists here make their brushes from squirrel hair, and the James Bond Movie "Octopussy" was shot there.

On the way, a lot of scrub land, low bushes, and narrow two-way traffic roads with an occasional tollway. The small towns are all starting to look alike: lots of garbage alongside the road, cattle, dogs, goats, and donkeys scattered about, with an occasional cow in the meridian or alongside the road, none very active, resting or nosing through the various garbage clusters. The shops in the towns are food, snack food, shoes, electronics or phone stores and clothing stores, multiples of all.

We also received clarification on the caste system; there are 4 general castes with sub-classes in each.

At one point, we stopped at a place where a bull was blindfolded, walking around an area grinding sesame seeds. The people were more than happy to let us take pictures and watch; Frank gave the driver a 100-real note for a bag sample. Yes, I know, we all knew that this was an uncooked product, but about half of us tried it; the oily mush was quite sweet and very tasty!

The Jain religion is one of the oldest. It has 24 prophets, and their main beliefs include hygiene, non-violence, no harm to people or animals, including bad words, no eating after dusk, no root plants, garlic, and onions (these create short tempers), and no eggs, dairy, meat or fish. This religion comprises only 0.4 % of the Indian population. (Our guide is a member of the Jain faith.)

Morning is for worship, that is why the temple is only open from noon to dusk, in the temple there are 1444 carved pillars, and you must remove shoes and all leather products before entering.

We were at the temple just a hair past noon, left everything leather in the bus, including wallets and belts, and hiked up to the temple. There was a rack to deposit shoes outside the temple; we were instructed to explore all we wanted, those that wanted to take pictures inside paid 200 rupees more for the privilege, and not to take a picture of the main prophet inside. The inside is incredible, everything is carved, everything is marble, and it is intricate, multi leveled, and just amazing, I took quite a few pictures to try to show the detail, some of the lower borders where dragon heads, (that looked like monkey heads) similar to the guardian monkeys we saw in Tibet! (I later asked our guide, he said those were dragon heads??)

I was one of the last folks out to retrieve my shoes, and was there at 12:45; however, I drifted over for some close-up flower shots and to talk with some students, and when I looked back, the group was gone… I headed back to the bus, talked to some more students, took some more flower shots and arrived at the bus at 1:05, to a cheering ovation…. the first time I was ever late! Argggghhh! I took the beating and we were off to lunch. The lunch was to last no longer than ½ hour including potty break; I was NOT the last one this time, someone else was but she only got a tepid cheer from everyone.

The bus trip was 58 miles of small towns, two-way streets, and an occasional tollway; we did see a number of Lemur Monkeys with black faces and long tails at several spots, a tree that had upper branches with black leaves (bats sleeping) but I didn't get a picture of that! We also stopped by a well with a system of pails on a wheel that was turned by oxen to bring up the water for washing clothes, drinking, and irrigation. I got that picture!

It was too late to get to the boat, so we stopped at a botanical garden to explore the flowers and fountains there. We were promised a visit to an art school also, but that was canceled due to the traffic being too heavy and our time, so the boat cruise was pushed off till the next day.

We checked into our hotel. This was not the one we had reserved, but a wedding party had booked the entire hotel for three days, and this was the substitute that was arranged, still 5-star and very opulent.

I asked about the WIFI and was told it was complimentary, and that our bags would be brought to our rooms. Went to the room, Frank had some intestinal problems, but was OK to go for the cocktails arranged at 7:15.

The drinks came, appetizers were few and far between and we called it a night at 8:30. This time the roadrunner worked! I caught up with Lynn on what happened on thanksgiving and told her that I was actually missing her already! Finished the daily journaling, put out clothes for tomorrow, and off to bed.

Monday, November 28th, 2016, another busy day. We have an ancient temple scheduled first. This was the festival temple, abandoned long ago, the carvings were very intricate, the grass /moss that surrounded the temple was very much like the soft carpet feel of the mix in the Iceland lava fields. No railing steps, begging kids, but we didn't have to take off our shoes, and only two other couples not in our group, so not crowded at all! This is a relatively small temple, but the carvings are still mostly intact, and very detailed.

The second temple we visited was only 2 kilometers away, but it is an active temple. NO shoes or socks to enter, no pictures inside the temple, people were selling flowers as offerings just inside the gate. This temple was dedicated to the Lord Shiva in 734 A.D. and is still active! In this complex, there are 108 temples, besides no shoes and socks, no water bottles, cameras, or bags were allowed. I did buy 2 pictures to show how extensive this was, everything carved inside, two statues of cows, and when you passed a central location two people were collecting the flower offerings.

The last morning attraction was the royal palace. It cost an additional 200 rupees to bring in a camera. As we approached the long drive the bus could not go up, the gate doors had the heads of pikes embedded in it, this was to prevent elephants from smashing down the gates, and I never saw this before. We were warned extensive walking, extensive stairs, close quarters, and a wedding was being prepared for later on this week.

As we enter the inside gates, to the right is an active fountain, and the royal family residence. The fountain being active signifies that the royal family is there now. This is the longest dynasty in the world, dating back to 1706. We move in, enter several courtyards, and then start going up stairs, to various chambers, hallways, and courtyards. The halls at times were very close, the stairs vary in height, all doorways have high thresholds, and low door heights, you may go up a flight of stairs with two across, and then get to a courtyard, then down a narrow staircase where only one person can do at a time, some with, some without rails. There are mosaics of pheasants, and paintings. Many of the paintings showed battles, the elephants were actually trained to swing a sword in its trunk in combat! Horses and mounted soldiers were used to confuse the elephants during battles; there was even a statue of a famous horse in one of the hallways. Looking out over the man-made lake we see two islands. One was the royal families retreat, and the other was a son's retreat that was created in spite of the family. This second island palace complex is now a 5-star hotel and also featured in the James Bond Movie "Octopussy".

Lunch was brief, another ½ hour event, very similar Indian selection, and we needed to be back on the bus promptly. We went back to the hotel to pick up the people who opted not to go with us previously to join us on a lake open boat tour.

We were quickly joined, and on the way to the lake, we picked up the travel host's family, his wife, and two children, a 7-year-old precious, bright daughter and a 5 ½ yr. An old son who was supposedly naughty and had a hard time smiling.

We loaded the boat for a tour of the artificial lake, found out that the wedding being set up in the palace was also being set up on the private island, (Magar Ghats) it seems that this wedding will cost in excess of 1 BILLION Rupees, encompasses both locations and has blocked out entire 5-star hotels for guests, and a carnival was even erected for the guests! We had a closer look at the Octopussy Hotel Island, and we even landed to walk the grounds of the Royal Island and witness the preparation there! There were hundreds of people between the palace and island, kitchens, flowers galore, statues, tents, it was truly overwhelming.

After the boat tour, we headed back to the hotel, cocktails at 7:15 with appetizers, tomorrow we fly out to our final India destination, so we all needed to pack up, suitcases on the bus before 7:00 and off by 7:45 for the 10:30 flight to Mumbai. We finished the cocktail hour, went back to the room, packed and set out for the next day, journaled and wrapped everything by 10:30. Tomorrow will be a travel day…

again.

November 29th, 2016, Tuesday. The hotel opened up the breakfast room at 6:30 to accommodate us, and the bus arrived at 6:50. We were all fed, all on the bus and gratuities and thank-yous' were given out. The bus promptly left at 7:15 as scheduled, and we were at the airport within an hour. It is a small airport, and they were not prepared for 23 people all at once, but we got our luggage scanned and tagged, then took the luggage to the ticket counter, had the non-carry-ons weighted, and checked, then to the metal detectors and wands.

There were no signs regarding shoes, belts, or electronics to be pulled, so almost everyone's carry-on was flagged, all electronics including chargers and cameras had to be removed, and then through the scanner again.... what a mess!

Bob, the group leader was detained due to the international satellite phone he was carrying; he told them just to throw it away if it was a problem, however, it turned out that he would be delayed until after the flight, so he asked me to take over for him.

The flight to Mumbai was only a little over an hour; I gathered everyone in an open area, made sure to relay to them what was going on, and then set an area aside where we all could meet and find the hotel representative.

The representative found us, I asked him how far the hotel was, he relayed one hour, so I told everyone to use the rest room, that the trip was an hour or so, and when re-assembled and counted; We followed the representative out to the bus. Kept the group together, halted what traffic I could for them, got them on the bus, recounted, and then told them the plan after discussing it with the tour connection.

When we got to the hotel, I had them gather away from the desk so that the representative could check them in and give us the keys to distribute. I asked about lunch, when and where, and assumed that it would be picked up by Bob, and also assumed that the beer and wine would be included, so I signed everything, distributed the information, got room numbers, so that I could forward the cocktail hour time and place, along with where the lunch was to be held.

Everyone got their assigned rooms, and we all met in the dining room where there was an area set aside for us. Discussed final things needed by the maître de for dinner (only three wanted dinner) after the cocktails and appetizers, signed the bill, and returned to the room to coordinate information with those that had left before I received the information.

I thought I had Bob's e-mail in my address book, but it wasn't there, I did get a call from one of the group relaying that they had forwarded my room number to Bob, and that he should be arriving tonight between 6:30 and 7. Frank went out for a walk with others, he soon came back, it is humid and over 90; Got his swim suit and off to the pool he went, I kept updating, repacking, and catching up on journaling and e-mails, we only have CNN here, and Trump is being bashed all the time, it is so one sided, the second thing out of people when they have the courage is where are you from, and then what do you think of Trump!

Went with Frank to the Executive club for appetizers and drinks, some still insisted on a meal afterward and Vagabonds picked it up. Bob did show up here, thanked me, and stated he would take over everything from now on. After appetizers and drinks (closes at 8:30P.M.), we came back to the room, Frank washed out some clothes, I threw out some, and off to bed, a busy day tomorrow!

Wednesday November 30th, 2016 a busy day scheduled. We left at 09:00 Mumbai is blanketed in smog/fog, the property on the inlet is going for $3000 per square foot, the first stop, a freedom park where freedom fighters were hanged was explored.

It must have been nice a couple of years ago, but the filth of the city is encroaching on it, the 24 million population stresses the resources, and it shows, city workers sitting on steps, others casually sweeping dirt off the sidewalks, shanties just outside the gates selling food and also a food pantry providing to a majority of women a stew, on stainless steel plates.

We explored both sides of the park for a good half-hour, the design was very artistic, had some very nice flower shots, but the care doesn't seem to be there; what a shame, lots of signs regarding keeping the park clean, but these seem to be ignored, plus simple up-keep seems to be poor.

The next stop was a temple, this one was dedicated to three gods, we parked outside a lower class neighborhood, and walked into the inner streets, There was no real place to deposit our shoes, just on the street next to a low dividing railing, We were to take off our shoes, then walk a quarter block to the temple, and then upstairs into the temple, I, and a number of folks, had seen a number of temples, and decided to keep our shoes on and explore the shops around the temple.

It was early, many of the shops had the same stuff, (no baskets, lamps, or tigers) and not what we wanted. We looked over the offerings, walked to the next busy street and then back to the bus, we did ask those that did go in, and there was nothing new to be seen, so we counted ourselves as lucky to view the locals rather than another temple.

Fresh water is a problem here, due to the population and the only fresh water available is from an artificial lake, it is quite expensive. Spices are offered in bulk, very intense reds, blood reds, and different shades of gold and brown. We are driven past one of the most expensive residences in the world. One is owned by the fourth richest man in the world, costs $3.5 Billion dollars for the building that only four people live in.

We are also treated to an explanation of the Indian flag; this one is, the top orange represents the Hindu religion, the white peace and tranquility, and the last green represents the Muslim faith, with the circle in the middle representing the lower caste. This is a different explanation than we heard before; I guess it depends on your faith... the first was from a guide in the Jain religion.

India was under Communist rule for 37 years, and finally got rid of that, was conquered by the Portuguese (Mumbai means "good day" in Portuguese), then displaced by the British.

Sundays here, on the main beach is called " Yoga Day". As in Rio, the main street is blocked off, so that people have a few hours to enjoy the sea without the hum drum and noise of traffic.

We stopped and walked through a fruit and grocery market and tiny shops (over 200). there were several areas that didn't smell right, small thin aisles, and yes, there were even some trying to get through on bicycles, scooters, and smaller motorcycles. I was finally able to find a basket for Lynn!

A photo op at Victoria Station, it is one of the largest employers of India, employing millions of people, 5 million people take the train daily. Another slow drive along "fashion street" where over 250 vendors sell modern clothes, again all very small open-air shops, lined up for blocks on the sidewalk.

In the garment district, the jobs are handed down in the families, parent to son or daughter, or a widowed wife or husband, so positions may have been filled for generations! One of the most common languages here is Hindi; it is not unusual for an Indian to know several languages fluently.

We were to stop for a half-hour dinner; it took 15 minutes just for the first course, and then someone ordered dessert. By the time it was over, we were there for over an hour, which messed with the schedule for the rest of the afternoon.

Noah

We received mixed communication on the bus; some heard we were to take everything, others just that was needed, for the elephant Island excursion. This was not handy, especially transferring to and from the ferry. A few of the group are getting increasingly "test-ee", many still ask if the dish is "spicy" and all expect beer or wine to be included with lunch and dinners.

We were hurriedly walked three blocks to the wharf, to be wanded and metal detected (this is getting really old too!) in separate lines, men, and women...

The ferries carry about 100 people, so we all find an unbroken old chair on the top deck or main deck for the one-hour ride, to the island, this inlet from the ocean is called the Arabian Sea. It is hot and muggy, but the ferry moves along at a good pace, the breeze feels great!

As in Mumbai, fresh water is at a premium, none sold on the boat, or on the island, it is the same as a soft drink. One of the guides purchased some snacks to feed to the gulls, the gulls would hover close to the boat, many would catch the treat in midair, fun to watch, and I do believe I got a few pictures.

As we moor next to another ferry, we transfer through that ferry to the pier. The pier is about 300-500 meters, and for a small fee, you can ride a miniature train to take you to the mainland. Restrooms on the island cost a few rupees, then the long trek up.

Elephanta Caves are early Hindus which succeeded Buddhism as a major religion here. The estimated time of creation of this is 600-650 A.D. It was dedicated to the God Siva, "the creator and destroyer of the Universe." The island is 2.5 km by 173 meters, and the people on the island live by selling souvenirs, farming, and fishing.

The stairs up are in groups of 3,5, or7 to a small landing, then an upward sloping landing and a few more steps. From the bottom to top, on both sides, vendors have their wares, and are hawking them, usually no hand holds due to the merchandise; if you do stop to catch your breath, or rest, as they request, it is an automatic sales job on you. The stairs are covered with a tarp, an occasional monkey will jump on it and scare the crap out of those just below.

The island was named Elephanta by the Portuguese in 1535 due to the huge stone elephant they found on the island.

The center cave is the largest of a number of caves and each has shrines, alcoves, and reliefs of deities. All of them have been damaged by soldiers who had different faiths, or others that had no respect for other beliefs. The trip down the steps was easier and faster. We only had a half hour in the caves since we got there so late, and the last tourist ferry left at 5:30.

The hour-long trip back was refreshing, with a beautiful sunset, and a cool breeze off the bay. We made it back to the bus, through the crowds, and were returned to the hotel. It was past 7, so quite a few complained that the Hor de' Orvs and drinks were not enough, so Bob arranged pizza in the dining room for them, a few of us sated by the appetizers and drinks, went back up to our respective rooms to relax and finish the day, the rest went down to gobble up the pizza.

Thursday December 1st, 2016. Slept in till 7, went down and tried the eggs Benedict and we were both pleasantly surprised. A number of folks wanted to go shopping yet, a time to meet was set, and we walked the three-quarter mile to the shopping district. Most found what they wanted as we walked block after block of back alley, sidewalk, and store-front shops. An hour and a half later, the sun hotter, humidity climbing we took a census, Frank wanted to continue, the rest of us, crossed the street and headed back. When we approached the circle to head back to the hotel, most opted to take a cab back, one of the women decided to hoof it, I asked her twice if she felt safe to do it alone, she assured me she would, so I and the last woman of the group grabbed a cab, and for 50 rupees plus 10-rupee tip, got a cab back. The approximately 85 cents was worth it.

Back at the hotel, breakfast was great and plentiful, so lunch wasn't necessary. I decided to go out to the pool for a swim. The water was cool, being in the shadow of the building. After an hour or so, I went up to the room, showered, and hung the suit to dry. A few minutes later, Frank came up to the room, said Fran wanted to walk, check out the bank, so we all met in the lobby at 4:00. We hoofed it to the bank, nope, bank hours here are 10:00 A.M. to 3:30 P.M., they were already closed… we found one other bank, same story. We went down to the beach, in front of the wall are concrete jacks, to prevent erosion, as the fog lifted, you could see the skyscrapers across the bay.

We walked a distance, then decided to come back another way, and discovered the subway. We went down and into the underground, found that the subway cars here are almost twice as wide as American, Russian, and the Chinese ones we saw in Hong Kong!

After exploring the subway, we exited a different way, and across the street was a Burger King! Fran sprung the rupees for some French fries, here even fast food is VAT taxed at 20.5 %. We ate the fries, they were as good as home, and made our way back to the hotel, crossing streets now is a little easier, but you still have plenty of the annoying horn beeping, as a matter of fact, the horns start blaring the second the lights change…unbelievable!

Cocktails again, at 6:30-8: 30 with appetizers, then a special meal at 8:35 with the same.

Bob arranged a visit to a local government school, so I was nominated to provide the speech and collection for school supplies for the kids. I made the pitch and collected on the bus arriving at the school. I looked up our Vagabond address to give them with the voluntary donation.

We had one of the best meals in India that night, but it was way too much, and everyone left, full, and waddled to the elevators for a full day on Friday.

Educating Noah...Travelin'

Friday, December 2, 2016, our last full day in India, and it will be busy!

There has been a welcome change in schedule; today we are visiting a government grade school! All the kids in government and private schools are required to master three languages, the State language, Hindi, and English; when they move on to High school, they can add French or Spanish. In this school, there were 2000 students, and there are 50-80 students per class, class lasts 35 minutes, uniforms are required. Girls participate in many, if not all sports, the playground was rather small, the rooms cramped and the students were very curious.

We are told while waiting outside for class changes that they do not see white people in person, that we could not only be from another part of the world but from outer space! We talked to the principal and two senior teachers. Since this is a government school, the teachers and staff are all government employees. The advantage of being a teacher is that you have off 90 days out of the year (just like here); the pay for teachers is not the best, though; for government schools, it is about $500.00 US per month. For private school teachers, it is twice that. However, the govt. Pension and benefits are better than the private sector.

Most teachers keep the occupation for life.

The unguarded door to the playground that was enclosed with a four-foot wall, then a wire fence, and the top of that barbed wire, was dead bolted and locked, the front entrance had two guards on duty. We were able to briefly interact with two classes, the questions asked were smart, the classes were attentive, and very courteous; Most students smiled easily, when I made several funny gestures, they giggled and laughed.

I had collected $50.00 worth of dollars and rupees, put them all in an envelope with the Vagabond address and presented it to the principal; they were very impressed and shocked.

As we went back to the bus, we thought this town was one of the cleanest towns we had been in, but there was still a lot of litter. The next stop was Mahakam Railway station, delayed by a stop back at the hotel for a bathroom break. Then we got off the bus and watched the distribution of Tiffin boxes;

These Tiffin boxes are sorted and placed on bicycles or a wooden crate and then distributed all over the station, containing a hot lunch from home to the workers, some even supper. We lifted one. It was named, color-coded, and warm; this was not a light lunch; the container must be 4-5 pounds!

We then proceeded across the street (no small feat) to Church gate station, the one we stumbled on yesterday. We were given a briefing as to the schedule, we actually got in line to buy round trip tickets for 10 Rupees ($.16), but then there was confusion in the group. The guide said he was going to buy the tickets, then some did not want to go inside, and then some did not want to ride to and back from North Mumbai. Bob, our leader, stepped in and just stopped the confusion by saying "no" to the ride, we were running late, not on schedule, and no coordination between those wanting the experience and not ... so most of us went on the platform, watched one take off, with passengers running and jumping in, and another coming in, with the same, passengers jumping off before the train stopped. There are women cars, and men cars, and a 1st class car ($.10 more) if too many women, they can go on the men's car but no to the men on the women's car.

Our guide tells us that about 30 people die each month from accidents with the train, he actually lost a brother last year who fell off the train.

Since we were already an hour plus behind schedule, we did not visit the open-air Laundry known as DHOBI GHAT. And proceeded north by bus to a lunch stop. It took a good two hours, traffic is that bad, and I can see why the trains are used so heavily!

Lunch was to last only ½ hour since we were still way behind schedule, which turned into an hour (dessert was put out late, and most HAD to have that!) Off to Bollywood. We didn't have any star houses pointed out, but we were let into the gate. We were shown a number of sets, Yes, there is a picture of me and several others behind bars, a hospital set, a courtroom set (I was the witness), and we were able to watch a scene being played, with cut, after cut, action, cut, action, and so forth. We went up to the sound room and were given a tour of the circuit board, blending, and dubbing. A few of the group attempted to sing, but it was not well coordinated and was not pleasant... I suggested everyone sing the song in "cat," meow, meow, etc....

We then went into a screening room and were treated to a number of dance routines put on by four dancers. Lots of fun, especially when we were all invited down to dance with the dancers, most of us participated, what fun!

Outside the screening room, they had statues and awards; I volunteered to put on a too-small robe but also got to wear a turban and a sword! Another two of the girls dressed up, and we all posed for additional pictures.

Back on the bus, another two hours of horrible traffic to a restaurant called Ali Baba's. A nice sit-down with chicken, fish, green peas and beans, rice, sauces, and a very good caramel ice cream.

Walked to the bus, a short ride home. Frank went down to see if he could scarf up a dessert; I went up to the room. Guess what? The key no longer worked... I went down to the desk and had the key recoded. It seems all the vagabond's rooms were decoded; it must have been a subtle hint!

Tomorrow is another day of leisure; we have extended room privileges along with breakfast, so we may check out that laundry in the morning. We leave for the airport at 4:15, then go home.

Saturday, December 3,

On the is my last day in India, I will leave for home tonight. We both slept in till 7 and went down for our final breakfast. We treated ourselves to full breakfasts so that there would be no need for lunch.

After breakfast, I checked with the concierge to find out the distance and location of the outdoor laundry we had missed on Friday. I was told it was a 20-minute cab ride, and when asked, I was told the cab would cost 300-400 rupees.

I then went up to the room, waited for Frank, and read the paper. He showed up just as I finished, we agreed to go, added the rupees we had left (besides the 1000 rupee notes I had that no one would take, and agreed to take a cab to the laundry by taking the 270 rupees we had between us.

We talked to three cabbies, then one agreed to do the job for the sum, and off we went. The trip was a good 20 minutes, and the view from the cab was a bit more exciting. One guy did bounce off the hood, but he signaled it was his fault, no dent, no harm. Both smiled and waved.

The cabbie volunteered to take us in. He said this was the poor side of town. Most, if not all, understood English and would be of no help if we got lost. So, we agreed to the tour and to drop us off in the side of town that could take U.S. dollars.

It was located behind some shabby little stores made of old sheet metal, the alley was narrow, and of course, we shared the route with bicycles and motorbikes with white-wrapped bundles of clothing. Once in, there was a field of concrete stalls; each stall had someone in, some aside a concrete table soaping and scrubbing, and others were dancing on top of clothes like an agitator of a washing machine. There were also three stories of wash lines, all with wash hanging out to dry.

Under a porch, there were several men spinning clothes in a tub to remove most of the water. On the way out, we saw people folding clothes that had been laundered.

We asked how they kept track of which clothes went where, and our guide told us about a small tag put on the inside of each item. We went into the foray, we were ignored, the folks doing the work were too busy to be concerned with us, we made way in the aisles, and they made way for us, a very smooth, well-organized, hectic operation.

Our cabbie then asked where next. Frank wanted a two-faced ivory owl, and we were driven to one place with no agreed price. I told the cabbie to "just get us within a kilometer of the hotel in a shopping district," and we would settle up. He did just that. I gave him the agreed 370 rupees plus a $5.00 bill, but he said that wasn't enough. I said that was all he was going to get from me and to see what he could get from Frank. Frank agreed to another five bucks, and we were on our own.

We walked up and down a number of streets; we both bought a few more items at reasonable prices and started to head back home. Frank's sense of direction was not as good as he claimed, but between us, we were back at the hotel before 1 P.M. We went up to the room; Frank decided to go to the pool for one last swim, I wanted to pack, weigh, and journal, rest the hip and right arm, and prepare for the trip back.

Everyone was on time to leave for home. Numbers were counted, luggage was loaded onto the bus, and we were on the way. Even though the airport is in Mumbai, and we took a tollway and main streets, it was 2 hours before we arrived at the airport.

Passports were checked before entering, got in line to get our tickets and check in the luggage, find the TSA, this one, shoes and belts off, phones and computers OK, men in one scanner line, women in another, everyone gets wanded after going through the scanner, then on to passport control, no separation of lines except for crews and business class, everything asked, questioned as to where and why, stamp, stamp, and off to the gates. A two hour wait for our fight to get on, the gate opens 40 minutes before the flight, the hordes crowd the gate, business, kids and disabled follow, then the free for all.

The flight actually takes off 45 minutes late, so we have already been in the jet an hour; the flight is two hours, and aisle seats give a little extra armroom; however, that side must be bumped or rubbed by most passengers or attendants as they progress up and down the aisle. As the plane taxis to a stop, aisle people are propelled up so that some in the back don't push themselves ahead to be first off to wait for their luggage TWO SECONDS earlier than others.

We exit the plane, gather outside to re-group, then off to passport control, but first x-rays and wanding, this time shoes on, belts off, computers out and turned on, and the 2 oz. of sanitizer put into separate plastic bags. Wanded; knees identified, frisked, and off again. Down a hall, staircases, transfer to the USA, enter passport control, answer a number of questions, have a picture taken, then to another agent, questions, answers, release, then up to a waiting area for a three-hour wait for the last plane home.

Forty minutes before the scheduled flight, the gates open, business, then kids and disabled fight through the crowd at the gate to get in to line, then a gate agent yells at everyone to stand back and load from group A, the B, then C, then gives up and says D & E. Push, shove, we all get on the plane, overhead storage is at a premium, since most have carry-ons one at maximum size and a large purse or additional bag take up most of the space, one passenger decided that my carry-on was in the way for his, he puts it in various places in the bin and repeatedly shoves his carry on into the too small place, He then pulls his out and goes to another bin, I voice my dissatisfaction of abusing my bag, and find it compressed in the back of the bin.

We finally take off, only 15 minutes late, the flight lasts…14 ½ hours! Argggghhh, person in front reclines fully, my seat is broken does not recline, too bad, means eating cramped, with only half of the tray unfolded, all meals have a variation of rice with… plus additional beverage, and yes, the continual bump and rub as attendants and passengers go to and from the bathroom three seats up.

Off the plane, actually, there was less push and shove on this exit than all the rest; we gathered together before collecting our luggage, and it took a good hour from arrival to leaving the luggage area for the bus.

It is Sunday morning. In a little over an hour, we are in the parking lot of the motel to be picked up by our loved ones or pick up our cars. Lynn is there; Suzy (our Subaru) has been washed and has on her Christmas antlers and nose (the car, not Lynn!). We loaded her up, dropped off the ladies we had picked up when we left, and headed for home. Another great adventure comes to a close.

Noah

It is harder and harder to readjust after a vacation; I definitely prefer to vacation with Lynn without the drama of a group. I believe the next four cruises should finish the world for us, and we will have our fill of exploring and traveling. Believe it or not, this, too, I am tired of!?!?, of course, there are several locations we will explore, but

Educating Noah…Travelin'

one to two travels a year! Then to learn a new vocation, I am looking forward to that too!

I am having increasing problems with my right shoulder. Now, the left hip is making it difficult to get into and out of a tub for bathing. I have an appointment tomorrow about that, new tattoos next Wednesday, and babysat for Gordon, our neighbor, again today. I am still dragging from returning and long flights!

I had an appointment with the VA, and they had the order to x-ray my knees? I asked why? The doctor in training said it was the follow-up. I told him my right shoulder was getting worse and let's treat the cause, not the symptom. He had a discussion with the surgeon and then agreed with me to proceed with a fix. I asked him to schedule my x-rays while I was still there, and he also scheduled an MRI before another appointment in two weeks. Hopefully, this will be done soon after our return from Antarctica.

I also decided to switch carriers and finally dump Time Warner for TV, Internet, and Phone. I am still maintaining a landline and want consistent contact with home, and Roadrunner failed us, both in Russia and India.

Well, it has been three weeks since we returned from India; we switched from Time Warner to ATT. It took me hours, and I had to finally get my printer to work with the ATT router after 45 minutes of useless support from ATT. Now we are in the midst of an ATT outage….23 hours and counting, no phone, internet, or TV.

I guess the younger set would have been driven mad by now. I have the basement TV on rabbit ears so Lynn can watch the Packer Game, and I also have the main stereo on the antenna, so the house is filled with Christmas music.

My tattoos are on, and I like them. I had x-rays, an MRI, and a CAT scan, and scheduled a shoulder replacement in March. The only other health concern is my left hip. I am now limping, and I don't trust the hip. It generates heat on the surface of the leg. I have stumbled a couple times and have difficulty picking up items on the floor on that side. This one feels like the other one did just before replacement, and I am having difficulties far faster with this than I will admit to anyone! (I guess the 3+ million steps I put in after the first hip replacement didn't help!!)

Ma was emboldened by the rejection of Thanksgiving with the family and refused to come to the family gathering for Christmas. She is lonely, wants more attention, and is progressively depressed and feeling sorry for herself. She will not go down to live with Ted, my brother, and is getting short with him on the phone. I will have to have some more encouraging talks with her before leaving on our next adventure. We will see.

Chapter five
2017

It took a few weeks, increased visits, heated conversations, visits to her regular doctor, and two visits to her orthopedic doctor for shots in her left arm and left knee. She is planning to go shopping at Pick and Save again with the group, promised to at least watch her group play mini golf, may help another at Bingo, and is walking the halls with her friend Hatti.

I gave her three choices including moving down with Ted, having in home assistance, and assisted care. More talking, more discussions, more clarification resulted in her not really now wanting to go to assisted care and having a care giver twice a week. She is smiling again, and she is visiting others in the building; a good start!

I have been driving for the DAV at least two times a week because a good number of the drivers are snowbirds and live down south in December, January, and February. Still, sit with the neighbor on the first Wednesday of the month and have actually finished packing less than two weeks before leaving.

I also installed Uber on Lynn's phone, so we have a back-up ride to and from the bus station.

Took my mother in to emergency care on Sunday, they admitted her, Monday, they are giving her angioplasty tomorrow after we told him I am leaving Thursday. I will be checking in at the hospital tomorrow after driving for the DAV and hopefully will have good news as to when I take her home!!

More drama just before our Antarctica trip…I really don't need this!!!

Noah

Argentina and Antarctica February, 2017

In a few days, we will be leaving on our first adventure for 2017. I am all packed, the weather has been checked both in Chicago and in Atlanta, and it looks good. We sent the info to the kids, Lynn this time is in charge of the cab to the bus station, she is also packing tomorrow, and both of us are ready to go again.

I did buy the internet package; I have been working with my mother who had a serious bout with pain and depression. We visited the ortho doctor twice, and she now has a helper two times a week from Synergy. It has been a significant improvement and will just have the internet access as a fail-safe.

Then three days before we left, she called and I took her to the Emergency Room at the hospital, they admitted her, and after extensive tests, including an angiogram, installed a stent, and discharged her TWENTY hours before we were to leave. Hattie, her great friend volunteered to look over her, so she will be receiving post cards from as many ports as we can! I left final instructions for Tiffany, reminded her to check on Ma every few days and water our stuff, when we are gone, the next entry will be in Buenos Aires!

Our cab ride didn't show at 10:15, we called, they had called to confirm at 10, but Lynn had turned off her phone; everything worked, cab was dispatched, picked us up at 10:25, and we were at the bus station by 10:50, our bus schedule was 11:10. No problems driving down to O'Hare, customs and TSA the fastest yet, the counter clerk asked why I did not use the Kiosk, I told her the last two times I went overseas it was rejected do to Visa requirements, she proceeded but asked that I check every time. So much for consistency!

We found our gate, waited for our flight, it was on time, loaded, the compartment above was full, so we tucked our nap sacks under the seat. Two-hour flight to Atlanta Georgia, de-planed not as push and shove as other countries, found the bus to the international airport, found our next gate, grabbed a bite to eat, and boarded the flight to Buenos Aires at 8:30 PM; we had two seats together on the 777; the extra leg room with premium economy paid off...It is a 10-hour flight.

Neither of us sleeps well on planes, maybe two hours sleep between both of us, with Lynn sleeping about twice what I did.

We arrived at 8:30 a.m. their time, three planes unloaded and swamped immigration, the lines moved pretty fast, basically we presented passports, provided a thumb print (yes, had to try numerous times with the agent telling me to "press harder", and me heating my fingers with my hot breath, fourth time it was accepted!) Both of us took off our glasses and presented ourselves for a photo.

Picked up our luggage, located our connection, and off to the hotel. We stayed at the NH Buenos Aires, located right downtown. There were only two couples on the plane for the transfer, at the hotel we filled out the registration, gave passports for copies and found our room. Both of us showered, and I set the alarm for 4 P.M. just in case. Two hours was all that was needed, we got dressed and walked the downtown area.

There was a demonstration going on for something so we avoided that street. On the way back, the demonstration was over, the street was full of garbage, trash and litter, like at home, except for the tea party ones I attended where everything was picked up, no trash left behind, and everything looked as good if not better than when they started. (Funny how only one group in the world actually took responsibility for their actions.)

We found a local souvenir shop for our first purchases and breaking down of the large bills, this hotel didn't offer that service.

We stopped at a small café, had churros, Pepsi and a beer (Patagonia) it was good and cold, outside it was in the 80's, sunny and humid, a little different than home on the 3rd of February! The streets run in various angles, yes, we did get a little lost, but the map in the back pocket helped a lot, we asked a local teenager for directions, two blocks from the hotel, (we found out soon) she didn't have a clue.... her English was good though!

This was the night we had the "Argentine Experience". We had the desk call us a cab; the restaurant was about a half hour drive away. The city has some beautiful buildings and quite a few parks, there were people in all of the parks, and the parks were all clean, green, and welcoming.

The restaurant door was locked; we rang the bell and were greeted shortly by a young man in a chef's hat. I looked over my shoulder, and the cab driver had actually waited to see if we got in, I thought that was very nice, I gave him the thumbs up, and he waved and drove away.

We were shown to a medium sized room on the second floor, two tables, with each table set with ten place settings. We each had an apron and chef's hat we put on, we were the last to show up, and there was only one set of place settings that went unused for the night. We were served a fruity cocktail, and then the wine started, just after the beginning orientation.

During the three hours, we were served four wines, both red and white. Malbec is the signature wine of Argentina. An appetizer of trout prepared ceviche style with lemon or lime on a toast sliver.

We were then shown how to make empanadas; meat is made one way, cheese another. We were given several platters with dough rounds, cheese and sun-dried tomato stuffing, and steak tenderloin roasted for hours stuffing. We then made one each; they were labeled and taken to the kitchen to bake so that we could enjoy the fruits of our labor later. (They should be lightly brown and puffy.)

We then were taught the Spanish words for how the steak was to be prepared and placed our orders.

Argentina brags that Argentine beef is the best in the world, and we are also told that Argentinean's are affectionate, greet one another with cheek kisses rather than handshakes, men to men, women to women, and women to men. Spanish is the official language as in all of South America except for Brazil, and that is Portuguese. After World War II, 4 million Italians came to Argentina, which, we are told, contributes to the extensive use of hand gestures.

Next, we are asked to be creative, to make the most interesting empanada of the group. I made a lily flower on a lily pad; Lynn made a boob and stuffed it with cheese. Neither of us won, the winner made hers a palm tree; they were all cooked also to accompany the steaks.

Baked root vegetables were then brought out; we were taught to use lemon, and lime, with a rosemary stem to spread a lemon aioli lightly on top. Each of us had a portion; the 6-ounce steaks done perfectly to our requests were also served.

The meal finished with a cheese and fruit tart, and a cookie with caramel in the center, to be dipped in warm chocolate and coconut flakes. Yummo!!

We also were shown the mate' tea, how it is to be stirred, etc., Lynn did not care for it, I finished mine. Our three hours were up, they called cabs for everyone, and we were back at the hotel just before midnight.

Saturday morning

We were up by 6:30, dressed, and went to check out the breakfast room. This was a typical European feast: loaves of bread, cold cuts and cheeses, yogurt, fruits, cereals, loose scrambled eggs, and small sausages; of course, coffee and a small assortment of juices.

We then went to the desk and had them call us a cab. The cab arrived but was confused as to where to take us. I kept saying the cruise ship terminal, door # 4 but I don't know if cruise ship or terminal connected.

One of the desk clerks came out and tried also to explain, but we were all going nowhere. I got out the city map and pointed to an area number 4 on the map, and he agreed to take us there. He dropped us off, and we went in. Luckily, I always plan extra time. We went to an excursion office a block away, and after going back and forth, he called the main office and told us we had to go to the terminal door number 4 (sound familiar) and that we would have to get a taxi because the location was a little better than a half mile away, and we only had about 20 minutes to get there.

Off we went, as we left the yard, I flagged down a cab, gave him the slip of paper that agent had written in Spanish as to where to go, and off we went, delivered to door 14, the cab was not allowed to enter. We walked to door #4 and asked around to find the group.

We did make the 9:30 start time, but the bus didn't show up till after 10 o'clock, so we really didn't have to sweat it! The bus came, and the tour started.

The ride to the river boat was about 22 kilometers, we drove past one of the largest stadiums in this country it could seat 80,000 people; we also went through a town that is home to the national rugby team. Argentina got its name from the Latin word for silver, "argentums". We stopped at a small park, grabbed some water and gelato and used the rest rooms. We checked out the vendors but did not purchase anything. Back on the bus, drove the remaining miles to a town called Tigre. It is also known as the "Venice of Argentina".

After a half hour wait on the dock, the excursion boat arrived, off loaded, and we were allowed to board. It was hot and muggy, we opted to sit on the main enclosed lightly air-conditioned deck; many of the group still went on top in the fresh air.

Our boat was larger than most of them, some were like elongated wooden Chris-craft style inboards, open air with a canopy. There were also quite a few kayaks that you could rent to go up and down the river, along with various-sized power boats.

We passed by a group of kayaks in the water as we motored down the river and passed a rowing club dock. This is also the location of thirty-five-acre water and amusement park, the largest in Argentina, and may be in South America.

There were many homes along this river. The Tigre is also called the "Silver River" because they expected to find silver in it, but they never did. The river looks dirty and polluted but is relatively clean. The color is due to the muddy bed, runoff, and clay. The homes along the river cost $30k to $150K American dollars. There are also many tributaries where the homes are much cheaper, and there are river services /supply boats.

The professional services include doctors and dentists, as well as supply boats as in grocery boats, hardware boat, even an ice cream boat available to residents, on a weekly basis. There are two schools, a grade school and a high school serving this delta and collection of islands. The teachers and students are picked up and returned by a school boat. (The school bus didn't work well on water!)

At one time, the president had a home there; it has been encased in glass to preserve it from the heat and humidity.

Today was 35 degrees Celsius (95 F) and high humidity, summer is usually humid, and the temperature 25-35 Celsius. We did see a number of people swimming in the river by their docks. Most homeowners have boat lifts. There is quite a wake created by the excursion boats and relatively heavy traffic during the warm seasons.

We did see quite a lot of huge, half sunk rusting ocean-going ships, barges, and hulks into or next to the shoreline. Some even had 10-12-foot trees growing out of the middle of them. They may have been left there to protect the shoreline from the erosion problem they have here. (Not the prettiest sight though!!)

The bus took the freeway back to the city. We had three stops to choose from. Two were for monuments, and one was for the shopping district. Guess which one Lynn wanted? It was the shopping center, Florida Street.

We walked, shopped, and ate. We did some great shopping. The shopping district/street is about 12 blocks long. It began with a one-legged woman who was selling pens, and took off from there, we walked the entire twelve blocks plus a few more to our hotel.

Not only were there all kinds of stores, malls, and a shopping center on this street, but we also saw a chalk mural by an artist, a tango dancer who looked like she was going to promote a tango show. Her outfit was short, black, and sexy; she was in full makeup and high heels. We had seen some street people in a few of the parks; this was also where we were hit up by some beggars. The buildings around this area are beautiful, and yes, I took pictures!

We were back at the hotel a little after four, tired, hot, and done for the day. We asked the desk clerk about where and when the pick-up was for the transfer to the ship, and if we could mail a post card. They mailed the card and we are to have luggage out at 10:30, leave at 11. We went up to the room, took showers and relaxed the rest of the evening, tomorrow starts the next phase.

Sunday, we go to the ship; luggage out at 10:30, we leave the room and check out; now is the start of hurry up and wait. We struck up a conversation with a pilot in the elevator and continued our talk in the lounge. He is a native Australian and flying for Air Europe. On the elevator, he quietly stated, "Aussie, Aussie, Aussie….and waited (the proper response was to be Oui, Oui, Oui!). So, when we talked in the lounge, I asked him why he didn't respond; he told me it was another urban legend…probably promoted by "expats." So, I apologized, and he let it go.

On vacations, he takes his child to different counties; I told him about Nadine when we went to Europe with Robert and Nicky Dragon and how the school was upset that she missed school for those two weeks. We agreed that the education received in traveling to different cultures and countries is far more valuable than just book learning.

He then told us that in England, if the child is pulled out of school for travel during the time school is in session, the parents are fined every day! I guess there are closed minds everywhere! He was then called for his ride and we drifted to another couple we met at breakfast. We discussed the captains' conversation, and we were told that they had a 5-year-old who was exposed to another language and had no problem at all picking up both English and French. I commented that it would have been nice to be bilingual; too bad this stuff isn't incorporated in today's USA curriculum!

Our two busses arrived; we loaded in with our luggage and were off to the terminal. We were amazed at all the statues in this town, and the modern versus classic buildings, they even have a bottle opener building like in Shanghai! (The bottle opener building had the world's fastest elevator until 2 years ago, and it has an open space at the top with a glass floor so you can look down to the lower level and surrounding buildings.)

This is a small harbor; they were loading both a Celebrity and a Norwegian Cruise ship at once with only 5 metal detectors. It was crowded and slow, then checked into the ship line, processed through immigration, down to a bus, and brought out to the ship. Oh, it was raining now and windy. However, we were greeted at the bus by Celebrity staff with umbrellas, a very nice touch!

The rooms were not ready, so we went up to the cafeteria for lunch and started checking out where everything was.

Lunch involved a large selection of salads, cold cuts, a pizza counter, and some fish, roast beef, and pork, a really nice selection.

The rooms opened up, we met our attendant, asked for two

programs every day, rested, and unpacked for the next two weeks. This is home.

We toured the ship and found the theatre, the dining room, and the easiest way to navigate the ship.

Muster was at 5:30, Then supper, and we had a table for eight; we were the first there, waited until 6:30 (1/2 hour) for a couple of women to be seated at the table, and waited some more. Finally, Lynn got up and talked to the Maître's, and the waiter came to take our order; the other four people never showed up. We were done at 7:15; Lynn went off to watch the Super Bowl, and I went to the desk to get my internet code and set up my computer, then back to the room to diary and set up the schedule for the next day.

We weighed anchor at 8 p.m. The water was a bit choppy and brown, both at the dock and outside the harbor; at the lecture the next day, we were told that we were actually in a major river mouth on the Plate River, the mouth of which is 163 miles wide! The average depth is 15 feet, not much depth for the cruise ships; when we did finally clear the river, the water was again green. There were no forecasts in the daily program as far as weather or sea condition, thought that was odd, nothing on the ships channel either.

On the first day at sea

Last night, the ship was rocking. Lynn put on her sickness bracelet; we both slept well, up for breakfast, then off to our various activities.

The first lecture was a general picture of where, when, and what to look for on this cruise. Of the 14 days on the ship, 9 are sea days. We are told the following: some of this may be repeated later, but that is good memory enforcement!

There is a sunrise club for those who want the total experience, so I will be in that cluster; deck 4 is the best to observe in that it is the closest to the water. I asked about putting a foot on the land mass/ice but was told that ships carrying over 1500 passengers could not land passengers. However, the water under the keel is considered Antarctica, so technically, we will be there.

Only 32,000 people visit Antarctica per year, with a world of 7.5 billion. It is a rather exclusive club! Celebrity does only one cruise here a year; other cruise lines only have a few, if any.

Cape Horn was named in 1616. It is actually an island, the Island of Hornos; trivia fact: the center of this island divides the Atlantic and Pacific oceans. This is also called the "end of the World."

After we finish Cape Horn, we travel south, 56 degrees to the south, through "the Furious Fifties," known as the Drake Passage, also known as the roughest water in the world. The closest we get to the Arctic Circle is 564.50.335 degrees. The Arctic Circle is at a longitude of 566.30.000. (About 118 miles from it)

In the summertime, the ice heats up and swells. If the camera catches the red color in the ice, that is ice algae. Krill, a very small yellow shrimp-like animal, is what sustains and provides protein to Antarctic animals, from whales to birds.

If the whole of Antarctica were to melt, the oceans would rise 200-220 feet from where they are now. When the ice melts a bit in the summer, the freshwater floats on top of the salt water.

Penguins have more feathers per centimeter than any other bird (around 15) and dive the deepest, some as far as 565 meters! Emperor Penguins are the only permanent members of the penguin family that make the Antarctic their exclusive home.

The song "Yankee Doodle" by Feather in the Hat, called Macaroni, is from the macaroni penguin that has yellow feathers on top of their heads. (That is for those trivia people we know!)

Lunch, then a discussion on other birds found in the area, how to identify whales, and what to look for on our upcoming shore excursion.

I attended an information seminar in acupuncture, Lynn participated in an on-deck line dancing session, then read in one of the lounges, met for trivia with our new teammates, and then went down to the excursion office for any information on our cruise in October.

The steward there had run off all the excursions associated with that cruise. Now, all we had to do was go through the extensive list to see which ones we would be interested in and buy a few with the discount offered. I went back to the cabin, cleared e-mails, and relaxed, then dressed for dinner. This was the first dress-up night.

The ship has been rolling since we left port, the swells are 6-7 feet, people are swaying in the aisles, some are definitely showing signs of seasickness, and we are days from the "rough" seas! (Lynn is wearing her wristbands all the time now.)

Another couple showed up at our table for eight. They were very nice, but he was getting ill, and one of the women from the other couple was slowly spiraling down also; she actually left shortly after two-three forks full of her entrée. I advised the other guy to go down to the third level, amidships, and just relax for a while. He wasn't doing much better than the one that left.

The show was jammed with people. It was a 60s- 70s show, dancing, singing to all the "old" favorites, lots of fun, good memories, and smiles all around. Then, we stopped at the casino for a raffle drawing. Lynn got to pick a ticket, but neither of us won anything.

On to the Martini Lounge, where everyone checked out a set of headphones, with neon lights flashing, and danced with their partners; kind of different in that you had no idea what the other partner was listening to, and when you took off the headsets, it was quiet, but everyone was dancing…. fun!!

Tuesday, February 7th, another day at sea.

The ocean is calm, the sun is out and bright, the breeze is easy, and the temperature is in the 60s.

Today, we are passing the Peninsula Valdez. It looks like a stingray on the map, one of the easiest locations to find in South America, but we are too far out at sea to see it; the other significance of today is that we are crossing out of the continental shelf, this is where the average depth goes from 500 ft. to 3280 ft. quite a drop!!

We are also informed the longest days will be from 4:45 a.m. to 11:00 p.m., and the southern lights are rarely seen at this time. (I really never heard of the southern lights!) At the true South Pole, the polar night is 187 days long, and the polar day is 187 days long. The lowest temperature recorded is -128.6 degrees Fahrenheit, much colder than the North Pole because it is completely surrounded by water, whereas the North Pole is surrounded by land, then water to a smaller scale; it also has one of the 7 highest peaks in the world, 16,000 feet.

Antarctica is 5th in size of the seven continents. Antarctica is the highest, driest, coldest, windiest place in the world and the largest wilderness on earth.

There are Southern Lights, also called Aurora Austral, but they are rarely seen from the Earth. They are easily seen from space, though. The landing on Antarctica is rare except for scientists; since we will be in the territorial waters for a few days, we can claim to have been here.

The ice in Antarctica is 800,000 years old, determined by core samples; Antarctica holds 68% of the world's fresh water and 90% of all the ice in the world. Antarctica is both the driest and wettest place on earth and the windiest; winds have been measured to be over 200 mph, and 70% of the world's freshwater is trapped in the ice here.

Animals: This is home to many. The longest migratory birds are the Sooty Shearwater, which migrates 40,000 miles round trip, and the Arctic Tern, 91,000 miles round trip per year; given this bird has an average lifespan of 30 years, it flies about 2.4 million kilometers in a lifetime. There are also albatrosses, penguins, whales, seals, sea lions, and much more. I will touch on these as we observe them, provided for by the food of the ocean.

We are also to look for Mirages like those in the deserts and halos that are called "sun dogs."

In the afternoon, we attended the two regular trivia sessions with our team of six, played officers vs. guests in Musical Madness, attended the Solomon Jaye show at the theatre, a solo very talented singer, and went up to the Lounge to the Groove' 60's Interactive Theme Party with the dancers and singers on the dance floor…very fun. Looking over the ocean east, we saw more than 100 fishing boats, all brightly lit; these were squid trawlers, and the strong light attracts the squid for them to net. Never knew that before!

Wednesday

This day is another sea day, but tomorrow we actually go into port, Ushuaia, Argentina, the end of the world! It is the end of the Andes Mountain range and the Pan American Highway.

Attended two more back-to-back lectures, identification of different whales, birds, and penguins, the history of Cape Horn, that it actually took some ships up to 3 months to round it (Blame Australia for the weather)

We were also given the history of the National Park Service, started by President Grant, with Yellowstone and the Grand Canyon. This set the precedence of the government preserving lands for the population of the country for ours and other countries.

The lecture included the retreats in glaciers in Alaska, where one major glacier retreated 35 miles from 1778 to 1892. He pushed for global warming but didn't offer an answer for the "science" that claimed global cooling 40 years ago and that there was virtually no fossil fuel burning in the 1800s to cause the glacial retreat. He also brought up the banning of DDT but then mentioned that some mosquitoes had started to become immune and that there are still quite a few people dying in the world due to Malaria. Selective preaching, but what do you expect from a retired park ranger?

The sea otter has the densest fur of all animals (the penguins are birds, and they have feathers), which makes them comfortable in very cold water. Otters also sleep floating on their back if the seas are rough; they entangle themselves in seaweed to stay in one place.

I then joined Lynn for a class on cooking a perfect steak. The main criterion is the slow defrosting of the meat and the quality of the cut. Try coffee grounds as seasoning along with favorites next time.

Another method for checking the condition of the steak: Inside the bottom of the thumb raw, touch the thumb to the first finger, medium rare, the second finger to the thumb, medium; middle finger and top of the thumb, medium well and why would you go any further?

At just before noon, we entered a fog bank; we could only see about 200 feet, and everything above the ocean green was grey.

That evening, Lynn was a contestant in a singing contest. She was up on stage with seven other guests. The game entailed singing a song when you were pointed at, sometimes you sang a few words, sometimes a few verses. This is a quick-fire game. If you repeat a song, you lose. Lynn made it to second place! What a gal! What she won was a Celebrity hat and applause from the rest of us.

February 9th, Ushuaia.

Ushuaia, Argentina, located at the southern end of Tierra del Fuego Island, "The End of the World," 750 miles north of Antarctica. (There are a few communities to the south, but none has a current population of more than 2000.)

The town is located just inside an inlet along the Beagle Canal. Hungry? The restaurants here specialize in lamb and spider crabs.

We docked a little after 9:00 in the morning, and we met in the theatre at 8:30. The crowd just to get in was pure mayhem; the line goes back through the Casino that is a midships; every one after three days at sea, want to get off the ship! And yes, people try to cut in, blend in, and most in line don't say anything, which just encourages it.

Finally, we get our bus assigned and sit in a full theatre. I still don't get what is happening on this ship; the dining room is very crowded, the handling of this excursion/port is poor and not well organized, as agreeing with another fellow passenger, they "kind of cheapen out" on this, fewer waiters, entertainers, and on-board options.

We are one of the last on the bus, so we get the back seat; there is not an empty seat on this bus! It is a good 45-minute drive to Tierra del Fuego National Park; we stop once for 20 minutes for a photo opportunity on the coast that turns into a half-hour due to a couple that thought the time was "too short." …

This is the end of the Pan American Highway; pictures of signs in English and Spanish, note this. The park has several varieties of Beech trees. As we progress south, trees disappear due to the winds; even here, there are many trees with trunk widths of 3-4 feet uprooted. The reason is that the root systems are shallow. The soil to bedrock is thin, thereby having no support. In the trees are balls of mistletoe, which may have different tones of green and brown.

We finish after three stops of landscape pictures to board a powered catamaran. This, too, was at capacity. Nice views; you have to see the photos I took, including snowcapped mountains, glaciers, and ocean.

After an hour, we come upon an island (actually two) that has the promised wide life: Imperial Sags, small penguins, and seals, tons of them! Yes, pictures were taken, and then after circling the islands, we came back to our original port and docked forward of the cruise ship. The reason for the crowding is today, there are five cruise ships in this small port!

We take a short walk into town, we apply for our "End of the World" official certificates (They ran out of paper ones, so they will e-mail one to us), buy souvenirs (nothing is cheap in this town), and find a mailbox to send the postcards. The certificates were e-mailed on 12-02-18…better than never!!

There was a craft stall alley we walked through, and I posed with a prisoner and jailer on the sidewalk. This town was also home to a severe and desolate prison that closed 40 years ago, similar to Devils Island, Alcatraz, and others, now converted to a maritime museum.

That was enough; we walked the quarter mile back to the ship and had an hour to rest before our 6 PM dinner time.

After dinner, a "one minute to beat the officer activity," a juggler show, then a Motown review in the forward lounge.

Friday, February 10th

We were up at 05:30. We are at the Cape! It is misty, the temperature is in the upper 40's, and the seas are relatively calm. I joined the early risers for the event; there are about 100 people in the forward lounge, all of the window seats are taken, and coffee and pastries have been set out. An introduction of where we are and what to look for is on the loudspeaker: average yearly temperature is 42 F, 278 days a year some form of precipitation, including snow, a year, no more trees.

The lighthouse is pointed out to us; the albatross monument sits to the right of the lighthouse. The Albatross Monument is a dedication to the sailors who lost their lives crossing and buried at sea, something to mark their loss. It is two triangles pointing upward. It is called the Albatross monument because the sailors believed that God sent the albatross to carry their souls to heaven.

This is the most hazardest crossings in the world; between 1850 and 1900, more than 100 ships have been lost here. Many ships took weeks to get past this point. Sails ripped apart, sails coated with ice, and waves exceeded 20 meters (65 feet) in height! When attempting to sail south to bypass the difficulties, the wind and current keep getting worse, from "the roaring 40s to the furious 50s, to the screaming 60s. The losses included engine ships.

I moved from inside to outside. It is misting, lots of people hogging the rails just looking (after they took their pictures!) and taking an occasional picture. I travel from side to side, go up in front of the ship, and as high as I can go, grab a quick shot when I can get close to the railing.

The ship doughnuts around the Cape for an hour so everyone could see it, then we headed south to Antarctica.

As soon as we clear the Cape, the swells increase in size, and the ship starts to sway a bit again; let's hope our luck holds and the seas stay relatively calm. A few albatrosses come and go, but that is all the wildlife we see.

I attended three 45-minute lectures, one regarding rescuing trapped ships with an icebreaker. The main thing the Ice breaker does is bring fuel and provisions and then lead the ship out; it is not uncommon for the ice to reform within 6 minutes after the ship passes.

We were asked to guess the time when we saw the first of Antarctica, Snip Island. One of the lecturer's children, about a 6-year-old girl, handed out post-it notes for those who wanted to guess the time; she was very cute and took her job very seriously, making sure everyone who wanted a guess got a note. On the note, we needed to put the following:

Cabin #   6064

Name: Noah Borkenhagen

Time: 04:35, 37 secs

He gave us the following parameters: 270-350 miles, average speeds the last three times: 24.3 miles per hour. Turns out I was off by about 3 hours!

The early afternoon talk was during lunch hour; the "herd" was feeding, and so only a little over 10 of us were there. I felt kind of bad. He was interested in telling us about his progress and experiences as a Hollywood screenwriter and actor.

He did bring up the Carter years and the oil embargo, which led us to try to become energy independent, what the young people do not understand or care about being innovative with environmental activism.

We went to another trivia game and watched a version of the Newlywed game. One of the couples had met only two weeks ago and decided to take a cruise together, we thought that was odd…and, yes, they lost, only knowing someone for two weeks doesn't really prepare one for questions regarding habits and relatives but they were fun!!

We were joined by another couple, a retired Air Force Colonel, and now the dinner table is full! That night was a production number with all the singers and dancers, very well put together. A trapeze act was incorporated, and it was lots of fun.

Saturday, February 11th

Got an e-mail from Tiffany regarding Ma setting off her alarm. The rescue squad came and took her to Wheaton; the doctor says it may have been caused by the blood thinner he prescribed. I thanked Tiffany and forwarded her Ted's email to keep him in the loop.

Noah

This morning, we go into the Antarctica waters, the Schollart Channel, and Paradise Bay; it is heavily clouded outside at 06:00 a.m. By 08:15, the fog had cleared up again. This is one of the two harbors in Antarctica. This harbor is inactive. Paradise Bay was named by the Whalers. With calm, sheltered waters, it was an ideal place to butcher and process the whales.

We are coming to a few places where we should see some whales, seals, and penguins. We had some very nice land shots, including some various glaciers. We passed several icebergs and saw the blue color on some and red on others. Some folks saw whale spouts, and some saw some penguins skipping over the waves. I was all over the ship, both sides, top, $4^{th,}$ and 5th decks, too, but just landscapes. The water temperature and the air temperature are the same, 30 F, the seas are calm, and the sun peaked through for an hour or two, then back to haze and fog.

The cold and wind have their effect; our next viewing is Elephant Island (named for the elephant seals that live there), which is from 1-4 tomorrow, so no early rise for us tomorrow!

Factoid for today: Sunlight starts to fade around 200 meters (656 feet) below the surface of the ocean. At 1,000 meters (3,280 feet), practically no light can penetrate.

Sunday February 12th, Antarctica. I put the room thermostat two notches below the highest temperature, and it is comfortable. As we travel east last night through the morning, fog and mist prevail, hard to see farther than a few hundred feet, islands are there, we just can't see them. This morning the temperature is mid 30's and windy c-c-c-cold!

The first lecture (the theatre was full!) is on the discovery of Antarctica, attributed to Captain Cook in 1773, who also discovered South Georgia Island, and the Sandwich Islands (named after the Duke of Sandwich). England at that time did not have a Navy, so they commissioned ships and captains to explore for England.

The news of an abundance of seals here led to a flurry of ships hunting seals, and in 10 years all of the seals for practical purposes were wiped out, estimated population of 100,000.

Elephant Island is home of two types of penguins, the Macaroni, and the chin strapped, along with the elephant seal. I saw a few very small penguin heads bobbing, as they swam away, believing the ship is a predator, but still no pictures! I struck a deal with a friend on board to send me those of animals she caught with her telephoto lens as we watched, came in to warm up, watched, went in and so on!!

We did stop the ship a little after 2 pm to the edge of some sheet ice, this stuff forms at a rate of 2 miles per hour! We were also on the other side of the island where the Shanklin experience occurred, where the ship from the Shanklin expedition got caught in the ice, crushed, and the captain, took a small boat with a few from the crew to find help, and two months later returned to rescue his crew. We can also see three glaciers, I would have never thought I would say "oh, just another glacier" especially when it was only last year when we stepped on our very first one in Jasper, Canada!

In the afternoon, we started to attend a seminar about where art treasures went, but we couldn't get interested. We then went hunting for materials for Lynn's egg drop entry, mine are mostly acquired, tomorrow I will get most of the rest I need, then the day after the balance; can't wait to see if my over-engineered project works!

After supper, we entered a guess the carat weight…I was the closest! I guessed 247 carats, actual was 232, everyone else were almost 100 over (one guy) or 100 carats under (all the rest). What did I win? A tiny gold charm…….

Tonight's show was a piano player, good show, lots of audience participation, a stand-up performance.

Noah

Monday, 02-13-14, another day at sea. The first lecture was a brief on what to expect on the Falkland Islands tomorrow, seems they have lots of penguins and seals. After the Falkland war of the United Kingdom versus Argentina, the people on the Island voted to be a territory of England, under British rule.

We are told the major places to go, and what to look for, we have left the Arctic Ocean, From Schollart Channel to past Elephant Island a total of 469 miles, or 754 kilometers, so I believe we qualify as being "in" Antarctica.

Antarctica doubles in size in the winter, and although the Park ranger disagrees, we are currently overdue for a "cold spell" and just shifting weather patterns may be what we are experiencing; I guess it depends on how open minded you are, or who is funding your beliefs.

Penguins actually predate dinosaurs, haven't changed in eons…I guess they are the perfect bird! Penguins were known as having only one mate, but it seems that after coming home, cleaning up the nest, and setting the table, if she doesn't return after a while someone else can take her place………. They live about 30 years if they are lucky, some whales live over 200 years old, dated by the weapons found in the remains when they die.

Attended the Art auction to get our "free" print, many items over $1500; some over $15,000, yes dollars!! A set of trivia games, I put caution tape across friend's door, even told the desk, but no coordination, the room steward took it down before they both saw it; however, one did see, and I took the picture.

The comedian at the show was very good, clean jokes and an easy style. We are promised weather in the 50's tomorrow, what a difference that will be! Our excursion leaves first thing tomorrow at 07:45, so we set the alarm and went to bed after the comedian.

Tuesday, February 14th, the Falkland Islands, we were promised penguins. We got up early to monitor going into the harbor, it is shallow, and so we have to be ferried in. I looked for the penguins or seals promised, and may have seen some, but they were only specks, even with the telephoto maxed; just another disappointment.

We do lower anchor out in the bay, there is another cruise ship behind us, and so it will be hectic at the dock. Breakfast was nice; the constant opening of the aft deck doors was tolerable due to the 50's weather. We slow walked the perimeter looking for wild life....... nothing. We did see the squid boats up close; they are all Chinese, and the nets are continuous fore to aft with tons of lights mounted high on both sides.

We are on the first tender (that is a first!), and it only takes twenty minutes to get to the dock. A bus is waiting for us and we are told that the ride to the farm is an hour there, an hour back, and two hours there. Our guide has a very clever and dry sense of humor, very entertaining, providing information on the Falkland's and other snip-its.

He tells us that the war of 1812 between the USA and England, it wasn't the English that burned down our white house it was the Canadian attachment, more stuff not learned in books....

The roads are very narrow, just two lanes, so we do have to stop several times to let others go the other way or pass our bus. The first roads transverse the island was cut in 1980! Most of them gravel, small stretches have asphalt. It is clear, sunny, and in the upper 50's, we are told that yesterday the winds were so high, that one of the squid trawlers was grounded.

The main industries of these islands are fishing, agriculture (65 farms), and tourism. The tourism caters to 100 cruise ships a year, us and the other cruise ship comprised of 2% of this year's tourist season!

We arrived at the farm and walk out to the peat area, as we walk over some uneven bog; I noticed small plants close to the ground, with tiny red berries. Took a picture to share, then went to watch how peat is harvested, cut with a "peat" shovel into bricks, and tossed up on top for the ground to dry for at least three days, then collected and placed inside a sheltered area to age for two months. The deeper the peat, the more the compression, and the better the burn, these bogs were formed by the glaciers.

We then moved to a pen where some sheep were waiting for us. The owner of the farm introduced us to her border collie, (we could pet her if we wanted to, yes, I did!), then she unleashed her dog, and told her to bring in the sheep, the dog jumped into action, she walked over to a pen gate, opened it up, and blew a whistle, within three minutes the sheep were in the pen, WOW!

Next, we were taken to a shearing barn, we are shown a wool baler, a bale weighs 200 kilos, and it takes 40-45 sheared sheep wool to make a bale.

We are treated to a complete sheering of a sheep, it took him a little more than five minutes to shave the wool, and the sheep was well aware when he was finishing and started fighting to get loose. When he released the sheep, the animal bolted into the chute to join his buddies, all the wool was gathered, and placed on a table to determine the grade, A- Fine, b-Medium, and C-Coarse.

All the sheep have color tags on their ears; this tells everyone the age of the sheep. The land is so bad here, pasture so sparse that a common ranch is 19,000 acres! (Most of the land reminds us of Iceland, barren and with very little grazing land.) We tour the farmhouse, are treated to tea and cookies, walk around the garden, visit the two horses, find whale bones used as decoration, an extensive flower garden, and visit with the family regarding the windmill for electricity and living in the Island, this is the third generation on this farm, and she is 65 years old!

Back on the bus, we are told that the tax rate here is 21% on all wages, 26% on wages over 60,000, there is no VAT tax, but he was unclear as to property tax.

Trees are few and far between, few higher than three meters high (about 9 feet) and all the shrubs and trees are bent due to the strength and constant winds.

The hills all have stone runs, these are "rivers" of rock created by the glaciers, and the thaw and refreezing of the land. There is a lot of red colored stone, the problem, is when that stone is exposed to the atmosphere, it bleaches. There is one traffic light on the island, and yes it was red on the way out…. go figure!

We passed an area where boots are displayed on sticks; one boot is to represent "I will be back" two boots, "I'm outta here!"

Back in town, we get a map, and buy tickets to "Go to Gypsy Cove" to finally see some penguins. It is only a ten-minute wait, and we are on the mini bus and taken out to the cove in a quick 15-minute drive. When we arrive, we see a long line of folks waiting to go back, a concern, in that the last tender leaves at 5 P.M., and it is 2:30 now. Lynn and I walk the path to the first viewing point, down below, about 100 yards is a group of the southern Rock Hopper penguins. It turns out this is as close as we can get due to penguin protection, and the possibility of land mines.

Lynn decides to head back to get a place in line for the return, I continue up the path, find another penguin colony, again over 100 yards away, and also some nesting wild geese. No seals or whales in sight. On the way, back down the path, I did find one little penguin, he was molting, standing by himself, and posing for pictures…got him!!

I joined Lynn in the line, she was only about a third from the front, and we were back in town by 3:30. I walked over to see if I could get a picture of the church with the whale bone structure in front, and maybe find a flightless steamer duck or two, but none close enough to get a photo.

We checked out some yards with native flowers and plants,

checked out the souvenir shops, and joined the line forming for the tenders back to the ship.

This is dress up night, poached scallops, lobster tail on the menu, and tomorrow is egg drop day and acupuncture, should be interesting. We are skipping the show, catching up on journaling, repacking, evaluation each of our egg drop plans and bed before 10:30!!

Wednesday 02-15-17; a lazy at sea day. The night was overcast so the Southern Cross was not visible. We were warned about high waves and rough seas, but that did not happen. The morning greeted us with bright sun and a 5-10 mph cool breeze. We got up late today, didn't finish breakfast till after nine. Gathered the remaining stuff for our egg drop except for the eggs, went to a trivia, then I had an acupuncture session for pain and diet. Agreed to another session, met Lynn for collection of raw eggs, finished our delivery devices and went to lunch.

After lunch, not much going on, went back to the room for a little siesta and then, after three, headed down to the egg drop!

Results of the egg drop.... Lynn, missed the target, but both eggs survived, mine hit the target, but BOTH eggs broke, I was devastated! One of our new friends did win; he made a contraption out of straws! It was in target, and both eggs survived! Afterword, played two trivia performed badly on both, dinner, attended a brief on the port tomorrow, and watched a "liars club" performance which was quite good. Journaled the day, the one bright spot was the magnificent sundown, which I did catch, tomorrows another day.

Thursday, February 16th, f. The port we are at early is Puerto Madryn, Argentina, and we dock before 7 A.M.

Our excursion is to the Punta Luona sheep ranch, and a visit to a seal beach. We left the theatre and out to the bus, all loaded and rolling at 8:20. On the dock are pallets of aluminum ingots, it seems this port and Argentina are the largest exporter of aluminum in the world! Half of the production goes to the U.S.A., the balance to Europe. This port is natural harbor that is also a teeming collection of marine animals, including the southern elephant seal, southern sea lion, dolphins, killer whales, right whales, penguins, and various shore and sea birds.

Factoid: Oceans are home to as many as 100 million species- from the largest animal that has ever lived on earth, the Blue whale, to the tiniest bacteria.

Our first stop is about 10 miles out of town. It is a bluff overlooking two bays, both have extensive seals, albatrosses, other sea birds and penguin colonies, they again are about 1000 yards away. The paved roads stop about 5 miles out of town, then two-lane gravel, not really suitable for a bus, but after the Falkland Islands, we are getting used to dust and poor roads. The land is barren, very similar to the Falkland's also, nothing really but scrub, sparse scrub, and nothing else. After 20 minutes at the bluff, we reloaded the bus and off to the ranch.

The ranch like the one on the Falkland's, is in the middle of nowhere; the ranch consists of three relatively small buildings, on several thousand acres of scrub. This is simple country, and it shows. We have about twenty minutes to walk around, use the rest room facilities, and pet the sheep dogs, take pictures of a pet baby Guanaco (like a small llama) and pose with one of the owners dressed like a Gaucho.

We are all herded into a shearing area with bleachers. Three sheep are brought in from the corral by 12 volunteers. (Four per sheep) The sheering station is equipped with four stations. An employee then proceeds to sheer on sheep. We are told males produce thicker and more wool; females produce less (5kg. vs. 4kg.), and the wool is courser. Only one ewe per year, they are shorn once a year after sheering, and they are given a shot of antibiotics and vitamins to help them recover from the ordeal.

Noah

The farmers here also no longer sheer their own sheep, but rely on professionals that do the complete herd, more effectively, both in cost, and quality. A sheep is good for 7 years of wool production. The biggest threat to the herd is feral domesticated dogs. Since sheep are grazers, and the types of plants they eat are not really compatible with their tooth structure, they uproot the entire plant, when the females give birth, they can produce more than 2 liters of milk a day, and sheep produce more manure than cows.

After the second sheep is sheered, we were treated to a crescent roll made with ham and cheese baked inside, a beignet, and a fruit-filled empanada. This with coffee or the special tea they called Mata. I liked the tea, and Lynn doesn't.

We also watched a cook who butchered a sheep, cut his own wood, and set up the meat for roasting in an open fire.

Interesting people, answered all the questions we had, we were all full from lunch, time to head back to the ship. We arrived to the dock about 1:30, and the shuttle bus was still on the dock so we then loaded on to the shuttle bus and took the 20-minute ride to town. We explored several souvenirs shops and caught the next bus back to the dock. There are a number of ships beached and rusting hulls, but it does not seem to concern the town.

On the ship, two more games of Trivia, (we stink), then I had a very good conversation with one of the friends of our trivia partners who was sent to Israel at the age of 16 to join a cabal. I needed to find out about this life style, and her progression.

It seems these are the purest forms of socialism; there are fewer and fewer because when there are no longer rich or rich sponsors, the cabal fails. (This coincides with the Margaret Thatcher phrase: "socialism works until the outside money is gone")

Her mother was also raised by a Kabul and she chimed in that that was much different than her daughter's experience.

Educating Noah...Travelin'

In Israel women, most serve in the military for 2 years, boys, 3 years. The exception for women is if they have children or are pregnant. She is now a pastry chef and is engaged to be married in Israel. She is very self-confident, and she agrees that a good part of the confidence came from being in the military.

Dinner, watched a game show put on by the crew vs. guests, take-off, where guests perform with crew. Then watched an excellent "3 Almost Tenors" show. This was one of the best shows and following that was the Dancing with the Stars where crew members are the stars, very entertaining, very energetic, and one of our new-found friends ended up in the top three.

Friday, we are at sea all day, another acupuncture session, talked to one of the presenters regarding photos, and photo share, three games of Trivia, an amateur show with the crew and guests singing or dancing, even an interpretive dance by a Chinese in full outfit.

Congratulated our friend on his placing in the Dancing with the Stars, production show after dinner, just bounced around the ship, the temperature is in the 60's and full sun, great day for a cruise!

Saturday February 16th, our last port before returning to Buenos Aires; Montevideo, Uruguay.

We dock at 8:30 and are on the tour bus by 9:30. This was a tour of the town highlights, and shopping at the end. We are told that we must be back on the ship by 4:00 P.M.; the tour is about 4 hours, so there should be no problem at all!

We have a very friendly and informative guide, who talks rather fast, with a Uruguayan accent, but we can make out most of what he says. There are no natives left in this country, there were only about 20,000 to begin with, but with the European invasions, the introduction of alcohol, syphilis, and venereal disease, they were wiped out completely. Uruguay is now 100% immigrants, the only country in South America that is 100% immigrants. There are 14 million cows, 3 million people, and half of the country's population lives here in Montevideo.

It is warm (mid 70's) and humid (upper 80's). The flag of this country is blue and white, with a sun of yellow in the upper right corner.

These folks, as in other lower South American countries, have siesta from 2P.M. to 6 P.M., they start at 10 A.M., and close around 8 p.m., then go out or eat late.

Everything is organic in this country, no pesticides, no fertilizer needed due to the natural cow pie fertilizer. Speaking of fertilizer, everything here is just center of right, or center left politically. The president is a medical doctor, so health is promoted, and there is a heavy tax on cigarettes.

Mate', as in Argentina, is the drink (tea) of choice. You carry a hot thermos with you and your Mate' cup to keep drinking as long as you want. Our guide had a Mate' Watch, which sent up a high flame when a button was pushed. This is to warm your tea.

At restaurants, you have to ask for bread and any condiments, as they are otherwise not provided.

The one tall modern building is their telephone company.

Abortion is legal and free, but you must be evaluated by a shrink first. We are told that Uruguay people are very laid back and almost consider working on weekends a crime. The economy is growing vs. Brazil and Argentina because there is much more corruption in those governments than here, and they welcome Venezuelans along with others that want to come. (For the last 6 months Venezuela economy is in very bad condition.)

The health care is free to everyone; no I.D. is required for care. More than 50% of the citizen's work for the government, the government owns more than 1/2 of the economy and industry. The minimum wage here is $450-750 per month; those that graduate from college have an additional tax on their income to help others graduate from college. Apartments on the ocean run $250,000-$350,000; but just a half hour drive the suburbs, small houses run as low as $60-65,000. Everyone loves to have their own garden, so most if not, all private homes have gardens. "A house without a garden is not a home".

Marijuana is legal here, but it is no longer "cool" and since there is such a stigma set on smoking here, there is little use any longer.

Living with someone, male or female, provides the same benefits as those that are married; everyone is required to vote in elections, and all high schools are voting places.

We stopped at a number of places in the city, including the park, with a local market, a number of statues, high end neighbor hoods and middle-class neighborhoods, again, all very clean and neat. Some graffiti but not as much as we have seen in most other countries.

The beach here is almost as long, and as clean as that one in Rio. We also stopped on a bluff where a sculpture was dedicated to H. G. Wells. In the trees were large nests, these were parrot nests, and we could hear them screeching. There are a number of Casinos here also, and "there are more casinos than schools."

Beef is the choice of food," fish" is everything that comes out of the sea except tuna, so everything is easily classified, but you may get something from the sea you are not familiar with when ordering "fish".

The waters are not heavily fished, there is a problem with illegal fishing by the Chinese and Korea; they are addressing this, the harbor has a number of ships half sunk and abandoned rusting away, not worth the cost of scrapping.

The Tango was originally a very sexual dance, and only

performed by men, but women did get involved and it is the dance in this country. Everyone seems to be carrying their mate' thermos and cup, it is like a tea, and you will see many pictures with the locals holding these items...

We are dropped off two blocks from the ship, to explore one more local market and eatery. The meat is so tender, this and Argentina beef has got to be the best in the world.

We checked out the booths and shops, and then followed the green path back to the ship. We had a quick lunch, and then organized everything so that we could pack; we leave the ship Sunday morning at 07:30, luggage out by 8:30 P.M. Saturday. One final show, then everyone off after our final night on board.

We were up at 6, dressed, checked all the drawers again, the safe, and closet. The luggage was set out early last night so all we had are back packs. Breakfast was crowded since all the late sleepers didn't this morning.

We were to meet in one of the lounges at 7:15, at five after 7 the line to check in was all the way out in the hall, and no directions, of course since all the excursions were to be handled here?? There were no seats. I deposited Lynn in a corner with the carry-ons, got in line and got our group stickers, rejoined Lynn and waited for our group to be called.

We were the third group called and made our way to our bus. As soon as everyone was on, we took off to our first stop, a cemetery, per our guide, "The Rich Peoples Cemetery". This was an exclusive mausoleum cemetery, beautiful marble, stone and wrought iron, including steeples and statues, peeking inside, all you see are caskets on top another. We walk the cobblestone roads peek in a few that have open internal doors, and then shown Eva Peron' (Evita) mausoleum. Her grave was the only one that had fresh flowers. Her body was in Italy for a number of years and then brought back to her beloved

Argentina. At one site, a young girl's bronze was posted with her dog. Like in Russia, rubbing a dog statue nose mean good luck, the top of the dog's nose was rubbed bright bronze, the rest a weathered dark brown.

Back on the bus, we are told more about Argentina and its people. We are told there is no middle, no grey areas; you are either right or wrong! (Or left and wrong??) A year or so ago, the government stopped issuing dollars, similar to India now, due to black money, and corruption. 10 Argentine pesos are worth 67 cents American, where the Argentine Peso used to be par with the dollar.

The second stop was an artist, crafty area with shops and an open-air vending park, it was only 9:30 when we arrived, and in this culture 10:00 is actually the common opening time, so many of the stores were not open, only one vendor in the open area. This was one of the places all the tourist busses stopped, it is a four-block area, and as we walked through it more and more of the shops opened. I didn't find the souvenirs to be cheap, but I guess that is how they make their money!

We were there for about 45 minutes, by the time we left most of the shops were open, many carrying the same items at about the same price, all converted to American dollars when asked, and all had American dollar change. There was no parking for the busses, so when they dropped us off, the bus disappeared, in total, there were 8 busses that stopped and unloaded while we were there, and our bus showed up promptly at 10:15.

On the bus to our next stop, more information was provided. The river that flows through to the ocean is bragged by both the Uruguay's and Argentinean's as being the widest mouth river in the world, it is a combination of salt and fresh water, in that it does empty in to the Atlantic Ocean.

To attend the universities, it costs a family $500.00 per month or about 4000 pesos; there are no dorms, so everyone goes to the university that is the closest to home, and commutes.

Half way to our third stop we pulled into a souvenir shop and gas station for a potty break (we are an old bunch that cannot hold water long!) As we are starting to exit, there were three busses ahead of us, and a line for the rest rooms was almost out the opposite door when we arrived, after everyone did their business and did some additional shopping (about 20 minutes) we got back on the bus, there were two new busses that came after us and one more pulling in when we left.

There were several toll booths we went through, but after this last one, we were pulled over by the military, a soldier sauntered over, and entered the bus, walked down the aisle to the back, looking at everyone, then left giving the guide the O.K.; we were not told why we were stopped, just that this was military, not police....

We soon reached the La Bompa Province, Gaucho territory. As we are closing in on our third and final stop before the Airport, we are told that the gaucho dance was basically done by men only, then women were added years ago, very similar to the Tango; Fancy foot work, a high-energy fancy and dramatic dance.

The number of cattle has declined 50%, since the best cuts are exported the poorer cuts sold locally, the government imposed a heavy tax on the exported beef (35%) to incentivize the growing of soy beans rather than raise beef cattle 20 years ago, but when the prices for soy beans went down, the beef export tax was lowered again (15%) to incentivize exporting beef again, so the cattle population is again on the rise.

Unemployment has improved the last 10 years; it is now standing at only 10%.

The national drink Mate' tea is a mixture of herbs, which are placed in a mate' cup, and drunk through a metal straw that has a filter on the lower spoon shaped end. The guide passed around a cup of it, invited everyone to take a sip, it is customary here in Argentina, to drink from the same straw as a sign of friendship, most just pretended to sip without putting their lips on the straw, but a few of us including me tried it, it tasted like a strong herbal tea.

At the ranch, we are greeted at the gate by a gaucho in gaucho dress and horseback for pictures, as we enter the gate, we are served water, or wine, plus a small empanada, there is a small stage set up, and we are treated to a gaucho dance, then a couple dance, then the gaucho and his partner invited different folks from the crowd to dance with them, about ½ of the folks did turn them down, but a number did dance to a dance similar to a waltz.

We are then invited to walk through the house, and back to the corral where you could either ride in a wagon or horseback, about 30% were interested, and the rest watched. After everyone that wanted to ride was done, we were shown to a large dining hall. We are started out with rolls, wine, sparking water, and beer, a tapenade (a bit spicy for most) was supplied for spreading on the rolls.

Then came the food, starting with potato salad, salad, beef, and chicken, large portions served to each plate, and more if asked, then a dessert. Half way through the meal, we were treated to more dancing on a stage.

I ducked out after the main course, with a couple of rolls, to feed the peacocks, ducks, and chickens walking around outside. At one time, I had over thirty birds waiting for a treat!

Everything was done by 3:00 PM; we woke our drivers up to leave (you know it was their siesta time!) and off we went to the airport. It was a three-quarter hour drive to the airport. Some left in terminal 3, others terminal 1, to the guide's credit, he said we could get our luggage and load it on to the bus, and they would drive us there (about four blocks). The luggage for all the excursions was outside the third terminal, all the luggage which we all tagged 1-7 was mixed, complete disorganization; people trying to get their luggage out, others directing spouses, and others confused. Another failure of Celebrity!

I did locate our luggage, brought it back to the bus, along with the other half of the bus. We were driven to the #1 terminal, and looked for the kiosks to expedite boarding, but the ones I looked at did not have Delta. I started to walk away, but then a Delta representative approached. She said she could help and assisted in getting us pre-booked at the desk.

Then into another line, about 30 people deep, one priority and the other common folk. What time was it? A little after 4; all the luggage agents were in a meeting, after another half hour, wheel chair and people with kids were formed in a separate line for pre-priority, and the line behind us going back 2/3rds of the terminal, the meeting was ended, and they started checking us in.

After getting boarding passes, I went to the security check, shoes, off, electronics in separate trays, and yes, I was wanded only one knee showed up?? Then, to immigration, another set of lines, I got a smile out of the agent, only two attempts with the thumb to make it work, then to the gate.

We waited about two hours, and then 17 agents came to the gate area, set up tables, and set up for the lines where, as we finally started to load, all carry-ons were inspected again. Lynn asked, and the agent said they were looking for liquids??

The ten-hour flight back, even with the extended space, was not pleasant, the guy sitting next to me hogged the arm rest, and if I leaned out toward the aisle, I was bumped and rubbed as crew and passengers passed. (at least it was an aisle seat).

Atlanta, we breezed through immigration, but had to collect our luggage, then took our luggage to domestic to drop off for the flight to Chicago. Took the subway to the domestic terminal, found our gate, and waited another two hours. We were assigned a window and aisle seat, the person sitting between us was very nice, but the seats were again very narrow, we were assigned group 3, this means we were the last group to enter the plane, and yes, no room in the bins above, so we had to store under the seat ahead of us. It was not comfortable, the guy in front of me tilted his seat back, my knees were touching his chair, to begin with, and no room under his seat because of my carry on.... but the flight was just over an hour, and we were back to Chicago in no time.

The person between us was a stewardess flying standby. She has been a stewardess for 30 years, loved the job, and admitted the airlines have gotten progressively worse, especially after 911. She remarked that it was nice that we had traveled outside the U.S., and smelled good?? And that her husband and she had never traveled outside the U.S. Go figure!!

We disembarked, got our luggage, went to the bus stop, and within 10 minutes were on the bus to home, when we got to the bus terminal, Lynn tried to use her phone, it didn't work, so the Uber ride we had planned on didn't happen, the bus terminal agent called us a cab, and we were home at 1:00 P.M.

We brought up the luggage, took showers, and a nap, we had been flying or in airport 22 hours; another adventure accomplished!

Noah

It will be a while before we will be eating escargot in garlic butter, and bagel with lox for breakfast. I even saw Lynn ordering the snails one evening…go figure!

We both went through after travel with-drawl (ATW), jet lag, cough, malaise; then back to life.

I was to get my right shoulder replaced, called a radical replacement, it takes 4-6 months to schedule, then you have series of tests, and consultations. I had a problem with low red blood count, anemia, so they scheduled me for a colonoscopy, and an EGD. They found a 1.5 cm ulcer in my stomach (probably from the Naproxen (Advil)) for the pain.

I checked with Ortho and Ambulatory Surgery Friday morning to confirm the Surgery on Monday at 9:30 am; They confirmed and said they would call if the time was changed.

I showed up at Monday at 8 AM; Lynn had dropped me off, only VA I.D. on me; no jewelry, no wallet, and an extra change of clothes, and off she went to work. I reported in, the receptionist said I wasn't on the schedule, and that someone else had my slot. I was a bit upset; she had the surgeon come out and talk to me. He told me that since I had that ulcer and that I was a bit anemic he did not want to fix my shoulder, oh, and he was sorry he didn't call me to cancel.

I now needed to get back into the que; I went back down to the Ortho department to talk. In the VA, you need to schedule a consult with a doctor, I got an appointment in 6 weeks. I also discussed my left hip, and maybe get that replaced first. I told her I had requested another hip x-ray with the pre-shoulder surgery x-ray, and she also told me I would need a pelvic x-ray. She set that up right away, I thanked her, got the x-ray and then went down to the DAV to see about a ride home.

Oh, yeah, we were in the middle of a snow storm, late in season, so all the roads were horrible. I got the ride, so there I sat, I called my

NP and she ordered IV Iron for me to get my blood count up and provided an acid neutralizer to help heal the ulcer. I discontinued using any pain killers; and had a four-day adjustment problem with pain and difficulty sleeping being a side sleeper with a right shoulder and left hip both aching, badly.

I also got on the schedule to drive for the DAV on Fridays; looked up natural cures for ulcers and started drinking cabbage and honey slurries. I discovered that "Bio Freeze" works well to get me mobile, and to get to sleep; I just hope that my body doesn't acclimate to it too fast! The iron infusions do affect me, I do get skin irritation, (I itch), but there are only four infusions to go through.

Ma had another fall, she called me first, and I went over to the apartment to pick her off the floor and took her to the hospital to be checked out. Nothing seemed to be wrong, but on the way home we discussed her condition and she finally admitted that an assisted care facility should be looked into.

I asked, and she wanted to go to the assisted living facility that was just south of her building. They just happened to be advertising tours, I called, and we toured the place, with two different rooms currently available. We surveyed the facility, the rooms are spacious, and efficient. It happened that the director of the place recognized my name, and it seems that I had made a favorable impression when I was working. (One of my hospice patients was here.)

We made arrangements after talking to the current apartment manager, the assisted care facility, and expediting everything. We put in our notice March 31st and they agreed to having us pay for only April and May for the apartment; we made arrangements to be into the assisted living facility by April 15th.

By April 14th, she was completely moved, the apartment cleaned out and keys turned in, with the help of my two daughters, Lynn, Tiffany's former husband, Mike, her new man friend and the

Salvation Army. Her apartment looks like she has lived there for a year, Tiffany did a great job of setting it up, she has a new lounge chair, a trundle bed, and all set for the next phase of her life! Just in time for us to get our stuff together for our second trip this year including the Caribbean and Western Mexico. Not bad for a guy with a shoulder and left hip both begging to be replaced if I do say so myself!!

It is the week before our next adventure, the third day of now being at ma's new place settled; It took a total of a week and a half, very draining!!

I go for another stomach inspection and blood work, and finally another discussion with Ortho regarding my deteriorating joints!

The Three C's Adventure April 2017

Our flight out was 05:30 on Tuesday. We had my daughter drop us off at the bus terminal for the last bus out to O'Hare at 8:10 PM the night before. Three blocks after we left the bus terminal, the bus was stopped by a guy claiming luggage was falling out of the bus. The driver checked, and everything seemed to be on board, so we continued the trip.

We arrived at the terminal. It was 9:45 P.M. and promptly walked to the economy customer service. There was no line; we were feelin' pretty good, until we were called up to the counter. They looked at the printed boarding passes, and said they couldn't check us in until 3:30 A.M. I objected, since there is nothing out here, everything is inside the terminal, no seating, restaurants, or even chairs!

I protested again, they just shrugged, closed the counter, and said they would be back at 3:30 AM, so much for customer service, customer care, we sat down in the disabled chairs, it will be a long 5 hours, yeah, I was pissed!!

O'Hare closes down at 10, at least in this terminal; we watched the taking down of the corals, the buffing of the floors, and the parade of "different" travelers looking for another place to go.... (and probably somewhere to sit)

At about 2:50 A.M. some folks started showing up, the corral crowd guides were put out again, then everyone from American disappeared. (The three or four of them.) I asked a passing guard, and she told me that they would start coming out between three and three thirty, of the fifteen to twenty stations, some folks started lining up in the "Disney" queuing aisles, hoping the counter would open there.

Around 3:20 A.M. two agents appeared, and the line grew quickly. Then another agent came and directed those that had pre-confirmed and had boarding passes to use the kiosks for the luggage. We got out of line and went over, entered exactly the same info that was asked when I confirmed Monday except now it charged for our luggage, yep, $25.00 each. I tried to pay three times, card not accepted; Called over assist, everything re-done, this time the card was accepted, we thanked the attendant, and then into another line to have the suitcases weighted, and checked in.

It is now 3:50 a.m, Progress!! Get in line for the TSA precheck. It opens at 4:00, shoes stay on, no electronics out, and yeah, I had to be wanded, but it was quick, and we were out to find our gate.

The airport is coming alive, few of the stores or restaurants are open, we find restrooms, and wait to board, we are in group 6, there are 9 groups!!

The flight went well, we left on time, both Lynn and I got about a half hour sleep, and we landed early, 9:30 EST.

Finding our luggage was an adventure in itself, escalators broken, poor signage, a people mover train, more walking, finally after walking "about 50 miles" we found not only our connection with the transportation to the ship, but our luggage!

Noah

Wait for a gathering of people, and at 10:30 we load on to a bus for the seven-mile trip to the port. Here we found seats for another check- in and wait. Finally, we goad one of the anxious one's in the group, to push for opening up, we encourage a few other couples to follow us, and we descended on the counters, and finally they opened up!!

Information exchanged, this was the first time in all of our travels that my credit card was rejected because it had "debit" on it...I told them it was both, but they insisted on another, luckily Lynn had one, then on to the ship.

We were told the rooms were not ready till 3P.M., so we went up to eat lunch. The buffet was small but very upscale, if help was needed to take more than one plate the first run it was offered. White linen tables, attentive staff, and of course, the "free", included wine was offered and dispensed.

After lunch, yes, it was excellent! We went to the pool area, found a chaise lounge for each of us, and tried to nap. Yes, a bit of napping, but we were both zombies, sweaty, irritable, headaches, and beat, we gave up trying to sleep, and went down to find our room. It was ready, and the luggage was already placed on the bed for unpacking!

This is a small (700 passenger) deluxe ship, every room is a suite, all have balconies, generous bathrooms, and a walk-in closet! Queen sized bed, couch, desk, and chairs....and very attractive trim.

I showered, and unpacked, Lynn just crashed. By 5:30 we had unpacked, gotten some rest, and just returned from the mandatory muster for the lifeboats. We changed and headed down for the first complimentary specialty meal at Prime 7 the steakhouse restaurant.

Lynn was slow with her make-up, so we agreed to meet at the restaurant at 6:30, our assigned time, I stopped at a bar outside, and ordered a martini, yeah, alcohol and wine were included in the package, during the entire cruise except for specific, high-end alcohol.

We always ask for a large table. We were soon joined by two other couples, introduced ourselves, and a great conversation ensued, along with fork tender steak, unique compliments like steak tartar, goose liver, and ahi tuna; veggies including truffle asparagus and creamed spinach, all in quantities enough to share with the entire table!!

At 8:45 we finished up the desserts, waddled to our room, and ended the day, looking forward to a good night's sleep. Tomorrow is a sea day, so we plan on sleeping in!

Wednesday, April 26th, the first day at sea. We wake up just after 8 A.M., and both of us are refreshed and functioning well! I get dressed, and start the journaling, Lynn reads a while, and we slowly get ready and familiarize ourselves with the room, the TV guide provides when and where the daily activities are to take place.

Nine o'clock we head up to see what is for breakfast. We found a table on the aft deck, and like last night, the selection is tasteful, and one needs to restrain a lot not to overindulge, the coffee is of course served by roaming servers.

After breakfast, we went to our first lecture; it was presented by a traveling Smithsonian doctor specializing in Caribbean history.

In the 15th and 16th centuries, there were two main ports in the Caribbean, ruled essentially by Spain: Havana, Cuba, and Cartagena, Columbia.

These "explorers" had mixed missions, their main purpose was to discover, plunder, and claim property, so they would be called conquistadors, Corsairs, buccaneer, privateer, or pirate depending on the country served, or origin. Burn and ransom were common techniques, and this was followed by torture and sacking.

Definitions and origins: Grog = water and rum, Criollo (Creole) = homebred or local indigenous

On Columbus's second trip of three to the Caribbean, he brought

17 ships, and 1700 conquistadors to conquer and plunder more of the Caribbean in 1499; others that fought for the riches and plunder including Francis Drake, Jean Baptiste, (French), Henry Morgan (known as the Butcher Privateer (English)); all looking for riches to be shared for their respective countries and fame and honor when they returned to their homeland.

Odd names for wars, including the war of Jenkins's Ear and Assassin Succession, to name two of them!

Venezuela is named after Venice, Italy, due to the local homes and huts all built on stilts and poles over the water.

New Granada became Columbia, and Aspinall became Colon.

Colon, Panama, was a "sailor town," which meant there were mostly saloons and brothels. Colon has suffered significant setbacks recently; 1964, there was rioting and political discourse; in 1999, the U.S. Naval base closed, and Colon is yet to recover.

To transverse from the eastern coast to the western coast, the progression was from trails, to roads, then stagecoach to railroad, and finally to the Panama Canal. This area is the largest free trade zone in the Western Hemisphere (FTZ), Hong Kong is the Eastern.

After the lecture, I signed up for the boat building and started thinking of the design. I asked the room steward to find me some empty water bottles and some large pieces of cardboard; we were supplied with string, markers, scissors, and a t-shirt for each member of our team (Lynn and me!)

Up on deck for a half hour of sun front and then back, the Mojito was very good, actually both of them (gotta keep hydrated), and of course, they were included!

Afternoon, I started working on the ship, Lynn found a number of activities, and we met at the trivia observation deck and played our first round of trivia, with a couple originally from Scotland, and another originally from England.

This was another formal night, and our second at a specialty restaurant, this one was French. We were seated at a table with two other couples, one was both Chiropractic doctors, and the other was a HR Specialist and his wife, still working, consulting for American Express. The conversation was lively, and the 2 ½ hours went quickly. We left to find a seat at the show, it was a single lady singer, that put on a very good one-person show, what I didn't understand was that there were only about 200 people there, this was the only show, and the enthusiasm was tepid; no standing ovation, although she was quite good.

We toured the ship to find the night life, which seemed even less attended than any other ship we had been on, and after a few songs at a bar, we went back to the cabin, showered and called it a day.

Thursday, April 27th, another at sea day. It is windy, warm, and the ship is rocking' much more than before. Breakfast, we are getting into a routine, the aft deck is where we seem to go, it is windy, and we have to mind our napkins, and anything light.

After breakfast Lynn goes to seek out things with the activity staff, I turn in some duplicate excursion tickets, and get a small roll of packaging tape. I check out the ship, enter into the knowledge quiz, and head to the lecture on the Panama Canal.

The theatre had more people here than for the entertainment; 275-300 people, last night, 200 tops!

The Panama Canal was the second man-made trench and connection to bodies of water, the Suez Canal finished in 1869 was the first in modern day.

The French started the 400-mile-long project, the soil make-up of lava, stone, and clay was a problem with mud slides, and then there was Yellow fever, Malaria, Typhoid, pneumonia, and dysentery.

Of every 100 people brought in to work, 20 died and only 20 were fully able to work after a year, the whole project involved at least 20,000 workers dying before the project went bankrupt in 1889.

Besides the mosquito problem there was a constant ant problem. So, small dishes of water were placed at the bed posts at night, to prevent the ants from crawling up the bed posts; little did they know, this helped breed the mosquitoes that carried most of the disease! Once the mosquito was discovered as the carrier, the swamps were drained, open water was limited, and those bed dishes removed.

America originally wanted to build a canal in Nicaragua; but seeing the progress made by the French, assisted in the independence of Panama from Columbia with Teddy Roosevelt, and the availability of American shovels and cranes that dwarfed the European equipment, the U.S. was involved now. Construction was from 1904-1914; it took 43,000 people to build and required 10,000 people to maintain.

Those giant cranes made by Bucyrus Erie, in Milwaukee, (My home town) were one of the major factors in completing this task along with the railroads and innovative ideas to move earth and keep it from sliding.

Gatun Lake has the world's largest earth dam, and is the largest man-made lake in the world, at 164 square miles.

All the locks work on gravity, the first ship passage was on 8-15-1914, but from then until the 1930's regular passage was interrupted frequently by land-slides, it finally becoming reliable in the 1930's. During World War Two, America was actually planning to expand the canal involving nuclear bombs!

The treaty with Panama was signed by President Carter, and the Canal was turned over to the Panama people in 1999. The Chinese presently are contracted to run the canal.

Educating Noah...Travelin'

The canal transports 4% of world trade, 16% of total waterborne trade, between 13-14,000 ships use it every year, and with every ship, 55 million gallons of fresh water is dumped into the ocean, bring up concerns from the global crowd.

After the lecture, I checked out the boat building coordinator, there are three boat builders signed up so far, and I also acquired some packing tape from the front desk (I had to sign it out??).

I went up to the top deck to work on my tan, my back was beet red yesterday, so 20 minutes on the front, only 15 on the back this time, today's lunch is with a Greek theme, I am already cutting back, 1/2 plate, one water and one Dos Equis beer. Many of these folks have obviously never gone through a deli line, sloooow, many take some of everything, and pile that dish high with food...then leave 1/3 of it for the fishes... arghhhhhhh!!

Back to the room, found out that they want to charge for the "free" internet, and worked a little more on the boat, need to wait for the glue to dry now! I did not accept the charge for internet, so I went down to the reception desk, they took the charge sheet and gave me another to sign on for internet w/o charge, it was mid-afternoon, and there must have been too many devices running, I will check again tonight! (TWC Road Runner doesn't work outside America, I found this out in Russia, and I thought it was a fluke, no, it wasn't, so anyone using Road Runner should have an alternative e-mail.)

Four thirty Trivia with the two other couples (we are a team now) both husbands have been working for NASA for years in the U.S. We lost...again. The dinner (long pants needed after 6 on this ship, was again excellent (I will probably mention this a number of times) but way too much, appetizer, soup/salad, main course, and desert; all done to perfection served with wine, and all of the highest standards in both taste and presentation.

The show was a comedian; one man show, very clever, very

polished, and yes, very entertaining, one joke after another; he was a "clean" comic, which I found very refreshing! The crowd was larger than for the singer, but not like the lecture.

Friday, April 28th; our first port since leaving Miami, is Cartagena, Columbia.

The excursions were included with this cruise; they just didn't tell us that there were a maximum number of seats per choice. Luckily, I had signed up 3 months before with first and standby selections, two standbys became available, and I turned in the 2nd choice tickets for others to use.

The excursion we had was a bus tour, walking tour through the old section, and shopping. The bus tour went fine, the shopping for 20 minutes went well, but when we came out to the area where we were to meet, no one was there. One of the vendors walked us up two streets and pointed to a group way down the street and told us that was "Franks Group". We hurried as much as we could, and finally did catch up. It seems two other people had joined the group, and after walking a few blocks were discovered and sent back to the shopping area…and he wasn't concerned about us??

It was 95 degrees and the humidity in the 80's, a beautiful city, notes to follow, we were back on the ship by 12:30, I refused to tip that jerk that left us behind, Lynn slipped him a couple of bucks.

Information on Cartagena, Columbia: There are five major cultures in Columbia. The wall surrounding the original settlement, 480 years old, was 7 miles long. It is still 5.5 miles long and in fairly good condition. (The use of coral and strategically placed expansion holes contributed to this stability.) Cartagena is the safest town in Columbia, has the most events, and averages 6 inches above sea level. The ocean has receded about 300 yards from the walls in the last 400 years, and roads and sidewalks are now there. April and May are the rainy season, with year-round temperatures 77 to 95 degrees(F) and humidity 60-85%; we were told this is a "less-dry" decade.

The average work day is 8 a.m. to 6 p.m. with an hour siesta. There is no income tax, just property tax, and that is only $400.00 US average; the town has a population of 1.2 million people, there is no welfare, the unemployment rate is 9.8 %, you don't work, you don't eat.

35% of income is from fishing, 35% from tourism; there is a good amount of coal (one of the largest producers in the world) and of the oil, 10% of the oil is sold to the U.S.A.

Although Bogota is the capital, this is the most progressive city, traffic is a problem; 80,000 motorbikes, 14,000 taxis; all cars are imported, the bus fare is $1.00 U.S. (I am giving the amounts in the U.S. the conversion here is 28,000 Columbian pesos to $1.00 U.S.).

The second and fourth Friday of every month are designated "no bike days" to ease congestion, the police ride two up on the motorcycles, they are all State police, and have the authority to pat search and detain anyone, anytime. ("No one messes with the police" our tour guide warns.)

School starts at 4 years old; the public university has a capacity of 16,000, and private Universities cost $2,000-10,000 US per year.

This is one of the few countries with Atlantic and Pacific sides, Columbia exports five million flowers to the U.S annually.

The heat, humidity, and my shoulder and hip along with my lobster-boy look took its toll! I had to have a siesta this time, Lynn went out and participated in some of the activities, I went up and toured the ship, had a small sandwich (there is free food, water, drinks all over this ship, from 11:00 on!) and later joined Lynn and the group for our trivia.

I wasn't up to snuff, we went back to the room rested, and then went to the Italian restaurant for dinner. Not really in the mood for conversation, we took a table for two. The menu was tempting, Lynn ordered from that and had the best meal yet, I ate off the antipasto bar and salad, everything offered, again, exceptional!

After a few more touches on the boat building, it was early to bed for me, Lynn explored the ship, and that concluded the day.

Saturday, Colon, Panama. We were scheduled to dock at 9 a.m.; slept till 7:30, refreshed, I caught up on some of the journaling, worked on the boat, and joined Lynn for a breakfast on the aft of the ship. Yes, warm and muggy, our Gambia Aerial Tram Experience doesn't start until 13:00 (1 P.M.) so the morning is ours, we agree to meet for lunch at 11:30 and we are off. I checked about sending postcards, the desk will send them with postage for $1.00 each, so although no one gets one from Columbia, some will go from here on.

Back to the room for working on the boat; tomorrow is at sea, Panama Canal Day, so I will start applying the paper Mache to the hull so the boat will start looking like a boat after tomorrow!

The Gambia Aerial Tram experience. Quick lunch before our 1:00 P.M. start, I know we usually take the first tour out, but this was offered, and we took it!

Everything went smoothly; I couldn't get over the free water offered before and after leaving the ship! The trip to Gambia and the tram was a little over an hour by bus, so we were educated on the way.

Ciara is our guide, the tram is located in a resort complex, that includes the tram, a butterfly sanctuary, a frog sanctuary, and an orchid farm, and maybe, if we are lucky, some natives selling their unique wares from the jungles.

Panama is 75,500 kilometers long (times 0.6 for miles) The natives say Panama means "an abundant place", abundant fish, abundant trees, and abundant butterflies.

Days are either dry or rainy. Today, it started out dry, but it may rain when we are in a rainforest! We are reminded…

Panama is a natural bridge to North and South America, the newest animal, is the coyote, and they are adapting to this. The national bird is the Harpy Eagle, national flower is the orchid; (represents the Holy Spirit) and the national religion is Catholic. There were/are seven indigenous tribes of people before the Spaniards came.

The native wares use different parts of the trees and seeds, we did stop, and I bought Lynn a bird dish, a length of material, and a Toucan carved from a seed for me.

It was raining hard when we got to the tram; we had to wait almost an hour before the rain let up enough to travel to and from the observation tower with 5 people and one guide per tram. I put Lynn in one of the groups and I joined another, most did not want to split up husband and wife, and it got kind of stupid for the guides to ask over and over again, for one person to complete a tram! (The tram ride to and from the observation tower was only 10-15 minutes long each way!)

The rain let up, and off we went, the odd person shared the seat with the guide, which I thought was a bonus! (Both Lynn and I got this position!) A number of items were pointed out in the lush forest below, termite nests in trees here, and kill the tree, and ants also nest in the trees but do not kill the trees. Some fruits only certain animals can eat and some trees are the only one's animals utilize, like the Koala, only liking one species of eucalyptus trees; the sloths only climb and eat the fruit of the trumpet trees here.

After the rain, we saw a few toucans (both large and small) and a few parrots. Lynn saw a large rodent, and we both saw a sloth moving slowly up a tree.

We would go 100-200 feet, stop, and let the next gondola fill, which gave the guide enough time to point out different points of interest trees, and provide information about the fruits and flowers the foliage had to offer. One plant looks exactly like African/Jamaican hair braiding! I have pictures!!

At the top, we exit our gondola and walk a few 100 feet to the tower. This tower is all ramps! (No steps!) It must be at least 10-12 stories and give a breathtaking view of the Canal and a 360 degree of the surrounding forest. I did get a toucan picture (The toucans were calling, which in turn starts the frogs croaking; I thought that was kind of neat!) and a sloth picture, along with ant and termite nests, fruits, and flowers, and great panoramic views!

Back on the bus, we were an hour late; we stopped at the butterfly sanctuary. There at 17,000 species of butterflies in Panama, and only 2,000 are active during the day. The balance is nocturnal!

Most of the butterflies we saw in the sanctuary were the ones with the owl's eyes; when they flew, the top of the wings was iridescent blue. There were a few bright oranges and some yellow, but none came within camera range, and yes, there were some jerk tourists who hogged the point-and-shoot opportunities for minutes, adjusting their phone cameras and NOT turning off the flashes!! Argggghhh!!!

We were able to stop by the natives and yes, I bought as mentioned before, they were not used to people wanting to barter, however, I did get $5.00 off the purchase which made both of us happy!

We were late; it was Saturday, and they closed the frog sanctuary, but we did get to walk the orchid garden.

They provided a ham sandwich, water, and a sweet muffin on the trip back. They seem to love mangos here, along with avocados. By the way, mangos come from China; it's funny how Kiwis came from China, and now New Zealand produces the most, and mangos came from China, and Central and South America produce most of them now.

Educating Noah...Travelin'

We were back on the ship by 7:30 P.M. We showered and decided to watch a movie and call it a day.

Sunday, we go through the Panama Canal Day, and it will take most of the day. It is overcast with intermittent rain, so it will be a perfect day to stay in, watch the sides of the canal, work on the boat, and Lynn flit between different activities and earn some more points. I pestered the front desk for more tape and was given a new roll of duct tape, so I was quite busy with the paper Mache and then the duct tape to finish the hull. Our team is The Odd Ducks, and the boat's name is "Ducky."

The whole day, over the P.A. system, was explanations of the locks, the progress we were making, and where we were. Since we have done this before, only a few photos for the album and very few activities were scheduled. The meals are all excellent, and we are both "feelin'" like stuffed pigs, and we are not filling our plates like everyone else! Not much else to note.

Monday, a day at sea, we are now in the Pacific Ocean. It is cooler, and the humidity is way down. Bright and sunny, calm seas, as we progress north, up the coast. Lynn had trouble sleeping last night. I found that the shower water was hot in the A.M., I could get on the internet in the early morning, and I could also get some work done on Ducky; what a great start!

A little after 8, a pod of dolphins was swimming next to us. They were dark grey and white, only about four-foot-long, but fun to watch! There were about a dozen or so with some young ones. The show lasted about ten minutes, then they turned back toward the stern.

We had breakfast at the coffee shop. Yes, it was like a Starbucks, barista and all, and like everything else, complementary. I filled out the daily trivia sheet, glanced at the newspaper, and obtained more string for Ducky.

The lecture today was on Costa Rica vs. Nicaragua, a contrast.

Costa Rica, the "Rich Coast," where 97% of the population is literate, vs. Nicaragua, the land of revolution. Both were of the original United States of Central America, along with Guatemala, Honduras, and El Salvador. The United States of Central America was dissolved in 1838.

The population of Costa Rica is 4.3 million, and most of them live in 6% of the country; Nicaragua is twice the size and has 6.2 million people.

The main exports of both countries are bananas and coffee. Bananas were introduced in the U.S.A. in the early 1900s, when the United Fruit Company discovered using white boats to transport fruit, and later, with refrigeration, the fruit could be brought to the U.S. with minimum, if any, spoilage. They were known as the white fleet!

United Fruit then branched out into carrying passengers; our government broke up the company as a monopoly in 1961. United Foods and Chiquita Banana are two of the pieces. After the lecture, I joined Lynn for a game of majority wins. We both placed second.

It is beautiful, warm in the 80's and sunny, with a light cool breeze. Lunch on deck, then I went back to boat building, Lynn, to find some games; there isn't much to do today, but I made the rudder and mounted it, put on both wings and worked on rigging and the sail.

Lunch, Lynn found the pizza window. She's happy; the Lobster boy is still red, so the shirt stays on…

We both played a second game of majority rules. Lynn won 1st place, and I got second. I found out there is a rather big following of the bridge card game, so besides staying in their cabin, eating, and drinking, they (the rest of the passengers) play bridge!

Did horrible at trivia, but I had a light supper this evening, just a few appetizers. The show was the first production show of the cruise. It was a 50's theme, a good show if you like Sinatra and his ilk. (This was the fullest I have seen in the theatre, a good 250-300 people, all with drinks in hand.) Lynn went to check out the R&B band show in the lounge, ten to twelve people. I called it a day.

Tuesday, May 2nd, Puntarenas, Costa Rica

Today, our excursion is the Macaw Sanctuary and Puntarenas Highlights. It is partly cloudy, mid-80s, and a bit humid.

We decided on a brief breakfast at the coffee shop and then waited our turn for our excursion. We now have Lynn go ahead and save a seat on the bus. The back of the bus all the time gets tiring, and being the last off gets me the look from the driver, especially when I have difficulty getting this hip working with this. Sometimes good, most of the time, bad right shoulder!

We got a seat fairly close to the front and settled in for the hour and twenty minutes to the sanctuary. Jose is our tour guide; he laughs easily and is at ease with us. "Punt Remes" means all is well and used extensively.

Costa Rica was formed by volcanic activity and is part of the Pacific Rim of Fire, including far-reaching areas such as Japan and Hawaii. A volcanic ash and sand bar formed a land bridge for animals and birds to migrate from North America to South America. The beach sand is dark grey.

The schools are very important; they have a very high literacy rate, but the colleges are producing too many doctors, and they are concentrating on private practice rather than working for the government social health program due to the significant difference in pay.

There are seven provinces and eight regions for coffee production; we again drive on the Pan American Highway. Their definition of highway is much different than ours, and it is the best road in this country, mostly 4 lanes here. (Two each way)

Noah

When we arrive at the sanctuary, we are greeted by a guide, and all are shown to the restrooms. We are then shown two boards of rules: no loud sounds, keep conversations kept to a minimum, stay on the trail, stay together with your group, and don't touch or feed the animals or birds. This is a rescue center, and we find many of the birds are outside the cages as well as inside!

As we passed blooming flowers, odd seed pods, and ferns, I took pictures of everything I thought was beautiful or odd, and there was a lot. There are many different bird species and animals, from macaws, parrots, and even solitary toucans to tapirs, jaguars, and monkeys. (I got a picture of the world's smallest monkey, and he is cute!)

There are more termites and ant nests in the trees. With the termite nest, there are always black tendrils that hang from the tree. This is to protect the termites; exposure to direct sunlight will actually burn the termite up due to the sensitivity of the exoskeleton, so this is the way for the termites to get to the ground and back inside the tendrils.

A third of the way through the tour, we are treated to cold water, watermelon, and mango slices. It is getting "steamier" and humid, and in the high eighties, everyone is slowing down. It is getting a little irritating trying to take a picture on a small path with people standing in the middle of the path and taking minutes to shoot multiple pictures with their point-and-shoot cameras.

I also talked to one of the guides. She is from Germany and will be volunteering here for four weeks, then at another sanctuary for another four weeks as part of a German program similar to our Peace Corp., with similar perks when she finishes her volunteer work.

There was a small souvenir shop at the end, very reasonable stuff, and the money went to support the sanctuary, so everyone dropped a couple bucks there, too!

The air conditioning on the bus felt good; we passed several shantytowns, and some of the dwellings had no walls!

Running water and sewer are only dreams, sometimes extensive clusters of corrugated metal roof dwellings. As we approached Puntarenas, we were given a bus tour indicating the points of interest, the extensive beach, and the best places for food and souvenirs, then dropped off in front of the ship.

Lynn wanted to head back to look over the souvenir shops, so we walked back on the pier, explored the various little shops, and threw money at them for stuff we "needed."

Back on the boat, lunch, then a game of crazy golf, I took second place, Lynn took third, and four people took 1st place. Back to the room, rest, and cool down.

Trivia at 4:30; change for dinner. Tonight we eat in the dining room. We were seated at a table for six, good conversation with folks who wanted to talk to other folks, but these are "properly served" dinners, so another 2 ½ hours easily passed.

Two of us ordered fish, and yes, there was a server that expertly boned the fish, skeleton completely intact.

Wednesday, another port and another country: San Juan Del Sur, Nicaragua. We were anchored by 7 a.m., and we will be tendered to shore. The forecast is 92 degrees and partly sunny…hot and humid.

We were to leave the ship at 8:00, and I always like to be there at least 15 minutes early, "The rule" was not broken, but the theatre was full!

It seems that the wind has picked up, and there is a lot of trouble loading the tenders. We are cautioned that the captain recommends anyone with any disability, handicap, or mobility issue to reconsider going ashore. Some of our new-found friends did bow out, but it will be a cold day in hell if we do!

SOOO, we waited, and finally, 45 minutes late, we were called. Yes, there were a lot of problems aligning the tender with the shipping platform, and due to the swells, it took over 20 minutes just to load, loading 1 to 2 at a time and then trying to realign again. What an adventure!

We loaded up about 45 people, hot and stuffy, crammed tight for the ten-minute run to shore. The getting off went reasonably well. We were headed through security to get on our assigned bus.

This was a first; as we passed one security officer, our temperature was taken. This was never done before, but we all seemed to pass and off to the bus. This is the largest port on the Pacific side; there is one pier, very few small boats, and no commercial boats of other ships.

Ray, our guide, introduced himself to us Nicaragua style, first and last name, the last name of his mother, and the last name of his father last.

Nicaragua is the largest of the Central American countries; natives on the Pacific coast were mostly Mestizos. There was a large immigration of Germans from the 1920s to the 1940s; they were followed by the British, who set up on the East Coast with their colonial-style houses, followed by the Jamaicans. These folks were well known for their pot use, and it is overlooked if the quantity is less than a pound. (That's 16 ounces!!)

The main meal in this country is beans and rice with corn tortillas, no wheat for bread, or flour tortillas; with small variations, the staples are different, especially on the coasts, where sea food is plentiful. Sundays are special, and that would be the only variation. Otherwise, the same staples are morning, noon, and night.

Except for the English side, there are no formal restaurants. Every block will have local sidewalk restaurants, but in the capital, there are Burger King, Pizza Hut, and McDonald's.

There are 425 volcanic structures in Nicaragua, and boasting 75 volcanoes. Central America is known as the land of lakes and volcanoes. The main freshwater lake, Lake Nicaragua, is as large as Costa Rica and remains fairly pristine. This being a socialist republic, the emphasis is going green by the government. I saw only three small street vendors for tourists in the main port city; there are no resorts or tourist complexes on the lake.

Chocolate beans used to be the main currency; the currency here is the NIO Nicaraguan Cordoba, the main religion is Catholic, and Spanish is the official language. Two seasons: November to May is the dry season, May to November is the rainy season, and temperatures are stable, mid-70s to mid-90s year-round.

One of the most significant flowering trees we found is called the golden shower in English. The whole tree is covered in yellow flowers, and I hope I got a few pictures of one or two.

President Clinton was the only U.S. President to visit this country. Coca-Cola here tastes different due to the use of cane sugar; sugar cane is a commodity, and the burning of sugar cane stalks supplies power, along with windmills; they are working with Iceland for geothermal power production by 2025.

We arrived at the Hacienda after a little over an hour; it is a single-story building, mostly open and set up for tourists, within walking distance of the beach of Lake Nicaragua. We are treated first to a tortilla demonstration and tasting, a walk past five vendors, then a milking of a cow demonstration where people are invited to try; a walk down to the beach to run our feet in the warm fresh water, this lake has a variety of fish, bull sharks, and crocodiles!

There is not a commercial fisher on site, but there is a nice view of two of the major volcanoes!

Back at the Hacienda, we were treated to a little show. I danced with a few of them (the guy who was dressed up like an old woman), and Lynn and I danced with two other couples in a small competition; we came in second!

We were all treated to a typical meal. The heat is starting to get oppressive; there is shade but little wind away from the lake. We, along with a couple other couples, headed for the air-conditioned buses. We did miss a small dancing horse presentation, but from what we found, it was only a short 10-minute show and only one horse.

Back to the pier, the road here is two lanes, and in only "OK" repair, the water has calmed down. We load much easier to the tender, but the inside is very stuffy and hot, and we all thanked one of the deckhands when he opened a small window. The ten-minute trip back to the ship was bearable; the windows were salted up, and although the winds were down, it took a while to disembark.

We met another interesting couple at dinner. Seems a lot of second marriages and a lot of professionals or business owners in this upper 70-plus crowd. The entertainment that night was a very good ventriloquist. On the way back to the cabin, we found some couples just finishing up supper! (10:45 PM)

Thursday, May 4th

We will not be at our next port in Guatemala until after lunch, so it is a slow morning. A mandatory drill refresher is the main thing scheduled for this morning. I made the sail and finished most of the deck for "Ducky." I had some dark thoughts yesterday, so we checked to make sure she would fit through the door. Yes, with 2-3 inches to spare, I was so relieved!!

We docked in Puerto Quetzal, Guatemala, just a bit early, and what a contrast to yesterday,

Here, we had a dock; here, there were other cargo ships, multiple loading docks, a yard filled with trailers and cranes, and other cruise ships. Yesterday, one tender dock was the largest Pacific dock in Nicaragua! Makes you wonder why capitalism is shunned. Socialism promoted in America with socialism always seems to lead to revolt, revolution, and people being much happier when it is ended?

Educating Noah...Travelin'

I guess a good education still needs to be promoted, the problem is those teaching are indoctrinating, and not educating. What a shame.

Our excursion today is an open zoo; animals come right up to the vehicle. Auto Safari Chapin, we leave the ship a little after 1400, (2 P.M.) we should be back around 6:30 P.M. or 18:30.

The drive like most of these excursions will be 45 minutes to a little over an hour so we get filled in on the country. Hugo is our guide; Walter is the driver. There are 22 different languages here, Spanish is the official language; there are two seasons, raining and pouring! 16 million people more than 50% under 40, why do these Central American countries have such a young population? ... Revolution and Civil War! This has been much better here with peace and the new government for the last 30 years.

There are 33 volcanoes, 3 actives; bananas, 6 million tons exported a month, coffee (seems all these countries have the "best") (McDonald's, is the largest single customer) and chocolate beans.

On coffee, North Americans prefer medium roast, Europeans prefer the high mountain coffee.

We are told that many of the animals have their names due to Julius Caesar; for knowing that the closest relative of the Hippo is a whale, I won a kid's toy!

All of the people were given woven bracelets by the guide, The Pan American Highway here is four lanes, and well maintained.

The Mayan word for water is "Ha". They are still here. There was no nation; every city had their own king, who was considered a god ("A-How"), "Co-coon-a-how" means "Sacred Lord of Providence." Their pyramids are the highest in the world, and they were constructed as podiums and worship sites instead of grave sites like in Egypt.

The political election is every three years no re-elections, only one term! (What a great idea!!)

Noah

The sugar fields are burned to harvest the sugar cane, there is a problem with snakes and vipers, some called "two steps" once bitten, two steps later your dead! I did get it.

The money here is plastic, and yes, I did get a sample for my barber! Guatemala imports over a million used cars a year, much cheaper, they fix them up and sell them, they also recycle school buses.

When we arrived, we were greeted with beer or soda and French fries. The tour was through the park, some giraffes approach our vehicle, we are told they like to lick the windows for the salt. Yes, they were very close! We were also close to most of the rest of the animals, including a pair of lions, small deer crossed in front of us, peacocks, ducks, mocking birds, iguanas everywhere, monkeys in trees, some actually posing!

We then left the bus and took a walking tour of a number of caged birds, an alligator just off the path, and monkeys in the trees. It was reinforced that the toucans are shy, and very hard to get a close-up view. In a small lake, there were tons of bullheads; waiting for someone to put a quarter into the food venders and feed them...you could see the open whiskered mouths just below the surface!

As we headed back to the bus, we were told we should be back in port by 6:45. I got some shots of locals and poor housing. There was no shopping during this trip,

And nothing at the port, this was a working port mostly industrial, so no post cards from here!

We changed, had a little dinner, and joined in with a ship activity. Our team of 6 was against 6 other teams of 6 (the largest showing yet!) we WON! Then, back to the room, Lynn wanted to watch a movie, and I wanted to get the paper Mache, on Ducky,

Both of us beat, tomorrow is a day at sea, no alarm set.

Educating Noah…Travelin'

Friday, May 5th, even though the ship is rockin', we slept till 7:30!! Lynn put on a scope patch; waves are from the left starboard and about 5-6 feet high. I checked out the three laundry rooms, all being used, so we decided on trying again at 11:45.

Lynn went off for games, I touched up Ducky and journaled, then joined Lynn for one of the games, we met later, waited a bit for a washer, then dryer, to get some wash done.

This afternoon was to be "Fair Day" on deck, but the ship is rolling, we thought the fair was a no-go but we were wrong, the fair must go on!

Every department of the ship had little contests for skill sets, this included completion between passengers in identifying spices from the kitchen, racing to put pillows in pillow cases, a wind-up horse race, hoops over crew members in the pool and so forth. You accumulated tickets, and after the event, the prizes were given to the lucky ticket holders, we participated, both Lynn and I won in the waiter completion, I won the hoop game, tossing all 5 hoops over crew members in the pool, Lynn won at a make-up game, I just lost a housekeeping game, and I did very well on a game similar to "Operation" with the crew engineers. Everyone got a number of tickets for participation, and gifts raffled out by number on the tickets, the more tickets you had the better the chance, Lynn had 35, I had earned 37, but we still didn't win, but everyone had fun!

Ducky is done! She has feather accents, inside and out. On judgment day, I will try to get the use of one on the carts the cleaners use, to transport her to the pool area.

Later this afternoon, the sun came out, but the wind did not die, most of the chairs are stacked on the deck, most of the people are inside. We are going to tea at 4, grab a cup with a small sandwich, and then wait for the show at 9:30; it is the second show of the ventriloquist.

Noah

Saturday, May 6th, 2017. We are in port, Acapulco, Mexico. The trip to the cliff divers is less than an hour, and even at 8:30 in the morning, traffic is reasonable, I guess it being a Saturday morning helped quite a bit though!!

Mexico is actually the United States of Mexico, there are 31 states. Oil is the number one export, in Mexico; Mexico City is the 3rd largest city in the world at 23 million people, and Mexico is also part of the world ring of fire along with its Southern Central American countries.

Education is from 6 years old till high school, since President Vicente Fox, English is also taught or available grades 7, 8, and 9. College is $60.00 ($U.S.) per semester, but to qualify for this, you must be in the top 10% of your graduating class. Otherwise, private and that costs considerably more.

The average income depends on the State, those States producing oil, and those with big tourist exposure have the highest.

Now, Acapulco, in general, Spanish translation of the native words for "The place of broken bamboo"; here, tourism is the most income, silver is second, and third is agriculture. We passed by the smallest beach in Acapulco, called La Costa Beach.

There was a well know hacienda on the cliffs overlooking the beach, the owner was asked to leave after a few years due to the numerous and noisy parties, his name: Frank Sinatra. The house was sold to Dolores Deliria; there is also an estate owned by Ricardo Montevon, and other Hollywood stars, this area known as the "Hollywood section".

Hedy Lamar had a restaurant down the road, next to the cliffs and the ocean. She was not only known as an actress, but an engineer and contributed to the sonar program for submarines. Her restaurant was not doing as well as she wished, she observed some young boys jumping off the cliffs into the water below.

She promoted them as entertainment, with an evening show having them dive at 10:30 at night with torches, and the practice continues today.

This is where the show is! We watched from the restaurant, they were engaged to jump just for the tourists this morning and this afternoon, no one discloses what they are paid, but they did greet us as we left for pictures and tips. We watched eight divers in all, the highest dove from 136 feet up, the water averages in depth from 4-12 feet, and it is 5 feet away from water's edge to the cliff, so they must jump out and down.

No one has died from jumping, (although there has been broken arms and legs), the divers quit when they believe it is time, the oldest one to date was 65-years-old, and his last jump caused him to pass out. He came too after four hours and told his companions it was time to quit! The divers rotate positions on the cliff, and only dive two or three times per week...

Here, prescriptions for drugs are needed only for antibiotics, prescription costs 20 pesos (about a $1.00 U.S.) The Spanish fort was erected in the 1600's and September 15, 1810, The United States of Mexico gained its independence from Spain.

Fishing both sport and commercial is very good off the coast, except the day after a full moon. All the beaches are public, if you use one of the beach umbrellas, the rent charged pays for those that clean the beach daily. It is sunny 347 days a year here, if it does rain, it mostly rains at night, the exceptional day rains only last a half hour or so. VW Bug taxis in the city; the crossing rule of "run or die" still applies except in the few crosswalks that are controlled.

We also passed sites where other Hollywood elites had investments and partnerships, including the old Los Flamingo's Hotel jointly owned by John Wayne, and Johnny Weissmuller. Sylvester Stallone has a mansion here, there is a white and pink hotel where every room has its own pool, and transportation provided by a pink and white jeep, per room. Jacque Cousteau named one of the coves, Cortez Bay "The largest outdoor swimming pools" the calm waters invite all water sports.

The tour ended just after noon, the guide was excellent, and we headed back to the ship to hydrate (even though every place we stopped, offered free water, beer, and Pina' Collates).

Lunch, Lynn off to games, and mail postcards, I found the room attendant and arranged for a laundry cart to transport Ducky on judgment day, and caught up on the journaling, Ducky is finished, awaiting the completion! I joined Lynn for the games in the afternoon, we met an interesting couple at a table for four, listened to a duo after supper, joined into the "60's and 70's Live Dance Party" that was crowded, (30-40 people!) lively! We had lots of fun!

My right shoulder started to throb, I went to the room, and Lynn went to karaoke to finish up her night.

Sunday, May 7th, 2017 another day at sea. We slept in till 8! Had breakfast, then Lynn went down to work on the communal jig saw puzzle, I explored the library, the WIFI is poor, at best, sometimes I can get my Gmail account, most the time the roadrunner account times out before opening. I would say about 1/3 of the people on board have either phones or notepads they carry with them. I found this amazing with an average age of 95! (Or 105!?!)

I went to join Lynn for the first on-board game, oops, we were supposed to turn our clocks back last night, and so I was an hour early! Back to the library, changed watch, and joined her and now a growing consistent group of about 25 in on ship activities, this being bowling!

Back to the room to catch up on the journaling, add some finishing touches to Ducky, and plan out the rest of the day.

Trivia, we got third place, a light supper, a game of Name That

Tune, and a Burt Baccarat production show and I was done. Lynn went off to a music show.

Believe it or not both of us are tired of food and drinks, from 6:30 A.M. till midnight there is some kind of food out, breakfast, or doughnuts or cookies, coffee and hot chocolate, just use the machines that are always stocked; Drinks (alcohol, soda, coffee, as much as you want) start about 11:30, served to you, even some pretty top shelf liquors brought to you or belly up to a number of bars and they are yours, with snacks!

Monday May 7th, Mazatlán, Mexico, our tour starts at 9:00 AM. I went early for a light breakfast at the coffee bar with Lynn to see why I couldn't get out on the Wi-Fi the last two days. The computer expert showed up, asked what suite, nodded, did something on his computer, and asked me to try again…it worked…seems there was a glitch two day ago, only affecting certain parts of the ship….

Lynn took the computer back to the room; we met at the crossword puzzle and then got in line for the excursion.

As we leave the terminal, we are cautioned that there are no pedestrians in Mexico, just survivors! Always watch, always cross only in the crosswalks, and always watch…Matalan has a population of 600,000, about the same as Milwaukee, and of the 600,000 30% are retired from Canada and the U.S., the cost of living here is very low.

This is the home of Pacifica beer; it is owned by Corona. The main industries are:

1. Fishing and shrimping
2. Tourism
3. Agriculture
4. Pacifica beer

Most of the downtown is in ruin, the rich moved out for larger homes, yards, and land. The Hass family (of Avocado fame) has built (donated) both the hospital here and the theatre. The beach is 12 miles long, (all open to the public, and the hotels must provide access to the beach from the sidewalk) most of it is shallow and rocky, there are 15 islands off the coast, all are Federally owned, and there is no staying on any of them over night.

Wild animals include goats, deer, and many birds, sea lions come here all the way from San Diego, they are protected and the fishermen and everyone else are forbidden to kill them.

The cabs are open air, white fiberglass bodies like golf carts with VW engines, no meters, so you must negotiate price before getting in or you are at the mercy of the cab driver.

The town is on the San Andres fault, it was invaded by France twice, and the biggest holiday here is Mardi gras.

This used to be a big spring break town, but some kids dropped ash trays one on top of the hotel owners Mercedes, so the hotel owners petitioned the city "no more Spring Break crowds" and yes, they won!

First stop was a silver store for shopping; we went across the street to a Senior Frog's store to pick up a few "needed" souvenirs. After a half hour, we all board the bus and proceed to the cliff where three cliff divers dive for us, this time it is unpaid brothers, so everyone chips in to pay them, and yes it was worth it, this time they were even closer to the side of the cliff!

The road has cliff on one side, beach on another, pass a cave with gates called "Diablo" we can smell a sulfur smell as we pass.

We stop at the shrimp market, our guide goes out and shows us samples of the catch, the more transparent the shrimp, the fresher; they are selling them, $1.50-$4.50 U.S. is per kilo or 2.2 pounds!!

After the shrimp market, we are dropped off for an hour to explore the main church, 93% of Mexico is Catholic.

The Catholics actually started running out of money after most of this church was completed, the Jewish community stepped up and helped finish the church, in exchange, on top all of the stained-glass windows are a stained-glass star of David. (Talk about getting along!)

We look inside, beautiful! Then explore a local bakery and buy a small treat for making the restroom available to us, we still had a little time, so Lynn and I struck out to explore the one block square market place, we find fresh food, seafood, and souvenirs.

We go back to the meeting place and are directed to walk back to the bus next to the still-operation Woolworth store. I did take a picture of a public phone on a pole. Also, a guy in one of those fiberglass white VW taxis posed for me!

We have one photo op concerning two white rocks, these are to represent two local guys fighting for the same woman, in the picture, there is a lower observation deck shaped like a heart, she ended up marrying a sailor…go figure!!

Back on the ship, a couple games played, and dinner with a very interesting couple, and then we went back to the room, watched a movie and called it a day.

Tuesday May 9th, 2017, Cabo San Lucas! We are anchored by 8:00 AM; this is another tender port; our excursion leaves at 9:30. Cabo San Lucas is on the 1,000-mile tip of Baja California ending as El Arco. The sea of Cortez or Gulf of Baja is the world's youngest body of water and contains more than 100 uninhabited islands; this is still an active geological zone. Los Cabo is actually two villages merged.

We tendered in and actually saw a sea lion swimming alongside the tender for a while. This happened on the way back to the ship. We will be looking for whales, both Grays and Humpbacks (some of these whales average 40-50 feet!), along with sea lions on our way to San Diego, but back to our day.

The excursion was called Salsa-Salsa. We were given two options as far as drink that were included, Margarita's or Hibiscus water, both very good, I opted for one, Lynn the other, and both were continuously filled throughout the event.

What we accomplished was assembling 6 salsas and a margarita, and there were two contests, one on mild salsa, the other on spicy salsas, in both contests there was no winner, however, I was in the spicy contest, and the tour guide pulled me aside and confirmed I made the best!

The salsas we made were as follows:

1. Garlic, onion, salt, lime, tomato, and cilantro
2. Garlic, onion and tomato
3. The above (2) plus avocado
4. Tomato, onion, cilantro
5. Pineapple, tomato, salt, and lime
6. Apple, pineapple, and nun rum

After tasting each, we took group pictures, and danced several Salsas' with judges determining which couple were most graceful, most improved, and best dancers.

It seemed as though everyone had fun, I made a suggestion to have the name of the restaurant on the chef's hats we were issued and sell them. If they use the idea, they will send us a couple, we gave them our card!

Back on the boat by three, I took a nap, Lynn played some games, dinner, name that tune, and a magic show finished the day.

Educating Noah…Travelin'

There is no longer a jig saw puzzle out, books are all locked up, no menu holders for dinner or drinks, a few people have diarrhea, and there is nothing to be handled commonly. There is staff to provide what you want with gloved hands, I asked to keep our menu, just to show one night's extensive offerings and the quality and quantity available, this includes a white or red wine selection offered and included, or the offer from anything the bar offers.

Wednesday May 10th, 2017. My stamina is failing, the hip and arm are working against me, and using alcohol as an analgesic is tiring. We set our clocks back again last night, another time zone changes, our next port of call is San Diego, and we received notice of agents coming aboard on Thursday for everyone to go through customs, we will also get our passports back at that time.

Last night a pod of small dolphins played off the ship, the magician was very practiced, a good comedian, and highly entertaining. Today is a day at sea; I will try to use their computers to open my roadrunner account, with all the spam I bet it is full in just three days. Road runner is not a good choice for travelers, I had the same problem in Russia, it will not load, and thank goodness, I also have a g-mail account. Funny how Time Warner keeps on failing with service, must be that kinda' monopoly thing! We will be working the ship activities, the lecture series is a Smithsonian professor that explains everything through art…no interest in this, I will take a peek and see if is actually interesting to other fossils!?! I did, maybe 100 people showed up. It is in the upper 60's, (temperature, not passengers!) and winds gusting in the teens, bright and cold.

No self-serve, no books, menu holders, not even self-serve with utensils, no salt and pepper shakers, jackets are being worn, few people on deck.

We participated in the entertainment staff events. A consistent group of about 18-20 now shows up, congenial, and we know everyone by their first name.

Noah

I received show time information for our Friday boat contest, due to the winds we had today, I changed the sail configuration to allow it to be raised and lowered, like a real one. Dinner with the Drs., nice couple; the show was kind of bland, mostly singing, didn't recognize a number of the songs, went back to the cabin, shoulder really acting up, Lynn joined me, few people at venues after the show.

Thursday May 11th, 2017. We have to go through passport inspection. Lazy morning, breakfast at leisure, played a number of games with Lynn, and the staff, (Lynn actually played against a staff person and won with zeros, he had negative points!!) lunch was on the open deck. We headed back to our room to wait for our turn to go through customs. I thought it would be interesting, to add some pipe cleaner people to Ducky, while waiting, I had enough pipe cleaners to make 7 people, two were guys, 5 women; I thought I would have them point out which were the guys and which girls! Also, I soaked a stir stick to make an anchor.

Our excursion was called, the inspection went very well, and we received our passports, got a quick look-over, and off to the theatre to wait for our bus to be cued.

We had the San Diego city tour; it was to start at 1:30 and last about 4 hours. The tour included four main sections, the suburb of La Joila; Old San Diego, a park; and a tour of the downtown district.

Our ship was moored next to the USS Midway aircraft carrier, now a museum, which seemed to be smaller than we imagined, out to the busses and into town.

La Joella is an exclusive suburb, (known as the "Jewel of the Pacific") one of five cities (San Diego, Chula Vista, Imperial, Coronado, and National) linked together on these 40 miles Cull Du Sac bay, all beaches are public except for a small percentage used by Sea World.

Springtime means blooming trees. One of the most outstanding was the Jacaranda tree covered in purple flowers; there are also bushes and trees with bright yellows, oranges, pinks, and reds. The average rainfall is 9 ½ inches per year. The water from the Colorado River also provides water to the area, and a desalination plant contributes to the lushness and beauty.

We pass by a gigantic Mormon tabernacle and see many Catholic churches, Jewish temples, and a Mosque, showing the diversity of this city. The first stop is on the coast, where caves are cut into the shoreline; there are a number of sea lions sunning themselves, a large gathering of kormans, and frigates. As we walked the area, more and more clusters of animals and birds were sunning themselves in the warm sun. The water here is about the same as the air temperature at 74 degrees; a few whales have been sited off this point, mostly grey whales. By the way, whale milk is 53% fat, and the mother squeezes the milk into the baby whale's mouth.

One of the problems with the whales now, is that they are getting used to humans, and approach boats including fishing boats. When they do get caught in the nets, there is a special number to call, and divers will come out to free the whales from the nets.

I asked the housing prices of this area, because it seemed to be rather "high-end", and was told lots start about $500,000, many houses in the millions! There are public toilets here, we are an older crowd, and we re-enter the bus to check out Old San Diego.

Old San Diego was just a number of craft and gift shops; we explored, compared prices and moved on. Many of the trees here and in California were imported by the railroads, for rail ties, but the Eucalyptus trees proved to split too easily so they were left alone, and they thrived. (No Koalas though!!)

Next stop was Balboa Park. On the way, California got its name from Queen Talia (?) and was the 31st State admitted. The Mormons taught Californians to bake bricks so that they would last.

Noah

The land for this park, 1400 acres, was in exchange to Alonzo Horton, who agreed to import trees from around the world; he did it too, for over ten years! He also was the person who planned Hortonville, Wisconsin, this small world is amazing for one thing, and the demonizing of the rich still puzzles me!

Balboa Park was part of the 1916 Exposition Panama California that began with an opening lasting two year. We walked through an anthem theatre that has the world's largest outdoor organ, donated by the Sprinklers family; there are fifteen museums on the property, and all the buildings have been rebuilt from the bottom up to make them as earthquake proof as possible. One of the museums was some aeronautics building, with a jet that could land on water, and also one of the Black Bird supersonic jets. It is interesting to note that the Black bird is made primarily of titanium, and most of the titanium was purchased from the Soviet Union.

Blackbird, fastest plane, 3X the speed of sound, London to New York in less than two hours.

On the way back to the ship, we toured the downtown by bus, the popular gas light district, China Town, the old red-light district that has been cleaned up, everything was very clean, inviting, and a significant selection of entertainment and food.

Back on the boat, changed for dinner, had dinner with another interesting couple, attended the last magician show, Martin Lewis (very practiced, smooth, and entertaining), then we met a group for Karaoke, Lynn and I sang "I Got You Babe" and we got most of the small crowd up to sing Neil Diamond's "Sweet Caroline". I headed back to the room; Lynn hung out with others, and finally got back at 1 A.M. The neighbors immediately noticed the yellow tape on their door, and the next morning we had a sign on ours indicating Banjos (Men's room) in Spanish.

Friday, May 12, 2017, our last day at sea, tomorrow the cruise is over. We slept in, had a good breakfast, came back to the room finished up on the boat, and took it down first to the desk, to show them as promised, then up to the outside deck.

Winds were 12-15 knots, white capped seas, not good for a sailing ship! There were three entries, Ducky was three times the size of the two others. We were the first to show her, after that they let me lower the sail. All the boats passed the float test, and the pool test, the waves were over a foot high in the pool!

WE WON!! The officers gave us the best mark but made it a point to tell me that the rudder should have been on the port side, not starboard. We got a certificate as master boat builders, two visors, two hats, two sets of golf balls, two long sleeve, two short sleeve shirts and two decks of cards. Plus, all the gloating we could muster.

We had a small lunch, I was called by the event manager to run the sail back up for display by the concierge desk, which I did; played two more event games, and trivia, we dressed for our final meal on the ship, went down and requested a group table, after we were sitting for about 15 minutes, we were joined by Martin Lewis, the magician! Another couple, a pharmacist and his wife from Tasmania! The meal lasted almost three hours, what great conversation! Then we excused ourselves, packed, and put out our main luggage by 11:00. The "show" was a movie, back to the room to re-check everything; we leave the ship at 9 A.M.

Saturday May 13, 2017. We both were up by 6:45 and out of the room by 7:15, the cruise included gratuities but we left a little extra for the room stewards.

Breakfast, then waited, we were finally called around 9 A.M., this was the fastest disembarkation, turned in card key, declaration of what was bought, picked up our luggage and were out finding our tour guide at 9:10.

We are part of a four-person post-cruise excursion; we were

picked up with the other couple and whisked away in a Mercedes custom van to the Golden Gate Bridge. We took our pictures by a cross-section of one of the cables and strolled on to the bridge to take some more pictures. Although flowers are mostly past peak, there was still plenty of beauty to be taken.

We were to go to the Cline Cellars winery next, but the other couple thought it would be OK to stop in the pavilion for a bathroom break. They finally showed up at the car, and we left. Now we were late, a phone call was made, and the winery accommodated us being late, but the pre-tour restroom break promised did not materialize, and for some reason, I actually made it to a time where I could break away…that is when the other couple decided to pick up a couple sandwiches before the wine tasting……yeah, really considerate folks!

The tour was great, a beautiful vineyard, built on a mission, tasted their 5 best wines, toured the gift shop, and off we went to Sonoma. This was our lunch stop, we were on our own for an hour and 15 minutes, ate at a bakery that was recommended by our guide, and toured the town, much like a door county town.

Sheep are kept, they are let out to graze between the vines, they eat all the grass and the lower grape leaves, making it easier for the harvesters to gather the grapes. Grapes taste sour to sheep, and they don't touch them!

Back on the bus, everyone actually showed up on time, and off to Napa Valley, to explore the Domaine Taittinger Sparkling wines.

The tour gave us how sparkling wines are made and some facts to share, and here they are:

1. The smaller the bubble, the better the Champaign or sparkling wine.
2. Foil was to cover the top for variations of how full the bottle was. This has been changed, if fewer than 750 ml,

Educating Noah...Travelin'

heavy state fine, if over, additional taxes levied.

3. To rid the sediment or Leeds the bottles used to be inserted in snow, upside-down, and then the frozen sediment was taken out; now it is done with cooling agent. Spain and Portugal, running out of cork trees, trees last up to 300 years, but the cork that can be used must come from a tree that is at least 50 years old.

5. Bottles cost about thirty-five cents, cork now costs fifty cents to $1.25; that is why cheap wines going to synthetic or screw on tops.

6. Wine will only age in corked bottles. (They can breathe)

7. The quiet pop when opening a bottle of Champaign or Sparkling wine is known as a nun's fart.

8. The foil top and wire that holds in the cork is called "the cage".

9. Roses were planted on the end of the vine rows to detect any disease or insects, but they became more resilient so they are really just for ornamental use now.

10. Napa Valley, the 40 X 40-mile area most resembles the growing conditions as that in France; and the wine here is in some cases judged the best in the world!

Samples of all wines were given, including some $100.00 plus bottles; after the tour and presentation we were taken to our hotel, in downtown Napa Valley, this will be our home tonight, and after the train ride tomorrow. Supper on us, hot shower and small meal were welcome!

Sunday, May 14th, Mother's Day, and second day in Napa Valley California.

We both couldn't keep our eyes open, both of us asleep by 9:30

last night. The day started out slow and easy, we both took our time to dress and get ready for breakfast. We were down to eat at 7:45 to a ghost town, two other couples, but that was it! We both ordered simple one egg breakfasts, but the bill was still almost $40 bucks; no free breakfast here! (But we found that any upscale hotel we stayed at, you not only pay a premium for a room, but the "free-be's" are gone too!)

Back to the room, collected some rocks for those rock friends, and walked the three blocks to the Wine Train!

The Napa Valley Wine Train was the brain child of Vincent DE Domenico, the same guy that came up with Rice-a-Roni and Ghirardelli Chocolates. (Talk about the Midas touch!) It was started in 1989 featuring a World Class Chef, serving 333 meals a day, made-to-order, and fresh from scratch. (I kept the menu!)

We were told to be there by 10, but when we got there, we found the train leaves at 11:30, so again, hurry and wait. We explored the souvenir stores, and walked around the station, gathering more pictures of flowers in bloom, this may be the album with the most flowers!!

The bridge to the trains has many locks, like many of the bridges in Europe, when I asked the person in the souvenir shop why there wasn't any for sale, she told me they stopped selling them a couple weeks ago...I gave her "that look", and she whole heartedly agreed! I guess they were running out of room on the bridge and not enough profit margins in locks!!

We left promptly at 11:30; we shared the table with the other couple from our "group" and got acquainted. She was a school teacher, he a builder both in Poland and in the U.S.A... We were in the observation car, 1st Class; first to load, preferred table etc.

We were served sparkling wine, gourmet choices in appetizer, soup or salad, main course, and dessert. The train travels slowly to take in the countryside, the hour and a half provided adequate time to

Educating Noah...Travelin'

eat, talk, and observe. The waiter was very informative, and although we were told tips were included, the menu discreetly stated that a gratuity of $10-$15 each would be appreciated, yeah, I left the $30; but I don't think the other couple did!

When we reached the town of St. Helena, we were led through the entire train of nine cars to observe the other classes, the kitchen, and the other folks on the train. We were loaded on a small bus and taken with a group of about fifteen to Castello di Amoroso. (Castle of Love)

This is the 10th year anniversary of the completion, all the materials were imported from Italy, and the design was to make this as 13th century Tuscan castle as authentic as possible! 121,000 square feet, 106 rooms, complete with a maze of caves and caverns below, high walls, five defensive towers, and 30 acres (here) of vineyards!

The tour included visiting the court yard, a grand dining room, a chapel; examples of old wine presses, then through a maze of caverns with thousands of filled wine casks. We are treated to sampling of a barrel, the pipette they use is called a "wine thief", and we are all given a sample. Then we go to a tasting room for more samplings, including wines made here selling for more than $100.00/bottle; discounts are offered along with special multi bottle cases for taking on commercial flights. They will sell you a complete barrel and all for a little over $1,000., if you like.

The end of the tour left everyone in a mellow mood; we had a 30-minute motor-coach ride back to the train station and a short walk back to the hotel for a little nap, journaling for me and preparing for a light supper. This would not be complete without some wine stuff:

1. Amoroso bypassed the prohibition days by claiming their wine was actually for medicinal purposes only. (I have used this excuse in the past myself!)

2. What did the white grape say to the purple grape? "Breath!!"

3. What is all you can expect from weak grapes? "Just a little whine"

4. And for the olive lovers…. Where do you get extra virgin olive oil? "Ugly olives"; extra extra virgin olive oil?? "Ugly olives that can't cook!!"

We walked a couple blocks to the Oxbow market district to GOTT'S, a hamburger joint mentioned on Guy Fierri's Dinner's Drive-in's and Dives (Triple D's). I kept this menu also, a burger, garlic fries, and two root beers came to a little more than $20.00, but I guess in California that is cheap! The food was good, and of course the menus have a large beer and wine menu.

Walk back to the hotel, Lynn commented there was a real "safe" feeling in walking back along the river to the hotel.

Showers, re-packs, and planning for check-out for tomorrow, and we called it a night, another great experience!

Monday, May 15th, 2017 Lynn's Birthday; We started off with being the only two in the breakfast area, and then joined by others who were eating off a private buffet; it took over 20 minutes to get our breakfast, this was the second morning I needed the Imodium after breakfast….

We had the original instructions, and did not update the new times, so we were an hour early checking out and sitting in the lobby…hurry up and wait…

We were picked up by our escort and driver and preceded to Sausalito. This was our first stop on the way back to San Francisco. This is an art community just outside of San Francisco, (actually it was where the Liberty Ships were built during WWII; all of that is gone now).

We stopped here to look at San Francisco across the bay, use the rest room facilities and explore a few of the shops. Yes, we contributed to the community, none of the prices are given with sales tax, and that tax here, is...., wait for it...; 9.3%!! This town also has a large house boat (400+) community, mooring fees average $700/month.

Back on the van, we see a Lane Zipper, this is used to add lanes during rush hour, taking one away from outgoing lanes and adding one to incoming lanes to accommodate rush traffic.

We attempted another high view, but the county blocked all the overlook parking areas without notifying anyone or signs out, go figure!

San Francisco, it is sunny, but cool, in the 60's. We stop on top of Lombard Street; this is the Crooked Street. We start at the top and slowly work our way down, it is steep, steps are 1/2 regular height but lots of them! The street is at least four blocks long, pictures taken on the way down, top and bottom, then we walked down an additional 4 blocks to stop and have a noon snack before progressing to the pier.

Alcatraz is our next destination; the tickets have been reserved for the 1 o'clock sail of the ferry. We get in line, board the ferry, and arrive on the island in about twenty minutes.

A ranger gathers us up, briefs us as to what to explore, and indicates where a people mover for walking challenged to take. It was afternoon; I and Lynn had walked that crooked ½ plus mile, so we opted to take the mover. (I think I was the most slowed down, everyone else was off and gone by the time I had my left hip set!)

The tour of the inside of the prison is on recordings, and a self-guided tour. Very thorough, very interesting, and it takes you through everything, cells, corridors, offices, guard's quarters, dining room, kitchens, and exercise yards. The tour lasts over an hour, is complete, and in looking back, there didn't seem to be really that many cells!

We took an earlier ferry back and grabbed a bite on the dock while waiting for the other couple and our ride. The winds have picked up, 15-20 mph and cold!

Our guide joined us, the van appeared, we were given a ride through China town; there is also a Russian town, an Italian section, so why is Milwaukee labeled as the most segregated town?? Just more promotion of division I guess…more bending of facts...

We check into the hotel, have to ask for breakfast tickets, have a nice supper in the hotel, and prepare for the journey home tomorrow. Problems with the internet connection, after four people and a half hour finally get that working, the rewards card didn't work either for dinner, so hopefully everything will be worked out by check-out tomorrow!

Tuesday May 16th, 2017; we are going home! We went down for breakfast, packed-up, and checked out, after having them apply the credit for the internet promised the night before, so much for Hilton!

Our driver met us in the lobby below; the traffic wasn't too bad especially during rush hour. Lynn and I agreed, we are not big city people, San Francisco, New York, and Chicago…no thanks!!

Our wait at the airport went well, except the loud talking on cell phones is so irritating!

Our flight arrived 20 minutes early, luggage was easy to get, and we trekked to the bus pick-up, and made it with 2-3 minutes to spare!

Traffic home was bearable, the bus was full! Tiffany picked us up; we were home, luggage upstairs by 8 PM! Not bad for leaving San Francisco at 11 A.M.

Another venture completed, now to finish the documentation, go through the over 700 pictures taken, get ready for the hip replacement and check up on Ma!

It took less than a week to finish the writing, finish the photo album, check on Ma, three appointments to finalize the left hip replacement, catch up on mail, e-mails, and lodge the complaint with Hilton on how poor their service was. I also started reviewing the excursions for Japan coming up in October, e-mailed back and forth with an interested party in the time share, that is sold, just check and paperwork, the lot may have an offer next week, that should be gone soon also!

The only glaring observation I have regarding the last cruise, is that you can actually get tired of excellent food and being served all the time! Actually, not take the custom blend coffee, perfect cocktails, and constant variety of well -presented food! Good to be home, good to drive the car, good to shop for food and look at the bill!!

I did get another debit card from the travel agency, this now pays me back plus for the 500 shares I bought last year, so the shares are now free, and I have some extra bucks in my pocket!

My left hip replacement went extremely well; this time it was done anteriorly. I showed up at 7AM, taken in at 7:20, prepped and waited my turn for the 10:00, my operation time. I was back to the world by 1:45! I have a puffy upper leg, little pain, and actually walked by 6:30 that evening! Compare that to when I had my right hip done!

I was discharged at 10:00 on FRIDAY…48 hours after the start of the replacement!

We had set up the spare bedroom for these occasions, within two weeks, I had eliminated the toilet riser, and started using my tub shower. I started walking consistently, the right shoulder actually hurts more than the healing hip some days, I refused to take any pain meds, I do not want to jeopardize the right shoulder replacement! I attained 5000 steps per day, walking up the stairs several times, and have agreed to work for the DAV a day a week in July!

With all this time on my hands, I worked on the 2018 trips, made arrangements for the Doro River in Spain and Portugal for October 2018, looking at England, Scotland and Wales, and Cuba with Jamaica.

The shoulder is getting worse, took two Oxytocin today just to function. We did a cross state run to a place in Prairie Du Chen; that bragged about different jerkies. A 3-hour drive each way, Cruz did not care for long drives, especially when the internet on his phone quit, a grandson of a neighbor came along but both were on their phones the way over and back, I bought jerky for both, they refused to try the fish jerky (it was very tastee) and bought them lunch also.

That evening was the show and tell from the India trip group. My picture album was the highlight, and a few more asked for the write-up. Lynn did not come along, drinks and dinner were included, good to see those folks again, but I do prefer traveling with Lynn and folks we don't know.

I am visiting ma once a week, have most of her bills on auto withdrawl, taking her to doctor, dentist, and shopping. She still has Hatti visit at least twice a week and others from the senior apartments also visit on occasion. She is eating regularly, walks to and from the dining room, and knows most of the residents, and all the help.

Lynn signed me up to be in the fourth of July parade riding in the veteran's trolley, it was fun, there were 14 of us, three from Vietnam and the others from Korea and WWII; we were the youngest. We were all presented with quilts from the women of Quilts for Vets, nice gesture! Lynn and I brought $30.00 worth of tootsie rolls and the driver let us sit in the stairwell to toss the candy; I couldn't believe the number of kids!! It was great!

The problem of these waits for the next surgery is that I don't trust the surgeons; and anything negative may stop the replacement. I went to 5 appointments as a preliminary for the shoulder replacement and have hounded my provider since to make sure the blood levels are

OK; One nurse practitioner did find and enlarged lymph gland in my neck, I told him that I had a sore throat, but another appointment was arranged with an eyes, ears, and throat specialist just before surgery, so now I am taking Nyquil AM and PM ....it is driving me nuts!!

The shoulder replacement went off with only a 2-hour delay, but it took place!

A reverse replacement was not necessary, a lot of arthritis was removed, but just the socket was needed.... I was determined to leave the next day. Tuesday morning the doctor came, told me what went on and agreed that if I got OT and PT to release me, I could go home.

OT came first, I dressed without assistance from her, and showed her I could go to the bathroom without help; she gave me an A-OK, then the wait. Since I had used the arm a lot, I was in a ton of pain. Pushed the call button and told the desk that I needed pain relief. After 45 minutes, I walked down the corridor to the desk, I requested what happened to the nurse? They apologized and said they would have someone find her and attend to the pain. She came ten minutes later, provided the pills, and confirmed that if O.T. (Occupational Therapy) O.K.-ed me I could leave, and promised to bring an ice bag for the swelling. Of the three ice bags, I requested while there for 24 hours, I received only one, the first one; both the nurse and the aide "forgot" the second and third....... I walked down with the aide to OT, went through the test, passed, and he released me, I told him I did not need an aide to return to my room and left, with his blessing. I stopped at the nursing desk on the way back to the room, let them know I had all the clearances and to let the nurse know to finalize the paperwork so that I could leave by 3:30; Lynn picked me up, everything was cleared and back home I was!!!

It has been 4 weeks, I have a chair that exercises the arm, I spend hours in that chair, along with walks, and a pulley system on a door. This has been more painful than the knees and hips, go figure.

We also went on a trip with the Franklin Seniors for a tour of Chicago. It involved a 1 ½ hour river cruise exploring thee architectural icons of Chicago, a lunch at Harry Carrie's and then a bus tour of 7-8 neighborhoods.

We left Franklin by 9AM, and returned at 7PM, a great tour, learned a lot and were pleasantly surprised by how clean the neighborhoods were, and the lack of graffiti. The restaurant housed the late Frank Nitti's vault, and the whole experience was excellent, there was two bus-loads of us, over 100 people!

It is a little over a month to the next adventure. We also plan to see the ARK in Kentucky, a full-sized recreation, and I told the therapist that he only had 4 weeks to get me ready!! Hopefully, the troubles with North Korea will be resolved. Lynn is getting a bit nervous!! (South Korea has two stops on our Japan cruise later this year.)

The Ark Encounter

The Ark adventure started early on a Friday morning. The traffic was tolerable, a few lane sitters but we averaged a good 70 plus mph. Lunch was at a dairy complex that looked interesting from the interstate, had a lunch, picked up some Christmas gifts at the gift shop, and continued on our way.

We did change time zones, so we pulled into the La Quinta an hour later than planned, but the Cracker Barrel was just across the street. Dinner caught us up on southern food, with Okra, grits, cornbread, and shrimp for me. Lynn had roast beef; regular portions are now too much for both of us, and we walked out stuffed! The beds were comfortable, the breakfast plentiful, and we left the motel to arrive at the Ark Encounter by 9:30 a.m.

It was located just off the highway but hidden due to the rolling hills. The parking lot seemed sparsely full, we parked by a light pole to locate the car. We could see the Ark from the parking lot, you had

Educating Noah...Travelin'

to go to a bank of ticket booths, then take a park bus for a 5-10-minute trip to the Ark.

We were both surprised at the size of the thing! The people were very friendly, very similar to the Disney personnel, the area around the Ark contains a restaurant, craft shops, where fair-traded items are sold, and a pond, all surrounded by flowers and vegetation. In the background is a zip line for those wanting to fly by the seat of their pants!

We walked around the pond, some topiary animals, and flowers ending their bloom season. You enter the Ark from below the bow, there is a ramp and side door about half way up, but that was only for staff. Inside you progress past the obligatory photo ($34.00 for the cheapest package, we passed) Then into the Ark. There is an open area stem to stern about 10 feet wide and top to below deck for lighting, plus lamps inside. On the sides and in the middle, are storage areas for food, oil, and water, there were two theatres where there were presentations very cleverly done as interviews of Noah and his family before the flood. There were a number of areas explaining science vs bible, different ages and even how waste both solid and liquid from people and animals may have been addressed.

Time lines, as far as the time of the flood, correlations and verifications from around the world, and the answers to questions about the sea dwellers and how the fresh and salt water animals survived; It is also thought the time in the Ark was about a year! It RAINED 40 days and 40 nights....

It took us a good 2 1/2 hours to work our way through the Ark, there were a lot of Amish there, everyone was pleasant, kids all well behaved, at times crowded at an exhibit, but it seemed all were aware of others, and accommodated one another.

On the way out, you had to pass through the gift shop (imagine that!) and we were on the road by noon. We stopped for lunch, and just before Wisconsin, stopped at a seafood restaurant (Captain Porky's on Hwy. 41; It was on our "must stop" list) for supper, home and unpacked by 7:00 p.m. A great two-day trip!

Two months since the right shoulder replacement; saw the MD; will see me again in late November; this is taking a lot longer than I ever thought, I can get the right arm up about chest high; I need to exercise more; push it!! I will get instructions for exercises while on the Far East cruise, hopefully I will "wow" both OT and MD in November…no matter how it hurts!!

Now, on to the next adventure, said "bye" to mom and assisted living crew, instructions to both kids, Tiffany is taking the lead, she will also drop us off at the bus station.

The Far East Adventure October-2017

Tiffany promptly picked us up at 7:19 so that we could be ready for the 8:00 o'clock bus to O'Hare. Due to traffic the bus was behind schedule, so we arrived at the airport a half hour later than we planned.

Our tickets were through American Airlines, with a sub text Japan Air; we tried the KIOSK at American International, didn't recognize us, we called over the attendant, and she directed us to Japan Air where we could actually check in, typical airline confusion, then we had to go through regular TSA since Japan Air doesn't recognize Trusted Travelers, the line did go fast but since I had a problem lifting my right arm high enough for the scan, they gave me a complete pat down.

The loading of the plane was very orderly, with no push and shove. We had premium economy seats on two, four, and two patterns, so the seats were window and aisle. They were also the most spacious we have had, with ample leg room and seat comfort. The food was generous, tasty, and hot, the flight attendants were friendly and helpful, and we were supplied with slippers, Sony headsets, eye covers, toothbrushes, toothpaste, and earplugs. (There is a BIG difference between Japan Airlines and ANY American airline!!)

It was from The flight path from Chicago to upper Alaska, across to Russia and down, crossing the dateline, and touched down on the 4th at 3:30 PM Tokyo time. We were in daylight the entire trip. We got through customs, got our bags, and met with the group for our 1 ½ hour drive to the hotel for the night. It started getting dark at 5:30 P.M.

We checked into the hotel, got our welcoming envelopes with directions for pick-up tomorrow for the ship, breakfast, and room keys. We found our room, each country has unique lighting for the rooms, and we figured ours out fairly quickly without having to call room service...showers, travel socks off, first travel day done! A loooong day, both of us beat!

October 5th, yeah, we crossed the date line yesterday, we went to bed early, and slept till about I A.M. then struggled to go back to sleep and slept till 6:30 to re-set our internal clocks.

Took some A.M. pictures out of the room window, we are both quickly getting spoiled with toilets that have warmed seats and bidet. We went down for the complimentary buffet western breakfast, this one included a doughnut and bread table, an egg and roast beef section, and a huge round table with at least 50 different breakfast offerings, including fish, fruit, eggs, cold cuts, cheeses and more.

Ours was the first bus to the ship of six buses, leaving at 11:00, so we went back to the room to watch local TV and wait.

It seems that there are 42 nuclear reactors on the Japanese islands (we thought only that one that went down in 2011!) The new electric cars that they are designing have motors at the wheels, they will be able to park by turning sideways, and they will have magnetic brakes which are more efficient than the disc brakes today.

At ten, we left the room and checked out. Lynn stayed in the lobby, and I went for a walk. The silence was mind-blowing. There was very little traffic noise and no noise inside the room or the hotel!

The 45-minute bus ride to the pier was also very interesting. Everything was spotless, with no dirt or trash. We asked and were told that the Japanese are a very clean people; streets are not swept by the city, there is no trash outside, and even in the public bathrooms, you are reminded to wipe the sink when you are done for the next person.

We were told that in school, the oldest student in the class is responsible for the class to leave the room clean, and this is carried forward in adult life. Very nice to see, no graffiti, even the lack of trash barrels, they were not needed; people take care of their own trash!!

"Tokyo e Yokoso!" (Welcome to Tokyo) A little bit about Tokyo. Over the past 500 years, the little fishing village of Edo has changed into the most populated urban area of the world, with 13 million in the city alone and an estimated 37 million, including the metropolitan area. One US dollar currently equals 100.8 yen (JPY). Japan only takes its own currency. It is not customary to tip in Japan; it is considered rude, and tipping will only confuse the server. Handy words to know:

Hello, is "Konnichiwa," Yes is"hai," No is "iie," bathroom is "toire," Thanks a lot "Domo arigato."

Goodbye "sayonara" How much? "ikura"

We were on the ship by 12:00; (actually the ship is moored in Yokohama), rooms are not ready till 1P.M., so we checked with the head waiter regarding dinner, then went up to have lunch, to the room to unpack, go over the ship layout, and check the excursion tickets for the cruise. I did find an extra set of tickets and turned them in at the excursion deck. I also checked about the internet, I was given a password and instructions, back to the room, still feeling the effects of jet drag. Evening meal and watched a movie at the theater. This is an older and "smaller" cruise ship, launched in 2000, with a crew of 957, and a guest capacity of 2120.

Friday, October 6th

A full-day excursion and we are on the bus by 8:00. It will take an easy hour to get to our first destination, so here are some interesting things we learned;

Count to ten in Japanese: Itchy, knee, sun, yawn, go, ruck, nana, hutch, Q, Jew; that's 1-10 phonetically.

Typical Japanese breakfast: raw fish, raw egg, rice and soy sauce, with fermented (spoiled) soy bean curd on the side. (Yum!)

We drove on bridges (one was 800 meters long) and through tunnels and elevated tollways. "Anything shortening transit time is tolled"; to own a car in Tokyo, you must prove you have a parking space for it. These spaces range from $100-$400/month; gas is $1.40 per liter; they only produce 1% of the oil and gas they need and only have a 6-month supply on hand.

Housing is expensive, a house outside the city goes for about a million dollars, most rent, and an apartment of about 300 sq. meters is $1500.00/month. Seems like Copenhagen!!)

We passed by the bullet train, it reaches 210 MPH, there is a magnetic train designed for the future that will exceed 380 MPH; there is a lot of discussion about the need.

As we approach our first stop, we enter The Ginza Strip, the high-end shopping street. It is about a half hour before the stores open, and there are employees washing down the sidewalks in front of the stores, scrubbing and squeegee them, including the gutters!

The first stop is The Sen Soji Temple, also called Asakusa Kannon Temple. This temple, founded in the 7th Century, is the oldest extant temple in Tokyo.

Noah

It stands at the end of Nakamise-dori, the oldest street of inside shops, more of an alley lined on both sides with food, souvenir, and gift shops, and actually more food shops! (They were the busiest!) We spent an hour and a half exploring the temple, nosing around the shops and vendors, and then back to the bus for a Western-style lunch.

We did learn that Tokyo is the birthplace of sushi. Tokyo is the largest city in Japan and the capital. 69-70% of the students attend college and there is no military draft.

Lunch was served in a restaurant located in one of the better hotels. The lunch consisted of soup, salad, baked chicken, and a dessert plate, all very tasty!

Back to the bus and on to the next stop, Meiji Shrine, if there is a gate, it is not Buddhist, none of the gates had doors, there was an extensive forest where 10,000 trees were imported to form a quiet, peaceful environment. A lot of walking, peaceful, but it was even more humid under the trees!

The last stop was The Imperial Plaza. This is where Royalty lives. This area is surrounded by a moat, and many trimmed Mogo Pines. Yes, I got pictures! Also, a statue of a Sho-Gun warrior, and the neat thing about this, was the royal family personally had to harvest the rice from the rice patty, fish from the pond, and work with silk from silk worm cocoons kept on-premise to "relate to the common man."

Back to the bus and on the way home to the ship. My eyes have been watering since we de-planed after arriving here, the humidity is very high, the upper 80s and 90s, it sprinkled on and off during the day, and everyone's arthritis was "talkin'," all my artificial joints let me know they weren't happy either!

Both of us dragged ourselves back to the room, safety muster at 5; we opted for dinner at the café, lunch was too big, trivia, and we called it a day!

Saturday, Oct. 6th

We slept in, up at 7, and had breakfast at 7:45—peak time, hard to find a table! We are docked in Shimizu, Japan, the closest port to Mt. Fuji. As we docked, we were treated to a full orchestra greeting our arrival, vendors setting up on the dock, and guides and security taking pictures of themselves at their assigned posts and buses. Our tour starts at 9 A.M. As with yesterday, the buses started loading early. Everyone was on the bus by 9, so off we went!

The drive to the Schirato Waterfalls was about an hour, so here is more about the Japanese culture, relayed by our hostess, KIMI. She wears yellow for identification, and that makes her stand out. This is contrary to the sodalities of the Japanese, but she doesn't care. She is 67 and a black belt, was a nursing teacher and also a guide, and studied English from 6th grade on. Two months ago, she had the honor of guiding Arnold Schwarzenegger; she said he was very kind and pleasant.

There is a total of four major islands that Japan is made of, 70% wood and 120 million people. Patience, modesty, politeness, quiet, family, and independence are to be aspired to, with no reliance on others outside the family or the government. Lucky or good numbers are 3, 5, 7, and 9. The typical Japanese house has one main room, with only a low table for furniture. The usual household has three generations. It is hard for the Japanese to pronounce "Rs" and "Ls," and frogs symbolize Happiness or returning home safely.

We were shown a package of spotted or cherry scrimp, which you heat up and throw on your noodles (very small and unshelled). We drove past green tea plantings, all neatly trimmed, weeded, and in perfect rows. Green tea is supposed to prevent stomach cancer, among other things.

Oh, by the way, the Japanese drive on the left side of the road seems clumsy on many of the turns, but I guess it is from whose perspective!!

Our first stop was the falls. Every place we have gone, we leave the bus and have a 10-15-minute hike to the attraction, this was about 20 minutes, we get 15 minutes to enjoy, and then back to the bus...tough time schedules!!

The first stop was the public toilet. We were warned not to press a button and look into the toilet because it may be the bidet! Also, in the women's room, there is a button to push when using the toilet that makes the sound of a waterfall to mask the sound of "tinkle." There was nothing like that in the men's room!! Oh, in Japan, people carry their own towels, so don't count on any paper towels or drying devices in the restrooms!

After the hike it was 120 steps down to the falls, yep, took pictures, very nice, cruised the shops on the way back, had two ice cream cones, one green tea flavored ice cream, the other wasabi flavored, guess who ate which! The wasabi was subtle and very good!! The green tea was OK...

As we got back on the bus, I asked the driver if he wanted to change places... he was with two other drivers. They thought that was funny but declined.

The next stop was a Shinto shrine. This is the native religion and has eight million gods! (Buddhism was introduced to Japan from China and Korea in the 6th century.) Christianity, 1-10 % of the population. However, Christian weddings are very popular and big events (you can be married in a Christian ceremony), and you can have several faiths here. When you are on the grounds of a shrine, look for a straw rope with white paper; this indicates a sacred spot.

For 200 years, Japan was closed to all countries except China, Korea, and Holland. This was the Shogun era. There are no specific days of worship; January 1, 2, and 3 are the official holidays, and the average commute time to work is 1 hour and 40 minutes ☹; In this area, there is a festival in May, a horseback archery festival.

While at the shrine, we both learned to make proper wishes with bowing protocol and briefly watched a wedding from outside; the bride was all in white, and two small children dressed in traditional clothes (I did get a picture of the boy!) The bride's head is covered in white; this is to "hide her horns" to show that she may be mild, but when provoked, WATCH OUT!

The kimono is very expensive, usually handed down from generation to generation, with ten layers of silk cloth. Single women wear brighter colors, and after marriage, the kimono is dark. Kimonos, like wedding dresses, can be rented; some, if bought, may cost over 1,000,000 yen or $10,000 US.

Kids: 33 days after birth for girls, thirty-four days after birth for boys, are presented at the shrine, then again at three years, and at seven years, the girls are dressed up and presented again, the boys, at five years.

The crane is the symbol of longevity; Christmas in Japan means KFC! Yes, Kentucky Fried Chicken...long lines, they do run out!!

The average life span is 80 for men and 86 for women. Over 85 is not unusual. 1 in 4 at that age has ALS.

The trains stop running after 9 p.m. If you are caught in town, you can rent a sleeping capsule for $30.00 per night; there are some now for women, but they are a bit more expensive, and those areas are exclusively female.

Our last stop was a half-mile walk to a black sand beach for a view of Mt. Fuji, and if you had the urge, dip your foot into the ocean. On the way back, we saw a woman cleaning her driveway on hands and knees, a procession, a ceremony dedicated to the fishermen, including a man dressed as a fisherman in a stylized boat carried by a number of men proceeded by Girl Scouts, other distinctive organizations and costumed actors. The ancient Cyprus trees banking the path had bark that, with a little imagination, looked like dragon scales!

Back to the dock, we grabbed a late lunch just before an early cast-off. We were treated to another demonstration of Japanese Drummers on the pier! Our stateroom faced the pier, so we enjoyed the show from our balcony.

Trivia with a couple from Australia and another from Oregon... we actually won this time, which made everyone on the team happy, then we were kicked out (gabbing too long) so the area could be set up for an exclusive party, no, we were not on the list...none of us!!

Formal night for dinner, tuxes no longer needed, suits or sports coats requested, but long sleeve shirts and dress pants are acceptable now. I had dinner with a couple from New Mexico and another from Canada; a good match. I broke it up after 2 hours of talking and eating, then went to the first production show, song, and dance, and wrapped up the evening.

Sunday, Oct. 8th.

We both woke up early. We received disembarking requests from the desk, so I made copies of what we had and took them down to the desk. Since this is a back-to-back Cruise, we had to let them know whether or not we would be getting off the ship in Shanghai due to customs, and also, in the end, how we were going to return to where we came from! I wanted to beat the crowd, and I did. Back to the room, went over our schedules, set a time to meet for a late breakfast, and caught up on my diary Lynn, on her book.

Our 5-hour excursion started at 11:45, so we had some time to ourselves early today... I went to a lecture on Japan; Lynn explored the library for a new book.

The lecture was presented by Michael Malagan, the retired business owner turned lecturer since he spent most of his life traveling the world, visiting over 200 countries and territories. He married a Japanese woman, and that also gave him a perspective on Japanese culture.

He had a company not connected with Disney but used the Disney name. Disney charges 8-15 % for the trademark, and according to Mr. Malagan, it was well worth it. On to Japan:

This is a shortened history from the feudal to Industrial to the current Japanese free market economy. From 1636, for two hundred years, Japan practiced isolation; they did not want to be American. In Japan, if you left Japan, you could not come back, under penalty of not only ostracism but death!

"John" was taken to America; in 1841, he was a refugee. In 1848, during the gold rush in America, he traveled to the West Coast; in 1851, he returned to Japan with Admiral Perry as an interpreter; in 1853, he became the official Japanese English interpreter,

When Japan determined to become Westernized, they needed to upgrade their military. They say that England had the best navy, so they sent sailors to England and bought English ships. The military was best represented by Prussia, so soldiers were sent to Prussia to learn; the military was one of the best, if not the best, with 200,000 soldiers.

War with China over Korea; China lost; war with Russia over Korea; Russia lost; World War I, Japan allies with Britain, the war is won. In the Treaty of Verse, Japan felt cheated; in 1924, America prevented any immigration from Japan, and Japan was humiliated. 1933 Japan quits the League of Nations, 1935 Japan quits the Roosevelt embargo… little of any of this was taught in school…

One last thing, at the beginning of every school day, all classes have a recitation very similar to what we used to do with the pledge of allegiance. Theirs is a litany of qualities, including Bushido, Integrity, Respect, Duty, Loyalty, and so on.

Noah

As we came into the dock, we were greeted by a fire boat spraying different colors of water to welcome us as we passed by, and white and blue balloons were released as we moored. What a welcome! Then, a Japanese Drum ensemble played as the ship was secured, another great welcome. This is the 150th year of this port being open to the world.

Excursion at 11:45, we were all on the bus and gone by then! It is another good hour on the bus before we get to our first stop, so here is more Japan from a local:

Kobe beef the cows are pastured in the low mountains and pampered with massages daily, and classical music fills the air for a perfectly marbled beef; the name Kobe Beef was from the foreigners. Japanese eat little beef, mainly exported or served at high-end restaurants here. There is another very good beef called WAGYO; this beef is fed beer!

There are 47 "states" or territories; Kewpie is a mayonnaise company (We saw a large logo and advertising sign and asked); 900 tons of trash is processed here daily!

The average salary is around $42,000 US; many of the wives now work due to the high cost of living in Japan; many men find jobs outside of Japan due to the very low unemployment and need to maintain a good life style.

Our first stop is Osaka Castle. It has been rebuilt, and it was discovered that the original was built on top of a Buddhist temple. If the Emperor moves to another city, as he did, that new city becomes the capital of Japan. Kobe is the 6th largest city in Japan. The castle is surrounded by a moat; Lynn saw how far the Castle was away and decided to stay by the moat. It is a good 1/3rd mile hike just to the castle, then ¼ mile inside the walls to the castle. My knees were giving out, so I was lucky enough to get an elevator ride to the top 8th floor. Then worked my way to the surrounding balcony and maneuvered to the edge to take a couple photos…by the way, this was a holiday weekend, tons of people, very crowded, polite, but very close, and you had to take a narrow staircase down…all eight stories with 1000's of other people; The view was okay, it wasn't really worth the effort; I re-joined Lynn, and everyone was back on the bus and ready to go on time.

The next stop was Sumiyoshi Taisha, the guardian deity for sailors and prosperity. There was an orange bridge with reflection, again, lots of people, many women in kimonos, a wedding, little kids dressed up, saw our first yellow Koi in the pools, a wall stacked high with empty sake barrels, and a market just closing up. We walked the grounds, made some more wishes, and threw in some coins. We easily made it back to the bus for the ride home.

Osaka is Japan's center for rice distribution due primarily to the multiple rivers for transportation. One small section in Kobe had graffiti, and that was the only place so far we have seen that. The streets in that area were not as clean as everywhere else, so I guess there are always exceptions!!

Everything is a bridge; all bridges have concave enclosures 10-20 feet high and translucent in residential areas, the barriers for noise control and modesty for the people. There are multiple layers of bridges, and they are EVERYWHERE! It is hard to find clothes made in Japan except for the Kimonos; there is very little crime (although there is a Japanese Mafia… shhhh), no rent–a-bikes, but lots of bikes and scooters everywhere (little or no parking on main streets). Men are more patient than women (watch those married women horns!), and after 40 years old, there is an additional tax on individuals to cover advanced elderly care.

Back on the boat, we had dinner with two new couples, one from England and the other from Seattle. Lively discussions, a good 2 ½ hours, played Wheel of Fortune, actually won some more points, and ended the evening with a fantastic Japanese Drum Show put on by a world-famous Japanese drummer!

<u>Monday, Oct. 9th</u>

Another all-day excursion is called the Highlights of Kyoto with lunch. The temperature is still in the 80s but not quite as humid as yesterday for a guy who doesn't sweat much; I was soaked yesterday, not to mention arthritis and knees not wanting to work well.

As it seems to be standard now, they are calling for loading the buses about a ½ hour before what the ticket says, so I had Lynn wait at the gangway, and I got the numbers and met her there as soon as our bus was called, we still met a bus that was already ½ full of people??

The driver introduced himself in Japanese and smiled, and then our guide introduced both of them and relayed that both had sore throats and raspy voices…Back on the tollways, this ride is estimated at over an hour. It is still a holiday, and expect crowds and traffic...both came true.

On the way: three license plate colors: green trucks and buses, white cars/vehicles over 660cc, yellow cars/vehicles under 660cc. New drivers have a bi-colored "V" on the back of the vehicle, and over 70 drivers have a multicolored clover leaf.

The phoenix is considered a symbol of longevity. There are 2.5 million vending machines in Japan, which would average about one vending machine for every 50 people!

This is a three-day holiday, Sports Day, from when the Olympics was played in Japan three days, Saturday, Sunday, and Monday.

Bullet trains run every ten minutes but do not run late at night. The rest stops away from the pier are oriental, with a few western toilets in the women's room. Most are squat holes; many of the women did not realize this the first time, and yes, there were no towels to dry hands.

Educating Noah...Travelin'

Kyoto, the cultural center of Japan, with lots of shrines, was the capital of Japan from 1867 (the end of the Shogun period)-1964. It is also big in industry, including weaving silk for kimonos (actually started as the place for the Royal Kimonos) and handicrafts (we even saw a university for handicrafts), electronics for games like Nintendo, and Pokémon, medical equipment and Japanese whiskey is made here, not nearly as popular as sake or plum wine but it is catching on, and no I did not get a taste...yet!

The first stop is the Golden Palace, originally a Buddhist (Toji) temple, then converted to a Zen temple, basically a pagoda with a gold leaf covering, originally built in 1397, burned down twice, and last rebuilt in 1995 after an arson fire. The surrounding acreage is a manicured garden, a beautiful setting, cultivated gardens, and extensive. It is crowded; crowd control at the best photo spots, especially where the reflection in the lagoon can be captured, but most people are cooperative, and most "get the photo shot" ... with patience! The stroll through lasted about an hour, cool under the trees... then off to the included lunch.

Like the previous tour with lunch, the restaurant is set in a very exclusive hotel; this one had an artificial stream from the front of the building, alongside, under a bridge, falling to a lower pond, all landscaped and peaceful. The dinner was served and included vegetable sushi, a very fresh salad, squash soup, grilled pork with potato and broccoli, and even a freshly baked roll! (I don't usually see bread in a Japanese restaurant), with a pudding for dessert, coffee, or tea. Everything was individually perfectly presented and well attended by staff...wow.

Last stop, another temple, lots of walking, many steps without railings, and yes, lots of people. We are given almost two hours to explore the grounds, take in the various temples, the beautiful views, and, this time, a few blocks of streets lined with vendors. Deposited Lynn halfway, explored the upper temples and vistas, took pictures, and rejoined Lynn for the shopping. I was looking for a spice that the host of Bizarre Foods always carries with him for my son-in-law, Kelly, and our guide indicated the shop that would have it. I did taste it subtly; I also bought a spice for myself. Bought some more Knick knacks, and only yen was accepted along with credit cards.

A little over an hour's drive back to the port, dropped a little more cash at the shops there and boarded the ship. We were still full from lunch so we ate a little at the café, the entertainment was a singer who won on "The Voice," and was also on America's Got Talent; great voice, powerful songs, and a good show! Next was Wheel of Fortune, guests vs. officers; our team won! We all got necklaces and bragging rights. The other team came close to winning, but the officers beat them (too classy to gloat), but they also won a consolation prize, guess…. Necklaces!

At 10:30 a Rhythm and Blues show and dance on deck, I lasted through the show, Lynn stayed to dance a bit, another great day!

Tuesday October 10th, our first day at sea, catch-up time!

We had our own programs, went our ways and decided when to meet for lunch. One of my first missions was to find out how I can buy an hour's worth of internet time, since this first cruise was in many different ports and only two sea days. Front desk couldn't help, but they told me to be in the computer lab at 9. I went for breakfast, had an "everything" omelet, picked up the notebook, and re-found the lab. (It is not on the ships maps or indicated on any of the directories). There were three couples ahead of me, then I had to fight for my turn.

From there it was the use of a different number on the key card, and you had to place "login.com" where the computer searches for the browser. Checked my e-mails, nothing from the kids; asked them to call grandma and let them know I would check again on the 16th. I also checked my roadrunner e-mail, it took a full 5 minutes to load, and then 2-6 minutes to delete 1 message, so I delete 6, gave up, and took the laptop back to the room.

The lecture today was on Hiroshima and the atomic bomb. We were given two book referrals, "Japan Subdued" and "Longest Day". The name of Hiroshima is derived from Hiro (5) Shima (islands.)

The atomic bomb was developed by three physicists Otto Han, Lise Meitner (a female Jew, who later converted to Christianity) and Fritz Stresemann. Otto Han got all the credit, Lise fled Germany due to her Jewish background, and afraid her Austrian nationality wouldn't protect her from the Nazi's and ended up in Sweden. Although they were all working in Germany, both Otto and Lise were anti-Nazi.

They contacted Albert Einstein regarding cracking the relativity code and feasibility of a nuclear bomb. Einstein then met with Roosevelt, the English were strapped for money, and England was too dangerous to develop the bomb on English soil, so the Manhattan Project was initiated. The project was secretly picked up through a presidential slush fund to bypass congress, Little Boy with one mechanism to explode the uranium, and Big Boy another.

Due to war atrocities in China by the Japanese, Roosevelt also embargoed all the oil to Japan, so not only were they humiliated by the US with no immigration, and not permitting immigrant Japanese kids in school, now Japan had no oil.

Battles in Manila, other islands, and the last big battle in Okinawa convinced the U.S. that the Japanese would rather die than give up; many soldiers thought suicide was compulsory if they were captured, and the Kamikazes though only 14 % hit ships, there were 2800 attacks, and 47 ships sunk. Most of the pilots were boys fresh out of high school with 3-6 months training, the mission was basically only one way, and just to crash the aircraft into a ship! Other loss of life compared to Hiroshima was the Tokyo firebombing where Napalm was used killing 80,000 to 130,000 people and the Dresden bombing, all three horrific as to people killed.

Interesting Japanese words and definitions:

Fu-shi (no death)

Kami (spirits)

Bonsai (10,000 years of long life!)

Kikusui (floating chrysanthemum) Medieval Japanese Battle Standard

Katsu-Go (Defend Japan to the death!)

Sherman Carpets: little children trained to roll under tanks and blow themselves up with explosives tied around their waists.

The reasoning for the bombs was to keep the monarchy in place, so that guerrilla warfare would not happen and extend the confrontation, Japan still had 4 million soldiers, and 2400 kamikaze planes and pilots, plus there was the matter of $2 billion spent on producing the bombs. There was also the growing distrust of Stalin's Soviet Union becoming increasingly communistic and aggressive.

The two bombs did turn the proud Japanese with Hirohito staying in power and breaking the vote to surrender presented by the military Generals.

I talked to the lecturer after the discussion, I wanted the woman's name that was key in the physic research, and asked why Japan is so far in debt, having a surplus in the mid 80's! He looked up and provided the name, and what did in the Japanese was the bubble of 1989, the internet bubble. This, with infrastructure, all those bridges and highways, and an aging population. They started to add taxes both to retire the debt and contribute to the care of the elderly, starting at 3% and in less than 20 years will soon be 10% of income in addition to all the other taxes.

Watched a close-up magic demonstration, I may get the CD later, participated in the paper airplane contest, neither plane placed! Riddles trivia, defeated again!

Dinner in the dining room, two new couples one from Texas, the other from New Zealand, I lamented that when we travel, we need to experience the different foods, and with this cruise line, no Japanese entrees were offered! One wife cornered the Maître' de; asked about them, and he promised that tomorrow night, our table would be eating Japanese, everyone at the table was excited!

Majority rules game show at 8, lost again, and the Abba Mania trivia and sing along at 10:15.

Wednesday, Oct.11th. Hiroshima, our tour is "A Trip to Miyajima". Early excursion must be in the auditorium by 7:30, so the clock was set, we beat the clock again, and turned it off. Outside the coast is misty, warm, and no wind, and yes, the humidity is there too!

The city has been completely rebuilt since the devastation of the atomic bomb, a park and one tower remain with a museum to remind people of the aristocracies of war, Millions of people perished at the explosion, and millions died from the radiation exposure afterward. Too depressing to visit on a vacation, but it seems the lesson is never learned! Hiroshima now famous for oysters, and conga eels, there are 6800 islands in this area!

It was a short 12-minute ferry ride to the island, and that was after a short 20-minute drive to the ferry dock! The 50-foot-tall Orange Torii gate setting in the water before the shrine is made of Camphor wood to withstand the salt water; the last time this was replaced was 140 years ago. Ago. This is a sacred island, no people live on the island, and it has both Buddhist (introduced in the 6th century) and Shinto shrines (original religion), kinda nice how religions can get together. Since this is a sacred land, there is no digging, thereby no graves. There are quite a few deer on the island, they are wild, but used to deliver messages. Everyone showed up on time, ferry back, loaded bus, and we were back at the dock by 12:30.

There was a small booth in the terminal where three women invited others to try on a Kimono, so yes, Lynn tried it. Three women fussing; Lynn's boobs were a little in the way, layers of silk, different belts, and fastenings It took three women 15 minutes to dress her. (It took less than 5 minutes to un-wrap her; I think there was some male influence there!) She looked great, pictures; I offered a tip, for sodas or tea, but they refused, after offering three times I gave up and bowed. I also asked about thimbles for one of the folks I bring souvenirs back, and told they use buttons to push the needle through, no thimbles being sold…

On the ship, lunch, then Lynn had her nails done, and I had my first ever pedicure, both of us enjoyed, and had a good time with the manicurists. After that I had an acupuncture session for my shoulder, felt great afterwards, and back to the room, Lynn played the Trivia, the team lost again, but only by two points!

The Dinner tonight was the promised Japanese meal, everyone showed up on time, we confirmed the meal with the waiter and the matre' de came over and asked if we were ready, we all were!

I ordered sake, offered dry or sweet, I chose sweet, it was served as a wine, and as sweet as an Italian Modella, delicious! Appetizer was two pork dumplings with a very unique soy sauce on the side. By the way, our last excursion today, we explored a soy souse shop. There were samples but everything, labels and descriptions were in Japanese's so we left! The second course was shrimp tempura on a bed of black seaweed and rice noodles, different, and good, the main course was grilled salmon with grilled asparagus with a side of rice with vegetables, best salmon ever, and the asparagus was perfectly grilled! This followed by a regular dessert menu, what a treat!

Next was 60 seconds or less with crew vs guests, four challenges to be done in 60 seconds or less. The first was cup stacking, 6,5,4,3,2,1, and then collapse them all into a single stack in less than a minute, guest won, hat with two tea bags, object was to flip both bags onto the visor only, guest won, third, pennies in pantyhose I can explain if you want, crew member won, and last was chopstick flip, start with two chopsticks on the back of a hand, flip up and catch, the goal is to get to 16 chopsticks! The best was 8, by a guest!

The show was a production sing and dance, one of the smoothest we have seen, well done and very professional, that wrapped it up for the day.

Thursday, October 12th

We dock in Kagoshima, Japan; this city has only 606,000 residents. This town is the "Naples of the Orient" due to the sunshine, beautiful ocean, and bright blue sky! (Today, high of 86F, bright and sunny) Our excursion was not till 11, but I have another acupuncture at 8, another busy day. There was a "Best of Nagasaki tour," but again, seeing reminders of the second atomic bomb was not on our list. However, we were told by guests who took the tour only a very small reminder remains: the entire area was revised and makes what happened indistinguishable!

Our guide "Hiroko" which means rich and nice in Japanese was one of the best guides to date. The ride to the first attraction is only about 45 minutes, so not too much additional culture information to start with.

This was a Kids Day holiday; the carp flag/wind sock is displayed wishing kids to be healthy and strong, activities emphasizing kids around the area.

Japan has 4 major islands, and 6400 smaller islands (yes, I realized some of this is repeat, but I still can't get over how many little islands!) The population is 10X the USA, and 100X Australia.

A condo apt. Costs $300K-700K US; requires 10-20% down on a 30-year loan. The current loan rate is 1%!! I asked her to confirm, and she did, 1% for a home loan!!

Rainy season is June, summer is May, June, and July; rice farming here, 2000 years, Japan is also home to 10% (110) of the world's active volcanoes. There are 2000 hot springs, 10 different types, if family, no swim suits, if communal, swim suits only if mixed male and female.

The Bullet train was started in 1964 for the first Olympic hosting, there has never been a bad accident associated with this train, and a super bullet train is planned for the next Olympics that will be about twice as fast.

Sweet potatoes are big here, with 30 different kinds; the main ones are white, purple, yellow, and orange. One of the interesting products besides chips is purple sweet potato ice cream, an alcoholic drink made from sweet potatoes; I tried the ice cream, not the booze…yet! (Ice cream was like the other green tea and wasabi flavored.) and now orange sweet potato, the flavoring is "subtle."

In 1593, Japan started opening up mostly due to self-defense, the then most powerful country; hand guns changed the world as far as warfare; at the same time Christianity was introduced to Japan.

First stop was a traditional Japanese garden at Seng an-en. Everything meticulously trimmed an easy walk, Koi pond with large Koi; we fed them, a large house with paper walls and very sparse furniture, a nice departure from the bustle on the highway just a block away!

Our next stop was Sakurajima, a mildly active volcano that has erupted 30 times in recorded history. The last eruption was 1/12/1914 when 58 died, 2,000 houses were destroyed, ashes in some places 24,000 feet high, two lava cracks appeared, and 3 billion tons of lava flowed at a rate as high as 25 mph. There are no animals on the island.

Educating Noah...Travelin'

There are 5,000 inhabitants. The island is called a living museum; radishes grow very large, they are sweet, and there is a "biggest radish" contest every year. There are no gutters or downspouts on the buildings. Grave sites are covered with roofs to protect the grave from acid rain. Fish is cooked with volcanic ash; there is no "fish" smell, and cooking this way is called "Hobojhi Fish." Cherry blossoms symbolize Japan. (Bloom in April)

We had to take a ferry across the bay, (24hrs. a day); the entire bus was loaded on for the 15-minute ride. The bay has warm and cold areas, and it is inhabiting with many types of familiar and strange flora and animals, we were shown a picture of an animal that has no mouth, no eyes, nothing like any animal, more like a plant! There is also a pod of 150 Dolphins that live there; a dolphin eats 10 kilograms of fish a day! The "tour" consisted of driving up ¾ to the top of one of the peaks, walking around to take in the vistas and rock formations and then back to the bus; another treat was a bottle of mango soda, very refreshing! Back on the bus, drove back on the ferry and back to the ship. On the way back, we noticed grass planted in the middle of the street around the trolley tracks, this is to keep the tracks cool, and the grass is planted over ashes, and watered with acid water. The businesses on both sides of the road maintain the trimming, weeding, and upkeep after midnight when the trolleys are not running, they are not paid, this is just expected, and not questioned. I did also get a picture of the statue of the last Samurai.

A rest room is called a "Happy House"; Tangerines are grown here also and given as gifts for Christmas. Even though Christianity is only 2-10% of the population, Christmas is celebrated by most!! The two rice's used in the households, are Table and Saki; Gifts are wrapped in material, (called Kurashiki) instead of paper; this is from the Samurai era, the cloth is also folded to make many things including a hat, scarf, wrapping a gift bottle or even a hand bag.

This is called the dolphin port, there is even a bus made to look a little like a dolphin, yes, I took the picture!

Back to the ship, dressed for dinner, and met one new couple of women from New Zealand, and the couple from Canada we met the first night also joined us. We had a great time, 2 ½ hours passed, one woman walked past just as we were finishing up and told us we were too loud but it didn't faze anyone at the table, good times had by all (except her… (prude!)).

English pub night, with English music trivia, we stunk, lost horribly. Then on to the Show. Tonight, was "Lazybonz"; two guys doing silly things for 45 minutes, extremely entertaining, had everyone in stitches, full house!

The last event was three couples picked for "The Marriage Game" one of the couples was a gay two men couple, and they almost won! The couple that did win was married only a few months!

We were locked out of our room, neither card worked, called down to the desk, they sent up an officer and maintenance. The officer arrived first and opened the door with a key, opened it twice, then tried both cards everything works again. The maintenance man showed up, he re-checked everything, and told us it was a glitch in the program, in talking to the crew, it happens to them also. At the end of the cruises, the locks are re-scrambled, so when we continue in Singapore, we will have to get new cards.

That was it for today, tomorrow would be the last day in Japan, and notice was sent out that everyone had to go through customs before the ship left port.

Friday the 13th, Nagasaki, Japan, Japan's closest port city to the Asian mainland. This morning started with another acupuncture treatment, the shoulder is definitely improving, a late breakfast, journaling, another trivia…stunk again, toured the ship, it is only in the 70's and quite a difference than the last week!

Educating Noah...Travelin'

We had an early lunch, then on to the panoramic bus tour of Nagasaki, the 35-minute ride (not a bridge in site!) to the top of one of the close mountains consisted of many hair-pin turns, and very narrow streets, we could not or did not stop at the peak (there was a small parking lot) but the driver did slow the bus to take some shots of the city.

If a family wants to take a hot springs bath, the cost is 1200 yen (about a dollar US) It is said if you take a hot spring bath once a year, you will live an additional year, 2/years 2 years, and three...Do to the lack of space, rooftops are used for parking. The USA provided dogwood trees after the war. The government wanted free enterprise, and were strongly against Communism, this was insisted on under the terms of surrender. I know what I said before, but this tour included the atomic bomb site, park and ground zero. Nagasaki was the second city after Hiroshima to be destroyed by the atom bomb. (Actually, it was an alternative target, the second target was actually protected by cloud cover, and Nagasaki was a munitions area that supplied the torpedoes for Pearl Harbor.)

North Korea's prime minister toured Japan and stated "there was no longer a Japan after the war"; this did not go over well with the Japanese government or its people! The tour was to be 4 ½ hours but due to us leaving Japan and customs, we were back at the dock in 2 ½ hours.

The tour did include the park and monuments; we were also treated to a short talk from an 86-year-old survivor. He told us after the initial bomb took its toll, there was no water. People were dehydrated and starving, the USA and the world came through and sent food and water. All children in the womb during the bombs were given $3300 yen per year if they survived, plus free health care for life. (Many think health cares are "free" in most countries, here, taxes start from earned dollar one and a specific amount are dedicated to health care, plus there are always the private health care for the wealthy or those that prefer better treatment.) The bomb actually detonated 500 meters above the ground, thereby no crater, and the temperature generated was 4000 degrees Centigrade! The sun is about 6000 degrees Centigrade! The majority of Japanese people have accepted the disaster of the two bombs to be prayers for peace in the future to learn and not hate. There is still a lot of cancer in the aged, but many are in their 80's and 90's yet! The birthrate is a concern due to the aging population; it has dropped from 1.4 to 1.29, couples are encouraged to have more children.

The schools are both public and private; the tour guide relayed a story about a child that was adopted from a geisha. The child was adopted, had a hard life, tried to commit suicide, and then traveled abroad, and turned into Madame Butterfly from which the play was written.

She (tour guide) also says her Nissan speaks to her, tells her not to drink and drive, tells her to pull over when she is tired, and forget the phone! She also told us that she is a retired English teacher, never been outside Japan and is 67 years old, and loves her job! The bullet train costs $3000 yen (about $30 US) one way; (unless you have a Japan Air charge card, then you can use points and have a reduced rate of $1600 yen) and many Japanese women carry umbrellas, they have light skin, sun sensitive and do not want darkened skin from tanning or sun exposure.

Back through customs, on the ship by 3:30 rested in the room and waited till the next activity at 4 P.M. We joined a British family; between the four of them, they knew every answer, we scored a perfect 20/20!

As the ship prepared to leave, we were sent off by a full orchestra next to the ship, talk about welcoming!

Dinner was shared by only one new couple, the restaurant was sparse till about 6:45, nice couple from Florida, and they had a

Educating Noah...Travelin'

Goldwing trike, and now travel with a travel van.

Trivia, lost; the show started out with a ballerina, then went to a magician couple, very clever, and ended with an acrobatic scarf ballet.

The activity afterward in the lounge was S.A.F.E. archery in the lounge. This consisted of a blow-up target area with three balls held up with streams of air. A regular bow and arrows with soft tips, the size of a small juice concentrate can. Everyone that wanted to try, got three arrows; my shoulder wasn't ready, the guests won against the officers.

Lynn was too tired to continue, so off to the room to end another day.

Saturday Oct. 14th, Jeju Island, South Korea. We have a four-hour City Highlights tour at 9:15, so Lynn slept in. Today and tomorrow will be in South Korea. We had some reservations about this since the ruler of North Korea was sending up missiles, and threatening bomb tests, but we were assured by the cruise line that it should not affect us. So here we are, south, with fingers crossed! Forecast is mid 60's, light rain in the afternoon.

Jeju is the largest island of South Korea and was known to the Europeans as Quelea. The island has a volcano and many lava tubes, sand and dirt all black. I had talked to the shore excursion folks about front reserved seating for Lynn, and this morning there were bus tags for us at the door! We ate breakfast, and then started down early. Entering South Korea, everyone had to go through immigration, since most of the ship goes on the excursions or explore off the ship, the line was very long, it took us over a half hour, and we were in the early group! By the way, the crew has special dispensation, the entire crew list is provided to each country before the ship sails with arrival and departure schedules.

The line for the money exchange was too long so we decided to wing it with American dollars.

Noah

We were first on the bus, so it gave us a little time to talk to the guide. When they greet people here, it is a bow and a handshake. Here again, it is a very clean country. We are assured that the bus trips are no longer than 20 minutes from site to site, and there are 4 sites today in 4 hours,

The South Korean language has difficulty pronouncing F, P, L and R in the English language; there are no Korean sounds similar (Like Chinese and Japanese rice and lice hard to say).

The population of 600,000 of the Island, is far fewer than the main city of Seoul, Korea on the mainland which is 10,000,000; the Island is 75X33 kilometers. This is the closest to China, and the Chinese use it at a honeymoon destination, the mountain Hela, is the highest in Korea. We now see phone booths, and rent–a- bikes. There are 368 volcanoes on this island, more per square kilometer than anywhere else given the size of this island! Income here first, is tourism, second tangerines, yes, we tried them, and they are full of flavor and very sweet.

A group of high school kids passed by, one spoke to Lynn, and Lynn answered, we think he was practicing his English, and she wanted to confirm it was quite good!

First stop was a museum site, showing a primitive village, at an individual home, there are stone pillars at the front, about 1 ½ meters apart, with 3 - 4" X 2-meter tree limbs to be inserted, none across, "we are home", one across "we will be back soon", two across "will be back in half day", three across "gone for a while/far away". There was no theft, no beggars; all were related in some way.

The primitive out house sat high, with the contents flowing into the pig pen, needless to say; lot of disease difficulties… in the granary two horses were hitched to turn the grinding stones, female in front of male, the male had incentive to pull forward…

Red sculpture at front of the museum complex was to represent the grandfather, patriarch of the village cluster, and also represents a connection to the earth. There are small horses on the island, residents they eat horse meat, learned from the Mongolian's. Genghis Kahn also visited the island. The deer here are also small, about ½ the size of the Wisconsin deer. They are famous for black pork, the main meal is fish, however, they marinate the fish first, no raw or shichimi like the Japanese.

At one time they were known for the female divers who would go out every day to harvest from the ocean, trained at 6/7 years old, the current AVERAGE age now is 65. Some men now also dive, but the culture is changing.

Examples of lava rock with holes through them, and a statue of a woman with a jug on their back, representing the women who walked 1-2 kilometers a day for fresh water, the jugs with water weighing 15-20 kilograms (2.2 lbs. per kilo)!

The next stop was an inlet, or outlet, depending on how you look at it; picturesque and involved a suspension bridge that swayed and lava rock formations. A footpath on one side had dragons imprinted in the large tiles, and the path down to the bridge was embedded with rope to ensure traction. This was right on the ocean, all rocks and sand black lava.

Third stop was a rock formation just a short walking distance from the inlet, called Dragon Rock; it did resemble a dragon, the road dead ended here, and the concrete pylons to stop traffic were concrete little old men, yep, another picture opportunity showing we were there.

Last stop was a shopping area, ½ food, ½ shopping, maybe more food…they would only take the "wan" (pronounced like in wand) 1012 wan equals $1 US.

The bus was to pick us up at the entrance at 11:50 but was late; we saw a row of what looked like fire hose connectors in the side of the river edge. Upon a bit of nosing around I found a plaque indicating a water show from 12-12:30 every day but Sunday, so I told Lynn and we positioned ourselves for watching. It turned out to be a water fountain show to music much like the Bellagio in Las Vegas; the fountains played to various songs, some jets up to 6 stories high, and all the water contained within the river bed. The guide arranged for us to watch most of the show before heading back to the ship.

The rest rooms here again clean, mostly western toilets, and hand towels or hot blow dryers for drying hands are in each bathroom. Here, the driver or guide does not offer assistance to those having difficulty boarding or leaving the bus.

After clearing customs again, back on the ship, quick lunch, then we attended an activity where we were given a chance to control a small drone. I tried twice, kind of got the hang of it, but the controls are very sensitive, and I did not impress!

Later, Flags of the World Trivia... our team won! Acupuncture at 5 (shoulder actually responding) Dinner with two other couples, had a great time, after dinner, battle of the sexes, the women won; a musical game show trivia of the '80s (our team lost); ending the night with the house party band specializing in the songs of the '80s.

Sunday, October 15th, Busan.

It is cool and overcast, low to mid 60's; again immigration, we left for the bus early today to secure seats in the front of the bus. The money exchange was also open without a line so I was able to convert some cash.

Busan is the second largest city in South Korea, with a population of 3.6 million. It has the longest river and beach in Korea and worlds fifth (in tonnage) busiest port, located on the southeastern tip of Korea. There are 30 buses in the parking lot behind the immigration building, plus regular buses, and cabs.

Our guide speaks excellent English we are to call her "So-Hey" as she outlines the three areas we are to visit. Due to it being Sunday, she arranged for us to go to the tower first, then the fish market, and ending up going through the international market.

Our first stop, the tower, originally a light house, converted to an observatory for tourists to view the city and harbor. Only eight people on the elevator at a time, then after looking at the panoramic view, taking picture, and looking at the small souvenir shop, you had to go down a very narrow set of stairs (so narrow, my shoulders almost touched the sides), to the 7th floor where you waited for the elevator (same one) to take you to the bottom; a beautiful garden, then on to the bus.

Being Sunday morning, the fish market opens later, so the delay was well planned. We arrived and were dropped off on the main street, about two blocks off the waterfront. As we approached many small shops had their tanks cleaned with an assortment of fish, mostly kept alive in the tanks along with shell fish, octopus, squid, and sea cucumbers and what someone called a sea penis (it was muted orange, hairless, scale-less, about 6" long and basically, no front or back 1 ½ inch in diameter), we entered the fish market we saw rows of stalls with fish tanks, all with running salt water packed with crabs, fish, octopus, with vendors offering to sell, live, or clean and gut them for you. We stopped at a vendor and the guide purchased a live abalone and octopus, the vendor butchered both live, put on a plate with a squirt of hot sauce, and the plate taken out to a benches, we were offered to take a piece of live squirming octopus or abalone, of course I tried both, neither had much taste, but the octopus was rather active, in my mouth, a new sensation, chewy and kind of odd, the abalone had slightly more taste, but at least it wasn't squirming in my mouth as I chomped down on it.

We finished the market and walked back to the main street, crossed it and were at the international marketplace formally known as cannery row, due to vendor selling left over cans of G.I. rations.

Again, every other or more store front sold food, we were directed to a vendor that sold pancake sized bread deep fried and then cut open and stuffed with a sesame paste…delicious! Other vendors had showcases of food that was literally mouthwatering, walk and eat food!

We walked into an upscale department store, prices were similar to the prices at home, street food, $2-$3 US each item, there was a McDonalds; three stories, you put in order and then went to wait or went up to second or third store where a vertical conveyor provided the food when prepared. There were also three motor scooters that delivered McDonalds orders off premises…. will soon be in the USA!

Back to the port, immigration was a breeze, but then the line to get back on the ship was extensive! Poor planning, 10-15 minutes just to enter the ship, in the drizzle and cold, what a shame!

We grabbed a late bite to eat, Trivia at 4, and off to dinner. One new couple, and the other we had dined with again, the 2-2 1/2 hours went way too fast, a walk through the store level, the show was a Stevie Wonder imitation, extremely good, then to the silent Disco, and finally the Full Moon Party.

Monday Oct.16th; our second and last day at sea, tomorrow, the first half of the cruise is over, we must change rooms, and the instructions are murky at best. I have my last acupuncture today at 8 A.M. Lynn was really pissed about the room change and the "limbo" involved, we are promised this will be addressed. I had to catch up on the diary, then another trivia, followed by a lecture.

The lecture started out about the history of Shanghai and the Soong sisters. The history basically, about the turmoil between various factions in China, the communists, and Japan. It seems every time the communists are mentioned, the philosophy sounds good and "fair" for the working class against the wealthy, then when implemented the standard of living is lowered for all except the ruling class, funny how history repeats, and doesn't seem to be learned. The more people are promised, the more they want as long as "others" pay for it, and yet nothing improves, those subscribing to communism do not progress or degenerate, while the rest of the world improves. Enough preaching, lunch, Lynn said it was supposed to be American Bar-B-Q, turned out it was yesterday with hot dogs and chicken…no ribs, no brisket, no cobs of corn…. I am unhappy with the selections, yes, a pasta bar, a pizza bar, and a salad bar, offered every day; however, neither restaurants or buffet offered regional food, neither Japanese or Korean; I found this tragic, what a lost experience!

I caught up on my journaling, bought another hour of WIFI to touch basis at home, then the World Wildlife Walk was cancelled for weather, medium winds, rain, and cold on deck. A meeting for those going on with the back-to-back cruise looked like about 25%.

Passports were collected, information to be given out that evening as where to meet for new key cards, immigration, and guest count.

Another Trivia, another close, but loss, then a table was set up to cash in winning points acquired during the cruise for winning; Lynn had enough for a shirt.

Dinner with a new couple and a past couple, tip envelopes handed out, and we wished a good time off to our waiter.

Participated in the "yes or no" Game; you had to participate in a conversation with the host trying to have you say or indicate yes or no. I was 3rd worse, thank you…saved by two other guys.

Another production show: "Boogie Nights", well performed, good audience participation, and polished singing and dancing.

The last activity for this cruise, "Frisky Feud," an R-rated family feud, Lynn and I, plus another couple, won! The total distance traveled by ship during this half of the cruise is 2100 nautical miles. (1 nautical mile = 1.15 land miles)

Noah

Tuesday October 17ᵗʰ, Shanghai

Depart from the first cruise by ¾ of the passengers, new key cards, immigration for the rest of us, plus some of us had a room change. The ship was delayed at sea due to the wind and high seas. Actually, the port closed! So, we arrived 5 hours later than planned.

It is utter chaos when timing is off on this ship. We were packed and out of the room by 8:30 a.m.; we were told initially that the switched rooms would be a priority and we could unpack after 1 p.m. Even though most if not all were out of their rooms by 8:30, but I kinda worked my way through the shut doors, and unpacked at 2:30 using the attendants key, we actually weren't processed until 5:30, so we sat around the ship all day boring... no activities, couldn't use either old or new room, most excursions if not all were severely delayed and shortened by at least half, of course, no refunds offered even when asked., Those leaving the ship had to wait past 4 P.M. and the new passengers were finally let on about 5:30. Poor if any communication, we went to the regular restaurant at 5:45 and asked when that would open (regular hours 5:30-9:30) and they did not know, so we went up to the buffet, and back to the room, muster, no one at the desk knows, but it will be before the evening ends.

We expressed our dissatisfaction on the room change, the placing of food way back so many put their heads over the food, and the lack of specialty foods; with the late arrival, nothing was addressed, confusion ruled, under communication with staff frustrated all!

History on the Seven Seas...This phrase can be traced through many cultures and different times, in Greek literature the seven seas were Aegean, Adriatic, Mediterranean, Black, Red, and Caspian Seas, including the Persian Gulf as a "sea"; In Medieval European literature, it was the North Sea, Baltic, Atlantic, Mediterranean, Black, Red, and Arabian seas. After North America was "discovered" mariners referred to the seven seas as today, Arctic, Atlantic, Indian, Pacific, the Mediterranean, Caribbean, and the Gulf of Mexico.

Wednesday Oct.18, sea day. Yesterday was horrible, we lost an hour last night, and the muster was from 10:00 to 10:30 P.M.; many were nodding off, many just getting into their rooms afterwards. The only good thing was Lynn met and talked to one of the dancers; he was from Moldavia, and very nice, good sense of humor.

Thursday, Oct.19th; Busan, South Korea, we arrived on time, everything back on schedule. Since we were here before, we elected to stay on board today. Trivia and putting, we were the only ones; only 248 passengers on the ship today, everyone else went on to explore South Korea. Had lunch, and we arranged for Lynn to have a massage, we are in port so the normally astronomical charges were down to expensive, but we had more credits than I thought, so it was "treating" day for Lynn!

I went to the gym, then changed, and had the therapy pool and hot tub to myself! Then I went up to the top deck, to watch The Last Sammari with Tom Cruise on the open deck. It is only in the upper 60's, a bit cool but in the sun, it is comfortable. What a great movie! Then I was making my way down, and a woman with a walker needed to get down. I found some officers on a lower deck, and made sure they assisted her, they did, she was happy! Took a nap waiting for Lynn to return all loose and supple!

Trivia, dinner with two new couples, very nice and a lot of fun, the singer at the show, Monique DeHaney, was one of the best one-woman shows we have seen, another trivia with friends, and ending the evening with Karaoke I did Neil diamond Sweet Caroline (I need to practice a bit!!), Our friends did a number of songs.

Friday, October 20th; a sea day.

I tried the audio guided meditation, of the 2000 plus guests, there were maybe 10 of us. The twenty minutes or so with headsets would have been nice with a little soothing music, but no, someone complained, so that was gone, and the woman in the back decided to have loud conversation 15 feet away from the meditation area…; two Trivia's, our team won both!

Flash mob rehearsal, Lynn and I participated, I dropped out about ½ way, I may join them again later, three more practices, we will see, it is a pretty complicated routine, and a lot of upper arm involvement. Lynn went on to line dancing. After lunch we stuck around for the poolside question, it was "Guess the playing card in the envelope", for a hat; we both lost, but we did get some vitamin D and probably a little tan!

Slow afternoon, caught up on journaling, and we also sat through a presentation on chocolate diamonds; and yet another Trivia. The participation in these games is way less than on other ships, maybe 35-40 at most, sometimes less than 20. I asked about ship building and egg drop, ship building discontinued for lack of participation, egg drop not on this ship, not a high enough area to drop the eggs. We are seeing more and more with their noses in phones or I-pads breakfast to night…

We did stop by the shore excursion office, asked why no help at the bus and no whisper guides. The answer should be no surprise, they were sued twice, one by a guest that was dropped while being assisted, and once by an employee injured helping someone. For the actions of a few, many suffer!

The whisper guides for guide and guests to actually hear what the guide says when not right by them are not used in the Far East, we are told, only in Europe.

I did buy an hour of internet for $25.00, to check on any updates on my mother, nothing, then cleaned up my g-mail account, wrote a note to Tiffany regarding "Tiffany Twisted" in the song Hotel California, and started a critique of the first half of the cruise, when my hour ran out, I will find out if the information was saved when I buy another hour on Sunday.

Dinner with partners in some of the trivia's, went to the Stevie Wonder impersonator show, it was the same as we saw a week ago, but still good, our dinner companions both fell asleep during the show, and bowed out to further activity after-words. Friendly Feud with the officers, many of the same questions, we were the only four people willing to participate; so, we won by default (they basically asked the same questions, we still lost, …great memories!) The final activity for the day was the Love and Marriage game show, we were not picked, three couples, better participation, fun, time to retire.

October 21, Saturday; Keelung (Taipei), Taiwan. Standing on the balcony, it feels perfect, the temperature today 67-74 F, overcast, chance of rain. The Japanese acquired Taiwan in the Sino-Japanese war in 1895, after the WWII defeat of Japan; the Chinese took over the island.

Our tour starts at 10:10, we got our bus stickers in advance and assigned seat for Lynn due to her asthma, and back. The day prior, we had to turn in our passports again, and in the morning, we had copies of our passports stamped with a visitor authorization we needed to carry with us during our visit. We were the third couple on the bus even though we left when the group before us was called, the bus has steps to go up into the guest area, curtains, sun screens, very nice, except the seating made for smaller people, like a little less room (width of seat and leg room) as economy airlines. There were also two bottles of water at the window seat, plus a number of umbrellas stored in the front…have never seen that before!

There are three destinations today, The Fairy Tale rock formations, in Yehlid Geopark, the Bisha Fishing Port and fish market, and finally Chung Cheng Park with a panoramic view of the city, under a 74-foot statue in gleaming white of the Goddess of Mercy.

It is a 30-minute drive to our first destination, so here is some info on Taiwan; The tour guide (heavy accent hard to understand, with a nervous laugh) warned us that there were many Chinese visitors, and they tend to push ahead and ignore cues, the name Taiwan comes from Keeling which means sea shell. Sixty five percent of Taiwan is mountains, the mountains are all green, and protect the valleys from the typhoons and heavy storms. The history for this island starts with the Dutch, at first the Europeans were beheaded to honor them, after that the island was settled by the Dutch, lasting about 10 years, then the Portuguese, then the Spanish. Most goods are imported, real estate is relatively inexpensive due to landslides; most of the inhabitants rent, very few live in the country or outside the cities, pigs, and chickens along with small crops are grown locally, no sheep, or beef, a few goats, fish, the main staple is expensive, but there is a great variety and very fresh. Beef is imported, but less expensive than the fish, no oil here; the main exports are machinery and semi-conductors; currency is the yen, 30/$1 US. Many stray dogs on this island, wild boars, bears, and a number of poisonous snakes. There are a million Chinese workers here; unemployment is currently 3.5 %, which is high here, usually 2% or better. School required English starting in middle school for hours, high school English study more mandatory hours per week, the main language (indigenous) is Mandarin. The religion, mostly from India, Buddhism, and Taoism. There are about 15% Christian, as in South Korea, and Japan, there is a great tolerance for religious beliefs. The cemeteries are very colorful; many graves have colorful shrines over them. There is no subway here, just buses for public transportation. Lots of motorbikes and scooters, very few places to park in town, streets are narrow, it seems every nook and cranny has a car of bike parked in it. Taiwan is safe, little crime, no pickpockets, and little if any theft. All shops open from 10 A.M. to 10 P.M.

Our first stop is an area where the winds are quite high, and there are various rock formations carved from the wind and corresponding waves and rain. Various names assigned for imagination, including camel rock, queen's head, fairy shoe, and candlestick. The path is about 8-foot-wide, tiled with tiles that are non-slip, even with the ocean spray. It is crowded, and there is pushing from behind, and both sides. The path at times has no railings, steps also, and some people actually pushing strollers. Lynn decided to stay put when the railing disappeared, there are many places sprayed with sea water when various waves hit the shore, and the path is also wavy, following the contour of the land. I braved it, the wind was persistent and at times even I felt the strength of the wind! Yes, there was crowding, lots of selfies, lots of people with point and shoot phones that just had to have the right magnification, but I was able to get the shots I wanted, returned to find Lynn, then watch for the tour guide. The tour guide was good enough to get us there, and back to the bus, the 5-6 people around him were the only ones to hear.

Next stop was the fish market; this time I bought a package of sesame honey fish, raw not sure, sweet, and tastee, just a little "fish" taste at the end. Lynn stated that they would not allow food back on the ship, so I ate about half of it, then gave the rest of the bag to the driver of the bus, with a little persuasion, he took it.

The last stop was Chung Chang Park, high on a mountain top, great entrance with two full-sized male and female white elephant sculptures. My camera then informed me of a full card! We toured, I found postcards, then back to the bus, and returned to the ship. In case you wonder, yes, with both knees, hips, and right shoulder replaced, I get wanded every time!

Back on board, a little lunch, another trivia (don't ask!) then dinner. Dinner was interesting, the captain made an announcement that we had left port to outrun a storm, the ship was rocking pretty good, and we noticed quite a difference in attendance at dinner. We shared the table with the couple we had last night, compared excursions, and then joined them in the lounge for a game of Majority Rules; nope, didn't win again!

The show was a magician couple, very good, I wanted to buy the

CD last cruise, but didn't find it, this time I bought from them, and he signed both copies. (One copy shows how to do some tricks; the other is of a complete show in Vegas.) We then went to an interactive theme party afterwards, Motown, included the house band, and dancers and singers. After the mini show we were invited to dance with the performers and staff, many of us did, that lasted about three songs, then the crowd rapidly dwindled to less than 30, and we decided to leave and retire to the room. The ship had basically stabilized during the magic show, so not too much problems with sea sickness.

Sunday Oct.22; another day at sea. Lynn woke up with diarrhea, so I brought her breakfast before the medication kicked in, this morning I turned in the room questionnaires, post cards, and checked out the sales in the shops. We then proceeded to turn in the immunization questionnaires for our Philippians ports of call Monday and Tuesday.

Attended a lecture on the foundations of Islam and Isis. This was pretty factual as to the beginning of the major religion today. But just like many things, a small minority of radicals has sprung up, supported by oil money and the want for power. I did put in another complaint, they will soon write me off as a complainer, that half way through the presentation, the sounds of power tools in the background was very distracting. I found it disrespectful to both the presenter and the audience, thought someone should know!

Checked out and bought wildlife t-shirts, lunch, Lynn went to the flash-mob rehearsal, we both went to another trivia and SAFE archery, I did get 1/3 targets Lynn also, the arm is getting better!

I attended a reflexology class, she along with the acupuncture doctor insisted that I talk to my doctor regarding my hypothyroid condition. Met Lynn who was relaxing in the cabin, dress for a formal night. This evening we had guests from three European countries, England, Scotland, and Ireland, and although we try to keep away from politics it did come up, discussions as to opinions of Trump and

Obama; and yes, the only news they had was how wonderful and polished President Obama was, had no idea of any negativity, and of course how bad President Trump was, so we had to explain an alternate point of view. Healthcare was brought up, for those touting government health care in the US, all three expressed disappointment in theirs, especially in pediatric care, any mental or psychological problems for kids have an 18 month wait for diagnosis, Ireland and Scotland higher, then treatment after has a long waiting list, and this is for kids! I guess that grass on the other side of the fence is not so green after all. Speaking of fences, they too have immigration problems, all were turning back people at the ports, and now the immigrants are coming in the "back door". Denmark is actually identifying them and putting them on a plane back to where they came from or claim to come from, funny how we don't hear this in the States.

After dinner Lynn went to the production show, I watched a nature show on the outside theatre, we met in the disco lounge, took pictures of the DJ and his sound board/mixer, over 1000 songs, he showed me how to work it, very interesting.

We listened for a while and decided to call it a night.

Monday Oct 23, today is Manila in the Philippine Islands. Forecast today, 77-89 degrees F, and humid. Our arrival is scheduled for 11 A.M. Our excursion is to start soon after docking. We had time for a trivia, there were actually 6 teams, and that is good for this cruise, yep, we lost.

Overcast, hot and humid to start, off the ship quickly, no one inspected those passport copies and immunization declarations, no time for money exchange, so on to find the buses. On the way we pass three different school bands with native instruments, and each in different native dress. Lots of smiles and enthusiasm, today is a work and school holiday due to a major cab strike.

Noah

The trip to the first stop is twenty minutes away, so we get a little info about the Philippians. Our guide has a sore throat, and heavy accent, so hard to understand, plus a microphone that only works sometimes. So, this will be abbreviated and this trip will be without pictures, the camera got dropped, and ruined. I did get the card out when we returned and was able to save the pictures taken!

The Philippians' peso is about 50 to $1; the history goes back 333 years when they were occupied by Spain. The 101 million population is 97% Catholic, and strict, no divorce here.

The first stop was the walled city of Intramuros, the traffic here was worse than India, then add MORE cars, buses, trucks and triple the motorbikes and motorcycles, And Extended Jeepee's, these no longer had tussled fringes and open sides, they are now fully enclosed with room for about 8 passengers. Stop signs are run, turns from the wrong lanes, everything you can imagine happened in front of the bus, yet, no accidents, and the cars, trucks, and buses were in very good shape, no dents??? As we exited the bus, we were assaulted by street vendors, after shaking them off, we were on a walking tour inside the gates. It had a draw bridge, that is gone, but the walls still stand over 300 years! One sad note, they opened one of the dungeons and found 600 bodies of Philippine's, locked and left to die by the Japanese. There is a monument to those so brutally killed.

Next was a church /convent, a 200-year-old building, interesting artifacts, clean and spacious. Then it started to rain and rain hard. We had to wait for the bus, we found some cover, but everyone got wet. Finally, our bus came, we loaded in the drizzle that the downpour had turned into, and then a quick stop at another church, only half the bus got out, it wasn't open. Since everyone was wet, we were given the option of returning to the ship, those that stayed, would be taken to the Mall of Asia, to shop for an hour. One half of the bus got off, the rest of us taken to the mall.

At least ½ of the mall was food! We walked the first floor then the upper level, looking for a soccer shirt for the grandson, still no shirt, along with no thimbles for someone else, so far, this entire trip! We did stop at a bakery called "Bread Talk" and bought 3 pastries, they were very good! The bus showed up and took us back to the ship, with one quick stop for photos at the monument for a Philippine hero.

Showers for both of us, clothes out to dry, and dinner in the cafeteria. A "Port vs. starboard" quiz activity and a Folkloric show, (there are 7102 islands in the Philippians at high tide, 7106 islands at low tide). I went to the buffet, got a doughnut and jelly for Lynn and myself due to the early excursion the next day, and that ended the day for me, Lynn went up to the Karaoke show, and then spent a little time at the Hot Latin Heat Party poolside. Oh, I also cautioned taped some of our new friend's room…

October 24th Tuesday, the forecast is partly cloudy, chance of rain and upper 80's both in temperature and humidity. The excursion had us report at 6:45 A.M. for a start time of 7:00 A.M. I set the alarm for 5:45 so that I could have everything done before opening up the room and giving Lynn a whole ½ hour. What was not expected was no water; neither hot nor cold, I did what I could w/o water, and then opened the faucet on full, and the shower, nothing…then at 6 A.M gurgling, spurts of water, then brown water. I left it run till it cleared, both hot and cold, shaved and brushed, then turned the WORKING bathroom over to Lynn. We both ate our breakfasts, and were out the door by 6:35, out of the ship and on the bus (after a K-9 dog sniff of the bus, first time we have seen that!).

The excursion today was called Villa Escudero Plantation Resort visit. An eight-hour excursion, including a water buffalo drawn carriage ride, a museum tour, and lunch in a stream, yes, I said stream, the tables are set up in a shallow river produced by a man-made dam.

The 90-kilometer drive to the plantation is estimated at 2 ½ hours. During this time, we witnessed again horrible traffic, more of the city, and a drive into the country. The only rule is "DON'T TOUCH", so in the city it is jockeying for position, and "chicken"; lots of hurry up, slow down, lane change, pass on left and right, watch for motorcycles, and be bold. Many times, just inches from vehicle in front, too much space, motorcycle or car will nose in; so, the ride out of the city was a lot of braking, shifting and horn honking. We have never seen this aggressive driving with so little regard to stop signs and signals including Mexico and Italy!

The guide is pleasant, funny, and very polished. He also gave us a lot of information, which I will try to document, although on the bus, in the city, it was very hard to take notes! There are two seasons in the Philippines, wet and dry; this area in the world is known as the Pacific Ring of Fire. Ten million Philippines', mostly women, work somewhere else in the world and send money back home. The ratio of men to women here is 5 to 1 (women to men), and women are in more demand in the labor force here (mostly call centers). There are 8 different languages, Borneo, Indonesian, Macedonian, Indian, Chinese, Islam, and Spanish spoken here, with a strong emphasis on English as a second language. (Most signage and billboards have English at least as an alternate conveyance.) When the Spanish conquered, all the last names were changed to reflect the area the people lived in. The president can only serve one 6-year term. Gold is one of their exports, and they are the world's tenth-largest exporter of the metal. The land is owned by the government; you can either rent or buy a condo. Fast food restaurants, Mcdonalds (35 pesos for a hamburger), KFC, and Shakey's are the most popular. Here is a local chain called Jolli Bee.

1974, the Miss America Pageant was held here, Ms. Spain won!

Observing an inland lake where freshwater fish are farmed and a volcano in the distance, we are told there are hot springs at its base, making it a favorite meeting place for locals... Many towns, many Jeepee's, (converted US Army jeeps, much different than when I was here 40 years ago when they were jeeps with elaborate decorated soft

Educating Noah...Travelin'

tops and auto bodies to now, an eight-passenger totally enclosed vehicle with only the original jeep hood, the balance running gear Toyota, the body totally fabricated locally at a rate of about 7/week), tricycles, a motorcycle with sidecar, again extensively modified with enclose sidecar, and many enclose the motorcycle. Both of these have local service areas; Philippino's will take a Jeepee's or these for only two blocks! Fares are on the honor system; most operators know the clients, and most clients are "regulars." License plate numbers indicate the days you can have that vehicle on the road and the day it should not be on the road. The average commute to work here is two hours.

Gas prices are 48.35 pesos per liter, 50 pesos to a US dollar, when figured out, about a dollar more per gallon than the current US prices. The highways, along with the police departments, are privately owned in order to keep government costs down and expedite growth. Do cat poop coffee beans produce the best coffee?

We arrive just in time to end the coffee taste comparison! The plantation consists of 4,000 acres of coconut trees, a museum, and a resort, including a man-made dam with a stream below outfitted with tables and benches in the water. Our first stop was the welcoming center; most used the restroom after that 2 ½ hour drive! Then, a leisurely walk to the museum, two floors of artifacts, pottery, displays of all the indigenous animals, ceremony clothes made of pineapple fiber, and weaponry. Anything showing the past of the Philippians is extensive and informative, especially as a private collection.

We then gathered in the garden to an area where we were picked up and driven to the restaurant by water buffalo cart. (They are all female, males, too aggressive). It was extremely smooth, and very comfortable, the buffalo didn't seem to strain at all, the trip is accompanied with a singer and guitar player in the back seat. We are dropped off by two paths, the first we took to a large open drawn carts, the name of the buffalo is posted in front of the area dining hall, covered but no sides, used to view the river above a dam and to be utilized in the event of rain.

Then, we went down the other path, to a series of steps taking us down to the river's edge. There are shelves to deposit your shoes, and a ramp to enter the water. This area can accommodate up to 1,000 people, all with metal picnic tables and benches covered with oil cloth, mid-stream. We selected a spot, then waded over to the buffet line (the water was cool, a little slippery, but not bad, and the underwater bed was smooth) where we were handed a woven plate covered with a banana leaf, the selection as follows: hard boiled eggs chopped, radish slices, potato salad, squash, okra, eggplant, a shrimp paste, prepared rice and noodles, grilled banana, chicken, pork, fish, and beef, a vegetable soup with slices of pineapple. We were offered coconut milk or coke to drink, the coconut milk was provided in a coconut, cut with a lid to prevent flies entering, and a straw. Everything was delicious. It was nice and calm, the cool water up to our ankles, and the waterfall, not only the sound, but the visual from a "head on" perspective.

After the dinner, we went back up to the area where we were waiting to be picked up by the carts, Lynn found a gift shop (she can find these faster than anyone), where we spent the last of our pesos. Cart ride back to the bus, then the 3-hour ride back to the ship.

Since the toll roads are private, there were about 7 tolls we had to go through, some tour buses had motorcycle escorts to weave through the traffic. These bikes had red and blue lights; I suspect this is a part time job for some of the private police force.

U.S. military bases are closed now; the main sport here is basketball. Lynn has been trying desperately to find gifts of soccer shirts, and I have been trying to find thimbles so far but have been unsuccessful... Most of the colleges are catholic, no public education after high school, and many prefer to send the kids to private elementary schools. The guides work for the travel agencies until the tourist season arrives, then act as guides; Manila gets about 60 ships a year (305 days), staying 1-2 days. We see a lot of Christmas decorations; the guide tells us Christmas here is in all months ending in "er." You have to be 18 to get a driver's license.

Today, all aboard at 3:30, we arrived at 3:05, and several buses pulled in just at 3:30 or right after. Trivia game, dinner with a couple from Oregon and an English couple, interesting perspectives; show by a violinist, Yoomia (excellent one-woman show), then British Pub night, this was not too successful, most of the Brits were on one side, and their participation was poor at best... Lynn went to a flash mob warm-up. I did some journaling and tried to take pictures of Lynn dancing, but there was confusion as to when the flash mob would happen. After ½ hour, I went back to the room and called it a night. Lynn showed up about an hour later.

Wednesday, October 25th, a day at sea.

The forecast was clear, low eighties, a nice relaxing day aboard ship. I have been disappointed with the progress on this shoulder, so I went to the gym to see how far I can push it! I did what I could. I will be going back to the gym when I return and to keep up the progress.

I went to a sushi demonstration; this was the first time that after a demonstration of food preparation, samples were not offered. Yes, I filled out another complaint form; this is the cheapest ship we have been on. I even compared them to Carnival!

Trivia, met Lynn and the trivia team we formed...second place, no cigar! Lynn was off to line dancing, and I went to a Captain's welcome to repeaters, met Lynn for lunch, got ½ hour of sun, another trivia, and then we split up again. Lynn read, I caught up on diarying and also bought an hour on the internet to check if anything new back home. We attended another trivia (We are consistent regulars...have you noticed) before dressing for dinner, dinner with a repeat couple from Perth, Australia, and a couple from Israel. It was a good conversation, but the Israeli couple were soft-spoken, and neither Lynn nor I could really participate in conversation with them. The violinist had a show in the foyer. We listened to her and the disc jockey, checked with the desk regarding our visas for the next trip, and went back to the room to rest till the next event.

Participated in another game show, and then the function turned into a dance party to the 80's music; joints working, we danced two dances, listened for a while, and then called it a night.

Thursday, Oct. 26th, Vietnam; Da Nang, (Chan May) Vietnam.

The weather forecast is a chance of rain, 75-84 F, muggy. Arrived at the port at 9 a.m., our excursion, Rural Traditions, starts at 9:45 and is projected to be 8 hours, including lunch. As with the last day in Manila, the excursion takes us up to the time the ship leaves the port at 6:30 P.M.

The port is a small working port about 20 miles outside Da Nang. We got our bus numbers early (It was already 83F with matching humidity), so we were quickly one of the first on the bus. We took the second seat, in case there were others worse than Lynn, leaving two seats. The fifth or sixth couple did not see a reserved sign, so they sat in the front seat, with ¾ of the bus full. A second couple boarded and took the guide's seat. He claimed the guide didn't need one, moved the microphone to the divider behind the driver, and planted himself and his wife, knowing the guide would not risk a tip. (This left the guide to sit on a 5-gallon bucket when not talking; so much for consideration and safety of others!) He also asked if the WIFI was working on the bus, and then this clown made it a point of walking to the back of the bus to inform them and tell them the password. So much for taking in the countryside of a place you have never been to!

The trip to our first destination, Hua Chau, was about a 30-minute drive, so here are some perspectives from a Vietnam resident…The name of the country Vietnam is literally South Man. In Vietnam, many restrooms are not marked. Women are always on the left, men on the right.

We pass the Perfume River and Hue, previously known as "Forbidden Purple City," called the Citadel. We are also about 20km (12 miles) from the Marble Mountains. Mining has been stopped, but as we progress down a major road, rows of stores are selling marble figures (examples of another era, the Indianite Cham civilization.), some full size, and many others much larger, in all shades of white and pastels. There are 90 million people here, 70% are farmers, 54 different nationalities, Hinduism and Buddhism. Da Nang is the 3rd largest city. This is a very poor country. Many in the city $200/ month pay. In the country, $20-$40/month pay; no free school or healthcare.

There are scooters, Vespas, and small motorcycles everywhere, about 16 million, and we have seen up to four on these bikes, (our guide claims he has had his whole family including himself of five in his motorbike) and yes, the same "no hit" rules apply, so they are seen going the wrong way, between cars, trucks and buses, and passing between curb and vehicle. You need to be 18 to get a license.

New houses are formed of concrete, and three styles dominate: Vietnamese, Chinese, and Japanese. There are a lot of new hotels being erected. This is not Japan, with garbage along the road and filth in the streets. Like most major cities we have been in, what a shame…

We traveled through a tunnel that had to be 2-3 miles long. It took 5 years to build and seemed to go on forever at least 4-5 minutes! (However, it was very clean! One lane each way)

Hua Chou is a small town with one main street and a few others. We visit the local private temple, a cultivated lemon grass patch, a walk down the street, poor two-room homes, and small storefront stores, and then we have a tour of one of the prominent family houses. Beautiful flower garden tiles, and actually consisted of two small buildings, one with three small rooms for living and eating, and another three small rooms with two bedrooms, one for parents and the other for the two children. This is the 4th and 5th generation in this home. The two little girls posed for pictures to add a little sunshine to the flower pics in the photo album! This is a holiday for the kids, so no visit to a promised kindergarten took place.

Back on the bus, now on to the promised Vietnamese lunch, so more info on the place and culture. The divorce rate is about 5%; Egret is the symbol of the farmer. The cemeteries have elaborate tombs; anyone can open a business with little licenses, if any. The Vietnam War cost the Vietnamese the most; three million died. Four crops of rice can be grown a year.

At the restaurant and shopping stop, Hoi An, the food was served family style and included one beer or soda. Here is what we had: Vegetable soup, Pomelo salad with prawn and pork, shrimp crackers, "Hoi An" White Rose Dumplings plus spring rolls, Sautéed chicken with cashew nuts, sautéed fish in sweet, sour sauce, stir-fried cabbage with mushrooms, steamed rice, and fresh watermelon as dessert. No one went away hungry!

A few steps to the market, we sat through a presentation on a three-hundred-year-old house we were in, then shown fine embroidery, then we were given an hour to meander through streets lined with open-faced stores, and the best shopping on this adventure, bar none! We spent all the cash-less tips for the driver. I bargained a wood carver down on two pieces, and once we agreed on a price, I gave him an extra buck, telling him he deserved it. The smile and gratefulness was fantastic!

Back to the bus, one more market stop in the middle of Da Nang. This was only 20-30 minutes, way too crowded, and again, everything you could ask for and very good prices. Hour drive back to the dock, we arrived at 5:50, all aboard was 6:30, turned in our visas, and back up to the room. Our room was port side and facing the dock; there were still buses returning while we changed for supper. We had dinner with a couple from San Francisco, watched an activities challenge, and then attended a vocalist. She was a bit too operatic for us; we were both extremely tired from the heat, walking, and humidity, lasted ½ the show, decided to go back to the room, and crashed for the night.

Friday, Oct.27th, last day at sea

With high 70s, mid-humidity, and a light breeze, it is a perfect day! It was a "catch-up" day, so we slept till 7 in the morning. We went our different ways. I went to the gym and attended a discussion on the Opium Wars, Lynn Trivia, line dance, and flash mob practice. After lunch, a music challenge, a bit of sunbathing, and then the flash mob performance, Lynn had me record her dancing. Socializing with other guests, another trivia, dinner, meeting another couple from England, Karaoke with friends, bringing pastry and sandwich to room for the early excursion on Saturday, exchanging print gifts at an art gallery, and another day is done.

Saturday, Oct.28th, we are docked in Hong Kong.

Forecast low 80s, medium humidity, partly sunny. Hong Kong is located on China's south coast on the Pearl River Delta, has a population of around 7 million people, and is the most densely populated area in the world.

We had the first excursion, meeting time 7:30 a.m.; most people had caught on, half the bus full when we got there, and we had our number tags before everyone else. There was no reserved seat for the impaired. One front-seat couple offered, but we were happy with 2nd seat; the other couple sat and planted in the guide's seat, forcing him to stand the entire tour a second time! (Yeah, I am getting tired of "tourists"). We have a 40-minute drive to the Tai O Fishing Village, so here is some more local "info."

Of the 1100 square kilometers of island, 900 sq. kilos are mountains. The dock where we parked is brand new and used to be the airport. Hong Kong outgrew the airport, and it was not friendly to the planes needing longer runways, so they built one on the other side of the island, on reclaimed land. The transfer from the old to the new airport happened in 12 hours, complete! There are only two runways at present, but another is in the "works" to handle the increasing present 1000 flights/day and 70 million passengers per year.

As in America, industry followed cheap labor, so this is mostly service and headquarters. Apartment space is at a premium, 400 sq. ft apt. or less $1.2 million US; half the population is in government-subsidized apartments, so the family is only required to pay $200-$300 US equivalent per month. Hong Kong is the most populated and best-known of this island cluster of 250 islands. Actually, of the 250, only 23 are populated. One is a prison island!

In 1998, the world's largest /longest suspension bridge currently opened here. It swings up to 5 meters with strong winds!

The current population is 7.15 million, and May through October is typhoon season. The British occupied till the late 90's, their judicial system still in place, and yes, they drive on the left side of the road. You must be 18 to drive, you must get a permit to drive outside of the Island, and one to get back in. Public education is free through high school, but college is not.

Macau, to the south, now is the largest gambling complex in the world, exceeding Las Vegas since the late 90s; Chinese people must get a visa to visit Macau, and nothing else is required. It is about an hour by hydroplane from Hong Kong to Macau, and 40 million visitors a year, of which 70% are Chinese.

The fishing village (known as Hong Kong's Little Venice) has narrow, crowded streets (one canal). Our group is warned to keep a path open for carts and others going the other way or from behind (which, of course, is ignored by some and has to be constantly reminded by the guide.) Fishermen were the lowest income class along with farmers, just that farmers had land, many families grew up on the fishing boat that was home, and many families had more than a few kids. It was a very hard life, but the kids were needed to help with the fishing. The streets are lined with fresh fish, dried fish, and everything animal or vegetable from the sea. Some venues offered the fish to be prepared, some offered dried fish, all fresh! We walked through the streets to a temple, got the spiel on this 400-year-old temple, paid our respects, got 20 minutes to look around, and met back on the bus.

Next, the world's largest seated outdoor bronze Buddha (it is 34 meters high; it took 12 years to build.), which was adjacent to the Po Lin Monastery, where we were to have an included vegetarian lunch. (Buddhists are vegetarian). The Buddha is made up of 202 cast bronze pieces. Two make up the head, and 200 the body.

There was a back road to the Buddha and the building he sits on, so we were able to forgo the 100-plus steps from the front. Inside the building was a museum with ancient painted scenes, a bell, statues, and, of course, a few religious and not-so-religious remembrance shops that would take US or HK monies. No photos inside.

Lunch was amazing, including generous plates, served family style with a Lazy Susan in the middle of the table. Rice flour bread, rice, and vegetables, corn soup, two different varieties of stir fry, one with tofu (looked a lot like pork, not bad…), Hot green tea, no dessert, but everyone at the table had eaten their limit! All loved the meal without exception.

The last part of this excursion was a 20-minute cable car ride. It was a bit hazy, but it did provide great views of Hong Kong, Lantau Island, Kowloon, and a bird's eye view of the airport. The claim here is that it is the longest cable car ride in the world…

A few more "snip its" of info: We asked why they were so busy so late in the day on a Saturday, and we were told that the Chinese like to sleep late on their days off, 10-11 a.m is common, so on days off, their day starts just after noon; most men work two jobs, women also work. 3% inflation, 3 % unemployment. Back on the ship, both of us now have "colds"; Lynn blames those filling up their tea thermoses in the cafeteria on the ship. It was signed but ignored (rules are for those who obey the rules), so we napped a little. The luggage was to be out by 10 p.m., so we also packed our suitcases. After 5-6 weighings, Lynn's was at 49.5#, mine at 48.6#, and I now have a "purse" with my carry-on!

Last formal dinner, I had to have that escargot one more time, gave out the tips, and took names so we could mention them all in the comments when the evaluation was sent just after the cruise.

Played one final game with our friends, and there were only 6 of us who showed up. We did the game, and all of us were awarded a prize!

Enough was enough. I went back to the cabin, took a hot shower, set the alarm, and the last day on the ship was over.

<u>Sunday Oct.29th, disembarkation day</u>.

Our meeting time to wait was 9:45. We were to be completely out of the room by 8 a.m. and packed our last things in the carry-ons, up to the cafeteria for my last bagel and lox, and hug from May, the greeter and sanitizer girl.

We finished breakfast, picked up our carry-ons, gave the attendant his tip, and then went off to the meeting place. We were told to proceed. We did, found our connection, and loaded onto the bus for the hotel. Waited for everyone to load (about 40 minutes), then driven to the Park Hotel. (Currently under renovation) Our escort stored our luggage, and we were directed to the 4th floor for check-in. The rooms would not be ready till 2 p.m. It was 9:45 a.m., so they secured our carry-ons and luggage, and off we went to explore Hong Kong on foot.

Educating Noah…Travelin'

Crowded streets, crowded sidewalks, stores, food, up-scale stores, organic food stores, pharmacies, massage services, fine dining, storefront dining, Korean dining, any kind of food you can find here, any service, any brand, plus custom tailoring overnight. After walking a few blocks, we needed a break from the bustling crowd, so we opened the map and set a course for a large park. This park in the heart of Hong Kong is also on the edge of a Mosque, so the park is filled with a large number of Islamists lounging on the benches and in the shade, there are small groups practicing Tai Quan Doo, beautiful trees, flowers, butterflies, and a pond that has lots of turtles competing for space on tree roots and branches sticking out of the water.

Lynn was tiring out fast and needed food and drink and a covered place, so against my objections, we grabbed a table at a very busy restaurant…McDonald's. I had exchanged some money and bought 2 cokes, a cheeseburger, and fries for Lynn. We shared the table with an Indian couple and their son and answered their questions about our new president. After explaining our position, I asked them to name one good thing that they had heard or read about him. They could not, and then I told them that is exactly the point! Nice folks, they moved from India for an opportunity 13 years ago and enjoy living in Hong Kong.

Walked through the park, found our way back to the hotel, got our room, picked out our luggage, and we were set; the meeting time for the airport was 8:30 a.m. Lynn went to the room with the carry-ons and jumped into bed. The luggage came to the room right after I arrived; Lynn was coughing way too much, so off I went to find a drugstore. Found one about a block away, got her some Robitussin, and settled down for the last entries before the 14-hour flight home. Lynn felt better, but in no shape to go out for dinner, so off I went. What I brought back was one chocolate milk, one lemon juice, one pastry with two eyes in the shape of a dark brown crawler (white pastry eyes), another tan pastry with two eyes and a breakfast sausage in the middle, and the last, no eyes but had tuna and corn inside. (That was a surprise!) I also picked up some magnets to use up the money I had exchanged. S30 US, we had McDonalds, lunch, a small supper, 4 magnets, change for my foreign money collector, and some loose change combined with some American for a tip tomorrow at the airport! Not bad!!

The room did include WIFI on a smartphone; the guest (us) was encouraged to take the phone while exploring Hong Kong! On the phone was a map, recommendations of restaurants and attractions, plus local and worldwide phone calling, all included; another something to look forward to here in the States! This room must have a key in a slot to activate the lighting; you need to find that slot, then the different light panels and controls. Just a regular toilet, nice shower stall, free bottled water…and yes, I checked, tap water is not safe to drink.

The flight home was direct, Hong Kong to O'Hare; 14 hours on Cathay Pacific Airways, special economy, great seats, lots of leg room, and even though both people in front of us fully reclined, we both still had plenty of room! We left at 12:30 p.m. Monday, Oct.30, and with the 14-hour flight and time and date changes, arrived at O'Hare at 1:30 p.m., so the 30th turned into a 37-hour day.

We picked up our luggage, and the Wisconsin Coach Lines bus was there to take us home. Then we tried Uber to get home from there. Everything worked well. We are both beat! It was 4:15 p.m., and another adventure was done.

Educating Noah…Travelin'

We called the kids and found out that my mother had fallen early that afternoon and was in the hospital. I quickly changed and went off to the hospital.

She had severe hemorrhaging in the head, and they wanted her to see a cerebral specialist, but she refused intubation for transportation to the hospital specializing in head injuries. I talked with the doctor, and we agreed to put her in Hospice.

The next day, she was no longer talking gibberish and seemed to respond well. However, I did sign the paperwork for Hospice.

By Friday, she had gone from oral morphine to morphine injections and then to a pump. I received a call from the hospice social worker asking which option we wanted: keep her in the hospital and take her off Hospice, or move her, or keep her in the hospital, on Hospice, and pay the daily hospital day and board rate.

I told him it was really kind of horrible to offer these options on a Friday afternoon without any warning. We agreed to stop hospice and keep her there, then I called the doctor and left a message with the hospice company to have the nurse contact me.

On Saturday afternoon, the doctor came into the room and explained that he had called the hospice and had them extend the coverage till Ma was moved on Monday. The nurse never contacted me. On Monday early afternoon, the social worker contacted me and said I had to take my mother's bed out of the room so that he could arrange a hospital bed there. I told him it would be out that night. I called my ex-son-in-law for help and arranged a time to meet. We did. The facility aides had already moved the bed to a vacant room, so we loaded it into the VW bus and left it at Tiffany's place.

My brother flew in from Nevada and spent the next ten days with us, visiting her daily. I fired the Ascension Hospice with the help of Ma's facility and replaced them with a competent Hospice. It has been three weeks to date, and there is no word from the Hospice as to why they were fired; it reminds me of "fish stink from the head back." They should not be in business!!

Little progress with ma, little appetite, little will to take care of herself, or effort to improve. She does have her hair done, and with much encouragement, does get out of bed with assistance and has eaten meals in the dining room twice since returning.

Since she had stabilized, Lynn and I went up to our timeshare, spent four days touring the area and Door County, and then paid them $2500.00 to terminate the timeshare. I was tired of the promises of buyback sites, plus the various up-front money demand scams. Time to get it over and done with!

Back to ma, organized all of her papers, made copies of the will, power of attorney, and the checking account and investment account in trust, and presented it to an attorney to set up the estate when the time comes.

Everything stabilized, and Ma bounced back again! We had Thanksgiving with Tiffany and her friend Victor; Cruz, Camille, and Kelly were with others. December was uneventful; visiting Ma two times per week, she will not be joining us anymore for meals, the stairs are too hard for her, and she is even refusing to pedal with the wheelchair to her table for meals. However, her spirits are good, her eyes are failing, but she has more visitors than anyone else in the building.

Our next adventure is a 10-week cruise from Miami to Singapore, January 3rd through March 15th. I set up authority for Tiffany with Ma, and she promised to take good care of her, so we left after letting Ma know if she finally gave up, she could.

The lot in Nevada is also gone; that "great opportunity" turned into a great loss, but it is gone for a $40,000 loss to offset market gains for years!

Noah

Cruise Lines and Where

1. Caribbean — Royal Caribbean (RC) 1
2. Alaska — Regency Cruises (1)
3. South America — Norwegian Cruise Lines NCL (1)
4. Mediterranean — NCL (2+3)
5. Quebec to New York — NCL (4)
6. France Seine (River cruise) — Viking (1)
7. Brazil -Amazon (River cruise) — Iberia (1)
8. Atlantic Crossing — Mediterranean Ship Co. (MSC)(1)
9. Scandinavia — Royal Caribbean (RC) (2)
10. Caribbean — Holland America (HA) (1)
11. Caribbean — NCL (5)
12. Caribbean — Celebrity Cruise Line (1)
13. New Zealand/ Australia/ Bali — Celebrity (back to back) (2+3)
14. China/Tibet (River cruise) — Viking (2)
15. Caribbean — NCL (6)
16. Greece — Regent (1)
17. Russia (river cruise) — Viking (3)
18. Argentina/Falkland/Antarctica — Celebrity (4)
19. Caribbean/Panama Canal/Central America — Celebrity (5)
20. Japan/Korea/ S. Vietnam — Celebrity (6)
21. Carib/Africa/India/Myanmar/ — Oceania (1)
22. Portugal/Spain (River cruise) — Viking (4)

23. Alaska (second time)　　　　Oceania (2)

24. Cuba　　　　　　　　　　　Azamara (1)

25. Polynesia (Bora Bora/Tahiti/Easter Island)　　Oceania (3)

26. Holy Land/ Jordan/Suez/Egypt /Oman　　Silver seas (1)

27. Eastern Europe (Poland/Transylvania) (River cruise)　　Vantage (1)

28. Netherlands to Switzerland (River Cruise)　　Amadeus (1)

29. Columbia River　　　　　　American Steamboat Co. (1)

30. Great lakes　　　　　　　　Pearl Seas (1)

Noah

Countries and States visited:

All the states have been visited, Hawaii four islands, Oahu, Maui, Hawaii, Kauai, twice, and plus the Highway to Hana, and Alaska twice, including the Yukon territory.

Countries and Islands:

Alsace; Antarctica; Argentina; Australia; Austria; Belize; Brazil; Bulgaria; Canada (All the drivable territories); Chile; China; Costa Rica; Columbia; Croatia; Czech Republic; Denmark; Ecuador; England; Egypt; Finland; France; Germany; Greece; Guatemala; Holland; Hungary; Iceland; India; Indonesia; Ireland; Israel; Italy; Japan; Jordan; Mexico; Monaco; Montenegro; Morocco; Myanmar; Newfoundland; Netherlands, New Zealand; Nicaragua; Namibia; Norway; Nova Scotia; Oman; Panama; Peru; Poland; Portugal; Romania; Russia; Scotland; Serbia; Sicily; Singapore; Slovakia; South Korea; Spain; Sweden; Switzerland; Tanzania; Tibet; Thailand; Tunisia; Turkey; United Arab Emirs; Uruguay; Vatican; Vietnam; Wales , (72)

Islands:

Antigua; Apostle; Aruba; Bahamas; Bali; Barbados; Bonaire: Bora Bora; British Columbia; Canary Islands; Cuba; Curacao; Devil's Island; Easter Island (observed, harbor was closed) Fakarava; Galapagos Islands: (Isla Santa Cruz; Isla Santa Fe; Isla Bartolome; Seymour Norte); Grand Cayman; Falkland Islands; Grand Cayman Islands; Guam; Hawaii: (Maui; Kauai; Oahu; and Hawaii); Honduras; Jamaica; Madeira; Maldives; Papeete (Tahiti); Pitcairn Islands; Philippines; Raiatea; Puerto Rico; Principe; Sao Tome; Seychelles; St. Johns; St. Thomas; St. Martin (43)

Educating Noah…Travelin'

Picture albums of most:

http://theyaregoneagain.shutterfly.com

The seven natural Wonders of the World:

1. Grand Canyon — done
2. Victoria Falls S. Africa
3. Mt. Everest (saw from plane when we went to Tibet) — done
4. The Great Barrier Reef (snorkeled it in 2014) — done
5. Harbor of Rio De Jannero (stayed just off the beach) — done
6. Paricutin Volcano (Mexico)
7. Northern Lights (Ivalo, Finland, glass Igloo 2016) — done
8. Swiss Alp's experience — done
9. Amazon river experience — done

Rivers of the world: Ganga, Amazon, Rio Grande, Rio Negro, Doro, Nile, Yangtze, Yellow, Volga, Thames, Mississippi, Columbia, Rhine, Danube, Seine

Destinations left: Greenland, Bermuda, Western Russia, Madagascar, Shri Lanka, Laos

www.ingramcontent.com/pod-product-compliance
Lightning Source LLC
Chambersburg PA
CBHW041315110526
44591CB00021B/2791